Doing
Business

2012

Doing business in a
more transparent world

A COPUBLICATION OF THE WORLD BANK AND THE INTERNATIONAL FINANCE CORPORATION

THE DOING BUSINESS WEBSITE

Current features
News on the *Doing Business* project
http://www.doingbusiness.org

Rankings
How economies rank—from 1 to 183
http://www.doingbusiness.org/Rankings

Doing Business reforms
Short summaries of DB2011 reforms, lists of reforms
since DB2008
http://www.doingbusiness.org/Reforms

Historical data
Customized data sets since DB2004
http://www.doingbusiness.org/Custom-Query

Methodology and research
The methodology and research papers underlying
Doing Business
http://www.doingbusiness.org/Methodology
http://www.doingbusiness.org/Research

Download reports
Access to *Doing Business* reports as well as
subnational and regional reports, reform case studies
and customized economy and regional profiles
http://www.doingbusiness.org/Reports

Subnational and regional projects
Differences in business regulations at the
subnational and regional level
http://www.doingbusiness.org/Subnational-Reports

Law library
Online collection of laws and regulations relating to
business and gender issues
http://www.doingbusiness.org/Law-library
http://wbl.worldbank.org

Local partners
More than 9,000 specialists in 183 economies who
participate in *Doing Business*
*http://www.doingbusiness.org/Local-Partners/
Doing-Business*

Business Planet
Interactive map on the ease of doing business
http://rru.worldbank.org/businessplanet

Doing Business
THE WORLD BANK IFC
2012

Contents

Doing Business 2012 is the ninth in a series of annual reports investigating the regulations that enhance business activity and those that constrain it. *Doing Business* presents quantitative indicators on business regulation and the protection of property rights that can be compared across 183 economies—from Afghanistan to Zimbabwe—and over time.

Regulations affecting 11 areas of the life of a business are covered: starting a business, dealing with construction permits, getting electricity, registering property, getting credil, protecting investors, paying taxes, trading across borders, enforcing contracts, resolving insolvency (formerly closing a business) and employing workers. The employing workers data are not included in this year's ranking on the ease of doing business.

Data in *Doing Business 2012* are current as of June 1, 2011. The indicators are used to analyze economic outcomes and identify what reforms of business regulation have worked, where and why. Chapters exploring these issues for each of the 11 *Doing Business* topics—as well as showing global trends—are being published online this year. The chapters are available on the *Doing Business* website at http://www.doingbusiness.org.

The methodology for the dealing with construction permits, getting credit and paying taxes indicators changed for *Doing Business 2012*. See the data notes for details.

Preface

Enabling private sector growth—and ensuring that poor people can participate in its benefits—requires a regulatory environment where new entrants with drive and good ideas, regardless of their gender or ethnic origin, can get started in business and where firms can invest and grow, generating more jobs. *Doing Business 2012* is the ninth in a series of annual reports benchmarking the regulations that enhance business activity and those that constrain it. The report presents quantitative indicators on business regulation and the protection of property rights for 183 economies—from Afghanistan to Zimbabwe. The data are current as of June 2011.

A fundamental premise of *Doing Business* is that economic activity requires good rules—rules that establish and clarify property rights and reduce the cost of resolving disputes; rules that increase the predictability of economic interactions and provide contractual partners with certainty and protection against abuse. The objective is regulations designed to be efficient, accessible to all and simple in their implementation. In some areas *Doing Business* gives higher scores for regulation providing stronger protection of investor rights, such as stricter disclosure requirements in related-party transactions.

Doing Business takes the perspective of domestic, primarily smaller companies and measures the regulations applying to them through their life cycle. This year's report ranks economies on the basis of 10 areas of regulation—for starting a business, dealing with construction permits, getting electricity, registering property, getting credit, protecting investors, paying taxes, trading across borders, enforcing contracts and resolving insolvency (formerly closing a business). In addition, data are presented for regulations on employing workers.

Doing Business is limited in scope. It does not attempt to measure all costs and benefits of a particular law or regulation to society as a whole. Nor does it measure all aspects of the business environment that matter to firms and investors or affect the competitiveness of an economy. Its aim is simply to supply business leaders and policy makers with a fact base for informing policy making and to provide open data for research on how business regulations and institutions affect such economic outcomes as productivity, investment, informality, corruption, unemployment and poverty.

Through its indicators, *Doing Business* has tracked changes to business regulation around the world, recording more than 1,750 improvements since 2004. Against the backdrop of the global financial and economic crisis, policy makers around the world continue to reform business regulation at the level of the firm, in some areas at an even faster pace than before.

These continued efforts prompt questions: How has business regulation changed around the world—and how have the changes affected firms and economies? Drawing on a now longer time series, the report introduces a measure to illustrate how the regulatory environment for business has changed in absolute terms in each economy over the 6 years since *Doing Business 2006* was published in 2005. The "distance to frontier" measure, which assesses the level of change in each economy's regulatory environment as measured by *Doing Business*, complements the aggregate ranking on the ease of doing business, which benchmarks each economy's current performance on the indicators against that of all other economies in the

Doing Business sample (for more detail, see the chapter on the ease of doing business and distance to frontier).

There still remains an unfinished agenda for research into what regulations constitute binding constraints, what package of regulatory reforms is most effective and how these issues are shaped by the context in an economy. To stimulate new research in this area, *Doing Business* plans a conference for the fall of 2012. Its aim will be to deepen our understanding of the connections between business regulation reforms and broader economic outcomes.

Doing Business would not be possible without the expertise and generous input of a network of more than 9,000 local experts, including lawyers, business consultants, accountants, freight forwarders, government officials and other professionals routinely administering or advising on the relevant legal and regulatory requirements in the 183 economies covered. In particular, the Doing Business team would like to thank its global contributors: Allen & Overy LLP; Baker & McKenzie; Cleary Gottlieb Steen & Hamilton LLP ; Ernst & Young; Ius Laboris, Alliance of Labor, Employment, Benefits and Pensions Law Firms; KPMG; the Law Society of England and Wales; Lex Mundi, Association of Independent Law Firms; Panalpina; PwC; Raposo Bernardo & Associados; Russell Bedford International; SDV International Logistics; and Toboc Inc.

The project also benefited throughout the past year from advice and input from governments and policy makers around the world. In particular, the team would like to thank the governments of the Republic of Korea, the former Yugoslav Republic of Macedonia, Mexico and the United Kingdom for providing input and feedback on the economy case studies. The team would also like to thank the more than 60 governments that contributed detailed information on business regulation reforms in 2010/11.

This volume is a product of the staff of the World Bank Group. The team would like to thank all World Bank Group colleagues from the regional departments and networks for their contributions to this effort.

Janamitra Devan
Vice President and Head of Network
Financial & Private Sector Development
The World Bank Group

Executive summary

Over the past year a record number of governments in Sub-Saharan Africa changed their economy's regulatory environment to make it easier for domestic firms to start up and operate. In a region where relatively little attention was paid to the regulatory environment only 8 years ago, regulatory reforms making it easier to do business were implemented in 36 of 46 economies between June 2010 and May 2011. That represents 78% of economies in the region, compared with an average of 56% over the previous 6 years (figure 1.1).

Worldwide, regulatory reforms aimed at streamlining such processes as starting a business, registering property or dealing with construction permits are still the most common. But more and more economies are focusing their reform efforts on strengthening legal institutions such as courts and insolvency regimes and enhancing legal protections of investors and property rights. This shift has been particularly pronounced in low- and lower-middle-income economies,

where 43% of all reforms recorded by *Doing Business* in 2010/11 focused on aspects captured by the getting credit, protecting investors, enforcing contracts and resolving insolvency indicators (figure 1.2).

Overall in 2010/11, governments in 125 economies implemented 245 institutional and regulatory reforms as measured by *Doing Business*—13% more than in the previous year (box 1.1). A faster pace of regulatory reform is good news for entrepreneurs in developing economies. Starting a business is a leap of faith under any circumstances. For the poor, starting a business or finding a job is an important way out of poverty.[1] In most parts of the world small and medium-size businesses are often the main job creators.[2] Yet entrepreneurs in developing economies tend to encounter greater obstacles than their counterparts in high-income economies. Finding qualified staff and dealing with lack of adequate infrastructure are among the challenges. Overly burdensome regulations and inefficient institutions that

discourage the creation and expansion of businesses compound the problems.

Through indicators benchmarking 183 economies, *Doing Business* measures and tracks changes in the regulations applying to domestic companies in 11 areas in their life cycle (box 1.2). A fundamental premise of *Doing Business* is that economic activity requires good rules that are transparent and accessible to all. Such regulations should be efficient, striking a balance between safeguarding some important aspects of the business environment and avoiding distortions that impose unreasonable costs on businesses. Where business regulation is burdensome and competition limited, success depends more on whom you know than on what you can do. But where regulations are relatively easy to comply with and accessible to all who need to use them, anyone with talent and a good idea should be able to start and grow a business in the formal sector.

FIGURE 1.1 A large number of economies in Sub-Saharan Africa reformed business regulation in 2010/11
Share of economies with at least 1 *Doing Business* reform making it easier to do business

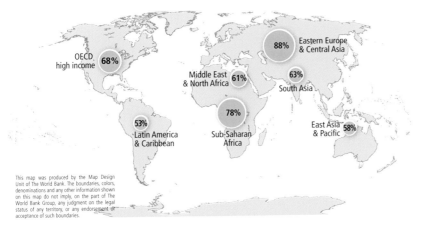

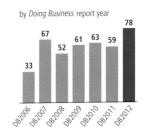

Source: *Doing Business* database.

Across regions, entrepreneurs in developing economies face a regulatory environment that is on average less business-friendly than those in OECD high-income economies. This means costlier and more bureaucratic procedures to start a business, deal with construction permits, register property, trade across borders and pay taxes. Getting an electricity connection, a new dimension in this year's ease of doing business ranking, costs more on average in Sub-Saharan Africa than in any other part of the world—more than 5,400% of income per capita (the average in OECD high-income economies is 93% of income per capita). Local businesses complete more complex formalities to get an electricity connection in many Eastern European and Central Asian economies than anywhere else in the world. But it is not just about complex formalities or red tape. A less business-friendly regulatory environment also means weaker legal protections of minority shareholders and weaker collateral laws and institutions such as courts, credit bureaus and collateral registries.

Globally, more efficient regulatory processes often go hand in hand with stronger legal institutions and property rights protections. There is an association between the strength of legal institutions and property rights protections in an economy as captured by several sets of *Doing Business* indicators (getting credit, protecting investors, enforcing contracts and resolving insolvency) and the complexity and cost of regulatory processes as captured by several others (starting a business, dealing with construction permits, getting electricity, registering property, paying taxes and trading across borders). OECD high-income economies, by a large margin, have the world's most business-friendly environment on both dimensions (figure 1.3). At the other end of the spectrum, economies in Sub-Saharan Africa and South Asia are most likely to have both weaker legal institutions and more complex regulatory processes as measured by *Doing Business*.

Some regions break away from the general trend. One is the Middle East and North Africa, a region where reform efforts over the past 6 years have focused mainly on simplifying regulation. Today economies in the region often combine relatively weaker legal institutions

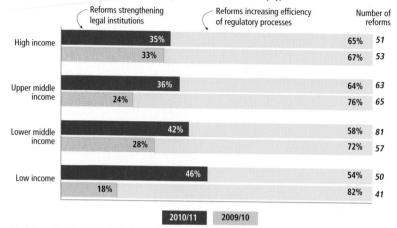

FIGURE 1.2 In 2010/11 economies worldwide increasingly focused reform efforts on strengthening legal institutions and property rights protections

Doing Business reforms making it easier to do business by type

Note: Reforms strengthening legal institutions are those in the areas of getting credit, protecting investors, enforcing contracts and resolving insolvency. Reforms increasing efficiency of regulatory processes are those in the areas of starting a business, dealing with construction permits, getting electricity, registering property, paying taxes and trading across borders.

Source: Doing Business database.

BOX 1.1 Key findings in this year's report

- In Sub-Saharan Africa 36 of 46 governments improved their economy's regulatory environment for domestic businesses in 2010/11—a record number since 2005. This is good news for entrepreneurs in the region, where starting and running a business is still costlier and more complex than in any other region of the world.

- Worldwide, 125 economies implemented 245 reforms making it easier to do business in 2010/11, 13% more than in the previous year. In low- and lower-middle-income economies a greater share of these changes were aimed at strengthening courts, insolvency regimes and investor protections than in earlier years. The pickup in the pace of regulatory reform is especially welcome for small and medium-size businesses, the main job creators in many parts of the world.

- Against the backdrop of the global financial and economic crisis, more economies strengthened their insolvency regime in 2010/11 than in any previous year. Twenty-nine economies implemented insolvency reforms, up from 16 the previous year and 18 the year before. Most were OECD high-income economies or in Eastern Europe and Central Asia. Research has shown that effective insolvency systems can influence the cost of debt, access to credit, and both the ability of an economy to recover from a recession and the speed of its recovery.

- New data show the importance of access to regulatory information. Fee schedules, documentation requirements and information relating to commercial cases and insolvency proceedings are most easily accessible in OECD high-income economies and least accessible in Sub-Saharan Africa and the Middle East and North Africa. The rise in e-government initiatives around the world provides an opportunity to increase access to information and transparency.

- A new measure shows that over the past 6 years, 94% of 174 economies covered by *Doing Business* have made their regulatory environment more business-friendly. These economies moved closer to the "frontier," a synthetic measure based on the most business-friendly regulatory practices across 9 areas of business regulation—from starting a business to resolving insolvency.

- A broad, sustained approach to managing business regulation is common among the 20 economies that have the most business-friendly regulatory environment today and among those that made the greatest progress toward the "frontier" over the past 6 years. This year's report highlights the experiences of the Republic of Korea, the former Yugoslav Republic of Macedonia, Mexico and the United Kingdom. Korea just joined the top 10 economies on the ease of doing business after streamlining business entry, tax administration and contract enforcement. FYR Macedonia is among the economies that improved the most in the ease of doing business over the past year.

- The economies that improved the most in the ease of doing business in 2010/11—with improvements in 3 or more areas of regulation measured by *Doing Business*—are Morocco, Moldova, FYR Macedonia, São Tomé and Príncipe, Latvia, Cape Verde, Sierra Leone, Burundi, the Solomon Islands, Korea, Armenia, and Colombia.

FIGURE 1.3   Stronger legal institutions and property rights protections are associated with more efficient regulatory processes
Average ranking on sets of *Doing Business* indicators

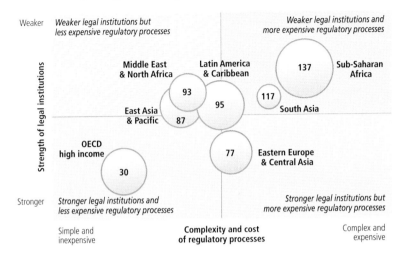

Note: Strength of legal institutions refers to the average ranking in getting credit, protecting investors, enforcing contracts and resolving insolvency. *Complexity and cost of regulatory processes* refers to the average ranking in starting a business, dealing with construction permits, getting electricity, registering property, paying taxes and trading across borders. The size of the bubble reflects the number of economies in each region and the number is the average ranking on the ease of doing business for the region. Correlation results for individual economies are significant at the 1% level after controlling for income per capita.

Source: Doing Business database.

BOX 1.2   Measuring regulation through the life cycle of a local business

This year's aggregate ranking on the ease of doing business is based on indicator sets that measure and benchmark regulations affecting 10 areas in the life cycle of a business: starting a business, dealing with construction permits, getting electricity, registering property, getting credit, protecting investors, paying taxes, trading across borders, enforcing contracts and resolving insolvency. *Doing Business* also looks at regulations on employing workers, which are not included in this year's aggregate ranking.

Doing Business encompasses 2 types of data and indicators. One set of indicators focuses on the strength of property rights and investor protections as measured by the treatment of a case scenario according to the laws and regulations on the books. *Doing Business* gives higher scores for stronger property rights and investor protections, such as stricter disclosure requirements in related-party transactions. The second set of indicators focuses on the cost and efficiency of regulatory processes such as starting a business, registering property and dealing with construction permits. Based on time-and-motion case studies from the perspective of the business, these indicators measure the procedures, time and cost required to complete a transaction in accordance with all relevant regulations. Any interaction of the company with external parties such as government agencies counts as 1 procedure. Cost estimates are recorded from official fee schedules where these apply. For a detailed explanation of the *Doing Business* methodology, see the data notes and the chapter "About *Doing Business*: measuring for impact."

---

with relatively more efficient regulatory processes. In Eastern Europe and Central Asia, by contrast, economies have on average slightly stronger legal institutions and less efficient regulatory processes. In this region reform efforts over the past 6 years have put greater emphasis on strengthening legal institutions and protection of property rights than those in the Middle East and North Africa.[3]

Policy makers worldwide recognize the role that entrepreneurs play in creating economic opportunities for themselves and for others, and often take measures to improve the investment climate and boost productivity growth. Investments in infrastructure—ports, roads, telecommunications—are seen as a vital ingredient of private sector development. In an increasingly complex global economy, investments

in education and training are critical. These investments typically take time to bear fruit. But economies that have made the transition from developing to high-income status have generally done so by boosting the skills and capabilities of their labor force. A critical way for policy makers to encourage entrepreneurship is by creating a regulatory environment conducive to the creation and growth of businesses—one that promotes rather than inhibits competition.[4]

OPPORTUNITIES FOR GREATER ACCESS TO INFORMATION IN BUSINESS REGULATION

Institutions play a major role in private sector development. Courts, registries, tax agencies and credit information bureaus are essential to make markets work. How efficient and transparent they are matters greatly to business. To improve the efficiency of processes and institutions, governments around the world—regardless of national income level—are making greater use of technology. More than 100 of the 183 economies covered by *Doing Business* use electronic systems for services ranging from business registration to customs clearance to court filings.[5] This saves time and money for business and government alike. It also provides new opportunities to increase transparency as well as to facilitate access to information and compliance with regulation. But not all economies take advantage of the opportunities for openness provided by the new technologies. And at times fiscal constraints and budgetary priorities have prevented faster adoption of the latest technologies to improve the quality of public services.

This year *Doing Business* researched how businesses can access information essential for complying with regulations and formalities, such as documentation requirements for trade or fee schedules for business start-up, construction permitting or electricity connections. Because some economies lack fully developed information technology infrastructure, the research also explored whether economies used other means to make such information easily accessible, such as posting fee schedules at the relevant agency or disseminating them through public notices.

The findings are striking. In the majority of economies in Sub-Saharan Africa and the Middle East and North Africa, obtaining such information requires a meeting with an official. In all OECD high-income economies documentation requirements for trade are accessible online, at an agency or through public notices (figure 1.4). In the Middle East and North Africa this is the case in only about 30% of economies, and in Sub-Saharan Africa in less than 50% of economies. Documentation requirements for building permits are available online or through public notices in only about 40% of economies in these 2 regions.

Easier access to fee schedules and lower fees tend to go hand in hand. In economies where fee schedules are easily accessible, starting a business costs 18% of income per capita on average; where they are not, it costs 66% of income per capita on average (figure 1.5).

Beyond information that businesses need to comply with regulation, institutions such as courts provide information that helps increase transparency in the marketplace. Efficient and fair courts are essential for creating the trust needed for businesses to build

WHAT WERE THE TRENDS IN BUSINESS REGULATION REFORMS AROUND THE WORLD IN 2010/11?

In Sub-Saharan Africa measures to improve the regulatory environment for local businesses in 2010/11 included the first overhaul of a body of harmonized commercial laws in the region. The legal reform by the Organization for the Harmonization of Business Law in Africa (OHADA) required the consensus of its 16 member states.[1] This first stage simplified business entry and strengthened secured transaction laws.

Overall in Sub-Saharan Africa, regulatory reform agendas have been broadening. Thirteen economies implemented reforms making it easier to do business in 3 or more areas measured by *Doing Business*—from business entry to exit—including postconflict economies such as Burundi, Liberia and Sierra Leone. South Africa introduced a new company act streamlining business incorporation and a new reorganization procedure facilitating the rehabilitation of financially distressed companies.

Against the backdrop of the global economic and financial crisis, changes to insolvency regimes continued across Europe and among OECD high-income economies elsewhere.[2] Worldwide, 29 economies improved insolvency regimes in 2010/11, more than in any previous year. These included Austria, Denmark, France, Italy, Poland, Slovenia and Switzerland as well as Bulgaria, Latvia, Lithuania, the former Yugoslav Republic of Macedonia, Moldova, Montenegro, Romania, Serbia and Ukraine. Iceland tightened approval requirements for related-party transactions. Greece, Portugal and Spain simplified business start-up.

In other regions the pace of regulatory reform was uneven. In the Middle East and North Africa 61% of economies implemented regulatory changes making it easier to do business. In Latin America and the Caribbean the 3 economies with the most business-friendly regulatory environments, Chile, Peru and Colombia, made them more so—each through regulatory reforms in 3 areas measured by *Doing Business*. But there were no such reforms in Ecuador or the majority of the Caribbean states.[3]

Malaysia was one of the economies that took the lead in East Asia and the Pacific, introducing electronic filing in its courts, setting up specialized civil and commercial courts in Kuala Lumpur and merging company, tax, social security and employment fund registrations at the one-stop shop for business start-up. Several small island states—the Solomon Islands, Tonga and Vanuatu—implemented regulatory reforms in 3 or more areas, often supported by donor programs. In South Asia the pace of regulatory reform remained steady over the past year. Sri Lanka and Bhutan were the most active. Sri Lanka implemented tax changes and tightened disclosure requirements for transactions involving a conflict of interest. Bhutan launched a public credit registry and streamlined business start-up.

1. OHADA is a system of common business laws and implementing institutions adopted by treaties among 16 West and Central African nations. It was created by 14 initial member economies on October 17, 1993, in Port Louis, Mauritius.
2. According to the International Monetary Fund (IMF 2009), the financial crisis resulted in a sharp increase in corporate and household defaults and firm bankruptcies.
3. No reforms making it easier to do business were recorded for Antigua and Barbuda, The Bahamas, Dominica, Grenada, Haiti, Jamaica, St. Lucia, St. Vincent and the Grenadines, Suriname or Trinidad and Tobago in 2010/11.

FIGURE 1.4   Access to documentation requirements for building permits and trading across borders easiest in OECD high-income economies

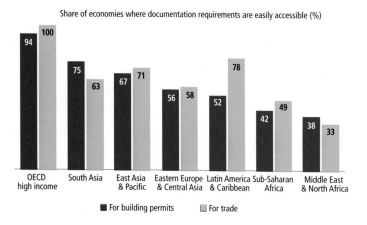

Share of economies where documentation requirements are easily accessible (%)

- OECD high income: 94, 100
- South Asia: 75, 63
- East Asia & Pacific: 67, 71
- Eastern Europe & Central Asia: 56, 58
- Latin America & Caribbean: 52, 78
- Sub-Saharan Africa: 42, 49
- Middle East & North Africa: 38, 33

■ For building permits   □ For trade

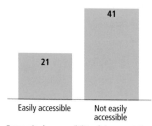

Average time to import goods (days)

- Easily accessible: 21
- Not easily accessible: 41

Economies by accessibility of documentation requirements for trade

Note: Documentation requirements are considered easily accessible if they can be obtained through the website of the relevant authority or another government agency or through public notices, without a need for an appointment with an official. The data sample for building permits includes 159 economies, and that for trade 175 economies. Differences in the second panel are statistically significant at the 5% level after controlling for income per capita.

Source: Doing Business database.

FIGURE 1.5   Easier access to fee schedules and lower fees tend to go hand in hand

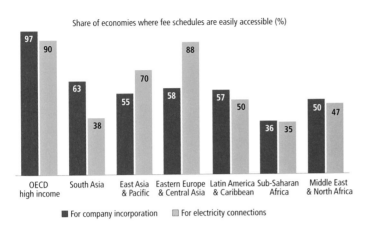

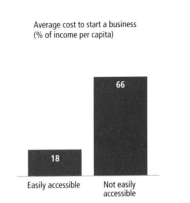

Note: Fee schedules are considered easily accessible if they can be obtained through the website of the relevant authority or another government agency or through public notices, without a need for an appointment with an official. The data sample for incorporation includes 174 economies, and that for electricity connections 181 economies. Differences in the second panel are statistically significant at the 5% level after controlling for income per capita.

Source: Doing Business database.

new relationships and expand their markets—and for investors to invest. But it is not only their role in efficient enforcement that matters. *Doing Business* finds that in close to 75% of a sample of 151 economies, courts are required by law to publicize the initiation of insolvency proceedings.

HOW THE TOP 20 ECONOMIES MANAGE BUSINESS REGULATION

The 20 economies with the most business-friendly regulation as reflected in their ranking on the ease of doing business are Singapore; Hong Kong SAR, China; New Zealand; the United States; Denmark; Norway; the United Kingdom; the Republic of Korea; Iceland; Ireland; Finland; Saudi Arabia; Canada; Sweden; Australia; Georgia; Thailand; Malaysia; Germany; and Japan (table 1.1). As noted elsewhere in this report, an economy's ranking on the ease of doing business does not tell the whole story about its business environment. The underlying indicators do not account for all factors important to doing business, such as macroeconomic conditions, market size, workforce skills and security. But they do capture some key aspects of the regulatory and institutional environment that matter for firms. These 20 economies have implemented effective yet streamlined procedures for regulatory processes such as starting a business and dealing with construction

permits as well as strong legal protections of property rights. They also periodically review and update business regulations as part of a broader competitiveness agenda and take advantage of new technologies through e-government initiatives.

Only 2 decades ago some of these 20 economies faced challenges similar to those in many lower-income economies today. Consider Norway's property registry. Today it is one of the world's most efficient. But in 1995 its paper records required 30 kilometers of shelving and were growing at a rate of 1 kilometer a year. Norway took steps to change this. First it merged the land department and survey information, then digitized title certificates. In 2002 it amended the 50-year-old Land Transfer Act to allow online titling. Online registration has been required by law since 2008.

Sweden undertook a systematic review of all regulations in the 1980s. Any unjustified requirements were cut in a "guillotine" initiative. (Mexico took a similar approach in the 1990s.) In Korea the Presidential Council on National Competitiveness, created in 2008, identified regulatory reform as 1 of 4 pillars to improve the economy's competitiveness, along with public sector innovation, investment promotion, and legal and institutional advancement. Reviewing Korea's business

regulations, the council found that 15% had not been revised since 1998. The council applied sunset clauses to more than 600 regulations and 3,500 administrative rules (see the case study on Korea).

Policy makers in some economies today consider regulatory reform a continual process and create dedicated committees or agencies such as Actal in the Netherlands and the Better Regulation Executive in the United Kingdom. These agencies not only routinely assess existing regulations. They also pay increasing attention to managing the flow of new regulations.

In the United Kingdom in 2005–10 a program reduced the burden of regulatory compliance on businesses by 25% according to the government.[6] That amounted to savings for firms equivalent to £3.5 billion. New initiatives are under way, such as the "one in, one out" system and the Red Tape Challenge (see the case study on the United Kingdom). The European Union has also targeted a 25% reduction in the administrative burden that regulation imposes on business. The underlying principle is to have "smart" regulation, dispensing with cumbersome and costly regulations that impair the private sector's capacity to innovate and grow while maintaining regulations that promote a level playing field.[7]

TABLE 1.1   Rankings on the ease of doing business

DB2012 rank	DB2011 rank[a]	Economy	DB2012 reforms	DB2012 rank	DB2011 rank[a]	Economy	DB2012 reforms	DB2012 rank	DB2011 rank[a]	Economy	DB2012 reforms
1	1	Singapore	0	62	59	Poland	2	123	119	Uganda	1
2	2	Hong Kong SAR, China	2	63	60	Ghana	0	124	123	Swaziland	1
3	3	New Zealand	1	64	70	Czech Republic	2	125	127	Bosnia and Herzegovina	2
4	4	United States	0	65	64	Dominica	0	126	120	Brazil	1
5	5	Denmark	1	66	69	Azerbaijan	0	127	125	Tanzania	1
6	7	Norway	0	67	71	Kuwait	0	128	130	Honduras	2
7	6	United Kingdom	1	68	76	Trinidad and Tobago	0	129	126	Indonesia	1
8	15	Korea, Rep.	3	69	91	Belarus	3	130	131	Ecuador	0
9	13	Iceland	2	70	67	Kyrgyz Republic	0	131	128	West Bank and Gaza	0
10	8	Ireland	0	71	73	Turkey	2	132	139	India	1
11	14	Finland	1	72	65	Romania	2	133	133	Nigeria	0
12	10	Saudi Arabia	1	73	68	Grenada	0	134	136	Syrian Arab Republic	1
13	12	Canada	1	74	81	Solomon Islands	4	135	135	Sudan	0
14	9	Sweden	0	75	66	St. Vincent and the Grenadines	0	136	134	Philippines	1
15	11	Australia	1	76	75	Vanuatu	3	137	144	Madagascar	2
16	17	Georgia	4	77	72	Fiji	0	138	138	Cambodia	1
17	16	Thailand	1	78	74	Namibia	1	139	132	Mozambique	0
18	23	Malaysia	3	79	78	Maldives	0	140	137	Micronesia, Fed. Sts.	0
19	19	Germany	0	80	79	Croatia	1	141	150	Sierra Leone	4
20	20	Japan	0	81	99	Moldova	4	142	146	Bhutan	2
21	31	Latvia	4	82	77	Albania	1	143	142	Lesotho	1
22	34	Macedonia, FYR	4	83	86	Brunei Darussalam	1	144	140	Iran, Islamic Rep.	0
23	21	Mauritius	0	84	80	Zambia	0	145	141	Malawi	2
24	18	Estonia	0	85	82	Bahamas, The	0	146	148	Mali	2
25	24	Taiwan, China	2	86	89	Mongolia	1	147	152	Tajikistan	1
26	22	Switzerland	2	87	83	Italy	1	148	143	Algeria	1
27	25	Lithuania	2	88	85	Jamaica	0	149	145	Gambia, The	3
28	27	Belgium	2	89	98	Sri Lanka	2	150	151	Burkina Faso	3
29	26	France	1	90	107	Uruguay	2	151	155	Liberia	3
30	30	Portugal	2	91	87	China	0	152	149	Ukraine	4
31	29	Netherlands	0	92	88	Serbia	2	153	147	Bolivia	0
32	28	Austria	1	93	92	Belize	1	154	157	Senegal	4
33	35	United Arab Emirates	2	94	115	Morocco	3	155	161	Equatorial Guinea	1
34	32	Israel	2	95	84	St. Kitts and Nevis	1	156	160	Gabon	1
35	36	South Africa	3	96	95	Jordan	2	157	156	Comoros	1
36	38	Qatar	2	97	93	Guatemala	0	158	153	Suriname	0
37	37	Slovenia	3	98	90	Vietnam	1	159	162	Mauritania	1
38	33	Bahrain	0	99	94	Yemen, Rep.	1	160	154	Afghanistan	1
39	41	Chile	3	100	101	Greece	2	161	165	Cameroon	2
40	49	Cyprus	1	101	97	Papua New Guinea	0	162	158	Togo	2
41	39	Peru	3	102	100	Paraguay	2	163	174	São Tomé and Príncipe	4
42	47	Colombia	3	103	109	Seychelles	2	164	159	Iraq	0
43	42	Puerto Rico (U.S.)	2	104	103	Lebanon	1	165	163	Lao PDR	0
44	45	Spain	1	105	96	Pakistan	0	166	164	Uzbekistan	1
45	50	Rwanda	3	106	102	Marshall Islands	0	167	170	Côte d'Ivoire	3
46	40	Tunisia	0	107	110	Nepal	1	168	169	Timor-Leste	2
47	58	Kazakhstan	1	108	105	Dominican Republic	1	169	177	Burundi	4
48	43	Slovak Republic	1	109	106	Kenya	1	170	167	Djibouti	1
49	53	Oman	3	110	108	Egypt, Arab Rep.	0	171	168	Zimbabwe	0
50	44	Luxembourg	0	111	104	Ethiopia	0	172	171	Angola	2
51	46	Hungary	0	112	112	El Salvador	1	173	172	Niger	1
52	48	St. Lucia	0	113	114	Argentina	0	174	166	Haiti	0
53	54	Mexico	3	114	113	Guyana	1	175	173	Benin	2
54	52	Botswana	0	115	111	Kiribati	0	176	181	Guinea-Bissau	2
55	61	Armenia	5	116	116	Palau	0	177	175	Venezuela, RB	0
56	56	Montenegro	3	117	117	Kosovo	0	178	176	Congo, Dem. Rep.	3
57	51	Antigua and Barbuda	0	118	122	Nicaragua	3	179	179	Guinea	1
58	62	Tonga	3	119	129	Cape Verde	3	180	178	Eritrea	0
59	57	Bulgaria	2	120	124	Russian Federation	4	181	180	Congo, Rep.	1
60	55	Samoa	0	121	121	Costa Rica	2	182	183	Central African Republic	3
61	63	Panama	1	122	118	Bangladesh	0	183	182	Chad	2

Note: The rankings for all economies are benchmarked to June 2011 and reported in the country tables. This year's rankings on the ease of doing business are the average of the economy's rankings on the 10 topics included in this year's aggregate ranking.
[a] Last year's rankings, shown in italics, are adjusted: they are based on 10 topics and reflect data corrections. The number of reforms excludes those making it more difficult to do business.
Source: Doing Business database.

Other initiatives share the objective of making business regulation effective at the lowest possible cost for business. In Sweden the government recently commissioned the Swedish Agency for Growth Policy Analysis to conduct studies on the effect of rules on the enterprise sector.[8] Canada and the United States have introduced impact assessments to prevent the introduction of regulations considered too costly to society.

At all levels, much attention is being paid to transparent policy making. Governments are making business regulation and the regulatory process accessible, helped in many cases by e-government initiatives. The United Kingdom invites comment on regulatory proposals on the website of the Better Regulation Executive.[9] Canada and the United States publish guidelines on the evaluation process underlying the cost-benefit analysis of new regulations.

DIFFERENCES IN PERFORMANCE ACROSS AREAS OF BUSINESS REGULATION

The economies making such continued efforts, often over decades, often compare well with others across all 10 areas of business regulation included in this year's ease of doing business ranking—and they do so over time, reflecting a more consistent and comprehensive approach to business regulation. In many of the other economies, by contrast, the degree to which regulations and institutions are business-friendly varies fairly widely across different areas of regulation.[10]

This shows up in comparisons of an economy's 3 highest rankings on *Doing Business* topics with its 3 lowest rankings (figure 1.6). For example, Malaysia's top 3 rankings (on getting credit, protecting investors and trading across borders) average 11, while its lowest 3 (on dealing with construction permits, getting electricity and registering property) average 77.

For some economies this variance is due in part to the rapid pace of reform in some areas of business regulation. One such area is business entry: more than 80% of the 183 economies covered by *Doing Business* have made it easier to start a business since 2003. Among them is the Arab Republic of

Egypt, where starting a business is reasonably straightforward thanks to the implementation of an efficient one-stop shop. But dealing with construction permits takes about 7 months, and enforcing a contract through the courts takes almost 3 years on average. Egypt's top 3 rankings (on starting a business, getting credit and trading across borders) average 54, while its lowest 3 (on dealing with construction permits, paying taxes and enforcing contracts) average 149.

Indeed, reforms simplifying business entry have been high on the agenda since early on—particularly in common markets such as the European Union, where businesses are free to start and operate in any of the member states. Over time such business regulation reforms have increasingly been undertaken by low- and lower-middle-income economies. Many have been helped by peer learning among policy makers, which has picked up around the world. Every year corporate registrars from 31 economies meet to discuss challenges and solutions.[11] Representatives from Canada, which ranks number 3 on the ease of starting a business, are now advising economies as diverse as Indonesia and Peru. In 2010/11, 53 economies made it easier to start a business (figure 1.7). Since 2005 the number of economies where starting a business takes 20 days or less has increased from 41 to 98.

Improving the regulatory environment for business can be difficult and take time, particularly if the improvements involve substantial institutional or legal changes. Some require difficult political trade-offs. Outside pressures may be needed to push through legislative changes. So it is no surprise that times of crisis have often proved to be a time of opportunity. Against the backdrop of the global economic and financial crisis, the number of insolvency reforms increased over the past 3 years, particularly in Europe and among OECD high-income economies elsewhere.[12] In 2010/11, 29 economies around the world reformed their insolvency systems, more than in any previous year. Most focused on improving reorganization proceedings to allow viable firms to continue operating.

Differences across areas of business regulation provide an opportunity for policy makers interested in regulatory reform. Not surprisingly, different areas of business regulation interact. Some research suggests that business regulation reforms have greater impact if combined with effective regulation in other areas. For example, when India dismantled a strict licensing regime controlling business entry and production, the benefits were greater in states that had more flexible labor regulations. These states saw real output gains 17.8% larger than those in other states.[13] In Mexico researchers found that a municipal license reform across states increased new firm registrations by 5% and employment by 2.2%.[14] The effect was greater in states with less corruption and better governance.[15]

Beyond these country-specific studies, cross-country analysis found that a 10-day reduction in the time to start a business was associated with a 0.3 percentage point increase in the investment rate and a 0.36% increase in the GDP growth rate in relatively poor and well-governed economies.[16] Another study points to synergistic effects between institutional reforms that reduce the costs of high-quality production and trade reforms. In many developing economies production of high-quality output is a precondition for firms to become exporters. Institutional deficiencies that raise the costs of high-quality production therefore limit the positive effect that trade facilitation can have on income.[17]

CLOSING THE GAP—A GLOBAL TREND TOWARD BUSINESS-FRIENDLY REGULATION

Policy makers often keep an eye on relative rankings that compare economies at a point in time. But they increasingly recognize the importance of improvements within economies over time. And results from recent years are encouraging. In the past 6 years policy makers in 163 economies made domestic regulations more business-friendly (figure 1.8). They lowered barriers to entry, operation and exit and strengthened protections of property and investor rights. Only a few economies moved in the opposite direction. República Bolivariana de Venezuela

FIGURE 1.6   An economy's regulatory environment may be business-friendly in some areas, less so in others

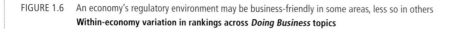

Within-economy variation in rankings across *Doing Business* topics

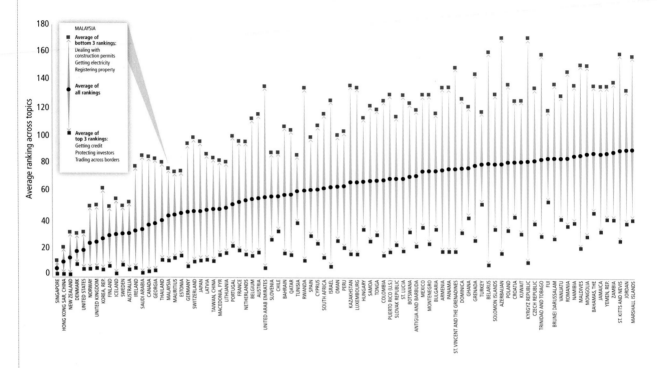

FIGURE 1.7   Reforms making it easier to start a business were most common in 2010/11—and have shown results over time

Number of *Doing Business* reforms making it easier to do business in 2010/11, by topic

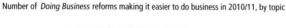

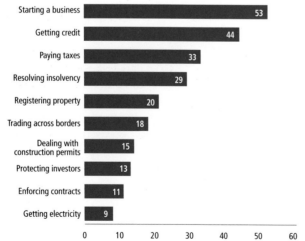

Topic	Number
Starting a business	53
Getting credit	44
Paying taxes	33
Resolving insolvency	29
Registering property	20
Trading across borders	18
Dealing with construction permits	15
Protecting investors	13
Enforcing contracts	11
Getting electricity	9

Number of economies by time to start a business

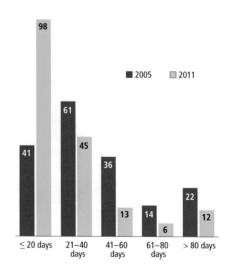

Note: The data in the second panel refer to the 174 economies included in *Doing Business 2006* (2005). Additional economies were added in subsequent years.

Source: Doing Business database.

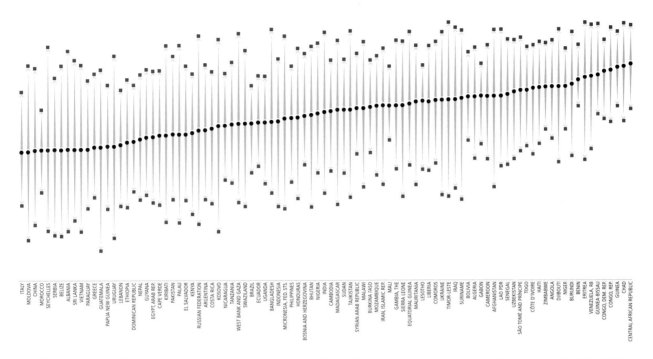

Note: Figure illustrates the variability in the degree to which an economy's regulatory environment is business-friendly compared with other economies across different areas of regulation. The vertical bars show the distance between the average of the highest 3 topic rankings and the average of the lowest 3 for each of 183 economies across the 10 topics included in this year's aggregate ranking.

Source: Doing Business database.

and Zimbabwe went the furthest in making business regulation less business-friendly.

Some economies have gone particularly far in closing the gap with the regulatory systems of top-performing economies such as Singapore, New Zealand and the Northern European economies (figure 1.9). Many of them are developing economies that started off with relatively high levels of bureaucracy and weak protections of property rights as measured by *Doing Business*. In narrowing the gap, all these economies are moving closer to the frontier—a synthetic measure based on the most efficient practice or highest score observed for each indicator. For starting a business, for example, the bar is set by New Zealand on the time (1 day), Canada and New Zealand on the number of procedures (1), Denmark and Slovenia on the cost (0). Georgia, Norway, Portugal, Sweden and the United Arab Emirates set the bar on the number of procedures for register- ing property (1), France on the documents

required to export (2), Singapore on the time to enforce contracts (150 days). The frontier is thus a proxy for global good practice across all indicators.

Economies making the greatest progress toward the frontier have been able to do so thanks to broad regulatory reform programs covering multiple areas of regulation and embedded in a long-term competitiveness strategy (figure 1.10). China, for example, im- plemented policy changes across 9 areas of business regulation in the years since 2005. The changes included a new company law in 2005, a new credit registry in 2006 and, in 2007, the first bankruptcy law regulating the bankruptcy of private enterprises since 1949 (figure 1.11).

More economies are taking this broad approach. In 2010/11, 35 economies implemented reforms making it easier to do business in 3 or more areas measured by *Doing Business*—12 of them in 4 or more

areas. Four years before, only 10 reformed in 3 or more areas.

Also new are the comprehensive approach and high level of coordination and commit- ment that some developing and emerging market economies are bringing to regulatory reform. More than 2 dozen economies have put in place regulatory reform committees, often reporting directly to the president or prime minister—as in Colombia, Malaysia and Rwanda.[18] And they have not shied away from radical legal reforms. Economies mak- ing the greatest strides in creating a more business-friendly regulatory environment have been revamping their regulatory and administrative systems in multiple areas to encourage private sector activity (box 1.3).

That more and more developing economies are serious about business regulation reform is encouraging. Such broad thinking is good news for entrepreneurs and governments alike.

FIGURE 1.8   In the past 6 years 163 economies moved closer to the frontier in regulatory practice

Distance to frontier, 2005 and 2011

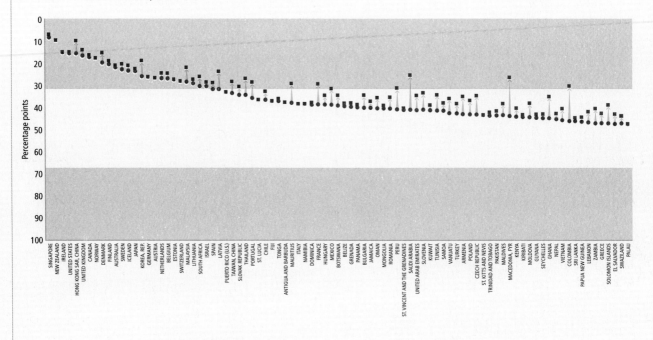

FIGURE 1.9   Who advanced the most in closing the gap to the frontier?

Progress in narrowing distance to frontier, 2005–11

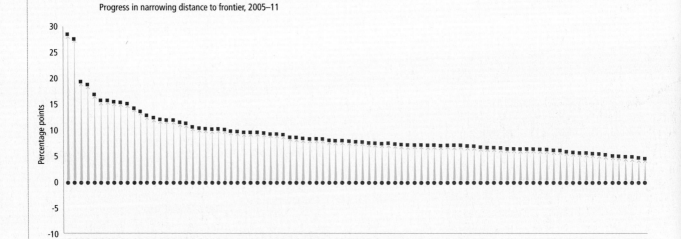

● 2005   ■ 2011

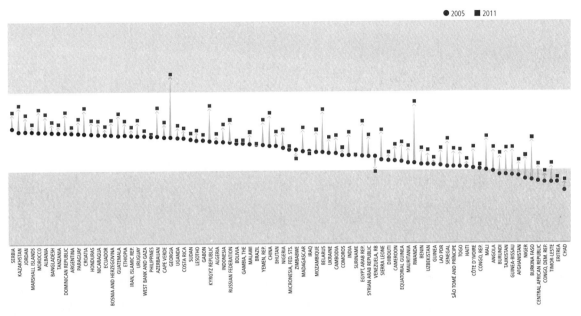

Note: The distance to frontier measure illustrates the distance of an economy to the "frontier"—a synthetic measure based on the most efficient practice or highest score achieved by any economy on each of the indicators in 9 *Doing Business* indicator sets (excluding the employing workers and getting electricity indicators) since 2005. The vertical axis represents the distance to the frontier, and 0 the most efficient regulatory environment (frontier practice). The data refer to the 174 economies included in *Doing Business 2006* (2005). Additional economies were added in subsequent years.

Source: Doing Business database.

● 2005   ■ 2011

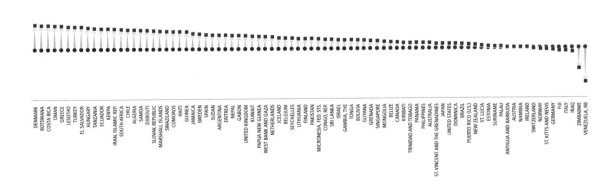

Note: Figure shows the absolute difference for each economy between its distance to frontier in 2005 and that in 2011.

Source: Doing Business database.

FIGURE 1.10   Economies with broader and more sustained business regulation reforms moved a greater distance toward the frontier

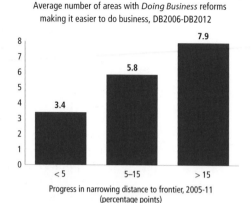

Average number of areas with *Doing Business* reforms making it easier to do business, DB2006-DB2012

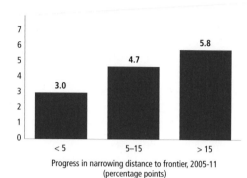

Average number of years with *Doing Business* reforms making it easier to do business, DB2006-DB2012

Note: The data refer to the 174 economies included in *Doing Business 2006* (2005). Additional economies were added in subsequent years.

Source: Doing Business database.

BOX 1.3   Broad approach to regulatory reform over time in Rwanda and Georgia

Rwanda's broad and sustained approach to regulatory reform shows up in progress toward the frontier in a range of areas (see figure on Rwanda). The economy has undertaken ambitious land and judicial reforms, often years in the making. Since 2001 it has introduced new corporate, insolvency, civil procedure and secured transactions laws. And it has streamlined and remodeled institutions and processes for starting a business, registering property, trading across borders and enforcing a contract through the courts.

Rwanda's broad approach to making regulation business-friendly

Distance to frontier, 2005 and 2011

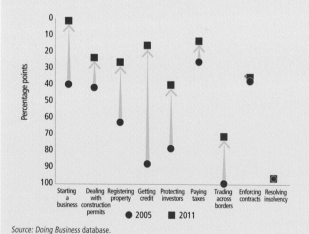

Source: Doing Business database.

Georgia too has pursued broad-ranging business regulation reform (see figure on Georgia). Since 2005 the economy has introduced a new company law and customs code. A new property registry replaced a confusing system requiring duplicate approvals by multiple agencies. The economy's first credit information bureau and large-scale judicial reforms followed.

In 2008 Georgian firms recognized the low levels of bureaucracy and flexible business environment in enterprise surveys. Senior managers

reported spending less than 2% of their time dealing with government regulations, down from about 10% in 2002 and the smallest share among economies in Eastern Europe and Central Asia. Only 4% of firms expected to make informal payments to public officials to get things done, compared with a regional average of 17%.

Georgian firms participating in survey rounds in both 2005 and 2008 reported adding an average of 23 permanent workers (increasing the average from 61 to 84) during that period.[1] They also reported a big drop in visits from or required meetings with tax officials, from an average of 8 in 2005 to only 0.4 in 2008. This result may be related to a new tax code that took effect at the start of 2005, reducing the categories of taxes from 21 to 9.

Yet more remains to be done to improve the overall business environment. Enterprise surveys show that security and infrastructure remain among the top concerns of businesses in Georgia.

How Georgia is closing the distance to the frontier

Distance to frontier, 2005 and 2011

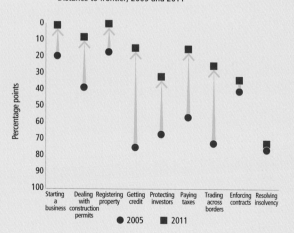

Source: Doing Business database.

1. World Bank 2009c.

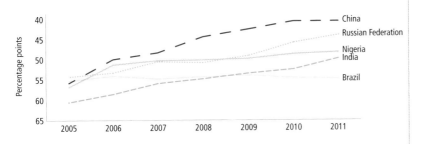

FIGURE 1.11 China has been making steady progress toward the frontier
Distance to frontier, 2005–11

Source: Doing Business database.

A friendly competition has emerged as economies adopt proven regulatory practices from others. Lessons from others have proved invaluable for such economies as Colombia, Georgia, the former Yugoslav Republic of Macedonia and Rwanda. Within larger economies good practices can often be found across state borders (see the case study on Mexico).

Practitioners interested in learning from others have more resources to turn to. This year's topic chapters provide the basis for web content and a new online database on practices and experiences in business regulation reform around the world. A series of case studies will explore how economies have integrated regulatory reform into broader competitiveness strategies or approached regulatory reform more generally. This year's report presents the cases of Korea, FYR Macedonia, Mexico and the United Kingdom.

These expanding resources, including a growing time series of data on business regulation, are allowing more empirical research that sheds light on synergies among different areas of regulation and on the effect of regulatory reform on such economic outcomes as informality, corruption, employment and economic growth. The evidence is encouraging. It suggests that if key bottlenecks

Among the 12 economies improving the most in the ease of doing business in 2010/11, two-thirds are low- or lower-middle-income economies. All implemented regulatory reforms making it easier to do business in 3 or more of the 10 areas included in this year's aggregate ranking (table 1.2).

THE ADVANTAGE OF BEING A LATE STARTER

Many economies have the advantage today of being able to learn from the experience of others. And many are already adopting good practices from other economies (table 1.3). To help identify such practices, this year *Doing Business* is electronically publishing topic chapters that provide an overview

of what has worked and why in 11 areas of business regulation, from business entry to exit. These chapters also provide insights into the importance of each area and show global trends.[19]

WHAT TO EXPECT NEXT?

Doing Business has been measuring and tracking business regulation around the world for the past 9 years. During this time most economies have made their regulatory environment for local firms more business-friendly. Firms create jobs, and policy makers play a key role in creating a regulatory environment that encourages their creation, growth and investment.

TABLE 1.2	Economies that improved the most across 3 or more areas measured by *Doing Business* in 2010/11												
	Ease of doing business rank			Reforms making it easier to do business										
	DB2012	DB2011	Improvement	Starting a business	Dealing with construction permits	Getting electricity	Registering property	Getting credit	Protecting investors	Paying taxes	Trading across borders	Enforcing contracts	Resolving insolvency
1 Morocco	94	115	-21		√				√	√			
2 Moldova	81	99	-18	√				√				√	√
3 Macedonia, FYR	22	34	-12		√		√	√					√
4 São Tomé and Príncipe	163	174	-11	√	√		√				√		
5 Latvia	21	31	-10	√		√	√						√
Cape Verde	119	129	-10				√	√					√
6 Sierra Leone	141	150	-9					√			√	√	√
7 Burundi	169	177	-8		√				√	√			√
8 Solomon Islands	74	81	-7	√			√		√				√
Korea, Rep.	8	15	-7	√							√	√	
9 Armenia	55	61	-6	√	√			√		√			√
10 Colombia	42	47	-5	√							√		√

Note: Economies are ranked on the number of their net reforms and on how much they improved in the ease of doing business ranking. First, Doing Business selects the economies that implemented reforms making it easier to do business in 3 or more of the 10 topics included in this year's aggregate ranking (see box 1.2). Regulatory reforms making it more difficult to do business are subtracted from the number of those making it easier to do business. Second, Doing Business ranks these economies on the increase in their ranking on the ease of doing business from the previous year using comparable rankings. The larger the improvement, the higher the ranking as the most improved.

Source: Doing Business database.

TABLE 1.3	Good practices around the world, by *Doing Business* topic		
Topic	Practice	Economiesª	Examples
Making it easy to start a business	Putting procedures online	110	Hong Kong SAR, China; Kuwait; FYR Macedonia; New Zealand; Peru; Puerto Rico (U.S.); Singapore
	Having a one-stop shop	83	Bahrain; Burkina Faso; Georgia; Republic of Korea; Uruguay; Vietnam
	Having no minimum capital requirement	82	Kenya; Madagascar; Portugal; Rwanda; United Arab Emirates; United Kingdom
Making it easy to deal with construction permits	Having an organized set of building rules	116	Croatia; Kenya; New Zealand; Republic of Yemen
	Using risk-based building approvals	86	Armenia; Germany; Mauritius; Singapore
	Having a one-stop shop	26	Bahrain; Chile; Hong Kong SAR, China; Rwanda
Making it easy to register property	Using an electronic database for encumbrances	108	Jamaica; Sweden; United Kingdom
	Setting effective time limits for registration	54	Botswana; Guatemala; Indonesia
	Offering cadastre information online	50	Denmark; Lithuania; Malaysia
	Offering expedited procedures	16	Azerbaijan; Bulgaria; Georgia
	Setting fixed transfer fees	15	New Zealand; Russian Federation; Rwanda
Making it easy to get credit	Allowing out-of-court enforcement	123	Australia; India; Nepal; Peru; Russian Federation; Serbia; Sri Lanka; United States
	Distributing data on loans below 1% of income per capita	119	Brazil; Bulgaria; Germany; Kenya; Malaysia; Sri Lanka; West Bank and Gaza
	Distributing both positive and negative credit information	100	China; Croatia; India; Italy; Jordan; Panama; South Africa
	Allowing a general description of collateral	91	Cambodia; Canada; Chile; Nigeria; Romania; Singapore; Vanuatu; Vietnam
	Maintaining a unified registry	68	Bosnia and Herzegovina; Guatemala; Honduras; Marshall Islands; Federated States of Micronesia; Montenegro; New Zealand; Romania; Solomon Islands
	Distributing credit information from retailers, trade creditors or utilities as well as financial institutions	54	Fiji; Lithuania; Nicaragua; Rwanda; Saudi Arabia; Spain
Protecting investors	Allowing rescissionᵇ of prejudicial related-party transactions	70	Brazil; Mauritius; Rwanda; United States
	Regulating approval of related-party transactions	60	France; Iceland; Indonesia; Lebanon; United Kingdom
	Requiring detailed disclosure	52	Hong Kong SAR, China; Israel; New Zealand; Singapore
	Allowing access to all corporate documents during the trial	45	Chile; Ireland; Morocco; Peru; Poland
	Defining clear duties for directors in case of related-party transactions	45	Colombia; Malaysia; Mexico; United States; Vietnam
	Requiring external review of related-party transactions	41	Australia; Burundi; Arab Republic of Egypt; Norway
	Allowing access to all corporate documents *before* the trial	31	Greece; Japan; South Africa; Sweden
Making it easy to pay taxes	Allowing self-assessment	145	Argentina; Canada; China; Arab Republic of Egypt; Rwanda; Sri Lanka; Turkey
	Allowing electronic filing and payment	66	Australia; Colombia; India; Lithuania; Mauritius; Singapore; Tunisia
	Having one tax per tax base	49	Hong Kong SAR, China; FYR Macedonia; Morocco; Namibia; Paraguay; United Kingdom
Making it easy to trade across bordersᶜ	Using electronic data interchange	130ᵈ	Belize; Chile; Estonia; Pakistan; Turkey
	Using risk-based inspections	97	Morocco; Nigeria; Palau; Suriname; Vietnam
	Providing a single window	49ᵉ	Colombia; Ghana; Republic of Korea; Singapore
Making it easy to enforce contracts	Making judgments publicly available	122ᶠ	Australia; Austria; Chile; Dominican Republic; Greece; Mozambique; Nigeria; Uruguay
	Maintaining specialized commercial court, division or judge	87	Burkina Faso; France; Lesotho; Saudi Arabia; Sierra Leone; Singapore
	Allowing electronic filing of complaints	16	Australia; Republic of Korea; Malaysia; Russian Federation; United Kingdom
Making it easy to resolve insolvency	Allowing creditors' committees a say in relevant decisions	103	Bulgaria; Philippines; South Africa
	Requiring professional or academic qualifications for insolvency administrators by law	64	Cape Verde; Namibia
	Providing a legal framework for out-of-court workouts	45	Italy; Philippines

Note: Good practices making it easy to get electricity will be included in *Doing Business 2013.*

a. Among 183 economies surveyed, unless otherwise specified.
b. The right of parties involved in a contract to return to a state identical to that before they entered into the agreement.
c. Among 159 economies surveyed for electronic data interchange, 152 for risk-based inspections and 150 for single window.
d. Twenty-six have a full electronic data interchange system, 104 a partial one.
e. Twenty have a single-window system that links all relevant government agencies, 29 a system that does not.
f. Among 175 economies surveyed.

Source: Doing Business database; for starting a business, also World Bank (2009b).

are identified, targeted changes can have a substantial effect on new firm creation, productivity and employment. Because many regulations interact, implementing regulatory reform in several areas has synergistic effects. It is also important to recognize that regulatory reforms can take time to translate into changes in the economy. [20]

Other World Bank Group initiatives provide data complementing the *Doing Business* resources. Two global data sets support the exploration of other areas of analysis—one focusing on laws and regulations specific to women's participation in the economy and the other on those relating to foreign companies' engagement in the domestic economy.[21] Enterprise surveys covering 125 economies over 9 years allow researchers and policy makers to assess what the private sector looks like in an economy at a given time—in terms of firm size, sector of activity and geographic location.[22] Through direct interviews with more than 130,000 firms around the world, these surveys examine a range of issues relating to the business environment, including the biggest constraints as perceived by businesses.

The agenda for research into what regulations constitute binding constraints, what package of regulatory reforms is most effective and how these issues are shaped by the context in an economy is still unfinished. To stimulate new research in this area, *Doing Business* plans to hold a conference in the fall of 2012. Its aim will be to deepen our understanding of the links between business regulation reforms and broader economic outcomes.

NOTES

1. Narayan and others 2000.

2. Ayyagari, Demirgüç-Kunt and Maksimovic 2011.

3. Only 27% of all regulatory reforms recorded by *Doing Business* for economies in the Middle East and North Africa over the past 6 years were in the areas of getting credit, protecting investors, enforcing contracts and resolving insolvency. In Eastern Europe and Central Asia 38% of all regulatory reforms recorded were in these areas.

4. Research shows that business regulations of the type measured by *Doing Business* affect the creation of new firms in the local market, the productivity levels of those firms and the creation of employment. Cross-country studies show that greater ease of entry is associated with a higher firm entry rate and greater business density on average. Encouraging evidence from economies as diverse as Colombia, India, Mexico and Portugal also supports these findings. For more on this and other relevant research, see the chapter "About *Doing Business*: measuring for impact."

5. Public procurement, while not covered by any of the *Doing Business* indicators, is another area in which a growing number of governments are using electronic platforms. The aim is to increase transparency in the relationships between public officials and suppliers.

6. Nineteen U.K. government departments participated in the program, which started with an extensive quantification exercise in the summer of 2005. In May 2010 the target was met: a total cost reduction for businesses of £3.5 billion. Based on this experience, a new target was set: to cut the ongoing costs of regulation by another £6.5 billion by 2015 (http://www.bis.gov.uk).

7. European Commission 2011.

8. The assignment was to compile the latest research findings on regulatory burden, regulatory simplification and regulatory impact on business and to examine what effects direct and indirect costs have on businesses and the economy (Swedish Agency for Growth Policy Analysis 2010).

9. http://www.businesslink.gov.uk.

10. This pattern of relatively large variation across indicator sets is not specific to *Doing Business*. A similar pattern can be discerned in, for example, the World Economic Forum's Global Competitiveness Index, a broader measure capturing such factors as macroeconomic stability, the soundness of

public institutions, aspects of human capital and the sophistication of the business community. The United States and Japan, as leaders in technology, score extremely well on measures of innovation. But with large budget deficits and high levels of public debt, they do less well on measures of macroeconomic stability.

11. Some members of the Corporate Registrars Forum are Australia; Bangladesh; Bermuda; Botswana; the British Virgin Islands; Burkina Faso; Canada; the Cook Islands; Croatia; Hong Kong SAR, China; India; Jordan; FYR Macedonia; Malawi; Malaysia; Mauritius; Nepal; the Netherlands; New Zealand; Nigeria; Pakistan; Rwanda; Samoa; Singapore; South Africa; Sri Lanka; Tunisia; the United Arab Emirates; the United Kingdom; and Vanuatu. (http://www.corporateregistersforum.org/member-jurisdictions).

12. See also World Bank (2009a, 2010a).

13. Aghion and others 2008.

14. Bruhn 2011.

15. Kaplan, Piedra and Seira 2007.

16. Eifert 2009.

17. Rauch 2010.

18. These include economies across regions: In East and South Asia, India; Malaysia; Sri Lanka; Taiwan, China; Thailand; and Vietnam. In the Middle East and North Africa, Egypt; Morocco; Saudi Arabia; the United Arab Emirates; and the Republic of Yemen. In Eastern Europe and Central Asia, Georgia; Kazakhstan; the Kyrgyz Republic; Moldova; and Tajikistan. In Sub-Saharan Africa, Botswana; Burundi; the Central African Republic; the Comoros; the Democratic Republic of Congo; Kenya; Liberia; Malawi; Mali; and Zambia. And in Latin America, Guatemala; Mexico; and Peru.

19. Topic chapters are available on the *Doing Business* website (http://www.doing business.org).

20. For more information on relevant research, see the chapter "About *Doing Business*: measuring for impact."

21. The databases are Women, Business and the Law (http://wbl.worldbank.org/) and Investing Across Borders (http://iab.worldbank.org/).

22. World Bank Enterprise Surveys (http://www.enterprisesurveys.org).

About *Doing Business*: measuring for impact

A vibrant private sector—with firms making investments, creating jobs and improving productivity—promotes growth and expands opportunities for poor people. To foster a vibrant private sector, governments around the world have implemented wide-ranging reforms, including price liberalization and macroeconomic stabilization programs. But governments committed to the economic health of their country and opportunities for its citizens focus on more than macroeconomic conditions. They also pay attention to the quality of laws, regulations and institutional arrangements that shape daily economic activity.

Until 10 years ago, however, there were no globally available indicator sets for monitoring such microeconomic factors and analyzing their relevance. The first efforts to address this gap, in the 1980s, drew on perceptions data from expert or business surveys that capture often one-time experiences of businesses. Such surveys can be useful gauges of economic and policy conditions. But few perception surveys provide indicators with a global coverage that are updated annually.

The *Doing Business* project takes a different approach from perception surveys. It looks at domestic, primarily small and medium-size companies and measures the regulations applying to them through their life cycle. Based on standardized case studies, it presents quantitative indicators on business regulation that can be compared across 183 economies and over time. This approach complements the perception surveys in exploring the major constraints for businesses, as experienced by the businesses themselves and as set out in the regulations that apply to them.

Rules and regulations are under the direct control of policy makers—and policy makers intending to change the experience and behavior of businesses will often start by changing rules and regulations that affect them. *Doing Business* goes beyond identifying that a problem exists and points to specific regulations or regulatory procedures that may lend themselves to reform (table 2.1). And its quantitative measures of business regulation enable research on how specific regulations affect firm behavior and economic outcomes.

The first *Doing Business* report, published in 2003, covered 5 indicator sets and 133 economies. This year's report covers 11 indicator sets and 183 economies. Ten topics are included in the aggregate ranking on the ease of doing business and other summary measures.[1] The project has benefited from feedback from governments, academics, practitioners and reviewers.[2] The initial goal remains: to provide an objective basis for understanding and improving the regulatory environment for business.

WHAT *DOING BUSINESS* COVERS

An entrepreneur's willingness to try a new idea may be influenced by many factors, including perceptions of how easy (or difficult) it will be to deal with the array of rules that define and underpin the business environment. Whether the entrepreneur decides to move forward with the idea, to abandon it or to take it elsewhere might depend in large part on how simple it is to comply with the requirements for opening a new business or getting a construction permit and how efficient the mechanisms are for resolving commercial disputes or dealing with insolvency. *Doing Business* provides quantitative measures of regulations for starting a business, dealing with construction permits, getting electricity, registering property, getting credit, protecting investors, paying taxes, trading across borders, enforcing contracts and resolving insolvency—as they apply to domestic small and medium-size enterprises.[3] It also looks at regulations on employing workers.

A fundamental premise of *Doing Business* is that economic activity requires good rules. These include rules that establish and clarify property rights and reduce the cost of resolving disputes, rules that increase the predictability of economic interactions and rules that provide contractual partners with core protections against abuse. The objective: regulations designed to be simple and efficient in implementation and accessible

TABLE 2.1	*Doing Business* methodology allows an objective but limited global comparison
Advantages	**Limitations**
Transparent, based on *factual information* about laws and regulations (with an element of judgment on time estimates)	*Limited in scope*: focuses on 11 areas of regulation affecting local businesses; does not measure all aspects of business environment or all areas of regulation
Comparison and *benchmarking* valid thanks to *standard assumptions*	Based on *standardized case*: transactions described in case scenario refer to specific set of issues and type of company
Inexpensive and easily replicable	Focuses on *formal sector*
Actionable: data highlight extent of specific obstacles, identify source, point to what might be changed	Only *reforms related to indicators* can be tracked
Multiple interactions with local respondents to clarify potential misinterpretation	Assumes that business has full information on what is required and does not waste time when completing procedures
Nearly complete *coverage of world's economies*	Part of data obtained refer to an economy's *largest business city only*

to all who need to use them. Accordingly, some *Doing Business* indicators give a higher score for more regulation, such as stricter disclosure requirements in related-party transactions. Some give a higher score for a simplified way of implementing existing regulation, such as completing business start-up formalities in a one-stop shop.

The *Doing Business* project encompasses 2 types of data. The first come from readings of laws and regulations by both the local expert respondents and *Doing Business*. The second are time-and-motion indicators that measure the efficiency in achieving a regulatory goal (such as granting the legal identity of a business). Within the time-and-motion indicators, cost estimates are recorded from official fee schedules where applicable. A regulatory process such as starting a business or registering property is broken down into clearly defined steps and procedures. The time estimates for each procedure are based on the informed judgment of expert respondents who routinely administer or advise on the relevant regulations.[4] Here, *Doing Business* builds on Hernando de Soto's pioneering work in applying the time-and-motion approach first used by Frederick Taylor to revolutionize the production of the Model T Ford. De Soto used the approach in the 1980s to show the obstacles to setting up a garment factory on the outskirts of Lima.[5]

WHAT *DOING BUSINESS* DOES NOT COVER

Just as important as knowing what *Doing Business* does is to know what it does not do—to understand what limitations must be kept in mind in interpreting the data.

Limited in scope

Doing Business focuses on 11 topics, with the specific aim of measuring the regulation relevant to the life cycle of a domestic firm (table 2.2). Accordingly:

• *Doing Business* does not measure all aspects of the business environment that matter to firms or investors—or all factors that affect competitiveness. It does not, for example, measure security, corruption, market size, macroeconomic stability, the state of the financial system, the labor skills of the population or all aspects of the quality of infrastructure. Nor does it focus on regulations specific to foreign investment.

• While *Doing Business* focuses on the quality of the regulatory framework, it is not all-inclusive; it does not cover all regulations in any economy. As economies and technology advance, more areas of economic activity are being regulated. For example, the European Union's body of laws (*acquis*) has now grown to no fewer than 14,500 rule sets. *Doing Business*

covers 11 areas of a company's life cycle, through 11 specific sets of indicators. These indicator sets do not cover all aspects of regulation in the area of focus. For example, the indicators on starting a business or protecting investors do not cover all aspects of commercial legislation. The employing workers indicators do not cover all areas of labor regulation. The current set of indicators does not, for example, include measures of regulations addressing safety at work or the right of collective bargaining.

• *Doing Business* also does not attempt to measure all costs and benefits of a particular law or regulation to society as a whole. The paying taxes indicators, for example, measure the total tax rate, which is a cost to business. The indicators do not measure, nor are they intended to measure, the social and economic programs funded through tax revenues. Measuring business laws and regulations provides one input into the debate on the regulatory burden associated with achieving regulatory objectives. Those objectives can differ across economies.

Based on standardized case scenarios

Doing Business indicators are built on the basis of standardized case scenarios with specific assumptions, such as the business being located in the largest business city of the economy. Economic indicators commonly make limiting assumptions of this kind. Inflation statistics, for example, are often based on prices of a set of consumer goods in a few urban areas.

Such assumptions allow global coverage and enhance comparability. But they come at the expense of generality. *Doing Business* recognizes the limitations of including data on only the largest business city. Business regulation and its enforcement, particularly in federal states and large economies, may differ across the country. Recognizing governments' interest in such variation, *Doing Business* has complemented its global indicators with subnational studies in a range of economies (box 2.1). This year *Doing Business* also conducted a pilot study on the second largest city in 3 large economies to assess within-country variations.

TABLE 2.2	*Doing Business*—measuring 11 areas of business regulation		
Start-up	**Expansion**	**Operations**	**Insolvency**
• Starting a business *Minimum capital requirement* *Procedures, time and cost*	• Registering property *Procedures, time and cost* • Getting credit *Credit information systems* *Movable collateral laws* • Protecting investors *Disclosure and liability in related-party transactions* • Enforcing contracts *Procedures, time and cost to resolve a commercial dispute*	• Dealing with construction permits *Procedures, time and cost* • Getting electricity *Procedures, time and cost* • Paying taxes *Payments, time and total tax rate* • Trading across borders *Documents, time and cost* • Employing workers	• Resolving insolvency *Time, cost and recovery rate*

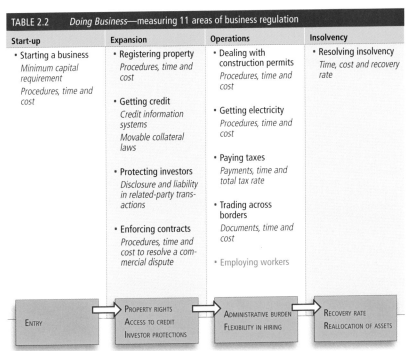

In areas where regulation is complex and highly differentiated, the standardized case used to construct the *Doing Business* indicator needs to be carefully defined. Where relevant, the standardized case assumes a limited liability company or its legal equivalent. This choice is in part empirical: private, limited liability companies are the most prevalent business form in many economies around the world. The choice also reflects one focus of *Doing Business*: expanding opportunities for entrepreneurship. Investors are encouraged to venture into business when potential losses are limited to their capital participation.

Focused on the formal sector

In constructing the indicators, *Doing Business* assumes that entrepreneurs are knowledgeable about all regulations in place and comply with them. In practice, entrepreneurs may spend considerable time finding out where to go and what documents to submit. Or they may avoid legally required procedures altogether—by not registering for social security, for example.

Where regulation is particularly onerous, levels of informality are higher. Informality comes at a cost: firms in the informal sector typically grow more slowly, have poorer access to credit and employ fewer workers— and their workers remain outside the protections of labor law.[6] All this may be even more so for female-owned businesses, according to country-specific research.[7] Firms in the informal sector are also less likely to pay taxes. *Doing Business* measures one set of factors that help explain the occurrence of informality and give policy makers insights into potential areas of regulatory reform. Gaining a fuller understanding of the broader business environment, and a broader perspective on policy challenges, requires combining insights from *Doing Business* with data from other sources, such as the World Bank Enterprise Surveys.[8]

WHY THIS FOCUS

Doing Business functions as a kind of cholesterol test for the regulatory environment for domestic businesses. A cholesterol test does not tell us everything about the state of our health. But it does measure something important for our health. And it puts us on watch to change behaviors in ways that will improve not only our cholesterol rating but also our overall health.

One way to test whether *Doing Business* serves as a proxy for the broader business environment and for competitiveness is to look at correlations between the *Doing Business* rankings and other major economic benchmarks. Closest to *Doing Business* in what it measures is the set of indicators on product market regulation compiled by the Organisation for Economic Co-operation and Development (OECD). These indicators are designed to help assess the extent to which the regulatory environment promotes or inhibits competition. They include measures of the extent of price controls, the licensing and permit system, the degree of simplification of rules and procedures, the administrative burdens and legal and regulatory barriers, the prevalence of discriminatory procedures and the degree of government control over business enterprises.[9] The rankings on these indicators—for the 39 countries that are

---

BOX 2.1   Comparing regulation within economies: subnational *Doing Business* indicators and a multicity pilot study

Subnational *Doing Business* studies are conducted at the request of a government and capture differences in business regulation across cities within the same economy or region. They build local capacity by involving government partners and local think tanks. Since 2005 subnational *Doing Business* reports have compared business regulation in states and cities within such economies as Brazil, China, Colombia, Egypt, India, Indonesia, Kenya, Mexico, Morocco, Nigeria, Pakistan and the Philippines.[1]

Subnational studies increasingly are being periodically updated to measure progress over time or to expand geographic coverage to additional cities. This year that is the case for the subnational studies in the Philippines; the regional report in Southeast Europe; the ongoing studies in Italy, Kenya and the United Arab Emirates; and the projects implemented jointly with local think tanks in Indonesia, Mexico and the Russian Federation.

In 2011 *Doing Business* published subnational indicators for the Philippines and a regional report for 7 economies in Southeast Europe (Albania, Bosnia and Herzegovina, Kosovo, FYR Macedonia, Moldova, Montenegro and Serbia) that covers 22 cities. It also published a city profile for Juba, in the Republic of South Sudan.

To further explore variations in business regulation within economies, *Doing Business* this year collected data on all 10 indicator sets included in the ease of doing business ranking in an additional city in 3 large economies: in Rio de Janeiro in Brazil (in addition to São Paulo), Beijing in China (in addition to Shanghai) and St. Petersburg in the Russian Federation (in addition to Moscow). Subnational studies usually cover only a subset of indicators.

The results show no variation between cities within each economy in areas governed by laws or regulations such as the civil procedure code, listing rules for companies and incorporation rules. For rules governing secured transactions, for example, entrepreneurs in Brazil all refer to the Civil Code of 2002, those in China to the Property Rights Law of 2007 and those in Russia to the Civil Code of 1994 and Law on Pledge of 1992.

But the efficiency of regulatory processes—such as starting a business or dealing with construction permits—and that of institutions do differ across cities, because of differences either in local regulations or in the capacity of institutions to respond to business demand. In Russia, dealing with construction permits is more complex in Moscow than in St. Petersburg. In Brazil, starting a business, dealing with construction permits and getting electricity take less time in Rio de Janeiro than in the larger São Paulo. But property registration is slightly more efficient in São Paulo than in Rio de Janeiro. This is thanks to São Paulo's digitized cadastre.

In all 3 economies the number of taxes and contributions varies between cities. In China businesses in both cities have to comply with 3 state-administered taxes (value added tax, corporate tax and business tax). But while companies in Beijing need to comply with 6 locally administered taxes, those in Shanghai must comply with 7. Distance to the port plays a role in the time to import and export. The cities housing a main port—Rio de Janeiro, Shanghai and St. Petersburg—have faster and cheaper inland transport than those where entrepreneurs need to hire someone to go to another city to ship or receive their cargo— São Paulo (to Santos), Beijing (to Tianjin) and Moscow (to St. Petersburg).

1. Subnational reports are available on the *Doing Business* website at http://www.doingbusiness.org/reports/subnational-reports.

covered, several of them large emerging markets—are highly correlated with those on the ease of doing business (the correlation here is 0.72; figure 2.1).

Similarly, there is a high correlation (0.82) between the rankings on the ease of doing business and those on the World Economic Forum's Global Competitiveness Index, a much broader measure capturing such factors as macroeconomic stability, aspects of human capital, the soundness of public institutions and the sophistication of the business community (figure 2.2).[10] Economies that do well on the *Doing Business* indicators tend to do well on the OECD market regulation indicators and the Global Competitiveness Index and vice versa.

A bigger question is whether the issues on which *Doing Business* focuses matter for development and poverty reduction. The World Bank study *Voices of the Poor* asked 60,000 poor people around the world how they thought they might escape poverty.[11] The answers were unequivocal: women and men alike pin their hopes above all on income from their own business or wages earned in employment. Enabling growth—and ensuring that poor people can participate in its benefits—requires an environment where new entrants with drive and good ideas, regardless of their gender or ethnic origin, can get started in business and where good firms can invest and grow, generating more jobs.

Small and medium-size enterprises are key drivers of competition, growth and job creation, particularly in developing economies. But in these economies up to 80% of economic activity takes place in the informal sector. Firms may be prevented from entering the formal sector by excessive bureaucracy and regulation. Even firms operating in the formal sector might not have equal access to transparent rules and regulations affecting their ability to compete, innovate and grow.

Where regulation is burdensome and competition limited, success tends to depend more on whom you know than on what you can do.[12] But where regulation is transparent, efficient and implemented in a simple way, it becomes easier for any aspiring entrepreneurs, regardless of their connections, to

FIGURE 2.1   A strong correlation between *Doing Business* rankings and OECD rankings on product market regulation

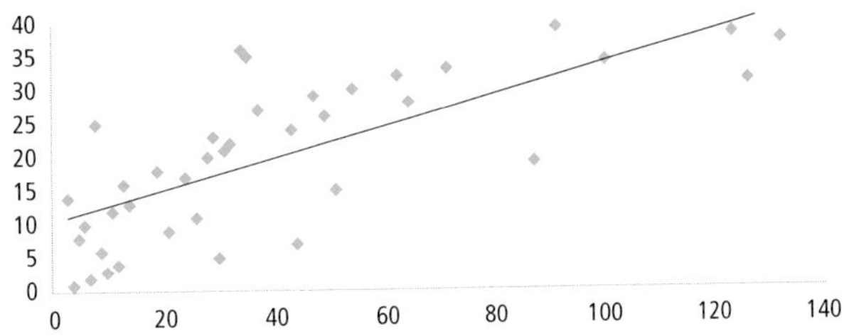

Ranking on OECD product market regulation indicators

Note: Correlation is significant at the 5% level when controlling for income per capita.
Source: Doing Business database; OECD data.

FIGURE 2.2   A similarly strong correlation between *Doing Business* rankings and World Economic Forum rankings on global competitiveness

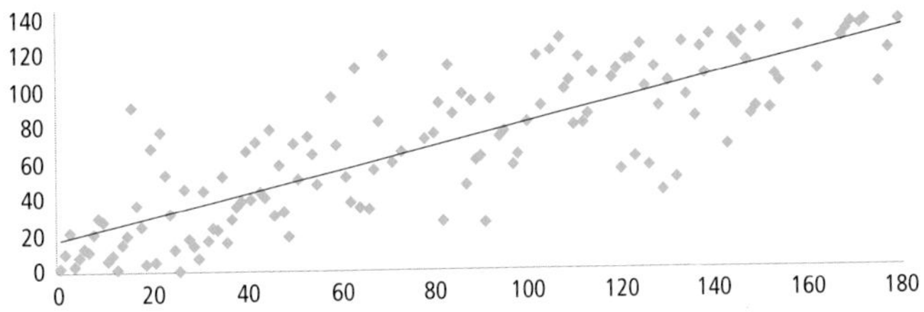

Ranking on Global Competitiveness Index

Note: Correlation is significant at the 5% level when controlling for income per capita.
Source: Doing Business database; WEF 2010.

operate within the rule of law and to benefit from the opportunities and protections that the law provides. Not surprisingly, higher rankings on the ease of doing business—based on 10 areas of business regulation measured by *Doing Business*—are correlated with better governance and lower levels of perceived corruption.[13]

In this sense *Doing Business* values good rules as a key to social inclusion. It also provides a basis for studying effects of regulations and their application. For example, *Doing Business 2004* found that faster contract enforcement was associated with perceptions of greater judicial fairness—suggesting that justice delayed is justice denied.[14]

DOING BUSINESS AS A BENCHMARKING EXERCISE

Doing Business, in capturing some key dimensions of regulatory regimes, has been found useful for benchmarking—an aspect allowing decision makers to make more

considered judgments on the policy options available, enhancing the ability to assess progress over time and make meaningful international comparisons, and contributing to public debate and the promotion of greater accountability.

Since 2006 *Doing Business* has provided 2 takes on the data it collects: it presents "absolute" indicators for each economy for each of the 11 regulatory topics it addresses, and it provides rankings of economies for 10 topics, both by topic and in aggregate.[15] In addition, as noted in the executive summary, this year's report introduces a new measure—the distance to frontier measure—that illustrates how an economy's regulatory environment has changed over time.[16] Judgment is required in interpreting all these measures for any economy and in determining a sensible and politically feasible path for regulatory reform.

Reviewing the *Doing Business* rankings in isolation may reveal unexpected results. Some economies may rank unexpectedly high on some topics. And some economies that have had rapid growth or attracted a great deal of investment may rank lower than others that appear to be less dynamic.

As economies develop, they strengthen and add to regulations to protect investor and property rights. Meanwhile, they find more efficient ways to implement existing regulations and cut outdated ones. One finding of *Doing Business*: dynamic and growing economies continually reform and update their business regulations and their way of implementing them, while many poor economies still work with regulatory systems dating to the late 1800s.

For reform-minded governments, how much the regulatory environment for local entrepreneurs improves in absolute terms matters more than their economy's relative ranking on the overall ease of doing business. The distance to frontier measure aids in assessing such improvements over time by showing the distance of each economy to the "frontier," which represents the highest performance observed on each of the *Doing Business* indicators across all economies and years included since 2005. Comparing the measure for an economy at 2 points in time allows users to assess how much the economy's regulatory environment as measured by *Doing Business* has changed over time—how far it has moved toward (or away from) the most efficient practices and strongest regulations in the areas covered by *Doing Business*. The distance to frontier measure complements the yearly ease of doing business rankings that compare economies with one another at a point in time.

Each indicator set covered by *Doing Business* measures a different aspect of the business regulatory environment. The rankings of each economy vary, sometimes significantly, across the indicator sets. A quick way to assess the variability of an economy's regulatory performance across the different areas of business regulation is to look at the topic rankings (see the country tables). Korea, for example, stands at 8 in the overall ease of doing business ranking. Its ranking is 2 on the ease of enforcing contracts, 4 on the ease of trading across borders and 8 on the ease of getting credit. At the same time, it

has a ranking of 24 on the ease of starting a business, 26 on the ease of dealing with construction permits, 38 on the ease of paying taxes and 71 on the ease of registering property. Variation in performance across the indicator sets reflects the different priorities that governments give to particular areas of business regulation as well as economy-specific circumstances that may allow a faster pace of reform in some areas than in others.

WHAT RESEARCH SHOWS ON THE EFFECTS OF BUSINESS REGULATION

Nine years of *Doing Business* data, together with other data sets, have enabled a growing body of research on how specific areas of business regulation—and regulatory reforms in those areas—relate to social and economic outcomes. Some 873 articles have been published in peer-reviewed academic journals, and about 2,332 working papers are available through Google Scholar.[17]

Much attention has been given to exploring links to microeconomic outcomes, such as firm creation and employment. Recent research focuses on how business regulations affect the behavior of firms by creating incentives (or disincentives) to register and operate formally, to create jobs, to innovate and to increase productivity.[18] Many studies have also looked at the role played by courts, credit bureaus, and insolvency and collateral laws in providing incentives for creditors and investors to increase access to credit. The literature has produced a range of findings.

Lower costs for business registration encourage entrepreneurship and enhance firm productivity. Economies with efficient business registration have a higher entry rate by new firms as well as greater business density.[19] Economies where registering a new business takes less time have seen more businesses register in industries where the potential for growth is greatest, such as those that have experienced expansionary shifts in global demand or technology.[20] Reforms making it easier to start a business tend to have a significant positive effect on investment in product market industries such as transport, communications and utilities, which are often sheltered from competition.[21] There is also evidence that more efficient business entry

regulations improve firm productivity and macroeconomic performance.[22]

Simpler business registration translates into greater employment opportunities in the formal sector. Reducing start-up costs for new firms was found to result in higher take-up rates for education, higher rates of job creation for high-skilled labor and higher average productivity because new firms are often set up by high-skilled workers.[23] Lowering entry costs can boost legal certainty: businesses entering the formal sector gain access to the legal system, to the benefit of both themselves and their customers and suppliers.[24]

Assessing the impact of policy reforms poses challenges. While cross-country correlations can appear strong, it is difficult to isolate the effect of regulations given all the other potential factors that vary at the country level. Generally, cross-country correlations do not show whether a specific outcome is caused by a specific regulation or whether it coincides with other factors, such as a more positive economic situation. So how do we know whether things would have been different without a specific regulatory reform? Some studies have been able to test this by investigating variations within an economy over time. Other studies have investigated policy changes that affected only certain firms or groups. Several country-specific impact studies conclude that simpler entry regulations encourage the establishment of more new firms:

- In Mexico one study found that a program that simplified municipal licensing led to a 5% increase in the number of registered businesses and a 2.2% increase in wage employment, while competition from new entrants lowered prices by 0.6% and the income of incumbent businesses by 3.2%.[25] Other research found that the same licensing reform directly led to a 4% increase in new start-ups and that the program was more effective in municipalities with less corruption and cheaper additional registration procedures.[26]

- In India the progressive elimination of the "license raj" led to a 6% increase in new firm registrations, and highly productive firms entering the market saw larger increases in real output than less productive firms.[27] Simpler entry regulation and labor market flexibility were found to be complementary. States with more flexible employment regulations saw a 25% larger decrease in informal firms and 17.8% larger gains in real output than states with less flexible labor regulations.[28] The same licensing reform led to an aggregate productivity improvement of around 22% for firms affected by the reform.[29]

- In Colombia new firm registrations increased by 5.2% after the creation of a one-stop shop for businesses.[30]
- In Portugal the introduction of a one-stop shop for businesses led to a 17% increase in new firm registrations and 7 new jobs for every 100,000 inhabitants compared with economies that did not implement the reform.[31]

A sound regulatory environment leads to stronger trade performance. Efforts to streamline the institutional environment for trade (such as by increasing the efficiency of customs) have been shown to have positive effects on trade volumes.[32] One study found that an inefficient trade environment was among the main factors in poor trade performance in Sub-Saharan African countries.[33] Similarly, another study identified the government's ability to formulate and implement sound policies and regulations that promote private sector development, customs efficiency, quality of infrastructure and access to finance as important factors in improving trade performance.[34] The same study found that economies with more constrained access to foreign markets benefit more from improvements in the investment climate than those with easier access.

Research also shows that an economy's ability to enforce contracts is an important determinant of its comparative advantage in the global economy: among comparable economies, those with good contract enforcement tend to produce and export more customized products than those with poor contract enforcement.[35] Another study shows that in many developing economies production of high-quality output is a precondition for firms to become exporters: institutional reforms that lower the cost of high-quality production increase the positive effect that trade facilitation can have on income.[36] Research shows that removing

barriers to trade needs to be accompanied by other reforms, such as making labor markets more flexible, to achieve higher productivity and growth.[37]

Regulations and institutions that form part of the financial market infrastructure—including courts, credit information systems, and collateral, creditor and insolvency laws—play a role in easing access to credit. Enterprise surveys conducted by the World Bank show that access to credit is a major constraint to businesses around the world.[38] Good credit information systems and strong collateral laws can help alleviate financing constraints. Analysis in 12 transition economies found that reforms strengthening collateral laws increased the supply of bank loans by 13.7% on average.[39] Creditor rights and the existence of credit registries, whether public or private, are both associated with a higher ratio of private credit to GDP.[40] And greater information sharing through credit bureaus is associated with higher bank profitability and lower bank risk.[41]

Country-specific research assessed the effect of efficient debt recovery and exit processes in determining conditions of credit and in ensuring that less productive firms are either restructured or exit the market:

- The establishment of specialized debt recovery tribunals in India sped up the resolution of debt recovery claims and allowed lenders to seize more collateral on defaulting loans. It also increased the probability of repayment by 28% and lowered interest rates on loans by 1–2 percentage points.[42]
- Following a broad bankruptcy reform in Brazil in 2005 that, among other things, improved the protection of creditors, the cost of debt fell by 22% and the aggregate level of credit rose by 39%.[43]
- The introduction of improved insolvency regimes that streamlined mechanisms for reorganization reduced the number of liquidations by 8.4% in Belgium and by 13.6% in Colombia as more viable firms opted for reorganization instead.[44] In Colombia the new law better distinguished viable from nonviable firms, making survival more likely for financially distressed but viable firms.

HOW GOVERNMENTS USE *DOING BUSINESS*

Quantitative data and benchmarking can be useful in stimulating debate about policy, both by exposing potential challenges and by identifying where policy makers might look for lessons and good practices. For governments, a common first reaction to the *Doing Business* data is to ask questions about the quality and relevance of the data and about how the results are calculated. Yet the debate typically proceeds to a deeper discussion exploring the relevance of the data to the economy and areas where business regulation reform might make sense.

Most reformers start out by seeking examples, and *Doing Business* helps in this (boxes 2.2 and 2.3). For example, Saudi Arabia used the company law of France as a model for revising its own. Many countries in Africa look to Mauritius—the region's strongest performer on *Doing Business* indicators—as a source of good practices for business regulation reform. In the words of Luis Guillermo Plata, the former minister of commerce, industry and tourism of Colombia,

> It's not like baking a cake where you follow the recipe. No. We are all different. But we can take certain things, certain key lessons, and apply those lessons and see how they work in our environment.

Over the past 9 years there has been much activity by governments in reforming the regulatory environment for domestic businesses. Most reforms relating to *Doing Business* topics have been nested in broader programs of reform aimed at enhancing economic competitiveness, as in Colombia, Kenya and Liberia, for example. In structuring their reform programs for the business environment, governments use multiple data sources and indicators.[45] And reformers respond to many stakeholders and interest groups, all of whom bring important issues and concerns to the reform debate. World Bank Group dialogue with governments on the investment climate is designed to encourage critical use of the data, sharpening judgment, avoiding a narrow focus on improving *Doing Business* rankings and encouraging broad-based reforms that enhance the investment climate. The World

To ensure the coordination of efforts across agencies, such economies as Colombia and Rwanda have formed regulatory reform committees, reporting directly to the president, that use the *Doing Business* indicators as one input to inform their programs for improving the business environment. More than 25 other economies have formed such committees at the interministerial level. These include economies across regions: In East and South Asia, India; Malaysia; Sri Lanka; Taiwan, China; Thailand; and Vietnam. In the Middle East and North Africa, Egypt; Morocco; Saudi Arabia; the United Arab Emirates; and the Republic of Yemen. In Eastern Europe and Central Asia, Georgia; Kazakhstan; the Kyrgyz Republic; Moldova; and Tajikistan. In Sub-Saharan Africa, Botswana; Burundi; the Central African Republic; the Comoros; the Democratic Republic of Congo; Kenya; Liberia; Malawi; Mali; and Zambia. And in Latin America, Guatemala; Mexico; and Peru. Governments have reported more than 300 regulatory reforms that have been informed by *Doing Business* since 2003.

The Asia-Pacific Economic Cooperation (APEC) organization uses *Doing Business* to identify potential areas of regulatory reform, to champion economies that can help others improve and to set measurable targets. In 2009 APEC launched the Ease of Doing Business Action Plan with the goal of making it 25% cheaper, faster and easier to do business in the region by 2015.[1] The action plan sets specific targets, such as making it 25% faster to start a business by reducing the average time by 1 week.

Drawing on a firm survey, planners identified 5 priority areas: starting a business, getting credit, enforcing contracts, trading across borders and dealing with construction permits. APEC economies then selected 6 "champion economies" for the priority areas: New Zealand and the United States (starting a business), Japan (getting credit), Korea (enforcing contracts), Singapore (trading across borders) and Hong Kong SAR, China (dealing with construction permits). In 2010 and 2011 several of the champion economies organized workshops to develop programs for building capacity in their area of expertise.

1. APEC 2010.

Bank Group uses a vast range of indicators and analytics in this policy dialogue, including its Global Poverty Monitoring indicators, World Development Indicators, Logistics Performance Indicators and many others. With the open data initiative, all indicators and data are available to the public at http://data.worldbank.org.

METHODOLOGY AND DATA

Doing Business covers 183 economies—including small economies and some of the poorest economies, for which little or no data are available in other data sets. The *Doing Business* data are based on domestic laws and regulations as well as administrative requirements. (For a detailed explanation of the *Doing Business* methodology, see the data notes.)

Information sources for the data

Most of the *Doing Business* indicators are based on laws and regulations. In addition, most of the cost indicators are backed by official fee schedules. *Doing Business* respondents both fill out written questionnaires and provide references to the relevant laws, regulations and fee schedules, aiding data checking and quality assurance. Having representative samples of respondents is not an issue, as the texts of the relevant laws and regulations are collected and answers checked for accuracy.

For some indicators—for example, those on dealing with construction permits, enforcing contracts and resolving insolvency—the time component and part of the cost component (where fee schedules are lacking) are based on actual practice rather than the law on the books. This introduces a degree of judgment. The *Doing Business* approach has therefore been to work with legal practitioners or professionals who regularly undertake the transactions involved. Following the standard methodological approach for time-and-motion studies, *Doing Business* breaks down each process or transaction, such as starting and legally operating a business, into separate steps to ensure a better estimate of time. The time estimate for each step is given by practitioners with significant and routine experience in the transaction.

The *Doing Business* approach to data collection contrasts with that of firm surveys, which capture often one-time perceptions and experiences of businesses. A corporate lawyer registering 100–150 businesses a year will be more familiar with the process than an entrepreneur, who will register a business only once or maybe twice. A bankruptcy attorney or judge dealing with dozens of cases a year will have more insight into bankruptcy than a manager of a company who may have never undergone the process.

Doing Business respondents

Over the past 9 years more than 12,000 professionals in 183 economies have assisted in providing the data that inform the *Doing Business* indicators. This year's report draws on the inputs of more than 9,000 professionals. Table 4.1 in the data notes lists the number of respondents for each indicator set. The *Doing Business* website indicates the number of respondents for each economy and each indicator. Respondents are professionals or government officials who routinely administer or advise on the legal and regulatory requirements covered in each *Doing Business* topic. They are selected on the basis of their expertise in the specific areas covered by *Doing Business*. Because of the focus on legal and regulatory arrangements, most of the respondents are legal professionals such as lawyers, judges or notaries. The credit information survey is answered by officials of the credit registry or bureau. Freight forwarders, accountants, architects and other professionals answer the surveys related to trading across borders, taxes and construction permits.

Development of the methodology

The methodology for calculating each indicator is transparent, objective and easily replicable. Leading academics collaborated in the development of the indicators, ensuring academic rigor. Eight of the background papers underlying the indicators have been published in leading economic journals.[46]

Doing Business uses a simple averaging approach for weighting component indicators and calculating rankings. Other approaches were explored, including using principal components and unobserved components.[47] They turn out to yield results nearly identical to those of simple averaging. Thus *Doing Business* uses the simplest method: weighting all topics equally and, within each topic, giving equal weight to each of the topic components.[48]

Inclusion of getting electricity indicators

This year's ease of doing business ranking includes getting electricity as a new topic. The getting electricity indicators were introduced as a pilot in *Doing Business 2010* and *Doing Business 2011*, which presented the results in an annex. During the pilot phase the methodology was reviewed by experts, and data on the time, cost and procedures to obtain an electricity connection were collected for the full set of 183 economies. To avoid double counting, procedures related to getting an electricity connection have been removed from the dealing with construction permits indicators.[49]

Improvements to the methodology

The methodology has undergone continual improvement over the years.[50] Changes have been made mainly in response to suggestions providing new insights. For enforcing contracts, for example, the amount of the disputed claim in the case study was increased from 50% to 200% of income per capita after the first year of data collection, as it became clear that smaller claims were unlikely to go to court.

Another change relates to starting a business. The minimum capital requirement can be an obstacle for potential entrepreneurs. Initially *Doing Business* measured the required minimum capital regardless of whether it had to be paid up front or not. In many economies only part of the minimum capital has to be paid up front. To reflect the actual potential barrier to entry, the paid-in minimum capital has been used rather than the required minimum capital.

This year's report includes improvements in the methodology for the employing workers indicators and the getting credit (legal rights) indicators, in addition to the removal of the procedures related to getting an electricity connection from the dealing with construction permits indicators. It also

includes changes in the ranking methodology for paying taxes.

Employing workers methodology. With the aim of better capturing the balance between worker protection and efficient employment regulation that favors job creation, *Doing Business* has made a series of amendments to the methodology for the employing workers indicators over the past 4 years.

In addition, the World Bank Group has been working with a consultative group—including labor lawyers, employer and employee representatives, and experts from civil society, the private sector, the International Labour Organization (ILO) and the OECD—to review the methodology and explore future areas of research.[51] The consultative group completed its work this year, and its guidance has provided the basis for several changes in methodology (see also the data notes). A full report with the conclusions of the consultative group is available on the *Doing Business* website.[52]

Follow-on work is continuing to explore the measurement of worker protection to complement the measurement of the cost to employers of labor regulations. The data on worker protection will serve as a basis for the development of a joint analysis of worker protection by the World Bank Group and the ILO.

Pending further progress on research in this area, this year's report does not present rankings of economies on the employing workers indicators or include the topic in the aggregate ranking on the ease of doing business. It does present the data on the employing workers indicators. Additional data on labor regulations collected in 183 economies are available on the *Doing Business* website.[53]

Paying taxes methodology. *Doing Business* has benefited from dialogue with external stakeholders, including participants in the International Tax Dialogue, on the survey instrument and methodology for the paying taxes indicators. As a result of these consultations, this year's report introduces a threshold for the total tax rate for the purpose of calculating the ranking on the ease of paying taxes. All economies with a total tax rate below the threshold (which

will be calculated and adjusted on a yearly basis) will now receive the same ranking on the total tax rate indicator. Since the total tax rate is 1 of 32 indicators included in the ranking on the overall ease of doing business, this change has minimal effects on the overall rankings. The correlation between rankings on the ease of paying taxes with and without this threshold is 99%.

The threshold is not based on any underlying theory. Instead, it is meant to emphasize the purpose of the indicator: to highlight economies where the tax burden on business is high relative to the tax burden in other economies. Giving the same ranking to all economies whose total tax rate is below the threshold avoids awarding economies in the scoring for having an unusually low total tax rate, often for reasons unrelated to government policies toward enterprises. For example, economies that are very small or that are rich in natural resources do not need to levy broad-based taxes. For more details on the calculation of the threshold, see the data notes.

In addition, this year *Doing Business* collected data on labor taxes and social security contributions paid by employees as well as employers. These data will be made available on the *Doing Business* website to enable analysis of the distribution of these contributions between employers and employees.

Getting credit methodology. The strength of legal rights index measures certain rights of borrowers and lenders with respect to secured transactions. The index describes how well collateral and bankruptcy laws facilitate lending by measuring 10 aspects of these laws.

One aspect of collateral law that is measured relates to whether secured creditors can continue individual court actions after a debtor starts a court-supervised reorganization procedure or whether they are subject to an automatic stay or a moratorium. Previously only economies where secured creditors can continue a court action in these circumstances were rewarded in the scoring for the strength of legal rights index. Now economies where secured creditors must stop individual court actions but their rights remain protected through other means are also rewarded (see the data notes for more details). The change aligns the methodology for this indicator with guidelines of the United Nations Commission on International Trade Law (UNCITRAL) and the World Bank Group.

Data adjustments

All changes in methodology are explained in the data notes as well as on the *Doing Business* website. In addition, data time series for each indicator and economy are available on the website, beginning with the first year the indicator or economy was included in the report. To provide a comparable time series for research, the data set is back-calculated to adjust for changes in methodology and any revisions in data due to corrections. The data set is not back-calculated for year-to-year changes in income per capita. The website also makes available all original data sets used for background papers.

Information on data corrections is provided in the data notes and on the website. A transparent complaint procedure allows anyone to challenge the data. If errors are confirmed after a data verification process, they are expeditiously corrected.

NOTES

1. For more details on how the aggregate rankings are created, see the chapter on the ease of doing business and distance to frontier.

2. This has included a review by the World Bank Independent Evaluation Group (2008) as well as ongoing input from the International Tax Dialogue.

3. The resolving insolvency indicators measure the time, cost and outcome of insolvency proceedings involving domestic entities. In previous reports this indicator set was referred to as closing a business. *Resolving insolvency* more accurately reflects the outcomes that are measured: a judicial procedure aimed at reorganization or rehabilitation, a judicial procedure aimed at liquidation or winding up, and debt enforcement or foreclosure (in or outside the courts).

4. Local experts in 183 economies are surveyed annually to collect and update the data. The local experts for each economy are listed on the *Doing Business* website (http://www .doingbusiness.org).

5. De Soto 2000.

6. Schneider 2005; La Porta and Shleifer 2008.

7. Amin 2011.

8. http://www.enterprisesurveys.org.

9. OECD, "Indicators of Product Market Regulation," http://www.oecd.org/. The measures are aggregated into 3 broad families that capture state control, barriers to entrepreneurship and barriers to international trade and investment. The 39 countries included in the OECD market regulation indicators are Australia, Austria, Belgium, Brazil, Canada, Chile, China, the Czech Republic, Denmark, Estonia, Finland, France, Germany, Greece, Hungary, Iceland, India, Ireland, Israel, Italy, Japan, Korea, Luxembourg, Mexico, the Netherlands, New Zealand, Norway, Poland, Portugal, Russia, the Slovak Republic, Slovenia, South Africa, Spain, Sweden, Switzerland, Turkey, the United Kingdom and the United States.

10. The World Economic Forum's *Global Competitiveness Report* uses *Doing Business* data sets on starting a business, employing workers, protecting investors and getting credit (legal rights), representing 7 of a total of 113 different indicators (or 6.2%).

11. Narayan and others 2000.

12. Hallward-Driemeier, Khun-Jush and Pritchett (2010) analyze data from World Bank Enterprise Surveys for Sub-Saharan Africa and show that broadly de jure measures such as *Doing Business* indicators are not correlated with ex post firm-level responses. While countries that do better according to *Doing Business* generally perform better on enterprise surveys, for the majority of economies in the sample there is no correlation. Further, the authors find that the gap between de jure and de facto conditions grows with the formal regulatory burden. This suggests that more burdensome processes in Africa open up more space for making deals and that firms may not incur the official costs of compliance, but they still pay to avoid them. A few differences in the underlying methodologies should be kept in mind. The *Doing Business* methodology focuses on the main business city, while enterprise surveys typically cover the entire country. *Doing Business* gathers the considered views of experts who examine the laws and rules underlying the business regulatory framework in a narrow set of areas; enterprise surveys collect the views of enterprise managers and the question posed to the manager is seldom identical to the one being addressed by *Doing Business* contributors, which is in reference to a particular standardized case. World Bank Enterprise Surveys, available at http://www.enterprisesurveys.org, collect business data on more than 100,000 firms in 125 economies, covering a broad range of business environment topics.

13. The correlation coefficient between the ease of doing business ranking and the ranking on the Control of Corruption Index is 0.62, and that between the ease of doing business ranking and the ranking on the Transparency International Corruption Perceptions Index 0.77. The positive correlation is statistically significant at the 5% level.

14. World Bank 2003.

15. This year's report does not present rankings of economies on the employing workers indicators. Nor does it include this topic in the aggregate ranking on the ease of doing business.

16. For further details on the construction of the indicators, the aggregate rankings and the distance to frontier measure, see the data notes and the chapter on the ease of doing business and distance to frontier.

17. According to searches on Google Scholar (http://scholar.google.com) and the Social Science Citation Index.

18. Djankov and others 2002; Alesina and others 2005; Perotti and Volpin 2005; Klapper, Laeven and Rajan 2006; Fisman and Sarria-Allende 2010; Antunes and Cavalcanti 2007; Barseghyan 2008; Eifert 2009; Klapper, Lewin and Quesada Delgado 2009; Djankov, Freund and Pham 2010; Klapper and Love 2011; Chari 2011; Bruhn 2011.

19. Klapper, Lewin and Quesada Delgado 2009. *Entry rate* refers to newly registered firms as a percentage of total registered firms. *Business density* is defined as the total number of businesses as a percentage of the working-age population (ages 18–65).

20. Ciccone and Papaioannou 2007.

21. Alesina and others 2005.

22. Loayza, Oviedo and Sérven 2005; Barseghyan 2008.

23. Dulleck, Frijters and Winter-Ebmer 2006; Calderon, Chong and Leon 2007; Micco and Pagés 2006.

24. Masatlioglu and Rigolini 2008; Djankov 2009.

25. Bruhn 2011.

26. Kaplan, Piedra and Seira 2007.

27. Aghion and others 2008.

28. Sharma 2009.

29. Chari 2011.

30. Cardenas and Rozo 2009.

31. Branstetter and others 2010.

32. Djankov, Freund and Pham 2010.

33. Iwanow and Kirkpatrick 2009.

34. Seker 2011.

35. Nunn 2007.

36. Rauch 2010.

37. Chang, Kaltani and Loayza 2009; Cuñat and Melitz 2007.

38. http://www.enterprisesurveys.org.

39. Haselmann, Pistor and Vig 2010. The countries studied were Bulgaria, Croatia, the Czech Republic, Estonia, Hungary, Latvia, Lithuania, Poland, Romania, the Slovak Republic, Slovenia and Ukraine.

40. Djankov, McLiesh and Shleifer 2007; Houston and others 2010.

41. Djankov, McLiesh and Shleifer 2007; Houston and others 2010.

42. Visaria 2009.

43. Funchal 2008.

44. Dewaelheyns and Van Hulle (2008) on Belgium; Giné and Love (2010) on Colombia.

45. One recent study using *Doing Business* indicators illustrates the difficulties in using highly disaggregated indicators to identify reform priorities (Kraay and Tawara 2011).

46. All background papers are available on the *Doing Business* website (http://www.doingbusiness.org).

47. For more details, see the chapter on the ease of doing business and distance to frontier.

48. A technical note on the different aggregation and weighting methods is available on the *Doing Business* website (http://www.doingbusiness.org).

49. Previous years' data on dealing with construction permits are adjusted to reflect this change. They are made available on the *Doing Business* website under "historical data" (http://www.doingbusiness.org).

50. All changes in methodology are explained in the data notes in this year's report and in previous years' reports back to *Doing Business 2007* (data notes and previous years' reports are available at http://www.doingbusiness.org).

51. For the terms of reference and composition of the consultative group, see World Bank, "Doing Business Employing Workers Indicator Consultative Group," http://www.doingbusiness.org.

52. http://www.doingbusiness.org/methodology/employing-workers.

53. http://www.doingbusiness.org.

Economy case studies

KOREA: BETTER BUSINESS REGULATION AND IMPROVED COMPETITIVENESS

Rapid growth over the past 3 decades transformed Korea into the world's 13th largest economy.[1] Exports were a big driver of that growth, which averaged 6.4% a year between 1981 and 2009.[2] Exports and imports together amounted to 83% of GDP in 2007, and by 2008 Korea had become the world's 7th largest trader.[3] But the economy's heavy reliance on foreign trade made it especially vulnerable to the global economic crisis of 2008-09. During the height of the crisis, in the fall of 2008, the economy contracted by 15% as exports, hit by poor credit conditions and declining investor confidence, plunged by 34%.[4]

The government's policy response to the global economic crisis recognized the larger role played by small and medium-size enterprises, especially in employment—in contrast to before the 1997–98 East Asian financial crisis, when the large conglomerates known as *chaebol* dominated. At the end of 2008 Korea's 3 million small and medium-size enterprises accounted for 99.9% of all companies in the economy, almost 90% of employment and about 50% of production.[5] In the wake of the crisis the government took steps to reduce the tax and regulatory burden on these businesses, building on reforms begun earlier in the decade.

Many of the reforms of business regulation, such as the launch of an online system for business registration and the introduction of an electronic single window to facilitate trade, reflect Korea's broader push toward e-government. A road map adopted in 2003 to create the "world's best open e-government" included targets such as putting 85% of public services online.[6] Korea's advanced e-government provided the foundation for implementing several of the recent reforms in business regulation.

The institutional framework

In 2008 newly elected President Lee Myung-bak established the Presidential Council on National Competitiveness with a broad mandate to revive the economy by improving Korea's competitiveness. Regulatory reform was identified as 1 of 4 pillars for the initiative, along with public sector innovation, investment promotion, and legal and institutional advancement.

The council's ambition in 2008 was "to achieve a potential economic growth rate of 6–7% and a national competitiveness rank of 15 globally by 2012."[7] The council noted early on that of the economy's 5,189 business regulations, 800 (15%) had not been revised in the 10 years since 1998. In an effort to bring regulations up to date, the council applied sunset clauses to more than 600 regulations and 3,500 administrative rules.[8]

For the past 3 years the council has been holding meetings twice a month to discuss Korea's competitiveness strategy, bringing together representatives from the Employers Federation, trade unions, the Chamber of Commerce, the Federation of SMEs, the Ministry of Strategy and Finance, academia and the private sector. The Ministry of Strategy and Finance is responsible for improving the business environment by planning and implementing economic regulation, simplifying administrative procedures and reducing related costs. The Small & Medium Business Administration, created in 1996, focuses on promoting small and medium-size enterprises as the backbone of the economy.[9]

To further support the reform initiative, in 2008 the government, in collaboration with the Korean Chamber of Commerce, established the public-private Regulatory Reform Task Force to monitor and resolve difficulties faced by businesses. Every year the council reports statistics on the issues the task force investigates and resolves through cooperation with relevant authorities.[10]

Multipronged regulatory reform

In recent years Korea has been implementing reforms that affect several areas of business regulation, including taxation, trade, investor protections, bankruptcy and business registration.

Lower and simpler taxes

As part of a stimulus package following the global crisis, Korea accelerated its 5-year corporate income tax reduction program to a 3-year program. It reduced the highest corporate tax rate from 25% to 22% in 2009, and the lowest rate from 11% to 10% in 2010. The plan is to further reduce the highest rate in 2012, from 22% to 20%.

Korea also undertook efforts to lighten the administrative burden of taxes. In 1997 it had already implemented a system allowing taxpayers to file taxes electronically.[11] In 2002 it launched a new one, the Hometax system.[12] In 2010, thanks to increased use of the new system, the time to comply with tax obligations was reduced by 14% as measured by *Doing Business*. In parallel with introducing online taxation, Korea reorganized its tax administration, shifting from an organization by type of tax (such as personal income tax and corporate income tax) to one by tax function (collection, audit and so on). The introduction of online taxation and the functional reorganization of tax administration have substantially reduced the need for informal contact between government officials and taxpayers.

In 2010 and 2011 Korea took further steps to ease the administrative burden of taxes. It amended the Local Tax Law twice in 2010 to merge 4 local taxes into 2. And effective January 1, 2011, it made the National Health Insurance Corporation the consolidated collector for pension, health, unemployment and industrial accident insurance payments. This allows joint filing and payment for 4 different labor taxes and contributions.

As Korea started to recover from the crisis, the revenue collected from corporate income tax rose, exceeding the 2008 level in both 2009 and 2010. The number of companies registered for corporate income tax also rose, increasing by 7% from 2008 to 2009 and by 10% from 2009 to 2010.

Easier trade

In 2008 the Korea Customs Service launched a comprehensive reform plan aimed at establishing the world's best customs clearance system.[13] By 2009 the agency had moved from an "E-customs system"—an electronic data interchange system with access for subscribers only—to a "U-customs system"—a global internet-based customs portal linking financial institutions, customs agencies, logistics companies and 23 government agencies.[14]

This international single window, known as UNI-PASS, allows importers and exporters to handle customs declarations and other trade-related requirements from anywhere at any time. UNI-PASS is one of the world's few 100% electronic clearance portals. Its introduction reduced the average time to export from 11 days to 8, and the average time to import from 10 days to 8, as measured by *Doing Business 2009*. The Korea Customs Service estimates that it spent about $7.7 million in total on the single window in 2006–10, generating cost savings of about $70.5 million in 2010 alone.[15]

Greater protections for investors and creditors

Already in 2005 Korea had begun to adopt a range of measures to improve corporate governance, including supporting the nascent shareholder rights movement by giving minority shareholders more rights. Korea's class action law came into effect in January 2005. Minority investors can now file class actions for negligent external audits of a listed company, for insider trading and market manipulation and for false disclosure in the prospectuses or quarterly, semiannual and annual reports of listed companies.

In October 2009 Korea amended its 2006 bankruptcy law in an effort to keep more companies operating during the global economic crisis. By the second half of 2008 both export and domestic companies had begun to feel the effect of the decline in international demand due to the global crisis and rising oil prices.[16] Much as it had done after the East Asian financial crisis, Korea modified its bankruptcy law to favor restructuring over liquidation, launched workout plans to save ailing financial institutions and enhanced transparency among foreign and domestic creditors—a strategy that according to research helped to gradually revive investor confidence.[17]

Under Korea's new bankruptcy law, creditors lending money to distressed companies receive "superpriority" over other secured creditors. This makes it easier for such companies to obtain new loans and continue operating. The law also encourages reorganization by simplifying rules and allowing management to stay onboard to administer the company's turnaround—while balancing creditors' interests by allowing them to establish creditors' committees during bankruptcy.[18]

By 2010 more companies were able to continue operating. The number of reorganization filings in Korea rose from 366 in 2008 to 630 in 2010 (table 3.1). More important, the number of companies that kept operating after filing for reorganization increased from 73 in 2008 to 223 in 2010, while the number filing for liquidation grew by much less (from 191 in 2008 to 253 in 2010).

Easier and cheaper business start-up

In 2009 Korea made starting a business easier, particularly for joint stock companies, or *jusik hoesa*, which account for more than 90% of Korean companies.[19] For these companies the minimum capital requirement was abolished, and the cost to start a business reduced from 17% of income per capita to 14.57%. Since 2009 notaries have no longer been required, strict time limits have applied for value added tax registration, and entrepreneurs have been able to pay registration taxes online. Online payment is very accessible in Korea, which has the world's highest wireless broadband penetration rate.[20]

In February 2010 Korea made start-up even easier and less costly through an online system, Start-Biz Online, which is managed by the Small & Medium Business Administration.[21] In the past, entrepreneurs starting a company had to manually fill out more than 30 forms and visit 6 different agencies—which led 96% of company founders to hire a lawyer as their agent. Now they enter information once, and the online system automatically distributes it. Entrepreneurs can use the system to

TABLE 3.1	Reorganization and liquidation filings in the Republic of Korea, 2008–10					
	Companies filing for reorganization		Companies that kept operating after filing for reorganization		Companies filing for liquidation	
Year	Seoul	All of Korea	Seoul	All of Korea	Seoul	All of Korea
2008	111	366	11	73	74	191
2009	192	669	54	257	122	226
2010	155	630	35	223	122	253

Source: Ministry of Justice of Korea.

TABLE 3.2	New companies registering and exiting in the Republic of Korea, 2008–10							
	Jusik hoesa registering		Jusik hoesa exiting		Yuhan hoesa registering		Yuhan hoesa exiting	
Year	Seoul	All of Korea	Seoul	All of Korea	Seoul	All of Korea	Seoul	All of Korea
2008	17,567	47,739	10,801	26,175	538	2,766	284	359
2009	19,313	52,976	12,344	29,783	998	3,361	224	295
2010	20,789	57,828	15,062	35,795	838	2,765	276	383

Note: Jusik hoesa are joint stock companies. *Yuhan hoesa* are limited liability companies.
Source: Supreme Court of Korea.

conduct name searches, register a company, pay local taxes and the corporate registration tax—and more.

As Korea started recovering from the crisis, the number of newly registered joint stock companies began steadily increasing. It grew by about 9% between 2009 and 2010 (table 3.2). More than a third of the new companies are located in Seoul.

Besides making start-up easier for all companies, Korea plans to relax or abolish many industry-specific barriers to entry, in an effort to promote new business and revitalize the economy. For example, it will no longer restrict businesses selling petroleum to operate only in a specific region.[22]

Smoother permitting

Korea also strengthened construction permitting, updating its building code in 2005/06. In May 2006 small construction projects were exempted from the requirement to apply for an advance building permit.[23] This allows regulators to focus their energy on the more complex projects.

In 2010 Korea started a general licensing reform (this does not yet apply to matters such as construction permitting). Until recently Korean licensing laws had "prohibition of a license" as the principle and "permission for license" as the exception. Permission became the principle in 2010.[24] The goal for the coming years is to establish a licensing council, a one-stop shop that will bring together all administrative agencies and process applications within 20 days as a general rule.

Conclusion

In 2010, as the world economy slowly recovered from the crisis, Korea's growth rate reached 6.1%, the highest among OECD members and up sharply from the 0.2% rate in 2009.[25] The government aims to continue the regulatory reform process. At the October 2010 meeting of the Presidential Council on National Competitiveness, President Lee Myung-bak said, "In the process of recovery of the world economy, the competition will be fiercer. Therefore, we need to make an effort to be more competitive. We have to endeavor to make a country good for enterprise and investment."

NOTES

1. Based on 2010 GDP measured by purchasing power parity (PPP) exchange rates. Data are from the International Monetary Fund, World Economic Outlook Database, http://www.imf.org/.
2. World Bank, World Development Indicators database, http://data.worldbank.org/.
3. World Bank, World Development Indicators database, http://data.worldbank.org/. The OECD average for exports and imports is about 50% of GDP.
4. See Bernanke (2009, p. 15); and Asian Development Bank (2009, pp. 172–76).
5. Small & Medium Business Administration, "Statistics," http://eng.smba.go.kr/ (accessed July 2011).
6. Between 2003 and 2007, 31 new e-government initiatives were implemented. In 2010 Korea ranked number 1 globally on the United Nations E-government Development Index (United Nations Department of Economic and Social Affairs 2010).
7. PCNC (2009) cites Korea's "national competitiveness ranking on IMD's World Competitiveness Yearbook (31 out of 55 in 2008), WEF's Global Competitiveness report (13 out of 134) and WBG's Doing Business report (23 out of 178)" (p. 11).
8. PCNC 2011.
9. Small & Medium Business Administration, http://eng.smba.go.kr/.
10. The statistics are included in annual reports of the Presidential Council on National Competitiveness. In 2009 the task force undertook on-site inspections of companies in 30 areas and held 67 sectoral meetings, revealing 785 issues. It resolved 559 issues through cooperation with relevant authorities.
11. In 2009, 95% of corporate income tax returns, 80% of individual income tax returns and 78% of value added tax returns were filed electronically.
12. The Hometax system is available at http://www.hometax.go.kr.
13. Korea Customs Service 2009b.
14. The U-customs system is being used as a model by several economies seeking to improve their trade systems, including Dominica and Ecuador.
15. The cost of the single window fell after the initial investment in 2006. The share of Korean export and import transactions processed through the single window increased from about 67% in 2009 to about 92% in 2010 (Korea Customs Service 2009a, 2010).
16. Kim 2009, p. 279.
17. See Cirmizi, Klapper and Uttamchandani (2010); and Oh and Haliday (2009).
18. See Eunjai Lee and Wan Shik Lee, "Restructuring and Insolvency: South Korea," http://www.practicallaw.com/.
19. About 10% of companies are small or medium-size limited liability companies, or *yuhan hoesa*. In 2006–09 an average of 2,500 new *yuhan hoesa* a year were created in Korea.
20. OECD 2010.
21. http://www.startbiz.go.kr.
22. PCNC 2011, p. 14.
23. World Bank 2006b.
24. PCNC 2011.
25. See PCNC (2011), which cites International Monetary Fund data on 2010 growth rates in major economies.

FYR MACEDONIA: MAJOR CHANGES SPURRED BY REGIONAL INTEGRATION

Regional integration efforts such as the accession process of the European Union can help drive reforms in business regulation. This has been the case in FYR Macedonia, which launched a comprehensive reform agenda after applying for EU membership. FYR Macedonia signed the Stabilization and Association Agreement with the European Union in April 2001 and received candidate country status in November 2005.[1] Its reform agenda has been driven largely by requirements to ensure that the country's laws are in line with the EU legal framework (*acquis*) and to fulfill certain macroeconomic criteria. Equally important has been the desire to attract investment and develop business activity to create jobs and achieve economic growth. Since 2004 the parliament has made important changes to legislation, including business regulations.

The efforts are showing results. FYR Macedonia is among the 10 economies that made the biggest strides in creating a regulatory environment more favorable to business in the past 6 years.[2] It moved up in the global ranking on the ease of doing business from 81 in *Doing Business 2006* to 22 in this year's report.[3] Besides improving in the relative ranking, FYR Macedonia is also among the economies that closed the gap to the frontier the most in the past 6 years (see figure 1.9 in the executive summary).[4]

In addition to the EU *acquis*, FYR Macedonia has used the *Doing Business* reports to benchmark good practices and promote improvements to its regulatory framework to make it easier to do business. External assistance has contributed to the sustained success. The World Bank, the European Commission and the U.S. Agency for International Development (USAID) have provided funds and technical assistance for drafting new laws and implementing administrative reforms.

The institutional framework

The government of FYR Macedonia has been the driving force behind the reforms, with the reform agenda receiving support at the highest political levels. The cabinet of the deputy prime minister for economic affairs has provided coordination to streamline the reform efforts, and the Ministries of Finance, Justice, Economy, and Transport and Communications have joined initiatives for reforming the legal and regulatory framework.

Along with political will and capacity, there has been strong collaboration among ministries, particularly at the operational level. As the government pushed for change, its efforts triggered initiatives in ministries and agencies. Since November 2006 the government has implemented 3 phases of a "regulatory guillotine" project aimed at reducing the regulatory burden and cutting red tape and bureaucracy. As part of this, the Ministry of Transport and Communications initiated several legal reforms to simplify and speed up the process of obtaining a building permit.[5] And the Customs Administration introduced several measures to increase the speed and efficiency of trade.

In another initiative, the National Bank helped strengthen the financial system by establishing a public credit registry in 2008. Thanks to a more recent effort initiated by the Ministry of Finance, a private credit bureau was formed by the association of commercial banks and started operating in 2011.

E-government provided the platform for many of the reforms in the business regulatory environment. The government set out to transform public administration processes by establishing the Ministry of Information Society and Administration and implementing a number of e-government projects. The aim was to create more modern, integrated, efficient, transparent and secure processes. The first step was to establish the infrastructure; the second was to roll out the e-services.[6] Support was provided by USAID, which has funded the development of e-government through 11 projects so far.[7] Achievements have included an electronic tax system created in 2008 to streamline the filing and payment of taxes, an electronic cadastre for property registration introduced in 2010 and an online system for business registration that began operating in 2011.

The government also implemented tax changes. In 2008 it reduced the corporate income tax rate to 10%. The following year it reduced rates for social security contributions and integrated their payment with that of other taxes.

Judicial reforms

A comprehensive information technology system was introduced in 2007 as part of the government's 2007–10 information technology strategy. This provided a foundation for reforms in judicial processes, especially through the introduction of electronic case management. Before reforms, the judicial system was plagued by inefficiencies. Procedures were slow, delaying access to justice. Getting final decisions enforced was a long and difficult process. Courts were overburdened with minor cases, and case management was unorganized. There was too little use of information technology—and qualified human resources were scarce.[8] FYR Macedonia tackled these inefficiencies through several reform initiatives for which EU legislation provided a framework.

Modernizing the courts

Judicial reforms began in 2003, with the donor-funded Macedonia Court Modernization Project. The project introduced new practices in pilot courts with the aim of demonstrating modern case management methods, increasing proactive court management by judges and administrative staff and showing how courts could improve access for the public by reducing case backlogs and eliminating unnecessary delays.[9]

In a separate initiative starting in 2004, the Ministry of Justice developed a judicial reform strategy focused on building capacity, strengthening court infrastructure and improving information technology systems. The ministry set up an advisory body made up of representatives of judicial institutions to review and provide input on the strategy. It also organized several public debates, as well as roundtables giving representatives of the legal and judicial professions an opportunity to provide feedback and suggestions.

Changing laws to speed up court proceedings

Enacting and amending laws on civil procedure and enforcement of judgments has also played an important part in improving the judicial environment. A new law on enforcement, coming into force on June 1, 2006, and amended in 2011, enabled creditors to initiate the process through private enforcement agents. This enforcement model has served as inspiration for other economies in the region, including Croatia.

Overall, the changes have produced results. The time to enforce a contract fell from 509 days in 2004 to 370 days in 2009, as measured by *Doing Business*. A 2011 amendment to the law on civil procedure, the result of an analysis of court cases by the Ministry of Justice, is aimed at further reducing the cost and duration of court proceedings. The law sets deadlines for the different steps in a court case. One tool helping to meet those deadlines is software supporting electronic case management.[10]

While courts are more efficient and the case backlog smaller, the backlog still remains a major problem. But the Ministry of Justice estimates that the latest amendments to the law on enforcement—with the expected transfer of 402,000 cases from the courts to notaries or enforcement agents—will soon reduce the number of cases in the courts by more than 80% compared with 2006. That will allow faster enforcement of contracts and speedier reduction of the large case backlog.

Reforming bankruptcy

FYR Macedonia's 2006 Bankruptcy Law greatly reduced the average duration of bankruptcy cases. According to the Ministry of Economy, concluding cases took an average of 1.4 years under the 2006 law—compared with 6.6 years under the 1997 Bankruptcy Law and 13.8 years under the 1989 Law on Forced Settlement, Bankruptcy and Liquidation.[11]

Recent amendments to the 2006 law are aimed at making the bankruptcy process even faster. The amended law, which came into force in 2011, requires bankruptcy trustees to use an electronic system to record all phases and actions during bankruptcy proceedings, increasing transparency. Trustees can log on to the system to upload documents and track cases. The amendments to the law reduced the legal time frame for

trustees to sell all the assets of the bankrupt company and conclude the bankruptcy case to a maximum of 18 months.

Administrative reforms

Through the regulatory guillotine project, the government of FYR Macedonia has undertaken several reforms to streamline administrative processes, reduce costs and introduce the "silence is consent" rule. The most important achievements include reducing the complexity, time and cost of starting a business and registering property and speeding up the export and import process.

Making business registration one stop

As a first step to streamline business registration, FYR Macedonia launched a central registry on January 1, 2006. A 2005 law had transferred business registration out of the courts—where the process was slow, expensive and overly complex—and made the registry the only body in the country responsible for registering companies.[12]

The government created a one-stop shop at the central registry, unifying and simplifying the procedures to register a company and its employees. This cut the number of procedures to start a business from 13 in 2004 to 3 in 2010, and the time from 48 days to 3, as measured by *Doing Business*. The new registry, along with legal changes such as abolishing the minimum capital requirement, enabled FYR Macedonia to join the top 6 economies worldwide on the ease of starting a business.

In April 2011 the government further streamlined and reduced the cost of business registration by introducing an online system. Now there is no need to get corporate documents and signatures notarized. By July 2011 only a few applications for business registration had been received through the online system. But use of the system is expected to grow as its existence becomes more widely known.

Making property registration faster and easier

A series of changes at the real estate cadastre in Skopje have made registering property faster and easier. A 2008 law streamlined procedures and set time limits. The number

of property cases awaiting registration in Skopje shrank from 15,035 in 2005 to 2,082 in May 2011. The average time to process applications fell from 60 days in 2004 to 5 in 2011. All fees were cut by 50% in 2007 as part of the regulatory guillotine project and by another 10–72% in January 2010. These accomplishments won the cadastre an award of excellence from the World Bank in June 2010.[13]

The cadastre has introduced performance standards to motivate staff to work more efficiently. Staff exceeding the average can receive a salary increase of up to 25%. The cadastre has also worked to improve its public image, by holding "open days," opening "hotlines" to answer questions and meeting with citizens in the municipalities of Skopje. A customer asked about his recent experience reported having to wait in line outside the cadastre for 4 hours in the summer heat—but considered that a huge improvement over a few years ago, when transferring property took several months.

The most recent efforts to increase efficiency and effectiveness include launching an electronic cadastre and front desk in 2010. The "e-cadastre" is aimed at improving management of the workload and providing real-time dissemination and exchange of data. The "e-front desk," supported by the Netherlands, includes electronic conveyance, recording and processing of applications. Among other things, it allows notaries to check information on encumbrances and the status of applications.

Increasing the speed and efficiency of trade

The Customs Administration has undertaken a range of measures to make importing and exporting faster and more efficient. In 2002 it introduced a risk-based inspection system to minimize the time to process customs declarations and prevent unnecessary delays in customs terminals. The Customs Administration uses various information technology systems for risk management and has continued to introduce guidelines for risk management in customs controls since 2005.[14]

By using risk profiling, risk-based inspection systems can focus only on the riskier containers, reducing the need for physical inspections of cargo and allowing most traders to get their goods cleared more quickly. After analyzing potential risk factors, these systems typically direct containers through a "red channel" (for physical inspection), "yellow channel" (inspection of documents only) or "green channel" (no additional inspections). Since 2009 FYR Macedonia has also used a "blue channel" allowing goods to be released from customs without inspection and instead to undergo postclearance control. Imports going through the yellow channel are cleared in 1 hour on average, and exports in 23 minutes on average.

In 2008 the Customs Administration introduced an electronic single window that allows traders to submit customs documents online. Early in the same year it introduced 4 mobile scanners and rationalized the customs fee schedule and permit structure. As a result of these changes, the time required to export fell from 19 days to 17 in 2008, and the time to import from 17 days to 15, as measured by *Doing Business*.

Conclusion

It takes time for reforms to translate into changes in the economy. But FYR Macedonia has shown that it is on the right path—and more changes are soon to come. To make resolving insolvency faster and easier, FYR Macedonia plans to implement an electronic system for the sale of assets of bankrupt companies. The Ministry of Transport and Communications aims to launch an electronic process for building permit applications by July 2012. The cadastre continues to improve its operations and has several

ongoing projects with international donors to digitize all property records and to establish a national geoportal allowing citizens to see the location of land plots and their surroundings online, a useful tool for builders and developers.

But the process of EU accession will demand broader changes. The European Commission reported in 2010 that "limited progress" had been made in reforming the judiciary, a key priority of the accession partnership and a key remaining challenge to EU accession. It identified other areas of "limited progress" as social policy, employment and corruption. It also reported that implementation of the anticorruption legal framework remained deficient.[15] But there is good reason to be hopeful. FYR Macedonia has already shown itself capable of overcoming obstacles that are part of every reform process—through political will, a desire to change and coordination with stakeholders.

NOTES

1. European Commission 2005.

2. FYR Macedonia was among the 10 economies that improved the most in the ease of doing business as measured in *Doing Business 2008* and in *Doing Business 2010*.

3. The ease of doing business ranking cited from *Doing Business 2006* is the ranking published in the report, not a back-calculated ranking that has been adjusted for changes in methodology and data revisions.

4. For details on the distance to frontier measure, see the data notes.

5. The Law on Spatial and Urban Planning (amended February 14, 2011) and Law on Construction (amended February 14, 2011) have streamlined the construction permitting process. Among other things, the amendments set deadlines for the approval

process and introduce a "silence is consent" rule for cases where the deadlines are missed.

6. Armenski, Gusev and Spasov 2007.

7. E-gov Project, http://www.egov.org.mk.

8. FYR Macedonia, Ministry of Justice 2005.

9. Between November 2003 and March 2006 the number of cases pending for more than 1 year in the pilot courts fell by 19%, and the number pending for more than 3 years by 48%. The Macedonia Court Modernization Project (2006) attributes these results to judges and lawyers working harder and focusing on older cases as well as new ones; measures to discourage multiple court appearances; the project's employment of court coordinators to work with the judges and staff; the establishment of case flow committees in each pilot court; a yearly backlog reduction plan tailored to the needs of each local court; the circulation of results from all pilot courts; and monthly tracking of pending and closed cases.

10. Following the introduction of electronic case management, the Automated Court Case Management Information System (ACCMIS) software was introduced in 2009 and became fully operational in January 2010.

11. FYR Macedonia, Ministry of Economy 2011.

12. Under judicial authority the registration process required filing documents and forms at several different institutions, leading to higher fees and longer wait times (USAID 2009).

13. Agency for Real Estate Cadastre Skopje 2011.

14. An automated risk-based inspection system, CDPS Risk-Based Selection for Red, Yellow, Green and Blue Channel Inspection, has been in place since 2002. Other information technology systems in place include the South-East European Messaging System, created by the European Commission's EuropeAid Co-operation (AIDCO) and the European Union's Customs and Fiscal Assistance Office (CAFAO).

15. European Commission 2010.

MEXICO: UNLEASHING REGULATORY REFORM AT THE LOCAL LEVEL

Governments around the world face challenges when pursuing broad regulatory reform: identifying bottlenecks, obtaining political support, getting the resources needed, gaining buy-in from stakeholders, bringing agencies together in one coordinated effort. Mexico illustrates the challenges of regulatory policy making when it involves different levels of government and regulation.

Mexico's 31 states and 2,441 municipalities, along with Mexico City, have extensive regulatory powers, allowing them to design, implement and enforce regulations.[1] So regulatory reform has required not only horizontal coordination among ministries, agencies, and legislative and judicial bodies at the federal level, but vertical coordination with entities at the state and municipal levels. The regulatory reform initiative in Mexico has used an exercise of benchmarking business regulation in all 31 states and Mexico City to support this coordination and stimulate change.

Gathering momentum

Regulatory reform efforts started as early as the 1980s as Mexico, seeking rapid integration with the global economy, joined large international trade agreements and the OECD. Greater openness to international markets and increased competition required measures to lower the cost of doing business for its 75 million people.[2] In the early 1990s the reform initiative was led by the Office of the President and a small group of technical advisers. The consequences of the 1994–95 economic crisis helped intensify the focus on small and medium-size enterprises as an engine of employment growth.

But the success of the reform efforts was undermined by lack of effective monitoring, transparency and public support. Changes in the political landscape after the 1997 midterm elections weakened the government's support in Congress, where the president's party lost its 68-year majority in the lower chamber. Now none of the 3 major political parties had an absolute majority. In this fragmented political environment the unilateral top-down approach was seen as

no longer viable. Compounding the problem was the lack of outreach to other stakeholders: Congress, the judiciary and the public administration.[3]

In 2000 the Office of the President set up the Federal Commission for Regulatory Improvement (known by its Spanish acronym Cofemer) with the aim of establishing a long-lasting reform effort and a systematic approach to regulation. But while this agency became the main driver of change, continuing political obstacles at the local and national levels limited its effectiveness. In late 2003 the first *Doing Business* report ranked Mexico above the global average on the ease of doing business. Yet Mexico trailed behind such competitors as Chile, Malaysia and Thailand—and even further behind OECD high-income economies such as the United Kingdom, Australia and Germany.

The Office of the President saw an opportunity to use the *Doing Business* report to drive improvements. But because the president's support in Congress eroded even further in the 2003 midterm elections, reforms failed to pass. With a national presidential election looming in mid-2006, the Office of the President simply did not have the political clout to carry out broad reforms, which usually take several years to plan and implement.

Thanks to Mexico's federal structure, however, states could start reform efforts immediately. In 2005 the Office of the President requested a subnational *Doing Business* report that would go beyond Mexico City. The first such report, launched in 2005, benchmarked 12 states in addition to Mexico City. A second one extended coverage to all 31 states in 2006. A third report repeated the benchmarking in 2008. A fourth is under way.

What has worked?

The subnational *Doing Business* reports, by providing a fact-based set of indicators that capture differences in local regulation and local implementation of national laws, prompted first dialogue and then action on regulatory reform. Along the way they have also led to the sharing of experience, to competition and to collaboration, all of which have helped to promote and sustain change.

Sharing experience

The subnational *Doing Business* project has provided a vehicle for peer-to-peer learning and sharing of good practices among Mexican states. Cofemer organizes a conference twice a year at which plenary sessions allow every state to share its experiences with regulatory reform, as well as lessons learned. Peer learning also takes place even more informally, on visits by policy makers to good performers such as Aguascalientes and Guanajuato. A visit to Sinaloa, where policy makers learned more about how this state issues land use authorizations electronically, led Colima to set up a similar system on its own website.

Sharing experience makes sense, because differences across states in what entrepreneurs encounter in doing business can point to opportunities for improvement. For example, *Doing Business in Mexico 2007* showed that business registration fees varied greatly from state to state. In Michoacán the registration cost for companies was the equivalent of $16; in Chihuahua it was $1,035, more than 60 times as much. And while some states set fixed fees, others charged percentage-based fees, calculated on the basis of the company's capital.[4] The 5 states with the most expensive business start-up processes used percentage-based fees.[5] The story was similar for property transfer fees. Yet a company registration or property transfer takes the same amount of work regardless of the size of the company's capital or the value of the property.

The many similarities across states—such as bottlenecks faced by entrepreneurs trying to start or expand a business—provided just as much reason for sharing experience. In registering a business or transferring property, the biggest hurdle was filing documents with the company or property registry. *Doing Business in Mexico 2007* reported that the property registration procedures with the public registry took between 73% and 87% of the total time for registering property. But *Doing Business in Mexico 2009* could report that 13 states had focused on updating their property and commercial registries. Many states have also been working to consolidate procedures in one place. Most now have a one-stop shop that centralizes procedures and provides advice to entrepreneurs.

Creating competition

Competition between states was the biggest catalyst for reform. Faced by almost identical federal regulations, mayors and governors had difficulty explaining why it took longer or cost more to start a business or register property in their city or state. States that did poorly could not justify their poor performance, and they were inspired by the reform efforts of other states.

This showed up in an accelerating pace of change. *Doing Business in Mexico 2007* reported that 9 of 12 states (75%) had implemented reforms in at least one area measured by the report. Two years later, *Doing Business in Mexico 2009* reported that 28 of 31 states (90%) as well as Mexico City had implemented *Doing Business* reforms. Mexican states were improving their regulatory environments, and the impulse for regulatory reform persisted even through changes in government.

The pace of reform was maintained thanks in part to the regulatory reform units that states were beginning to create. Puebla set up the first, in 2003. By 2005, 5 states had regulatory reform units. Today about 20 states do. Nuevo León created the most recent one, in 2010. All the units have been created at the state's initiative, with technical assistance from the federal government through Cofemer.

Promoting collaboration

Delegating the reform agenda to local authorities proved to be an essential part of the national reform effort. This fostered commitment, a sense of collaboration and better communication among federal, state and municipal authorities.

Early on in the reform process the federal government collaborated with the states to improve business registration through the Rapid Business Opening System (SARE). A system of one-stop shops for local procedures, SARE was created to coordinate municipal procedures so that low-risk companies could get their license and start operating in a few days. The improved

collaboration through Cofemer helped expand the system to more municipalities across more states.

Today the system has been implemented in 186 municipalities across 30 states.[6] According to a recent study, the SARE initiative has had a significant impact.[7] After the introduction of SARE's one-stop shops, the number of registered businesses increased by 5% and wage employment by 2.2%.

After a few years of steady improvement at the state and municipal levels, the Office of the President saw a need for broad regulatory reforms at the federal level. One impetus was a perception that the subnational reform efforts needed another boost. Mexico City's poor performance in the subnational rankings on the ease of doing business pushed the federal government to collaborate more closely with Mexico City's 16 boroughs to coordinate reform efforts. A second impetus was Mexico's performance in the global rankings. While several regulatory reform programs had been introduced at the federal level in 2005–09, these had not been enough to propel Mexico into the ranks of the best performers—such as New Zealand, Korea and Denmark, which were then among the top 35 on the ease of doing business.

In September 2009 the Office of the President announced its intention to transform Mexico's regulatory environment. The aims were to build a regulatory framework centered on and involving the citizen, to increase competitiveness and to promote development. The Mexican government secured technical assistance from the World Bank Group to identify opportunities for regulatory reform and to provide expert advice.

The initiative has already produced results in business registration. Previously there had been little coordination between federal agencies and the state and municipal organizations involved in the process. Now an online one-stop shop, Tuempresa, launched in August 2009, coordinates the federal procedures and is adding state and municipal procedures.[8] Public notaries have been granted access. Today the online system processes about 100 new business registrations a month in Mexico City, or 7% of the

total. Mexico has also improved construction permitting, by merging and streamlining procedures related to zoning and utilities.

More areas are being worked on. Reforms continue in trade, construction permitting, and business, property and collateral registration.

Seeing results

There are encouraging signs that strengthening different areas of the business environment at the same time produces better overall results for business creation. A study performed after the introduction of SARE in several states found that the program had a significantly greater effect on the number of new businesses created in areas with a better overall investment climate.[9]

Changes are also apparent for firms. The share of senior management's time spent dealing with requirements imposed by government regulations fell from 20% in 2005 to 14% in 2009. During the same period the share of businesses that had applied for an operating license increased from 4% to 23%.[10]

Conclusion

Regulatory reform in Mexico has become an ongoing process. The government has taken steps to continue the subnational *Doing Business* project. In a first for such projects, the methodology is being transferred to a reputable, independent think tank in Mexico, which expects to continue to do the study every 2–3 years. The federal and state governments have taken the lead on the funding side as well. The first *Doing Business in Mexico* reports were financed in part by donors (such as USAID) and the World Bank Group and in part by the Mexican government. The fourth is being fully funded by the federal and state finance ministries.

The hope is that by tracking progress over time, continued periodic benchmarking by an independent third party will create incentives to maintain the reform effort through changes in government. The *Doing Business in Mexico* reports, capturing the progress of regulatory reform over time, show that it was not a one-time initiative—but instead an effort that has strengthened with continued benchmarking.

NOTES

1. García Villarreal 2010. Information on the number of municipalities is from National Institute for Federalism and Municipal Development (INAFED), "Los últimos municipios creados," http://www.e-local .gob.mx/.
2. Population in 1985 from World Bank 2010b.
3. Cordova and Haddou-Ruiz 2008.
4. World Bank 2006a.
5. World Bank 2008a.
6. Information provided by Cofemer.
7. Bruhn 2011.
8. http://tuempresa.gob.mx.
9. Kaplan, Piedra and Seira 2007.
10. World Bank Enterprise Surveys (http://www .enterprisesurveys.org).

THE UNITED KINGDOM: RETHINKING REGULATION

The United Kingdom has consistently performed well on the *Doing Business* indicators—and this year again stands high in the ranking on the overall ease of doing business, at 7. But the new government believes that more can be done to relieve business from burdensome regulation. Because of the effects of the global financial crisis, the public sector has limited scope to use spending to enable economic growth. While the government has made the difficult decisions necessary to reduce the deficit and stabilize debt levels to create the conditions for sustainable growth,[1] it has also adopted a complementary strategy based on the idea that by simplifying the regulatory system, it can free up the private sector's capacity to innovate, diversify and expand.[2]

Regulation has a role in the modern economy. A framework of rules is necessary to promote competition and stability and to ensure transparency in market interactions. Well-targeted and sensibly designed regulations can deal with market failures, promote a level playing field for businesses and support government objectives. The challenge is to do so in a way that does not impair the ability of businesses to operate, to create jobs and to grow.

Striking the right balance between these objectives can also create a better balance of responsibility between the state, the business community and civil society. Where regulation is needed, the U.K. government intends to more closely scrutinize how regulations are designed and enforced.

Reducing the stock and flow of regulations

The new government has taken a number of steps aimed at reducing the burden of regulation since taking office in early 2010. These have included abolishing regulations that are seen as impeding growth, introducing new regulations only where there are no sensible alternatives and as a last resort, reducing the volume of new regulations and reducing regulatory costs for business.

One in, one out

The government's strategy for easing the burden of regulation is aimed at the flow of new regulations as well as the existing stock. The "one in, one out" system requires government departments to assess the net cost to business of complying with any new regulation that is proposed (an "in"). These calculations are validated by the independent Regulatory Policy Committee.[3] If a new regulation means a cost to business, a deregulatory measure (an "out") must be found that reduces the net cost by at least the same amount.[4] One such "out" is a measure permitting credit unions to communicate with their members electronically. This is estimated to reduce the net cost to business by about £10.4 million, a calculation validated by the Regulatory Policy Committee.[5]

Other initiatives support the one-in, one-out system. For example, the government has introduced review and sunset clauses for new regulations. This means that policy makers must review the relevance of new regulations after a maximum of 7 years and justify their continuation rather than simply leaving them on the statute books.[6]

The one-in, one-out system focuses on domestic regulation. European Union regulations and directives as well as international agreements to which the United Kingdom is a party are managed through a different strand of work. The one-in, one-out system also excludes fiscal measures aimed at reducing the budget deficit, regulatory measures aimed at addressing systemic financial risk, civil emergency regulations or fees, and charges imposed by state bodies for cost recovery purposes only.

In another measure, on April 1, 2011, the government introduced a 3-year moratorium on new domestic regulation affecting micro-enterprises (businesses with fewer than 10 employees, which account for half of total employment in the economy) and start-ups. Any breaches of the moratorium—allowed only in exceptional circumstances and if supported by a compelling argument—will require cabinet-level approval and sign-off by the Economic Affairs Committee, which is chaired by the chancellor of the exchequer.

The Red Tape Challenge

The government has also launched a first-time initiative to scrutinize the entire stock of inherited regulations. The country has more than 21,000 regulations and statutory instruments on the books, spanning virtually the entire spectrum of economic activity and imposing a huge cost on business.[7] Some of these have been on the books since World War II (those related to "trading with the enemy," for example). Many have become obsolete or are otherwise not binding and serve no useful public policy purpose. In areas such as consumer protection the law has become complicated and confusing.

The government estimates that in recent years an average of 6 regulations have been introduced every working day, with a particularly heavy burden in employment law, tax administration, and health and safety. According to a recent government review, "evidence also suggests that Government does not do all it can to support business when introducing new regulations. Often guidance is poorly designed, not provided, or provided late (i.e., after the regulation has come into force)."[8] The same government review reports that a typical small enterprise spends 34 hours a month dealing with red tape and complying with regulations. When businesses need to hire consultants for expert advice on regulatory compliance, this adds to an already heavy cost burden.

The government has begun to tackle the stock of regulation through the Red Tape Challenge. This comprehensive review is aimed at identifying regulations that could be removed, simplified or approached in a different way. Using a public website, the government is gathering the views of the business community and the public and inviting practical suggestions for alternatives. The feedback from those affected by regulation will inform government decision making. This exercise presumes that burdensome regulations will be removed if there are no good reasons for retaining them.

A watchful eye on EU legislation

The government is also taking steps to reduce the cost to U.K. business from EU legislation and continues to work with European partners to ensure that there is appropriate downward pressure on the volume and impact of EU regulations. For example, although the Red Tape Challenge focuses on domestic regulation, the public is also being encouraged to comment on how EU regulations and directives are implemented in the United Kingdom. The government will review any previous instances of "gold plating"—where U.K. regulation has gone beyond the minimum required by the EU legislation, imposing an unnecessary burden on U.K. businesses.

This complements a wider government effort to end the gold plating of EU legislation, under the "Guiding Principles for EU Legislation."[9] Government departments responsible for implementing an EU law must satisfy the cabinet that they have identified the aims of the law and the relevant government policies and will harmonize them in a way that does not cause unintended consequences in the United Kingdom and that minimizes the cost to business. The government is also working with businesses to identify good practices for implementing EU rules and ways to make EU laws friendlier to economic growth.

Transforming regulatory enforcement

The U.K. government believes that reforming the implementation and enforcement of regulations is as important as reducing their stock and flow—and has promised to end the culture of unthinking "tick box" regulation, adopted purely to satisfy convention rather than to ensure the right outcomes. Its aim is to find new ways of achieving compliance that contribute to economic growth and remove unnecessary burdens on businesses and individuals.

The government has already started to reform some of the most disproportionate enforcement systems and has commissioned independent external reviews to examine specific areas in detail. For example, it is adopting Lord Young's proposals to reform the implementation of health and safety law and is reviewing the enforcement of employment law. And the government recently received the recommendations of the Farming Regulation Task Force on ways to ease heavy-handed enforcement of regulation in agriculture and food processing.

The United Kingdom's Primary Authority scheme plays a key part in changing how businesses experience regulatory inspections and enforcement. Businesses operating multiple sites in different local authority jurisdictions can find themselves subject to varying—and at times contradictory—regulatory advice or judgments. To help resolve problems with inconsistent enforcement, the Primary Authority scheme allows businesses to partner with a single local authority that will operate as their sole point of advice and assured guidance. The aim is to support both business compliance and economic growth.

In the first 2 years of the scheme's operation, businesses initiated more than 1,000 Primary Authority partnerships, far exceeding original projections. Building on this success and the initial experience, the government proposes to extend the scheme to allow more businesses access to assured regulatory advice. The emphasis will be on extending the benefits to micro, small and medium-size enterprises.

Thinking more creatively about regulation

Underpinning all these government measures is the idea that policy makers need to think more creatively about whether the traditional "command and control" approach to regulation—with its many unintended consequences—is the most effective way to achieve desired policy outcomes. Against the backdrop of a rapidly changing global economy, the policy papers supporting these initiatives ask whether a combination of non-regulatory policy instruments can achieve policy objectives more effectively, at lower cost and with less coercion.

There are a range of alternatives. One is to use industry codes of conduct or other negotiated codes as mechanisms of self-regulation or (if some level of government involvement is seen to be necessary) coregulation. Another is to make more active use of information and education—supported by rating systems, better labeling and greater disclosure—to enable consumers to make informed decisions. And governments have sometimes used taxes, subsidies, quotas, auctions and other such instruments to

align incentives in ways that support public policy objectives. This approach relies on a consideration of costs and benefits—rather than the coercive power of rigid, sometimes difficult-to-enforce regulation—to shape decisions by individuals and businesses.

As the U.K. authorities implement their strategy, one challenge they will face is to allay public concerns about whether adequate regulations remain in place to ensure stability in the financial system, whose shortcomings are seen by many as a precipitating factor in the 2008–09 financial crisis. Another need is to meet the challenges of climate change.

Conclusion

The government sees this new approach to business regulation as part of a broader effort to boost the competitiveness of the United Kingdom. This has been prompted by concerns about the rapidly rising levels of public debt brought about by the financial crisis,[10] the declining performance of British students in international rankings of excellence in science and mathematics, the erosion of manufacturing output and employment and the economy's declining share of world exports.[11]

Public policies in the medium term are geared to reversing some of these trends. A comprehensive rethinking of the role of business regulation in empowering the private sector to boost productivity, innovation and growth is a key part of this effort.

NOTES

1. See IMF (2011a).

2. U.K. Department for Business, Innovation and Skills 2110b.

3. Regulatory Policy Committee website, http://regulatorypolicycommittee .independent.gov.uk/.

4. U.K. Department for Business, Innovation and Skills 2011a.

5. U.K. Department for Business, Innovation and Skills 2011a, annex D, p. 18.

6. U.K. Department for Business, Innovation and Skills 2010a.

7. U.K. Department for Business, Innovation and Skills 2011b, p. 20.

8. U.K. Department for Business, Innovation and Skills 2011b, p. 51.

9. U.K. Department for Business, Innovation and Skills, "Guiding Principles for EU Legislation," http://www.bis.gov.uk/.

10. According to the IMF (2011b), public debt levels rose from 42.1% of GDP in 2005 to an estimated 77.2% in 2010 and are projected to rise to 83% in 2011.

11. U.K. Department for Business, Innovation and Skills 2011b, p. 3.

References

Agency for Real Estate Cadastre Skopje. 2011. "Overview of the Real Estate Cadastre." Skopje, FYR Macedonia.

Aghion, Philippe, Robin Burgess, Stephen Redding and Fabrizio Zilibotti. 2008. "The Unequal Effects of Liberalization: Evidence from Dismantling the License Raj in India." *American Economic Review* 98 (4): 1397–412.

Alesina, Alberto, Silvia Ardagna, Giuseppe Nicoletti and Fabio Schiantarelli. 2005. "Regulation and Investment." *Journal of the European Economic Association* 3 (4): 791–825.

Amin, Mohammad. 2011. "Labor Productivity, Firm-Size and Gender: The Case of Informal Firms in Argentina and Peru." Enterprise Note 22, Enterprise Analysis Unit, World Bank Group, Washington, DC. http://www.enterprisesurveys.org/.

Antunes, Antonio, and Tiago Cavalcanti. 2007. "Start Up Costs, Limited Enforcement, and the Hidden Economy." *European Economic Review* 51 (1): 203–24.

APEC (Asia-Pacific Economic Cooperation). 2010. "APEC Ease of Doing Business Action Plan (2010–2015)." http://aimp.apec.org/.

Armenski, Goce, Marjan Gusev and Dejan Spasov. 2007. "Growth of eGovernment Services in Macedonia." *Informatica* 31: 397–406.

Asian Development Bank. 2009. *Asian Development Outlook 2009*. Manila: Asian Development Bank. http://www.adb.org/.

Ayyagari, Meghana, Asli Demirgüç-Kunt and Vojislav Maksimovic. 2011. "Small vs. Young Firms across the World: Contribution to Employment, Job Creation, and Growth." Policy Research Working Paper 5631, World Bank, Washington, DC.

Barseghyan, Levon. 2008. "Entry Costs and Cross-Country Differences in Productivity and Output." *Journal of Economic Growth* 13 (2): 145–67.

Bernanke, Ben. 2009. "Asia and the Global Financial Crisis." In *Asia and the Global Financial Crisis*, ed. Reuven Glick and Mark Spiegel. San Francisco, CA: Federal Reserve Bank of San Francisco. http://www.frbsf.org/.

Botero, Juan Carlos, Simeon Djankov, Rafael La Porta, Florencio López-de-Silanes and Andrei Shleifer. 2004. "The Regulation of Labor." *Quarterly Journal of Economics* 119 (4): 1339–82.

Branstetter, Lee G., Francisco Lima, Lowell J. Taylor and Ana Venâncio. 2010. "Do Entry Regulations Deter Entrepreneurship and Job Creation? Evidence from Recent Reforms in Portugal." NBER Working Paper 16473, National Bureau of Economic Research, Cambridge, MA.

Bruhn, Miriam. 2011. "License to Sell: The Effect of Business Registration Reform on Entrepreneurial Activity in Mexico." *Review of Economics and Statistics* 93 (1): 382–86.

Calderon, César, Alberto Chong and Gianmarco Leon. 2007. "Institutional Enforcement, Labor-Market Rigidities, and Economic Performance." *Emerging Markets Review* 8 (1): 38–49.

Cardenas, Mauricio, and Sandra Rozo. 2009. "Firm Informality in Colombia: Problems and Solutions." *Desarrollo y Sociedad*, no 63: 211–43.

Chang, Roberto, Linda Kaltani and Norman Loayza. 2009. "Openness Can Be Good for Growth: The Role of Policy Complementarities." *Journal of Development Economics* 90: 33–49.

Chari, Anusha. 2011. "Identifying the Aggregate Productivity Effects of Entry and Size Restrictions: An Empirical Analysis of License Reform in India." *American Economic Journal: Economic Policy* 3: 66–96.

Ciccone, Antonio, and Elias Papaioannou. 2007. "Red Tape and Delayed Entry." *Journal of the European Economic Association* 5 (2–3): 444–58.

Cirmizi, Elena, Leora Klapper and Mahesh Uttamchandani. 2010. "The Challenges of Bankruptcy Reform." Policy Research Working Paper 5448, World Bank, Washington, DC.

Cordova, Cesar, and Ali Haddou-Ruiz. 2008. "Regulatory Transformation in Mexico, 1988–2000: Case Studies on Reform Implementation Experience." FIAS, World Bank Group, Washington, DC. http://www.ifc.org/.

Cuñat, Alejandro, and Marc J. Melitz. 2007. "Volatility, Labor Market Flexibility, and the Pattern of Comparative Advantage." NBER Working Paper 13062, National Bureau of Economic Research, Cambridge, MA.

de Soto, Hernando. 2000. *The Mystery of Capital: Why Capitalism Triumphs in the West and Fails Everywhere Else*. New York: Basic Books.

Dewaelheyns, Nico, and Cynthia Van Hulle. 2008. "Legal Reform and Aggregate Small and Micro Business Bankruptcy Rates: Evidence from the 1997 Belgian Bankruptcy Code." *Small Business Economics* 31 (4): 409–24.

Djankov, Simeon. 2009. "The Regulation of Entry: A Survey." *World Bank Research Observer* 24 (2): 183–203.

Djankov, Simeon, Caroline Freund and Cong S. Pham. 2010. "Trading on Time." *Review of Economics and Statistics* 92 (1): 166–73.

Djankov, Simeon, Caralee McLiesh and Andrei Shleifer. 2007. "Private Credit in 129 Countries." *Journal of Financial Economics* 84 (2): 299–329.

Djankov, Simeon, Oliver Hart, Caralee McLiesh and Andrei Shleifer. 2008. "Debt Enforcement around the World." *Journal of Political Economy* 116 (6): 1105–49.

Djankov, Simeon, Rafael La Porta, Florencio López-de-Silanes and Andrei Shleifer. 2002. "The Regulation of Entry." *Quarterly Journal of Economics* 117 (1): 1–37.

___. 2003. "Courts." *Quarterly Journal of Economics* 118 (2): 453–517.

___. 2008. "The Law and Economics of Self-Dealing." *Journal of Financial Economics* 88 (3): 430–65.

Djankov, Simeon, Darshini Manraj, Caralee McLiesh and Rita Ramalho. 2005. "Doing Business Indicators: Why Aggregate, and How to Do It." World Bank, Washington, DC.

Djankov, Simeon, Tim Ganser, Caralee McLiesh, Rita Ramalho and Andrei Shleifer. 2010. "The Effect of Corporate Taxes on Investment and Entrepreneurship." *American Economic Journal: Macroeconomics* 2 (3): 31–64.

Dulleck, Uwe, Paul Frijters and R. Winter-Ebmer. 2006. "Reducing Start-up Costs for New Firms: The Double Dividend on the Labor Market." *Scandinavian Journal of Economics* 108: 317–37.

Eifert, Benjamin. 2009. "Do Regulatory Reforms Stimulate Investment and Growth? Evidence from the Doing Business Data, 2003–07." Working Paper 159, Center for Global Development, Washington, DC.

European Commission. 2005. *The Commission Recommends Candidate Status for the Former Yugoslav Republic of Macedonia*. IP/05/1391. Brussels: European Commission.

___. 2010. "Former Yugoslav Republic of Macedonia 2010 Progress Report." SEC (2010) 1332. Brussels.

___. 2011. "Smart Regulation: Action Programme for Reducing Administrative Burdens in the EU." http://ec.europa.eu/.

Fisman, Raymond, and Virginia Sarria-Allende. 2010. "Regulation of Entry and the Distortion of Industrial Organization." *Journal of Applied Economics* 13 (1): 91–120.

Funchal, Bruno. 2008. "The Effects of the 2005 Bankruptcy Reform in Brazil." *Economics Letters* 101: 84–86.

FYR Macedonia, Ministry of Economy. 2011. "Information about the Current Trends in the Bankruptcy Area in the Republic of Macedonia." Internal presentation. Skopje.

FYR Macedonia, Ministry of Justice. 2005. "The Reform of the Judicial System in the Republic of Macedonia." Skopje. Available at http://siteresources.worldbank.org/INTECA/Resources/Macedoniastrategija.pdf.

García Villarreal, Jacobo P. 2010. "Successful Practices and Policies to Promote Regulatory Reform and Entrepreneurship at the Sub-national Level." OECD Working Papers on Public Governance, no. 18, OECD, Paris. http://www.oecd.org/.

Giné, Xavier, and Inessa Love. 2010. "Do Reorganization Costs Matter for Efficiency? Evidence from a Bankruptcy Reform in Colombia." *Journal of Law and Economics* 53 (4): 833–64.

Hallward-Driemeier, Mary, Gita Khun-Jush and Lant Pritchett. 2010. "Deals versus Rules: Policy Implementation Uncertainty and Why Firms Hate It." NBER Working Paper 16001, National Bureau of Economic Research, Cambridge, MA.

Haselmann, Rainer, Katharina Pistor and Vikrant Vig. 2010. "How Law Affects Lending." *Review of Financial Studies* 23 (2): 549–80.

Houston, Joel, Chen Lin, Ping Lin and Yue Ma. 2010. "Creditor Rights, Information Sharing, and Bank Risk Taking." *Journal of Financial Economics* 96 (3): 485–512.

IMF (International Monetary Fund). 2009. *World Economic Outlook, April 2009*. Washington, DC: IMF. http://www.imf.org/.

___. 2011a. "United Kingdom: 2011 Article IV Consultation—Staff Report." IMF Country Report 11/220. http://www.imf.org/.

___. 2011b. *World Economic Outlook, April 2011*. Washington, DC: IMF. http://www.imf.org/.

Iwanow, Thomasz, and Colin Kirkpatrick. 2009. "Trade Facilitation and Manufacturing Exports: Is Africa Different?" *World Development* 37 (6): 1039–50.

Kaplan, David, Eduardo Piedra and Enrique Seira. 2007. "Entry Regulation and Business Start-Ups: Evidence from Mexico." Policy Research Working Paper 4322, World Bank, Washington, DC.

Kim, Kyungsoo. 2009. "Global Financial Crisis and the Korean Economy." In *Asia and the Global Financial Crisis*, ed. Reuven Glick and Mark Spiegel. San Francisco, CA: Federal Reserve Bank of San Francisco. http://www.frbsf.org/.

Klapper, Leora, and Inessa Love. 2011. "The Impact of Business Environment Reforms on New Firm Registration." Policy Research Working Paper 5493, World Bank, Washington, DC.

Klapper, Leora, Luc Laeven and Raghuram Rajan. 2006. "Entry Regulation as a Barrier to Entrepreneurship." *Journal of Financial Economics* 82 (3): 591–629.

Klapper, Leora, Anat Lewin and Juan Manuel Quesada Delgado. 2009. "The Impact of the Business Environment on the Business Creation Process." Policy Research Working Paper 4937, World Bank, Washington, DC.

Kraay, Aart, and Norikazu Tawara. 2011. "Can Disaggregated Indicators Identify Governance Reform Priorities?" Policy Research Working Paper 5254, World Bank, Washington, DC.

Korea Customs Service. 2009a. "The Embodiment of Business-Friendly Environment by KCS Challenges." http://www.customs.go.kr.

___. 2009b. "World Best Korea Customs." http://www.customs.go.kr.

___. 2010. "The Embodiment of Business-Friendly Environment by KCS Challenges." http://www.customs.go.kr.

La Porta, Rafael, and Andrei Shleifer. 2008. "The Unofficial Economy and Economic Development." Tuck School of Business Working Paper 2009-57. Available at http://ssrn.com/abstract=1304760.

Loayza, Norman, Ana Maria Oviedo and Luis Servén. 2005. "Regulation and Macroeconomic Performance." Policy Research Working Paper 3469, World Bank, Washington, DC.

Macedonia Court Modernization Project. 2006. *Macedonia Court Modernization Project Newsletter* (USAID) 4 (2).

Masatlioglu, Yusufcan, and Jamele Rigolini. 2008. "Informality Traps." *B.E. Journal of Economic Analysis & Policy* 8 (1).

Micco, Alejandro, and Carmen Pagés. 2006. "The Economic Effects of Employment Protection: Evidence from International Industry-Level Data." IZA Discussion Paper 2433, Institute for the Study of Labor (IZA), Bonn, Germany.

Narayan, Deepa, Robert Chambers, Meera Kaul Shah and Patti Petesh. 2000. *Voices of the Poor: Crying Out for Change*. Washington, DC: World Bank.

Nunn, Nathan. 2007. "Relationship-Specificity, Incomplete Contracts, and the Pattern of Trade." *Quarterly Journal of Economics* 122 (2): 569–600.

OECD (Organisation for Economic Co-operation and Development). 2010. "OECD Broadband Statistics (December 2010)." Press release. http://www.oecd.org/.

Oh, Soogeun, and Terence Haliday. 2009. "Rehabilitating Korea's Corporate Insolvency Regime, 1992-2007." In *Regulation in Asia: Pushing Back on Globalization*, ed. John Gillespie and Randall Peerenboom. London and New York: Routledge.

PCNC (Presidential Council on National Competitiveness). 2009. *PCNC Annual Report 2008*. Seoul.

___. 2011. *PCNC Annual Report 2010*. Seoul.

Perotti, Enrico, and Paolo Volpin. 2005. "The Political Economy of Entry: Lobbying and Financial Development." Paper presented at the American Finance Association 2005 Philadelphia Meetings.

Rauch, James. 2010. "Development through Synergistic Reforms." *Journal of Development Economics* 93 (2): 153–61.

Schneider, Friedrich. 2005. "The Informal Sector in 145 Countries." Department of Economics, University Linz, Austria.

Seker, Murat. 2011. "Trade Policies, Investment Climate, and Exports." MPRA Paper 29905, University Library of Munich, Germany.

Sharma, Siddharth. 2009. "Entry Regulation, Labor Laws and Informality: Evidence from India." Enterprise Survey Working Paper, Enterprise Analysis Unit, World Bank Group, Washington, DC.

Swedish Agency for Growth Policy Analysis. 2010. "The Economic Effects of the Regulatory Burden." Report 2010: 14. Östersund.

U.K. Department for Business, Innovation and Skills. 2010a. "Business Plan 2011-2015." London.

___. 2010b. "Reducing Regulation Made Simple—Less Regulation, Better Regulation and Regulation as a Last Resort." Better Regulation Executive. London.

___. 2011a. "One-in, One-out: Statement of New Regulation." London.

___. 2011b. "The Plan for Growth." London.

UNCITRAL (United Nations Commission on International Trade Law). 2004. *Legislative Guide on Insolvency Law*. New York: United Nations.

___. 2007. *Legislative Guide on Secured Transactions*. New York: United Nations.

United Nations Department of Economic and Social Affairs. 2010. *United Nations E-government Survey 2010*. New York: United Nations. http://www2.unpan.org/.

USAID (U.S. Agency for International Development). 2009. "Macedonia's Agenda for Action." Business Climate Legal and Institutional Reform Diagnostic, Final Report. http://www.bea.org.mk/.

Visaria, Sujata. 2009. "Legal Reform and Loan Repayment: The Microeconomic Impact of Debt Recovery Tribunals in India." *American Economic Journal: Applied Economics* 1 (3): 59–81.

WEF (World Economic Forum). 2010. *The Global Competitiveness Report 2010–2011*. Geneva: WEF.

World Bank. 2003. *Doing Business in 2004: Understanding Regulation*. Washington, DC: World Bank Group.

___. 2006a. *Doing Business in Mexico 2007*. Washington, DC: World Bank Group.

___. 2006b. *Doing Business in 2007: How to Reform*. Washington, DC: World Bank Group.

___. 2007. *Doing Business 2008*. Washington, DC: World Bank Group.

___. 2008a. *Doing Business in Mexico 2009*. Washington, DC: World Bank Group.

___. 2008b. *Doing Business 2009*. Washington, DC: World Bank Group.

___. 2009a. *Doing Business 2010: Reforming through Difficult Times*. Washington, DC: World Bank Group.

___. 2009b. *How Many Stops in a One-Stop Shop?* Washington, DC: World Bank Group.

___. 2009c. "Running a Business in Georgia." Country Note 6, Enterprise Analysis Unit, World Bank Group, Washington, DC. http://www.enterprisesurveys.org/.

___. 2010a. *Doing Business 2011: Making a Difference for Entrepreneurs*. Washington, DC: World Bank Group.

___. 2010b. *World Development Indicators 2010*. Washington, DC: World Bank.

___. 2011a. "Principles for Effective Creditor Rights and Insolvency Systems." Revised draft, January 20. http://siteresources.worldbank.org/INTGILD/Resources/ICRPrinciples_Jan2011.pdf.

___. 2011b. *World Development Indicators 2011*. Washington, DC: World Bank.

World Bank Independent Evaluation Group. 2008. *Doing Business: An Independent Evaluation—Taking the Measure of the World Bank-IFC Doing Business Indicators*. Washington, DC: World Bank.

Data notes

The indicators presented and analyzed in *Doing Business* measure business regulation and the protection of property rights—and their effect on businesses, especially small and medium-size domestic firms. First, the indicators document the complexity of regulation, such as the number of procedures to start a business or to register and transfer commercial property. Second, they gauge the time and cost of achieving a regulatory goal or complying with regulation, such as the time and cost to enforce a contract, go through bankruptcy or trade across borders. Third, they measure the extent of legal protections of property, for example, the protections of investors against looting by company directors or the range of assets that can be used as collateral according to secured transactions laws. Fourth, a set of indicators documents the tax burden on businesses. Finally, a set of data covers different aspects of employment regulation.

The data for all sets of indicators in *Doing Business 2012* are for June 2011.[1]

METHODOLOGY

The *Doing Business* data are collected in a standardized way. To start, the *Doing Business* team, with academic advisers, designs a questionnaire. The questionnaire uses a simple business case to ensure comparability across economies and over time—with assumptions about the legal form of the business, its size, its location and the nature of its operations. Questionnaires are administered through more than 9,028 local experts, including lawyers, business consultants, accountants, freight forwarders, government officials and other professionals routinely administering or advising on legal and regulatory requirements (table 4.1). These experts have several rounds of interaction with the *Doing Business* team, involving

conference calls, written correspondence and visits by the team. For *Doing Business 2012* team members visited 40 economies to verify data and recruit respondents. The data from questionnaires are subjected to numerous rounds of verification, leading to revisions or expansions of the information collected.

The *Doing Business* methodology offers several advantages. It is transparent, using factual information about what laws and regulations say and allowing multiple interactions with local respondents to clarify potential misinterpretations of questions. Having representative samples of respondents is not an issue; *Doing Business* is not a statistical survey, and the texts of the relevant laws and regulations are collected and answers checked for accuracy. The methodology is inexpensive and easily replicable, so data can be collected in a large sample of economies. Because standard assumptions are used in the data collection, comparisons and benchmarks are valid across economies. Finally, the data not only highlight the extent of specific regulatory obstacles to business but also identify their source and point to what might be reformed.

TABLE 4.1	How many experts does *Doing Business* consult?
Indicator set	Contributors
Starting a business	1,755
Dealing with construction permits	837
Getting electricity	782
Registering property	1,257
Getting credit	1,277
Protecting investors	1,139
Paying taxes	1,276
Trading across borders	868
Enforcing contracts	1,088
Resolving insolvency	1,044
Employing workers	1,092

ECONOMY CHARACTERISTICS

Gross national income (GNI) per capita

Doing Business 2012 reports 2010 income per capita as published in the World Bank's *World Development Indicators 2011*. Income is calculated using the Atlas method (current US$). For cost indicators expressed as a percentage of income per capita, 2010 GNI in U.S. dollars is used as the denominator. Data were not available from the World Bank for Afghanistan; Australia; The Bahamas; Bahrain; Brunei Darussalam; Canada; Cyprus; Djibouti; the Islamic Republic of Iran; Kuwait; New Zealand; Oman; Puerto Rico (territory of the United States); Qatar; Saudi Arabia; Suriname; Taiwan, China; the United Arab Emirates; West Bank and Gaza; and the Republic of Yemen. In these cases GDP or GNP per capita data and growth rates from the International Monetary Fund's World Economic Outlook database and the Economist Intelligence Unit were used.

Region and income group

Doing Business uses the World Bank regional and income group classifications, available at http://www.worldbank.org/data/countryclass. The World Bank does not assign regional classifications to high-income economies. For the purpose of the *Doing Business* report, high-income OECD economies are assigned the "regional" classification *OECD high income*. Figures and tables presenting regional averages include economies from all income groups (low, lower middle, upper middle and high income).

Population

Doing Business 2012 reports midyear 2010 population statistics as published in *World Development Indicators 2011*.

LIMITS TO WHAT IS MEASURED

The *Doing Business* methodology has 5 limitations that should be considered when interpreting the data. First, the collected data refer to businesses in the economy's largest business city and may not be representative of regulation in other parts of the economy. To address this limitation, subnational *Doing Business* indicators were created (box 4.1). Second, the data often focus on a specific business form—generally a limited liability company (or its legal equivalent) of a specified size—and may not be representative of the regulation on other businesses, for example, sole proprietorships. Third, transactions described in a standardized case scenario refer to a specific set of issues and may not represent the full set of issues a business encounters. Fourth, the measures of time involve an element of judgment by

the expert respondents. When sources indicate different estimates, the time indicators reported in *Doing Business* represent the median values of several responses given under the assumptions of the standardized case.

Finally, the methodology assumes that a business has full information on what is required and does not waste time when completing procedures. In practice, completing a procedure may take longer if the business lacks information or is unable to follow up promptly. Alternatively, the business may choose to disregard some burdensome procedures. For both reasons the time delays reported in *Doing Business 2012* would differ from the recollection of entrepreneurs reported in the World Bank Enterprise Surveys or other perception surveys.

CHANGES IN WHAT IS MEASURED

The methodology for 3 of the *Doing Business* topics was updated this year—getting credit, dealing with construction permits and paying taxes.

First, for getting credit, the scoring of one of the 10 components of the strength of legal rights index was amended to recognize additional protections of secured creditors and borrowers. Previously the highest score of 1 was assigned if secured creditors were not subject to an automatic stay or moratorium on enforcement procedures when a debtor entered a court-supervised reorganization procedure. Now the highest score of 1 is also assigned if the law provides secured creditors with grounds for relief from an automatic stay or moratorium (for example, if the movable property is in danger) or sets a time limit for the automatic stay.

Second, because the ease of doing business index now includes the getting electricity indicators, procedures, time and cost related to obtaining an electricity connection were removed from the dealing with construction permits indicators.

Third, a threshold has been introduced for the total tax rate for the purpose of calculating the ranking on the ease of paying taxes. All economies with a total tax rate below the threshold (which will be calculated and adjusted on a yearly basis) will now receive the

same ranking on the total tax rate indicator. The threshold is not based on any underlying theory. Instead, it is meant to emphasize the purpose of the indicator: to highlight economies where the tax burden on business is high relative to the tax burden in other economies. Giving the same ranking to all economies whose total tax rate is below the threshold avoids awarding economies in the scoring for having an unusually low total tax rate, often for reasons unrelated to government policies toward enterprises. For example, economies that are very small or that are rich in natural resources do not need to levy broad-based taxes.

DATA CHALLENGES AND REVISIONS

Most laws and regulations underlying the *Doing Business* data are available on the *Doing Business* website at http://www.doing business.org. All the sample questionnaires and the details underlying the indicators are also published on the website. Questions on the methodology and challenges to data can be submitted through the website's "Ask a Question" function at http://www.doingbusiness.org.

Doing Business publishes 8,967 indicators each year. To create these indicators, the team measures more than 52,000 data points, each of which is made available on the *Doing Business* website. Historical data for each indicator and economy are available on the website, beginning with the first year the indicator or economy was included in the report. To provide a comparable time series for research, the data set is back-calculated to adjust for changes in methodology and any revisions in data due to corrections. The website also makes available all original data sets used for background papers. The correction rate between *Doing Business 2011* and *Doing Business 2012* is 7%.

STARTING A BUSINESS

Doing Business records all procedures that are officially required for an entrepreneur to start up and formally operate an industrial or commercial business. These include obtaining all necessary licenses and permits and completing any required notifications,

FIGURE 4.1   Starting a business: getting a local limited liability company up and running
Rankings are based on 4 indicators

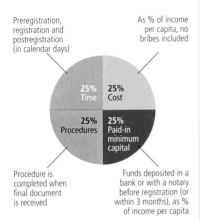

Preregistration, registration and postregistration (in calendar days)

As % of income per capita, no bribes included

| 25% Time | 25% Cost |
| 25% Procedures | 25% Paid-in minimum capital |

Procedure is completed when final document is received

Funds deposited in a bank or with a notary before registration (or within 3 months), as % of income per capita

verifications or inscriptions for the company and employees with relevant authorities. The ranking on the ease of starting a business is the simple average of the percentile rankings on its component indicators (figure 4.1).

After a study of laws, regulations and publicly available information on business entry, a detailed list of procedures is developed, along with the time and cost of complying with each procedure under normal circumstances and the paid-in minimum capital requirements. Subsequently, local incorporation lawyers, notaries and government officials complete and verify the data.

Information is also collected on the sequence in which procedures are to be completed and whether procedures may be carried out simultaneously. It is assumed that any required information is readily available and that all agencies involved in the start-up process function without corruption. If answers by local experts differ, inquiries continue until the data are reconciled.

To make the data comparable across economies, several assumptions about the business and the procedures are used.

Assumptions about the business

The business:

• Is a limited liability company (or its legal equivalent). If there is more than one type of limited liability company in the economy, the limited liability form most popular among domestic firms is chosen. Information on the most popular form is obtained from incorporation lawyers or the statistical office.

• Operates in the economy's largest business city.

• Is 100% domestically owned and has 5 owners, none of whom is a legal entity.

• Has start-up capital of 10 times income per capita at the end of 2010, paid in cash.

• Performs general industrial or commercial activities, such as the production or sale to the public of products or services. The business does not perform foreign trade activities and does not handle products subject to a special tax regime, for example, liquor or tobacco. It is not using heavily polluting production processes.

• Leases the commercial plant and offices and is not a proprietor of real estate.

• Does not qualify for investment incentives or any special benefits.

• Has at least 10 and up to 50 employees 1 month after the commencement of operations, all of them nationals.

• Has a turnover of at least 100 times income per capita.

• Has a company deed 10 pages long.

Procedures

A procedure is defined as any interaction of the company founders with external parties (for example, government agencies, lawyers, auditors or notaries). Interactions between company founders or company officers and employees are not counted as procedures. Procedures that must be completed in the same building but in different offices are counted as separate procedures. If founders have to visit the same office several times for different sequential procedures, each is counted separately. The founders are assumed to complete all procedures themselves, without middlemen, facilitators, accountants or lawyers, unless the use of such a third party is mandated by law. If the services of professionals are required, procedures conducted by such professionals on behalf of the company are counted separately. Each electronic procedure is counted separately. If 2 procedures can be completed through the same website but

TABLE 4.2	What do the starting a business indicators measure?
Procedures to legally start and operate a company (number)	
Preregistration (for example, name verification or reservation, notarization)	
Registration in the economy's largest business city	
Postregistration (for example, social security registration, company seal)	
Time required to complete each procedure (calendar days)	
Does not include time spent gathering information	
Each procedure starts on a separate day	
Procedure completed once final document is received	
No prior contact with officials	
Cost required to complete each procedure (% of income per capita)	
Official costs only, no bribes	
No professional fees unless services required by law	
Paid-in minimum capital (% of income per capita)	
Funds deposited in a bank or with a notary before registration (or within 3 months)	

require separate filings, they are counted as 2 procedures.

Both pre- and postincorporation procedures that are officially required for an entrepreneur to formally operate a business are recorded (table 4.2).

Procedures required for official correspondence or transactions with public agencies are also included. For example, if a company seal or stamp is required on official documents, such as tax declarations, obtaining the seal or stamp is counted. Similarly, if a company must open a bank account before registering for sales tax or value added tax, this transaction is included as a procedure. Shortcuts are counted only if they fulfill 4 criteria: they are legal, they are available to the general public, they are used by the majority of companies, and avoiding them causes substantial delays.

Only procedures required of all businesses are covered. Industry-specific procedures are excluded. For example, procedures to comply with environmental regulations are included only when they apply to all businesses conducting general commercial or industrial activities. Procedures that the company undergoes to connect to electricity, water, gas and waste disposal services are not included.

Time

Time is recorded in calendar days. The measure captures the median duration that incorporation lawyers indicate is necessary in practice to complete a procedure with minimum follow-up with government agencies and no extra payments. It is assumed that the minimum time required for each procedure is 1 day. Although procedures may take place simultaneously, they cannot start on the same day (that is, simultaneous procedures start on consecutive days). A procedure is considered completed once the company has received the final document, such as the company registration certificate or tax number. If a procedure can be accelerated for an additional cost, the fastest procedure is chosen. It is assumed that the entrepreneur does not waste time and commits to completing each remaining procedure without delay. The time that the entrepreneur spends on gathering information is ignored. It is assumed that the entrepreneur is aware of all entry requirements and their sequence from the beginning but has had no prior contact with any of the officials.

Cost

Cost is recorded as a percentage of the economy's income per capita. It includes all official fees and fees for legal or professional services if such services are required by law. Fees for purchasing and legalizing company books are included if these transactions are required by law. The company law, the commercial code and specific regulations and fee schedules are used as sources for calculating costs. In the absence of fee schedules, a government officer's estimate is taken as an official source. In the absence of a government officer's estimate, estimates of incorporation lawyers are used. If several incorporation lawyers provide different estimates, the median reported value is applied. In all cases the cost excludes bribes.

Paid-in minimum capital

The paid-in minimum capital requirement reflects the amount that the entrepreneur needs to deposit in a bank or with a notary before registration and up to 3 months following incorporation and is recorded as a percentage of the economy's income per capita. The amount is typically specified in the commercial code or the company law. Many economies require minimum capital but allow businesses to pay only a part of it before registration, with the rest to be paid after the first year of operation. In Italy in June 2011 the minimum capital requirement for limited liability companies was €10,000, of which at least €2,500 was payable before registration. The paid-in minimum capital recorded for Italy is therefore €2,500, or 9.9% of income per capita. In Mexico the minimum capital requirement was 50,000 pesos, of which one-fifth needed to be paid before registration. The paid-in minimum capital recorded for Mexico is therefore 10,000 pesos, or 8.4% of income per capita.

The data details on starting a business can be found for each economy at http://www .doingbusiness.org by selecting the economy in the drop-down list. This methodology was developed in Djankov and others (2002) and is adopted here with minor changes.

DEALING WITH CONSTRUCTION PERMITS

Doing Business records all procedures required for a business in the construction industry to build a standardized warehouse. These procedures include submitting all relevant project-specific documents (for example, building plans and site maps) to the authorities; obtaining all necessary clearances, licenses, permits and certificates; completing all required notifications; and receiving all necessary inspections. *Doing Business* also records procedures for obtaining connections for water, sewerage and a fixed telephone landline.[2] Procedures necessary to register the property so that it can be used as collateral or transferred to another entity are also counted. The survey divides the process of building a warehouse into distinct procedures and calculates the time and cost of completing each procedure. The ranking on the ease of dealing with construction permits is the simple average of the percentile rankings on its component indicators (figure 4.2).

Information is collected from experts in construction licensing, including architects, construction lawyers, construction firms, utility service providers and public officials

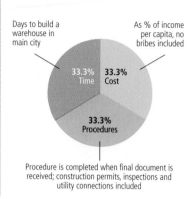

FIGURE 4.2   Dealing with construction permits: building a warehouse

Rankings are based on 3 indicators

Days to build a warehouse in main city

As % of income per capita, no bribes included

33.3% Time

33.3% Cost

33.3% Procedures

Procedure is completed when final document is received; construction permits, inspections and utility connections included

who deal with building regulations, including approvals and inspections. To make the data comparable across economies, several assumptions about the business, the warehouse project and the utility connections are used.

Assumptions about the construction company

The business (BuildCo):

- Is a limited liability company.
- Operates in the economy's largest business city.
- Is 100% domestically and privately owned.
- Has 5 owners, none of whom is a legal entity.
- Is fully licensed and insured to carry out construction projects, such as building warehouses.
- Has 60 builders and other employees, all of them nationals with the technical expertise and professional experience necessary to obtain construction permits and approvals.
- Has at least 1 employee who is a licensed architect and registered with the local association of architects.
- Has paid all taxes and taken out all necessary insurance applicable to its general business activity (for example, accidental insurance for construction workers and third-person liability).
- Owns the land on which the warehouse is built.

Assumptions about the warehouse

The warehouse:

- Will be used for general storage activities, such as storage of books or stationery. The warehouse will not be used for any goods requiring special conditions, such as food, chemicals or pharmaceuticals.
- Has 2 stories, both above ground, with a total surface of approximately 1,300.6 square meters (14,000 square feet). Each floor is 3 meters (9 feet, 10 inches) high.
- Has road access and is located in the periurban area of the economy's largest business city (that is, on the fringes of the city but still within its official limits).
- Is not located in a special economic or industrial zone. The zoning requirements for warehouses are met by building in an area where similar warehouses can be found.
- Is located on a land plot of 929 square meters (10,000 square feet) that is 100% owned by BuildCo and is accurately registered in the cadastre and land registry.
- Is a new construction (there was no previous construction on the land).
- Has complete architectural and technical plans prepared by a licensed architect.
- Will include all technical equipment required to make the warehouse fully operational.
- Will take 30 weeks to construct (excluding all delays due to administrative and regulatory requirements).

Assumptions about the utility connections

The water and sewerage connection:

- Is 10 meters (32 feet, 10 inches) from the existing water source and sewer tap.
- Does not require water for fire protection reasons; a fire extinguishing system (dry system) will be used instead. If a wet fire protection system is required by law, it is assumed that the water demand specified below also covers the water needed for fire protection.
- Has an average water use of 662 liters (175 gallons) a day and an average wastewater flow of 568 liters (150 gallons) a day.
- Has a peak water use of 1,325 liters (350 gallons) a day and a peak wastewater flow of 1,136 liters (300 gallons) a day.

- Will have a constant level of water demand and wastewater flow throughout the year.

The telephone connection:

- Is 10 meters (32 feet, 10 inches) from the main telephone network.
- Is a fixed telephone landline.

Procedures

A procedure is any interaction of the company's employees or managers with external parties, including government agencies, notaries, the land registry, the cadastre, utility companies, public and private inspectors and technical experts apart from in-house architects and engineers. Interactions between company employees, such as development of the warehouse plans and inspections conducted by employees, are not counted as procedures. Procedures that the company undergoes to connect to water, sewerage and telephone services are included. All procedures that are legally or in practice required for building a warehouse are counted, even if they may be avoided in exceptional cases (table 4.3).

Time

Time is recorded in calendar days. The measure captures the median duration that local experts indicate is necessary to complete a procedure in practice. It is assumed that the

TABLE 4.3	What do the dealing with construction permits indicators measure?
Procedures to legally build a warehouse (number)	
Submitting all relevant documents and obtaining all necessary clearances, licenses, permits and certificates	
Completing all required notifications and receiving all necessary inspections	
Obtaining utility connections for water, sewerage and a fixed telephone landline	
Registering the warehouse after its completion (if required for use as collateral or for transfer of the warehouse)	
Time required to complete each procedure (calendar days)	
Does not include time spent gathering information	
Each procedure starts on a separate day	
Procedure completed once final document is received	
No prior contact with officials	
Cost required to complete each procedure (% of income per capita)	
Official costs only, no bribes	

minimum time required for each procedure is 1 day. Although procedures may take place simultaneously, they cannot start on the same day (that is, simultaneous procedures start on consecutive days). If a procedure can be accelerated legally for an additional cost, the fastest procedure is chosen. It is assumed that BuildCo does not waste time and commits to completing each remaining procedure without delay. The time that BuildCo spends on gathering information is ignored. It is assumed that BuildCo is aware of all building requirements and their sequence from the beginning.

Cost

Cost is recorded as a percentage of the economy's income per capita. Only official costs are recorded. All the fees associated with completing the procedures to legally build a warehouse are recorded, including those associated with obtaining land use approvals and preconstruction design clearances; receiving inspections before, during and after construction; getting utility connections; and registering the warehouse property. Nonrecurring taxes required for the completion of the warehouse project are also recorded. The building code, information from local experts and specific regulations and fee schedules are used as sources for costs. If several local partners provide different estimates, the median reported value is used.

The data details on dealing with construction permits can be found for each economy at http://www.doingbusiness.org by selecting the economy in the drop-down list.

GETTING ELECTRICITY

Doing Business records all procedures required for a business to obtain a permanent electricity connection and supply for a standardized warehouse. These procedures include applications and contracts with electricity utilities, all necessary inspections and clearances from the utility and other agencies and the external and final connection works. The survey divides the process of getting an electricity connection into distinct procedures and calculates the time and cost of completing each procedure. The ranking on the ease of getting electricity is the simple average of the percentile rankings on its component indicators (figure 4.3).

Data are collected from the electricity distribution utility, then completed and verified by electricity regulatory agencies and independent professionals such as electrical engineers, electrical contractors and construction companies. The electricity distribution utility surveyed is the one serving the area (or areas) where warehouses are located. If there is a choice of distribution utilities, the one serving the largest number of customers is selected.

To make the data comparable across economies, several assumptions about the warehouse and the electricity connection are used.

Assumptions about the warehouse

The warehouse:

- Is owned by a local entrepreneur.
- Is located in the economy's largest business city.
- Is located within the city's official limits and in an area where other warehouses are located (a nonresidential area).
- Is not located in a special economic or investment zone; that is, the electricity connection is not eligible for subsidization or faster service under a special investment promotion regime. If several options for location are available, the warehouse is located where electricity is most easily available.
- Has road access. The connection works involve the crossing of a road (for excavation, overhead lines and the like), but they are all carried out on public land; that is, there is no crossing onto another owner's private property.
- Is located in an area with no physical constraints. For example, the property is not near a railway.
- Is used for storage of refrigerated goods.
- Is a new construction (that is, there was no previous construction on the land where it is located). It is being connected to electricity for the first time.
- Has 2 stories, both above ground, with a total surface area of approximately 1,300.6 square meters (14,000 square

feet). The plot of land on which it is built is 929 square meters (10,000 square feet).

Assumptions about the electricity connection

The electricity connection:

- Is a permanent one.
- Is a 3-phase, 4-wire Y, 140-kilovolt-ampere (kVA) (subscribed capacity) connection.
- Is 150 meters long. The connection is to either the low-voltage or the medium-voltage distribution network and either overhead or underground, whichever is more common in the economy and in the area where the warehouse is located. The length of any connection in the customer's private domain is negligible.
- Involves the installation of only one electricity meter. The monthly electricity consumption will be 0.07 gigawatt-hour (GWh). The internal electrical wiring has already been completed.

Procedures

A procedure is defined as any interaction of the company's employees or its main electrician or electrical engineer (that is, the one who may have done the internal wiring) with external parties such as the electricity distribution utility, electricity supply utilities, government agencies, electrical contractors and electrical firms.

TABLE 4.4   What do the getting electricity indicators measure?
Procedures to obtain an electricity connection (number)
Submitting all relevant documents and obtaining all necessary clearances and permits
Completing all required notifications and receiving all necessary inspections
Obtaining external installation works and possibly purchasing material for these works
Concluding any necessary supply contract and obtaining final supply
Time required to complete each procedure (calendar days)
Is at least 1 calendar day
Each procedure starts on a separate day
Does not include time spent gathering information
Reflects the time spent in practice, with little follow-up and no prior contact with officials
Cost required to complete each procedure (% of income per capita)
Official costs only, no bribes
Value added tax excluded

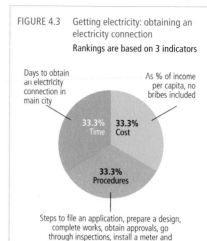

FIGURE 4.3   Getting electricity: obtaining an electricity connection

Rankings are based on 3 indicators

Days to obtain an electricity connection in main city

As % of income per capita, no bribes included

33.3% Time

33.3% Cost

33.3% Procedures

Steps to file an application, prepare a design, complete works, obtain approvals, go through inspections, install a meter and sign a supply contract

Interactions between company employees and steps related to the internal electrical wiring, such as the design and execution of the internal electrical installation plans, are not counted as procedures. Procedures that must be completed with the same utility but with different departments are counted as separate procedures (table 4.4).

The company's employees are assumed to complete all procedures themselves unless the use of a third party is mandated (for example, if only an electrician registered with the utility is allowed to submit an application). If the company can, but is not required to, request the services of professionals (such as a private firm rather than the utility for the external works), these procedures are recorded if they are commonly done. For all procedures, only the most likely cases (for example, more than 50% of the time the utility has the material) and those followed in practice for connecting a warehouse to electricity are counted.

Time

Time is recorded in calendar days. The measure captures the median duration that the electricity utility and experts indicate is necessary in practice, rather than required by law, to complete a procedure with minimum follow-up and no extra payments. It is also assumed that the minimum time required for each procedure is 1 day. Although procedures may take place simultaneously, they cannot start on the same day (that is, simultaneous procedures start on consecutive days). It is assumed that the company does not waste time and commits to completing each remaining procedure without delay. The time that the company spends on gathering information is ignored. It is assumed that the company is aware of all electricity connection requirements and their sequence from the beginning.

Cost

Cost is recorded as a percentage of the economy's income per capita. Costs are recorded exclusive of value added tax. All the fees and costs associated with completing the procedures to connect a warehouse to electricity are recorded, including those related to obtaining clearances from government agencies, applying for the connection, receiving inspections of both the site and the internal wiring, purchasing material, getting the actual connection works and paying a security deposit. Information from local experts and specific regulations and fee schedules are used as sources for costs. If several local partners provide different estimates, the median reported value is used. In all cases the cost excludes bribes.

Security deposit

Utilities require security deposits as a guarantee against the possible failure of customers to pay their consumption bills. For this reason the security deposit for a new customer is most often calculated as a function of the customer's estimated consumption.

Doing Business does not record the full amount of the security deposit. If the deposit is based on the customer's actual consumption, this basis is the one assumed in the case study. Rather than the full amount of the security deposit, *Doing Business* records the present value of the losses in interest earnings experienced by the customer because the utility holds the security deposit over a prolonged period, in most cases until the end of the contract (assumed to be after 5 years). In cases where the security deposit is used to cover the first monthly consumption bills, it is not recorded. To calculate the present value of the lost interest earnings, the end-2010 lending rates from the International Monetary Fund's *International Financial Statistics* are used. In cases where the security deposit is returned with interest, the difference between the lending rate

and the interest paid by the utility is used to calculate the present value.

In some economies the security deposit can be put up in the form of a bond: the company can obtain from a bank or an insurance company a guarantee issued on the assets it holds with that financial institution. In contrast to the scenario in which the customer pays the deposit in cash to the utility, in this scenario the company does not lose ownership control over the full amount and can continue using it. In return the company will pay the bank a commission for obtaining the bond. The commission charged may vary depending on the credit standing of the company. The best possible credit standing and thus the lowest possible commission are assumed. Where a bond can be put up, the value recorded for the deposit is the annual commission times the 5 years assumed to be the length of the contract. If both options exist, the cheaper alternative is recorded.

In Honduras in June 2011 a customer requesting a 140-kVA electricity connection would have had to put up a security deposit of 126,894 Honduran lempiras (L) in cash or check, and the deposit would have been returned only at the end of the contract. The customer could instead have invested this money at the prevailing lending rate of 18.87%. Over the 5 years of the contract this would imply a present value of lost interest earnings of L 73,423. In contrast, if the customer chose to settle the deposit with a bank guarantee at an annual rate of 2.5%, the amount lost over the 5 years would be just L 15,862.

The data details on getting electricity can be found for each economy at http://www.doing business.org.

REGISTERING PROPERTY

Doing Business records the full sequence of procedures necessary for a business (buyer) to purchase a property from another business (seller) and to transfer the property title to the buyer's name so that the buyer can use the property for expanding its business, use the property as collateral in taking new loans or, if necessary, sell the property to another business. The process starts with obtaining

the necessary documents, such as a copy of the seller's title if necessary, and conducting due diligence if required. The transaction is considered complete when it is opposable to third parties and when the buyer can use the property, use it as collateral for a bank loan or resell it. The ranking on the ease of registering property is the simple average of the percentile rankings on its component indicators (figure 4.4).

Every procedure required by law or necessary in practice is included, whether it is the responsibility of the seller or the buyer or must be completed by a third party on their behalf. Local property lawyers, notaries and property registries provide information on procedures as well as the time and cost to complete each of them.

To make the data comparable across economies, several assumptions about the parties to the transaction, the property and the procedures are used.

Assumptions about the parties

The parties (buyer and seller):
• Are limited liability companies.
• Are located in the periurban area of the economy's largest business city.
• Are 100% domestically and privately owned.
• Have 50 employees each, all of whom are nationals.
• Perform general commercial activities.

Assumptions about the property

The property:
• Has a value of 50 times income per capita. The sale price equals the value.
• Is fully owned by the seller.
• Has no mortgages attached and has been under the same ownership for the past 10 years.
• Is registered in the land registry or cadastre, or both, and is free of title disputes.
• Is located in a periurban commercial zone, and no rezoning is required.
• Consists of land and a building. The land area is 557.4 square meters (6,000 square feet). A 2-story warehouse of 929 square meters (10,000 square feet) is located on the land. The warehouse is 10 years old,

FIGURE 4.4   Registering property: transfer of property between 2 local companies
Rankings are based on 3 indicators

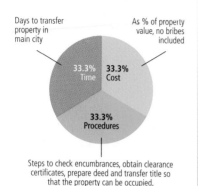

Days to transfer property in main city

As % of property value, no bribes included

33.3% Time   33.3% Cost

33.3% Procedures

Steps to check encumbrances, obtain clearance certificates, prepare deed and transfer title so that the property can be occupied, sold or used as collateral

is in good condition and complies with all safety standards, building codes and other legal requirements. The property of land and building will be transferred in its entirety.

• Will not be subject to renovations or additional building following the purchase.

• Has no trees, natural water sources, natural reserves or historical monuments of any kind.

• Will not be used for special purposes, and no special permits, such as for residential use, industrial plants, waste storage or certain types of agricultural activities, are required.

• Has no occupants (legal or illegal), and no other party holds a legal interest in it.

Procedures

A procedure is defined as any interaction of the buyer or the seller, their agents (if an agent is legally or in practice required) or the property with external parties, including government agencies, inspectors, notaries and lawyers. Interactions between company officers and employees are not considered. All procedures that are legally or in practice required for registering property are recorded, even if they may be avoided in exceptional cases (table 4.5). It is assumed that the buyer follows the fastest legal option available and used by the majority of property owners. Although the buyer may use lawyers or other professionals where necessary in the registration process, it is assumed

that the buyer does not employ an outside facilitator in the registration process unless legally or in practice required to do so.

Time

Time is recorded in calendar days. The measure captures the median duration that property lawyers, notaries or registry officials indicate is necessary to complete a procedure. It is assumed that the minimum time required for each procedure is 1 day. Although procedures may take place simultaneously, they cannot start on the same day. It is assumed that the buyer does not waste time and commits to completing each remaining procedure without delay. If a procedure can be accelerated for an additional cost, the fastest legal procedure available and used by the majority of property owners is chosen. If procedures can be undertaken simultaneously, it is assumed that they are. It is assumed that the parties involved are aware of all requirements and their sequence from the beginning. Time spent on gathering information is not considered.

Cost

Cost is recorded as a percentage of the property value, assumed to be equivalent to 50 times income per capita. Only official costs required by law are recorded, including fees, transfer taxes, stamp duties and any other payment to the property registry, notaries, public agencies or lawyers. Other taxes, such as capital gains tax or value added tax, are

TABLE 4.5	What do the registering property indicators measure?
Procedures to legally transfer title on immovable property (number)	
Preregistration procedures (for example, checking for liens, notarizing sales agreement, paying property transfer taxes)	
Registration procedures in the economy's largest business city	
Postregistration procedures (for example, filing title with municipality)	
Time required to complete each procedure (calendar days)	
Does not include time spent gathering information	
Each procedure starts on a separate day	
Procedure completed once final document is received	
No prior contact with officials	
Cost required to complete each procedure (% of property value)	
Official costs only, no bribes	
No value added or capital gains taxes included	

excluded from the cost measure. Both costs borne by the buyer and those borne by the seller are included. If cost estimates differ among sources, the median reported value is used.

The data details on registering property can be found for each economy at http://www .doingbusiness.org by selecting the economy in the drop-down list.

GETTING CREDIT

Doing Business measures the legal rights of borrowers and lenders with respect to secured transactions through one set of indicators and the sharing of credit information through another. The first set of indicators describes how well collateral and bankruptcy laws facilitate lending. The second set measures the coverage, scope and accessibility of credit information available through public credit registries and private credit bureaus. The ranking on the ease of getting credit is based on the percentile rankings on its component indicators: the depth of credit information index (weighted at 37.5%) and the strength of legal rights index (weighted at 62.5%) (figure 4.5).[3]

LEGAL RIGHTS

The data on the legal rights of borrowers and lenders are gathered through a survey of financial lawyers and verified through analysis of laws and regulations as well as public sources of information on collateral and bankruptcy laws. Survey responses are verified through several rounds of follow-up communication with respondents as well as by contacting third parties and consulting public sources. The survey data are confirmed through teleconference calls or on-site visits in all economies.

Strength of legal rights index

The strength of legal rights index measures the degree to which collateral and bankruptcy laws protect the rights of borrowers and lenders and thus facilitate lending (table 4.6). Two case scenarios, case A and case B, are used to determine the scope of the secured transactions system. The case scenarios involve a secured borrower, the company ABC, and a secured lender, BizBank. In certain

FIGURE 4.5 Getting credit: collateral rules and credit information
Rankings are based on 2 indicators

Scope, quality and accessibility of credit information through public and private credit registries

37.5% Depth of credit information index (0–6)

62.5% Strength of legal rights index (0–10)

Regulations on nonpossessory security interests in movable property

Note: Private bureau coverage and public registry coverage are measured but do not count for the rankings.

economies the legal framework for secured transactions means that only case A or case B can apply (not both). Both cases examine the same set of legal provisions relating to the use of movable collateral.

Several assumptions about the secured borrower and lender are used:

- ABC is a domestic, limited liability company.
- The company has 100 employees.
- ABC has its headquarters and only base of operations in the economy's largest business city.
- Both ABC and BizBank are 100% domestically owned.

TABLE 4.6	What do the getting credit indicators measure?
Strength of legal rights index (0–10)
Protection of rights of borrowers and lenders through collateral laws
Protection of secured creditors' rights through bankruptcy laws
Depth of credit information index (0–6)
Scope and accessibility of credit information distributed by public credit registries and private credit bureaus
Public credit registry coverage (% of adults)
Number of individuals and firms listed in a public credit registry as percentage of adult population
Private credit bureau coverage (% of adults)
Number of individuals and firms listed in largest private credit bureau as percentage of adult population

The case scenarios also involve assumptions. In case A, as collateral for the loan, ABC grants BizBank a nonpossessory security interest in one category of movable assets, for example, its accounts receivable or its inventory. ABC wants to keep both possession and ownership of the collateral. In economies where the law does not allow nonpossessory security interests in movable property, ABC and BizBank use a fiduciary transfer-of-title arrangement (or a similar substitute for nonpossessory security interests). The strength of legal rights index does not cover functional equivalents to security over movable assets (for example, leasing or reservation of title).

In case B, ABC grants BizBank a business charge, enterprise charge, floating charge or any charge that gives BizBank a security interest over ABC's combined movable assets (or as much of ABC's movable assets as possible). ABC keeps ownership and possession of the assets.

The strength of legal rights index includes 8 aspects related to legal rights in collateral law and 2 aspects in bankruptcy law. A score of 1 is assigned for each of the following features of the laws:

- Any business may use movable assets as collateral while keeping possession of the assets, and any financial institution may accept such assets as collateral.
- The law allows a business to grant a nonpossessory security right in a single category of movable assets (such as accounts receivable or inventory), without requiring a specific description of the collateral.
- The law allows a business to grant a nonpossessory security right in substantially all its movable assets, without requiring a specific description of the collateral.
- A security right may extend to future or after-acquired assets and may extend automatically to the products, proceeds or replacements of the original assets.
- A general description of debts and obligations is permitted in the collateral agreement and in registration documents; all types of debts and obligations can be secured between the parties, and the collateral agreement can include a

maximum amount for which the assets are encumbered.

- A collateral registry or registration institution for security interests over movable property is in operation, unified geographically and by asset type, with an electronic database indexed by debtors' names.
- Secured creditors are paid first (for example, before general tax claims and employee claims) when a debtor defaults outside an insolvency procedure.
- Secured creditors are paid first (for example, before general tax claims and employee claims) when a business is liquidated.
- Secured creditors either are not subject to an automatic stay or moratorium on enforcement procedures when a debtor enters a court-supervised reorganization procedure, or the law provides secured creditors with grounds for relief from an automatic stay or moratorium (for example, if the movable property is in danger) or sets a time limit for the automatic stay.[4]
- The law allows parties to agree in a collateral agreement that the lender may enforce its security right out of court.

The index ranges from 0 to 10, with higher scores indicating that collateral and bankruptcy laws are better designed to expand access to credit.

CREDIT INFORMATION

The data on credit information sharing are built in 2 stages. First, banking supervision authorities and public information sources are surveyed to confirm the presence of a public credit registry or private credit bureau. Second, when applicable, a detailed survey on the public credit registry's or private credit bureau's structure, laws and associated rules is administered to the entity itself. Survey responses are verified through several rounds of follow-up communication with respondents as well as by contacting third parties and consulting public sources. The survey data are confirmed through teleconference calls or on-site visits in all economies.

Depth of credit information index

The depth of credit information index measures rules and practices affecting the coverage, scope and accessibility of credit information available through either a public credit registry or a private credit bureau. A score of 1 is assigned for each of the following 6 features of the public credit registry or private credit bureau (or both):

• Both positive credit information (for example, outstanding loan amounts and pattern of on-time repayments) and negative information (for example, late payments, and number and amount of defaults and bankruptcies) are distributed.

• Data on both firms and individuals are distributed.

• Data from retailers and utility companies as well as financial institutions are distributed.

• More than 2 years of historical data are distributed. Credit registries and bureaus that erase data on defaults as soon as they are repaid obtain a score of 0 for this indicator.

• Data on loan amounts below 1% of income per capita are distributed. Note that a credit registry or bureau must have a minimum coverage of 1% of the adult population to score a 1 on this indicator.

• By law, borrowers have the right to access their data in the largest credit registry or bureau in the economy.

The index ranges from 0 to 6, with higher values indicating the availability of more credit information, from either a public credit registry or a private credit bureau, to facilitate lending decisions. If the credit registry or bureau is not operational or has a coverage of less than 0.1% of the adult population, the score on the depth of credit information index is 0.

In Lithuania, for example, both a public credit registry and a private credit bureau operate. Both distribute positive and negative information (a score of 1). Both distribute data on firms and individuals (a score of 1). Although the public credit registry does not distribute data from retailers or utilities, the private credit bureau does do so (a score of 1). Although the private credit bureau does not distribute more than 2 years of historical data, the public credit registry does do so (a score of 1). Although the public credit registry has a threshold of 50,000 litai, the private credit bureau distributes data on

loans of any value (a score of 1). Borrowers have the right to access their data in both the public credit registry and the private credit bureau (a score of 1). Summing across the indicators gives Lithuania a total score of 6.

Public credit registry coverage

The public credit registry coverage indicator reports the number of individuals and firms listed in a public credit registry with information on their borrowing history from the past 5 years. The number is expressed as a percentage of the adult population (the population age 15 and above in 2010 according to the World Bank's *World Development Indicators*). A public credit registry is defined as a database managed by the public sector, usually by the central bank or the superintendent of banks, that collects information on the creditworthiness of borrowers (individuals or firms) in the financial system and facilitates the exchange of credit information among banks and other regulated financial institutions. If no public registry operates, the coverage value is 0.

Private credit bureau coverage

The private credit bureau coverage indicator reports the number of individuals and firms listed by a private credit bureau with information on their borrowing history from the past 5 years. The number is expressed as a percentage of the adult population (the population age 15 and above in 2010 according to the World Bank's *World Development Indicators*). A private credit bureau is defined as a private firm or nonprofit organization that maintains a database on the creditworthiness of borrowers (individuals or firms) in the financial system and facilitates the exchange of credit information among creditors. Credit investigative bureaus and credit reporting firms that do not directly facilitate information exchange among banks and other financial institutions are not considered. If no private bureau operates, the coverage value is 0.

The data details on getting credit can be found for each economy at http://www.doingbusiness .org by selecting the economy in the dropdown list. This methodology was developed in Djankov, McLiesh and Shleifer (2007) and is adopted here with minor changes.

PROTECTING INVESTORS

Doing Business measures the strength of minority shareholder protections against directors' misuse of corporate assets for personal gain. The indicators distinguish 3 dimensions of investor protections: transparency of related-party transactions (extent of disclosure index), liability for self-dealing (extent of director liability index) and shareholders' ability to sue officers and directors for misconduct (ease of shareholder suits index). The data come from a survey of corporate and securities lawyers and are based on securities regulations, company laws, civil procedure codes and court rules of evidence. The ranking on the strength of investor protection index is the simple average of the percentile rankings on its component indicators (figure 4.6).

To make the data comparable across economies, several assumptions about the business and the transaction are used.

Assumptions about the business

The business (Buyer):

• Is a publicly traded corporation listed on the economy's most important stock exchange. If the number of publicly traded companies listed on that exchange is less than 10, or if there is no stock exchange in the economy, it is assumed that Buyer is a large private company with multiple shareholders.

• Has a board of directors and a chief executive officer (CEO) who may legally act on behalf of Buyer where permitted, even if this is not specifically required by law.

• Is a manufacturing company.

• Has its own distribution network.

Assumptions about the transaction

• Mr. James is Buyer's controlling shareholder and a member of Buyer's board of directors. He owns 60% of Buyer and elected 2 directors to Buyer's 5-member board.

• Mr. James also owns 90% of Seller, a company that operates a chain of retail hardware stores. Seller recently closed a large number of its stores.

• Mr. James proposes that Buyer purchase Seller's unused fleet of trucks to expand

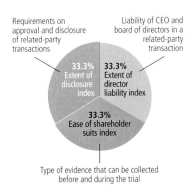

FIGURE 4.6   Protecting investors: minority shareholder rights in related-party transactions
Rankings are based on 3 indicators

Requirements on approval and disclosure of related-party transactions

Liability of CEO and board of directors in a related-party transaction

33.3% Extent of disclosure index

33.3% Extent of director liability index

33.3% Ease of shareholder suits index

Type of evidence that can be collected before and during the trial

Buyer's distribution of its products, a proposal to which Buyer agrees. The price is equal to 10% of Buyer's assets and is higher than the market value.

- The proposed transaction is part of the company's ordinary course of business and is not outside the authority of the company.
- Buyer enters into the transaction. All required approvals are obtained, and all required disclosures made (that is, the transaction is not fraudulent).
- The transaction causes damages to Buyer. Shareholders sue Mr. James and the other parties that approved the transaction.

Extent of disclosure index

The extent of disclosure index has 5 components (table 4.7):

- Which corporate body can provide legally sufficient approval for the transaction. A score of 0 is assigned if it is the CEO or the managing director alone; 1 if the board of directors or shareholders must vote and Mr. James is permitted to vote; 2 if the board of directors must vote and Mr. James is not permitted to vote; 3 if shareholders must vote and Mr. James is not permitted to vote.
- Whether immediate disclosure of the transaction to the public, the regulator or the shareholders is required.[5] A score of 0 is assigned if no disclosure is required; 1 if disclosure on the terms of the transaction is required but not on Mr. James's conflict of interest; 2 if disclosure on both the

terms and Mr. James's conflict of interest is required.

- Whether disclosure in the annual report is required. A score of 0 is assigned if no disclosure on the transaction is required; 1 if disclosure on the terms of the transaction is required but not on Mr. James's conflict of interest; 2 if disclosure on both the terms and Mr. James's conflict of interest is required.
- Whether disclosure by Mr. James to the board of directors is required. A score of 0 is assigned if no disclosure is required; 1 if a general disclosure of the existence of a conflict of interest is required without any specifics; 2 if full disclosure of all material facts relating to Mr. James's interest in the Buyer-Seller transaction is required.
- Whether it is required that an external body, for example, an external auditor, review the transaction before it takes place. A score of 0 is assigned if no; 1 if yes.

The index ranges from 0 to 10, with higher values indicating greater disclosure. In Poland, for example, the board of directors must approve the transaction and Mr. James is not allowed to vote (a score of 2). Buyer is required to disclose immediately all information affecting the stock price, including the conflict of interest (a score of 2). In its annual report Buyer must also disclose the terms of the transaction and Mr. James's ownership in Buyer and Seller (a score of

2). Before the transaction Mr. James must disclose his conflict of interest to the other directors, but he is not required to provide specific information about it (a score of 1). Poland does not require an external body to review the transaction (a score of 0). Adding these numbers gives Poland a score of 7 on the extent of disclosure index.

Extent of director liability index

The extent of director liability index has 7 components:[6]

- Whether a shareholder plaintiff is able to hold Mr. James liable for the damage the Buyer-Seller transaction causes to the company. A score of 0 is assigned if Mr. James cannot be held liable or can be held liable only for fraud or bad faith; 1 if Mr. James can be held liable only if he influenced the approval of the transaction or was negligent; 2 if Mr. James can be held liable when the transaction is unfair or prejudicial to the other shareholders.
- Whether a shareholder plaintiff is able to hold the approving body (the CEO or the members of the board of directors) liable for the damage the transaction causes to the company. A score of 0 is assigned if the approving body cannot be held liable or can be held liable only for fraud or bad faith; 1 if the approving body can be held liable for negligence; 2 if the approving body can be held liable when the transaction is unfair or prejudicial to the other shareholders.
- Whether a court can void the transaction upon a successful claim by a shareholder plaintiff. A score of 0 is assigned if rescission is unavailable or is available only in case of fraud or bad faith; 1 if rescission is available when the transaction is oppressive or prejudicial to the other shareholders; 2 if rescission is available when the transaction is unfair or entails a conflict of interest.
- Whether Mr. James pays damages for the harm caused to the company upon a successful claim by the shareholder plaintiff. A score of 0 is assigned if no; 1 if yes.
- Whether Mr. James repays profits made from the transaction upon a successful claim by the shareholder plaintiff. A score of 0 is assigned if no; 1 if yes.

TABLE 4.7	What do the protecting investors indicators measure?
Extent of disclosure index (0–10)	
Who can approve related-party transactions	
Disclosure requirements in case of related-party transactions	
Extent of director liability index (0–10)	
Ability of shareholders to hold interested parties and members of the approving body liable in case of related-party transactions	
Available legal remedies (damages, repayment of profits, fines and imprisonment)	
Ability of shareholders to sue directly or derivatively	
Ease of shareholder suits index (0–10)	
Direct access to internal documents of the company and use of a government inspector without filing suit in court	
Documents and information available during trial	
Strength of investor protection index (0–10)	
Simple average of the extent of disclosure, extent of director liability and ease of shareholder suits indices	

- Whether both fines and imprisonment can be applied against Mr. James. A score of 0 is assigned if no; 1 if yes.
- Whether shareholder plaintiffs are able to sue directly or derivatively for the damage the transaction causes to the company. A score of 0 is assigned if suits are unavailable or are available only for shareholders holding more than 10% of the company's share capital; 1 if direct or derivative suits are available for shareholders holding 10% or less of share capital.

The index ranges from 0 to 10, with higher values indicating greater liability of directors. Assuming that the prejudicial transaction was duly approved and disclosed, in order to hold Mr. James liable in Panama, for example, a plaintiff must prove that Mr. James influenced the approving body or acted negligently (a score of 1). To hold the other directors liable, a plaintiff must prove that they acted negligently (a score of 1). The prejudicial transaction cannot be voided (a score of 0). If Mr. James is found liable, he must pay damages (a score of 1) but he is not required to disgorge his profits (a score of 0). Mr. James cannot be fined and imprisoned (a score of 0). Direct or derivative suits are available for shareholders holding 10% or less of share capital (a score of 1). Adding these numbers gives Panama a score of 4 on the extent of director liability index.

Ease of shareholder suits index

The ease of shareholder suits index has 6 components:

- What range of documents is available to the shareholder plaintiff from the defendant and witnesses during trial. A score of 1 is assigned for each of the following types of documents available: information that the defendant has indicated he intends to rely on for his defense; information that directly proves specific facts in the plaintiff's claim; any information relevant to the subject matter of the claim; and any information that may lead to the discovery of relevant information.
- Whether the plaintiff can directly examine the defendant and witnesses during trial. A score of 0 is assigned if no; 1 if yes, with prior approval of the questions by the judge; 2 if yes, without prior approval.

- Whether the plaintiff can obtain categories of relevant documents from the defendant without identifying each document specifically. A score of 0 is assigned if no; 1 if yes.
- Whether shareholders owning 10% or less of the company's share capital can request that a government inspector investigate the Buyer-Seller transaction without filing suit in court. A score of 0 is assigned if no; 1 if yes.
- Whether shareholders owning 10% or less of the company's share capital have the right to inspect the transaction documents before filing suit. A score of 0 is assigned if no; 1 if yes.
- Whether the standard of proof for civil suits is lower than that for a criminal case. A score of 0 is assigned if no; 1 if yes.

The index ranges from 0 to 10, with higher values indicating greater powers of shareholders to challenge the transaction. In Greece, for example, the plaintiff can access documents that the defendant intends to rely on for his defense and that directly prove facts in the plaintiff's claim (a score of 2). The plaintiff can examine the defendant and witnesses during trial, though only with prior approval of the questions by the court (a score of 1). The plaintiff must specifically identify the documents being sought (for example, the Buyer-Seller purchase agreement of July 15, 2006) and cannot just request categories (for example, all documents related to the transaction) (a score of 0). A shareholder holding 5% of Buyer's shares can request that a government inspector review suspected mismanagement by Mr. James and the CEO without filing suit in court (a score of 1). Any shareholder can inspect the transaction documents before deciding whether to sue (a score of 1). The standard of proof for civil suits is the same as that for a criminal case (a score of 0). Adding these numbers gives Greece a score of 5 on the ease of shareholder suits index.

Strength of investor protection index

The strength of investor protection index is the average of the extent of disclosure index, the extent of director liability index and the ease of shareholder suits index. The index

ranges from 0 to 10, with higher values indicating more investor protection.

The data details on protecting investors can be found for each economy at http://www .doingbusiness.org by selecting the economy in the drop-down list. This methodology was developed in Djankov, La Porta and others (2008).

PAYING TAXES

Doing Business records the taxes and mandatory contributions that a medium-size company must pay in a given year as well as measures of the administrative burden of paying taxes and contributions. The project was developed and implemented in cooperation with PwC.[7] Taxes and contributions measured include the profit or corporate income tax, social contributions and labor taxes paid by the employer, property taxes, property transfer taxes, dividend tax, capital gains tax, financial transactions tax, waste collection taxes, vehicle and road taxes, and any other small taxes or fees.

The ranking on the ease of paying taxes is the simple average of the percentile rankings on its component indicators, with a threshold being applied to one of the component indicators, the total tax rate (figure 4.7). The threshold is defined as the highest total tax rate among the top 30% of economies in the ranking on the total tax rate. It will be calculated and adjusted on a yearly basis. This year's threshold is 32.5%. For all economies with a total tax rate below this threshold, the total tax rate is set at 32.5% this year. The threshold is not based on any underlying theory. Instead, it is intended to mitigate the effect of very low tax rates on the ranking on the ease of paying taxes.

Doing Business measures all taxes and contributions that are government mandated (at any level—federal, state or local) and that apply to the standardized business and have an impact in its financial statements. In doing so, *Doing Business* goes beyond the traditional definition of a tax. As defined for the purposes of government national accounts, taxes include only compulsory, unrequited payments to general government. *Doing Business* departs from this definition because it measures imposed charges that affect

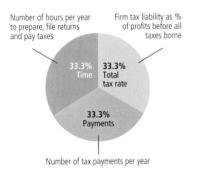

FIGURE 4.7 Paying taxes: tax compliance for a local manufacturing company

Rankings are based on 3 indicators

Number of hours per year to prepare, file returns and pay taxes — 33.3% Time

Firm tax liability as % of profits before all taxes borne — 33.3% Total tax rate

33.3% Payments

Number of tax payments per year

business accounts, not government accounts. One main difference relates to labor contributions. The *Doing Business* measure includes government-mandated contributions paid by the employer to a requited private pension fund or workers' insurance fund. The indicator includes, for example, Australia's compulsory superannuation guarantee and workers' compensation insurance. For the purpose of calculating the total tax rate (defined below), only taxes borne are included. For example, value added taxes are generally excluded (provided they are not irrecoverable) because they do not affect the accounting profits of the business—that is, they are not reflected in the income statement. They are, however, included for the purpose of the compliance measures (time and payments), as they add to the burden of complying with the tax system.

Doing Business uses a case scenario to measure the taxes and contributions paid by a standardized business and the complexity of an economy's tax compliance system. This case scenario uses a set of financial statements and assumptions about transactions made over the course of the year. In each economy tax experts from a number of different firms (in many economies these include PwC) compute the taxes and mandatory contributions due in their jurisdiction based on the standardized case study facts. Information is also compiled on the frequency of filing and payments as well as time taken to comply with tax laws in an economy. To make the data comparable across economies, several assumptions about the business and the taxes and contributions are used.

The methodology for the paying taxes indicators has benefited from discussion with members of the International Tax Dialogue and other stakeholders, which led to a refinement of the survey questions on the time to pay taxes, the collection of additional data on the labor tax wedge for further research and the introduction of a threshold applied to the total tax rate for the purpose of calculating the ranking on the ease of paying taxes (see discussion at the beginning of this section).

Assumptions about the business

The business:

- Is a limited liability, taxable company. If there is more than one type of limited liability company in the economy, the limited liability form most common among domestic firms is chosen. The most common form is reported by incorporation lawyers or the statistical office.
- Started operations on January 1, 2009. At that time the company purchased all the assets shown in its balance sheet and hired all its workers.
- Operates in the economy's largest business city.
- Is 100% domestically owned and has 5 owners, all of whom are natural persons.
- At the end of 2009, has a start-up capital of 102 times income per capita.
- Performs general industrial or commercial activities. Specifically, it produces ceramic flowerpots and sells them at retail. It does not participate in foreign trade (no import or export) and does not handle products subject to a special tax regime, for example, liquor or tobacco.
- At the beginning of 2010, owns 2 plots of land, 1 building, machinery, office equipment, computers and 1 truck and leases 1 truck.
- Does not qualify for investment incentives or any benefits apart from those related to the age or size of the company.
- Has 60 employees—4 managers, 8 assistants and 48 workers. All are nationals, and 1 manager is also an owner. The company pays for additional medical insurance for employees (not mandated by any law)

as an additional benefit. In addition, in some economies reimbursable business travel and client entertainment expenses are considered fringe benefits. When applicable, it is assumed that the company pays the fringe benefit tax on this expense or that the benefit becomes taxable income for the employee. The case study assumes no additional salary additions for meals, transportation, education or others. Therefore, even when such benefits are frequent, they are not added to or removed from the taxable gross salaries to arrive at the labor tax or contribution calculation.

- Has a turnover of 1,050 times income per capita.
- Makes a loss in the first year of operation.
- Has a gross margin (pretax) of 20% (that is, sales are 120% of the cost of goods sold).
- Distributes 50% of its net profits as dividends to the owners at the end of the second year.
- Sells one of its plots of land at a profit at the beginning of the second year.
- Has annual fuel costs for its trucks equal to twice income per capita.
- Is subject to a series of detailed assumptions on expenses and transactions to further standardize the case. All financial statement variables are proportional to 2005 income per capita. For example, the owner who is also a manager spends 10% of income per capita on traveling for the company (20% of this owner's expenses are purely private, 20% are for entertaining customers and 60% for business travel).

Assumptions about the taxes and contributions

- All the taxes and contributions recorded are those paid in the second year of operation (calendar year 2010). A tax or contribution is considered distinct if it has a different name or is collected by a different agency. Taxes and contributions with the same name and agency, but charged at different rates depending on the business, are counted as the same tax or contribution.

• The number of times the company pays taxes and contributions in a year is the number of different taxes or contributions multiplied by the frequency of payment (or withholding) for each tax. The frequency of payment includes advance payments (or withholding) as well as regular payments (or withholding).

Tax payments

The tax payments indicator reflects the total number of taxes and contributions paid, the method of payment, the frequency of payment, the frequency of filing and the number of agencies involved for this standardized case study company during the second year of operation (table 4.8). It includes consumption taxes paid by the company, such as sales tax or value added tax. These taxes are traditionally collected from the consumer on behalf of the tax agencies. Although they do not affect the income statements of the company, they add to the administrative burden of complying with the tax system and so are included in the tax payments measure.

The number of payments takes into account electronic filing. Where full electronic filing and payment is allowed and it is used by the majority of medium-size businesses, the tax is counted as paid once a year even if filings and payments are more frequent. For payments made through third parties, such as tax on interest paid by a financial institution or fuel tax paid by a fuel distributor, only one payment is included even if payments are more frequent.

Where 2 or more taxes or contributions are filed for and paid jointly using the same form, each of these joint payments is counted once. For example, if mandatory health insurance contributions and mandatory pension contributions are filed for and paid together, only one of these contributions would be included in the number of payments.

Time

Time is recorded in hours per year. The indicator measures the time taken to prepare, file and pay 3 major types of taxes and contributions: the corporate income tax, value added or sales tax, and labor taxes, including payroll taxes and social contributions. Preparation time includes the time to

collect all information necessary to compute the tax payable and to calculate the amount payable. If separate accounting books must be kept for tax purposes—or separate calculations made—the time associated with these processes is included. This extra time is included only if the regular accounting work is not enough to fulfill the tax accounting requirements. Filing time includes the time to complete all necessary tax return forms and file the relevant returns at the tax authority. Payment time considers the hours needed to make the payment online or at the tax authorities. Where taxes and contributions are paid in person, the time includes delays while waiting.

Total tax rate

The total tax rate measures the amount of taxes and mandatory contributions borne by the business in the second year of operation, expressed as a share of commercial profit. *Doing Business 2012* reports the total tax rate for calendar year 2010. The total amount of taxes borne is the sum of all the different taxes and contributions payable after accounting for allowable deductions and exemptions. The taxes withheld (such as personal income tax) or collected by the company and remitted to the tax authorities (such as value added tax, sales tax or goods and service tax) but not borne by the company are excluded. The taxes included can be divided into 5 categories: profit or corporate income tax, social contributions and labor taxes paid by the employer (in respect of which all mandatory contributions are included, even if paid to a private entity such as a requited pension fund), property taxes, turnover taxes and other taxes (such as municipal fees and vehicle and fuel taxes).

TABLE 4.8	What do the paying taxes indicators measure?
Tax payments for a manufacturing company in 2010 (number per year adjusted for electronic and joint filing and payment)	
Total number of taxes and contributions paid, including consumption taxes (value added tax, sales tax or goods and service tax)	
Method and frequency of filing and payment	
Time required to comply with 3 major taxes (hours per year)	
Collecting information and computing the tax payable	
Completing tax return forms, filing with proper agencies	
Arranging payment or withholding	
Preparing separate mandatory tax accounting books, if required	
Total tax rate (% of profit before all taxes)	
Profit or corporate income tax	
Social contributions and labor taxes paid by the employer	
Property and property transfer taxes	
Dividend, capital gains and financial transactions taxes	
Waste collection, vehicle, road and other taxes	

The total tax rate is designed to provide a comprehensive measure of the cost of all the taxes a business bears. It differs from the statutory tax rate, which merely provides the factor to be applied to the tax base. In computing the total tax rate, the actual tax payable is divided by commercial profit. Data for Norway illustrate (table 4.9).

Commercial profit is essentially net profit before all taxes borne. It differs from the conventional profit before tax, reported in financial statements. In computing profit before tax, many of the taxes borne by a firm are deductible. In computing commercial profit, these taxes are not deductible. Commercial profit therefore presents a clear picture of the actual profit of a business before any of the taxes it bears in the course of the fiscal year.

TABLE 4.9	Computing the total tax rate for Norway				
Type of tax (tax base)	Statutory rate r	Statutory tax base b NKr	Actual tax payable $a = r \times b$ NKr	Commercial profit* c NKr	Total tax rate $t = a/c$
Corporate income tax (taxable income)	28.1%	20,612,719	5,771,561	23,651,183	24.4%
Social security contributions (taxable wages)	14.1%	26,684,645	3,762,535	23,651,183	15.9%
Fuel tax (fuel price)	NKr 4 per liter	74,247 liters	297,707	23,651,183	1.3%
Total			9,831,803		41.6%

* Profit before all taxes borne.
Note: NKr is Norwegian kroner. Commercial profit is assumed to be 59.4 times income per capita.
Source: Doing Business database.

Commercial profit is computed as sales minus cost of goods sold, minus gross salaries, minus administrative expenses, minus other expenses, minus provisions, plus capital gains (from the property sale) minus interest expense, plus interest income and minus commercial depreciation. To compute the commercial depreciation, a straight-line depreciation method is applied, with the following rates: 0% for the land, 5% for the building, 10% for the machinery, 33% for the computers, 20% for the office equipment, 20% for the truck and 10% for business development expenses. Commercial profit amounts to 59.4 times income per capita.

The methodology for calculating the total tax rate is broadly consistent with the Total Tax Contribution framework developed by PwC and the calculation within this framework for taxes borne. But while the work undertaken by PwC is usually based on data received from the largest companies in the economy, *Doing Business* focuses on a case study for a standardized medium-size company.

The data details on paying taxes can be found for each economy at http://www.doingbusiness .org by selecting the economy in the drop-down list. This methodology was developed in Djankov, Ganser and others (2010).

TRADING ACROSS BORDERS

Doing Business measures the time and cost (excluding tariffs) associated with exporting and importing a standardized cargo of goods by ocean transport. The time and cost necessary to complete every official procedure for exporting and importing the goods—from the contractual agreement between the 2 parties to the delivery of goods—are recorded. All documents needed by the trader to export or import the goods across the border are also recorded. For exporting goods, procedures range from packing the goods into the container at the warehouse to their departure from the port of exit. For importing goods, procedures range from the vessel's arrival at the port of entry to the cargo's delivery at the warehouse. The time and cost for ocean transport are not included. Payment is made by letter of credit, and the time, cost and documents required for the issuance or advising of a letter of

credit are taken into account. The ranking on the ease of trading across borders is the simple average of the percentile rankings on its component indicators (figure 4.8).

Local freight forwarders, shipping lines, customs brokers, port officials and banks provide information on required documents and cost as well as the time to complete each procedure. To make the data comparable across economies, several assumptions about the business and the traded goods are used.

Assumptions about the business

The business:

- Has at least 60 employees.
- Is located in the economy's largest business city.
- Is a private, limited liability company. It does not operate in an export processing zone or an industrial estate with special export or import privileges.
- Is domestically owned with no foreign ownership.
- Exports more than 10% of its sales.

Assumptions about the traded goods

The traded product travels in a dry-cargo, 20-foot, full container load. It weighs 10 tons and is valued at $20,000. The product:

- Is not hazardous nor does it include military items.

TABLE 4.10 **What do the trading across borders indicators measure?**

Documents required to export and import (number)
Bank documents
Customs clearance documents
Port and terminal handling documents
Transport documents
Time required to export and import (days)
Obtaining all the documents
Inland transport and handling
Customs clearance and inspections
Port and terminal handling
Does not include ocean transport time
Cost required to export and import (US$ per container)
All documentation
Inland transport and handling
Customs clearance and inspections
Port and terminal handling
Official costs only, no bribes

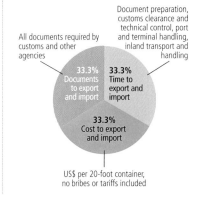

FIGURE 4.8   Trading across borders: exporting and importing by ocean transport

Rankings are based on 3 indicators

- Does not require refrigeration or any other special environment.
- Does not require any special phytosanitary or environmental safety standards other than accepted international standards.
- Is one of the economy's leading export or import products.

Documents

All documents required per shipment to export and import the goods are recorded (table 4.10). It is assumed that the contract has already been agreed upon and signed by both parties. Documents required for clearance by government ministries, customs authorities, port and container terminal authorities, health and technical control agencies, and banks are taken into account. Since payment is by letter of credit, all documents required by banks for the issuance or securing of a letter of credit are also taken into account. Documents that are renewed annually and that do not require renewal per shipment (for example, an annual tax clearance certificate) are not included.

Time

The time for exporting and importing is recorded in calendar days. The time calculation for a procedure starts from the moment it is initiated and runs until it is completed. If a procedure can be accelerated for an additional cost and is available to all trading companies, the fastest legal procedure is chosen. Fast-track procedures applying to firms located in an export processing zone are not taken into account because they are not available to all trading companies. Ocean transport time is not included. It is assumed that neither the exporter nor the importer wastes time and that each commits to completing each remaining procedure without delay. Procedures that can be completed in parallel are measured as simultaneous. The waiting time between procedures—for example, during unloading of the cargo—is included in the measure.

Cost

Cost measures the fees levied on a 20-foot container in U.S. dollars. All the fees associated with completing the procedures to export or import the goods are included. These include costs for documents, administrative fees for customs clearance and technical control, customs broker fees, terminal handling charges and inland transport. The cost does not include customs tariffs and duties or costs related to ocean transport. Only official costs are recorded.

The data details on trading across borders can be found for each economy at http://www .doingbusiness.org by selecting the economy in the drop-down list. This methodology was developed in Djankov, Freund and Pham (2010) and is adopted here with minor changes.

ENFORCING CONTRACTS

Indicators on enforcing contracts measure the efficiency of the judicial system in resolving a commercial dispute. The data are built by following the step-by-step evolution of a commercial sale dispute before local courts. The data are collected through study of the codes of civil procedure and other court regulations as well as surveys completed by local litigation lawyers and by judges. The ranking on the ease of enforcing contracts is the simple average of the percentile rankings on its component indicators (figure 4.9).

The name of the relevant court in each economy—the court in the largest business city with jurisdiction over commercial cases worth 200% of income per capita—is published at http://www.doingbusiness.org/ ExploreTopics/EnforcingContracts/.

Assumptions about the case

- The value of the claim equals 200% of the economy's income per capita.
- The dispute concerns a lawful transaction between 2 businesses (Seller and Buyer), located in the economy's largest business city. Seller sells goods worth 200% of the economy's income per capita to Buyer. After Seller delivers the goods to Buyer, Buyer refuses to pay for the goods on the grounds that the delivered goods were not of adequate quality.
- Seller (the plaintiff) sues Buyer (the defendant) to recover the amount under the sales agreement (that is, 200% of the economy's income per capita). Buyer opposes Seller's claim, saying that the quality of the goods is not adequate. The claim is disputed on the merits. The court cannot decide the case on the basis of documentary evidence or legal title alone.
- A court in the economy's largest business city with jurisdiction over commercial cases worth 200% of income per capita decides the dispute.
- Seller attaches Buyer's movable assets (for example, office equipment and vehicles) before obtaining a judgment because Seller fears that Buyer may become insolvent.
- An expert opinion is given on the quality of the delivered goods. If it is standard practice in the economy for each party to call its own expert witness, the parties each call one expert witness. If it is standard practice for the judge to appoint an independent expert, the judge does so. In this case the judge does not allow opposing expert testimony.
- The judgment is 100% in favor of Seller: the judge decides that the goods are of adequate quality and that Buyer must pay the agreed price.
- Buyer does not appeal the judgment. Seller decides to start enforcing the judgment as soon as the time allocated by law for appeal expires.
- Seller takes all required steps for prompt enforcement of the judgment. The money is successfully collected through a public sale of Buyer's movable assets (for example, office equipment and vehicles).

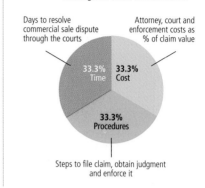

FIGURE 4.9   Enforcing contracts: resolving a commercial dispute through the courts

Rankings are based on 3 indicators

Days to resolve commercial sale dispute through the courts

Attorney, court and enforcement costs as % of claim value

33.3% Time   **33.3%** Cost

33.3% Procedures

Steps to file claim, obtain judgment and enforce it

Procedures

The list of procedural steps compiled for each economy traces the chronology of a commercial dispute before the relevant court. A procedure is defined as any interaction, required by law or commonly used in practice, between the parties or between them and the judge or court officer. This includes steps to file and serve the case, steps for trial and judgment and steps necessary to enforce the judgment (table 4.11).

The survey allows respondents to record procedures that exist in civil law but not common law jurisdictions and vice versa. For example, in civil law jurisdictions the judge can appoint an independent expert, while in

TABLE 4.11	What do the enforcing contracts indicators measure?
Procedures to enforce a contract through the courts (number)	
Any interaction between the parties in a commercial dispute, or between them and the judge or court officer	
Steps to file and serve the case	
Steps for trial and judgment	
Steps to enforce the judgment	
Time required to complete procedures (calendar days)	
Time to file and serve the case	
Time for trial and obtaining judgment	
Time to enforce the judgment	
Cost required to complete procedures (% of claim)	
No bribes	
Average attorney fees	
Court costs, including expert fees	
Enforcement costs	

common law jurisdictions each party submits a list of expert witnesses to the court. To indicate overall efficiency, 1 procedure is subtracted from the total number for economies that have specialized commercial courts, and 1 procedure for economies that allow electronic filing of the initial complaint in court cases. Some procedural steps that take place simultaneously with or are included in other procedural steps are not counted in the total number of procedures.

Time

Time is recorded in calendar days, counted from the moment the plaintiff decides to file the lawsuit in court until payment. This includes both the days when actions take place and the waiting periods between. The average duration of different stages of dispute resolution is recorded: the completion of service of process (time to file and serve the case), the issuance of judgment (time for the trial and obtaining the judgment) and the moment of payment (time for enforcement of the judgment).

Cost

Cost is recorded as a percentage of the claim, assumed to be equivalent to 200% of income per capita. No bribes are recorded. Three types of costs are recorded: court costs, enforcement costs and average attorney fees.

Court costs include all court costs and expert fees that Seller (plaintiff) must advance to the court, regardless of the final cost to Seller. Expert fees, if required by law or commonly used in practice, are included in court costs. Enforcement costs are all costs that Seller (plaintiff) must advance to enforce the judgment through a public sale of Buyer's movable assets, regardless of the final cost to Seller. Average attorney fees are the fees that Seller (plaintiff) must advance to a local attorney to represent Seller in the standardized case.

The data details on enforcing contracts can be found for each economy at http://www .doingbusiness.org by selecting the economy in the drop-down list. This methodology was developed in Djankov and others (2003) and is adopted here with minor changes.

RESOLVING INSOLVENCY (FORMERLY CLOSING A BUSINESS)

Doing Business studies the time, cost and outcome of insolvency proceedings involving domestic entities. *The name of this indicator set was changed from closing a business to resolving insolvency to more accurately reflect the content of the indicators. The indicators did not change in content or scope.* The data are derived from questionnaire responses by local insolvency practitioners and verified through a study of laws and regulations as well as public information on bankruptcy systems. The ranking on the ease of resolving insolvency is based on the recovery rate (figure 4.10).

To make the data comparable across economies, several assumptions about the business and the case are used.

Assumptions about the business

The business:

- Is a limited liability company.
- Operates in the economy's largest business city.
- Is 100% domestically owned, with the founder, who is also the chairman of the supervisory board, owning 51% (no other shareholder holds more than 5% of shares).
- Has downtown real estate, where it runs a hotel, as its major asset. The hotel is valued at 100 times income per capita or $200,000, whichever is larger.
- Has a professional general manager.
- Has 201 employees and 50 suppliers, each of which is owed money for the last delivery.
- Has a 10-year loan agreement with a domestic bank secured by a universal business charge (for example, a floating charge) in economies where such collateral is recognized or by the hotel property. If the laws of the economy do not specifically provide for a universal business charge but contracts commonly use some other provision to that effect, this provision is specified in the loan agreement.
- Has observed the payment schedule and all other conditions of the loan up to now.
- Has a mortgage, with the value of the mortgage principal being exactly equal to the market value of the hotel.

FIGURE 4.10 Resolving insolvency: time, cost and outcome of bankruptcy of a local company
Rankings are based on 1 indicator

Recovery rate is a function of time, cost and other factors such as lending rate and the likelihood of the company continuing to operate

100% Recovery rate

Note: Time and cost do not count separately for the rankings.

Assumptions about the case

The business is experiencing liquidity problems. The company's loss in 2010 reduced its net worth to a negative figure. It is January 1, 2011. There is no cash to pay the bank interest or principal in full, due the next day, January 2. The business will therefore default on its loan. Management believes that losses will be incurred in 2011 and 2012 as well.

The amount outstanding under the loan agreement is exactly equal to the market value of the hotel business and represents 74% of the company's total debt. The other 26% of its debt is held by unsecured creditors (suppliers, employees, tax authorities).

The company has too many creditors to negotiate an informal out-of-court workout. The following options are available: a judicial procedure aimed at the rehabilitation or reorganization of the company to permit its continued operation; a judicial procedure aimed at the liquidation or winding-up of the company; or a debt enforcement or foreclosure procedure against the company, enforced either in court (or through another government authority) or out of court (for example, by appointing a receiver).

Assumptions about the parties

The bank wants to recover as much as possible of its loan, as quickly and cheaply as possible. The unsecured creditors will do everything permitted under the applicable laws to avoid a piecemeal sale of the assets. The majority shareholder wants to keep the company operating and under its control. Management wants to keep the company operating and preserve its employees' jobs. All the parties are local entities or citizens; no foreign parties are involved.

Time

Time for creditors to recover their credit is recorded in calendar years (table 4.12). The period of time measured by *Doing Business* is from the company's default until the payment of some or all of the money owed to the bank. Potential delay tactics by the parties, such as the filing of dilatory appeals or requests for extension, are taken into consideration.

Cost

The cost of the proceedings is recorded as a percentage of the value of the debtor's estate. The cost is calculated on the basis of questionnaire responses and includes court fees and government levies; fees of insolvency administrators, auctioneers, assessors and lawyers; and all other fees and costs.

Outcome

Recovery by creditors depends on whether the hotel business emerges from the proceedings as a going concern or the company's assets are sold piecemeal. If the business keeps operating, no value is lost and the bank can satisfy its claim in full, or recover 100 cents on the dollar. If the assets

TABLE 4.12	What do the resolving insolvency indicators measure?
Time required to recover debt (years)
Measured in calendar years
Appeals and requests for extension are included
Cost required to recover debt (% of debtor's estate)
Measured as percentage of estate value
Court fees
Fees of insolvency administrators
Lawyers' fees
Assessors' and auctioneers' fees
Other related fees
Recovery rate for creditors (cents on the dollar)
Measures the cents on the dollar recovered by creditors
Present value of debt recovered
Official costs of the insolvency proceedings are deducted
Depreciation of furniture is taken into account
Outcome for the business (survival or not) affects the maximum value that can be recovered

are sold piecemeal, the maximum amount that can be recovered will not exceed 70% of the bank's claim, which translates into 70 cents on the dollar.

Recovery rate

The recovery rate is recorded as cents on the dollar recouped by creditors through reorganization, liquidation or debt enforcement (foreclosure) proceedings. The calculation takes into account the outcome: whether the business emerges from the proceedings as a going concern or the assets are sold piecemeal. Then the costs of the proceedings are deducted (1 cent for each percentage point of the value of the debtor's estate). Finally, the value lost as a result of the time the money remains tied up in insolvency proceedings is taken into account, including the loss of value due to depreciation of the hotel furniture. Consistent with international accounting practice, the annual depreciation rate for furniture is taken to be 20%. The furniture is assumed to account for a quarter of the total value of assets. The recovery rate is the present value of the remaining proceeds, based on end-2010 lending rates from the International Monetary Fund's *International Financial Statistics*, supplemented with data from central banks and the Economist Intelligence Unit.

No practice

If an economy had zero cases a year over the past 5 years involving a judicial reorganization, judicial liquidation or debt enforcement procedure (foreclosure), the economy receives a "no practice" ranking. This means that creditors are unlikely to recover their money through a formal legal process (in or out of court). The recovery rate for "no practice" economies is zero.

This methodology was developed in Djankov, Hart and others (2008) and is adopted here with minor changes.

EMPLOYING WORKERS

Doing Business measures flexibility in the regulation of employment, specifically as it affects the hiring and redundancy of workers and the rigidity of working hours. Since 2007 improvements have been made to align the methodology for the employing

workers indicators with the letter and spirit of the ILO conventions. Only 4 of the 188 ILO conventions cover areas measured by *Doing Business*: employee termination, weekend work, holiday with pay and night work. The *Doing Business* methodology is fully consistent with these 4 conventions. The ILO conventions covering areas related to the employing workers indicators do not include the ILO core labor standards—8 conventions covering the right to collective bargaining, the elimination of forced labor, the abolition of child labor and equitable treatment in employment practices.

Since 2009 the World Bank Group has been working with a consultative group—including labor lawyers, employer and employee representatives, and experts from the ILO, the OECD, civil society and the private sector—to review the employing workers methodology and explore future areas of research.[8]

The guidance of the consultative group has provided the basis for several changes in the methodology. The calculation of the minimum wage ratio was changed to ensure that no economy can receive the highest score if it has no minimum wage at all, if the law provides a regulatory mechanism for the minimum wage that is not enforced in practice, if there is only a customary minimum wage or if the minimum wage applies only to the public sector. A threshold was set for paid annual leave and a ceiling for working days allowed per week to ensure that no economy benefits in the scoring from excessive flexibility in these areas. Finally, the calculation of the redundancy cost and of the annual leave period for the rigidity of hours index was changed to refer to the average value for a worker with 1 year of tenure, a worker with 5 years and a worker with 10 years rather than the value for a worker with 20 years of tenure.

A full report with the conclusions of the consultative group is available at http://www.doingbusiness.org/methodology/employing-workers.

This year *Doing Business* collected additional data on regulations covering worker protection. The data will serve as a basis for developing a joint analysis of worker protection by the World Bank Group and the ILO and for developing measures of worker protection.

Doing Business 2012 does not present rankings of economies on the employing workers indicators or include the topic in the aggregate ranking on the ease of doing business. The report does present the data on the employing workers indicators. Detailed data collected on labor regulations are available on the *Doing Business* website (http://www.doingbusiness.org).

The data on employing workers are based on a detailed survey of employment regulations that is completed by local lawyers and public officials. Employment laws and regulations as well as secondary sources are reviewed to ensure accuracy. To make the data comparable across economies, several assumptions about the worker and the business are used.

Assumptions about the worker

The worker:

- Is a full-time, male, nonexecutive employee
- Earns a salary plus benefits equal to the economy's average wage during the entire period of his employment.
- Has a pay period that is the most common for workers in the economy.
- Is a lawful citizen who belongs to the same race and religion as the majority of the economy's population.
- Resides in the economy's largest business city.
- Is not a member of a labor union, unless membership is mandatory.

Assumptions about the business

The business:

- Is a limited liability company.
- Operates in the economy's largest business city.
- Is 100% domestically owned.
- Operates in the manufacturing sector.
- Has 60 employees.
- Is subject to collective bargaining agreements in economies where such agreements cover more than half the manufacturing sector and apply even to firms not party to them.

- Abides by every law and regulation but does not grant workers more benefits than mandated by law, regulation or (if applicable) collective bargaining agreement.

Rigidity of employment index

The rigidity of employment index is the average of 3 subindices: the difficulty of hiring index, rigidity of hours index and difficulty of redundancy index. Data and scores for Benin are provided as an example (table 4.13).

All the subindices have several components. And all take values between 0 and 100, with higher values indicating more rigid regulation.

The difficulty of hiring index measures (i) whether fixed-term contracts are prohibited for permanent tasks; (ii) the maximum cumulative duration of fixed-term contracts; and (iii) the ratio of the minimum wage for a trainee or first-time employee to the average value added per worker.[9] An economy is assigned a score of 1 if fixed-term contracts are prohibited for permanent tasks and a score of 0 if they can be used for any task. A score

of 1 is assigned if the maximum cumulative duration of fixed-term contracts is less than 3 years; 0.5 if it is 3 years or more but less than 5 years; and 0 if fixed-term contracts can last 5 years or more. Finally, a score of 1 is assigned if the ratio of the minimum wage to the average value added per worker is 0.75 or more; 0.67 for a ratio of 0.50 or more but less than 0.75; 0.33 for a ratio of 0.25 or more but less than 0.50; and 0 for a ratio of less than 0.25. A score of 0 is also assigned if the minimum wage is set by a collective bargaining agreement that applies to less than half the manufacturing sector or does not apply to firms not party to it, or if the minimum wage is set by law but does not apply to workers who are in their apprentice period. A ratio of 0.251 (and therefore a score of 0.33) is automatically assigned in 4 cases: if there is no minimum wage; if the law provides a regulatory mechanism for the minimum wage that is not enforced in practice; if there is no minimum wage set by law but there is a wage amount that is customarily used as a minimum; or if there is no minimum wage set by law in the private sector but there is one in the public sector.

TABLE 4.13 What do the employing workers indicators measure?		
	Data for Benin	Score for Benin
Rigidity of employment index (0–100)		**29.66**
Simple average of the difficulty of hiring, rigidity of hours and difficulty of redundancy indices		39 + 10 + 40
Difficulty of hiring index (0–100)		**39**
Fixed-term contracts prohibited for permanent tasks?	No	0
Maximum duration of fixed-term contracts	4 years	0.5
Ratio of minimum wage for trainee or first-time employee to value added per worker	0.58	0.67
Rigidity of hours index (0–100)		**10**
Restrictions on night work and weekend work?	No	0
Allowed maximum length of the workweek in days and hours, including overtime	6 days	0
Fifty-hour workweeks permitted for 2 months due to an increase in production?	Yes	0
Paid annual vacation days	24 days	0.5
Difficulty of redundancy index (0–100)		**40**
Redundancy allowed as grounds for termination?	Yes	0
Notification required for termination of a redundant worker or group of workers?	Yes	2
Approval required for termination of a redundant worker or group of workers?	No	0
Employer obligated to reassign or retrain and to follow priority rules for redundancy and reemployment?	Yes	2
Redundancy cost (weeks of salary)		**11.66**
Notice requirements, severance payments and penalties due when terminating a redundant worker, expressed in weeks of salary	Yes	11.66

Source: Doing Business database.

In Benin, for example, fixed-term contracts are not prohibited for permanent tasks (a score of 0), and they can be used for a maximum of 4 years (a score of 0.5). The ratio of the mandated minimum wage to the value added per worker is 0.58 (a score of 0.67). Averaging the 3 values and scaling the index to 100 gives Benin a score of 39.

The rigidity of hours index has 5 components: (i) whether there are restrictions on night work; (ii) whether there are restrictions on weekly holiday work; (iii) whether the workweek can consist of 5.5 days or is more than 6 days; (iv) whether the workweek can extend to 50 hours or more (including overtime) for 2 months a year to respond to a seasonal increase in production; and (v) whether the average paid annual leave for a worker with 1 year of tenure, a worker with 5 years and a worker with 10 years is more than 26 working days or fewer than 15 working days. For questions (i) and (ii), if restrictions other than premiums apply, a score of 1 is given. If the only restriction is a premium for night work or weekly holiday work, a score of 0, 0.33, 0.66 or 1 is given, depending on the quartile in which the economy's premium falls. If there are no restrictions, the economy receives a score of 0. For question (iii) a score of 1 is assigned if the legally permitted workweek is less than 5.5 days or more than 6 days; otherwise a score of 0 is assigned. For question (iv), if the answer is no, a score of 1 is assigned; otherwise a score of 0 is assigned. For question (v) a score of 0 is assigned if the average paid annual leave is between 15 and 21 working days, a score of 0.5 if it is between 22 and 26 working days and a score of 1 if it is less than 15 or more than 26 working days.

For example, Benin does not impose any restrictions either on night work (a score of 0) or on weekly holiday work (a score of 0), allows 6-day workweeks (a score of 0), permits 50-hour workweeks for 2 months (a score of 0) and requires average paid annual leave of 24 working days (a score of 0.5). Averaging the scores and scaling the result to 100 gives a final index of 10 for Benin.

The difficulty of redundancy index has 8 components: (i) whether redundancy is disallowed as a basis for terminating workers;

(ii) whether the employer needs to notify a third party (such as a government agency) to terminate 1 redundant worker; (iii) whether the employer needs to notify a third party to terminate a group of 9 redundant workers; (iv) whether the employer needs approval from a third party to terminate 1 redundant worker; (v) whether the employer needs approval from a third party to terminate a group of 9 redundant workers; (vi) whether the law requires the employer to reassign or retrain a worker before making the worker redundant; (vii) whether priority rules apply for redundancies; and (viii) whether priority rules apply for reemployment. For question (i) an answer of yes for workers of any income level gives a score of 10 and means that the rest of the questions do not apply. An answer of yes to question (iv) gives a score of 2. For every other question, if the answer is yes, a score of 1 is assigned; otherwise a score of 0 is given. Questions (i) and (iv), as the most restrictive regulations, have greater weight in the construction of the index.

In Benin, for example, redundancy is allowed as grounds for termination (a score of 0). An employer has to notify a third party to terminate a single redundant worker (a score of 1) as well as to terminate a group of 9 redundant workers (a score of 1), although the approval of a third party is not required in either of these cases (a score of 0). The law does not mandate any retraining or alternative placement before termination (a score of 0). There are priority rules for termination (a score of 1) and reemployment (a score of 1). Adding the scores and scaling to 100 gives a final index of 40.

Redundancy cost

The redundancy cost indicator measures the cost of advance notice requirements, severance payments and penalties due when terminating a redundant worker, expressed in weeks of salary. The average value of notice requirements and severance payments applicable to a worker with 1 year of tenure, a worker with 5 years and a worker with 10 years is used to assign the score. If the redundancy cost adds up to 8 or fewer weeks of salary and the workers can benefit from unemployment protection, a score of 0 is assigned, but the actual number of weeks is published. If the redundancy cost adds up

to 8 or fewer weeks of salary and the workers cannot benefit from any type of unemployment protection, a score of 8.1 is assigned, although the actual number of weeks is published. If the cost adds up to more than 8 weeks of salary, the score is the number of weeks. One month is recorded as 4 and 1/3 weeks.

In Benin, for example, an employer is required to give an average of 1 month's notice before a redundancy termination, and the average severance pay for a worker with 1 year of service, a worker with 5 years and a worker with 10 years equals 1.68 months of wages. No penalty is levied and the workers cannot benefit from any type of unemployment protection. Altogether, the employer pays the equivalent of 11.66 weeks of salary to dismiss a worker.

The data details on employing workers can be found for each economy at http://www .doingbusiness.org by selecting the economy in the drop-down list. The Doing Business *website provides historical data sets adjusted for changes in methodology to allow comparison of data across years. This methodology was developed in Botero and others (2004) and is adopted here with changes.*

NOTES

1. The data for paying taxes refer to January–December 2010.

2. Because the ease of doing business index now includes the getting electricity indicators, procedures, time and cost related to obtaining an electricity connection were removed from the dealing with construction permits indicators.

3. The ranking is based on a straight average of points from the strength of legal rights index and depth of credit information index.

4. The scoring on this aspect was revised this year to bring it into line with UNCITRAL (2004, 2007) and World Bank (2011a).

5. This question is usually regulated by stock exchange or securities laws. Points are awarded only to economies with more than 10 listed firms in their most important stock exchange.

6. When evaluating the regime of liability for company directors for a prejudicial related-party transaction, *Doing Business* assumes that the transaction was duly disclosed and approved. *Doing Business* does not measure director liability in the event of fraud.

7. *PwC* refers to the network of member firms of PricewaterhouseCoopers International Limited (PwCIL), or, as the context requires, individual member firms of the PwC network. Each member firm is a separate legal entity and does not act as agent of PwCIL or any other member firm. PwCIL does not provide any services to clients. PwCIL is not responsible or liable for the acts or omissions of any of its member firms nor can it control the exercise of their professional judgment or bind them in any way. No member firm is responsible or liable for the acts or omissions of any other member firm nor can it control the exercise of another member firm's professional judgment or bind another member firm or PwCIL in any way.

8. For the terms of reference and composition of the consultative group, see World Bank, "Doing Business Employing Workers Indicator Consultative Group," http://www.doingbusiness.org.

9. The average value added per worker is the ratio of an economy's GNI per capita to the working-age population as a percentage of the total population.

Ease of doing business and distance to frontier

This year's report presents results for 2 aggregate measures: the aggregate ranking on the ease of doing business and a new measure, the "distance to frontier." While the ease of doing business ranking compares economies with one another at a point in time, the distance to frontier measure shows how much the regulatory environment for local entrepreneurs in each economy has changed over time.

EASE OF DOING BUSINESS

The ease of doing business index ranks economies from 1 to 183. For each economy the ranking is calculated as the simple average of the percentile rankings on each of the 10 topics included in the index in *Doing Business 2012*: starting a business, dealing with construction permits, registering property, getting credit, protecting investors, paying taxes, trading across borders, enforcing contracts, resolving insolvency and, new this year, getting electricity. The employing workers indicators are not included in this year's aggregate ease of doing business ranking. In addition to this year's ranking, *Doing Business* presents a comparable ranking for the previous year, adjusted for any changes in methodology as well as additions of economies or topics.[1]

Construction of the ease of doing business index

Here is one example of how the ease of doing business index is constructed. In Korea it takes 5 procedures, 7 days and 14.6% of annual income per capita in fees to open a business. There is no minimum capital required. On these 4 indicators Korea ranks in the 18th, 14th, 53rd and 0 percentiles. So on average Korea ranks in the 21st percentile on the ease of starting a business. It ranks in the 12th percentile on getting credit, 25th percentile on paying taxes, 8th percentile on enforcing contracts, 7th percentile on resolving insolvency and so on. Higher rankings indicate simpler regulation and stronger protection of property rights. The simple average of Korea's percentile rankings on all topics is 21st. When all economies are ordered by their average percentile rankings, Korea stands at 8 in the aggregate ranking on the ease of doing business.

More complex aggregation methods—such as principal components and unobserved components—yield a ranking nearly identical to the simple average used by *Doing Business*.[2] Thus *Doing Business* uses the simplest method: weighting all topics equally and, within each topic, giving equal weight to each of the topic components.[3]

If an economy has no laws or regulations covering a specific area—for example, insolvency—it receives a "no practice" mark. Similarly, an economy receives a "no practice" or "not possible" mark if regulation exists but is never used in practice or if a competing regulation prohibits such practice. Either way, a "no practice" mark puts the economy at the bottom of the ranking on the relevant indicator.

The ease of doing business index is limited in scope. It does not account for an economy's proximity to large markets, the quality of its infrastructure services (other than services related to trading across borders and getting electricity), the strength of its financial system, the security of property from theft and looting, macroeconomic conditions or the strength of underlying institutions.

TABLE 5.1	Correlations between economy rankings on *Doing Business* topics								
	Dealing with construction permits	Registering property	Getting credit	Protecting investors	Paying taxes	Trading across borders	Enforcing contracts	Resolving insolvency	Getting electricity
Starting a business	0.39	0.32	0.45	0.59	0.37	0.45	0.42	0.45	0.28
Dealing with construction permits		0.22	0.19	0.25	0.36	0.45	0.20	0.33	0.40
Registering property			0.39	0.29	0.31	0.27	0.49	0.33	0.24
Getting credit				0.47	0.20	0.41	0.42	0.52	0.24
Protecting investors					0.37	0.39	0.29	0.37	0.20
Paying taxes						0.40	0.27	0.33	0.40
Trading across borders							0.35	0.50	0.56
Enforcing contracts								0.42	0.21
Resolving insolvency									0.32

Source: Doing Business database.

Variability of economies' rankings across topics

Each indicator set measures a different aspect of the business regulatory environment. The rankings of an economy can vary, sometimes significantly, across indicator sets. The average correlation coefficient between the 10 indicator sets included in the aggregate ranking is 0.36, and the coefficients between any 2 sets of indicators range from 0.19 (between dealing with construction permits and getting credit) to 0.59 (between starting a business and protecting investors). These correlations suggest that economies rarely score universally well or universally badly on the indicators (table 5.1).

Consider the example of Canada. It stands at 12 in the aggregate ranking on the ease of doing business. Its ranking is 3 on both starting a business and resolving insolvency, and 5 on protecting investors. But its ranking is only 59 on enforcing contracts, 42 on trading across borders and 156 on getting electricity.

Figure 1.6 in the executive summary illustrates the degree of variability in each economy's performance across the different areas of business regulation covered by *Doing Business*. The figure draws attention to economies with a particularly uneven performance by showing the distance between the average of the highest 3 topic rankings and the average of the lowest 3 for each of 183 economies across the 10 topics included in this year's aggregate ranking. While a relatively small distance between these 2 averages suggests a broadly consistent approach across the areas of business regulation measured by *Doing Business*, a relatively large distance suggests a more narrowly focused approach, with greater room for improvement in some areas than in others.

Variation in performance across the indicator sets is not at all unusual. It reflects differences in the degree of priority that government authorities give to particular areas of business regulation reform and the ability of different government agencies to deliver tangible results in their area of responsibility.

Economies that improved the most across 3 or more *Doing Business* topics in 2010/11

Doing Business 2012 uses a simple method to calculate which economies improved the most in the ease of doing business. First, it selects the economies that in 2010/11 implemented regulatory reforms making it easier to do business in 3 or more of the 10 topics included in this year's ease of doing business ranking.[4] Thirty economies meet this criterion: Armenia, Burkina Faso, Burundi, Cape Verde, the Central African Republic, Chile, Colombia, the Democratic Republic of Congo, Côte d'Ivoire, The Gambia, Georgia, Korea, Latvia, Liberia, FYR Macedonia, Mexico, Moldova, Montenegro, Morocco, Nicaragua, Oman, Peru, Russia, São Tomé and Príncipe, Senegal, Sierra Leone, Slovenia, the Solomon Islands, South Africa and Ukraine. Second, *Doing Business* ranks these economies on the increase in their ranking on the ease of doing business from the previous year using comparable rankings.

Selecting the economies that implemented regulatory reforms in at least 3 topics and improved the most in the aggregate ranking is intended to highlight economies with ongoing, broad-based reform programs.

DISTANCE TO FRONTIER MEASURE

This year's report introduces a new measure to illustrate how the regulatory environment for local businesses in each economy has changed over time. The distance to frontier measure illustrates the distance of an economy to the "frontier" and shows the extent to which the economy has closed this gap over time. The frontier is a score derived from the most efficient practice or highest score achieved on each of the component indicators in 9 *Doing Business* indicator sets (excluding the employing workers and getting electricity indicators) by any economy since 2005. In starting a business, for example, New Zealand has achieved the highest performance on the time (1 day), Canada and New Zealand on the number of procedures required (1), Denmark and Slovenia on the cost (0% of income per capita) and Australia on the paid-in minimum capital requirement (0% of income per capita).

Calculating the distance to frontier for each economy involves 2 main steps. First, individual indicator scores are normalized to a common unit. To do so, each of the 32 component indicators y is rescaled to $(y - min)/(max - min)$, with the minimum value (min) representing the frontier—the highest performance on that indicator across all economies since 2005. Second, for each economy the scores obtained for individual indicators are aggregated through simple averaging into one distance to frontier score. An economy's distance to the frontier is indicated on a scale from 0 to 100, where 0 represents the frontier and 100 the lowest performance.

The difference between an economy's distance to frontier score in 2005 and its score in 2011 illustrates the extent to which the economy has closed the gap to the frontier over time.

The maximum (max) and minimum (min) observed values are computed for the 174 economies included in the *Doing Business* sample since 2005 and for all years (from 2005 to 2011). The year 2005 was chosen as the baseline for the economy sample because it was the first year in which data were available for the majority of economies (a total of 174) and for all 9 indicator sets included in the measure. To mitigate the effects of extreme outliers in the distributions of the rescaled data (very few economies need 694 days to complete the procedures to start a business, but many need 9 days), the maximum (max) is defined as the 95th percentile of the pooled data for all economies and all years for each indicator.

Take Colombia, which has a score of 0.30 on the distance to frontier measure for 2011. This score indicates that the economy is 30 percentage points away from the frontier constructed from the best performances across all economies and all years. Colombia was further from the frontier in 2005, with a score of 0.46. The difference between the scores shows an improvement over time.

NOTES

1. In case of revisions to the methodology or corrections to the underlying data, the data are back-calculated to provide a comparable time series since the year the relevant economy or topic was first included in the data set. The time series is available on the *Doing Business* website (http://www.doingbusiness.org). The *Doing Business* report publishes yearly rankings for the year of publication as well as the previous year to shed light on year-to-year developments. Six topics and more than 50 economies have been added since the inception of the project. Earlier rankings on the ease of doing business are therefore not comparable.

2. See Djankov and others (2005). Principal components and unobserved components methods yield a ranking nearly identical to that from the simple average method because both these methods assign roughly equal weights to the topics, since the pairwise correlations among indicators do not differ much. An alternative to the simple average method is to give different weights to the topics, depending on which are considered of more or less importance in the context of a specific economy.

3. A technical note on the different aggregation and weighting methods is available on the *Doing Business* website (http://www .doingbusiness.org).

4. *Doing Business* reforms making it more difficult to do business are subtracted from the total number of those making it easier to do business.

Summaries of *Doing Business* reforms in 2010/11

245 reforms in 2010/11 made it easier to do business

Starting a business
53

Armenia
Benin
Bhutan
Bosnia and Herzegovina
Burkina Faso
Cameroon
Central African Republic
Chad
Chile
Colombia
Congo, Dem. Rep.
Côte d'Ivoire
Dominican Republic
Georgia
Greece
Guinea-Bissau
Guyana
Hong Kong SAR, China
Indonesia
Jordan
Korea, Rep.
Latvia
Liberia
Madagascar
Malaysia
Mali
Moldova
Montenegro
Oman
Panama
Peru
Portugal
Puerto Rico (U.S.)
Qatar
Rwanda
São Tomé and Príncipe
Saudi Arabia
Senegal
Solomon Islands
South Africa
Spain
Syrian Arab Republic
Taiwan, China
Tajikistan
Thailand
Timor-Leste
Tonga
Turkey
Ukraine
United Arab Emirates
Uruguay
Uzbekistan
Vanuatu

Dealing with construction permits
15

Armenia
Bosnia and Herzegovina
Burkina Faso
Burundi
Congo, Dem. Rep.
Macedonia, FYR
Mauritania
Mexico
Morocco
Paraguay
Portugal
Puerto Rico (U.S.)
São Tomé and Príncipe
Taiwan, China
United Kingdom

Getting electricity
9

Afghanistan
Brunei Darussalam
Gambia, The
Hong Kong SAR, China
Latvia
Lebanon
Russian Federation
Switzerland
Tonga

Registering property
20

Albania
Angola
Belarus
Belgium
Cape Verde
Central African Republic
Costa Rica
Czech Republic
Latvia
Macedonia, FYR
Nicaragua
Russian Federation
São Tomé and Príncipe
Serbia
Slovenia
Solomon Islands
South Africa
Swaziland
Uganda
Vanuatu

Getting credit
44

Algeria
Angola
Armenia
Benin
Bhutan
Brazil
Burkina Faso
Cambodia
Cameroon
Cape Verde
Central African Republic
Chad
Chile
Comoros
Congo, Rep.
Côte d'Ivoire
Croatia
Equatorial Guinea
Gabon
Georgia
Guinea
Guinea-Bissau
Honduras
Liberia
Macedonia, FYR
Madagascar
Malawi
Mali
Mexico
Moldova
Mongolia
Niger
Oman
Paraguay
Qatar
Rwanda
Senegal
Sierra Leone
Slovak Republic
Timor-Leste
Togo
Tonga
United Arab Emirates
Uruguay

Protecting investors
13

Belarus
Burundi
Cyprus
El Salvador
Georgia
Iceland
Kazakhstan
Lithuania
Morocco
Peru
Solomon Islands
Sri Lanka
Vietnam

Paying taxes
33

Armenia
Belarus
Belize
Burundi
Canada
Colombia
Congo, Dem. Rep.
Costa Rica
Côte d'Ivoire
Czech Republic
Finland
Gambia, The
Georgia
Greece
Iceland
India
Korea, Rep.
Mexico
Montenegro
Morocco
New Zealand
Nicaragua
Oman
Peru
Romania
Rwanda
Seychelles
Sri Lanka
St. Kitts and Nevis
Togo
Turkey
Ukraine
Yemen, Rep.

Trading across borders
18

Belgium
Bulgaria
Chile
Djibouti
Gambia, The
Honduras
Israel
Jordan
Liberia

Poland
Russian Federation
São Tomé and Príncipe
Senegal
Seychelles
Sierra Leone
Slovenia
Tanzania
Vanuatu

Enforcing contracts
11

Kenya
Korea, Rep.
Lesotho
Malaysia
Moldova
Nepal
Nicaragua
Russian Federation
Senegal
Sierra Leone
Ukraine

Resolving insolvency
29

Armenia
Australia
Austria
Bulgaria
Burundi
Cape Verde
Colombia
Denmark
France
Israel
Italy
Latvia
Lithuania
Macedonia, FYR
Malawi
Malaysia
Moldova
Montenegro
Namibia
Philippines
Poland
Romania
Serbia
Sierra Leone
Slovenia
Solomon Islands
South Africa
Switzerland
Ukraine

Source: Doing Business database.

Doing Business reforms affecting all sets of indicators included in this year's ranking on the ease of doing business, implemented between June 2010 and May 2011.

✔ *Doing Business* reform making it easier to do business

✘ *Doing Business* reform making it more difficult to do business

AFGHANISTAN

✔ **Getting electricity**

Afghanistan made getting electricity easier by improving the efficiency of the electricity department in Kabul and introducing a new fee schedule for connections.

ALBANIA

✘ **Dealing with construction permits**

In Albania dealing with construction permits became more difficult because the main authority in charge of issuing building permits has not met since April 2009.

✔ **Registering property**

Albania made property registration easier by setting time limits for the land registry to register a title.

ALGERIA

✔ **Getting credit**

Algeria improved its credit information system by guaranteeing by law the right of borrowers to inspect their personal data.

ANGOLA

✔ **Registering property**

Angola made transferring property less costly by reducing transfer taxes.

✔ **Getting credit**

Angola strengthened its credit information system by adopting new rules for credit bureaus and guaranteeing the right of borrowers to inspect their data.

ARGENTINA

✘ **Registering property**

Argentina made transferring property more difficult by adding a requirement that the notary obtain the tax agency's reference value for property before notarizing the sale deed.

ARMENIA

✔ **Starting a business**

Armenia made starting a business easier by establishing a one-stop shop that merged the procedures for name reservation, business registration and obtaining a tax identification number and by allowing for online company registration.

✔ **Dealing with construction permits**

Armenia made dealing with construction permits easier by eliminating the requirement to obtain an environmental impact assessment for small projects.

✔ **Getting credit**

Armenia improved its credit information system by introducing a requirement to collect and distribute information from utility companies.

✔ **Paying taxes**

Armenia made tax compliance easier for firms by reducing the number of payments for social security contributions and corporate income, property and land taxes and by introducing mandatory electronic filing and payment for major taxes.

✔ **Resolving insolvency**

Armenia amended its bankruptcy law to clarify procedures for appointing insolvency administrators, reduce the processing time for bankruptcy proceedings and regulate asset sales by auction.

AUSTRALIA

✔ **Resolving insolvency**

Australia clarified the priority of claims of unsecured creditors over all shareholders' claims and introduced further regulation of the profession of insolvency practitioners.

AUSTRIA

✔ **Resolving insolvency**

Austria passed a new law that simplifies restructuring proceedings and gives preferential consideration to the interests of the debtors.

BAHAMAS, THE

✘ **Registering property**

The Bahamas made transferring property more costly by increasing the applicable stamp duty fees.

BANGLADESH

✘ **Getting electricity**

Bangladesh made getting electricity more difficult by imposing a moratorium on new electricity connections from April 2010 to March 2011 because of an electricity supply shortage. This moratorium has led to long delays for customers and has increased the time to obtain an electricity connection.

BELARUS

✔ **Registering property**

Belarus simplified property transfer by doing away with the requirement to obtain the municipality's approval for transfers of most commercial buildings in Minsk.

✔ **Protecting investors**

Belarus strengthened investor protections by introducing requirements for greater corporate disclosure to the board of directors and to the public.

✔ **Paying taxes**

Belarus abolished several taxes, including turnover and sales taxes, and simplified compliance with corporate income, value added and other taxes by reducing the frequency of filings and payments and facilitating electronic filing and payment.

✘ **Enforcing contracts**

Belarus modified its code of economic procedure, altering the time frames for commercial dispute resolution.

BELGIUM

✔ **Registering property**

Belgium made property registration quicker for entrepreneurs by setting time limits and implementing its "e-notariat" system.

✔ **Trading across borders**

Belgium made trading across borders faster by improving its risk-based profiling system for imports.

BELIZE

✔ **Paying taxes**

Belize made paying taxes easier for firms by improving electronic filing and payment for social security contributions, an option now used by the majority of taxpayers.

BENIN

✔ **Starting a business**

Benin made starting a business easier by replacing the requirement for a copy of the founders' criminal records with one for a sworn declaration at the time of the company's registration.

✔ **Getting credit**

Access to credit in Benin was improved through amendments to the OHADA (Organization for the Harmonization of Business Law in Africa) Uniform Act on Secured Transactions that broaden the range of assets that can be used as collateral (including future assets), extend the security interest to the proceeds of the original asset and introduce the possibility of out-of-court enforcement.

BHUTAN

✔ **Starting a business**

Bhutan eased the process of starting a business by making its criminal records search electronic and making the rubber company stamps available on the local market.

✔ **Getting credit**

Bhutan improved its credit information system by launching the operation of a public credit registry.

BOLIVIA

✘ **Paying taxes**

Bolivia raised social security contribution rates for employers.

BOSNIA AND HERZEGOVINA

✔ **Starting a business**

Bosnia and Herzegovina made starting a business easier by replacing the required utilization permit with a simple notification of commencement of activities and by streamlining the process for obtaining a tax identification number.

✔ **Dealing with construction permits**

Bosnia and Herzegovina made dealing with construction permits easier by fully digitizing and revamping its land registry and cadastre.

BRAZIL

✔ **Getting credit**

Brazil improved its credit information system by allowing private credit bureaus to collect and share positive information.

BRUNEI DARUSSALAM

✔ **Getting electricity**

Brunei Darussalam made getting electricity easier by establishing a one-stop shop and reducing the time required to obtain an excavation permit.

BULGARIA

✔ **Trading across borders**

Bulgaria made trading across borders faster by introducing online submission of customs declaration forms.

✔ **Resolving insolvency**

Bulgaria amended its commerce act to extend further rights to secured creditors and increase the transparency of insolvency proceedings.

BURKINA FASO

✔ **Starting a business**

Burkina Faso made starting a business easier by replacing the requirement for a copy of the founders' criminal records with one for a sworn declaration at the time of the company's registration.

✔ **Dealing with construction permits**

Burkina Faso made dealing with construction permits less costly by reducing the fees to obtain a fire safety study.

✔ **Getting credit**

Access to credit in Burkina Faso was improved through amendments to the OHADA Uniform Act on Secured Transactions that broaden the range of assets that can be used as collateral (including future assets), extend the security interest to the proceeds of the original asset and introduce the possibility of out-of-court enforcement.

BURUNDI

✔ **Dealing with construction permits**

Burundi made dealing with construction permits easier by reducing the cost to obtain a geotechnical study.

✔ **Protecting investors**

Burundi strengthened investor protections by introducing new requirements for the approval of transactions between interested parties, by requiring greater corporate disclosure to the board of directors and in the annual report and by making it easier to sue directors in cases of prejudicial transactions between interested parties.

✔ **Paying taxes**

Burundi made paying taxes easier for companies by reducing the payment frequency for social security contributions from monthly to quarterly.

✔ **Resolving insolvency**

Burundi amended its commercial code to establish foreclosure procedures.

CAMBODIA

✔ **Getting credit**

Cambodia strengthened its credit information system through a new regulation allowing credit bureaus to collect and distribute positive as well as negative credit information.

CAMEROON

✔ **Starting a business**

Cameroon made starting a business easier by replacing the requirement for a copy of the founders' criminal records with one for a sworn declaration at the time of the company's registration, and by reducing publication fees.

✔ **Getting credit**

Access to credit in Cameroon was improved through amendments to the OHADA Uniform Act on Secured Transactions that broaden the range of assets that can be used as collateral (including future assets), extend the security interest to the proceeds of the original asset and introduce the possibility of out-of-court enforcement.

CANADA

✔ **Paying taxes**

Canada made paying taxes easier and less costly for companies by reducing profit tax rates, eliminating the Ontario capital tax and harmonizing sales taxes.

CAPE VERDE

✔ **Registering property**

Cape Verde made registering property faster by implementing time limits for the notaries and the land registry.

✔ **Getting credit**

Cape Verde improved its credit information system by introducing a new online platform and by starting to provide 5 years of historical data.

✔ **Resolving insolvency**

Cape Verde introduced qualification requirements for insolvency administrators and a shorter time frame for liquidation proceedings.

CENTRAL AFRICAN REPUBLIC

✔ **Starting a business**

The Central African Republic made starting a business easier by reducing business registration fees and by replacing the requirement for a copy of the founders' criminal records with one for a sworn declaration at the time of the company's registration.

✔ **Registering property**

The Central African Republic halved the cost of registering property.

✔ **Getting credit**

Access to credit in the Central African Republic was improved through amendments to the OHADA Uniform Act on Secured Transactions that broaden the range of assets that can be used as collateral (including future assets), extend the security interest to the proceeds of the original asset and introduce the possibility of out-of-court enforcement.

CHAD

✔ **Starting a business**

Chad made starting a business easier by eliminating the requirement for a medical certificate and by replacing the requirement for a copy of the founders' criminal records with one for a sworn declaration at the time of the company's registration.

✔ **Getting credit**

Access to credit in Chad was improved through amendments to the OHADA Uniform Act on Secured Transactions that broaden the range of assets that can be used as collateral (including future assets), extend the security interest to the proceeds of the original asset and introduce the possibility of out-of-court enforcement.

CHILE

✔ **Starting a business**

Chile made business start-up easier by starting to provide an immediate temporary operating license to new companies, eliminating the requirement for an inspection of premises by the tax authority before new companies can begin operations and allowing free online publication of the notice of a company's creation.

✔ **Getting credit**

Chile strengthened its secured transactions system by implementing a unified collateral registry and a new legal framework for non-possessory security interests.

✔ **Trading across borders**

Chile made trading across borders faster by implementing an online electronic data interchange system for customs operations.

COLOMBIA

✔ **Starting a business**

Colombia reduced the costs associated with starting a business, by no longer requiring upfront payment of the commercial license fee.

✔ **Paying taxes**

Colombia eased the administrative burden of paying taxes for firms by establishing mandatory electronic filing and payment for some of the major taxes.

✔ **Resolving insolvency**

Colombia amended regulations governing insolvency proceedings to simplify the proceedings and reduce their time and cost.

COMOROS

✔ **Getting credit**

Access to credit in the Comoros was improved through amendments to the OHADA Uniform

Act on Secured Transactions that broaden the range of assets that can be used as collateral (including future assets), extend the security interest to the proceeds of the original asset and introduce the possibility of out-of-court enforcement.

CONGO, DEM. REP.

✔ **Starting a business**

The Democratic Republic of Congo made business start-up faster by reducing the time required to complete company registration and obtain a national identification number.

✔ **Dealing with construction permits**

The Democratic Republic of Congo reduced the administrative costs of obtaining a construction permit.

✔ **Paying taxes**

The Democratic Republic of Congo made paying taxes easier for firms by replacing the sales tax with a value added tax.

CONGO, REP.

✘ **Registering property**

The Republic of Congo made registering property more expensive by reversing a previous law that reduced the registration fee.

✔ **Getting credit**

Access to credit in the Republic of Congo was improved through amendments to the OHADA Uniform Act on Secured Transactions that broaden the range of assets that can be used as collateral (including future assets), extend the security interest to the proceeds of the original asset and introduce the possibility of out-of-court enforcement.

COSTA RICA

✔ **Registering property**

Costa Rica made transferring property easier and quicker by making property certificates available online through a single website.

✔ **Paying taxes**

In Costa Rica online payment of social security contributions is now widespread and used by the majority of taxpayers.

CÔTE D'IVOIRE

✔ **Starting a business**

Côte d'Ivoire made starting a business easier by reorganizing the court clerk's office where entrepreneurs file their company documents.

✔ **Getting credit**

Access to credit in Côte d'Ivoire was improved through amendments to the OHADA Uniform Act on Secured Transactions that broaden the range of assets that can be used as collateral

(including future assets), extend the security interest to the proceeds of the original asset and introduce the possibility of out-of-court enforcement.

✔ **Paying taxes**

Côte d'Ivoire eliminated a tax on firms, the contribution for national reconstruction (*contribution pour la reconstruction nationale*).

CROATIA

✔ **Getting credit**

In Croatia the private credit bureau started to collect and distribute information on firms, improving the credit information system.

CYPRUS

✔ **Protecting investors**

Cyprus strengthened investor protections by requiring greater corporate disclosure to the board of directors, to the public and in the annual report.

CZECH REPUBLIC

✔ **Registering property**

The Czech Republic speeded up property registration by computerizing its cadastral office, digitizing all its data and introducing electronic communications with notaries.

✔ **Paying taxes**

The Czech Republic revised its tax legislation to simplify provisions relating to administrative procedures and relationships between tax authorities and taxpayers.

DENMARK

✔ **Resolving insolvency**

Denmark introduced new rules on company reorganization, which led to the elimination of the suspension-of-payments regime.

DJIBOUTI

✘ **Dealing with construction permits**

Djibouti made dealing with construction permits costlier by increasing the fees for inspections and the building permit and adding a new inspection in the preconstruction phase.

✔ **Trading across borders**

Djibouti made trading across borders faster by developing a new container terminal.

DOMINICAN REPUBLIC

✔ **Starting a business**

The Dominican Republic made starting a business easier by eliminating the requirement for a proof of deposit of capital when establishing a new company.

EL SALVADOR

✔ **Protecting investors**

El Salvador strengthened investor protections by allowing greater access to corporate information during the trial.

EQUATORIAL GUINEA

✔ **Getting credit**

Access to credit in Equatorial Guinea was improved through amendments to the OHADA Uniform Act on Secured Transactions that broaden the range of assets that can be used as collateral (including future assets), extend the security interest to the proceeds of the original asset and introduce the possibility of out-of-court enforcement.

ESTONIA

✘ **Paying taxes**

In Estonia a municipal sales tax introduced in Tallinn made paying taxes costlier for firms, though a later parliamentary measure abolished local sales taxes effective January 1, 2012.

ETHIOPIA

✘ **Getting electricity**

In Ethiopia delays in providing new connections made getting electricity more difficult.

FIJI

✘ **Starting a business**

Fiji made starting a business more difficult by adding a requirement to obtain a tax identification number when registering a new company.

FINLAND

✔ **Paying taxes**

Finland simplified reporting and payment for the value added tax and labor tax.

FRANCE

✔ **Resolving insolvency**

France passed a law that enables debtors to implement a restructuring plan with financial creditors only, without affecting trade creditors.

GABON

✔ **Getting credit**

Access to credit in Gabon was improved through amendments to the OHADA Uniform Act on Secured Transactions that broaden the range of assets that can be used as collateral (including future assets), extend the security

interest to the proceeds of the original asset and introduce the possibility of out-of-court enforcement.

GAMBIA, THE

✔ **Getting electricity**

The Gambia made getting electricity faster by allowing customers to choose private contractors to carry out the external connection works.

✔ **Paying taxes**

The Gambia reduced the minimum turnover tax and corporate income tax rates.

✔ **Trading across borders**

The Gambia made trading across borders faster by implementing the Automated System for Customs Data (ASYCUDA).

GEORGIA

✔ **Starting a business**

Georgia simplified business start-up by eliminating the requirement to visit a bank to pay the registration fees.

✔ **Getting credit**

Georgia expanded access to credit by amending its civil code to broaden the range of assets that can be used as collateral.

✔ **Protecting investors**

Georgia strengthened investor protections by introducing requirements relating to the approval of transactions between interested parties.

✔ **Paying taxes**

Georgia made paying taxes easier for firms by simplifying the reporting for value added tax and introducing electronic filing and payment of taxes.

GHANA

✘ **Starting a business**

Ghana increased the cost to start a business by 70%.

GREECE

✔ **Starting a business**

Greece made starting a business easier by implementing an electronic platform that interconnects several government agencies.

✔ **Paying taxes**

Greece reduced its corporate income tax rate.

GUINEA

✔ **Getting credit**

Access to credit in Guinea was improved through amendments to the OHADA Uniform

Act on Secured Transactions that broaden the range of assets that can be used as collateral (including future assets), extend the security interest to the proceeds of the original asset and introduce the possibility of out-of-court enforcement.

GUINEA-BISSAU

✔ **Starting a business**

Guinea-Bissau made starting a business easier by establishing a one-stop shop, eliminating the requirement for an operating license and simplifying the method for providing criminal records and publishing the registration notice.

✔ **Getting credit**

Access to credit in Guinea-Bissau was improved through amendments to the OHADA Uniform Act on Secured Transactions that broaden the range of assets that can be used as collateral (including future assets), extend the security interest to the proceeds of the original asset and introduce the possibility of out-of-court enforcement.

GUYANA

✔ **Starting a business**

Guyana made starting a business easier by reducing the time needed for registering a new company and for obtaining a tax identification number.

✘ **Getting electricity**

Guyana made getting electricity more expensive by tripling the security deposit required for a new connection.

✘ **Registering property**

In Guyana transferring property became slower because of a lack of personnel at the deed registry.

HAITI

✘ **Dealing with construction permits**

Haiti made dealing with construction permits costlier by increasing the fees to obtain a building permit.

HONDURAS

✔ **Getting credit**

Honduras strengthened its secured transactions system through a new decree establishing a centralized and computerized collateral registry and providing for out-of-court enforcement of collateral upon default.

✘ **Paying taxes**

Honduras made paying taxes costlier for firms by raising the solidarity tax rate.

✔ **Trading across borders**

Honduras made trading across borders faster by implementing a web-based electronic data interchange system and X-ray machines at the port of Puerto Cortes.

✘ **Enforcing contracts**

Honduras adopted a new civil procedure code that modified litigation procedures for enforcing a contract.

HONG KONG SAR, CHINA

✔ **Starting a business**

Hong Kong SAR, China, made starting a business easier by introducing online electronic services for company and business registration.

✔ **Getting electricity**

Hong Kong SAR, China, made getting electricity easier by increasing the efficiency of public agencies and streamlining the utility's procedures with other government agencies.

HUNGARY

✘ **Getting credit**

Hungary reduced the amount of credit information available from private credit bureaus by shortening the period for retaining data on defaults and late payments (if repaid) from 5 years to 1 year.

✘ **Paying taxes**

Hungary made paying taxes costlier for firms by introducing a sector-specific surtax.

ICELAND

✔ **Protecting investors**

Iceland strengthened investor protections by introducing new requirements relating to the approval of transactions between interested parties.

✔ **Paying taxes**

Iceland made paying taxes easier and less costly for firms by abolishing a tax.

INDIA

✔ **Paying taxes**

India eased the administrative burden of paying taxes for firms by introducing mandatory electronic filing and payment for value added tax.

INDONESIA

✔ **Starting a business**

Indonesia made starting a business easier by introducing a simplified application process allowing an applicant to simultaneously obtain both a general trading license and a business registration certificate.

✘ **Getting electricity**

Indonesia made getting electricity more difficult by increasing connection fees.

IRAQ

✘ **Starting a business**

In Iraq starting a business became more expensive because of an increase in the cost to obtain a name reservation certificate and in the cost for lawyers to draft articles of association.

ISRAEL

✔ **Trading across borders**

Israel made trading across borders easier by changing the method used to calculate port fees.

✔ **Resolving insolvency**

Israel amended its courts law to establish specialized courts for dealing with economic matters.

ITALY

✔ **Resolving insolvency**

Italy has introduced debt restructuring and reorganization procedures as alternatives to bankruptcy proceedings.

JAPAN

✘ **Dealing with construction permits**

Japan made dealing with construction permits costlier by increasing inspection fees.

JORDAN

✔ **Starting a business**

Jordan made starting a business easier by reducing the minimum capital requirement from 1,000 Jordanian dinars to 1 dinar, of which only half must be deposited before company registration.

✔ **Trading across borders**

Jordan made trading across borders faster by introducing X-ray scanners for risk management systems.

KAZAKHSTAN

✔ **Protecting investors**

Kazakhstan strengthened investor protections by regulating the approval of transactions between interested parties and making it easier to sue directors in cases of prejudicial transactions between interested parties.

KENYA

✔ **Enforcing contracts**

Kenya introduced a case management system that will help increase the efficiency and cost-effectiveness of commercial dispute resolution.

KOREA, REP.

✔ **Starting a business**

Korea made starting a business easier by introducing a new online one-stop shop, Start-Biz.

✔ **Paying taxes**

Korea eased the administrative burden of paying taxes for firms by merging several taxes, allowing 4 labor taxes and contributions to be paid jointly and continuing to increase the use of the online tax payment system.

✔ **Enforcing contracts**

Korea made filing a commercial case easier by introducing an electronic case filing system.

KYRGYZ REPUBLIC

✘ **Paying taxes**

The Kyrgyz Republic made paying taxes costlier for firms by introducing a real estate tax, though it also reduced the sales tax rate.

LATVIA

✔ **Starting a business**

Latvia made starting a business easier by reducing the minimum capital requirement and introducing a common application for value added tax and company registration.

✔ **Getting electricity**

Latvia made getting electricity faster by introducing a simplified process for approval of external connection designs.

✔ **Registering property**

Latvia made transferring property easier by allowing electronic access to municipal tax databases that show the tax status of property, eliminating the requirement to obtain this information in paper format.

✔ **Resolving insolvency**

Latvia adopted a new insolvency law that streamlines and expedites the insolvency process and introduces a reorganization option for companies.

LEBANON

✔ **Getting electricity**

Lebanon made getting electricity less costly by reducing the application fees and security deposit for a new connection.

LESOTHO

✔ **Enforcing contracts**

Lesotho made enforcing contracts easier by launching a specialized commercial court.

LIBERIA

✔ **Starting a business**

Liberia made starting a business easier by introducing a one-stop shop.

✔ **Getting credit**

Liberia strengthened its legal framework for secured transactions by adopting a new commercial code that broadens the range of assets that can be used as collateral (including future assets) and extends the security interest to the proceeds of the original asset.

✔ **Trading across borders**

Liberia made trading across borders faster by implementing online submission of customs forms and enhancing risk-based inspections.

LITHUANIA

✘ **Getting electricity**

Lithuania made getting electricity more difficult by abolishing the one-stop shop for obtaining technical conditions for utility services.

✔ **Protecting investors**

Lithuania strengthened investor protections by introducing greater requirements for corporate disclosure to the public and in the annual report.

✔ **Resolving insolvency**

Lithuania amended its reorganization law to simplify and shorten reorganization proceedings, grant priority to secured creditors and introduce professional requirements for insolvency administrators.

MACEDONIA, FYR

✔ **Dealing with construction permits**

FYR Macedonia made dealing with construction permits easier by transferring oversight processes to the private sector and streamlining procedures.

✔ **Registering property**

FYR Macedonia made registering property easier by reducing notary fees and enforcing time limits.

✔ **Getting credit**

FYR Macedonia improved its credit information system by establishing a private credit bureau.

✔ **Resolving insolvency**

FYR Macedonia increased the transparency of bankruptcy proceedings through amendments to its company and bankruptcy laws.

MADAGASCAR

✔ **Starting a business**

Madagascar made starting a business easier by eliminating the minimum capital requirement, but also made it more difficult by introducing a requirement to obtain a tax identification number.

✔ **Getting credit**

Madagascar improved its credit information system by eliminating the minimum threshold for loans included in the database and making it mandatory for banks to share credit information with the credit bureau.

MALAWI

✘ **Registering property**

Malawi did not sustain the previous year's improvement in processing times for the compliance certificate at the Ministry of Lands, leading to slower property registration.

✔ **Getting credit**

Malawi improved its credit information system by passing a new law allowing the creation of a private credit bureau.

✔ **Resolving insolvency**

Malawi adopted new rules providing clear procedural requirements and time frames for winding up a company.

MALAYSIA

✔ **Starting a business**

Malaysia made starting a business easier by merging company, tax, social security and employment fund registrations at the one-stop shop and providing same-day registration.

✘ **Paying taxes**

Malaysia made paying taxes costlier for firms by reintroducing the real estate capital gains tax—but also made tax compliance easier by improving electronic systems and the availability of software.

✔ **Enforcing contracts**

Malaysia continued to improve the computerization of its courts by introducing a system making it possible to file complaints electronically.

✔ **Resolving insolvency**

Malaysia established dedicated commercial courts to handle foreclosure proceedings.

MALI

✔ **Starting a business**

Mali made starting a business easier by adding to the services provided by the one-stop shop.

✔ **Getting credit**

Access to credit in Mali was improved through amendments to the OHADA Uniform Act on Secured Transactions that broaden the range of assets that can be used as collateral (including future assets), extend the security interest to the proceeds of the original asset and introduce the possibility of out-of-court enforcement.

MAURITANIA

✔ **Dealing with construction permits**

Mauritania made dealing with construction permits easier by opening a one-stop shop.

MEXICO

✔ **Dealing with construction permits**

Mexico made dealing with construction permits faster by consolidating internal administrative procedures.

✔ **Getting credit**

Mexico strengthened its secured transactions system by implementing a centralized collateral registry with an electronic database that is accessible online.

✔ **Paying taxes**

Mexico continued to ease the administrative burden of paying taxes for firms by ending the requirement to file a yearly value added tax return and reducing filing requirements for other taxes.

MOLDOVA

✔ **Starting a business**

Moldova made starting a business easier by implementing a one-stop shop.

✔ **Getting credit**

Moldova improved its credit information system by establishing its first private credit bureau.

✔ **Enforcing contracts**

Moldova made enforcement of judgments more efficient by introducing private bailiffs.

✔ **Resolving insolvency**

Moldova amended its insolvency law to grant priority to secured creditors.

MONGOLIA

✔ **Getting credit**

Mongolia improved its credit information system by eliminating the minimum threshold for loans included in the database.

MONTENEGRO

✔ **Starting a business**

Montenegro made starting a business easier by implementing a one-stop shop.

✔ **Paying taxes**

Montenegro made paying taxes easier and less costly for firms by abolishing a tax, reducing the social security contribution rate and merging several returns into a single unified one.

✔ **Resolving insolvency**

Montenegro passed a new bankruptcy law that introduces reorganization and liquidation proceedings, introduces time limits for these proceedings and provides for the possibility of recovery of secured creditors' claims and settlement before completion of the entire bankruptcy procedure.

MOROCCO

✔ **Dealing with construction permits**

Morocco made dealing with construction permits easier by opening a one-stop shop.

✔ **Protecting investors**

Morocco strengthened investor protections by allowing minority shareholders to obtain any nonconfidential corporate document during trial.

✔ **Paying taxes**

Morocco eased the administrative burden of paying taxes for firms by enhancing electronic filing and payment of the corporate income tax and value added tax.

MOZAMBIQUE

✘ **Getting electricity**

Mozambique made getting electricity more difficult by requiring authorization of a connection project by the Ministry of Energy and by adding an inspection of the completed external works.

NAMIBIA

✘ **Registering property**

Namibia made transferring property more expensive for companies.

✔ **Resolving insolvency**

Namibia adopted a new company law that established clear procedures for liquidation.

NEPAL

✔ **Enforcing contracts**

Nepal improved oversight and monitoring in the court, speeding up the process for filing claims.

NEW ZEALAND

✔ **Paying taxes**

New Zealand reduced its corporate income tax rate and fringe benefit tax rate.

NICARAGUA

✔ **Registering property**

Nicaragua made transferring property more efficient by introducing a fast-track procedure for registration.

✔ **Paying taxes**

Nicaragua made paying taxes easier for companies by promoting electronic filing and payment of the major taxes, an option now used by the majority of taxpayers.

✔ **Enforcing contracts**

Nicaragua raised the monetary threshold for commercial claims that can be brought to the Managua local civil court, leaving lower-value claims in the local courts, where proceedings are simpler and faster.

NIGER

✔ **Getting credit**

Access to credit in Niger was improved through amendments to the OHADA Uniform Act on Secured Transactions that broaden the range of assets that can be used as collateral (including future assets), extend the security interest to the proceeds of the original asset and introduce the possibility of out-of-court enforcement.

OMAN

✔ **Starting a business**

Oman introduced online company registration, reducing the time it takes to register a business.

✔ **Getting credit**

Oman improved its credit information system by launching the Bank Credit and Statistical Bureau System, which collects historical information on performing and nonperforming loans for both firms and individuals.

✔ **Paying taxes**

Oman enacted a new income tax law that redefined the scope of taxation.

PAKISTAN

✘ **Paying taxes**

Pakistan increased the profit tax rate for small firms.

PANAMA

✔ **Starting a business**

Panama extended the operating hours of the public registry, reducing the time required to register a new company.

PARAGUAY

✔ **Dealing with construction permits**

Paraguay made dealing with construction permits easier by implementing a risk-based approval system and a single window for obtaining construction permits.

✔ **Getting credit**

Paraguay improved its credit information system by establishing an online platform for financial institutions to exchange information with the public credit registry.

✘ **Paying taxes**

Paraguay made paying taxes more burdensome for companies by introducing new tax declarations that must be filed monthly.

PERU

✔ **Starting a business**

Peru made starting a business easier by eliminating the requirement for micro and small enterprises to deposit start-up capital in a bank before registration.

✔ **Protecting investors**

Peru strengthened investor protections through a new law allowing minority shareholders to request access to nonconfidential corporate documents.

✔ **Paying taxes**

Peru made paying taxes easier for companies by improving electronic filing and payment of the major taxes and promoting the use of the electronic option among the majority of taxpayers.

PHILIPPINES

✔ **Resolving insolvency**

The Philippines adopted a new insolvency law that provides a legal framework for liquidation and reorganization of financially distressed companies.

POLAND

✔ **Trading across borders**

Poland made trading across borders faster by implementing electronic preparation and submission of customs documents.

✔ **Resolving insolvency**

Poland amended its bankruptcy and reorganization law to simplify court procedures and extend more rights to secured creditors.

PORTUGAL

✔ **Starting a business**

Portugal made starting a business easier by allowing company founders to choose the amount of minimum capital and make their paid-in capital contribution up to 1 year after the company's creation, and by eliminating the stamp tax on company's share capital subscriptions.

✔ **Dealing with construction permits**

Portugal made dealing with construction permits easier by streamlining its inspection system.

PUERTO RICO (U.S.)

✔ **Starting a business**

Puerto Rico (territory of the United States) made starting a business easier by merging the name search and company registration procedures.

✔ **Dealing with construction permits**

Puerto Rico (territory of the United States) made dealing with construction permits easier by creating the Office of Permits Management to streamline procedures.

QATAR

✔ **Starting a business**

Qatar made starting a business easier by combining commercial registration and registration with the Chamber of Commerce and Industry at the one-stop shop.

✘ **Dealing with construction permits**

Qatar made dealing with construction permits more difficult by increasing the time and cost to process building permits.

✔ **Getting credit**

Qatar improved its credit information system by starting to distribute historical data and eliminating the minimum threshold for loans included in the database.

ROMANIA

✘ **Starting a business**

Romania made starting a business more difficult by requiring a tax clearance certificate for a new company's headquarters before company registration.

✔ **Paying taxes**

Romania made paying taxes easier for companies by introducing an electronic payment system and a unified return for social security contributions. It also abolished the annual minimum tax.

✔ **Resolving insolvency**

Romania amended its insolvency law to shorten the duration of insolvency proceedings.

RUSSIAN FEDERATION

✔ **Getting electricity**

Russia made getting electricity less costly by revising the tariffs for connection.

✔ **Registering property**

Russia made registering property transfers easier by eliminating the requirement to obtain cadastral passports on land plots.

✘ **Paying taxes**

Russia increased the social security contribution rate for employers.

✔ **Trading across borders**

Russia made trading across borders easier by reducing the number of documents needed for each export or import transaction and lowering the associated cost.

✔ **Enforcing contracts**

Russia made filing a commercial case easier by introducing an electronic case filing system.

RWANDA

✔ **Starting a business**

Rwanda made starting a business easier by reducing the business registration fees.

✘ **Registering property**

Rwanda made transferring property more expensive by enforcing the checking of the capital gains tax.

✔ **Getting credit**

In Rwanda the private credit bureau started to collect and distribute information from utility companies and also started to distribute more than 2 years of historical information, improving the credit information system.

✔ **Paying taxes**

Rwanda reduced the frequency of value added tax filings by companies from monthly to quarterly.

SÃO TOMÉ AND PRÍNCIPE

✔ **Starting a business**

São Tomé and Príncipe made starting a business easier by establishing a one-stop shop, eliminating the requirement for an operating license for general commercial companies and simplifying publication requirements.

✔ **Dealing with construction permits**

São Tomé and Príncipe made dealing with construction permits easier by reducing the time required to process building permit applications.

✔ **Registering property**

São Tomé and Príncipe made registering property less costly by lowering property transfer taxes.

✔ **Trading across borders**

São Tomé and Príncipe made trading across borders faster by adopting legislative, administrative and technological improvements.

SAUDI ARABIA

✔ **Starting a business**

Saudi Arabia made starting a business easier by bringing together representatives from the Department of Zakat and Income Tax and the General Organization of Social Insurance at the Unified Center to register new companies with their agencies.

SENEGAL

✔ **Starting a business**

Senegal made starting a business easier by replacing the requirement for a copy of the founders' criminal records with one for a sworn declaration at the time of the company's registration.

✔ **Getting credit**

Access to credit in Senegal was improved through amendments to the OHADA Uniform Act on Secured Transactions that broaden the range of assets that can be used as collateral (including future assets), extend the security interest to the proceeds of the original asset and introduce the possibility of out-of-court enforcement.

✔ **Trading across borders**

Senegal made trading across borders less costly by opening the market for transport, which increased competition.

✔ **Enforcing contracts**

Senegal made enforcing contracts easier by launching specialized commercial chambers in the court.

SERBIA

✔ **Registering property**

Serbia made transferring property quicker by offering an expedited option.

✔ **Resolving insolvency**

Serbia adopted legislation introducing professional requirements for insolvency administrators and regulating their compensation.

SEYCHELLES

✔ **Paying taxes**

The Seychelles made paying taxes less costly for firms by eliminating the social security tax.

✔ **Trading across borders**

The Seychelles made trading across borders faster by introducing electronic submission of customs documents.

✘ **Enforcing contracts**

The Seychelles expanded the jurisdiction of the lower court, increasing the time required to enforce contracts.

SIERRA LEONE

✔ **Getting credit**

Sierra Leone improved its credit information system by enacting a new law providing for the creation of a public credit registry.

✔ **Trading across borders**

Sierra Leone made trading across borders faster by implementing the Automated System for Customs Data (ASYCUDA).

✔ **Enforcing contracts**

Sierra Leone made enforcing contracts easier by launching a fast-track commercial court.

✔ **Resolving insolvency**

Sierra Leone established a fast-track commercial court in an effort to expedite commercial cases, including insolvency proceedings.

SLOVAK REPUBLIC

✔ **Getting credit**

The Slovak Republic improved its credit information system by guaranteeing by law the right of borrowers to inspect their own data.

SLOVENIA

✔ **Registering property**

Slovenia made transferring property easier and less costly by introducing online procedures and reducing fees.

✔ **Trading across borders**

Slovenia made trading across borders faster by introducing online submission of customs declaration forms.

✔ **Resolving insolvency**

Slovenia simplified and streamlined the insolvency process and strengthened professional requirements for insolvency administrators.

SOLOMON ISLANDS

✔ **Starting a business**

The Solomon Islands made starting a business easier by implementing an online registration process.

✔ **Registering property**

The Solomon Islands made registering property faster by separating the land registry from the business and movable property registries.

✔ **Protecting investors**

The Solomon Islands strengthened investor protections by increasing shareholder access to corporate information.

✔ **Resolving insolvency**

The Solomon Islands adopted a new law that simplified insolvency proceedings.

SOUTH AFRICA

✔ **Starting a business**

South Africa made starting a business easier by implementing its new company law, which eliminated the requirement to reserve a company name and simplified the incorporation documents.

✔ **Registering property**

South Africa made transferring property less costly and more efficient by reducing the transfer duty and introducing electronic filing.

✔ **Resolving insolvency**

South Africa introduced a new reorganization process to facilitate the rehabilitation of financially distressed companies.

SPAIN

✔ **Starting a business**

Spain made starting a business easier by reducing the cost and by reducing the minimum capital requirement.

SRI LANKA

✔ **Protecting investors**

Sri Lanka strengthened investor protections by requiring greater corporate disclosure on transactions between interested parties.

✔ **Paying taxes**

Sri Lanka made paying taxes less costly for businesses by abolishing the turnover tax and social security contribution and by reducing corporate income tax, value added tax and national building tax rates.

ST. KITTS AND NEVIS

✔ **Paying taxes**

St. Kitts and Nevis made paying taxes easier by introducing a value added tax.

SWAZILAND

✔ **Registering property**

Swaziland made transferring property quicker by streamlining the process at the land registry.

SWEDEN

✘ **Registering property**

Sweden increased the cost of transferring property between companies.

SWITZERLAND

✔ **Getting electricity**

Switzerland made getting electricity less costly by revising the conditions for connections.

✔ **Resolving insolvency**

Switzerland introduced a unified civil procedure code and made a number of changes to its federal bankruptcy law.

SYRIAN ARAB REPUBLIC

✔ **Starting a business**

Syria made starting a business less costly by reducing both the minimum capital requirement and the cost of publication for the registration notice.

TAIWAN, CHINA

✔ **Starting a business**

Taiwan, China, made starting a business easier by implementing an online one-stop shop for business registration.

✔ **Dealing with construction permits**

Taiwan, China, made dealing with construction permits easier by creating a one-stop center.

TAJIKISTAN

✔ **Starting a business**

Tajikistan made starting a business easier by allowing entrepreneurs to pay in their capital up to 1 year after the start of operations, thereby eliminating the requirements related to opening a bank account.

✘ **Getting credit**

Access to credit using movable property in Tajikistan became more complicated because the movable collateral registry stopped its operations in January 2011.

TANZANIA

✔ **Trading across borders**

Tanzania made trading across borders faster by implementing the Pre-Arrival Declaration (PAD) system and electronic submission of customs declarations.

THAILAND

✔ **Starting a business**

Thailand made starting a business easier by introducing a one-stop shop.

✘ **Registering property**

Thailand made registering property more expensive by increasing the registration fee.

TIMOR-LESTE

✔ **Starting a business**

Timor-Leste made starting a business faster by improving the registration process.

✔ **Getting credit**

Timor-Leste improved its credit information system by establishing a public credit registry.

TOGO

✔ **Getting credit**

Access to credit in Togo was improved through amendments to the OHADA Uniform Act on Secured Transactions that broaden the range of assets that can be used as collateral (including future assets), extend the security interest to the proceeds of the original asset and introduce the possibility of out-of-court enforcement.

✔ **Paying taxes**

Togo reduced its corporate income tax rate.

TONGA

✔ **Starting a business**

Tonga made starting a business easier by implementing an electronic system at the registry, which reduced the time required for verification of the uniqueness of the company name and for registration of the company. The costs for the name search, company registration and business license increased, however.

✔ **Getting electricity**

Tonga made getting electricity faster by implementing a time limit for the safety inspection.

✘ **Registering property**

Tonga made transferring property more costly.

✔ **Getting credit**

Tonga strengthened its secured transactions system by passing a new law that allows a general description of the obligation in the security agreement and gives secured creditors priority outside bankruptcy.

TRINIDAD AND TOBAGO

✘ **Dealing with construction permits**

Trinidad and Tobago made dealing with construction permits costlier by increasing the fees for building permit approvals.

TURKEY

✔ **Starting a business**

Turkey made starting a business less costly by eliminating notarization fees for the articles of association and other documents.

✔ **Paying taxes**

Turkey lowered the social security contribution rate for companies by offering them a 5% rebate.

UGANDA

✘ **Starting a business**

Uganda introduced changes that added time to the process of obtaining a business license, slowing business start-up. But it simplified registration for a tax identification number and for value added tax by introducing an online system.

✔ **Registering property**

Uganda increased the efficiency of property transfers by establishing performance standards and recruiting more officials at the land office.

UKRAINE

✔ **Starting a business**

Ukraine made starting a business easier by eliminating the requirement to obtain approval for a new corporate seal.

✔ **Paying taxes**

Ukraine made paying taxes easier and less costly for firms by revising and unifying tax legislation, reducing corporate income tax rates and unifying social security contributions.

✘ **Trading across borders**

Ukraine made trading across borders more difficult by introducing additional inspections for customs clearance of imports.

✔ **Enforcing contracts**

Ukraine amended legislation to streamline commercial dispute resolution and increase the efficiency of enforcement procedures.

✔ **Resolving insolvency**

Ukraine amended its legislation on enforcement, introducing more guarantees for secured creditors.

UNITED ARAB EMIRATES

✔ **Starting a business**

The United Arab Emirates made starting a business easier by merging the requirements to file company documents with the Department for Economic Development, to obtain a trade license and to register with the Dubai Chamber of Commerce and Industry.

✔ **Getting credit**

The United Arab Emirates improved its credit information system through a new law allowing the establishment of a federal credit bureau under the supervision of the central bank.

UNITED KINGDOM

✔ **Dealing with construction permits**

The United Kingdom made dealing with construction permits easier by increasing efficiency in the issuance of planning permits.

URUGUAY

✔ **Starting a business**

Uruguay made starting a business easier by establishing a one-stop shop for general commercial companies.

✔ **Getting credit**

Uruguay improved its credit information system by introducing a new online platform allowing access to credit reports for financial institutions, public utilities and borrowers.

UZBEKISTAN

✔ **Starting a business**

Uzbekistan made starting a business easier by reducing the minimum capital requirement, eliminating 1 procedure and reducing the cost of registration.

VANUATU

✔ **Starting a business**

Vanuatu made starting a business easier by reducing the time required for company registration at the Vanuatu Financial Services Commission and issuing provisional licenses at the Department of Customs.

✘ **Dealing with construction permits**

Vanuatu made dealing with construction permits more difficult by increasing the number of procedures and the cost to obtain a building permit.

✔ **Registering property**

Vanuatu made registering property easier by computerizing the land registry.

✔ **Trading across borders**

Vanuatu made trading across borders faster by upgrading Port-Vila's wharf infrastructure, which increased the efficiency of port and terminal handling activities.

VENEZUELA, RB

✘ **Paying taxes**

República Bolivariana de Venezuela made paying taxes costlier for firms by doubling the municipal economic activities tax (sales tax).

VIETNAM

✔ **Protecting investors**

Vietnam strengthened investor protections by requiring higher standards of accountability for company directors.

YEMEN, REP.

✔ **Paying taxes**

The Republic of Yemen enacted a new tax law that reduced the general corporate tax rate from 35% to 20% and abolished all tax exemptions except those granted under the investment law for investment projects.

ZAMBIA

✘ **Registering property**

Zambia made registering property more costly by increasing the property transfer tax rate.

Country tables

✔ Reform making it easier to do business   ✘ Reform making it more difficult to do business

AFGHANISTAN

Ease of doing business (rank)	160	South Asia		GNI per capita (US$)	517	
		Low income		Population (m)	30.6	
Starting a business (rank)	30	**Registering property** (rank)	172	**Trading across borders** (rank)	179	
Procedures (number)	4	Procedures (number)	9	Documents to export (number)	10	
Time (days)	7	Time (days)	250	Time to export (days)	74	
Cost (% of income per capita)	25.8	Cost (% of property value)	5.0	Cost to export (US$ per container)	3,545	
Minimum capital (% of income per capita)	0.0			Documents to import (number)	10	
		Getting credit (rank)	150	Time to import (days)	77	
Dealing with construction permits (rank)	162	Strength of legal rights index (0-10)	6	Cost to import (US$ per container)	3,830	
Procedures (number)	12	Depth of credit information index (0-6)	0			
Time (days)	334	Public registry coverage (% of adults)	0.0	**Enforcing contracts** (rank)	161	
Cost (% of income per capita)	4,876.4	Private bureau coverage (% of adults)	0.0	Procedures (number)	47	
				Time (days)	1,642	
✔ **Getting electricity** (rank)	104	**Protecting investors** (rank)	183	Cost (% of claim)	25.0	
Procedures (number)	4	Extent of disclosure index (0-10)	1			
Time (days)	109	Extent of director liability index (0-10)	1	**Resolving insolvency** (rank)	105	
Cost (% of income per capita)	3,956.8	Ease of shareholder suits index (0-10)	1	Time (years)	2.0	
		Strength of investor protection index (0-10)	1.0	Cost (% of estate)	25	
				Recovery rate (cents on the dollar)	26.5	
		Paying taxes (rank)	63			
		Payments (number per year)	8			
		Time (hours per year)	275			
		Total tax rate (% of profit)	36.4			

ALBANIA

Ease of doing business (rank)	82	Eastern Europe & Central Asia		GNI per capita (US$)	4,000	
		Upper middle income		Population (m)	3.2	
Starting a business (rank)	61	✔ **Registering property** (rank)	118	**Trading across borders** (rank)	76	
Procedures (number)	5	Procedures (number)	6	Documents to export (number)	7	
Time (days)	5	Time (days)	33	Time to export (days)	19	
Cost (% of income per capita)	29.0	Cost (% of property value)	11.9	Cost to export (US$ per container)	745	
Minimum capital (% of income per capita)	0.0			Documents to import (number)	8	
		Getting credit (rank)	24	Time to import (days)	18	
✘ **Dealing with construction permits** (rank)	183	Strength of legal rights index (0-10)	9	Cost to import (US$ per container)	730	
Procedures (number)	NO PRACTICE	Depth of credit information index (0-6)	4			
Time (days)	NO PRACTICE	Public registry coverage (% of adults)	12.0	**Enforcing contracts** (rank)	85	
Cost (% of income per capita)	NO PRACTICE	Private bureau coverage (% of adults)	0.0	Procedures (number)	39	
				Time (days)	390	
Getting electricity (rank)	154	**Protecting investors** (rank)	16	Cost (% of claim)	35.7	
Procedures (number)	6	Extent of disclosure index (0-10)	8			
Time (days)	177	Extent of director liability index (0-10)	9	**Resolving insolvency** (rank)	64	
Cost (% of income per capita)	585.6	Ease of shareholder suits index (0-10)	5	Time (years)	2.0	
		Strength of investor protection index (0-10)	7.3	Cost (% of estate)	10	
				Recovery rate (cents on the dollar)	40.2	
		Paying taxes (rank)	152			
		Payments (number per year)	44			
		Time (hours per year)	371			
		Total tax rate (% of profit)	38.5			

Note: Most indicator sets refer to a case scenario in the largest business city of each economy. For more details, see the data notes.

✔ Reform making it easier to do business   ✗ Reform making it more difficult to do business

ALGERIA

Ease of doing business (rank)	148	Middle East & North Africa Upper middle income		GNI per capita (US$) Population (m)		4,460 35.4
Starting a business (rank)	153	**Registering property** (rank)	167	**Trading across borders** (rank)		127
Procedures (number)	14	Procedures (number)	10	Documents to export (number)		8
Time (days)	25	Time (days)	48	Time to export (days)		17
Cost (% of income per capita)	12.1	Cost (% of property value)	7.1	Cost to export (US$ per container)		1,248
Minimum capital (% of income per capita)	30.6			Documents to import (number)		9
		✔ **Getting credit** (rank)	150	Time to import (days)		27
Dealing with construction permits (rank)	118	Strength of legal rights index (0-10)	3	Cost to import (US$ per container)		1,318
Procedures (number)	19	Depth of credit information index (0-6)	3			
Time (days)	281	Public registry coverage (% of adults)	0.3	**Enforcing contracts** (rank)		122
Cost (% of income per capita)	23.1	Private bureau coverage (% of adults)	0.0	Procedures (number)		45
				Time (days)		630
Getting electricity (rank)	164	**Protecting investors** (rank)	79	Cost (% of claim)		21.9
Procedures (number)	6	Extent of disclosure index (0-10)	6			
Time (days)	159	Extent of director liability index (0-10)	6	**Resolving insolvency** (rank)		59
Cost (% of income per capita)	1,579.0	Ease of shareholder suits index (0-10)	4	Time (years)		2.5
		Strength of investor protection index (0-10)	5.3	Cost (% of estate)		7
				Recovery rate (cents on the dollar)		41.7
		Paying taxes (rank)	164			
		Payments (number per year)	29			
		Time (hours per year)	451			
		Total tax rate (% of profit)	72.0			

ANGOLA

Ease of doing business (rank)	172	Sub-Saharan Africa Lower middle income		GNI per capita (US$) Population (m)		3,960 19.0
Starting a business (rank)	167	✔ **Registering property** (rank)	129	**Trading across borders** (rank)		163
Procedures (number)	8	Procedures (number)	7	Documents to export (number)		11
Time (days)	68	Time (days)	184	Time to export (days)		48
Cost (% of income per capita)	118.9	Cost (% of property value)	3.2	Cost to export (US$ per container)		1,850
Minimum capital (% of income per capita)	25.3			Documents to import (number)		8
		✔ **Getting credit** (rank)	126	Time to import (days)		45
Dealing with construction permits (rank)	115	Strength of legal rights index (0-10)	3	Cost to import (US$ per container)		2,690
Procedures (number)	11	Depth of credit information index (0-6)	4			
Time (days)	321	Public registry coverage (% of adults)	2.4	**Enforcing contracts** (rank)		181
Cost (% of income per capita)	180.3	Private bureau coverage (% of adults)	0.0	Procedures (number)		46
				Time (days)		1,011
Getting electricity (rank)	120	**Protecting investors** (rank)	65	Cost (% of claim)		44.4
Procedures (number)	8	Extent of disclosure index (0-10)	5			
Time (days)	48	Extent of director liability index (0-10)	6	**Resolving insolvency** (rank)		160
Cost (% of income per capita)	890.5	Ease of shareholder suits index (0-10)	6	Time (years)		6.2
		Strength of investor protection index (0-10)	5.7	Cost (% of estate)		22
				Recovery rate (cents on the dollar)		6.9
		Paying taxes (rank)	149			
		Payments (number per year)	31			
		Time (hours per year)	282			
		Total tax rate (% of profit)	53.2			

ANTIGUA AND BARBUDA

Ease of doing business (rank)	57	Latin America & Caribbean Upper middle income		GNI per capita (US$) Population (m)		10,610 0.1
Starting a business (rank)	80	**Registering property** (rank)	124	**Trading across borders** (rank)		71
Procedures (number)	8	Procedures (number)	7	Documents to export (number)		5
Time (days)	21	Time (days)	26	Time to export (days)		16
Cost (% of income per capita)	12.5	Cost (% of property value)	10.9	Cost to export (US$ per container)		1,202
Minimum capital (% of income per capita)	0.0			Documents to import (number)		5
		Getting credit (rank)	98	Time to import (days)		15
Dealing with construction permits (rank)	21	Strength of legal rights index (0-10)	8	Cost to import (US$ per container)		1,633
Procedures (number)	10	Depth of credit information index (0-6)	0			
Time (days)	134	Public registry coverage (% of adults)	0.0	**Enforcing contracts** (rank)		70
Cost (% of income per capita)	26.8	Private bureau coverage (% of adults)	0.0	Procedures (number)		45
				Time (days)		351
Getting electricity (rank)	16	**Protecting investors** (rank)	29	Cost (% of claim)		22.7
Procedures (number)	4	Extent of disclosure index (0-10)	4			
Time (days)	42	Extent of director liability index (0-10)	8	**Resolving insolvency** (rank)		81
Cost (% of income per capita)	150.1	Ease of shareholder suits index (0-10)	7	Time (years)		3.0
		Strength of investor protection index (0-10)	6.3	Cost (% of estate)		7
				Recovery rate (cents on the dollar)		35.0
		Paying taxes (rank)	135			
		Payments (number per year)	57			
		Time (hours per year)	207			
		Total tax rate (% of profit)	41.5			

Note: Most indicator sets refer to a case scenario in the largest business city of each economy. For more details, see the data notes.

✔ Reform making it easier to do business   ✘ Reform making it more difficult to do business

ARGENTINA

Ease of doing business (rank)	113	Latin America & Caribbean Upper middle income		GNI per capita (US$)	8,450		
				Population (m)	40.7		

Starting a business (rank)	146
Procedures (number)	14
Time (days)	26
Cost (% of income per capita)	11.9
Minimum capital (% of income per capita)	2.2

Dealing with construction permits (rank)	169
Procedures (number)	25
Time (days)	365
Cost (% of income per capita)	107.7

Getting electricity (rank)	58
Procedures (number)	6
Time (days)	67
Cost (% of income per capita)	20.4

✘ Registering property (rank)	139
Procedures (number)	7
Time (days)	53
Cost (% of property value)	7.0

Getting credit (rank)	67
Strength of legal rights index (0-10)	4
Depth of credit information index (0-6)	6
Public registry coverage (% of adults)	35.9
Private bureau coverage (% of adults)	100.0

Protecting investors (rank)	111
Extent of disclosure index (0-10)	6
Extent of director liability index (0-10)	2
Ease of shareholder suits index (0-10)	6
Strength of investor protection index (0-10)	4.7

Paying taxes (rank)	144
Payments (number per year)	9
Time (hours per year)	415
Total tax rate (% of profit)	108.2

Trading across borders (rank)	102
Documents to export (number)	7
Time to export (days)	13
Cost to export (US$ per container)	1,480
Documents to import (number)	7
Time to import (days)	16
Cost to import (US$ per container)	1,810

Enforcing contracts (rank)	45
Procedures (number)	36
Time (days)	590
Cost (% of claim)	16.5

Resolving insolvency (rank)	85
Time (years)	2.8
Cost (% of estate)	12
Recovery rate (cents on the dollar)	32.9

ARMENIA

Ease of doing business (rank)	55	Eastern Europe & Central Asia Lower middle income		GNI per capita (US$)	3,090
				Population (m)	3.1

✔ Starting a business (rank)	10
Procedures (number)	3
Time (days)	8
Cost (% of income per capita)	2.9
Minimum capital (% of income per capita)	0.0

✔ Dealing with construction permits (rank)	57
Procedures (number)	18
Time (days)	79
Cost (% of income per capita)	57.1

Getting electricity (rank)	150
Procedures (number)	6
Time (days)	242
Cost (% of income per capita)	257.8

Registering property (rank)	5
Procedures (number)	3
Time (days)	7
Cost (% of property value)	0.3

✔ Getting credit (rank)	40
Strength of legal rights index (0-10)	6
Depth of credit information index (0-6)	6
Public registry coverage (% of adults)	23.7
Private bureau coverage (% of adults)	46.6

Protecting investors (rank)	97
Extent of disclosure index (0-10)	5
Extent of director liability index (0-10)	2
Ease of shareholder suits index (0-10)	8
Strength of investor protection index (0-10)	5.0

✔ Paying taxes (rank)	153
Payments (number per year)	34
Time (hours per year)	500
Total tax rate (% of profit)	40.9

Trading across borders (rank)	104
Documents to export (number)	5
Time to export (days)	13
Cost to export (US$ per container)	1,815
Documents to import (number)	8
Time to import (days)	18
Cost to import (US$ per container)	2,195

Enforcing contracts (rank)	91
Procedures (number)	49
Time (days)	440
Cost (% of claim)	19.0

✔ Resolving insolvency (rank)	62
Time (years)	1.9
Cost (% of estate)	4
Recovery rate (cents on the dollar)	40.3

AUSTRALIA

Ease of doing business (rank)	15	OECD high income High income		GNI per capita (US$)	43,740
				Population (m)	22.3

Starting a business (rank)	2
Procedures (number)	2
Time (days)	2
Cost (% of income per capita)	0.7
Minimum capital (% of income per capita)	0.0

Dealing with construction permits (rank)	42
Procedures (number)	15
Time (days)	147
Cost (% of income per capita)	9.9

Getting electricity (rank)	37
Procedures (number)	5
Time (days)	81
Cost (% of income per capita)	9.2

Registering property (rank)	38
Procedures (number)	5
Time (days)	5
Cost (% of property value)	5.0

Getting credit (rank)	8
Strength of legal rights index (0-10)	9
Depth of credit information index (0-6)	5
Public registry coverage (% of adults)	0.0
Private bureau coverage (% of adults)	100.0

Protecting investors (rank)	65
Extent of disclosure index (0-10)	8
Extent of director liability index (0-10)	2
Ease of shareholder suits index (0-10)	7
Strength of investor protection index (0-10)	5.7

Paying taxes (rank)	53
Payments (number per year)	11
Time (hours per year)	109
Total tax rate (% of profit)	47.7

Trading across borders (rank)	30
Documents to export (number)	6
Time to export (days)	9
Cost to export (US$ per container)	1,060
Documents to import (number)	5
Time to import (days)	8
Cost to import (US$ per container)	1,119

Enforcing contracts (rank)	17
Procedures (number)	28
Time (days)	395
Cost (% of claim)	21.8

✔ Resolving insolvency (rank)	17
Time (years)	1.0
Cost (% of estate)	8
Recovery rate (cents on the dollar)	80.8

Note: Most indicator sets refer to a case scenario in the largest business city of each economy. For more details, see the data notes.

✔ Reform making it easier to do business ✘ Reform making it more difficult to do business

AUSTRIA

Ease of doing business (rank)	32	OECD high income / High income		GNI per capita (US$)		46,710
				Population (m)		8.4

Starting a business (rank)	134
Procedures (number)	8
Time (days)	28
Cost (% of income per capita)	5.2
Minimum capital (% of income per capita)	52.0

Dealing with construction permits (rank)	76
Procedures (number)	13
Time (days)	194
Cost (% of income per capita)	60.8

Getting electricity (rank)	21
Procedures (number)	5
Time (days)	23
Cost (% of income per capita)	110.8

Registering property (rank)	35
Procedures (number)	3
Time (days)	21
Cost (% of property value)	4.6

Getting credit (rank)	24
Strength of legal rights index (0-10)	7
Depth of credit information index (0-6)	6
Public registry coverage (% of adults)	1.7
Private bureau coverage (% of adults)	51.6

Protecting investors (rank)	133
Extent of disclosure index (0-10)	3
Extent of director liability index (0-10)	5
Ease of shareholder suits index (0-10)	4
Strength of investor protection index (0-10)	4.0

Paying taxes (rank)	82
Payments (number per year)	14
Time (hours per year)	170
Total tax rate (% of profit)	53.1

Trading across borders (rank)	25
Documents to export (number)	4
Time to export (days)	7
Cost to export (US$ per container)	1,180
Documents to import (number)	5
Time to import (days)	8
Cost to import (US$ per container)	1,195

Enforcing contracts (rank)	9
Procedures (number)	25
Time (days)	397
Cost (% of claim)	18.0

✔ Resolving insolvency (rank)	21
Time (years)	1.1
Cost (% of estate)	18
Recovery rate (cents on the dollar)	72.7

AZERBAIJAN

Ease of doing business (rank)	66	Eastern Europe & Central Asia / Upper middle income		GNI per capita (US$)		5,180
				Population (m)		8.9

Starting a business (rank)	18
Procedures (number)	6
Time (days)	8
Cost (% of income per capita)	2.7
Minimum capital (% of income per capita)	0.0

Dealing with construction permits (rank)	172
Procedures (number)	30
Time (days)	212
Cost (% of income per capita)	335.2

Getting electricity (rank)	173
Procedures (number)	9
Time (days)	241
Cost (% of income per capita)	677.6

Registering property (rank)	9
Procedures (number)	4
Time (days)	11
Cost (% of property value)	0.2

Getting credit (rank)	48
Strength of legal rights index (0-10)	6
Depth of credit information index (0-6)	5
Public registry coverage (% of adults)	15.6
Private bureau coverage (% of adults)	0.0

Protecting investors (rank)	24
Extent of disclosure index (0-10)	7
Extent of director liability index (0-10)	5
Ease of shareholder suits index (0-10)	8
Strength of investor protection index (0-10)	6.7

Paying taxes (rank)	81
Payments (number per year)	18
Time (hours per year)	225
Total tax rate (% of profit)	40.0

Trading across borders (rank)	170
Documents to export (number)	8
Time to export (days)	38
Cost to export (US$ per container)	2,905
Documents to import (number)	10
Time to import (days)	42
Cost to import (US$ per container)	3,405

Enforcing contracts (rank)	25
Procedures (number)	39
Time (days)	237
Cost (% of claim)	18.5

Resolving insolvency (rank)	95
Time (years)	2.7
Cost (% of estate)	8
Recovery rate (cents on the dollar)	29.7

BAHAMAS, THE

Ease of doing business (rank)	85	Latin America & Caribbean / High income		GNI per capita (US$)		21,879
				Population (m)		0.3

Starting a business (rank)	73
Procedures (number)	7
Time (days)	31
Cost (% of income per capita)	8.7
Minimum capital (% of income per capita)	0.0

Dealing with construction permits (rank)	79
Procedures (number)	17
Time (days)	181
Cost (% of income per capita)	29.5

Getting electricity (rank)	105
Procedures (number)	8
Time (days)	69
Cost (% of income per capita)	99.9

✘ Registering property (rank)	177
Procedures (number)	7
Time (days)	122
Cost (% of property value)	14.1

Getting credit (rank)	78
Strength of legal rights index (0-10)	9
Depth of credit information index (0-6)	0
Public registry coverage (% of adults)	0.0
Private bureau coverage (% of adults)	0.0

Protecting investors (rank)	111
Extent of disclosure index (0-10)	2
Extent of director liability index (0-10)	5
Ease of shareholder suits index (0-10)	7
Strength of investor protection index (0-10)	4.7

Paying taxes (rank)	56
Payments (number per year)	18
Time (hours per year)	58
Total tax rate (% of profit)	47.7

Trading across borders (rank)	48
Documents to export (number)	5
Time to export (days)	19
Cost to export (US$ per container)	930
Documents to import (number)	5
Time to import (days)	13
Cost to import (US$ per container)	1,405

Enforcing contracts (rank)	123
Procedures (number)	49
Time (days)	427
Cost (% of claim)	28.9

Resolving insolvency (rank)	34
Time (years)	5.0
Cost (% of estate)	4
Recovery rate (cents on the dollar)	54.7

Note: Most indicator sets refer to a case scenario in the largest business city of each economy. For more details, see the data notes.

✔ Reform making it easier to do business ✘ Reform making it more difficult to do business

BAHRAIN

Ease of doing business (rank)	38	Middle East & North Africa High income		GNI per capita (US$) Population (m)	20,475 0.8
Starting a business (rank)	82	**Registering property** (rank)	30	**Trading across borders** (rank)	49
Procedures (number)	7	Procedures (number)	2	Documents to export (number)	6
Time (days)	9	Time (days)	31	Time to export (days)	11
Cost (% of income per capita)	0.7	Cost (% of property value)	2.7	Cost to export (US$ per container)	955
Minimum capital (% of income per capita)	259.8			Documents to import (number)	7
		Getting credit (rank)	126	Time to import (days)	15
Dealing with construction permits (rank)	7	Strength of legal rights index (0-10)	4	Cost to import (US$ per container)	995
Procedures (number)	12	Depth of credit information index (0-6)	3		
Time (days)	43	Public registry coverage (% of adults)	0.0	**Enforcing contracts** (rank)	114
Cost (% of income per capita)	10.7	Private bureau coverage (% of adults)	40.0	Procedures (number)	48
				Time (days)	635
Getting electricity (rank)	49	**Protecting investors** (rank)	79	Cost (% of claim)	14.7
Procedures (number)	5	Extent of disclosure index (0-10)	8		
Time (days)	90	Extent of director liability index (0-10)	4	**Resolving insolvency** (rank)	25
Cost (% of income per capita)	63.6	Ease of shareholder suits index (0-10)	4	Time (years)	2.5
		Strength of investor protection index (0-10)	5.3	Cost (% of estate)	10
				Recovery rate (cents on the dollar)	66.0
		Paying taxes (rank)	18		
		Payments (number per year)	25		
		Time (hours per year)	36		
		Total tax rate (% of profit)	15.0		

BANGLADESH

Ease of doing business (rank)	122	South Asia Low income		GNI per capita (US$) Population (m)	640 164.4
Starting a business (rank)	86	**Registering property** (rank)	173	**Trading across borders** (rank)	115
Procedures (number)	7	Procedures (number)	8	Documents to export (number)	6
Time (days)	19	Time (days)	245	Time to export (days)	25
Cost (% of income per capita)	30.6	Cost (% of property value)	6.6	Cost to export (US$ per container)	965
Minimum capital (% of income per capita)	0.0			Documents to import (number)	8
		Getting credit (rank)	78	Time to import (days)	31
Dealing with construction permits (rank)	82	Strength of legal rights index (0-10)	7	Cost to import (US$ per container)	1,370
Procedures (number)	11	Depth of credit information index (0-6)	2		
Time (days)	201	Public registry coverage (% of adults)	0.6	**Enforcing contracts** (rank)	180
Cost (% of income per capita)	154.5	Private bureau coverage (% of adults)	0.0	Procedures (number)	41
				Time (days)	1,442
✘ **Getting electricity** (rank)	182	**Protecting investors** (rank)	24	Cost (% of claim)	63.3
Procedures (number)	7	Extent of disclosure index (0-10)	6		
Time (days)	372	Extent of director liability index (0-10)	7	**Resolving insolvency** (rank)	107
Cost (% of income per capita)	3,526.1	Ease of shareholder suits index (0-10)	7	Time (years)	4.0
		Strength of investor protection index (0-10)	6.7	Cost (% of estate)	8
				Recovery rate (cents on the dollar)	25.8
		Paying taxes (rank)	100		
		Payments (number per year)	21		
		Time (hours per year)	302		
		Total tax rate (% of profit)	35.0		

BELARUS

Ease of doing business (rank)	69	Eastern Europe & Central Asia Upper middle income		GNI per capita (US$) Population (m)	6,030 9.6
Starting a business (rank)	9	✔ **Registering property** (rank)	4	**Trading across borders** (rank)	152
Procedures (number)	5	Procedures (number)	2	Documents to export (number)	9
Time (days)	5	Time (days)	10	Time to export (days)	15
Cost (% of income per capita)	1.3	Cost (% of property value)	0.0	Cost to export (US$ per container)	2,210
Minimum capital (% of income per capita)	0.0			Documents to import (number)	10
		Getting credit (rank)	98	Time to import (days)	30
Dealing with construction permits (rank)	44	Strength of legal rights index (0-10)	3	Cost to import (US$ per container)	2,615
Procedures (number)	13	Depth of credit information index (0-6)	5		
Time (days)	140	Public registry coverage (% of adults)	49.5	✘ **Enforcing contracts** (rank)	14
Cost (% of income per capita)	41.0	Private bureau coverage (% of adults)	0.0	Procedures (number)	29
				Time (days)	275
Getting electricity (rank)	175	✔ **Protecting investors** (rank)	79	Cost (% of claim)	23.4
Procedures (number)	7	Extent of disclosure index (0-10)	7		
Time (days)	254	Extent of director liability index (0-10)	1	**Resolving insolvency** (rank)	82
Cost (% of income per capita)	1,383.8	Ease of shareholder suits index (0-10)	8	Time (years)	5.8
		Strength of investor protection index (0-10)	5.3	Cost (% of estate)	22
				Recovery rate (cents on the dollar)	33.5
		✔ **Paying taxes** (rank)	156		
		Payments (number per year)	18		
		Time (hours per year)	654		
		Total tax rate (% of profit)	62.8		

Note: Most indicator sets refer to a case scenario in the largest business city of each economy. For more details, see the data notes.

✔ Reform making it easier to do business ✘ Reform making it more difficult to do business

BELGIUM

| | | OECD high income | | GNI per capita (US$) | 45,420 |
| Ease of doing business (rank) | 28 | High income | | Population (m) | 10.9 |

Starting a business (rank)	36	✔ Registering property (rank)	174	✔ Trading across borders (rank)	36
Procedures (number)	3	Procedures (number)	8	Documents to export (number)	4
Time (days)	4	Time (days)	64	Time to export (days)	8
Cost (% of income per capita)	5.2	Cost (% of property value)	12.7	Cost to export (US$ per container)	1,429
Minimum capital (% of income per capita)	18.9			Documents to import (number)	5
		Getting credit (rank)	48	Time to import (days)	8
Dealing with construction permits (rank)	51	Strength of legal rights index (0-10)	7	Cost to import (US$ per container)	1,600
Procedures (number)	12	Depth of credit information index (0-6)	4		
Time (days)	169	Public registry coverage (% of adults)	72.6	Enforcing contracts (rank)	20
Cost (% of income per capita)	53.6	Private bureau coverage (% of adults)	0.0	Procedures (number)	26
				Time (days)	505
Getting electricity (rank)	87	Protecting investors (rank)	17	Cost (% of claim)	17.7
Procedures (number)	6	Extent of disclosure index (0-10)	8		
Time (days)	88	Extent of director liability index (0-10)	6	Resolving insolvency (rank)	8
Cost (% of income per capita)	95.3	Ease of shareholder suits index (0-10)	7	Time (years)	0.9
		Strength of investor protection index (0-10)	7.0	Cost (% of estate)	4
				Recovery rate (cents on the dollar)	87.3
		Paying taxes (rank)	77		
		Payments (number per year)	11		
		Time (hours per year)	156		
		Total tax rate (% of profit)	57.3		

BELIZE

| | | Latin America & Caribbean | | GNI per capita (US$) | 3,740 |
| Ease of doing business (rank) | 93 | Lower middle income | | Population (m) | 0.3 |

Starting a business (rank)	152	Registering property (rank)	137	Trading across borders (rank)	107
Procedures (number)	9	Procedures (number)	8	Documents to export (number)	6
Time (days)	44	Time (days)	60	Time to export (days)	21
Cost (% of income per capita)	51.2	Cost (% of property value)	4.7	Cost to export (US$ per container)	1,505
Minimum capital (% of income per capita)	0.0			Documents to import (number)	6
		Getting credit (rank)	98	Time to import (days)	21
Dealing with construction permits (rank)	9	Strength of legal rights index (0-10)	8	Cost to import (US$ per container)	1,650
Procedures (number)	8	Depth of credit information index (0-6)	0		
Time (days)	91	Public registry coverage (% of adults)	0.0	Enforcing contracts (rank)	168
Cost (% of income per capita)	29.1	Private bureau coverage (% of adults)	0.0	Procedures (number)	51
				Time (days)	892
Getting electricity (rank)	53	Protecting investors (rank)	122	Cost (% of claim)	27.5
Procedures (number)	5	Extent of disclosure index (0-10)	3		
Time (days)	66	Extent of director liability index (0-10)	4	Resolving insolvency (rank)	29
Cost (% of income per capita)	395.4	Ease of shareholder suits index (0-10)	6	Time (years)	1.0
		Strength of investor protection index (0-10)	4.3	Cost (% of estate)	23
				Recovery rate (cents on the dollar)	63.7
		✔ Paying taxes (rank)	55		
		Payments (number per year)	29		
		Time (hours per year)	147		
		Total tax rate (% of profit)	33.2		

BENIN

| | | Sub-Saharan Africa | | GNI per capita (US$) | 750 |
| Ease of doing business (rank) | 175 | Low income | | Population (m) | 9.2 |

✔ Starting a business (rank)	154	Registering property (rank)	130	Trading across borders (rank)	129
Procedures (number)	6	Procedures (number)	4	Documents to export (number)	7
Time (days)	29	Time (days)	120	Time to export (days)	30
Cost (% of income per capita)	149.9	Cost (% of property value)	11.8	Cost to export (US$ per container)	1,049
Minimum capital (% of income per capita)	280.4			Documents to import (number)	8
		✔ Getting credit (rank)	126	Time to import (days)	32
Dealing with construction permits (rank)	117	Strength of legal rights index (0-10)	6	Cost to import (US$ per container)	1,496
Procedures (number)	12	Depth of credit information index (0-6)	1		
Time (days)	372	Public registry coverage (% of adults)	10.7	Enforcing contracts (rank)	176
Cost (% of income per capita)	132.6	Private bureau coverage (% of adults)	0.0	Procedures (number)	42
				Time (days)	795
Getting electricity (rank)	140	Protecting investors (rank)	155	Cost (% of claim)	64.7
Procedures (number)	4	Extent of disclosure index (0-10)	6		
Time (days)	158	Extent of director liability index (0-10)	1	Resolving insolvency (rank)	127
Cost (% of income per capita)	15,205.3	Ease of shareholder suits index (0-10)	3	Time (years)	4.0
		Strength of investor protection index (0-10)	3.3	Cost (% of estate)	22
				Recovery rate (cents on the dollar)	20.2
		Paying taxes (rank)	170		
		Payments (number per year)	55		
		Time (hours per year)	270		
		Total tax rate (% of profit)	66.0		

Note: Most indicator sets refer to a case scenario in the largest business city of each economy. For more details, see the data notes.

✔ Reform making it easier to do business ✘ Reform making it more difficult to do business

BHUTAN

		South Asia		GNI per capita (US$)	1,920
Ease of doing business (rank)	142	Lower middle income		Population (m)	0.7
✔ **Starting a business** (rank)	83	**Registering property** (rank)	83	**Trading across borders** (rank)	169
Procedures (number)	8	Procedures (number)	3	Documents to export (number)	8
Time (days)	36	Time (days)	92	Time to export (days)	38
Cost (% of income per capita)	7.2	Cost (% of property value)	5.0	Cost to export (US$ per container)	2,230
Minimum capital (% of income per capita)	0.0			Documents to import (number)	12
		✔ **Getting credit** (rank)	126	Time to import (days)	38
		Strength of legal rights index (0-10)	3	Cost to import (US$ per container)	2,805
Dealing with construction permits (rank)	135	Depth of credit information index (0-6)	4		
Procedures (number)	22	Public registry coverage (% of adults)	6.4	**Enforcing contracts** (rank)	35
Time (days)	180	Private bureau coverage (% of adults)	0.0	Procedures (number)	47
Cost (% of income per capita)	108.6			Time (days)	225
		Protecting investors (rank)	147	Cost (% of claim)	0.1
Getting electricity (rank)	145	Extent of disclosure index (0-10)	4		
Procedures (number)	6	Extent of director liability index (0-10)	3	**Resolving insolvency** (rank)	183
Time (days)	101	Ease of shareholder suits index (0-10)	4	Time (years)	NO PRACTICE
Cost (% of income per capita)	1,265.4	Strength of investor protection index (0-10)	3.7	Cost (% of estate)	NO PRACTICE
				Recovery rate (cents on the dollar)	0.0
		Paying taxes (rank)	67		
		Payments (number per year)	6		
		Time (hours per year)	274		
		Total tax rate (% of profit)	40.8		

BOLIVIA

		Latin America & Caribbean		GNI per capita (US$)	1,790
Ease of doing business (rank)	153	Lower middle income		Population (m)	10.0
Starting a business (rank)	169	**Registering property** (rank)	138	**Trading across borders** (rank)	126
Procedures (number)	15	Procedures (number)	7	Documents to export (number)	8
Time (days)	50	Time (days)	92	Time to export (days)	19
Cost (% of income per capita)	90.4	Cost (% of property value)	4.8	Cost to export (US$ per container)	1,425
Minimum capital (% of income per capita)	2.3			Documents to import (number)	7
		Getting credit (rank)	126	Time to import (days)	23
		Strength of legal rights index (0-10)	1	Cost to import (US$ per container)	1,747
Dealing with construction permits (rank)	107	Depth of credit information index (0-6)	6		
Procedures (number)	14	Public registry coverage (% of adults)	11.8	**Enforcing contracts** (rank)	135
Time (days)	249	Private bureau coverage (% of adults)	35.9	Procedures (number)	40
Cost (% of income per capita)	77.5			Time (days)	591
		Protecting investors (rank)	133	Cost (% of claim)	33.2
Getting electricity (rank)	124	Extent of disclosure index (0-10)	1		
Procedures (number)	8	Extent of director liability index (0-10)	5	**Resolving insolvency** (rank)	65
Time (days)	42	Ease of shareholder suits index (0-10)	6	Time (years)	1.8
Cost (% of income per capita)	1,181.2	Strength of investor protection index (0-10)	4.0	Cost (% of estate)	15
				Recovery rate (cents on the dollar)	39.3
		✘ **Paying taxes** (rank)	179		
		Payments (number per year)	42		
		Time (hours per year)	1,080		
		Total tax rate (% of profit)	80.0		

BOSNIA AND HERZEGOVINA

		Eastern Europe & Central Asia		GNI per capita (US$)	4,790
Ease of doing business (rank)	125	Upper middle income		Population (m)	3.8
✔ **Starting a business** (rank)	162	**Registering property** (rank)	100	**Trading across borders** (rank)	108
Procedures (number)	12	Procedures (number)	7	Documents to export (number)	8
Time (days)	40	Time (days)	33	Time to export (days)	15
Cost (% of income per capita)	17.0	Cost (% of property value)	5.3	Cost to export (US$ per container)	1,240
Minimum capital (% of income per capita)	29.4			Documents to import (number)	9
		Getting credit (rank)	67	Time to import (days)	16
		Strength of legal rights index (0-10)	5	Cost to import (US$ per container)	1,200
✔ **Dealing with construction permits** (rank)	163	Depth of credit information index (0-6)	5		
Procedures (number)	18	Public registry coverage (% of adults)	35.3	**Enforcing contracts** (rank)	125
Time (days)	181	Private bureau coverage (% of adults)	39.6	Procedures (number)	37
Cost (% of income per capita)	1,112.9			Time (days)	595
		Protecting investors (rank)	97	Cost (% of claim)	40.4
Getting electricity (rank)	157	Extent of disclosure index (0-10)	3		
Procedures (number)	8	Extent of director liability index (0-10)	6	**Resolving insolvency** (rank)	80
Time (days)	125	Ease of shareholder suits index (0-10)	6	Time (years)	3.3
Cost (% of income per capita)	497.6	Strength of investor protection index (0-10)	5.0	Cost (% of estate)	9
				Recovery rate (cents on the dollar)	35.0
		Paying taxes (rank)	110		
		Payments (number per year)	40		
		Time (hours per year)	422		
		Total tax rate (% of profit)	25.0		

Note: Most indicator sets refer to a case scenario in the largest business city of each economy. For more details, see the data notes.

✔ Reform making it easier to do business ✘ Reform making it more difficult to do business

BOTSWANA

Ease of doing business (rank)	54	Sub-Saharan Africa Upper middle income		GNI per capita (US$) Population (m)	6,890 2.0

Starting a business (rank)	90	**Registering property** (rank)	50	**Trading across borders** (rank)	150
Procedures (number)	10	Procedures (number)	5	Documents to export (number)	6
Time (days)	61	Time (days)	16	Time to export (days)	28
Cost (% of income per capita)	1.8	Cost (% of property value)	5.0	Cost to export (US$ per container)	3,185
Minimum capital (% of income per capita)	0.0			Documents to import (number)	8
		Getting credit (rank)	48	Time to import (days)	41
Dealing with construction permits (rank)	132	Strength of legal rights index (0-10)	7	Cost to import (US$ per container)	3,420
Procedures (number)	22	Depth of credit information index (0-6)	4		
Time (days)	145	Public registry coverage (% of adults)	0.0	**Enforcing contracts** (rank)	65
Cost (% of income per capita)	203.0	Private bureau coverage (% of adults)	59.6	Procedures (number)	28
				Time (days)	625
Getting electricity (rank)	91	**Protecting investors** (rank)	46	Cost (% of claim)	28.1
Procedures (number)	5	Extent of disclosure index (0-10)	7		
Time (days)	121	Extent of director liability index (0-10)	8	**Resolving insolvency** (rank)	28
Cost (% of income per capita)	408.9	Ease of shareholder suits index (0-10)	3	Time (years)	1.7
		Strength of investor protection index (0-10)	6.0	Cost (% of estate)	15
				Recovery rate (cents on the dollar)	64.5
		Paying taxes (rank)	22		
		Payments (number per year)	19		
		Time (hours per year)	152		
		Total tax rate (% of profit)	19.4		

BRAZIL

Ease of doing business (rank)	126	Latin America & Caribbean Upper middle income		GNI per capita (US$) Population (m)	9,390 194.9

Starting a business (rank)	120	**Registering property** (rank)	114	**Trading across borders** (rank)	121
Procedures (number)	13	Procedures (number)	13	Documents to export (number)	7
Time (days)	119	Time (days)	39	Time to export (days)	13
Cost (% of income per capita)	5.4	Cost (% of property value)	2.3	Cost to export (US$ per container)	2,215
Minimum capital (% of income per capita)	0.0			Documents to import (number)	8
		✔ **Getting credit** (rank)	98	Time to import (days)	17
Dealing with construction permits (rank)	127	Strength of legal rights index (0-10)	3	Cost to import (US$ per container)	2,275
Procedures (number)	17	Depth of credit information index (0-6)	5		
Time (days)	469	Public registry coverage (% of adults)	36.1	**Enforcing contracts** (rank)	118
Cost (% of income per capita)	40.2	Private bureau coverage (% of adults)	61.5	Procedures (number)	45
				Time (days)	731
Getting electricity (rank)	51	**Protecting investors** (rank)	79	Cost (% of claim)	16.5
Procedures (number)	6	Extent of disclosure index (0-10)	6		
Time (days)	34	Extent of director liability index (0-10)	7	**Resolving insolvency** (rank)	136
Cost (% of income per capita)	130.3	Ease of shareholder suits index (0-10)	3	Time (years)	4.0
		Strength of investor protection index (0-10)	5.3	Cost (% of estate)	12
				Recovery rate (cents on the dollar)	17.9
		Paying taxes (rank)	150		
		Payments (number per year)	9		
		Time (hours per year)	2,600		
		Total tax rate (% of profit)	67.1		

BRUNEI DARUSSALAM

Ease of doing business (rank)	83	East Asia & Pacific High income		GNI per capita (US$) Population (m)	31,238 0.4

Starting a business (rank)	136	**Registering property** (rank)	107	**Trading across borders** (rank)	35
Procedures (number)	15	Procedures (number)	7	Documents to export (number)	6
Time (days)	101	Time (days)	298	Time to export (days)	19
Cost (% of income per capita)	11.8	Cost (% of property value)	0.6	Cost to export (US$ per container)	680
Minimum capital (% of income per capita)	0.0			Documents to import (number)	6
		Getting credit (rank)	126	Time to import (days)	15
Dealing with construction permits (rank)	83	Strength of legal rights index (0-10)	7	Cost to import (US$ per container)	745
Procedures (number)	31	Depth of credit information index (0-6)	0		
Time (days)	163	Public registry coverage (% of adults)	0.0	**Enforcing contracts** (rank)	151
Cost (% of income per capita)	4.2	Private bureau coverage (% of adults)	0.0	Procedures (number)	47
				Time (days)	540
✔ **Getting electricity** (rank)	28	**Protecting investors** (rank)	122	Cost (% of claim)	36.6
Procedures (number)	5	Extent of disclosure index (0-10)	3		
Time (days)	56	Extent of director liability index (0-10)	2	**Resolving insolvency** (rank)	44
Cost (% of income per capita)	42.9	Ease of shareholder suits index (0-10)	8	Time (years)	2.5
		Strength of investor protection index (0-10)	4.3	Cost (% of estate)	4
				Recovery rate (cents on the dollar)	47.2
		Paying taxes (rank)	20		
		Payments (number per year)	27		
		Time (hours per year)	96		
		Total tax rate (% of profit)	16.8		

Note: Most indicator sets refer to a case scenario in the largest business city of each economy. For more details, see the data notes.

✔ Reform making it easier to do business ✘ Reform making it more difficult to do business

BULGARIA

		Eastern Europe & Central Asia		GNI per capita (US$)	6,240
Ease of doing business (rank)	59	Upper middle income		Population (m)	7.6
Starting a business (rank)	49	**Registering property** (rank)	66	✔ **Trading across borders** (rank)	91
Procedures (number)	4	Procedures (number)	8	Documents to export (number)	5
Time (days)	18	Time (days)	15	Time to export (days)	21
Cost (% of income per capita)	1.5	Cost (% of property value)	3.0	Cost to export (US$ per container)	1,551
Minimum capital (% of income per capita)	0.0			Documents to import (number)	6
		Getting credit (rank)	8	Time to import (days)	17
Dealing with construction permits (rank)	128	Strength of legal rights index (0-10)	8	Cost to import (US$ per container)	1,666
Procedures (number)	23	Depth of credit information index (0-6)	6		
Time (days)	120	Public registry coverage (% of adults)	52.8	**Enforcing contracts** (rank)	87
Cost (% of income per capita)	317.0	Private bureau coverage (% of adults)	28.8	Procedures (number)	39
				Time (days)	564
Getting electricity (rank)	133	**Protecting investors** (rank)	46	Cost (% of claim)	23.8
Procedures (number)	6	Extent of disclosure index (0-10)	10		
Time (days)	130	Extent of director liability index (0-10)	1	✔ **Resolving insolvency** (rank)	90
Cost (% of income per capita)	366.6	Ease of shareholder suits index (0-10)	7	Time (years)	3.3
		Strength of investor protection index (0-10)	6.0	Cost (% of estate)	9
				Recovery rate (cents on the dollar)	31.4
		Paying taxes (rank)	69		
		Payments (number per year)	17		
		Time (hours per year)	500		
		Total tax rate (% of profit)	28.1		

BURKINA FASO

		Sub-Saharan Africa		GNI per capita (US$)	550
Ease of doing business (rank)	150	Low income		Population (m)	16.3
✔ **Starting a business** (rank)	116	**Registering property** (rank)	111	**Trading across borders** (rank)	175
Procedures (number)	3	Procedures (number)	4	Documents to export (number)	10
Time (days)	13	Time (days)	59	Time to export (days)	41
Cost (% of income per capita)	47.7	Cost (% of property value)	12.8	Cost to export (US$ per container)	2,412
Minimum capital (% of income per capita)	373.3			Documents to import (number)	10
		✔ **Getting credit** (rank)	126	Time to import (days)	49
✔ **Dealing with construction permits** (rank)	59	Strength of legal rights index (0-10)	6	Cost to import (US$ per container)	4,030
Procedures (number)	12	Depth of credit information index (0-6)	1		
Time (days)	98	Public registry coverage (% of adults)	1.8	**Enforcing contracts** (rank)	108
Cost (% of income per capita)	345.0	Private bureau coverage (% of adults)	0.0	Procedures (number)	37
				Time (days)	446
Getting electricity (rank)	139	**Protecting investors** (rank)	147	Cost (% of claim)	81.7
Procedures (number)	4	Extent of disclosure index (0-10)	6		
Time (days)	158	Extent of director liability index (0-10)	1	**Resolving insolvency** (rank)	103
Cost (% of income per capita)	13,356.8	Ease of shareholder suits index (0-10)	4	Time (years)	4.0
		Strength of investor protection index (0-10)	3.7	Cost (% of estate)	9
				Recovery rate (cents on the dollar)	27.3
		Paying taxes (rank)	147		
		Payments (number per year)	46		
		Time (hours per year)	270		
		Total tax rate (% of profit)	43.6		

BURUNDI

		Sub-Saharan Africa		GNI per capita (US$)	160
Ease of doing business (rank)	169	Low income		Population (m)	8.5
Starting a business (rank)	108	**Registering property** (rank)	109	**Trading across borders** (rank)	174
Procedures (number)	9	Procedures (number)	5	Documents to export (number)	9
Time (days)	14	Time (days)	94	Time to export (days)	35
Cost (% of income per capita)	116.8	Cost (% of property value)	5.6	Cost to export (US$ per container)	2,965
Minimum capital (% of income per capita)	0.0			Documents to import (number)	10
		Getting credit (rank)	166	Time to import (days)	54
✔ **Dealing with construction permits** (rank)	159	Strength of legal rights index (0-10)	3	Cost to import (US$ per container)	4,855
Procedures (number)	22	Depth of credit information index (0-6)	1		
Time (days)	135	Public registry coverage (% of adults)	0.3	**Enforcing contracts** (rank)	172
Cost (% of income per capita)	4,065.7	Private bureau coverage (% of adults)	0.0	Procedures (number)	44
				Time (days)	832
Getting electricity (rank)	151	✔ **Protecting investors** (rank)	46	Cost (% of claim)	38.6
Procedures (number)	4	Extent of disclosure index (0-10)	8		
Time (days)	188	Extent of director liability index (0-10)	6	✔ **Resolving insolvency** (rank)	183
Cost (% of income per capita)	34,477.0	Ease of shareholder suits index (0-10)	4	Time (years)	NO PRACTICE
		Strength of investor protection index (0-10)	6.0	Cost (% of estate)	NO PRACTICE
				Recovery rate (cents on the dollar)	0.0
		✔ **Paying taxes** (rank)	125		
		Payments (number per year)	24		
		Time (hours per year)	274		
		Total tax rate (% of profit)	46.2		

Note: Most indicator sets refer to a case scenario in the largest business city of each economy. For more details, see the data notes.

✔ Reform making it easier to do business ✘ Reform making it more difficult to do business

CAMBODIA

		East Asia & Pacific		GNI per capita (US$)	760
Ease of doing business (rank)	138	Low income		Population (m)	14.1
Starting a business (rank)	171	**Registering property** (rank)	110	**Trading across borders** (rank)	120
Procedures (number)	9	Procedures (number)	7	Documents to export (number)	9
Time (days)	85	Time (days)	56	Time to export (days)	22
Cost (% of income per capita)	109.7	Cost (% of property value)	4.3	Cost to export (US$ per container)	732
Minimum capital (% of income per capita)	31.3			Documents to import (number)	10
		✔ **Getting credit** (rank)	98	Time to import (days)	26
Dealing with construction permits (rank)	149	Strength of legal rights index (0-10)	8	Cost to import (US$ per container)	872
Procedures (number)	21	Depth of credit information index (0-6)	0		
Time (days)	652	Public registry coverage (% of adults)	0.0	**Enforcing contracts** (rank)	142
Cost (% of income per capita)	40.6	Private bureau coverage (% of adults)	0.0	Procedures (number)	44
				Time (days)	401
Getting electricity (rank)	130	**Protecting investors** (rank)	79	Cost (% of claim)	103.4
Procedures (number)	4	Extent of disclosure index (0-10)	5		
Time (days)	183	Extent of director liability index (0-10)	9	**Resolving insolvency** (rank)	149
Cost (% of income per capita)	3,062.5	Ease of shareholder suits index (0-10)	2	Time (years)	6.0
		Strength of investor protection index (0-10)	5.3	Cost (% of estate)	15
				Recovery rate (cents on the dollar)	12.6
		Paying taxes (rank)	54		
		Payments (number per year)	39		
		Time (hours per year)	173		
		Total tax rate (% of profit)	22.5		

CAMEROON

		Sub-Saharan Africa		GNI per capita (US$)	1,160
Ease of doing business (rank)	161	Lower middle income		Population (m)	20.0
✔ **Starting a business** (rank)	128	**Registering property** (rank)	154	**Trading across borders** (rank)	156
Procedures (number)	5	Procedures (number)	5	Documents to export (number)	11
Time (days)	15	Time (days)	93	Time to export (days)	23
Cost (% of income per capita)	45.5	Cost (% of property value)	19.2	Cost to export (US$ per container)	1,379
Minimum capital (% of income per capita)	182.9			Documents to import (number)	12
		✔ **Getting credit** (rank)	98	Time to import (days)	25
Dealing with construction permits (rank)	92	Strength of legal rights index (0-10)	6	Cost to import (US$ per container)	2,167
Procedures (number)	11	Depth of credit information index (0-6)	2		
Time (days)	147	Public registry coverage (% of adults)	3.6	**Enforcing contracts** (rank)	174
Cost (% of income per capita)	1,096.2	Private bureau coverage (% of adults)	0.0	Procedures (number)	43
				Time (days)	800
Getting electricity (rank)	66	**Protecting investors** (rank)	122	Cost (% of claim)	46.6
Procedures (number)	4	Extent of disclosure index (0-10)	6		
Time (days)	67	Extent of director liability index (0-10)	1	**Resolving insolvency** (rank)	147
Cost (% of income per capita)	1,854.5	Ease of shareholder suits index (0-10)	6	Time (years)	3.2
		Strength of investor protection index (0-10)	4.3	Cost (% of estate)	34
				Recovery rate (cents on the dollar)	13.6
		Paying taxes (rank)	171		
		Payments (number per year)	44		
		Time (hours per year)	654		
		Total tax rate (% of profit)	49.1		

CANADA

		OECD high income		GNI per capita (US$)	46,215
Ease of doing business (rank)	13	High income	○	Population (m)	34.2
Starting a business (rank)	3	**Registering property** (rank)	41	**Trading across borders** (rank)	42
Procedures (number)	1	Procedures (number)	6	Documents to export (number)	3
Time (days)	5	Time (days)	17	Time to export (days)	7
Cost (% of income per capita)	0.4	Cost (% of property value)	1.8	Cost to export (US$ per container)	1,610
Minimum capital (% of income per capita)	0.0			Documents to import (number)	4
		Getting credit (rank)	24	Time to import (days)	11
Dealing with construction permits (rank)	25	Strength of legal rights index (0-10)	7	Cost to import (US$ per container)	1,660
Procedures (number)	12	Depth of credit information index (0-6)	6		
Time (days)	73	Public registry coverage (% of adults)	0.0	**Enforcing contracts** (rank)	59
Cost (% of income per capita)	57.5	Private bureau coverage (% of adults)	0.0	Procedures (number)	36
				Time (days)	570
Getting electricity (rank)	156	**Protecting investors** (rank)	5	Cost (% of claim)	22.3
Procedures (number)	8	Extent of disclosure index (0-10)	8		
Time (days)	168	Extent of director liability index (0-10)	9	**Resolving insolvency** (rank)	3
Cost (% of income per capita)	143.9	Ease of shareholder suits index (0-10)	8	Time (years)	0.8
		Strength of investor protection index (0-10)	8.3	Cost (% of estate)	4
				Recovery rate (cents on the dollar)	90.7
		✔ **Paying taxes** (rank)	8		
		Payments (number per year)	8		
		Time (hours per year)	131		
		Total tax rate (% of profit)	28.8		

Note: Most indicator sets refer to a case scenario in the largest business city of each economy. For more details, see the data notes.

✔ Reform making it easier to do business ✘ Reform making it more difficult to do business

CAPE VERDE

Ease of doing business (rank)	119	Sub-Saharan Africa		GNI per capita (US$)		3,160
		Lower middle income		Population (m)		0.5
Starting a business (rank)	131	✔ **Registering property** (rank)	61	**Trading across borders** (rank)		61
Procedures (number)	8	Procedures (number)	6	Documents to export (number)		5
Time (days)	11	Time (days)	31	Time to export (days)		19
Cost (% of income per capita)	17.0	Cost (% of property value)	3.9	Cost to export (US$ per container)		1,200
Minimum capital (% of income per capita)	39.0			Documents to import (number)		5
		✔ **Getting credit** (rank)	126	Time to import (days)		18
Dealing with construction permits (rank)	116	Strength of legal rights index (0-10)	2	Cost to import (US$ per container)		1,000
Procedures (number)	17	Depth of credit information index (0-6)	5			
Time (days)	122	Public registry coverage (% of adults)	20.2	**Enforcing contracts** (rank)		37
Cost (% of income per capita)	523.8	Private bureau coverage (% of adults)	0.0	Procedures (number)		37
				Time (days)		425
Getting electricity (rank)	70	**Protecting investors** (rank)	133	Cost (% of claim)		19.8
Procedures (number)	5	Extent of disclosure index (0-10)	1			
Time (days)	58	Extent of director liability index (0-10)	5	✔ **Resolving insolvency** (rank)		183
Cost (% of income per capita)	1,121.3	Ease of shareholder suits index (0-10)	6	Time (years)		NO PRACTICE
		Strength of investor protection index (0-10)	4.0	Cost (% of estate)		NO PRACTICE
				Recovery rate (cents on the dollar)		0.0
		Paying taxes (rank)	104			
		Payments (number per year)	41			
		Time (hours per year)	186			
		Total tax rate (% of profit)	37.8			

CENTRAL AFRICAN REPUBLIC

Ease of doing business (rank)	182	Sub-Saharan Africa		GNI per capita (US$)		460
		Low income		Population (m)		4.5
✔ **Starting a business** (rank)	160	✔ **Registering property** (rank)	132	**Trading across borders** (rank)		182
Procedures (number)	7	Procedures (number)	5	Documents to export (number)		9
Time (days)	21	Time (days)	75	Time to export (days)		54
Cost (% of income per capita)	175.5	Cost (% of property value)	11.0	Cost to export (US$ per container)		5,491
Minimum capital (% of income per capita)	452.9			Documents to import (number)		17
		✔ **Getting credit** (rank)	98	Time to import (days)		62
Dealing with construction permits (rank)	136	Strength of legal rights index (0-10)	6	Cost to import (US$ per container)		5,554
Procedures (number)	18	Depth of credit information index (0-6)	2			
Time (days)	203	Public registry coverage (% of adults)	2.2	**Enforcing contracts** (rank)		173
Cost (% of income per capita)	112.2	Private bureau coverage (% of adults)	0.0	Procedures (number)		43
				Time (days)		660
Getting electricity (rank)	162	**Protecting investors** (rank)	133	Cost (% of claim)		82.0
Procedures (number)	6	Extent of disclosure index (0-10)	6			
Time (days)	102	Extent of director liability index (0-10)	1	**Resolving insolvency** (rank)		183
Cost (% of income per capita)	12,852.1	Ease of shareholder suits index (0-10)	5	Time (years)		4.8
		Strength of investor protection index (0-10)	4.0	Cost (% of estate)		76
				Recovery rate (cents on the dollar)		0.0
		Paying taxes (rank)	177			
		Payments (number per year)	54			
		Time (hours per year)	504			
		Total tax rate (% of profit)	54.6			

CHAD

Ease of doing business (rank)	183	Sub-Saharan Africa		GNI per capita (US$)		600
		Low income		Population (m)		11.5
✔ **Starting a business** (rank)	183	**Registering property** (rank)	143	**Trading across borders** (rank)		178
Procedures (number)	11	Procedures (number)	6	Documents to export (number)		8
Time (days)	66	Time (days)	44	Time to export (days)		75
Cost (% of income per capita)	208.5	Cost (% of property value)	18.1	Cost to export (US$ per container)		5,902
Minimum capital (% of income per capita)	345.0			Documents to import (number)		11
		✔ **Getting credit** (rank)	98	Time to import (days)		101
Dealing with construction permits (rank)	122	Strength of legal rights index (0-10)	6	Cost to import (US$ per container)		8,525
Procedures (number)	13	Depth of credit information index (0-6)	2			
Time (days)	154	Public registry coverage (% of adults)	1.0	**Enforcing contracts** (rank)		163
Cost (% of income per capita)	5,756.5	Private bureau coverage (% of adults)	0.0	Procedures (number)		41
				Time (days)		743
Getting electricity (rank)	117	**Protecting investors** (rank)	155	Cost (% of claim)		45.7
Procedures (number)	5	Extent of disclosure index (0-10)	6			
Time (days)	67	Extent of director liability index (0-10)	1	**Resolving insolvency** (rank)		183
Cost (% of income per capita)	13,123.8	Ease of shareholder suits index (0-10)	3	Time (years)		4.0
		Strength of investor protection index (0-10)	3.3	Cost (% of estate)		60
				Recovery rate (cents on the dollar)		0.0
		Paying taxes (rank)	180			
		Payments (number per year)	54			
		Time (hours per year)	732			
		Total tax rate (% of profit)	65.4			

Note: Most indicator sets refer to a case scenario in the largest business city of each economy. For more details, see the data notes.

✔ Reform making it easier to do business ✘ Reform making it more difficult to do business

CHILE

Ease of doing business (rank)	39	Latin America & Caribbean / Upper middle income		GNI per capita (US$)	9,940		
				Population (m)	17.1		

✔ **Starting a business** (rank) — 27
Procedures (number) — 7
Time (days) — 7
Cost (% of income per capita) — 5.1
Minimum capital (% of income per capita) — 0.0

Dealing with construction permits (rank) — 90
Procedures (number) — 17
Time (days) — 155
Cost (% of income per capita) — 79.0

Getting electricity (rank) — 41
Procedures (number) — 6
Time (days) — 31
Cost (% of income per capita) — 77.6

Registering property (rank) — 53
Procedures (number) — 6
Time (days) — 31
Cost (% of property value) — 1.3

✔ **Getting credit** (rank) — 48
Strength of legal rights index (0-10) — 6
Depth of credit information index (0-6) — 5
Public registry coverage (% of adults) — 35.6
Private bureau coverage (% of adults) — 25.8

Protecting investors (rank) — 29
Extent of disclosure index (0-10) — 8
Extent of director liability index (0-10) — 6
Ease of shareholder suits index (0-10) — 5
Strength of investor protection index (0-10) — 6.3

Paying taxes (rank) — 45
Payments (number per year) — 9
Time (hours per year) — 316
Total tax rate (% of profit) — 25.0

✔ **Trading across borders** (rank) — 62
Documents to export (number) — 6
Time to export (days) — 21
Cost to export (US$ per container) — 795
Documents to import (number) — 6
Time to import (days) — 20
Cost to import (US$ per container) — 795

Enforcing contracts (rank) — 67
Procedures (number) — 36
Time (days) — 480
Cost (% of claim) — 28.6

Resolving insolvency (rank) — 110
Time (years) — 4.5
Cost (% of estate) — 15
Recovery rate (cents on the dollar) — 25.5

CHINA

Ease of doing business (rank)	91	East Asia & Pacific / Upper middle income — GNI per capita (US$) 4,260; Population (m) 1,338.3

Starting a business (rank) — 151
Procedures (number) — 14
Time (days) — 38
Cost (% of income per capita) — 3.5
Minimum capital (% of income per capita) — 100.4

Dealing with construction permits (rank) — 179
Procedures (number) — 33
Time (days) — 311
Cost (% of income per capita) — 444.1

Getting electricity (rank) — 115
Procedures (number) — 5
Time (days) — 145
Cost (% of income per capita) — 640.9

Registering property (rank) — 40
Procedures (number) — 4
Time (days) — 29
Cost (% of property value) — 3.6

Getting credit (rank) — 67
Strength of legal rights index (0-10) — 6
Depth of credit information index (0-6) — 4
Public registry coverage (% of adults) — 82.5
Private bureau coverage (% of adults) — 0.0

Protecting investors (rank) — 97
Extent of disclosure index (0-10) — 10
Extent of director liability index (0-10) — 1
Ease of shareholder suits index (0-10) — 4
Strength of investor protection index (0-10) — 5.0

Paying taxes (rank) — 122
Payments (number per year) — 7
Time (hours per year) — 398
Total tax rate (% of profit) — 63.5

Trading across borders (rank) — 60
Documents to export (number) — 8
Time to export (days) — 21
Cost to export (US$ per container) — 500
Documents to import (number) — 5
Time to import (days) — 24
Cost to import (US$ per container) — 545

Enforcing contracts (rank) — 16
Procedures (number) — 34
Time (days) — 406
Cost (% of claim) — 11.1

Resolving insolvency (rank) — 75
Time (years) — 1.7
Cost (% of estate) — 22
Recovery rate (cents on the dollar) — 36.1

COLOMBIA

Ease of doing business (rank)	42	Latin America & Caribbean / Upper middle income — GNI per capita (US$) 5,510; Population (m) 46.3

✔ **Starting a business** (rank) — 65
Procedures (number) — 9
Time (days) — 14
Cost (% of income per capita) — 8.0
Minimum capital (% of income per capita) — 0.0

Dealing with construction permits (rank) — 29
Procedures (number) — 8
Time (days) — 46
Cost (% of income per capita) — 338.9

Getting electricity (rank) — 134
Procedures (number) — 5
Time (days) — 165
Cost (% of income per capita) — 1,081.3

Registering property (rank) — 51
Procedures (number) — 7
Time (days) — 15
Cost (% of property value) — 2.0

Getting credit (rank) — 67
Strength of legal rights index (0-10) — 5
Depth of credit information index (0-6) — 5
Public registry coverage (% of adults) — 0.0
Private bureau coverage (% of adults) — 71.2

Protecting investors (rank) — 5
Extent of disclosure index (0-10) — 8
Extent of director liability index (0-10) — 8
Ease of shareholder suits index (0-10) — 9
Strength of investor protection index (0-10) — 8.3

✔ **Paying taxes** (rank) — 95
Payments (number per year) — 9
Time (hours per year) — 193
Total tax rate (% of profit) — 74.8

Trading across borders (rank) — 87
Documents to export (number) — 5
Time to export (days) — 14
Cost to export (US$ per container) — 2,270
Documents to import (number) — 6
Time to import (days) — 13
Cost to import (US$ per container) — 2,830

Enforcing contracts (rank) — 149
Procedures (number) — 34
Time (days) — 1,346
Cost (% of claim) — 47.9

✔ **Resolving insolvency** (rank) — 12
Time (years) — 1.3
Cost (% of estate) — 1
Recovery rate (cents on the dollar) — 82.8

Note: Most indicator sets refer to a case scenario in the largest business city of each economy. For more details, see the data notes.

✔ Reform making it easier to do business ✘ Reform making it more difficult to do business

COMOROS

		Sub-Saharan Africa		GNI per capita (US$)	820
Ease of doing business (rank)	157	Low income		Population (m)	0.7
Starting a business (rank)	172	**Registering property** (rank)	74	**Trading across borders** (rank)	139
Procedures (number)	11	Procedures (number)	4	Documents to export (number)	10
Time (days)	24	Time (days)	30	Time to export (days)	30
Cost (% of income per capita)	176.2	Cost (% of property value)	10.5	Cost to export (US$ per container)	1,207
Minimum capital (% of income per capita)	252.9			Documents to import (number)	10
		✔ **Getting credit** (rank)	150	Time to import (days)	21
Dealing with construction permits (rank)	74	Strength of legal rights index (0-10)	6	Cost to import (US$ per container)	1,191
Procedures (number)	15	Depth of credit information index (0-6)	0		
Time (days)	155	Public registry coverage (% of adults)	0.0	**Enforcing contracts** (rank)	153
Cost (% of income per capita)	62.8	Private bureau coverage (% of adults)	0.0	Procedures (number)	43
				Time (days)	506
Getting electricity (rank)	100	**Protecting investors** (rank)	133	Cost (% of claim)	89.4
Procedures (number)	3	Extent of disclosure index (0-10)	6		
Time (days)	120	Extent of director liability index (0-10)	1	**Resolving insolvency** (rank)	183
Cost (% of income per capita)	2,685.1	Ease of shareholder suits index (0-10)	5	Time (years)	NO PRACTICE
		Strength of investor protection index (0-10)	4.0	Cost (% of estate)	NO PRACTICE
				Recovery rate (cents on the dollar)	0.0
		Paying taxes (rank)	99		
		Payments (number per year)	20		
		Time (hours per year)	100		
		Total tax rate (% of profit)	217.9		

CONGO, DEM. REP.

		Sub-Saharan Africa		GNI per capita (US$)	180
Ease of doing business (rank)	178	Low income		Population (m)	67.8
✔ **Starting a business** (rank)	148	**Registering property** (rank)	121	**Trading across borders** (rank)	167
Procedures (number)	10	Procedures (number)	6	Documents to export (number)	8
Time (days)	65	Time (days)	54	Time to export (days)	44
Cost (% of income per capita)	551.4	Cost (% of property value)	6.8	Cost to export (US$ per container)	3,055
Minimum capital (% of income per capita)	0.0			Documents to import (number)	9
		Getting credit (rank)	174	Time to import (days)	63
✔ **Dealing with construction permits** (rank)	77	Strength of legal rights index (0-10)	3	Cost to import (US$ per container)	3,285
Procedures (number)	11	Depth of credit information index (0-6)	0		
Time (days)	117	Public registry coverage (% of adults)	0.0	**Enforcing contracts** (rank)	170
Cost (% of income per capita)	1,670.7	Private bureau coverage (% of adults)	0.0	Procedures (number)	43
				Time (days)	610
Getting electricity (rank)	145	**Protecting investors** (rank)	155	Cost (% of claim)	151.8
Procedures (number)	6	Extent of disclosure index (0-10)	3		
Time (days)	58	Extent of director liability index (0-10)	3	**Resolving insolvency** (rank)	166
Cost (% of income per capita)	28,801.5	Ease of shareholder suits index (0-10)	4	Time (years)	5.2
		Strength of investor protection index (0-10)	3.3	Cost (% of estate)	29
				Recovery rate (cents on the dollar)	1.2
		✔ **Paying taxes** (rank)	165		
		Payments (number per year)	32		
		Time (hours per year)	336		
		Total tax rate (% of profit)	339.7		

CONGO, REP.

		Sub-Saharan Africa		GNI per capita (US$)	2,310
Ease of doing business (rank)	181	Lower middle income		Population (m)	3.8
Starting a business (rank)	175	✘ **Registering property** (rank)	156	**Trading across borders** (rank)	181
Procedures (number)	10	Procedures (number)	6	Documents to export (number)	11
Time (days)	160	Time (days)	55	Time to export (days)	50
Cost (% of income per capita)	85.2	Cost (% of property value)	20.6	Cost to export (US$ per container)	3,818
Minimum capital (% of income per capita)	88.0			Documents to import (number)	10
		✔ **Getting credit** (rank)	98	Time to import (days)	62
Dealing with construction permits (rank)	103	Strength of legal rights index (0-10)	6	Cost to import (US$ per container)	7,709
Procedures (number)	14	Depth of credit information index (0-6)	2		
Time (days)	186	Public registry coverage (% of adults)	8.2	**Enforcing contracts** (rank)	159
Cost (% of income per capita)	157.7	Private bureau coverage (% of adults)	0.0	Procedures (number)	44
				Time (days)	560
Getting electricity (rank)	152	**Protecting investors** (rank)	155	Cost (% of claim)	53.2
Procedures (number)	5	Extent of disclosure index (0-10)	6		
Time (days)	129	Extent of director liability index (0-10)	1	**Resolving insolvency** (rank)	134
Cost (% of income per capita)	5,224.0	Ease of shareholder suits index (0-10)	3	Time (years)	3.3
		Strength of investor protection index (0-10)	3.3	Cost (% of estate)	25
				Recovery rate (cents on the dollar)	17.9
		Paying taxes (rank)	182		
		Payments (number per year)	61		
		Time (hours per year)	606		
		Total tax rate (% of profit)	65.9		

Note: Most indicator sets refer to a case scenario in the largest business city of each economy. For more details, see the data notes.

✔ Reform making it easier to do business ✗ Reform making it more difficult to do business

COSTA RICA

Ease of doing business (rank)	121	Latin America & Caribbean		GNI per capita (US$)		6,580
		Upper middle income		Population (m)		4.6
Starting a business (rank)	122	✔ **Registering property** (rank)	46	**Trading across borders** (rank)		73
Procedures (number)	12	Procedures (number)	5	Documents to export (number)		6
Time (days)	60	Time (days)	20	Time to export (days)		13
Cost (% of income per capita)	11.1	Cost (% of property value)	3.4	Cost to export (US$ per container)		1,190
Minimum capital (% of income per capita)	0.0			Documents to import (number)		7
		Getting credit (rank)	98	Time to import (days)		15
		Strength of legal rights index (0-10)	3	Cost to import (US$ per container)		1,190
Dealing with construction permits (rank)	141	Depth of credit information index (0-6)	5			
Procedures (number)	20	Public registry coverage (% of adults)	25.5	**Enforcing contracts** (rank)		129
Time (days)	188	Private bureau coverage (% of adults)	78.9	Procedures (number)		40
Cost (% of income per capita)	164.5			Time (days)		852
		Protecting investors (rank)	166	Cost (% of claim)		24.3
Getting electricity (rank)	43	Extent of disclosure index (0-10)	2			
Procedures (number)	5	Extent of director liability index (0-10)	5	**Resolving insolvency** (rank)		121
Time (days)	62	Ease of shareholder suits index (0-10)	2	Time (years)		3.5
Cost (% of income per capita)	299.5	Strength of investor protection index (0-10)	3.0	Cost (% of estate)		15
				Recovery rate (cents on the dollar)		22.2
		✔ **Paying taxes** (rank)	138			
		Payments (number per year)	31			
		Time (hours per year)	246			
		Total tax rate (% of profit)	55.0			

CÔTE D'IVOIRE

Ease of doing business (rank)	167	Sub-Saharan Africa		GNI per capita (US$)		1,070
		Lower middle income		Population (m)		21.6
✔ **Starting a business** (rank)	170	**Registering property** (rank)	158	**Trading across borders** (rank)		161
Procedures (number)	10	Procedures (number)	6	Documents to export (number)		10
Time (days)	32	Time (days)	62	Time to export (days)		25
Cost (% of income per capita)	132.6	Cost (% of property value)	13.9	Cost to export (US$ per container)		1,969
Minimum capital (% of income per capita)	200.4			Documents to import (number)		9
		✔ **Getting credit** (rank)	126	Time to import (days)		36
		Strength of legal rights index (0-10)	6	Cost to import (US$ per container)		2,577
Dealing with construction permits (rank)	169	Depth of credit information index (0-6)	1			
Procedures (number)	18	Public registry coverage (% of adults)	2.6	**Enforcing contracts** (rank)		124
Time (days)	583	Private bureau coverage (% of adults)	0.0	Procedures (number)		33
Cost (% of income per capita)	204.8			Time (days)		770
		Protecting investors (rank)	155	Cost (% of claim)		41.7
Getting electricity (rank)	73	Extent of disclosure index (0-10)	6			
Procedures (number)	5	Extent of director liability index (0-10)	1	**Resolving insolvency** (rank)		70
Time (days)	33	Ease of shareholder suits index (0-10)	3	Time (years)		2.2
Cost (% of income per capita)	4,002.3	Strength of investor protection index (0-10)	3.3	Cost (% of estate)		18
				Recovery rate (cents on the dollar)		37.6
		✔ **Paying taxes** (rank)	159			
		Payments (number per year)	62			
		Time (hours per year)	270			
		Total tax rate (% of profit)	44.3			

CROATIA

Ease of doing business (rank)	80	Eastern Europe & Central Asia		GNI per capita (US$)		13,760
		High income		Population (m)		4.4
Starting a business (rank)	67	**Registering property** (rank)	102	**Trading across borders** (rank)		100
Procedures (number)	6	Procedures (number)	5	Documents to export (number)		7
Time (days)	7	Time (days)	104	Time to export (days)		20
Cost (% of income per capita)	8.6	Cost (% of property value)	5.0	Cost to export (US$ per container)		1,300
Minimum capital (% of income per capita)	13.8			Documents to import (number)		8
		✔ **Getting credit** (rank)	48	Time to import (days)		16
		Strength of legal rights index (0-10)	6	Cost to import (US$ per container)		1,180
Dealing with construction permits (rank)	143	Depth of credit information index (0-6)	5			
Procedures (number)	12	Public registry coverage (% of adults)	0.0	**Enforcing contracts** (rank)		48
Time (days)	317	Private bureau coverage (% of adults)	100.0	Procedures (number)		38
Cost (% of income per capita)	591.1			Time (days)		561
		Protecting investors (rank)	133	Cost (% of claim)		13.8
Getting electricity (rank)	56	Extent of disclosure index (0-10)	1			
Procedures (number)	5	Extent of director liability index (0-10)	5	**Resolving insolvency** (rank)		94
Time (days)	70	Ease of shareholder suits index (0-10)	6	Time (years)		3.1
Cost (% of income per capita)	328.6	Strength of investor protection index (0-10)	4.0	Cost (% of estate)		15
				Recovery rate (cents on the dollar)		29.7
		Paying taxes (rank)	32			
		Payments (number per year)	17			
		Time (hours per year)	196			
		Total tax rate (% of profit)	32.3			

Note: Most indicator sets refer to a case scenario in the largest business city of each economy. For more details, see the data notes.

✔ Reform making it easier to do business ✘ Reform making it more difficult to do business

CYPRUS

		Eastern Europe & Central Asia		GNI per capita (US$)		28,237
Ease of doing business (rank)	40	High income		Population (m)		0.9
Starting a business (rank)	33	**Registering property** (rank)	123	**Trading across borders** (rank)		19
Procedures (number)	6	Procedures (number)	6	Documents to export (number)		5
Time (days)	8	Time (days)	42	Time to export (days)		7
Cost (% of income per capita)	13.1	Cost (% of property value)	10.3	Cost to export (US$ per container)		790
Minimum capital (% of income per capita)	0.0			Documents to import (number)		7
		Getting credit (rank)	78	Time to import (days)		5
Dealing with construction permits (rank)	78	Strength of legal rights index (0-10)	9	Cost to import (US$ per container)		900
Procedures (number)	9	Depth of credit information index (0-6)	0			
Time (days)	677	Public registry coverage (% of adults)	0.0	**Enforcing contracts** (rank)		105
Cost (% of income per capita)	47.5	Private bureau coverage (% of adults)	0.0	Procedures (number)		43
				Time (days)		735
Getting electricity (rank)	96	✔ **Protecting investors** (rank)	29	Cost (% of claim)		16.4
Procedures (number)	5	Extent of disclosure index (0-10)	8			
Time (days)	247	Extent of director liability index (0-10)	4	**Resolving insolvency** (rank)		23
Cost (% of income per capita)	95.3	Ease of shareholder suits index (0-10)	7	Time (years)		1.5
		Strength of investor protection index (0-10)	6.3	Cost (% of estate)		15
				Recovery rate (cents on the dollar)		70.8
		Paying taxes (rank)	37			
		Payments (number per year)	27			
		Time (hours per year)	149			
		Total tax rate (% of profit)	23.1			

CZECH REPUBLIC

		OECD high income		GNI per capita (US$)		17,870
Ease of doing business (rank)	64	High income		Population (m)		10.5
Starting a business (rank)	138	✔ **Registering property** (rank)	34	**Trading across borders** (rank)		70
Procedures (number)	9	Procedures (number)	4	Documents to export (number)		4
Time (days)	20	Time (days)	25	Time to export (days)		17
Cost (% of income per capita)	8.4	Cost (% of property value)	3.0	Cost to export (US$ per container)		1,060
Minimum capital (% of income per capita)	30.7			Documents to import (number)		7
		Getting credit (rank)	48	Time to import (days)		20
Dealing with construction permits (rank)	68	Strength of legal rights index (0-10)	6	Cost to import (US$ per container)		1,165
Procedures (number)	33	Depth of credit information index (0-6)	5			
Time (days)	120	Public registry coverage (% of adults)	6.1	**Enforcing contracts** (rank)		78
Cost (% of income per capita)	10.9	Private bureau coverage (% of adults)	95.7	Procedures (number)		27
				Time (days)		611
Getting electricity (rank)	148	**Protecting investors** (rank)	97	Cost (% of claim)		33.0
Procedures (number)	6	Extent of disclosure index (0-10)	2			
Time (days)	279	Extent of director liability index (0-10)	5	**Resolving insolvency** (rank)		33
Cost (% of income per capita)	186.2	Ease of shareholder suits index (0-10)	8	Time (years)		3.2
		Strength of investor protection index (0-10)	5.0	Cost (% of estate)		17
				Recovery rate (cents on the dollar)		56.0
		✔ **Paying taxes** (rank)	119			
		Payments (number per year)	8			
		Time (hours per year)	557			
		Total tax rate (% of profit)	49.1			

DENMARK

		OECD high income		GNI per capita (US$)		58,980
Ease of doing business (rank)	5	High income		Population (m)		5.6
Starting a business (rank)	31	**Registering property** (rank)	11	**Trading across borders** (rank)		7
Procedures (number)	4	Procedures (number)	3	Documents to export (number)		4
Time (days)	6	Time (days)	16	Time to export (days)		5
Cost (% of income per capita)	0.0	Cost (% of property value)	0.6	Cost to export (US$ per container)		744
Minimum capital (% of income per capita)	25.0			Documents to import (number)		3
		Getting credit (rank)	24	Time to import (days)		5
Dealing with construction permits (rank)	10	Strength of legal rights index (0-10)	9	Cost to import (US$ per container)		744
Procedures (number)	5	Depth of credit information index (0-6)	4			
Time (days)	67	Public registry coverage (% of adults)	0.0	**Enforcing contracts** (rank)		32
Cost (% of income per capita)	59.1	Private bureau coverage (% of adults)	7.3	Procedures (number)		35
				Time (days)		410
Getting electricity (rank)	13	**Protecting investors** (rank)	29	Cost (% of claim)		23.3
Procedures (number)	4	Extent of disclosure index (0-10)	7			
Time (days)	38	Extent of director liability index (0-10)	5	✔ **Resolving insolvency** (rank)		9
Cost (% of income per capita)	120.6	Ease of shareholder suits index (0-10)	7	Time (years)		1.0
		Strength of investor protection index (0-10)	6.3	Cost (% of estate)		4
				Recovery rate (cents on the dollar)		87.3
		Paying taxes (rank)	14			
		Payments (number per year)	10			
		Time (hours per year)	135			
		Total tax rate (% of profit)	27.5			

Note: Most indicator sets refer to a case scenario in the largest business city of each economy. For more details, see the data notes.

✔ Reform making it easier to do business ✘ Reform making it more difficult to do business

DJIBOUTI

Ease of doing business (rank)	170	Middle East & North Africa Lower middle income		GNI per capita (US$) Population (m)	1,383 0.9
Starting a business (rank)	179	**Registering property** (rank)	148	✔ **Trading across borders** (rank)	37
Procedures (number)	11	Procedures (number)	7	Documents to export (number)	5
Time (days)	37	Time (days)	40	Time to export (days)	18
Cost (% of income per capita)	169.8	Cost (% of property value)	13.0	Cost to export (US$ per container)	836
Minimum capital (% of income per capita)	434.0			Documents to import (number)	5
		Getting credit (rank)	177	Time to import (days)	18
✘ **Dealing with construction permits** (rank)	142	Strength of legal rights index (0-10)	1	Cost to import (US$ per container)	911
Procedures (number)	15	Depth of credit information index (0-6)	1		
Time (days)	172	Public registry coverage (% of adults)	0.2	**Enforcing contracts** (rank)	160
Cost (% of income per capita)	2,285.7	Private bureau coverage (% of adults)	0.0	Procedures (number)	40
				Time (days)	1,225
Getting electricity (rank)	143	**Protecting investors** (rank)	179	Cost (% of claim)	34.0
Procedures (number)	4	Extent of disclosure index (0-10)	5		
Time (days)	180	Extent of director liability index (0-10)	2	**Resolving insolvency** (rank)	141
Cost (% of income per capita)	8,799.1	Ease of shareholder suits index (0-10)	0	Time (years)	5.0
		Strength of investor protection index (0-10)	2.3	Cost (% of estate)	18
				Recovery rate (cents on the dollar)	16.5
		Paying taxes (rank)	70		
		Payments (number per year)	35		
		Time (hours per year)	82		
		Total tax rate (% of profit)	38.7		

DOMINICA

Ease of doing business (rank)	65	Latin America & Caribbean Upper middle income		GNI per capita (US$) Population (m)	4,960 0.1
Starting a business (rank)	48	**Registering property** (rank)	116	**Trading across borders** (rank)	88
Procedures (number)	5	Procedures (number)	5	Documents to export (number)	7
Time (days)	14	Time (days)	42	Time to export (days)	13
Cost (% of income per capita)	21.8	Cost (% of property value)	13.2	Cost to export (US$ per container)	1,340
Minimum capital (% of income per capita)	0.0			Documents to import (number)	8
		Getting credit (rank)	78	Time to import (days)	15
Dealing with construction permits (rank)	18	Strength of legal rights index (0-10)	9	Cost to import (US$ per container)	1,350
Procedures (number)	9	Depth of credit information index (0-6)	0		
Time (days)	165	Public registry coverage (% of adults)	0.0	**Enforcing contracts** (rank)	167
Cost (% of income per capita)	10.8	Private bureau coverage (% of adults)	0.0	Procedures (number)	47
				Time (days)	681
Getting electricity (rank)	65	**Protecting investors** (rank)	29	Cost (% of claim)	36.0
Procedures (number)	5	Extent of disclosure index (0-10)	4		
Time (days)	61	Extent of director liability index (0-10)	8	**Resolving insolvency** (rank)	98
Cost (% of income per capita)	849.7	Ease of shareholder suits index (0-10)	7	Time (years)	4.0
		Strength of investor protection index (0-10)	6.3	Cost (% of estate)	10
				Recovery rate (cents on the dollar)	28.3
		Paying taxes (rank)	73		
		Payments (number per year)	37		
		Time (hours per year)	120		
		Total tax rate (% of profit)	37.5		

DOMINICAN REPUBLIC

Ease of doing business (rank)	108	Latin America & Caribbean Upper middle income		GNI per capita (US$) Population (m)	4,860 10.2
✔ **Starting a business** (rank)	140	**Registering property** (rank)	105	**Trading across borders** (rank)	45
Procedures (number)	7	Procedures (number)	7	Documents to export (number)	6
Time (days)	19	Time (days)	60	Time to export (days)	8
Cost (% of income per capita)	18.2	Cost (% of property value)	3.7	Cost to export (US$ per container)	1,040
Minimum capital (% of income per capita)	55.7			Documents to import (number)	7
		Getting credit (rank)	78	Time to import (days)	10
Dealing with construction permits (rank)	105	Strength of legal rights index (0-10)	3	Cost to import (US$ per container)	1,150
Procedures (number)	14	Depth of credit information index (0-6)	6		
Time (days)	216	Public registry coverage (% of adults)	35.9	**Enforcing contracts** (rank)	83
Cost (% of income per capita)	82.1	Private bureau coverage (% of adults)	54.3	Procedures (number)	34
				Time (days)	460
Getting electricity (rank)	123	**Protecting investors** (rank)	65	Cost (% of claim)	40.9
Procedures (number)	7	Extent of disclosure index (0-10)	5		
Time (days)	87	Extent of director liability index (0-10)	4	**Resolving insolvency** (rank)	154
Cost (% of income per capita)	356.7	Ease of shareholder suits index (0-10)	8	Time (years)	3.5
		Strength of investor protection index (0-10)	5.7	Cost (% of estate)	38
				Recovery rate (cents on the dollar)	9.5
		Paying taxes (rank)	94		
		Payments (number per year)	9		
		Time (hours per year)	324		
		Total tax rate (% of profit)	41.7		

Note: Most indicator sets refer to a case scenario in the largest business city of each economy. For more details, see the data notes.

✔ Reform making it easier to do business ✘ Reform making it more difficult to do business

ECUADOR

Ease of doing business (rank)	130	Latin America & Caribbean Upper middle income		GNI per capita (US$) Population (m)	4,510 13.8
Starting a business (rank)	164	**Registering property** (rank)	75	**Trading across borders** (rank)	123
Procedures (number)	13	Procedures (number)	9	Documents to export (number)	8
Time (days)	56	Time (days)	16	Time to export (days)	20
Cost (% of income per capita)	28.8	Cost (% of property value)	2.1	Cost to export (US$ per container)	1,455
Minimum capital (% of income per capita)	4.3			Documents to import (number)	7
		Getting credit (rank)	78	Time to import (days)	25
Dealing with construction permits (rank)	91	Strength of legal rights index (0-10)	3	Cost to import (US$ per container)	1,432
Procedures (number)	16	Depth of credit information index (0-6)	6		
Time (days)	128	Public registry coverage (% of adults)	0.0	**Enforcing contracts** (rank)	100
Cost (% of income per capita)	184.0	Private bureau coverage (% of adults)	57.9	Procedures (number)	39
				Time (days)	588
Getting electricity (rank)	128	**Protecting investors** (rank)	133	Cost (% of claim)	27.2
Procedures (number)	6	Extent of disclosure index (0-10)	1		
Time (days)	89	Extent of director liability index (0-10)	5	**Resolving insolvency** (rank)	139
Cost (% of income per capita)	785.3	Ease of shareholder suits index (0-10)	6	Time (years)	5.3
		Strength of investor protection index (0-10)	4.0	Cost (% of estate)	18
				Recovery rate (cents on the dollar)	17.2
		Paying taxes (rank)	88		
		Payments (number per year)	8		
		Time (hours per year)	654		
		Total tax rate (% of profit)	35.3		

EGYPT, ARAB REP.

Ease of doing business (rank)	110	Middle East & North Africa Lower middle income		GNI per capita (US$) Population (m)	2,340 84.5
Starting a business (rank)	21	**Registering property** (rank)	93	**Trading across borders** (rank)	64
Procedures (number)	6	Procedures (number)	7	Documents to export (number)	8
Time (days)	7	Time (days)	72	Time to export (days)	12
Cost (% of income per capita)	5.6	Cost (% of property value)	0.8	Cost to export (US$ per container)	613
Minimum capital (% of income per capita)	0.0			Documents to import (number)	9
		Getting credit (rank)	78	Time to import (days)	12
Dealing with construction permits (rank)	154	Strength of legal rights index (0-10)	3	Cost to import (US$ per container)	755
Procedures (number)	22	Depth of credit information index (0-6)	6		
Time (days)	218	Public registry coverage (% of adults)	3.5	**Enforcing contracts** (rank)	147
Cost (% of income per capita)	155.3	Private bureau coverage (% of adults)	13.7	Procedures (number)	41
				Time (days)	1,010
Getting electricity (rank)	101	**Protecting investors** (rank)	79	Cost (% of claim)	26.2
Procedures (number)	7	Extent of disclosure index (0-10)	8		
Time (days)	54	Extent of director liability index (0-10)	3	**Resolving insolvency** (rank)	137
Cost (% of income per capita)	455.5	Ease of shareholder suits index (0-10)	5	Time (years)	4.2
		Strength of investor protection index (0-10)	5.3	Cost (% of estate)	22
				Recovery rate (cents on the dollar)	17.7
		Paying taxes (rank)	145		
		Payments (number per year)	29		
		Time (hours per year)	433		
		Total tax rate (% of profit)	43.6		

EL SALVADOR

Ease of doing business (rank)	112	Latin America & Caribbean Lower middle income		GNI per capita (US$) Population (m)	3,360 6.2
Starting a business (rank)	136	**Registering property** (rank)	54	**Trading across borders** (rank)	69
Procedures (number)	8	Procedures (number)	5	Documents to export (number)	8
Time (days)	17	Time (days)	31	Time to export (days)	14
Cost (% of income per capita)	45.1	Cost (% of property value)	3.7	Cost to export (US$ per container)	845
Minimum capital (% of income per capita)	3.0			Documents to import (number)	8
		Getting credit (rank)	48	Time to import (days)	10
Dealing with construction permits (rank)	144	Strength of legal rights index (0-10)	5	Cost to import (US$ per container)	845
Procedures (number)	33	Depth of credit information index (0-6)	6		
Time (days)	157	Public registry coverage (% of adults)	23.9	**Enforcing contracts** (rank)	66
Cost (% of income per capita)	168.3	Private bureau coverage (% of adults)	81.1	Procedures (number)	34
				Time (days)	786
Getting electricity (rank)	130	✔ **Protecting investors** (rank)	166	Cost (% of claim)	19.2
Procedures (number)	7	Extent of disclosure index (0-10)	3		
Time (days)	78	Extent of director liability index (0-10)	0	**Resolving insolvency** (rank)	88
Cost (% of income per capita)	533.3	Ease of shareholder suits index (0-10)	6	Time (years)	4.0
		Strength of investor protection index (0-10)	3.0	Cost (% of estate)	9
				Recovery rate (cents on the dollar)	31.5
		Paying taxes (rank)	146		
		Payments (number per year)	53		
		Time (hours per year)	320		
		Total tax rate (% of profit)	35.0		

Note: Most indicator sets refer to a case scenario in the largest business city of each economy. For more details, see the data notes.

✔ Reform making it easier to do business ✗ Reform making it more difficult to do business

EQUATORIAL GUINEA

Ease of doing business (rank)	155

Sub-Saharan Africa
High income

GNI per capita (US$)	14,680
Population (m)	0.7

Starting a business (rank)	178	**Registering property** (rank)	80	**Trading across borders** (rank)	134	
Procedures (number)	21	Procedures (number)	6	Documents to export (number)	7	
Time (days)	137	Time (days)	23	Time to export (days)	29	
Cost (% of income per capita)	101.4	Cost (% of property value)	6.2	Cost to export (US$ per container)	1,411	
Minimum capital (% of income per capita)	14.6			Documents to import (number)	7	
		✔ **Getting credit** (rank)	98	Time to import (days)	48	
Dealing with construction permits (rank)	100	Strength of legal rights index (0-10)	6	Cost to import (US$ per container)	1,411	
Procedures (number)	15	Depth of credit information index (0-6)	2			
Time (days)	166	Public registry coverage (% of adults)	2.9	**Enforcing contracts** (rank)	74	
Cost (% of income per capita)	150.6	Private bureau coverage (% of adults)	0.0	Procedures (number)	40	
				Time (days)	553	
Getting electricity (rank)	88	**Protecting investors** (rank)	147	Cost (% of claim)	18.5	
Procedures (number)	5	Extent of disclosure index (0-10)	6			
Time (days)	106	Extent of director liability index (0-10)	1	**Resolving insolvency** (rank)	183	
Cost (% of income per capita)	571.1	Ease of shareholder suits index (0-10)	4	Time (years)	NO PRACTICE	
		Strength of investor protection index (0-10)	3.7	Cost (% of estate)	NO PRACTICE	
				Recovery rate (cents on the dollar)	0.0	
		Paying taxes (rank)	167			
		Payments (number per year)	46			
		Time (hours per year)	492			
		Total tax rate (% of profit)	46.0			

ERITREA

Ease of doing business (rank)	180

Sub-Saharan Africa
Low income

GNI per capita (US$)	340
Population (m)	5.2

Starting a business (rank)	182	**Registering property** (rank)	178	**Trading across borders** (rank)	165
Procedures (number)	13	Procedures (number)	11	Documents to export (number)	10
Time (days)	84	Time (days)	78	Time to export (days)	50
Cost (% of income per capita)	62.6	Cost (% of property value)	9.1	Cost to export (US$ per container)	1,431
Minimum capital (% of income per capita)	243.0			Documents to import (number)	12
		Getting credit (rank)	177	Time to import (days)	59
Dealing with construction permits (rank)	183	Strength of legal rights index (0-10)	2	Cost to import (US$ per container)	1,581
Procedures (number)	NO PRACTICE	Depth of credit information index (0-6)	0		
Time (days)	NO PRACTICE	Public registry coverage (% of adults)	0.0	**Enforcing contracts** (rank)	47
Cost (% of income per capita)	NO PRACTICE	Private bureau coverage (% of adults)	0.0	Procedures (number)	39
				Time (days)	405
Getting electricity (rank)	96	**Protecting investors** (rank)	111	Cost (% of claim)	22.6
Procedures (number)	5	Extent of disclosure index (0-10)	4		
Time (days)	59	Extent of director liability index (0-10)	5	**Resolving insolvency** (rank)	183
Cost (% of income per capita)	4,436.6	Ease of shareholder suits index (0-10)	5	Time (years)	NO PRACTICE
		Strength of investor protection index (0-10)	4.7	Cost (% of estate)	NO PRACTICE
				Recovery rate (cents on the dollar)	0.0
		Paying taxes (rank)	121		
		Payments (number per year)	18		
		Time (hours per year)	216		
		Total tax rate (% of profit)	84.5		

ESTONIA

Ease of doing business (rank)	24

OECD high income
High income

GNI per capita (US$)	14,360
Population (m)	1.3

Starting a business (rank)	44	**Registering property** (rank)	13	**Trading across borders** (rank)	3
Procedures (number)	5	Procedures (number)	3	Documents to export (number)	3
Time (days)	7	Time (days)	18	Time to export (days)	5
Cost (% of income per capita)	1.8	Cost (% of property value)	0.4	Cost to export (US$ per container)	725
Minimum capital (% of income per capita)	24.4			Documents to import (number)	4
		Getting credit (rank)	40	Time to import (days)	5
Dealing with construction permits (rank)	89	Strength of legal rights index (0-10)	7	Cost to import (US$ per container)	725
Procedures (number)	13	Depth of credit information index (0-6)	5		
Time (days)	148	Public registry coverage (% of adults)	0.0	**Enforcing contracts** (rank)	29
Cost (% of income per capita)	278.6	Private bureau coverage (% of adults)	33.1	Procedures (number)	35
				Time (days)	425
Getting electricity (rank)	48	**Protecting investors** (rank)	65	Cost (% of claim)	22.3
Procedures (number)	4	Extent of disclosure index (0-10)	8		
Time (days)	111	Extent of director liability index (0-10)	3	**Resolving insolvency** (rank)	72
Cost (% of income per capita)	222.5	Ease of shareholder suits index (0-10)	6	Time (years)	3.0
		Strength of investor protection index (0-10)	5.7	Cost (% of estate)	9
				Recovery rate (cents on the dollar)	36.9
		✗ **Paying taxes** (rank)	51		
		Payments (number per year)	8		
		Time (hours per year)	85		
		Total tax rate (% of profit)	58.6		

Note: Most indicator sets refer to a case scenario in the largest business city of each economy. For more details, see the data notes.

✔ Reform making it easier to do business ✗ Reform making it more difficult to do business

ETHIOPIA

		Sub-Saharan Africa		GNI per capita (US$)	380
Ease of doing business (rank)	111	Low income		Population (m)	85.0

Starting a business (rank)	99	**Registering property** (rank)	113	**Trading across borders** (rank)	157
Procedures (number)	5	Procedures (number)	10	Documents to export (number)	7
Time (days)	9	Time (days)	41	Time to export (days)	42
Cost (% of income per capita)	12.8	Cost (% of property value)	2.1	Cost to export (US$ per container)	1,760
Minimum capital (% of income per capita)	333.5			Documents to import (number)	9
		Getting credit (rank)	150	Time to import (days)	44
Dealing with construction permits (rank)	56	Strength of legal rights index (0-10)	4	Cost to import (US$ per container)	2,660
Procedures (number)	9	Depth of credit information index (0-6)	2		
Time (days)	128	Public registry coverage (% of adults)	0.2	**Enforcing contracts** (rank)	57
Cost (% of income per capita)	369.1	Private bureau coverage (% of adults)	0.0	Procedures (number)	37
				Time (days)	620
✗ **Getting electricity** (rank)	93	**Protecting investors** (rank)	122	Cost (% of claim)	15.2
Procedures (number)	4	Extent of disclosure index (0-10)	4		
Time (days)	95	Extent of director liability index (0-10)	4	**Resolving insolvency** (rank)	89
Cost (% of income per capita)	3,386.0	Ease of shareholder suits index (0-10)	5	Time (years)	3.0
		Strength of investor protection index (0-10)	4.3	Cost (% of estate)	15
				Recovery rate (cents on the dollar)	31.4
		Paying taxes (rank)	40		
		Payments (number per year)	19		
		Time (hours per year)	198		
		Total tax rate (% of profit)	31.1		

FIJI

		East Asia & Pacific		GNI per capita (US$)	3,610
Ease of doing business (rank)	77	Lower middle income		Population (m)	0.9

✗ **Starting a business** (rank)	119	**Registering property** (rank)	52	**Trading across borders** (rank)	113
Procedures (number)	9	Procedures (number)	3	Documents to export (number)	10
Time (days)	45	Time (days)	68	Time to export (days)	22
Cost (% of income per capita)	25.1	Cost (% of property value)	2.0	Cost to export (US$ per container)	655
Minimum capital (% of income per capita)	0.0			Documents to import (number)	10
		Getting credit (rank)	67	Time to import (days)	23
Dealing with construction permits (rank)	73	Strength of legal rights index (0-10)	7	Cost to import (US$ per container)	635
Procedures (number)	17	Depth of credit information index (0-6)	3		
Time (days)	148	Public registry coverage (% of adults)	0.0	**Enforcing contracts** (rank)	64
Cost (% of income per capita)	46.3	Private bureau coverage (% of adults)	67.6	Procedures (number)	34
				Time (days)	397
Getting electricity (rank)	110	**Protecting investors** (rank)	46	Cost (% of claim)	38.9
Procedures (number)	5	Extent of disclosure index (0-10)	3		
Time (days)	82	Extent of director liability index (0-10)	8	**Resolving insolvency** (rank)	126
Cost (% of income per capita)	2,147.9	Ease of shareholder suits index (0-10)	7	Time (years)	1.8
		Strength of investor protection index (0-10)	6.0	Cost (% of estate)	38
				Recovery rate (cents on the dollar)	20.5
		Paying taxes (rank)	80		
		Payments (number per year)	33		
		Time (hours per year)	163		
		Total tax rate (% of profit)	38.3		

FINLAND

		OECD high income		GNI per capita (US$)	47,170
Ease of doing business (rank)	11	High income		Population (m)	5.4

Starting a business (rank)	39	**Registering property** (rank)	25	**Trading across borders** (rank)	6
Procedures (number)	3	Procedures (number)	3	Documents to export (number)	4
Time (days)	14	Time (days)	14	Time to export (days)	8
Cost (% of income per capita)	1.0	Cost (% of property value)	4.0	Cost to export (US$ per container)	540
Minimum capital (% of income per capita)	7.3			Documents to import (number)	5
		Getting credit (rank)	40	Time to import (days)	8
Dealing with construction permits (rank)	45	Strength of legal rights index (0-10)	8	Cost to import (US$ per container)	620
Procedures (number)	16	Depth of credit information index (0-6)	4		
Time (days)	66	Public registry coverage (% of adults)	0.0	**Enforcing contracts** (rank)	11
Cost (% of income per capita)	66.6	Private bureau coverage (% of adults)	20.5	Procedures (number)	33
				Time (days)	375
Getting electricity (rank)	25	**Protecting investors** (rank)	65	Cost (% of claim)	13.3
Procedures (number)	5	Extent of disclosure index (0-10)	6		
Time (days)	53	Extent of director liability index (0-10)	4	**Resolving insolvency** (rank)	5
Cost (% of income per capita)	31.7	Ease of shareholder suits index (0-10)	7	Time (years)	0.9
		Strength of investor protection index (0-10)	5.7	Cost (% of estate)	4
				Recovery rate (cents on the dollar)	89.1
		✔ **Paying taxes** (rank)	28		
		Payments (number per year)	8		
		Time (hours per year)	93		
		Total tax rate (% of profit)	39.0		

Note: Most indicator sets refer to a case scenario in the largest business city of each economy. For more details, see the data notes.

✔ Reform making it easier to do business   ✗ Reform making it more difficult to do business

FRANCE

Ease of doing business (rank)	29

OECD high income	
High income	

GNI per capita (US$)	42,390
Population (m)	64.9

Starting a business (rank) — 25
Procedures (number) — 5
Time (days) — 7
Cost (% of income per capita) — 0.9
Minimum capital (% of income per capita) — 0.0

Registering property (rank) — 149
Procedures (number) — 8
Time (days) — 59
Cost (% of property value) — 6.1

Trading across borders (rank) — 24
Documents to export (number) — 2
Time to export (days) — 9
Cost to export (US$ per container) — 1,078
Documents to import (number) — 2
Time to import (days) — 11
Cost to import (US$ per container) — 1,248

Dealing with construction permits (rank) — 30
Procedures (number) — 10
Time (days) — 184
Cost (% of income per capita) — 13.6

Getting credit (rank) — 48
Strength of legal rights index (0-10) — 7
Depth of credit information index (0-6) — 4
Public registry coverage (% of adults) — 43.3
Private bureau coverage (% of adults) — 0.0

Enforcing contracts (rank) — 6
Procedures (number) — 29
Time (days) — 331
Cost (% of claim) — 17.4

Getting electricity (rank) — 62
Procedures (number) — 5
Time (days) — 123
Cost (% of income per capita) — 40.2

Protecting investors (rank) — 79
Extent of disclosure index (0-10) — 10
Extent of director liability index (0-10) — 1
Ease of shareholder suits index (0-10) — 5
Strength of investor protection index (0-10) — 5.3

✔ **Resolving insolvency** (rank) — 46
Time (years) — 1.9
Cost (% of estate) — 9
Recovery rate (cents on the dollar) — 45.8

Paying taxes (rank) — 58
Payments (number per year) — 7
Time (hours per year) — 132
Total tax rate (% of profit) — 65.7

GABON

Ease of doing business (rank)	156

Sub-Saharan Africa	
Upper middle income	

GNI per capita (US$)	7,760
Population (m)	1.5

Starting a business (rank) — 156
Procedures (number) — 9
Time (days) — 58
Cost (% of income per capita) — 17.3
Minimum capital (% of income per capita) — 26.4

Registering property (rank) — 134
Procedures (number) — 7
Time (days) — 39
Cost (% of property value) — 10.5

Trading across borders (rank) — 133
Documents to export (number) — 7
Time to export (days) — 20
Cost to export (US$ per container) — 1,945
Documents to import (number) — 8
Time to import (days) — 22
Cost to import (US$ per container) — 1,955

Dealing with construction permits (rank) — 58
Procedures (number) — 13
Time (days) — 201
Cost (% of income per capita) — 21.5

✔ **Getting credit** (rank) — 98
Strength of legal rights index (0-10) — 6
Depth of credit information index (0-6) — 2
Public registry coverage (% of adults) — 24.2
Private bureau coverage (% of adults) — 0.0

Enforcing contracts (rank) — 150
Procedures (number) — 38
Time (days) — 1,070
Cost (% of claim) — 34.3

Getting electricity (rank) — 137
Procedures (number) — 6
Time (days) — 160
Cost (% of income per capita) — 256.0

Protecting investors (rank) — 155
Extent of disclosure index (0-10) — 6
Extent of director liability index (0-10) — 1
Ease of shareholder suits index (0-10) — 3
Strength of investor protection index (0-10) — 3.3

Resolving insolvency (rank) — 144
Time (years) — 5.0
Cost (% of estate) — 15
Recovery rate (cents on the dollar) — 15.2

Paying taxes (rank) — 141
Payments (number per year) — 26
Time (hours per year) — 488
Total tax rate (% of profit) — 43.5

GAMBIA, THE

Ease of doing business (rank)	149

Sub-Saharan Africa	
Low income	

GNI per capita (US$)	440
Population (m)	1.8

Starting a business (rank) — 120
Procedures (number) — 8
Time (days) — 27
Cost (% of income per capita) — 206.1
Minimum capital (% of income per capita) — 0.0

Registering property (rank) — 119
Procedures (number) — 5
Time (days) — 66
Cost (% of property value) — 7.7

✔ **Trading across borders** (rank) — 78
Documents to export (number) — 6
Time to export (days) — 23
Cost to export (US$ per container) — 831
Documents to import (number) — 7
Time to import (days) — 21
Cost to import (US$ per container) — 885

Dealing with construction permits (rank) — 88
Procedures (number) — 14
Time (days) — 143
Cost (% of income per capita) — 192.9

Getting credit (rank) — 159
Strength of legal rights index (0-10) — 5
Depth of credit information index (0-6) — 0
Public registry coverage (% of adults) — 0.0
Private bureau coverage (% of adults) — 0.0

Enforcing contracts (rank) — 69
Procedures (number) — 33
Time (days) — 434
Cost (% of claim) — 37.9

✔ **Getting electricity** (rank) — 127
Procedures (number) — 5
Time (days) — 78
Cost (% of income per capita) — 6,070.8

Protecting investors (rank) — 174
Extent of disclosure index (0-10) — 2
Extent of director liability index (0-10) — 1
Ease of shareholder suits index (0-10) — 5
Strength of investor protection index (0-10) — 2.7

Resolving insolvency (rank) — 129
Time (years) — 3.0
Cost (% of estate) — 15
Recovery rate (cents on the dollar) — 19.3

✔ **Paying taxes** (rank) — 178
Payments (number per year) — 50
Time (hours per year) — 376
Total tax rate (% of profit) — 283.5

Note: Most indicator sets refer to a case scenario in the largest business city of each economy. For more details, see the data notes.

✔ Reform making it easier to do business ✘ Reform making it more difficult to do business

GEORGIA

Ease of doing business (rank)	16	Eastern Europe & Central Asia Lower middle income		GNI per capita (US$) Population (m)		2,690 4.4
✔ Starting a business (rank)	7	Registering property (rank)	1	Trading across borders (rank)		54
Procedures (number)	2	Procedures (number)	1	Documents to export (number)		4
Time (days)	2	Time (days)	2	Time to export (days)		10
Cost (% of income per capita)	4.3	Cost (% of property value)	0.1	Cost to export (US$ per container)		1,595
Minimum capital (% of income per capita)	0.0			Documents to import (number)		4
		✔ Getting credit (rank)	8	Time to import (days)		13
Dealing with construction permits (rank)	4	Strength of legal rights index (0-10)	8	Cost to import (US$ per container)		1,715
Procedures (number)	9	Depth of credit information index (0-6)	6			
Time (days)	74	Public registry coverage (% of adults)	0.0	Enforcing contracts (rank)		41
Cost (% of income per capita)	20.2	Private bureau coverage (% of adults)	29.6	Procedures (number)		36
				Time (days)		285
Getting electricity (rank)	89	✔ Protecting investors (rank)	17	Cost (% of claim)		29.9
Procedures (number)	5	Extent of disclosure index (0-10)	9			
Time (days)	97	Extent of director liability index (0-10)	6	Resolving insolvency (rank)		109
Cost (% of income per capita)	751.3	Ease of shareholder suits index (0-10)	6	Time (years)		3.3
		Strength of investor protection index (0-10)	7.0	Cost (% of estate)		4
				Recovery rate (cents on the dollar)		25.5
		✔ Paying taxes (rank)	42			
		Payments (number per year)	4			
		Time (hours per year)	387			
		Total tax rate (% of profit)	16.5			

GERMANY

Ease of doing business (rank)	19	OECD high income High income		GNI per capita (US$) Population (m)		43,330 81.6
Starting a business (rank)	98	Registering property (rank)	77	Trading across borders (rank)		12
Procedures (number)	9	Procedures (number)	5	Documents to export (number)		4
Time (days)	15	Time (days)	40	Time to export (days)		7
Cost (% of income per capita)	4.6	Cost (% of property value)	5.2	Cost to export (US$ per container)		872
Minimum capital (% of income per capita)	0.0			Documents to import (number)		5
		Getting credit (rank)	24	Time to import (days)		7
Dealing with construction permits (rank)	15	Strength of legal rights index (0-10)	7	Cost to import (US$ per container)		937
Procedures (number)	9	Depth of credit information index (0-6)	6			
Time (days)	97	Public registry coverage (% of adults)	1.3	Enforcing contracts (rank)		8
Cost (% of income per capita)	49.7	Private bureau coverage (% of adults)	100.0	Procedures (number)		30
				Time (days)		394
Getting electricity (rank)	2	Protecting investors (rank)	97	Cost (% of claim)		14.4
Procedures (number)	3	Extent of disclosure index (0-10)	5			
Time (days)	17	Extent of director liability index (0-10)	5	Resolving insolvency (rank)		36
Cost (% of income per capita)	49.9	Ease of shareholder suits index (0-10)	5	Time (years)		1.2
		Strength of investor protection index (0-10)	5.0	Cost (% of estate)		8
				Recovery rate (cents on the dollar)		53.8
		Paying taxes (rank)	89			
		Payments (number per year)	12			
		Time (hours per year)	221			
		Total tax rate (% of profit)	46.7			

GHANA

Ease of doing business (rank)	63	Sub-Saharan Africa Lower middle income		GNI per capita (US$) Population (m)		1,240 24.3
✘ Starting a business (rank)	104	Registering property (rank)	36	Trading across borders (rank)		90
Procedures (number)	7	Procedures (number)	5	Documents to export (number)		6
Time (days)	12	Time (days)	34	Time to export (days)		19
Cost (% of income per capita)	17.3	Cost (% of property value)	0.7	Cost to export (US$ per container)		1,013
Minimum capital (% of income per capita)	5.5			Documents to import (number)		7
		Getting credit (rank)	48	Time to import (days)		29
Dealing with construction permits (rank)	156	Strength of legal rights index (0-10)	8	Cost to import (US$ per container)		1,315
Procedures (number)	16	Depth of credit information index (0-6)	3			
Time (days)	218	Public registry coverage (% of adults)	0.0	Enforcing contracts (rank)		45
Cost (% of income per capita)	560.3	Private bureau coverage (% of adults)	3.3	Procedures (number)		36
				Time (days)		487
Getting electricity (rank)	68	Protecting investors (rank)	46	Cost (% of claim)		23.0
Procedures (number)	4	Extent of disclosure index (0-10)	7			
Time (days)	78	Extent of director liability index (0-10)	5	Resolving insolvency (rank)		106
Cost (% of income per capita)	1,218.5	Ease of shareholder suits index (0-10)	6	Time (years)		1.9
		Strength of investor protection index (0-10)	6.0	Cost (% of estate)		22
				Recovery rate (cents on the dollar)		26.0
		Paying taxes (rank)	90			
		Payments (number per year)	33			
		Time (hours per year)	224			
		Total tax rate (% of profit)	33.6			

Note: Most indicator sets refer to a case scenario in the largest business city of each economy. For more details, see the data notes.

✔ Reform making it easier to do business ✘ Reform making it more difficult to do business

GREECE

Ease of doing business (rank)	100

OECD high income
High income

GNI per capita (US$)	27,240
Population (m)	11.3

✔ Starting a business (rank)	135
Procedures (number)	10
Time (days)	10
Cost (% of income per capita)	20.1
Minimum capital (% of income per capita)	22.8

Registering property (rank)	150
Procedures (number)	11
Time (days)	18
Cost (% of property value)	12.0

Trading across borders (rank)	84
Documents to export (number)	5
Time to export (days)	20
Cost to export (US$ per container)	1,153
Documents to import (number)	6
Time to import (days)	25
Cost to import (US$ per container)	1,265

Dealing with construction permits (rank)	41
Procedures (number)	14
Time (days)	169
Cost (% of income per capita)	3.4

Getting credit (rank)	78
Strength of legal rights index (0-10)	4
Depth of credit information index (0-6)	5
Public registry coverage (% of adults)	0.0
Private bureau coverage (% of adults)	82.4

Enforcing contracts (rank)	90
Procedures (number)	39
Time (days)	819
Cost (% of claim)	14.4

Getting electricity (rank)	77
Procedures (number)	6
Time (days)	77
Cost (% of income per capita)	59.2

Protecting investors (rank)	155
Extent of disclosure index (0-10)	1
Extent of director liability index (0-10)	4
Ease of shareholder suits index (0-10)	5
Strength of investor protection index (0-10)	3.3

Resolving insolvency (rank)	57
Time (years)	2.0
Cost (% of estate)	9
Recovery rate (cents on the dollar)	41.8

✔ Paying taxes (rank)	83
Payments (number per year)	10
Time (hours per year)	224
Total tax rate (% of profit)	46.4

GRENADA

Ease of doing business (rank)	73

Latin America & Caribbean
Upper middle income

GNI per capita (US$)	5,560
Population (m)	0.1

Starting a business (rank)	60
Procedures (number)	6
Time (days)	15
Cost (% of income per capita)	25.1
Minimum capital (% of income per capita)	0.0

Registering property (rank)	154
Procedures (number)	8
Time (days)	47
Cost (% of property value)	7.4

Trading across borders (rank)	40
Documents to export (number)	5
Time to export (days)	10
Cost to export (US$ per container)	876
Documents to import (number)	5
Time to import (days)	12
Cost to import (US$ per container)	2,028

Dealing with construction permits (rank)	11
Procedures (number)	8
Time (days)	123
Cost (% of income per capita)	23.5

Getting credit (rank)	98
Strength of legal rights index (0-10)	8
Depth of credit information index (0-6)	0
Public registry coverage (% of adults)	0.0
Private bureau coverage (% of adults)	0.0

Enforcing contracts (rank)	162
Procedures (number)	47
Time (days)	688
Cost (% of claim)	32.6

Getting electricity (rank)	39
Procedures (number)	5
Time (days)	49
Cost (% of income per capita)	357.8

Protecting investors (rank)	29
Extent of disclosure index (0-10)	4
Extent of director liability index (0-10)	8
Ease of shareholder suits index (0-10)	7
Strength of investor protection index (0-10)	6.3

Resolving insolvency (rank)	119
Time (years)	3.0
Cost (% of estate)	25
Recovery rate (cents on the dollar)	22.7

Paying taxes (rank)	91
Payments (number per year)	30
Time (hours per year)	140
Total tax rate (% of profit)	45.3

GUATEMALA

Ease of doing business (rank)	97

Latin America & Caribbean
Lower middle income

GNI per capita (US$)	2,740
Population (m)	14.4

Starting a business (rank)	165
Procedures (number)	12
Time (days)	37
Cost (% of income per capita)	52.5
Minimum capital (% of income per capita)	22.3

Registering property (rank)	23
Procedures (number)	4
Time (days)	23
Cost (% of property value)	0.9

Trading across borders (rank)	119
Documents to export (number)	10
Time to export (days)	17
Cost to export (US$ per container)	1,127
Documents to import (number)	9
Time to import (days)	17
Cost to import (US$ per container)	1,302

Dealing with construction permits (rank)	151
Procedures (number)	19
Time (days)	165
Cost (% of income per capita)	541.7

Getting credit (rank)	8
Strength of legal rights index (0-10)	8
Depth of credit information index (0-6)	6
Public registry coverage (% of adults)	17.3
Private bureau coverage (% of adults)	8.9

Enforcing contracts (rank)	97
Procedures (number)	31
Time (days)	1,459
Cost (% of claim)	26.5

Getting electricity (rank)	30
Procedures (number)	4
Time (days)	39
Cost (% of income per capita)	624.9

Protecting investors (rank)	133
Extent of disclosure index (0-10)	3
Extent of director liability index (0-10)	3
Ease of shareholder suits index (0-10)	6
Strength of investor protection index (0-10)	4.0

Resolving insolvency (rank)	101
Time (years)	3.0
Cost (% of estate)	15
Recovery rate (cents on the dollar)	27.9

Paying taxes (rank)	124
Payments (number per year)	24
Time (hours per year)	344
Total tax rate (% of profit)	40.9

Note: Most indicator sets refer to a case scenario in the largest business city of each economy. For more details, see the data notes.

✔ Reform making it easier to do business ✘ Reform making it more difficult to do business

GUINEA

Ease of doing business (rank)	179

Sub-Saharan Africa	
Low income	

GNI per capita (US$)	380
Population (m)	10.3

Starting a business (rank)	181
Procedures (number)	12
Time (days)	40
Cost (% of income per capita)	118.0
Minimum capital (% of income per capita)	407.3

Registering property (rank)	152
Procedures (number)	6
Time (days)	59
Cost (% of property value)	14.4

Trading across borders (rank)	130
Documents to export (number)	7
Time to export (days)	35
Cost to export (US$ per container)	855
Documents to import (number)	9
Time to import (days)	32
Cost to import (US$ per container)	1,391

Dealing with construction permits (rank)	174
Procedures (number)	29
Time (days)	287
Cost (% of income per capita)	275.8

✔ Getting credit (rank)	150
Strength of legal rights index (0-10)	6
Depth of credit information index (0-6)	0
Public registry coverage (% of adults)	0.0
Private bureau coverage (% of adults)	0.0

Enforcing contracts (rank)	127
Procedures (number)	49
Time (days)	276
Cost (% of claim)	45.0

Getting electricity (rank)	119
Procedures (number)	5
Time (days)	69
Cost (% of income per capita)	10,421.7

Protecting investors (rank)	174
Extent of disclosure index (0-10)	6
Extent of director liability index (0-10)	1
Ease of shareholder suits index (0-10)	1
Strength of investor protection index (0-10)	2.7

Resolving insolvency (rank)	130
Time (years)	3.8
Cost (% of estate)	8
Recovery rate (cents on the dollar)	19.3

Paying taxes (rank)	176
Payments (number per year)	56
Time (hours per year)	416
Total tax rate (% of profit)	54.3

GUINEA-BISSAU

Ease of doing business (rank)	176

Sub-Saharan Africa	
Low income	

GNI per capita (US$)	540
Population (m)	1.6

✔ Starting a business (rank)	149
Procedures (number)	9
Time (days)	9
Cost (% of income per capita)	49.8
Minimum capital (% of income per capita)	398.7

Registering property (rank)	179
Procedures (number)	8
Time (days)	210
Cost (% of property value)	10.6

Trading across borders (rank)	117
Documents to export (number)	6
Time to export (days)	23
Cost to export (US$ per container)	1,448
Documents to import (number)	6
Time to import (days)	22
Cost to import (US$ per container)	2,006

Dealing with construction permits (rank)	107
Procedures (number)	12
Time (days)	170
Cost (% of income per capita)	1,032.7

✔ Getting credit (rank)	126
Strength of legal rights index (0-10)	6
Depth of credit information index (0-6)	1
Public registry coverage (% of adults)	1.0
Private bureau coverage (% of adults)	0.0

Enforcing contracts (rank)	142
Procedures (number)	40
Time (days)	1,715
Cost (% of claim)	25.0

Getting electricity (rank)	180
Procedures (number)	7
Time (days)	455
Cost (% of income per capita)	2,049.5

Protecting investors (rank)	133
Extent of disclosure index (0-10)	6
Extent of director liability index (0-10)	1
Ease of shareholder suits index (0-10)	5
Strength of investor protection index (0-10)	4.0

Resolving insolvency (rank)	183
Time (years)	NO PRACTICE
Cost (% of estate)	NO PRACTICE
Recovery rate (cents on the dollar)	0.0

Paying taxes (rank)	137
Payments (number per year)	46
Time (hours per year)	208
Total tax rate (% of profit)	45.9

GUYANA

Ease of doing business (rank)	114

Latin America & Caribbean	
Lower middle income	

GNI per capita (US$)	3,270
Population (m)	0.8

✔ Starting a business (rank)	87
Procedures (number)	8
Time (days)	26
Cost (% of income per capita)	14.6
Minimum capital (% of income per capita)	0.0

✘ Registering property (rank)	104
Procedures (number)	6
Time (days)	75
Cost (% of property value)	4.6

Trading across borders (rank)	82
Documents to export (number)	7
Time to export (days)	19
Cost to export (US$ per container)	730
Documents to import (number)	8
Time to import (days)	22
Cost to import (US$ per container)	745

Dealing with construction permits (rank)	28
Procedures (number)	8
Time (days)	195
Cost (% of income per capita)	17.5

Getting credit (rank)	166
Strength of legal rights index (0-10)	4
Depth of credit information index (0-6)	0
Public registry coverage (% of adults)	0.0
Private bureau coverage (% of adults)	0.0

Enforcing contracts (rank)	73
Procedures (number)	36
Time (days)	581
Cost (% of claim)	25.2

✘ Getting electricity (rank)	144
Procedures (number)	7
Time (days)	109
Cost (% of income per capita)	518.7

Protecting investors (rank)	79
Extent of disclosure index (0-10)	5
Extent of director liability index (0-10)	5
Ease of shareholder suits index (0-10)	6
Strength of investor protection index (0-10)	5.3

Resolving insolvency (rank)	138
Time (years)	3.0
Cost (% of estate)	29
Recovery rate (cents on the dollar)	17.6

Paying taxes (rank)	115
Payments (number per year)	35
Time (hours per year)	263
Total tax rate (% of profit)	36.1

Note: Most indicator sets refer to a case scenario in the largest business city of each economy. For more details, see the data notes.

✔ Reform making it easier to do business   ✘ Reform making it more difficult to do business

HAITI

Ease of doing business (rank)	174	Latin America & Caribbean / Low income		GNI per capita (US$)	650	
				Population (m)	10.0	
Starting a business (rank)	180	**Registering property** (rank)	131	**Trading across borders** (rank)	145	
Procedures (number)	12	Procedures (number)	5	Documents to export (number)	8	
Time (days)	105	Time (days)	301	Time to export (days)	33	
Cost (% of income per capita)	314.2	Cost (% of property value)	6.6	Cost to export (US$ per container)	1,185	
Minimum capital (% of income per capita)	23.2			Documents to import (number)	10	
		Getting credit (rank)	159	Time to import (days)	31	
✘ **Dealing with construction permits** (rank)	139	Strength of legal rights index (0-10)	3	Cost to import (US$ per container)	1,545	
Procedures (number)	9	Depth of credit information index (0-6)	2			
Time (days)	1,129	Public registry coverage (% of adults)	0.7	**Enforcing contracts** (rank)	96	
Cost (% of income per capita)	764.5	Private bureau coverage (% of adults)	0.0	Procedures (number)	35	
				Time (days)	530	
Getting electricity (rank)	75	**Protecting investors** (rank)	166	Cost (% of claim)	42.6	
Procedures (number)	4	Extent of disclosure index (0-10)	2			
Time (days)	66	Extent of director liability index (0-10)	3	**Resolving insolvency** (rank)	162	
Cost (% of income per capita)	4,032.8	Ease of shareholder suits index (0-10)	4	Time (years)	5.7	
		Strength of investor protection index (0-10)	3.0	Cost (% of estate)	30	
				Recovery rate (cents on the dollar)	5.8	
		Paying taxes (rank)	118			
		Payments (number per year)	46			
		Time (hours per year)	184			
		Total tax rate (% of profit)	40.8			

HONDURAS

Ease of doing business (rank)	128	Latin America & Caribbean / Lower middle income		GNI per capita (US$)	1,880
				Population (m)	7.6
Starting a business (rank)	150	**Registering property** (rank)	94	✔ **Trading across borders** (rank)	103
Procedures (number)	13	Procedures (number)	7	Documents to export (number)	6
Time (days)	14	Time (days)	23	Time to export (days)	18
Cost (% of income per capita)	46.7	Cost (% of property value)	5.7	Cost to export (US$ per container)	1,242
Minimum capital (% of income per capita)	17.0			Documents to import (number)	8
		✔ **Getting credit** (rank)	8	Time to import (days)	22
Dealing with construction permits (rank)	70	Strength of legal rights index (0-10)	8	Cost to import (US$ per container)	1,420
Procedures (number)	14	Depth of credit information index (0-6)	6		
Time (days)	94	Public registry coverage (% of adults)	16.3	✘ **Enforcing contracts** (rank)	177
Cost (% of income per capita)	309.8	Private bureau coverage (% of adults)	31.2	Procedures (number)	47
				Time (days)	920
Getting electricity (rank)	114	**Protecting investors** (rank)	166	Cost (% of claim)	35.2
Procedures (number)	8	Extent of disclosure index (0-10)	0		
Time (days)	33	Extent of director liability index (0-10)	5	**Resolving insolvency** (rank)	131
Cost (% of income per capita)	1,082.2	Ease of shareholder suits index (0-10)	4	Time (years)	3.8
		Strength of investor protection index (0-10)	3.0	Cost (% of estate)	15
				Recovery rate (cents on the dollar)	19.2
		✘ **Paying taxes** (rank)	140		
		Payments (number per year)	47		
		Time (hours per year)	224		
		Total tax rate (% of profit)	44.0		

HONG KONG SAR, CHINA

Ease of doing business (rank)	2	East Asia & Pacific / High income		GNI per capita (US$)	32,900
				Population (m)	7.0
✔ **Starting a business** (rank)	5	**Registering property** (rank)	57	**Trading across borders** (rank)	2
Procedures (number)	3	Procedures (number)	5	Documents to export (number)	4
Time (days)	3	Time (days)	36	Time to export (days)	5
Cost (% of income per capita)	1.9	Cost (% of property value)	4.1	Cost to export (US$ per container)	575
Minimum capital (% of income per capita)	0.0			Documents to import (number)	4
		Getting credit (rank)	4	Time to import (days)	5
Dealing with construction permits (rank)	1	Strength of legal rights index (0-10)	10	Cost to import (US$ per container)	565
Procedures (number)	6	Depth of credit information index (0-6)	5		
Time (days)	67	Public registry coverage (% of adults)	0.0	**Enforcing contracts** (rank)	5
Cost (% of income per capita)	17.8	Private bureau coverage (% of adults)	86.3	Procedures (number)	26
				Time (days)	280
✔ **Getting electricity** (rank)	4	**Protecting investors** (rank)	3	Cost (% of claim)	21.2
Procedures (number)	4	Extent of disclosure index (0-10)	10		
Time (days)	43	Extent of director liability index (0-10)	8	**Resolving insolvency** (rank)	16
Cost (% of income per capita)	1.7	Ease of shareholder suits index (0-10)	9	Time (years)	1.1
		Strength of investor protection index (0-10)	9.0	Cost (% of estate)	9
				Recovery rate (cents on the dollar)	81.2
		Paying taxes (rank)	3		
		Payments (number per year)	3		
		Time (hours per year)	80		
		Total tax rate (% of profit)	23.0		

Note: Most indicator sets refer to a case scenario in the largest business city of each economy. For more details, see the data notes.

✔ Reform making it easier to do business ✘ Reform making it more difficult to do business

HUNGARY

Ease of doing business (rank)	51	OECD high income High income		GNI per capita (US$) Population (m)		12,990 10.0
Starting a business (rank)	39	**Registering property** (rank)	43	**Trading across borders** (rank)		74
Procedures (number)	4	Procedures (number)	4	Documents to export (number)		6
Time (days)	4	Time (days)	17	Time to export (days)		16
Cost (% of income per capita)	7.6	Cost (% of property value)	5.0	Cost to export (US$ per container)		1,015
Minimum capital (% of income per capita)	9.7			Documents to import (number)		7
		✘ **Getting credit** (rank)	48	Time to import (days)		18
Dealing with construction permits (rank)	55	Strength of legal rights index (0-10)	7	Cost to import (US$ per container)		1,085
Procedures (number)	29	Depth of credit information index (0-6)	4			
Time (days)	102	Public registry coverage (% of adults)	0.0	**Enforcing contracts** (rank)		19
Cost (% of income per capita)	5.8	Private bureau coverage (% of adults)	16.1	Procedures (number)		35
				Time (days)		395
Getting electricity (rank)	103	**Protecting investors** (rank)	122	Cost (% of claim)		15.0
Procedures (number)	5	Extent of disclosure index (0-10)	2			
Time (days)	252	Extent of director liability index (0-10)	4	**Resolving insolvency** (rank)		66
Cost (% of income per capita)	120.3	Ease of shareholder suits index (0-10)	7	Time (years)		2.0
		Strength of investor protection index (0-10)	4.3	Cost (% of estate)		15
				Recovery rate (cents on the dollar)		39.2
		✘ **Paying taxes** (rank)	117			
		Payments (number per year)	13			
		Time (hours per year)	277			
		Total tax rate (% of profit)	52.4			

ICELAND

Ease of doing business (rank)	9	OECD high income High income		GNI per capita (US$) Population (m)		33,870 0.3
Starting a business (rank)	37	**Registering property** (rank)	11	**Trading across borders** (rank)		81
Procedures (number)	5	Procedures (number)	3	Documents to export (number)		5
Time (days)	5	Time (days)	4	Time to export (days)		19
Cost (% of income per capita)	3.3	Cost (% of property value)	2.4	Cost to export (US$ per container)		1,532
Minimum capital (% of income per capita)	12.6			Documents to import (number)		5
		Getting credit (rank)	40	Time to import (days)		14
Dealing with construction permits (rank)	34	Strength of legal rights index (0-10)	7	Cost to import (US$ per container)		1,674
Procedures (number)	17	Depth of credit information index (0-6)	5			
Time (days)	74	Public registry coverage (% of adults)	0.0	**Enforcing contracts** (rank)		3
Cost (% of income per capita)	20.6	Private bureau coverage (% of adults)	100.0	Procedures (number)		27
				Time (days)		417
Getting electricity (rank)	1	✔ **Protecting investors** (rank)	46	Cost (% of claim)		8.2
Procedures (number)	4	Extent of disclosure index (0-10)	7			
Time (days)	22	Extent of director liability index (0-10)	5	**Resolving insolvency** (rank)		11
Cost (% of income per capita)	13.6	Ease of shareholder suits index (0-10)	6	Time (years)		1.0
		Strength of investor protection index (0-10)	6.0	Cost (% of estate)		4
				Recovery rate (cents on the dollar)		84.5
		✔ **Paying taxes** (rank)	35			
		Payments (number per year)	29			
		Time (hours per year)	140			
		Total tax rate (% of profit)	31.8			

INDIA

Ease of doing business (rank)	132	South Asia Lower middle income		GNI per capita (US$) Population (m)		1,340 1,170.9
Starting a business (rank)	166	**Registering property** (rank)	97	**Trading across borders** (rank)		109
Procedures (number)	12	Procedures (number)	5	Documents to export (number)		8
Time (days)	29	Time (days)	44	Time to export (days)		16
Cost (% of income per capita)	46.8	Cost (% of property value)	7.3	Cost to export (US$ per container)		1,095
Minimum capital (% of income per capita)	149.6			Documents to import (number)		9
		Getting credit (rank)	40	Time to import (days)		20
Dealing with construction permits (rank)	181	Strength of legal rights index (0-10)	8	Cost to import (US$ per container)		1,070
Procedures (number)	34	Depth of credit information index (0-6)	4			
Time (days)	227	Public registry coverage (% of adults)	0.0	**Enforcing contracts** (rank)		182
Cost (% of income per capita)	1,631.4	Private bureau coverage (% of adults)	15.1	Procedures (number)		46
				Time (days)		1,420
Getting electricity (rank)	98	**Protecting investors** (rank)	46	Cost (% of claim)		39.6
Procedures (number)	7	Extent of disclosure index (0-10)	7			
Time (days)	67	Extent of director liability index (0-10)	4	**Resolving insolvency** (rank)		128
Cost (% of income per capita)	216.2	Ease of shareholder suits index (0-10)	7	Time (years)		7.0
		Strength of investor protection index (0-10)	6.0	Cost (% of estate)		9
				Recovery rate (cents on the dollar)		20.1
		✔ **Paying taxes** (rank)	147			
		Payments (number per year)	33			
		Time (hours per year)	254			
		Total tax rate (% of profit)	61.8			

Note: Most indicator sets refer to a case scenario in the largest business city of each economy. For more details, see the data notes.

✔ Reform making it easier to do business ✘ Reform making it more difficult to do business

INDONESIA

Ease of doing business (rank)	129	East Asia & Pacific Lower middle income		GNI per capita (US$) Population (m)		2,580 232.5

✔ **Starting a business** (rank)	155	**Registering property** (rank)	99	**Trading across borders** (rank)		39
Procedures (number)	8	Procedures (number)	6	Documents to export (number)		4
Time (days)	45	Time (days)	22	Time to export (days)		17
Cost (% of income per capita)	17.9	Cost (% of property value)	10.8	Cost to export (US$ per container)		644
Minimum capital (% of income per capita)	46.6			Documents to import (number)		7
		Getting credit (rank)	126	Time to import (days)		27
Dealing with construction permits (rank)	71	Strength of legal rights index (0-10)	3	Cost to import (US$ per container)		660
Procedures (number)	13	Depth of credit information index (0-6)	4			
Time (days)	158	Public registry coverage (% of adults)	31.8	**Enforcing contracts** (rank)		156
Cost (% of income per capita)	105.3	Private bureau coverage (% of adults)	0.0	Procedures (number)		40
				Time (days)		570
✘ **Getting electricity** (rank)	161	**Protecting investors** (rank)	46	Cost (% of claim)		122.7
Procedures (number)	7	Extent of disclosure index (0-10)	10			
Time (days)	108	Extent of director liability index (0-10)	5	**Resolving insolvency** (rank)		146
Cost (% of income per capita)	1,379.0	Ease of shareholder suits index (0-10)	3	Time (years)		5.5
		Strength of investor protection index (0-10)	6.0	Cost (% of estate)		18
				Recovery rate (cents on the dollar)		13.8
		Paying taxes (rank)	131			
		Payments (number per year)	51			
		Time (hours per year)	266			
		Total tax rate (% of profit)	34.5			

IRAN, ISLAMIC REP.

Ease of doing business (rank)	144	Middle East & North Africa Upper middle income		GNI per capita (US$) Population (m)		4,741 73.9

Starting a business (rank)	53	**Registering property** (rank)	163	**Trading across borders** (rank)		138
Procedures (number)	6	Procedures (number)	9	Documents to export (number)		7
Time (days)	8	Time (days)	36	Time to export (days)		25
Cost (% of income per capita)	3.8	Cost (% of property value)	10.5	Cost to export (US$ per container)		1,275
Minimum capital (% of income per capita)	0.7			Documents to import (number)		8
		Getting credit (rank)	98	Time to import (days)		32
Dealing with construction permits (rank)	164	Strength of legal rights index (0-10)	4	Cost to import (US$ per container)		1,885
Procedures (number)	16	Depth of credit information index (0-6)	4			
Time (days)	320	Public registry coverage (% of adults)	26.5	**Enforcing contracts** (rank)		50
Cost (% of income per capita)	355.6	Private bureau coverage (% of adults)	24.4	Procedures (number)		39
				Time (days)		505
Getting electricity (rank)	162	**Protecting investors** (rank)	166	Cost (% of claim)		17.0
Procedures (number)	7	Extent of disclosure index (0-10)	5			
Time (days)	140	Extent of director liability index (0-10)	4	**Resolving insolvency** (rank)		118
Cost (% of income per capita)	1,058.5	Ease of shareholder suits index (0-10)	0	Time (years)		4.5
		Strength of investor protection index (0-10)	3.0	Cost (% of estate)		9
				Recovery rate (cents on the dollar)		23.1
		Paying taxes (rank)	126			
		Payments (number per year)	20			
		Time (hours per year)	344			
		Total tax rate (% of profit)	44.1			

IRAQ

Ease of doing business (rank)	164	Middle East & North Africa Lower middle income		GNI per capita (US$) Population (m)		2,320 32.3

✘ **Starting a business** (rank)	176	**Registering property** (rank)	98	**Trading across borders** (rank)		180
Procedures (number)	11	Procedures (number)	5	Documents to export (number)		10
Time (days)	77	Time (days)	51	Time to export (days)		80
Cost (% of income per capita)	115.7	Cost (% of property value)	6.9	Cost to export (US$ per container)		3,550
Minimum capital (% of income per capita)	35.5			Documents to import (number)		10
		Getting credit (rank)	174	Time to import (days)		83
Dealing with construction permits (rank)	120	Strength of legal rights index (0-10)	3	Cost to import (US$ per container)		3,650
Procedures (number)	13	Depth of credit information index (0-6)	0			
Time (days)	187	Public registry coverage (% of adults)	0.0	**Enforcing contracts** (rank)		140
Cost (% of income per capita)	469.8	Private bureau coverage (% of adults)	0.0	Procedures (number)		51
				Time (days)		520
Getting electricity (rank)	46	**Protecting investors** (rank)	122	Cost (% of claim)		28.1
Procedures (number)	5	Extent of disclosure index (0-10)	4			
Time (days)	47	Extent of director liability index (0-10)	5	**Resolving insolvency** (rank)		183
Cost (% of income per capita)	609.9	Ease of shareholder suits index (0-10)	4	Time (years)		NO PRACTICE
		Strength of investor protection index (0-10)	4.3	Cost (% of estate)		NO PRACTICE
				Recovery rate (cents on the dollar)		0.0
		Paying taxes (rank)	49			
		Payments (number per year)	13			
		Time (hours per year)	312			
		Total tax rate (% of profit)	28.4			

Note: Most indicator sets refer to a case scenario in the largest business city of each economy. For more details, see the data notes.

✔ Reform making it easier to do business ✗ Reform making it more difficult to do business

IRELAND

Ease of doing business (rank)	10	OECD high income		GNI per capita (US$)	40,990	
		High income		Population (m)	4.5	
Starting a business (rank)	13	**Registering property** (rank)	81	**Trading across borders** (rank)	21	
Procedures (number)	4	Procedures (number)	5	Documents to export (number)	4	
Time (days)	13	Time (days)	38	Time to export (days)	7	
Cost (% of income per capita)	0.4	Cost (% of property value)	6.5	Cost to export (US$ per container)	1,109	
Minimum capital (% of income per capita)	0.0			Documents to import (number)	4	
		Getting credit (rank)	8	Time to import (days)	12	
		Strength of legal rights index (0-10)	9	Cost to import (US$ per container)	1,121	
Dealing with construction permits (rank)	27	Depth of credit information index (0-6)	5			
Procedures (number)	10	Public registry coverage (% of adults)	0.0	**Enforcing contracts** (rank)	62	
Time (days)	141	Private bureau coverage (% of adults)	100.0	Procedures (number)	21	
Cost (% of income per capita)	33.1			Time (days)	650	
		Protecting investors (rank)	5	Cost (% of claim)	26.9	
Getting electricity (rank)	90	Extent of disclosure index (0-10)	10			
Procedures (number)	5	Extent of director liability index (0-10)	6	**Resolving insolvency** (rank)	10	
Time (days)	205	Ease of shareholder suits index (0-10)	9	Time (years)	0.4	
Cost (% of income per capita)	91.1	Strength of investor protection index (0-10)	8.3	Cost (% of estate)	9	
				Recovery rate (cents on the dollar)	86.9	
		Paying taxes (rank)	5			
		Payments (number per year)	8			
		Time (hours per year)	76			
		Total tax rate (% of profit)	26.3			

ISRAEL

Ease of doing business (rank)	34	OECD high income		GNI per capita (US$)	27,340	
		High income		Population (m)	7.6	
Starting a business (rank)	43	**Registering property** (rank)	147	✔ **Trading across borders** (rank)	10	
Procedures (number)	5	Procedures (number)	7	Documents to export (number)	5	
Time (days)	34	Time (days)	144	Time to export (days)	10	
Cost (% of income per capita)	4.4	Cost (% of property value)	5.0	Cost to export (US$ per container)	610	
Minimum capital (% of income per capita)	0.0			Documents to import (number)	4	
		Getting credit (rank)	8	Time to import (days)	10	
		Strength of legal rights index (0-10)	9	Cost to import (US$ per container)	545	
Dealing with construction permits (rank)	137	Depth of credit information index (0-6)	5			
Procedures (number)	19	Public registry coverage (% of adults)	0.0	**Enforcing contracts** (rank)	94	
Time (days)	212	Private bureau coverage (% of adults)	100.0	Procedures (number)	35	
Cost (% of income per capita)	90.8			Time (days)	890	
		Protecting investors (rank)	5	Cost (% of claim)	25.3	
Getting electricity (rank)	93	Extent of disclosure index (0-10)	7			
Procedures (number)	6	Extent of director liability index (0-10)	9	✔ **Resolving insolvency** (rank)	45	
Time (days)	132	Ease of shareholder suits index (0-10)	9	Time (years)	4.0	
Cost (% of income per capita)	12.2	Strength of investor protection index (0-10)	8.3	Cost (% of estate)	23	
				Recovery rate (cents on the dollar)	47.2	
		Paying taxes (rank)	59			
		Payments (number per year)	33			
		Time (hours per year)	235			
		Total tax rate (% of profit)	31.2			

ITALY

Ease of doing business (rank)	87	OECD high income		GNI per capita (US$)	35,090	
		High income		Population (m)	60.6	
Starting a business (rank)	77	**Registering property** (rank)	84	**Trading across borders** (rank)	63	
Procedures (number)	6	Procedures (number)	7	Documents to export (number)	4	
Time (days)	6	Time (days)	27	Time to export (days)	20	
Cost (% of income per capita)	18.2	Cost (% of property value)	4.5	Cost to export (US$ per container)	1,245	
Minimum capital (% of income per capita)	9.9			Documents to import (number)	4	
		Getting credit (rank)	98	Time to import (days)	18	
		Strength of legal rights index (0-10)	3	Cost to import (US$ per container)	1,245	
Dealing with construction permits (rank)	96	Depth of credit information index (0-6)	5			
Procedures (number)	11	Public registry coverage (% of adults)	23.0	**Enforcing contracts** (rank)	158	
Time (days)	258	Private bureau coverage (% of adults)	100.0	Procedures (number)	41	
Cost (% of income per capita)	138.1			Time (days)	1,210	
		Protecting investors (rank)	65	Cost (% of claim)	29.9	
Getting electricity (rank)	109	Extent of disclosure index (0-10)	7			
Procedures (number)	5	Extent of director liability index (0-10)	4	✔ **Resolving insolvency** (rank)	30	
Time (days)	192	Ease of shareholder suits index (0-10)	6	Time (years)	1.8	
Cost (% of income per capita)	327.2	Strength of investor protection index (0-10)	5.7	Cost (% of estate)	22	
				Recovery rate (cents on the dollar)	61.1	
		Paying taxes (rank)	134			
		Payments (number per year)	15			
		Time (hours per year)	285			
		Total tax rate (% of profit)	68.5			

Note: Most indicator sets refer to a case scenario in the largest business city of each economy. For more details, see the data notes.

✔ Reform making it easier to do business ✘ Reform making it more difficult to do business

JAMAICA

		Latin America & Caribbean		GNI per capita (US$)		4,750
Ease of doing business (rank)	88	Upper middle income		Population (m)		2.7
Starting a business (rank)	23	**Registering property** (rank)	103	**Trading across borders** (rank)		97
Procedures (number)	6	Procedures (number)	6	Documents to export (number)		6
Time (days)	7	Time (days)	37	Time to export (days)		21
Cost (% of income per capita)	7.2	Cost (% of property value)	7.5	Cost to export (US$ per container)		1,410
Minimum capital (% of income per capita)	0.0			Documents to import (number)		6
		Getting credit (rank)	98	Time to import (days)		22
Dealing with construction permits (rank)	49	Strength of legal rights index (0-10)	8	Cost to import (US$ per container)		1,420
Procedures (number)	8	Depth of credit information index (0-6)	0			
Time (days)	145	Public registry coverage (% of adults)	0.0	**Enforcing contracts** (rank)		126
Cost (% of income per capita)	227.5	Private bureau coverage (% of adults)	0.0	Procedures (number)		35
				Time (days)		655
Getting electricity (rank)	112	**Protecting investors** (rank)	79	Cost (% of claim)		45.6
Procedures (number)	6	Extent of disclosure index (0-10)	4			
Time (days)	96	Extent of director liability index (0-10)	8	**Resolving insolvency** (rank)		26
Cost (% of income per capita)	354.6	Ease of shareholder suits index (0-10)	4	Time (years)		1.1
		Strength of investor protection index (0-10)	5.3	Cost (% of estate)		18
				Recovery rate (cents on the dollar)		65.3
		Paying taxes (rank)	172			
		Payments (number per year)	72			
		Time (hours per year)	414			
		Total tax rate (% of profit)	45.6			

JAPAN

		OECD high income		GNI per capita (US$)		42,150
Ease of doing business (rank)	20	High income		Population (m)		127.4
Starting a business (rank)	107	**Registering property** (rank)	58	**Trading across borders** (rank)		16
Procedures (number)	8	Procedures (number)	6	Documents to export (number)		3
Time (days)	23	Time (days)	14	Time to export (days)		10
Cost (% of income per capita)	7.5	Cost (% of property value)	5.7	Cost to export (US$ per container)		880
Minimum capital (% of income per capita)	0.0			Documents to import (number)		5
		Getting credit (rank)	24	Time to import (days)		11
✘ **Dealing with construction permits** (rank)	63	Strength of legal rights index (0-10)	7	Cost to import (US$ per container)		970
Procedures (number)	14	Depth of credit information index (0-6)	6			
Time (days)	193	Public registry coverage (% of adults)	0.0	**Enforcing contracts** (rank)		34
Cost (% of income per capita)	27.9	Private bureau coverage (% of adults)	99.0	Procedures (number)		30
				Time (days)		360
Getting electricity (rank)	26	**Protecting investors** (rank)	17	Cost (% of claim)		32.2
Procedures (number)	3	Extent of disclosure index (0-10)	7			
Time (days)	117	Extent of director liability index (0-10)	6	**Resolving insolvency** (rank)		1
Cost (% of income per capita)	0.0	Ease of shareholder suits index (0-10)	8	Time (years)		0.6
		Strength of investor protection index (0-10)	7.0	Cost (% of estate)		4
				Recovery rate (cents on the dollar)		92.7
		Paying taxes (rank)	120			
		Payments (number per year)	14			
		Time (hours per year)	330			
		Total tax rate (% of profit)	49.1			

JORDAN

		Middle East & North Africa		GNI per capita (US$)		4,350
Ease of doing business (rank)	96	Upper middle income		Population (m)		6.1
✔ **Starting a business** (rank)	95	**Registering property** (rank)	101	✔ **Trading across borders** (rank)		58
Procedures (number)	7	Procedures (number)	7	Documents to export (number)		6
Time (days)	12	Time (days)	21	Time to export (days)		13
Cost (% of income per capita)	13.9	Cost (% of property value)	7.5	Cost to export (US$ per container)		825
Minimum capital (% of income per capita)	0.0			Documents to import (number)		7
		Getting credit (rank)	150	Time to import (days)		15
Dealing with construction permits (rank)	93	Strength of legal rights index (0-10)	4	Cost to import (US$ per container)		1,335
Procedures (number)	17	Depth of credit information index (0-6)	2			
Time (days)	70	Public registry coverage (% of adults)	1.6	**Enforcing contracts** (rank)		130
Cost (% of income per capita)	534.2	Private bureau coverage (% of adults)	0.0	Procedures (number)		38
				Time (days)		689
Getting electricity (rank)	36	**Protecting investors** (rank)	122	Cost (% of claim)		31.2
Procedures (number)	5	Extent of disclosure index (0-10)	5			
Time (days)	43	Extent of director liability index (0-10)	4	**Resolving insolvency** (rank)		104
Cost (% of income per capita)	274.2	Ease of shareholder suits index (0-10)	4	Time (years)		4.3
		Strength of investor protection index (0-10)	4.3	Cost (% of estate)		9
				Recovery rate (cents on the dollar)		27.2
		Paying taxes (rank)	21			
		Payments (number per year)	25			
		Time (hours per year)	116			
		Total tax rate (% of profit)	27.7			

Note: Most indicator sets refer to a case scenario in the largest business city of each economy. For more details, see the data notes.

✔ Reform making it easier to do business ✘ Reform making it more difficult to do business

KAZAKHSTAN

Ease of doing business (rank)	47	Eastern Europe & Central Asia Upper middle income		GNI per capita (US$) Population (m)		7,440 16.3
Starting a business (rank)	57	**Registering property** (rank)	29	**Trading across borders** (rank)		176
Procedures (number)	6	Procedures (number)	4	Documents to export (number)		9
Time (days)	19	Time (days)	40	Time to export (days)		76
Cost (% of income per capita)	0.8	Cost (% of property value)	0.1	Cost to export (US$ per container)		3,130
Minimum capital (% of income per capita)	0.0			Documents to import (number)		12
		Getting credit (rank)	78	Time to import (days)		62
Dealing with construction permits (rank)	147	Strength of legal rights index (0-10)	4	Cost to import (US$ per container)		3,290
Procedures (number)	32	Depth of credit information index (0-6)	5			
Time (days)	189	Public registry coverage (% of adults)	0.0	**Enforcing contracts** (rank)		27
Cost (% of income per capita)	93.2	Private bureau coverage (% of adults)	37.6	Procedures (number)		36
				Time (days)		390
Getting electricity (rank)	86	✔ **Protecting investors** (rank)	10	Cost (% of claim)		22.0
Procedures (number)	6	Extent of disclosure index (0-10)	9			
Time (days)	88	Extent of director liability index (0-10)	6	**Resolving insolvency** (rank)		54
Cost (% of income per capita)	88.4	Ease of shareholder suits index (0-10)	9	Time (years)		1.5
		Strength of investor protection index (0-10)	8.0	Cost (% of estate)		15
				Recovery rate (cents on the dollar)		42.7
		Paying taxes (rank)	13			
		Payments (number per year)	7			
		Time (hours per year)	188			
		Total tax rate (% of profit)	28.6			

KENYA

Ease of doing business (rank)	109	Sub-Saharan Africa Low income		GNI per capita (US$) Population (m)		780 40.9
Starting a business (rank)	132	**Registering property** (rank)	133	**Trading across borders** (rank)		141
Procedures (number)	11	Procedures (number)	8	Documents to export (number)		8
Time (days)	33	Time (days)	64	Time to export (days)		26
Cost (% of income per capita)	37.8	Cost (% of property value)	4.3	Cost to export (US$ per container)		2,055
Minimum capital (% of income per capita)	0.0			Documents to import (number)		7
		Getting credit (rank)	8	Time to import (days)		24
Dealing with construction permits (rank)	37	Strength of legal rights index (0-10)	10	Cost to import (US$ per container)		2,190
Procedures (number)	8	Depth of credit information index (0-6)	4			
Time (days)	125	Public registry coverage (% of adults)	0.0	✔ **Enforcing contracts** (rank)		127
Cost (% of income per capita)	160.9	Private bureau coverage (% of adults)	4.5	Procedures (number)		40
				Time (days)		465
Getting electricity (rank)	115	**Protecting investors** (rank)	97	Cost (% of claim)		47.2
Procedures (number)	4	Extent of disclosure index (0-10)	3			
Time (days)	163	Extent of director liability index (0-10)	2	**Resolving insolvency** (rank)		92
Cost (% of income per capita)	1,419.2	Ease of shareholder suits index (0-10)	10	Time (years)		4.5
		Strength of investor protection index (0-10)	5.0	Cost (% of estate)		22
				Recovery rate (cents on the dollar)		30.9
		Paying taxes (rank)	166			
		Payments (number per year)	41			
		Time (hours per year)	393			
		Total tax rate (% of profit)	49.6			

KIRIBATI

Ease of doing business (rank)	115	East Asia & Pacific Lower middle income		GNI per capita (US$) Population (m)		2,010 0.1
Starting a business (rank)	141	**Registering property** (rank)	69	**Trading across borders** (rank)		85
Procedures (number)	7	Procedures (number)	5	Documents to export (number)		6
Time (days)	31	Time (days)	513	Time to export (days)		21
Cost (% of income per capita)	22.2	Cost (% of property value)	0.0	Cost to export (US$ per container)		1,120
Minimum capital (% of income per capita)	21.1			Documents to import (number)		7
		Getting credit (rank)	159	Time to import (days)		21
Dealing with construction permits (rank)	106	Strength of legal rights index (0-10)	5	Cost to import (US$ per container)		1,120
Procedures (number)	16	Depth of credit information index (0-6)	0			
Time (days)	170	Public registry coverage (% of adults)	0.0	**Enforcing contracts** (rank)		75
Cost (% of income per capita)	163.7	Private bureau coverage (% of adults)	0.0	Procedures (number)		32
				Time (days)		660
Getting electricity (rank)	159	**Protecting investors** (rank)	46	Cost (% of claim)		25.8
Procedures (number)	6	Extent of disclosure index (0-10)	6			
Time (days)	97	Extent of director liability index (0-10)	5	**Resolving insolvency** (rank)		183
Cost (% of income per capita)	5,162.7	Ease of shareholder suits index (0-10)	7	Time (years)		NO PRACTICE
		Strength of investor protection index (0-10)	6.0	Cost (% of estate)		NO PRACTICE
				Recovery rate (cents on the dollar)		0.0
		Paying taxes (rank)	6			
		Payments (number per year)	7			
		Time (hours per year)	120			
		Total tax rate (% of profit)	31.8			

Note: Most indicator sets refer to a case scenario in the largest business city of each economy. For more details, see the data notes.

✔ Reform making it easier to do business ✘ Reform making it more difficult to do business

KOREA, REP.

Ease of doing business (rank)	8	OECD high income / High income		GNI per capita (US$)	19,890
				Population (m)	48.9

✔ **Starting a business** (rank)	24
Procedures (number)	5
Time (days)	7
Cost (% of income per capita)	14.6
Minimum capital (% of income per capita)	0.0
Dealing with construction permits (rank)	26
Procedures (number)	12
Time (days)	30
Cost (% of income per capita)	79.5
Getting electricity (rank)	11
Procedures (number)	4
Time (days)	49
Cost (% of income per capita)	38.6

Registering property (rank)	71
Procedures (number)	7
Time (days)	11
Cost (% of property value)	5.1
Getting credit (rank)	8
Strength of legal rights index (0-10)	8
Depth of credit information index (0-6)	6
Public registry coverage (% of adults)	0.0
Private bureau coverage (% of adults)	100.0
Protecting investors (rank)	79
Extent of disclosure index (0-10)	7
Extent of director liability index (0-10)	2
Ease of shareholder suits index (0-10)	7
Strength of investor protection index (0-10)	5.3
✔ **Paying taxes** (rank)	38
Payments (number per year)	12
Time (hours per year)	225
Total tax rate (% of profit)	29.7

Trading across borders (rank)	4
Documents to export (number)	3
Time to export (days)	7
Cost to export (US$ per container)	680
Documents to import (number)	3
Time to import (days)	7
Cost to import (US$ per container)	695
✔ **Enforcing contracts** (rank)	2
Procedures (number)	33
Time (days)	230
Cost (% of claim)	10.3
Resolving insolvency (rank)	13
Time (years)	1.5
Cost (% of estate)	4
Recovery rate (cents on the dollar)	82.3

KOSOVO

Ease of doing business (rank)	117	Eastern Europe & Central Asia / Lower middle income		GNI per capita (US$)	3,300
				Population (m)	1.8

Starting a business (rank)	168
Procedures (number)	10
Time (days)	58
Cost (% of income per capita)	26.7
Minimum capital (% of income per capita)	104.6
Dealing with construction permits (rank)	171
Procedures (number)	17
Time (days)	301
Cost (% of income per capita)	775.8
Getting electricity (rank)	124
Procedures (number)	7
Time (days)	60
Cost (% of income per capita)	1,016.8

Registering property (rank)	73
Procedures (number)	8
Time (days)	33
Cost (% of property value)	0.6
Getting credit (rank)	24
Strength of legal rights index (0-10)	8
Depth of credit information index (0-6)	5
Public registry coverage (% of adults)	20.5
Private bureau coverage (% of adults)	0.0
Protecting investors (rank)	174
Extent of disclosure index (0-10)	3
Extent of director liability index (0-10)	2
Ease of shareholder suits index (0-10)	3
Strength of investor protection index (0-10)	2.7
Paying taxes (rank)	46
Payments (number per year)	33
Time (hours per year)	164
Total tax rate (% of profit)	15.4

Trading across borders (rank)	131
Documents to export (number)	8
Time to export (days)	17
Cost to export (US$ per container)	2,270
Documents to import (number)	8
Time to import (days)	16
Cost to import (US$ per container)	2,280
Enforcing contracts (rank)	157
Procedures (number)	53
Time (days)	420
Cost (% of claim)	61.2
Resolving insolvency (rank)	31
Time (years)	2.0
Cost (% of estate)	15
Recovery rate (cents on the dollar)	57.4

KUWAIT

Ease of doing business (rank)	67	Middle East & North Africa / High income		GNI per capita (US$)	36,412
				Population (m)	2.9

Starting a business (rank)	142
Procedures (number)	12
Time (days)	32
Cost (% of income per capita)	1.2
Minimum capital (% of income per capita)	71.8
Dealing with construction permits (rank)	121
Procedures (number)	24
Time (days)	130
Cost (% of income per capita)	121.8
Getting electricity (rank)	57
Procedures (number)	7
Time (days)	42
Cost (% of income per capita)	48.2

Registering property (rank)	88
Procedures (number)	8
Time (days)	47
Cost (% of property value)	0.5
Getting credit (rank)	98
Strength of legal rights index (0-10)	4
Depth of credit information index (0-6)	4
Public registry coverage (% of adults)	0.0
Private bureau coverage (% of adults)	29.0
Protecting investors (rank)	29
Extent of disclosure index (0-10)	7
Extent of director liability index (0-10)	7
Ease of shareholder suits index (0-10)	5
Strength of investor protection index (0-10)	6.3
Paying taxes (rank)	15
Payments (number per year)	15
Time (hours per year)	118
Total tax rate (% of profit)	15.5

Trading across borders (rank)	112
Documents to export (number)	7
Time to export (days)	16
Cost to export (US$ per container)	1,085
Documents to import (number)	10
Time to import (days)	19
Cost to import (US$ per container)	1,242
Enforcing contracts (rank)	117
Procedures (number)	50
Time (days)	566
Cost (% of claim)	18.8
Resolving insolvency (rank)	48
Time (years)	4.2
Cost (% of estate)	1
Recovery rate (cents on the dollar)	43.9

Note: Most indicator sets refer to a case scenario in the largest business city of each economy. For more details, see the data notes.

✔ Reform making it easier to do business ✘ Reform making it more difficult to do business

KYRGYZ REPUBLIC

Ease of doing business (rank)	70	Eastern Europe & Central Asia / Low income		GNI per capita (US$)		880
				Population (m)		5.4

Starting a business (rank)	17	**Registering property** (rank)	17	**Trading across borders** (rank)	171
Procedures (number)	2	Procedures (number)	4	Documents to export (number)	8
Time (days)	10	Time (days)	5	Time to export (days)	63
Cost (% of income per capita)	3.5	Cost (% of property value)	2.2	Cost to export (US$ per container)	3,210
Minimum capital (% of income per capita)	0.0			Documents to import (number)	9
		Getting credit (rank)	8	Time to import (days)	72
		Strength of legal rights index (0-10)	10	Cost to import (US$ per container)	3,450
Dealing with construction permits (rank)	62	Depth of credit information index (0-6)	4		
Procedures (number)	12	Public registry coverage (% of adults)	0.0	**Enforcing contracts** (rank)	48
Time (days)	142	Private bureau coverage (% of adults)	18.7	Procedures (number)	38
Cost (% of income per capita)	171.8			Time (days)	260
		Protecting investors (rank)	13	Cost (% of claim)	29.0
Getting electricity (rank)	181	Extent of disclosure index (0-10)	8		
Procedures (number)	7	Extent of director liability index (0-10)	7	**Resolving insolvency** (rank)	150
Time (days)	337	Ease of shareholder suits index (0-10)	8	Time (years)	4.0
Cost (% of income per capita)	2,545.6	Strength of investor protection index (0-10)	7.7	Cost (% of estate)	15
				Recovery rate (cents on the dollar)	11.7
		✘ **Paying taxes** (rank)	162		
		Payments (number per year)	52		
		Time (hours per year)	210		
		Total tax rate (% of profit)	69.0		

LAO PDR

Ease of doing business (rank)	165	East Asia & Pacific / Lower middle income		GNI per capita (US$)		1,010
				Population (m)		6.4

Starting a business (rank)	89	**Registering property** (rank)	72	**Trading across borders** (rank)	168
Procedures (number)	7	Procedures (number)	5	Documents to export (number)	9
Time (days)	93	Time (days)	98	Time to export (days)	44
Cost (% of income per capita)	7.6	Cost (% of property value)	1.1	Cost to export (US$ per container)	1,880
Minimum capital (% of income per capita)	0.0			Documents to import (number)	10
		Getting credit (rank)	166	Time to import (days)	46
		Strength of legal rights index (0-10)	4	Cost to import (US$ per container)	2,035
Dealing with construction permits (rank)	80	Depth of credit information index (0-6)	0		
Procedures (number)	23	Public registry coverage (% of adults)	0.0	**Enforcing contracts** (rank)	110
Time (days)	108	Private bureau coverage (% of adults)	0.0	Procedures (number)	42
Cost (% of income per capita)	52.4			Time (days)	443
		Protecting investors (rank)	182	Cost (% of claim)	31.6
Getting electricity (rank)	138	Extent of disclosure index (0-10)	2		
Procedures (number)	5	Extent of director liability index (0-10)	1	**Resolving insolvency** (rank)	183
Time (days)	134	Ease of shareholder suits index (0-10)	2	Time (years)	NO PRACTICE
Cost (% of income per capita)	2,381.6	Strength of investor protection index (0-10)	1.7	Cost (% of estate)	NO PRACTICE
				Recovery rate (cents on the dollar)	0.0
		Paying taxes (rank)	123		
		Payments (number per year)	34		
		Time (hours per year)	362		
		Total tax rate (% of profit)	33.3		

LATVIA

Ease of doing business (rank)	21	Eastern Europe & Central Asia / Upper middle income		GNI per capita (US$)		11,620
				Population (m)		2.2

✔ **Starting a business** (rank)	51	✔ **Registering property** (rank)	32	**Trading across borders** (rank)	15
Procedures (number)	4	Procedures (number)	5	Documents to export (number)	5
Time (days)	16	Time (days)	18	Time to export (days)	10
Cost (% of income per capita)	2.6	Cost (% of property value)	2.0	Cost to export (US$ per container)	600
Minimum capital (% of income per capita)	0.0			Documents to import (number)	6
		Getting credit (rank)	4	Time to import (days)	11
		Strength of legal rights index (0-10)	10	Cost to import (US$ per container)	801
Dealing with construction permits (rank)	112	Depth of credit information index (0-6)	5		
Procedures (number)	23	Public registry coverage (% of adults)	59.7	**Enforcing contracts** (rank)	17
Time (days)	205	Private bureau coverage (% of adults)	0.0	Procedures (number)	27
Cost (% of income per capita)	21.0			Time (days)	369
		Protecting investors (rank)	65	Cost (% of claim)	23.1
✔ **Getting electricity** (rank)	84	Extent of disclosure index (0-10)	5		
Procedures (number)	5	Extent of director liability index (0-10)	4	✔ **Resolving insolvency** (rank)	32
Time (days)	108	Ease of shareholder suits index (0-10)	8	Time (years)	3.0
Cost (% of income per capita)	439.1	Strength of investor protection index (0-10)	5.7	Cost (% of estate)	13
				Recovery rate (cents on the dollar)	56.2
		Paying taxes (rank)	67		
		Payments (number per year)	7		
		Time (hours per year)	290		
		Total tax rate (% of profit)	37.9		

Note: Most indicator sets refer to a case scenario in the largest business city of each economy. For more details, see the data notes.

✔ Reform making it easier to do business   ✘ Reform making it more difficult to do business

LEBANON

Ease of doing business (rank)	104	Middle East & North Africa		GNI per capita (US$)		9,020
		Upper middle income		Population (m)		4.3

Starting a business (rank)	109	**Registering property** (rank)	105	**Trading across borders** (rank)	93
Procedures (number)	5	Procedures (number)	8	Documents to export (number)	5
Time (days)	9	Time (days)	25	Time to export (days)	22
Cost (% of income per capita)	67.1	Cost (% of property value)	5.8	Cost to export (US$ per container)	1,050
Minimum capital (% of income per capita)	35.3			Documents to import (number)	7
		Getting credit (rank)	78	Time to import (days)	32
Dealing with construction permits (rank)	161	Strength of legal rights index (0-10)	4	Cost to import (US$ per container)	1,250
Procedures (number)	19	Depth of credit information index (0-6)	5		
Time (days)	219	Public registry coverage (% of adults)	11.0	**Enforcing contracts** (rank)	120
Cost (% of income per capita)	234.9	Private bureau coverage (% of adults)	0.0	Procedures (number)	37
				Time (days)	721
✔ **Getting electricity** (rank)	47	**Protecting investors** (rank)	97	Cost (% of claim)	30.8
Procedures (number)	5	Extent of disclosure index (0-10)	9		
Time (days)	75	Extent of director liability index (0-10)	1	**Resolving insolvency** (rank)	125
Cost (% of income per capita)	99.9	Ease of shareholder suits index (0-10)	5	Time (years)	4.0
		Strength of investor protection index (0-10)	5.0	Cost (% of estate)	22
				Recovery rate (cents on the dollar)	20.6
		Paying taxes (rank)	30		
		Payments (number per year)	19		
		Time (hours per year)	180		
		Total tax rate (% of profit)	30.2		

LESOTHO

Ease of doing business (rank)	143	Sub-Saharan Africa		GNI per capita (US$)		1,080
		Lower middle income		Population (m)		2.1

Starting a business (rank)	144	**Registering property** (rank)	150	**Trading across borders** (rank)	147
Procedures (number)	7	Procedures (number)	6	Documents to export (number)	8
Time (days)	40	Time (days)	101	Time to export (days)	31
Cost (% of income per capita)	24.9	Cost (% of property value)	8.0	Cost to export (US$ per container)	1,680
Minimum capital (% of income per capita)	11.2			Documents to import (number)	8
		Getting credit (rank)	150	Time to import (days)	35
Dealing with construction permits (rank)	157	Strength of legal rights index (0-10)	6	Cost to import (US$ per container)	1,665
Procedures (number)	12	Depth of credit information index (0-6)	0		
Time (days)	510	Public registry coverage (% of adults)	0.0	✔ **Enforcing contracts** (rank)	102
Cost (% of income per capita)	1,038.7	Private bureau coverage (% of adults)	0.0	Procedures (number)	40
				Time (days)	785
Getting electricity (rank)	141	**Protecting investors** (rank)	147	Cost (% of claim)	19.5
Procedures (number)	5	Extent of disclosure index (0-10)	2		
Time (days)	140	Extent of director liability index (0-10)	1	**Resolving insolvency** (rank)	71
Cost (% of income per capita)	2,456.7	Ease of shareholder suits index (0-10)	8	Time (years)	2.6
		Strength of investor protection index (0-10)	3.7	Cost (% of estate)	8
				Recovery rate (cents on the dollar)	37.4
		Paying taxes (rank)	61		
		Payments (number per year)	21		
		Time (hours per year)	324		
		Total tax rate (% of profit)	16.0		

LIBERIA

Ease of doing business (rank)	151	Sub-Saharan Africa		GNI per capita (US$)		190
		Low income		Population (m)		4.1

✔ **Starting a business** (rank)	35	**Registering property** (rank)	176	✔ **Trading across borders** (rank)	116
Procedures (number)	4	Procedures (number)	10	Documents to export (number)	10
Time (days)	6	Time (days)	50	Time to export (days)	15
Cost (% of income per capita)	68.4	Cost (% of property value)	13.1	Cost to export (US$ per container)	1,220
Minimum capital (% of income per capita)	0.0			Documents to import (number)	9
		✔ **Getting credit** (rank)	98	Time to import (days)	14
Dealing with construction permits (rank)	123	Strength of legal rights index (0-10)	7	Cost to import (US$ per container)	1,200
Procedures (number)	23	Depth of credit information index (0-6)	1		
Time (days)	75	Public registry coverage (% of adults)	0.6	**Enforcing contracts** (rank)	166
Cost (% of income per capita)	694.1	Private bureau coverage (% of adults)	0.0	Procedures (number)	41
				Time (days)	1,280
Getting electricity (rank)	153	**Protecting investors** (rank)	147	Cost (% of claim)	35.0
Procedures (number)	4	Extent of disclosure index (0-10)	4		
Time (days)	586	Extent of director liability index (0-10)	1	**Resolving insolvency** (rank)	158
Cost (% of income per capita)	4,455.2	Ease of shareholder suits index (0-10)	6	Time (years)	3.0
		Strength of investor protection index (0-10)	3.7	Cost (% of estate)	43
				Recovery rate (cents on the dollar)	8.4
		Paying taxes (rank)	98		
		Payments (number per year)	33		
		Time (hours per year)	158		
		Total tax rate (% of profit)	43.7		

Note: Most indicator sets refer to a case scenario in the largest business city of each economy. For more details, see the data notes.

✔ Reform making it easier to do business   ✘ Reform making it more difficult to do business

LITHUANIA

Ease of doing business (rank)	27	Eastern Europe & Central Asia — Upper middle income		GNI per capita (US$)		11,400
				Population (m)		3.3
Starting a business (rank)	101	**Registering property** (rank)	7	**Trading across borders** (rank)		28
Procedures (number)	6	Procedures (number)	3	Documents to export (number)		6
Time (days)	22	Time (days)	3	Time to export (days)		9
Cost (% of income per capita)	2.8	Cost (% of property value)	0.8	Cost to export (US$ per container)		870
Minimum capital (% of income per capita)	35.7			Documents to import (number)		6
		Getting credit (rank)	48	Time to import (days)		9
		Strength of legal rights index (0-10)	5	Cost to import (US$ per container)		980
Dealing with construction permits (rank)	47	Depth of credit information index (0-6)	6			
Procedures (number)	15	Public registry coverage (% of adults)	15.0	**Enforcing contracts** (rank)		15
Time (days)	142	Private bureau coverage (% of adults)	75.6	Procedures (number)		30
Cost (% of income per capita)	25.5			Time (days)		275
		Protecting investors (rank)	65	Cost (% of claim)		23.6
✘ **Getting electricity** (rank)	81	Extent of disclosure index (0-10)	7			
Procedures (number)	5	Extent of director liability index (0-10)	4	✔ **Resolving insolvency** (rank)		40
Time (days)	148	Ease of shareholder suits index (0-10)	6	Time (years)		1.5
Cost (% of income per capita)	63.3	Strength of investor protection index (0-10)	5.7	Cost (% of estate)		7
				Recovery rate (cents on the dollar)		50.9
		Paying taxes (rank)	62			
		Payments (number per year)	11			
		Time (hours per year)	175			
		Total tax rate (% of profit)	43.9			

LUXEMBOURG

Ease of doing business (rank)	50	OECD high income — High income		GNI per capita (US$)		79,510
				Population (m)		0.5
Starting a business (rank)	81	**Registering property** (rank)	134	**Trading across borders** (rank)		31
Procedures (number)	6	Procedures (number)	8	Documents to export (number)		5
Time (days)	19	Time (days)	29	Time to export (days)		6
Cost (% of income per capita)	1.9	Cost (% of property value)	10.1	Cost to export (US$ per container)		1,420
Minimum capital (% of income per capita)	21.2			Documents to import (number)		4
		Getting credit (rank)	150	Time to import (days)		6
		Strength of legal rights index (0-10)	6	Cost to import (US$ per container)		1,420
Dealing with construction permits (rank)	33	Depth of credit information index (0-6)	0			
Procedures (number)	12	Public registry coverage (% of adults)	0.0	**Enforcing contracts** (rank)		1
Time (days)	157	Private bureau coverage (% of adults)	0.0	Procedures (number)		26
Cost (% of income per capita)	19.5			Time (days)		321
		Protecting investors (rank)	122	Cost (% of claim)		9.7
Getting electricity (rank)	63	Extent of disclosure index (0-10)	6			
Procedures (number)	5	Extent of director liability index (0-10)	4	**Resolving insolvency** (rank)		49
Time (days)	120	Ease of shareholder suits index (0-10)	3	Time (years)		2.0
Cost (% of income per capita)	58.8	Strength of investor protection index (0-10)	4.3	Cost (% of estate)		15
				Recovery rate (cents on the dollar)		43.5
		Paying taxes (rank)	17			
		Payments (number per year)	23			
		Time (hours per year)	59			
		Total tax rate (% of profit)	20.8			

MACEDONIA, FYR

Ease of doing business (rank)	22	Eastern Europe & Central Asia — Upper middle income		GNI per capita (US$)		4,520
				Population (m)		2.1
Starting a business (rank)	6	✔ **Registering property** (rank)	49	**Trading across borders** (rank)		67
Procedures (number)	3	Procedures (number)	4	Documents to export (number)		6
Time (days)	3	Time (days)	40	Time to export (days)		12
Cost (% of income per capita)	2.4	Cost (% of property value)	3.1	Cost to export (US$ per container)		1,376
Minimum capital (% of income per capita)	0.0			Documents to import (number)		6
		✔ **Getting credit** (rank)	24	Time to import (days)		11
		Strength of legal rights index (0-10)	7	Cost to import (US$ per container)		1,380
✔ **Dealing with construction permits** (rank)	61	Depth of credit information index (0-6)	6			
Procedures (number)	10	Public registry coverage (% of adults)	34.3	**Enforcing contracts** (rank)		60
Time (days)	117	Private bureau coverage (% of adults)	0.0	Procedures (number)		37
Cost (% of income per capita)	552.7			Time (days)		370
		Protecting investors (rank)	17	Cost (% of claim)		31.1
Getting electricity (rank)	121	Extent of disclosure index (0-10)	9			
Procedures (number)	5	Extent of director liability index (0-10)	7	✔ **Resolving insolvency** (rank)		55
Time (days)	151	Ease of shareholder suits index (0-10)	5	Time (years)		2.0
Cost (% of income per capita)	847.4	Strength of investor protection index (0-10)	7.0	Cost (% of estate)		10
				Recovery rate (cents on the dollar)		42.0
		Paying taxes (rank)	26			
		Payments (number per year)	28			
		Time (hours per year)	119			
		Total tax rate (% of profit)	9.7			

Note: Most indicator sets refer to a case scenario in the largest business city of each economy. For more details, see the data notes.

✔ Reform making it easier to do business ✗ Reform making it more difficult to do business

MADAGASCAR

Ease of doing business (rank)	**137**	Sub-Saharan Africa		GNI per capita (US$)	**440**		
		Low income		Population (m)	**20.1**		

✔ **Starting a business** (rank)	20	**Registering property** (rank)	146	**Trading across borders** (rank)	111
Procedures (number)	3	Procedures (number)	6	Documents to export (number)	4
Time (days)	8	Time (days)	74	Time to export (days)	21
Cost (% of income per capita)	12.1	Cost (% of property value)	10.6	Cost to export (US$ per container)	1,197
Minimum capital (% of income per capita)	0.0			Documents to import (number)	9
		✔ **Getting credit** (rank)	177	Time to import (days)	24
Dealing with construction permits (rank)	131	Strength of legal rights index (0-10)	2	Cost to import (US$ per container)	1,555
Procedures (number)	16	Depth of credit information index (0-6)	0		
Time (days)	172	Public registry coverage (% of adults)	0.1	**Enforcing contracts** (rank)	155
Cost (% of income per capita)	422.2	Private bureau coverage (% of adults)	0.0	Procedures (number)	38
				Time (days)	871
Getting electricity (rank)	179	**Protecting investors** (rank)	65	Cost (% of claim)	42.4
Procedures (number)	6	Extent of disclosure index (0-10)	5		
Time (days)	450	Extent of director liability index (0-10)	6	**Resolving insolvency** (rank)	148
Cost (% of income per capita)	8,390.9	Ease of shareholder suits index (0-10)	6	Time (years)	2.0
		Strength of investor protection index (0-10)	5.7	Cost (% of estate)	30
				Recovery rate (cents on the dollar)	13.5
		Paying taxes (rank)	75		
		Payments (number per year)	23		
		Time (hours per year)	201		
		Total tax rate (% of profit)	36.6		

MALAWI

Ease of doing business (rank)	**145**	Sub-Saharan Africa		GNI per capita (US$)	**330**		
		Low income		Population (m)	**14.9**		

Starting a business (rank)	139	✗ **Registering property** (rank)	95	**Trading across borders** (rank)	164
Procedures (number)	10	Procedures (number)	6	Documents to export (number)	10
Time (days)	39	Time (days)	69	Time to export (days)	41
Cost (% of income per capita)	90.9	Cost (% of property value)	3.2	Cost to export (US$ per container)	1,675
Minimum capital (% of income per capita)	0.0			Documents to import (number)	9
		✔ **Getting credit** (rank)	126	Time to import (days)	51
Dealing with construction permits (rank)	167	Strength of legal rights index (0-10)	7	Cost to import (US$ per container)	2,570
Procedures (number)	18	Depth of credit information index (0-6)	0		
Time (days)	200	Public registry coverage (% of adults)	0.0	**Enforcing contracts** (rank)	121
Cost (% of income per capita)	1,077.5	Private bureau coverage (% of adults)	0.0	Procedures (number)	42
				Time (days)	312
Getting electricity (rank)	177	**Protecting investors** (rank)	79	Cost (% of claim)	94.1
Procedures (number)	6	Extent of disclosure index (0-10)	4		
Time (days)	244	Extent of director liability index (0-10)	7	✔ **Resolving insolvency** (rank)	132
Cost (% of income per capita)	9,665.8	Ease of shareholder suits index (0-10)	5	Time (years)	2.6
		Strength of investor protection index (0-10)	5.3	Cost (% of estate)	25
				Recovery rate (cents on the dollar)	18.5
		Paying taxes (rank)	23		
		Payments (number per year)	19		
		Time (hours per year)	157		
		Total tax rate (% of profit)	28.2		

MALAYSIA

Ease of doing business (rank)	**18**	East Asia & Pacific		GNI per capita (US$)	**7,900**		
		Upper middle income		Population (m)	**27.9**		

✔ **Starting a business** (rank)	50	**Registering property** (rank)	59	**Trading across borders** (rank)	29
Procedures (number)	4	Procedures (number)	5	Documents to export (number)	6
Time (days)	6	Time (days)	48	Time to export (days)	17
Cost (% of income per capita)	16.4	Cost (% of property value)	3.3	Cost to export (US$ per container)	450
Minimum capital (% of income per capita)	0.0			Documents to import (number)	7
		Getting credit (rank)	1	Time to import (days)	14
Dealing with construction permits (rank)	113	Strength of legal rights index (0-10)	10	Cost to import (US$ per container)	435
Procedures (number)	22	Depth of credit information index (0-6)	6		
Time (days)	260	Public registry coverage (% of adults)	49.4	✔ **Enforcing contracts** (rank)	31
Cost (% of income per capita)	7.1	Private bureau coverage (% of adults)	83.4	Procedures (number)	29
				Time (days)	425
Getting electricity (rank)	59	**Protecting investors** (rank)	4	Cost (% of claim)	27.5
Procedures (number)	6	Extent of disclosure index (0-10)	10		
Time (days)	51	Extent of director liability index (0-10)	9	✔ **Resolving insolvency** (rank)	47
Cost (% of income per capita)	95.5	Ease of shareholder suits index (0-10)	7	Time (years)	1.5
		Strength of investor protection index (0-10)	8.7	Cost (% of estate)	15
				Recovery rate (cents on the dollar)	44.6
		✗ **Paying taxes** (rank)	41		
		Payments (number per year)	13		
		Time (hours per year)	133		
		Total tax rate (% of profit)	34.0		

Note: Most indicator sets refer to a case scenario in the largest business city of each economy. For more details, see the data notes.

✔ Reform making it easier to do business ✘ Reform making it more difficult to do business

MALDIVES

Ease of doing business (rank)	79

South Asia
Upper middle income

GNI per capita (US$)	4,270
Population (m)	0.3

Starting a business (rank)	59
Procedures (number)	5
Time (days)	9
Cost (% of income per capita)	8.9
Minimum capital (% of income per capita)	3.5

Registering property (rank)	152
Procedures (number)	6
Time (days)	57
Cost (% of property value)	16.7

Trading across borders (rank)	137
Documents to export (number)	8
Time to export (days)	21
Cost to export (US$ per container)	1,550
Documents to import (number)	9
Time to import (days)	22
Cost to import (US$ per container)	1,526

Dealing with construction permits (rank)	20
Procedures (number)	8
Time (days)	174
Cost (% of income per capita)	12.7

Getting credit (rank)	166
Strength of legal rights index (0-10)	4
Depth of credit information index (0-6)	0
Public registry coverage (% of adults)	0.0
Private bureau coverage (% of adults)	0.0

Enforcing contracts (rank)	92
Procedures (number)	41
Time (days)	665
Cost (% of claim)	16.5

Getting electricity (rank)	132
Procedures (number)	6
Time (days)	101
Cost (% of income per capita)	708.8

Protecting investors (rank)	79
Extent of disclosure index (0-10)	0
Extent of director liability index (0-10)	8
Ease of shareholder suits index (0-10)	8
Strength of investor protection index (0-10)	5.3

Resolving insolvency (rank)	41
Time (years)	1.5
Cost (% of estate)	4
Recovery rate (cents on the dollar)	50.4

Paying taxes (rank)	1
Payments (number per year)	3
Time (hours per year)	-
Total tax rate (% of profit)	9.3

MALI

Ease of doing business (rank)	146

Sub-Saharan Africa
Low income

GNI per capita (US$)	600
Population (m)	15.4

✔ Starting a business (rank)	115
Procedures (number)	4
Time (days)	8
Cost (% of income per capita)	90.5
Minimum capital (% of income per capita)	348.3

Registering property (rank)	91
Procedures (number)	5
Time (days)	29
Cost (% of property value)	12.1

Trading across borders (rank)	146
Documents to export (number)	6
Time to export (days)	26
Cost to export (US$ per container)	2,202
Documents to import (number)	9
Time to import (days)	31
Cost to import (US$ per container)	3,067

Dealing with construction permits (rank)	95
Procedures (number)	11
Time (days)	179
Cost (% of income per capita)	439.3

✔ Getting credit (rank)	126
Strength of legal rights index (0-10)	6
Depth of credit information index (0-6)	1
Public registry coverage (% of adults)	3.7
Private bureau coverage (% of adults)	0.0

Enforcing contracts (rank)	132
Procedures (number)	36
Time (days)	620
Cost (% of claim)	52.0

Getting electricity (rank)	113
Procedures (number)	4
Time (days)	120
Cost (% of income per capita)	4,397.7

Protecting investors (rank)	147
Extent of disclosure index (0-10)	6
Extent of director liability index (0-10)	1
Ease of shareholder suits index (0-10)	4
Strength of investor protection index (0-10)	3.7

Resolving insolvency (rank)	111
Time (years)	3.6
Cost (% of estate)	18
Recovery rate (cents on the dollar)	24.9

Paying taxes (rank)	163
Payments (number per year)	59
Time (hours per year)	270
Total tax rate (% of profit)	51.8

MARSHALL ISLANDS

Ease of doing business (rank)	106

East Asia & Pacific
Lower middle income

GNI per capita (US$)	2,990
Population (m)	0.1

Starting a business (rank)	52
Procedures (number)	5
Time (days)	17
Cost (% of income per capita)	17.7
Minimum capital (% of income per capita)	0.0

Registering property (rank)	183
Procedures (number)	NO PRACTICE
Time (days)	NO PRACTICE
Cost (% of property value)	NO PRACTICE

Trading across borders (rank)	66
Documents to export (number)	5
Time to export (days)	21
Cost to export (US$ per container)	945
Documents to import (number)	5
Time to import (days)	25
Cost to import (US$ per container)	970

Dealing with construction permits (rank)	8
Procedures (number)	8
Time (days)	87
Cost (% of income per capita)	29.1

Getting credit (rank)	78
Strength of legal rights index (0-10)	9
Depth of credit information index (0-6)	0
Public registry coverage (% of adults)	0.0
Private bureau coverage (% of adults)	0.0

Enforcing contracts (rank)	63
Procedures (number)	36
Time (days)	476
Cost (% of claim)	27.4

Getting electricity (rank)	76
Procedures (number)	5
Time (days)	67
Cost (% of income per capita)	1,010.0

Protecting investors (rank)	155
Extent of disclosure index (0-10)	2
Extent of director liability index (0-10)	0
Ease of shareholder suits index (0-10)	8
Strength of investor protection index (0-10)	3.3

Resolving insolvency (rank)	135
Time (years)	2.0
Cost (% of estate)	38
Recovery rate (cents on the dollar)	17.9

Paying taxes (rank)	96
Payments (number per year)	21
Time (hours per year)	128
Total tax rate (% of profit)	64.9

Note: Most indicator sets refer to a case scenario in the largest business city of each economy. For more details, see the data notes.

✔ Reform making it easier to do business ✘ Reform making it more difficult to do business

MAURITANIA

Ease of doing business (rank)	159	Sub-Saharan Africa Lower middle income		GNI per capita (US$)	1,060	
				Population (m)	3.4	
Starting a business (rank)	159	**Registering property** (rank)	59	**Trading across borders** (rank)	143	
Procedures (number)	9	Procedures (number)	4	Documents to export (number)	8	
Time (days)	19	Time (days)	49	Time to export (days)	34	
Cost (% of income per capita)	48.3	Cost (% of property value)	4.7	Cost to export (US$ per container)	1,520	
Minimum capital (% of income per capita)	334.9			Documents to import (number)	8	
		Getting credit (rank)	166	Time to import (days)	38	
✔ **Dealing with construction permits** (rank)	64	Strength of legal rights index (0-10)	3	Cost to import (US$ per container)	1,523	
Procedures (number)	18	Depth of credit information index (0-6)	1			
Time (days)	119	Public registry coverage (% of adults)	0.2	**Enforcing contracts** (rank)	79	
Cost (% of income per capita)	49.9	Private bureau coverage (% of adults)	0.0	Procedures (number)	46	
				Time (days)	370	
Getting electricity (rank)	122	**Protecting investors** (rank)	147	Cost (% of claim)	23.2	
Procedures (number)	5	Extent of disclosure index (0-10)	5			
Time (days)	75	Extent of director liability index (0-10)	3	**Resolving insolvency** (rank)	152	
Cost (% of income per capita)	7,310.9	Ease of shareholder suits index (0-10)	3	Time (years)	8.0	
		Strength of investor protection index (0-10)	3.7	Cost (% of estate)	9	
				Recovery rate (cents on the dollar)	10.3	
		Paying taxes (rank)	175			
		Payments (number per year)	37			
		Time (hours per year)	696			
		Total tax rate (% of profit)	68.3			

MAURITIUS

Ease of doing business (rank)	23	Sub-Saharan Africa Upper middle income		GNI per capita (US$)	7,740	
				Population (m)	1.3	
Starting a business (rank)	15	**Registering property** (rank)	67	**Trading across borders** (rank)	21	
Procedures (number)	5	Procedures (number)	4	Documents to export (number)	5	
Time (days)	6	Time (days)	22	Time to export (days)	13	
Cost (% of income per capita)	3.6	Cost (% of property value)	10.6	Cost to export (US$ per container)	737	
Minimum capital (% of income per capita)	0.0			Documents to import (number)	6	
		Getting credit (rank)	78	Time to import (days)	13	
Dealing with construction permits (rank)	53	Strength of legal rights index (0-10)	6	Cost to import (US$ per container)	689	
Procedures (number)	16	Depth of credit information index (0-6)	3			
Time (days)	136	Public registry coverage (% of adults)	49.8	**Enforcing contracts** (rank)	61	
Cost (% of income per capita)	30.6	Private bureau coverage (% of adults)	0.0	Procedures (number)	36	
				Time (days)	645	
Getting electricity (rank)	44	**Protecting investors** (rank)	13	Cost (% of claim)	17.4	
Procedures (number)	4	Extent of disclosure index (0-10)	6			
Time (days)	91	Extent of director liability index (0-10)	8	**Resolving insolvency** (rank)	79	
Cost (% of income per capita)	328.5	Ease of shareholder suits index (0-10)	9	Time (years)	1.7	
		Strength of investor protection index (0-10)	7.7	Cost (% of estate)	15	
				Recovery rate (cents on the dollar)	35.1	
		Paying taxes (rank)	11			
		Payments (number per year)	7			
		Time (hours per year)	161			
		Total tax rate (% of profit)	25.0			

MEXICO

Ease of doing business (rank)	53	Latin America & Caribbean Upper middle income		GNI per capita (US$)	9,330	
				Population (m)	108.5	
Starting a business (rank)	75	**Registering property** (rank)	140	**Trading across borders** (rank)	59	
Procedures (number)	6	Procedures (number)	7	Documents to export (number)	5	
Time (days)	9	Time (days)	74	Time to export (days)	12	
Cost (% of income per capita)	11.2	Cost (% of property value)	5.3	Cost to export (US$ per container)	1,450	
Minimum capital (% of income per capita)	8.4			Documents to import (number)	4	
		✔ **Getting credit** (rank)	40	Time to import (days)	12	
✔ **Dealing with construction permits** (rank)	43	Strength of legal rights index (0-10)	6	Cost to import (US$ per container)	1,780	
Procedures (number)	10	Depth of credit information index (0-6)	6			
Time (days)	81	Public registry coverage (% of adults)	0.0	**Enforcing contracts** (rank)	81	
Cost (% of income per capita)	333.1	Private bureau coverage (% of adults)	98.1	Procedures (number)	38	
				Time (days)	415	
Getting electricity (rank)	142	**Protecting investors** (rank)	46	Cost (% of claim)	32.0	
Procedures (number)	7	Extent of disclosure index (0-10)	8			
Time (days)	114	Extent of director liability index (0-10)	5	**Resolving insolvency** (rank)	24	
Cost (% of income per capita)	395.5	Ease of shareholder suits index (0-10)	5	Time (years)	1.8	
		Strength of investor protection index (0-10)	6.0	Cost (% of estate)	18	
				Recovery rate (cents on the dollar)	67.1	
		✔ **Paying taxes** (rank)	109			
		Payments (number per year)	6			
		Time (hours per year)	347			
		Total tax rate (% of profit)	52.7			

Note: Most indicator sets refer to a case scenario in the largest business city of each economy. For more details, see the data notes.

✔ Reform making it easier to do business ✘ Reform making it more difficult to do business

MICRONESIA, FED. STS

Ease of doing business (rank)	140
Starting a business (rank)	102
Procedures (number)	7
Time (days)	16
Cost (% of income per capita)	142.8
Minimum capital (% of income per capita)	0.0
Dealing with construction permits (rank)	19
Procedures (number)	11
Time (days)	114
Cost (% of income per capita)	33.2
Getting electricity (rank)	40
Procedures (number)	3
Time (days)	75
Cost (% of income per capita)	456.9

East Asia & Pacific
Lower middle income

Registering property (rank)	183
Procedures (number)	NO PRACTICE
Time (days)	NO PRACTICE
Cost (% of property value)	NO PRACTICE
Getting credit (rank)	126
Strength of legal rights index (0-10)	7
Depth of credit information index (0-6)	0
Public registry coverage (% of adults)	0.0
Private bureau coverage (% of adults)	0.0
Protecting investors (rank)	174
Extent of disclosure index (0-10)	0
Extent of director liability index (0-10)	0
Ease of shareholder suits index (0-10)	8
Strength of investor protection index (0-10)	2.7
Paying taxes (rank)	92
Payments (number per year)	21
Time (hours per year)	128
Total tax rate (% of profit)	58.7

GNI per capita (US$) 2,700
Population (m) 0.1

Trading across borders (rank)	106
Documents to export (number)	5
Time to export (days)	30
Cost to export (US$ per container)	1,295
Documents to import (number)	6
Time to import (days)	30
Cost to import (US$ per container)	1,295
Enforcing contracts (rank)	146
Procedures (number)	34
Time (days)	885
Cost (% of claim)	66.0
Resolving insolvency (rank)	164
Time (years)	5.3
Cost (% of estate)	38
Recovery rate (cents on the dollar)	3.4

MOLDOVA

Ease of doing business (rank)	81
✔ **Starting a business** (rank)	88
Procedures (number)	7
Time (days)	9
Cost (% of income per capita)	9.1
Minimum capital (% of income per capita)	9.9
Dealing with construction permits (rank)	164
Procedures (number)	27
Time (days)	291
Cost (% of income per capita)	79.2
Getting electricity (rank)	160
Procedures (number)	7
Time (days)	140
Cost (% of income per capita)	660.6

Eastern Europe & Central Asia
Lower middle income

Registering property (rank)	18
Procedures (number)	5
Time (days)	5
Cost (% of property value)	0.9
✔ **Getting credit** (rank)	40
Strength of legal rights index (0-10)	8
Depth of credit information index (0-6)	4
Public registry coverage (% of adults)	0.0
Private bureau coverage (% of adults)	3.0
Protecting investors (rank)	111
Extent of disclosure index (0-10)	7
Extent of director liability index (0-10)	1
Ease of shareholder suits index (0-10)	6
Strength of investor protection index (0-10)	4.7
Paying taxes (rank)	83
Payments (number per year)	48
Time (hours per year)	228
Total tax rate (% of profit)	31.3

GNI per capita (US$) 1,810
Population (m) 3.6

Trading across borders (rank)	134
Documents to export (number)	6
Time to export (days)	32
Cost to export (US$ per container)	1,545
Documents to import (number)	7
Time to import (days)	35
Cost to import (US$ per container)	1,740
✔ **Enforcing contracts** (rank)	26
Procedures (number)	30
Time (days)	352
Cost (% of claim)	28.6
✔ **Resolving insolvency** (rank)	91
Time (years)	2.8
Cost (% of estate)	9
Recovery rate (cents on the dollar)	31.3

MONGOLIA

Ease of doing business (rank)	86
Starting a business (rank)	97
Procedures (number)	7
Time (days)	13
Cost (% of income per capita)	2.9
Minimum capital (% of income per capita)	36.0
Dealing with construction permits (rank)	119
Procedures (number)	19
Time (days)	208
Cost (% of income per capita)	50.1
Getting electricity (rank)	171
Procedures (number)	8
Time (days)	156
Cost (% of income per capita)	1,104.6

East Asia & Pacific
Lower middle income

Registering property (rank)	26
Procedures (number)	5
Time (days)	11
Cost (% of property value)	2.1
✔ **Getting credit** (rank)	67
Strength of legal rights index (0-10)	6
Depth of credit information index (0-6)	4
Public registry coverage (% of adults)	51.4
Private bureau coverage (% of adults)	0.0
Protecting investors (rank)	29
Extent of disclosure index (0-10)	5
Extent of director liability index (0-10)	8
Ease of shareholder suits index (0-10)	6
Strength of investor protection index (0-10)	6.3
Paying taxes (rank)	57
Payments (number per year)	41
Time (hours per year)	192
Total tax rate (% of profit)	24.6

GNI per capita (US$) 1,890
Population (m) 2.7

Trading across borders (rank)	159
Documents to export (number)	8
Time to export (days)	46
Cost to export (US$ per container)	2,265
Documents to import (number)	8
Time to import (days)	47
Cost to import (US$ per container)	2,400
Enforcing contracts (rank)	33
Procedures (number)	32
Time (days)	314
Cost (% of claim)	30.6
Resolving insolvency (rank)	124
Time (years)	4.0
Cost (% of estate)	8
Recovery rate (cents on the dollar)	21.1

Note: Most indicator sets refer to a case scenario in the largest business city of each economy. For more details, see the data notes.

✔ Reform making it easier to do business ✘ Reform making it more difficult to do business

MONTENEGRO

		Eastern Europe & Central Asia		GNI per capita (US$)	6,690
Ease of doing business (rank)	56	Upper middle income		Population (m)	0.6
✔ **Starting a business** (rank)	47	**Registering property** (rank)	108	**Trading across borders** (rank)	34
Procedures (number)	6	Procedures (number)	7	Documents to export (number)	6
Time (days)	10	Time (days)	71	Time to export (days)	14
Cost (% of income per capita)	1.8	Cost (% of property value)	3.1	Cost to export (US$ per container)	805
Minimum capital (% of income per capita)	0.0			Documents to import (number)	6
		Getting credit (rank)	8	Time to import (days)	14
Dealing with construction permits (rank)	173	Strength of legal rights index (0-10)	10	Cost to import (US$ per container)	915
Procedures (number)	17	Depth of credit information index (0-6)	4		
Time (days)	267	Public registry coverage (% of adults)	26.4	**Enforcing contracts** (rank)	133
Cost (% of income per capita)	1,469.9	Private bureau coverage (% of adults)	0.0	Procedures (number)	49
				Time (days)	545
Getting electricity (rank)	71	**Protecting investors** (rank)	29	Cost (% of claim)	25.7
Procedures (number)	5	Extent of disclosure index (0-10)	5		
Time (days)	71	Extent of director liability index (0-10)	8	✔ **Resolving insolvency** (rank)	52
Cost (% of income per capita)	533.4	Ease of shareholder suits index (0-10)	6	Time (years)	2.0
		Strength of investor protection index (0-10)	6.3	Cost (% of estate)	8
				Recovery rate (cents on the dollar)	43.3
		✔ **Paying taxes** (rank)	108		
		Payments (number per year)	42		
		Time (hours per year)	372		
		Total tax rate (% of profit)	22.3		

MOROCCO

		Middle East & North Africa		GNI per capita (US$)	2,850
Ease of doing business (rank)	94	Lower middle income		Population (m)	32.4
Starting a business (rank)	93	**Registering property** (rank)	144	**Trading across borders** (rank)	43
Procedures (number)	6	Procedures (number)	8	Documents to export (number)	6
Time (days)	12	Time (days)	75	Time to export (days)	11
Cost (% of income per capita)	15.7	Cost (% of property value)	4.9	Cost to export (US$ per container)	577
Minimum capital (% of income per capita)	10.7			Documents to import (number)	8
		Getting credit (rank)	98	Time to import (days)	16
✔ **Dealing with construction permits** (rank)	75	Strength of legal rights index (0-10)	3	Cost to import (US$ per container)	950
Procedures (number)	15	Depth of credit information index (0-6)	5		
Time (days)	97	Public registry coverage (% of adults)	0.0	**Enforcing contracts** (rank)	89
Cost (% of income per capita)	234.6	Private bureau coverage (% of adults)	14.6	Procedures (number)	40
				Time (days)	510
Getting electricity (rank)	107	✔ **Protecting investors** (rank)	97	Cost (% of claim)	25.2
Procedures (number)	5	Extent of disclosure index (0-10)	7		
Time (days)	71	Extent of director liability index (0-10)	2	**Resolving insolvency** (rank)	67
Cost (% of income per capita)	2,588.6	Ease of shareholder suits index (0-10)	6	Time (years)	1.8
		Strength of investor protection index (0-10)	5.0	Cost (% of estate)	18
				Recovery rate (cents on the dollar)	38.3
		✔ **Paying taxes** (rank)	112		
		Payments (number per year)	17		
		Time (hours per year)	238		
		Total tax rate (% of profit)	49.6		

MOZAMBIQUE

		Sub-Saharan Africa		GNI per capita (US$)	440
Ease of doing business (rank)	139	Low income		Population (m)	23.4
Starting a business (rank)	70	**Registering property** (rank)	156	**Trading across borders** (rank)	136
Procedures (number)	9	Procedures (number)	8	Documents to export (number)	7
Time (days)	13	Time (days)	42	Time to export (days)	23
Cost (% of income per capita)	11.7	Cost (% of property value)	8.7	Cost to export (US$ per container)	1,100
Minimum capital (% of income per capita)	0.0			Documents to import (number)	10
		Getting credit (rank)	150	Time to import (days)	28
Dealing with construction permits (rank)	126	Strength of legal rights index (0-10)	2	Cost to import (US$ per container)	1,545
Procedures (number)	13	Depth of credit information index (0-6)	4		
Time (days)	370	Public registry coverage (% of adults)	3.8	**Enforcing contracts** (rank)	131
Cost (% of income per capita)	123.0	Private bureau coverage (% of adults)	0.0	Procedures (number)	30
				Time (days)	730
✘ **Getting electricity** (rank)	172	**Protecting investors** (rank)	46	Cost (% of claim)	142.5
Procedures (number)	9	Extent of disclosure index (0-10)	5		
Time (days)	117	Extent of director liability index (0-10)	4	**Resolving insolvency** (rank)	143
Cost (% of income per capita)	2,558.0	Ease of shareholder suits index (0-10)	9	Time (years)	5.0
		Strength of investor protection index (0-10)	6.0	Cost (% of estate)	9
				Recovery rate (cents on the dollar)	15.5
		Paying taxes (rank)	107		
		Payments (number per year)	37		
		Time (hours per year)	230		
		Total tax rate (% of profit)	34.3		

Note: Most indicator sets refer to a case scenario in the largest business city of each economy. For more details, see the data notes.

✔ Reform making it easier to do business   ✘ Reform making it more difficult to do business

NAMIBIA

		Sub-Saharan Africa		GNI per capita (US$)	4,650
Ease of doing business (rank)	78	Upper middle income		Population (m)	2.2
Starting a business (rank)	125	✘ **Registering property** (rank)	145	**Trading across borders** (rank)	142
Procedures (number)	10	Procedures (number)	7	Documents to export (number)	9
Time (days)	66	Time (days)	39	Time to export (days)	29
Cost (% of income per capita)	17.2	Cost (% of property value)	13.7	Cost to export (US$ per container)	1,800
Minimum capital (% of income per capita)	0.0			Documents to import (number)	7
		Getting credit (rank)	24	Time to import (days)	24
		Strength of legal rights index (0-10)	8	Cost to import (US$ per container)	1,905
Dealing with construction permits (rank)	52	Depth of credit information index (0-6)	5		
Procedures (number)	12	Public registry coverage (% of adults)	0.0	**Enforcing contracts** (rank)	40
Time (days)	139	Private bureau coverage (% of adults)	61.5	Procedures (number)	33
Cost (% of income per capita)	103.0			Time (days)	270
		Protecting investors (rank)	79	Cost (% of claim)	35.8
Getting electricity (rank)	105	Extent of disclosure index (0-10)	5		
Procedures (number)	7	Extent of director liability index (0-10)	5	✔ **Resolving insolvency** (rank)	56
Time (days)	55	Ease of shareholder suits index (0-10)	6	Time (years)	1.5
Cost (% of income per capita)	525.8	Strength of investor protection index (0-10)	5.3	Cost (% of estate)	15
				Recovery rate (cents on the dollar)	41.9
		Paying taxes (rank)	102		
		Payments (number per year)	37		
		Time (hours per year)	375		
		Total tax rate (% of profit)	9.8		

NEPAL

		South Asia		GNI per capita (US$)	490
Ease of doing business (rank)	107	Low income		Population (m)	29.9
Starting a business (rank)	100	**Registering property** (rank)	24	**Trading across borders** (rank)	162
Procedures (number)	7	Procedures (number)	3	Documents to export (number)	9
Time (days)	29	Time (days)	5	Time to export (days)	41
Cost (% of income per capita)	37.4	Cost (% of property value)	5.0	Cost to export (US$ per container)	1,960
Minimum capital (% of income per capita)	0.0			Documents to import (number)	9
		Getting credit (rank)	67	Time to import (days)	35
		Strength of legal rights index (0-10)	7	Cost to import (US$ per container)	2,095
Dealing with construction permits (rank)	140	Depth of credit information index (0-6)	3		
Procedures (number)	13	Public registry coverage (% of adults)	0.0	✔ **Enforcing contracts** (rank)	137
Time (days)	222	Private bureau coverage (% of adults)	0.3	Procedures (number)	39
Cost (% of income per capita)	753.3			Time (days)	910
		Protecting investors (rank)	79	Cost (% of claim)	26.8
Getting electricity (rank)	99	Extent of disclosure index (0-10)	6		
Procedures (number)	5	Extent of director liability index (0-10)	1	**Resolving insolvency** (rank)	112
Time (days)	70	Ease of shareholder suits index (0-10)	9	Time (years)	5.0
Cost (% of income per capita)	1,995.8	Strength of investor protection index (0-10)	5.3	Cost (% of estate)	9
				Recovery rate (cents on the dollar)	24.5
		Paying taxes (rank)	86		
		Payments (number per year)	34		
		Time (hours per year)	326		
		Total tax rate (% of profit)	31.5		

NETHERLANDS

		OECD high income		GNI per capita (US$)	49,720
Ease of doing business (rank)	31	High income		Population (m)	16.6
Starting a business (rank)	79	**Registering property** (rank)	48	**Trading across borders** (rank)	13
Procedures (number)	6	Procedures (number)	5	Documents to export (number)	4
Time (days)	8	Time (days)	7	Time to export (days)	6
Cost (% of income per capita)	5.5	Cost (% of property value)	6.1	Cost to export (US$ per container)	895
Minimum capital (% of income per capita)	50.4			Documents to import (number)	5
		Getting credit (rank)	48	Time to import (days)	6
		Strength of legal rights index (0-10)	6	Cost to import (US$ per container)	975
Dealing with construction permits (rank)	99	Depth of credit information index (0-6)	5		
Procedures (number)	15	Public registry coverage (% of adults)	0.0	**Enforcing contracts** (rank)	28
Time (days)	176	Private bureau coverage (% of adults)	83.2	Procedures (number)	26
Cost (% of income per capita)	107.8			Time (days)	514
		Protecting investors (rank)	111	Cost (% of claim)	23.9
Getting electricity (rank)	67	Extent of disclosure index (0-10)	4		
Procedures (number)	5	Extent of director liability index (0-10)	4	**Resolving insolvency** (rank)	7
Time (days)	143	Ease of shareholder suits index (0-10)	6	Time (years)	1.1
Cost (% of income per capita)	30.7	Strength of investor protection index (0-10)	4.7	Cost (% of estate)	4
				Recovery rate (cents on the dollar)	87.7
		Paying taxes (rank)	43		
		Payments (number per year)	9		
		Time (hours per year)	127		
		Total tax rate (% of profit)	40.5		

Note: Most indicator sets refer to a case scenario in the largest business city of each economy. For more details, see the data notes.

✔ Reform making it easier to do business   ✘ Reform making it more difficult to do business

NEW ZEALAND

Ease of doing business (rank)	3	OECD high income High income		GNI per capita (US$) Population (m)		32,145 4.4

Starting a business (rank)	1
Procedures (number)	1
Time (days)	1
Cost (% of income per capita)	0.4
Minimum capital (% of income per capita)	0.0

Dealing with construction permits (rank)	2
Procedures (number)	6
Time (days)	64
Cost (% of income per capita)	34.4

Getting electricity (rank)	31
Procedures (number)	5
Time (days)	50
Cost (% of income per capita)	79.1

Registering property (rank)	3
Procedures (number)	2
Time (days)	2
Cost (% of property value)	0.1

Getting credit (rank)	4
Strength of legal rights index (0-10)	10
Depth of credit information index (0-6)	5
Public registry coverage (% of adults)	0.0
Private bureau coverage (% of adults)	100.0

Protecting investors (rank)	1
Extent of disclosure index (0-10)	10
Extent of director liability index (0-10)	9
Ease of shareholder suits index (0-10)	10
Strength of investor protection index (0-10)	9.7

✔ Paying taxes (rank)	36
Payments (number per year)	8
Time (hours per year)	172
Total tax rate (% of profit)	34.4

Trading across borders (rank)	27
Documents to export (number)	7
Time to export (days)	10
Cost to export (US$ per container)	855
Documents to import (number)	5
Time to import (days)	9
Cost to import (US$ per container)	825

Enforcing contracts (rank)	10
Procedures (number)	30
Time (days)	216
Cost (% of claim)	22.4

Resolving insolvency (rank)	18
Time (years)	1.3
Cost (% of estate)	4
Recovery rate (cents on the dollar)	78.8

NICARAGUA

Ease of doing business (rank)	118	Latin America & Caribbean Lower middle income		GNI per capita (US$) Population (m)		1,080 5.8

Starting a business (rank)	130
Procedures (number)	8
Time (days)	39
Cost (% of income per capita)	107.9
Minimum capital (% of income per capita)	0.0

Dealing with construction permits (rank)	150
Procedures (number)	16
Time (days)	218
Cost (% of income per capita)	428.7

Getting electricity (rank)	136
Procedures (number)	6
Time (days)	70
Cost (% of income per capita)	1,653.8

✔ Registering property (rank)	122
Procedures (number)	8
Time (days)	49
Cost (% of property value)	4.1

Getting credit (rank)	98
Strength of legal rights index (0-10)	3
Depth of credit information index (0-6)	5
Public registry coverage (% of adults)	10.5
Private bureau coverage (% of adults)	31.9

Protecting investors (rank)	97
Extent of disclosure index (0-10)	4
Extent of director liability index (0-10)	5
Ease of shareholder suits index (0-10)	6
Strength of investor protection index (0-10)	5.0

✔ Paying taxes (rank)	155
Payments (number per year)	42
Time (hours per year)	207
Total tax rate (% of profit)	66.8

Trading across borders (rank)	83
Documents to export (number)	5
Time to export (days)	24
Cost to export (US$ per container)	1,140
Documents to import (number)	5
Time to import (days)	23
Cost to import (US$ per container)	1,220

✔ Enforcing contracts (rank)	52
Procedures (number)	37
Time (days)	409
Cost (% of claim)	26.8

Resolving insolvency (rank)	78
Time (years)	2.2
Cost (% of estate)	15
Recovery rate (cents on the dollar)	35.1

NIGER

Ease of doing business (rank)	173	Sub-Saharan Africa Low income		GNI per capita (US$) Population (m)		360 15.9

Starting a business (rank)	163
Procedures (number)	9
Time (days)	17
Cost (% of income per capita)	114.4
Minimum capital (% of income per capita)	584.2

Dealing with construction permits (rank)	158
Procedures (number)	12
Time (days)	326
Cost (% of income per capita)	2,214.5

Getting electricity (rank)	111
Procedures (number)	4
Time (days)	120
Cost (% of income per capita)	4,211.8

Registering property (rank)	86
Procedures (number)	4
Time (days)	35
Cost (% of property value)	11.0

✔ Getting credit (rank)	126
Strength of legal rights index (0-10)	6
Depth of credit information index (0-6)	1
Public registry coverage (% of adults)	0.9
Private bureau coverage (% of adults)	0.0

Protecting investors (rank)	155
Extent of disclosure index (0-10)	6
Extent of director liability index (0-10)	1
Ease of shareholder suits index (0-10)	3
Strength of investor protection index (0-10)	3.3

Paying taxes (rank)	142
Payments (number per year)	41
Time (hours per year)	270
Total tax rate (% of profit)	43.8

Trading across borders (rank)	173
Documents to export (number)	8
Time to export (days)	59
Cost to export (US$ per container)	3,545
Documents to import (number)	10
Time to import (days)	64
Cost to import (US$ per container)	3,545

Enforcing contracts (rank)	139
Procedures (number)	39
Time (days)	545
Cost (% of claim)	59.6

Resolving insolvency (rank)	123
Time (years)	5.0
Cost (% of estate)	18
Recovery rate (cents on the dollar)	21.9

Note: Most indicator sets refer to a case scenario in the largest business city of each economy. For more details, see the data notes.

✔ Reform making it easier to do business ✘ Reform making it more difficult to do business

NIGERIA

Ease of doing business (rank)	133	Sub-Saharan Africa / Lower middle income		GNI per capita (US$)	1,180		
				Population (m)	158.3		
Starting a business (rank)	116	**Registering property** (rank)	180	**Trading across borders** (rank)	149		
Procedures (number)	8	Procedures (number)	13	Documents to export (number)	10		
Time (days)	34	Time (days)	82	Time to export (days)	24		
Cost (% of income per capita)	70.6	Cost (% of property value)	20.8	Cost to export (US$ per container)	1,263		
Minimum capital (% of income per capita)	0.0			Documents to import (number)	9		
		Getting credit (rank)	78	Time to import (days)	39		
Dealing with construction permits (rank)	84	Strength of legal rights index (0-10)	9	Cost to import (US$ per container)	1,440		
Procedures (number)	15	Depth of credit information index (0-6)	0				
Time (days)	85	Public registry coverage (% of adults)	0.1	**Enforcing contracts** (rank)	97		
Cost (% of income per capita)	504.8	Private bureau coverage (% of adults)	0.0	Procedures (number)	40		
				Time (days)	457		
Getting electricity (rank)	176	**Protecting investors** (rank)	65	Cost (% of claim)	32.0		
Procedures (number)	8	Extent of disclosure index (0-10)	5				
Time (days)	260	Extent of director liability index (0-10)	7	**Resolving insolvency** (rank)	99		
Cost (% of income per capita)	1,056.0	Ease of shareholder suits index (0-10)	5	Time (years)	2.0		
		Strength of investor protection index (0-10)	5.7	Cost (% of estate)	22		
				Recovery rate (cents on the dollar)	28.2		
		Paying taxes (rank)	138				
		Payments (number per year)	35				
		Time (hours per year)	938				
		Total tax rate (% of profit)	32.7				

NORWAY

Ease of doing business (rank)	6	OECD high income / High income		GNI per capita (US$)	85,380
				Population (m)	4.9
Starting a business (rank)	41	**Registering property** (rank)	8	**Trading across borders** (rank)	9
Procedures (number)	5	Procedures (number)	1	Documents to export (number)	4
Time (days)	7	Time (days)	3	Time to export (days)	7
Cost (% of income per capita)	1.8	Cost (% of property value)	2.5	Cost to export (US$ per container)	830
Minimum capital (% of income per capita)	19.4			Documents to import (number)	4
		Getting credit (rank)	48	Time to import (days)	7
Dealing with construction permits (rank)	60	Strength of legal rights index (0-10)	7	Cost to import (US$ per container)	729
Procedures (number)	11	Depth of credit information index (0-6)	4		
Time (days)	250	Public registry coverage (% of adults)	0.0	**Enforcing contracts** (rank)	4
Cost (% of income per capita)	33.1	Private bureau coverage (% of adults)	100.0	Procedures (number)	34
				Time (days)	280
Getting electricity (rank)	12	**Protecting investors** (rank)	24	Cost (% of claim)	9.9
Procedures (number)	4	Extent of disclosure index (0-10)	7		
Time (days)	66	Extent of director liability index (0-10)	6	**Resolving insolvency** (rank)	4
Cost (% of income per capita)	7.1	Ease of shareholder suits index (0-10)	7	Time (years)	0.9
		Strength of investor protection index (0-10)	6.7	Cost (% of estate)	1
				Recovery rate (cents on the dollar)	90.6
		Paying taxes (rank)	27		
		Payments (number per year)	4		
		Time (hours per year)	87		
		Total tax rate (% of profit)	41.6		

OMAN

Ease of doing business (rank)	49	Middle East & North Africa / High income		GNI per capita (US$)	18,657
				Population (m)	2.9
✔ **Starting a business** (rank)	68	**Registering property** (rank)	21	**Trading across borders** (rank)	47
Procedures (number)	5	Procedures (number)	2	Documents to export (number)	8
Time (days)	8	Time (days)	16	Time to export (days)	10
Cost (% of income per capita)	3.1	Cost (% of property value)	3.0	Cost to export (US$ per container)	745
Minimum capital (% of income per capita)	271.7			Documents to import (number)	8
		✔ **Getting credit** (rank)	98	Time to import (days)	9
Dealing with construction permits (rank)	64	Strength of legal rights index (0-10)	4	Cost to import (US$ per container)	680
Procedures (number)	14	Depth of credit information index (0-6)	4		
Time (days)	174	Public registry coverage (% of adults)	18.9	**Enforcing contracts** (rank)	107
Cost (% of income per capita)	45.7	Private bureau coverage (% of adults)	0.0	Procedures (number)	51
				Time (days)	598
Getting electricity (rank)	61	**Protecting investors** (rank)	97	Cost (% of claim)	13.5
Procedures (number)	6	Extent of disclosure index (0-10)	8		
Time (days)	62	Extent of director liability index (0-10)	5	**Resolving insolvency** (rank)	76
Cost (% of income per capita)	62.5	Ease of shareholder suits index (0-10)	2	Time (years)	4.0
		Strength of investor protection index (0-10)	5.0	Cost (% of estate)	4
				Recovery rate (cents on the dollar)	35.7
		✔ **Paying taxes** (rank)	9		
		Payments (number per year)	14		
		Time (hours per year)	62		
		Total tax rate (% of profit)	22.0		

Note: Most indicator sets refer to a case scenario in the largest business city of each economy. For more details, see the data notes.

✔ Reform making it easier to do business   ✘ Reform making it more difficult to do business

PAKISTAN

Ease of doing business (rank)	105	South Asia / Lower middle income		GNI per capita (US$) / Population (m)	1,050 / 173.4

Starting a business (rank)	90	**Registering property** (rank)	125	**Trading across borders** (rank)	75
Procedures (number)	10	Procedures (number)	6	Documents to export (number)	7
Time (days)	21	Time (days)	50	Time to export (days)	21
Cost (% of income per capita)	11.2	Cost (% of property value)	7.7	Cost to export (US$ per container)	660
Minimum capital (% of income per capita)	0.0			Documents to import (number)	8
		Getting credit (rank)	67	Time to import (days)	18
Dealing with construction permits (rank)	104	Strength of legal rights index (0-10)	6	Cost to import (US$ per container)	705
Procedures (number)	11	Depth of credit information index (0-6)	4		
Time (days)	222	Public registry coverage (% of adults)	6.9	**Enforcing contracts** (rank)	154
Cost (% of income per capita)	262.5	Private bureau coverage (% of adults)	2.0	Procedures (number)	46
				Time (days)	976
Getting electricity (rank)	166	**Protecting investors** (rank)	29	Cost (% of claim)	23.8
Procedures (number)	6	Extent of disclosure index (0-10)	6		
Time (days)	206	Extent of director liability index (0-10)	6	**Resolving insolvency** (rank)	74
Cost (% of income per capita)	1,346.0	Ease of shareholder suits index (0-10)	7	Time (years)	2.8
		Strength of investor protection index (0-10)	6.3	Cost (% of estate)	4
				Recovery rate (cents on the dollar)	36.4
		✘ **Paying taxes** (rank)	158		
		Payments (number per year)	47		
		Time (hours per year)	560		
		Total tax rate (% of profit)	35.3		

PALAU

Ease of doing business (rank)	116	East Asia & Pacific / Upper middle income		GNI per capita (US$) / Population (m)	6,460 / 0.02

Starting a business (rank)	124	**Registering property** (rank)	20	**Trading across borders** (rank)	124
Procedures (number)	8	Procedures (number)	5	Documents to export (number)	6
Time (days)	28	Time (days)	14	Time to export (days)	29
Cost (% of income per capita)	5.8	Cost (% of property value)	0.4	Cost to export (US$ per container)	1,070
Minimum capital (% of income per capita)	15.5			Documents to import (number)	10
		Getting credit (rank)	182	Time to import (days)	33
Dealing with construction permits (rank)	39	Strength of legal rights index (0-10)	1	Cost to import (US$ per container)	1,030
Procedures (number)	22	Depth of credit information index (0-6)	0		
Time (days)	71	Public registry coverage (% of adults)	0.0	**Enforcing contracts** (rank)	144
Cost (% of income per capita)	5.2	Private bureau coverage (% of adults)	0.0	Procedures (number)	38
				Time (days)	810
Getting electricity (rank)	80	**Protecting investors** (rank)	174	Cost (% of claim)	35.3
Procedures (number)	5	Extent of disclosure index (0-10)	0		
Time (days)	125	Extent of director liability index (0-10)	0	**Resolving insolvency** (rank)	61
Cost (% of income per capita)	145.9	Ease of shareholder suits index (0-10)	8	Time (years)	1.0
		Strength of investor protection index (0-10)	2.7	Cost (% of estate)	23
				Recovery rate (cents on the dollar)	40.5
		Paying taxes (rank)	97		
		Payments (number per year)	19		
		Time (hours per year)	128		
		Total tax rate (% of profit)	73.0		

PANAMA

Ease of doing business (rank)	61	Latin America & Caribbean / Upper middle income		GNI per capita (US$) / Population (m)	6,990 / 3.5

✔ **Starting a business** (rank)	29	**Registering property** (rank)	120	**Trading across borders** (rank)	11
Procedures (number)	6	Procedures (number)	8	Documents to export (number)	3
Time (days)	8	Time (days)	32	Time to export (days)	9
Cost (% of income per capita)	9.9	Cost (% of property value)	5.3	Cost to export (US$ per container)	615
Minimum capital (% of income per capita)	0.0			Documents to import (number)	4
		Getting credit (rank)	48	Time to import (days)	9
Dealing with construction permits (rank)	71	Strength of legal rights index (0-10)	5	Cost to import (US$ per container)	965
Procedures (number)	17	Depth of credit information index (0-6)	6		
Time (days)	113	Public registry coverage (% of adults)	0.0	**Enforcing contracts** (rank)	119
Cost (% of income per capita)	95.5	Private bureau coverage (% of adults)	53.8	Procedures (number)	31
				Time (days)	686
Getting electricity (rank)	15	**Protecting investors** (rank)	111	Cost (% of claim)	50.0
Procedures (number)	5	Extent of disclosure index (0-10)	1		
Time (days)	35	Extent of director liability index (0-10)	4	**Resolving insolvency** (rank)	83
Cost (% of income per capita)	15.4	Ease of shareholder suits index (0-10)	9	Time (years)	2.5
		Strength of investor protection index (0-10)	4.7	Cost (% of estate)	18
				Recovery rate (cents on the dollar)	33.3
		Paying taxes (rank)	169		
		Payments (number per year)	53		
		Time (hours per year)	482		
		Total tax rate (% of profit)	45.2		

Note: Most indicator sets refer to a case scenario in the largest business city of each economy. For more details, see the data notes.

✔ Reform making it easier to do business ✘ Reform making it more difficult to do business

PAPUA NEW GUINEA

Ease of doing business (rank)	101	East Asia & Pacific Lower middle income		GNI per capita (US$) Population (m)		1,300 6.9
Starting a business (rank)	84	**Registering property** (rank)	87	**Trading across borders** (rank)		99
Procedures (number)	6	Procedures (number)	4	Documents to export (number)		7
Time (days)	51	Time (days)	72	Time to export (days)		26
Cost (% of income per capita)	15.6	Cost (% of property value)	5.1	Cost to export (US$ per container)		664
Minimum capital (% of income per capita)	0.0			Documents to import (number)		9
		Getting credit (rank)	98	Time to import (days)		29
Dealing with construction permits (rank)	138	Strength of legal rights index (0-10)	5	Cost to import (US$ per container)		722
Procedures (number)	21	Depth of credit information index (0-6)	3			
Time (days)	219	Public registry coverage (% of adults)	0.0	**Enforcing contracts** (rank)		163
Cost (% of income per capita)	65.6	Private bureau coverage (% of adults)	1.8	Procedures (number)		42
				Time (days)		591
Getting electricity (rank)	20	**Protecting investors** (rank)	46	Cost (% of claim)		110.3
Procedures (number)	4	Extent of disclosure index (0-10)	5			
Time (days)	66	Extent of director liability index (0-10)	5	**Resolving insolvency** (rank)		116
Cost (% of income per capita)	66.9	Ease of shareholder suits index (0-10)	8	Time (years)		3.0
		Strength of investor protection index (0-10)	6.0	Cost (% of estate)		23
				Recovery rate (cents on the dollar)		23.7
		Paying taxes (rank)	106			
		Payments (number per year)	33			
		Time (hours per year)	194			
		Total tax rate (% of profit)	42.3			

PARAGUAY

Ease of doing business (rank)	102	Latin America & Caribbean Lower middle income		GNI per capita (US$) Population (m)		2,940 6.5
Starting a business (rank)	106	**Registering property** (rank)	64	**Trading across borders** (rank)		154
Procedures (number)	7	Procedures (number)	6	Documents to export (number)		8
Time (days)	35	Time (days)	46	Time to export (days)		33
Cost (% of income per capita)	47.2	Cost (% of property value)	1.9	Cost to export (US$ per container)		1,440
Minimum capital (% of income per capita)	0.0			Documents to import (number)		10
		✔ **Getting credit** (rank)	78	Time to import (days)		33
✔ **Dealing with construction permits** (rank)	66	Strength of legal rights index (0-10)	3	Cost to import (US$ per container)		1,750
Procedures (number)	12	Depth of credit information index (0-6)	6			
Time (days)	137	Public registry coverage (% of adults)	15.7	**Enforcing contracts** (rank)		106
Cost (% of income per capita)	239.9	Private bureau coverage (% of adults)	48.5	Procedures (number)		38
				Time (days)		591
Getting electricity (rank)	23	**Protecting investors** (rank)	65	Cost (% of claim)		30.0
Procedures (number)	4	Extent of disclosure index (0-10)	6			
Time (days)	53	Extent of director liability index (0-10)	5	**Resolving insolvency** (rank)		140
Cost (% of income per capita)	224.6	Ease of shareholder suits index (0-10)	6	Time (years)		3.9
		Strength of investor protection index (0-10)	5.7	Cost (% of estate)		9
				Recovery rate (cents on the dollar)		16.6
		✘ **Paying taxes** (rank)	132			
		Payments (number per year)	35			
		Time (hours per year)	387			
		Total tax rate (% of profit)	35.0			

PERU

Ease of doing business (rank)	41	Latin America & Caribbean Upper middle income		GNI per capita (US$) Population (m)		4,710 29.5
✔ **Starting a business** (rank)	55	**Registering property** (rank)	22	**Trading across borders** (rank)		56
Procedures (number)	5	Procedures (number)	4	Documents to export (number)		6
Time (days)	26	Time (days)	7	Time to export (days)		12
Cost (% of income per capita)	11.9	Cost (% of property value)	3.3	Cost to export (US$ per container)		860
Minimum capital (% of income per capita)	0.0			Documents to import (number)		8
		Getting credit (rank)	24	Time to import (days)		17
Dealing with construction permits (rank)	101	Strength of legal rights index (0-10)	7	Cost to import (US$ per container)		880
Procedures (number)	16	Depth of credit information index (0-6)	6			
Time (days)	188	Public registry coverage (% of adults)	28.5	**Enforcing contracts** (rank)		111
Cost (% of income per capita)	76.3	Private bureau coverage (% of adults)	36.0	Procedures (number)		41
				Time (days)		428
Getting electricity (rank)	82	✔ **Protecting investors** (rank)	17	Cost (% of claim)		35.7
Procedures (number)	5	Extent of disclosure index (0-10)	8			
Time (days)	100	Extent of director liability index (0-10)	5	**Resolving insolvency** (rank)		100
Cost (% of income per capita)	441.6	Ease of shareholder suits index (0-10)	8	Time (years)		3.1
		Strength of investor protection index (0-10)	7.0	Cost (% of estate)		7
				Recovery rate (cents on the dollar)		28.0
		✔ **Paying taxes** (rank)	85			
		Payments (number per year)	9			
		Time (hours per year)	309			
		Total tax rate (% of profit)	40.7			

Note: Most indicator sets refer to a case scenario in the largest business city of each economy. For more details, see the data notes.

✔ Reform making it easier to do business   ✘ Reform making it more difficult to do business

PHILIPPINES

		East Asia & Pacific		GNI per capita (US$)	2,050
Ease of doing business (rank)	136	Lower middle income		Population (m)	93.6
Starting a business (rank)	158	**Registering property** (rank)	117	**Trading across borders** (rank)	51
Procedures (number)	15	Procedures (number)	8	Documents to export (number)	7
Time (days)	35	Time (days)	39	Time to export (days)	15
Cost (% of income per capita)	19.1	Cost (% of property value)	4.8	Cost to export (US$ per container)	630
Minimum capital (% of income per capita)	5.2			Documents to import (number)	8
		Getting credit (rank)	126	Time to import (days)	14
Dealing with construction permits (rank)	102	Strength of legal rights index (0-10)	4	Cost to import (US$ per container)	730
Procedures (number)	30	Depth of credit information index (0-6)	3		
Time (days)	85	Public registry coverage (% of adults)	0.0	**Enforcing contracts** (rank)	112
Cost (% of income per capita)	110.5	Private bureau coverage (% of adults)	8.2	Procedures (number)	37
				Time (days)	842
Getting electricity (rank)	54	**Protecting investors** (rank)	133	Cost (% of claim)	26.0
Procedures (number)	5	Extent of disclosure index (0-10)	2		
Time (days)	50	Extent of director liability index (0-10)	2	✔ **Resolving insolvency** (rank)	163
Cost (% of income per capita)	762.0	Ease of shareholder suits index (0-10)	8	Time (years)	5.7
		Strength of investor protection index (0-10)	4.0	Cost (% of estate)	38
				Recovery rate (cents on the dollar)	4.7
		Paying taxes (rank)	136		
		Payments (number per year)	47		
		Time (hours per year)	195		
		Total tax rate (% of profit)	46.5		

POLAND

		OECD high income		GNI per capita (US$)	12,420
Ease of doing business (rank)	62	High income		Population (m)	38.2
Starting a business (rank)	126	**Registering property** (rank)	89	✔ **Trading across borders** (rank)	46
Procedures (number)	6	Procedures (number)	6	Documents to export (number)	5
Time (days)	32	Time (days)	152	Time to export (days)	17
Cost (% of income per capita)	17.3	Cost (% of property value)	0.4	Cost to export (US$ per container)	1,050
Minimum capital (% of income per capita)	14.0			Documents to import (number)	5
		Getting credit (rank)	8	Time to import (days)	16
Dealing with construction permits (rank)	160	Strength of legal rights index (0-10)	9	Cost to import (US$ per container)	1,000
Procedures (number)	30	Depth of credit information index (0-6)	5		
Time (days)	301	Public registry coverage (% of adults)	0.0	**Enforcing contracts** (rank)	68
Cost (% of income per capita)	53.6	Private bureau coverage (% of adults)	74.8	Procedures (number)	37
				Time (days)	830
Getting electricity (rank)	64	**Protecting investors** (rank)	46	Cost (% of claim)	12.0
Procedures (number)	4	Extent of disclosure index (0-10)	7		
Time (days)	143	Extent of director liability index (0-10)	2	✔ **Resolving insolvency** (rank)	87
Cost (% of income per capita)	209.3	Ease of shareholder suits index (0-10)	9	Time (years)	3.0
		Strength of investor protection index (0-10)	6.0	Cost (% of estate)	15
				Recovery rate (cents on the dollar)	31.5
		Paying taxes (rank)	128		
		Payments (number per year)	29		
		Time (hours per year)	296		
		Total tax rate (% of profit)	43.6		

PORTUGAL

		OECD high income		GNI per capita (US$)	21,860
Ease of doing business (rank)	30	High income		Population (m)	10.6
✔ **Starting a business** (rank)	26	**Registering property** (rank)	31	**Trading across borders** (rank)	26
Procedures (number)	5	Procedures (number)	1	Documents to export (number)	4
Time (days)	5	Time (days)	1	Time to export (days)	16
Cost (% of income per capita)	2.3	Cost (% of property value)	7.3	Cost to export (US$ per container)	685
Minimum capital (% of income per capita)	0.0			Documents to import (number)	5
		Getting credit (rank)	126	Time to import (days)	15
✔ **Dealing with construction permits** (rank)	97	Strength of legal rights index (0-10)	3	Cost to import (US$ per container)	899
Procedures (number)	14	Depth of credit information index (0-6)	4		
Time (days)	255	Public registry coverage (% of adults)	86.2	**Enforcing contracts** (rank)	22
Cost (% of income per capita)	47.2	Private bureau coverage (% of adults)	21.5	Procedures (number)	31
				Time (days)	547
Getting electricity (rank)	34	**Protecting investors** (rank)	46	Cost (% of claim)	13.0
Procedures (number)	5	Extent of disclosure index (0-10)	6		
Time (days)	64	Extent of director liability index (0-10)	5	**Resolving insolvency** (rank)	22
Cost (% of income per capita)	54.6	Ease of shareholder suits index (0-10)	7	Time (years)	2.0
		Strength of investor protection index (0-10)	6.0	Cost (% of estate)	9
				Recovery rate (cents on the dollar)	70.9
		Paying taxes (rank)	78		
		Payments (number per year)	8		
		Time (hours per year)	275		
		Total tax rate (% of profit)	43.3		

Note: Most indicator sets refer to a case scenario in the largest business city of each economy. For more details, see the data notes.

✔ Reform making it easier to do business ✘ Reform making it more difficult to do business

PUERTO RICO

Ease of doing business (rank)	43	Latin America & Caribbean High income		GNI per capita (US$) Population (m)	17,280 4.0
✔ **Starting a business** (rank)	12	**Registering property** (rank)	126	**Trading across borders** (rank)	101
Procedures (number)	6	Procedures (number)	8	Documents to export (number)	6
Time (days)	6	Time (days)	194	Time to export (days)	15
Cost (% of income per capita)	0.6	Cost (% of property value)	0.9	Cost to export (US$ per container)	1,300
Minimum capital (% of income per capita)	0.0			Documents to import (number)	10
		Getting credit (rank)	24	Time to import (days)	16
✔ **Dealing with construction permits** (rank)	152	Strength of legal rights index (0-10)	8	Cost to import (US$ per container)	1,300
Procedures (number)	18	Depth of credit information index (0-6)	5		
Time (days)	189	Public registry coverage (% of adults)	0.0	**Enforcing contracts** (rank)	97
Cost (% of income per capita)	369.1	Private bureau coverage (% of adults)	72.3	Procedures (number)	39
				Time (days)	620
Getting electricity (rank)	35	**Protecting investors** (rank)	17	Cost (% of claim)	25.6
Procedures (number)	5	Extent of disclosure index (0-10)	7		
Time (days)	32	Extent of director liability index (0-10)	6	**Resolving insolvency** (rank)	27
Cost (% of income per capita)	392.4	Ease of shareholder suits index (0-10)	8	Time (years)	3.8
		Strength of investor protection index (0-10)	7.0	Cost (% of estate)	8
				Recovery rate (cents on the dollar)	64.7
		Paying taxes (rank)	113		
		Payments (number per year)	16		
		Time (hours per year)	218		
		Total tax rate (% of profit)	63.1		

QATAR

Ease of doing business (rank)	36	Middle East & North Africa High income		GNI per capita (US$) Population (m)	76,168 1.5
✔ **Starting a business** (rank)	116	**Registering property** (rank)	37	**Trading across borders** (rank)	57
Procedures (number)	8	Procedures (number)	7	Documents to export (number)	5
Time (days)	12	Time (days)	13	Time to export (days)	21
Cost (% of income per capita)	8.3	Cost (% of property value)	0.3	Cost to export (US$ per container)	860
Minimum capital (% of income per capita)	64.0			Documents to import (number)	7
		✔ **Getting credit** (rank)	98	Time to import (days)	20
✘ **Dealing with construction permits** (rank)	24	Strength of legal rights index (0-10)	4	Cost to import (US$ per container)	730
Procedures (number)	17	Depth of credit information index (0-6)	4		
Time (days)	70	Public registry coverage (% of adults)	32.2	**Enforcing contracts** (rank)	95
Cost (% of income per capita)	1.1	Private bureau coverage (% of adults)	0.0	Procedures (number)	43
				Time (days)	570
Getting electricity (rank)	18	**Protecting investors** (rank)	97	Cost (% of claim)	21.6
Procedures (number)	3	Extent of disclosure index (0-10)	5		
Time (days)	90	Extent of director liability index (0-10)	6	**Resolving insolvency** (rank)	37
Cost (% of income per capita)	4.1	Ease of shareholder suits index (0-10)	4	Time (years)	2.8
		Strength of investor protection index (0-10)	5.0	Cost (% of estate)	22
				Recovery rate (cents on the dollar)	53.1
		Paying taxes (rank)	2		
		Payments (number per year)	3		
		Time (hours per year)	36		
		Total tax rate (% of profit)	11.3		

ROMANIA

Ease of doing business (rank)	72	Eastern Europe & Central Asia Upper middle income		GNI per capita (US$) Population (m)	7,840 21.4
✘ **Starting a business** (rank)	63	**Registering property** (rank)	70	**Trading across borders** (rank)	72
Procedures (number)	6	Procedures (number)	8	Documents to export (number)	5
Time (days)	14	Time (days)	26	Time to export (days)	12
Cost (% of income per capita)	3.0	Cost (% of property value)	1.2	Cost to export (US$ per container)	1,485
Minimum capital (% of income per capita)	0.8			Documents to import (number)	6
		Getting credit (rank)	8	Time to import (days)	13
Dealing with construction permits (rank)	123	Strength of legal rights index (0-10)	9	Cost to import (US$ per container)	1,495
Procedures (number)	16	Depth of credit information index (0-6)	5		
Time (days)	287	Public registry coverage (% of adults)	15.2	**Enforcing contracts** (rank)	56
Cost (% of income per capita)	73.0	Private bureau coverage (% of adults)	42.0	Procedures (number)	31
				Time (days)	512
Getting electricity (rank)	165	**Protecting investors** (rank)	46	Cost (% of claim)	28.9
Procedures (number)	7	Extent of disclosure index (0-10)	9		
Time (days)	223	Extent of director liability index (0-10)	5	✔ **Resolving insolvency** (rank)	97
Cost (% of income per capita)	556.9	Ease of shareholder suits index (0-10)	4	Time (years)	3.3
		Strength of investor protection index (0-10)	6.0	Cost (% of estate)	11
				Recovery rate (cents on the dollar)	28.6
		✔ **Paying taxes** (rank)	154		
		Payments (number per year)	113		
		Time (hours per year)	222		
		Total tax rate (% of profit)	44.4		

Note: Most indicator sets refer to a case scenario in the largest business city of each economy. For more details, see the data notes.

✔ Reform making it easier to do business   ✘ Reform making it more difficult to do business

RUSSIAN FEDERATION

Ease of doing business (rank)	120	Eastern Europe & Central Asia / Upper middle income		GNI per capita (US$)	9,910
				Population (m)	141.8
Starting a business (rank)	111	✔ **Registering property** (rank)	45	✔ **Trading across borders** (rank)	160
Procedures (number)	9	Procedures (number)	5	Documents to export (number)	8
Time (days)	30	Time (days)	43	Time to export (days)	36
Cost (% of income per capita)	2.0	Cost (% of property value)	0.2	Cost to export (US$ per container)	1,850
Minimum capital (% of income per capita)	1.6			Documents to import (number)	10
		Getting credit (rank)	98	Time to import (days)	36
Dealing with construction permits (rank)	178	Strength of legal rights index (0-10)	3	Cost to import (US$ per container)	1,800
Procedures (number)	51	Depth of credit information index (0-6)	5		
Time (days)	423	Public registry coverage (% of adults)	0.0	✔ **Enforcing contracts** (rank)	13
Cost (% of income per capita)	183.8	Private bureau coverage (% of adults)	35.8	Procedures (number)	36
				Time (days)	281
✔ **Getting electricity** (rank)	183	**Protecting investors** (rank)	111	Cost (% of claim)	13.4
Procedures (number)	10	Extent of disclosure index (0-10)	6		
Time (days)	281	Extent of director liability index (0-10)	2	**Resolving insolvency** (rank)	60
Cost (% of income per capita)	1,852.4	Ease of shareholder suits index (0-10)	6	Time (years)	2.0
		Strength of investor protection index (0-10)	4.7	Cost (% of estate)	9
				Recovery rate (cents on the dollar)	41.5
		✘ **Paying taxes** (rank)	105		
		Payments (number per year)	9		
		Time (hours per year)	290		
		Total tax rate (% of profit)	46.9		

RWANDA

Ease of doing business (rank)	45	Sub-Saharan Africa / Low income		GNI per capita (US$)	540
				Population (m)	10.3
✔ **Starting a business** (rank)	8	✘ **Registering property** (rank)	61	**Trading across borders** (rank)	155
Procedures (number)	2	Procedures (number)	5	Documents to export (number)	8
Time (days)	3	Time (days)	25	Time to export (days)	29
Cost (% of income per capita)	4.7	Cost (% of property value)	6.3	Cost to export (US$ per container)	3,275
Minimum capital (% of income per capita)	0.0			Documents to import (number)	8
		✔ **Getting credit** (rank)	8	Time to import (days)	31
Dealing with construction permits (rank)	84	Strength of legal rights index (0-10)	8	Cost to import (US$ per container)	4,990
Procedures (number)	12	Depth of credit information index (0-6)	6		
Time (days)	164	Public registry coverage (% of adults)	1.4	**Enforcing contracts** (rank)	39
Cost (% of income per capita)	312.0	Private bureau coverage (% of adults)	0.0	Procedures (number)	24
				Time (days)	230
Getting electricity (rank)	50	**Protecting investors** (rank)	29	Cost (% of claim)	78.7
Procedures (number)	4	Extent of disclosure index (0-10)	7		
Time (days)	30	Extent of director liability index (0-10)	9	**Resolving insolvency** (rank)	165
Cost (% of income per capita)	4,696.8	Ease of shareholder suits index (0-10)	3	Time (years)	3.0
		Strength of investor protection index (0-10)	6.3	Cost (% of estate)	50
				Recovery rate (cents on the dollar)	3.2
		✔ **Paying taxes** (rank)	19		
		Payments (number per year)	18		
		Time (hours per year)	148		
		Total tax rate (% of profit)	31.3		

SAMOA

Ease of doing business (rank)	60	East Asia & Pacific / Lower middle income		GNI per capita (US$)	2,930
				Population (m)	0.2
Starting a business (rank)	22	**Registering property** (rank)	26	**Trading across borders** (rank)	96
Procedures (number)	4	Procedures (number)	5	Documents to export (number)	7
Time (days)	9	Time (days)	15	Time to export (days)	27
Cost (% of income per capita)	9.7	Cost (% of property value)	1.6	Cost to export (US$ per container)	820
Minimum capital (% of income per capita)	0.0			Documents to import (number)	7
		Getting credit (rank)	126	Time to import (days)	31
Dealing with construction permits (rank)	68	Strength of legal rights index (0-10)	7	Cost to import (US$ per container)	848
Procedures (number)	21	Depth of credit information index (0-6)	0		
Time (days)	87	Public registry coverage (% of adults)	0.0	**Enforcing contracts** (rank)	80
Cost (% of income per capita)	59.2	Private bureau coverage (% of adults)	0.0	Procedures (number)	44
				Time (days)	455
Getting electricity (rank)	32	**Protecting investors** (rank)	29	Cost (% of claim)	19.7
Procedures (number)	4	Extent of disclosure index (0-10)	5		
Time (days)	34	Extent of director liability index (0-10)	6	**Resolving insolvency** (rank)	145
Cost (% of income per capita)	857.1	Ease of shareholder suits index (0-10)	8	Time (years)	2.5
		Strength of investor protection index (0-10)	6.3	Cost (% of estate)	38
				Recovery rate (cents on the dollar)	15.1
		Paying taxes (rank)	66		
		Payments (number per year)	37		
		Time (hours per year)	224		
		Total tax rate (% of profit)	18.9		

Note: Most indicator sets refer to a case scenario in the largest business city of each economy. For more details, see the data notes.

✔ Reform making it easier to do business ✘ Reform making it more difficult to do business

SÃO TOMÉ AND PRÍNCIPE

		Sub-Saharan Africa		GNI per capita (US$)	1,200
Ease of doing business (rank)	163	Lower middle income		Population (m)	0.2
✔ **Starting a business** (rank)	105	✔ **Registering property** (rank)	160	✔ **Trading across borders** (rank)	94
Procedures (number)	4	Procedures (number)	7	Documents to export (number)	8
Time (days)	10	Time (days)	62	Time to export (days)	26
Cost (% of income per capita)	24.5	Cost (% of property value)	8.9	Cost to export (US$ per container)	690
Minimum capital (% of income per capita)	336.0			Documents to import (number)	8
		Getting credit (rank)	177	Time to import (days)	28
✔ **Dealing with construction permits** (rank)	134	Strength of legal rights index (0-10)	2	Cost to import (US$ per container)	577
Procedures (number)	13	Depth of credit information index (0-6)	0		
Time (days)	211	Public registry coverage (% of adults)	0.0	**Enforcing contracts** (rank)	179
Cost (% of income per capita)	536.8	Private bureau coverage (% of adults)	0.0	Procedures (number)	43
				Time (days)	1,185
Getting electricity (rank)	74	**Protecting investors** (rank)	155	Cost (% of claim)	50.5
Procedures (number)	4	Extent of disclosure index (0-10)	3		
Time (days)	89	Extent of director liability index (0-10)	1	**Resolving insolvency** (rank)	159
Cost (% of income per capita)	1,252.8	Ease of shareholder suits index (0-10)	6	Time (years)	6.2
		Strength of investor protection index (0-10)	3.3	Cost (% of estate)	22
				Recovery rate (cents on the dollar)	7.4
		Paying taxes (rank)	113		
		Payments (number per year)	42		
		Time (hours per year)	424		
		Total tax rate (% of profit)	32.5		

SAUDI ARABIA

		Middle East & North Africa		GNI per capita (US$)	16,996
Ease of doing business (rank)	12	High income		Population (m)	26.0
✔ **Starting a business** (rank)	10	**Registering property** (rank)	1	**Trading across borders** (rank)	18
Procedures (number)	3	Procedures (number)	2	Documents to export (number)	5
Time (days)	5	Time (days)	2	Time to export (days)	13
Cost (% of income per capita)	5.9	Cost (% of property value)	0.0	Cost to export (US$ per container)	615
Minimum capital (% of income per capita)	0.0			Documents to import (number)	5
		Getting credit (rank)	48	Time to import (days)	17
Dealing with construction permits (rank)	4	Strength of legal rights index (0-10)	5	Cost to import (US$ per container)	686
Procedures (number)	9	Depth of credit information index (0-6)	6		
Time (days)	75	Public registry coverage (% of adults)	0.0	**Enforcing contracts** (rank)	138
Cost (% of income per capita)	19.4	Private bureau coverage (% of adults)	16.0	Procedures (number)	43
				Time (days)	635
Getting electricity (rank)	18	**Protecting investors** (rank)	17	Cost (% of claim)	27.5
Procedures (number)	4	Extent of disclosure index (0-10)	9		
Time (days)	71	Extent of director liability index (0-10)	8	**Resolving insolvency** (rank)	73
Cost (% of income per capita)	18.1	Ease of shareholder suits index (0-10)	4	Time (years)	1.5
		Strength of investor protection index (0-10)	7.0	Cost (% of estate)	22
				Recovery rate (cents on the dollar)	36.8
		Paying taxes (rank)	10		
		Payments (number per year)	14		
		Time (hours per year)	79		
		Total tax rate (% of profit)	14.5		

SENEGAL

		Sub-Saharan Africa		GNI per capita (US$)	1,050
Ease of doing business (rank)	154	Lower middle income		Population (m)	12.9
✔ **Starting a business** (rank)	93	**Registering property** (rank)	171	✔ **Trading across borders** (rank)	65
Procedures (number)	3	Procedures (number)	6	Documents to export (number)	6
Time (days)	5	Time (days)	122	Time to export (days)	11
Cost (% of income per capita)	68.0	Cost (% of property value)	20.3	Cost to export (US$ per container)	1,098
Minimum capital (% of income per capita)	203.0			Documents to import (number)	5
		✔ **Getting credit** (rank)	126	Time to import (days)	14
Dealing with construction permits (rank)	125	Strength of legal rights index (0-10)	6	Cost to import (US$ per container)	1,740
Procedures (number)	13	Depth of credit information index (0-6)	1		
Time (days)	210	Public registry coverage (% of adults)	4.5	✔ **Enforcing contracts** (rank)	145
Cost (% of income per capita)	435.2	Private bureau coverage (% of adults)	0.0	Procedures (number)	43
				Time (days)	780
Getting electricity (rank)	168	**Protecting investors** (rank)	166	Cost (% of claim)	26.5
Procedures (number)	6	Extent of disclosure index (0-10)	6		
Time (days)	125	Extent of director liability index (0-10)	1	**Resolving insolvency** (rank)	86
Cost (% of income per capita)	5,938.9	Ease of shareholder suits index (0-10)	2	Time (years)	3.0
		Strength of investor protection index (0-10)	3.0	Cost (% of estate)	7
				Recovery rate (cents on the dollar)	32.0
		Paying taxes (rank)	174		
		Payments (number per year)	59		
		Time (hours per year)	666		
		Total tax rate (% of profit)	46.0		

Note: Most indicator sets refer to a case scenario in the largest business city of each economy. For more details, see the data notes.

✔ Reform making it easier to do business ✘ Reform making it more difficult to do business

SERBIA

| Eastern Europe & Central Asia | | GNI per capita (US$) | 5,820 |
| Upper middle income | | Population (m) | 7.3 |

| Ease of doing business (rank) | 92 |

Starting a business (rank)	92
Procedures (number)	7
Time (days)	13
Cost (% of income per capita)	7.8
Minimum capital (% of income per capita)	6.0

✔ Registering property (rank)	39
Procedures (number)	6
Time (days)	11
Cost (% of property value)	2.8

Trading across borders (rank)	79
Documents to export (number)	6
Time to export (days)	12
Cost to export (US$ per container)	1,433
Documents to import (number)	6
Time to import (days)	14
Cost to import (US$ per container)	1,609

Dealing with construction permits (rank)	175
Procedures (number)	19
Time (days)	279
Cost (% of income per capita)	1,603.8

Getting credit (rank)	24
Strength of legal rights index (0-10)	8
Depth of credit information index (0-6)	5
Public registry coverage (% of adults)	0.0
Private bureau coverage (% of adults)	100.0

Enforcing contracts (rank)	104
Procedures (number)	36
Time (days)	635
Cost (% of claim)	31.3

Getting electricity (rank)	79
Procedures (number)	4
Time (days)	131
Cost (% of income per capita)	545.7

Protecting investors (rank)	79
Extent of disclosure index (0-10)	7
Extent of director liability index (0-10)	6
Ease of shareholder suits index (0-10)	3
Strength of investor protection index (0-10)	5.3

✔ Resolving insolvency (rank)	113
Time (years)	2.7
Cost (% of estate)	23
Recovery rate (cents on the dollar)	24.4

Paying taxes (rank)	143
Payments (number per year)	66
Time (hours per year)	279
Total tax rate (% of profit)	34.0

SEYCHELLES

| Sub-Saharan Africa | | GNI per capita (US$) | 9,490 |
| Upper middle income | | Population (m) | 0.1 |

| Ease of doing business (rank) | 103 |

Starting a business (rank)	113
Procedures (number)	10
Time (days)	39
Cost (% of income per capita)	16.0
Minimum capital (% of income per capita)	0.0

Registering property (rank)	63
Procedures (number)	4
Time (days)	33
Cost (% of property value)	7.0

✔ Trading across borders (rank)	33
Documents to export (number)	5
Time to export (days)	16
Cost to export (US$ per container)	876
Documents to import (number)	5
Time to import (days)	17
Cost to import (US$ per container)	876

Dealing with construction permits (rank)	54
Procedures (number)	17
Time (days)	126
Cost (% of income per capita)	30.3

Getting credit (rank)	166
Strength of legal rights index (0-10)	4
Depth of credit information index (0-6)	0
Public registry coverage (% of adults)	0.0
Private bureau coverage (% of adults)	0.0

✘ Enforcing contracts (rank)	84
Procedures (number)	37
Time (days)	915
Cost (% of claim)	15.4

Getting electricity (rank)	149
Procedures (number)	6
Time (days)	147
Cost (% of income per capita)	504.7

Protecting investors (rank)	65
Extent of disclosure index (0-10)	4
Extent of director liability index (0-10)	8
Ease of shareholder suits index (0-10)	5
Strength of investor protection index (0-10)	5.7

Resolving insolvency (rank)	183
Time (years)	NO PRACTICE
Cost (% of estate)	NO PRACTICE
Recovery rate (cents on the dollar)	0.0

✔ Paying taxes (rank)	16
Payments (number per year)	21
Time (hours per year)	76
Total tax rate (% of profit)	32.2

SIERRA LEONE

| Sub-Saharan Africa | | GNI per capita (US$) | 340 |
| Low income | | Population (m) | 5.8 |

| Ease of doing business (rank) | 141 |

Starting a business (rank)	72
Procedures (number)	6
Time (days)	12
Cost (% of income per capita)	93.3
Minimum capital (% of income per capita)	0.0

Registering property (rank)	169
Procedures (number)	7
Time (days)	86
Cost (% of property value)	11.8

✔ Trading across borders (rank)	132
Documents to export (number)	7
Time to export (days)	24
Cost to export (US$ per container)	1,573
Documents to import (number)	7
Time to import (days)	27
Cost to import (US$ per container)	1,639

Dealing with construction permits (rank)	167
Procedures (number)	20
Time (days)	238
Cost (% of income per capita)	272.6

✔ Getting credit (rank)	126
Strength of legal rights index (0-10)	7
Depth of credit information index (0-6)	0
Public registry coverage (% of adults)	0.0
Private bureau coverage (% of adults)	0.0

✔ Enforcing contracts (rank)	141
Procedures (number)	39
Time (days)	515
Cost (% of claim)	149.5

Getting electricity (rank)	174
Procedures (number)	8
Time (days)	137
Cost (% of income per capita)	2,466.3

Protecting investors (rank)	29
Extent of disclosure index (0-10)	6
Extent of director liability index (0-10)	7
Ease of shareholder suits index (0-10)	6
Strength of investor protection index (0-10)	6.3

✔ Resolving insolvency (rank)	155
Time (years)	2.6
Cost (% of estate)	42
Recovery rate (cents on the dollar)	9.2

Paying taxes (rank)	76
Payments (number per year)	29
Time (hours per year)	357
Total tax rate (% of profit)	32.1

Note: Most indicator sets refer to a case scenario in the largest business city of each economy. For more details, see the data notes.

✔ Reform making it easier to do business ✘ Reform making it more difficult to do business

SINGAPORE

		East Asia & Pacific		GNI per capita (US$)	40,920
Ease of doing business (rank)	1	High income		Population (m)	5.1
Starting a business (rank)	4	**Registering property** (rank)	14	**Trading across borders** (rank)	1
Procedures (number)	3	Procedures (number)	3	Documents to export (number)	4
Time (days)	3	Time (days)	5	Time to export (days)	5
Cost (% of income per capita)	0.7	Cost (% of property value)	2.8	Cost to export (US$ per container)	456
Minimum capital (% of income per capita)	0.0			Documents to import (number)	4
		Getting credit (rank)	8	Time to import (days)	4
Dealing with construction permits (rank)	3	Strength of legal rights index (0-10)	10	Cost to import (US$ per container)	439
Procedures (number)	11	Depth of credit information index (0-6)	4		
Time (days)	26	Public registry coverage (% of adults)	0.0	**Enforcing contracts** (rank)	12
Cost (% of income per capita)	18.1	Private bureau coverage (% of adults)	53.8	Procedures (number)	21
				Time (days)	150
Getting electricity (rank)	5	**Protecting investors** (rank)	2	Cost (% of claim)	25.8
Procedures (number)	4	Extent of disclosure index (0-10)	10		
Time (days)	36	Extent of director liability index (0-10)	9	**Resolving insolvency** (rank)	2
Cost (% of income per capita)	31.1	Ease of shareholder suits index (0-10)	9	Time (years)	0.8
		Strength of investor protection index (0-10)	9.3	Cost (% of estate)	1
				Recovery rate (cents on the dollar)	91.3
		Paying taxes (rank)	4		
		Payments (number per year)	5		
		Time (hours per year)	84		
		Total tax rate (% of profit)	27.1		

SLOVAK REPUBLIC

		OECD high income		GNI per capita (US$)	16,220
Ease of doing business (rank)	48	High income		Population (m)	5.4
Starting a business (rank)	76	**Registering property** (rank)	10	**Trading across borders** (rank)	95
Procedures (number)	6	Procedures (number)	3	Documents to export (number)	6
Time (days)	18	Time (days)	17	Time to export (days)	17
Cost (% of income per capita)	1.8	Cost (% of property value)	0.0	Cost to export (US$ per container)	1,560
Minimum capital (% of income per capita)	20.9			Documents to import (number)	7
		✔ **Getting credit** (rank)	24	Time to import (days)	17
Dealing with construction permits (rank)	50	Strength of legal rights index (0-10)	9	Cost to import (US$ per container)	1,540
Procedures (number)	11	Depth of credit information index (0-6)	4		
Time (days)	286	Public registry coverage (% of adults)	2.6	**Enforcing contracts** (rank)	71
Cost (% of income per capita)	7.2	Private bureau coverage (% of adults)	56.1	Procedures (number)	32
				Time (days)	565
Getting electricity (rank)	102	**Protecting investors** (rank)	111	Cost (% of claim)	30.0
Procedures (number)	5	Extent of disclosure index (0-10)	3		
Time (days)	177	Extent of director liability index (0-10)	4	**Resolving insolvency** (rank)	35
Cost (% of income per capita)	242.2	Ease of shareholder suits index (0-10)	7	Time (years)	4.0
		Strength of investor protection index (0-10)	4.7	Cost (% of estate)	18
				Recovery rate (cents on the dollar)	54.3
		Paying taxes (rank)	130		
		Payments (number per year)	31		
		Time (hours per year)	231		
		Total tax rate (% of profit)	48.8		

SLOVENIA

		OECD high income		GNI per capita (US$)	23,860
Ease of doing business (rank)	37	High income		Population (m)	2.1
Starting a business (rank)	28	✔ **Registering property** (rank)	79	✔ **Trading across borders** (rank)	50
Procedures (number)	2	Procedures (number)	5	Documents to export (number)	6
Time (days)	6	Time (days)	110	Time to export (days)	16
Cost (% of income per capita)	0.0	Cost (% of property value)	2.0	Cost to export (US$ per container)	710
Minimum capital (% of income per capita)	43.6			Documents to import (number)	8
		Getting credit (rank)	98	Time to import (days)	15
Dealing with construction permits (rank)	81	Strength of legal rights index (0-10)	4	Cost to import (US$ per container)	765
Procedures (number)	13	Depth of credit information index (0-6)	4		
Time (days)	199	Public registry coverage (% of adults)	3.3	**Enforcing contracts** (rank)	58
Cost (% of income per capita)	64.9	Private bureau coverage (% of adults)	100.0	Procedures (number)	32
				Time (days)	1,290
Getting electricity (rank)	27	**Protecting investors** (rank)	24	Cost (% of claim)	12.7
Procedures (number)	5	Extent of disclosure index (0-10)	3		
Time (days)	38	Extent of director liability index (0-10)	9	✔ **Resolving insolvency** (rank)	39
Cost (% of income per capita)	119.1	Ease of shareholder suits index (0-10)	8	Time (years)	2.0
		Strength of investor protection index (0-10)	6.7	Cost (% of estate)	4
				Recovery rate (cents on the dollar)	51.1
		Paying taxes (rank)	87		
		Payments (number per year)	22		
		Time (hours per year)	260		
		Total tax rate (% of profit)	34.7		

Note: Most indicator sets refer to a case scenario in the largest business city of each economy. For more details, see the data notes.

✔ Reform making it easier to do business ✘ Reform making it more difficult to do business

SOLOMON ISLANDS

Ease of doing business (rank)	74	East Asia & Pacific Lower middle income		GNI per capita (US$) Population (m)	1,030 0.5

✔ Starting a business (rank)	110
Procedures (number)	7
Time (days)	43
Cost (% of income per capita)	34.1
Minimum capital (% of income per capita)	0.0

Dealing with construction permits (rank)	36
Procedures (number)	9
Time (days)	58
Cost (% of income per capita)	347.8

Getting electricity (rank)	42
Procedures (number)	4
Time (days)	39
Cost (% of income per capita)	1,982.1

✔ Registering property (rank)	168
Procedures (number)	10
Time (days)	87
Cost (% of property value)	4.9

Getting credit (rank)	78
Strength of legal rights index (0-10)	9
Depth of credit information index (0-6)	0
Public registry coverage (% of adults)	0.0
Private bureau coverage (% of adults)	0.0

✔ Protecting investors (rank)	46
Extent of disclosure index (0-10)	3
Extent of director liability index (0-10)	7
Ease of shareholder suits index (0-10)	8
Strength of investor protection index (0-10)	6.0

Paying taxes (rank)	25
Payments (number per year)	33
Time (hours per year)	80
Total tax rate (% of profit)	26.2

Trading across borders (rank)	86
Documents to export (number)	7
Time to export (days)	24
Cost to export (US$ per container)	1,030
Documents to import (number)	5
Time to import (days)	21
Cost to import (US$ per container)	1,237

Enforcing contracts (rank)	108
Procedures (number)	37
Time (days)	455
Cost (% of claim)	78.9

✔ Resolving insolvency (rank)	115
Time (years)	1.0
Cost (% of estate)	38
Recovery rate (cents on the dollar)	23.8

SOUTH AFRICA

Ease of doing business (rank)	35	Sub-Saharan Africa Upper middle income		GNI per capita (US$) Population (m)	6,100 50.0

✔ Starting a business (rank)	44
Procedures (number)	5
Time (days)	19
Cost (% of income per capita)	0.3
Minimum capital (% of income per capita)	0.0

Dealing with construction permits (rank)	31
Procedures (number)	13
Time (days)	127
Cost (% of income per capita)	21.2

Getting electricity (rank)	124
Procedures (number)	4
Time (days)	226
Cost (% of income per capita)	1,651.5

✔ Registering property (rank)	76
Procedures (number)	6
Time (days)	23
Cost (% of property value)	5.6

Getting credit (rank)	1
Strength of legal rights index (0-10)	10
Depth of credit information index (0-6)	6
Public registry coverage (% of adults)	0.0
Private bureau coverage (% of adults)	52.0

Protecting investors (rank)	10
Extent of disclosure index (0-10)	8
Extent of director liability index (0-10)	8
Ease of shareholder suits index (0-10)	8
Strength of investor protection index (0-10)	8.0

Paying taxes (rank)	44
Payments (number per year)	9
Time (hours per year)	200
Total tax rate (% of profit)	33.1

Trading across borders (rank)	144
Documents to export (number)	8
Time to export (days)	30
Cost to export (US$ per container)	1,531
Documents to import (number)	8
Time to import (days)	32
Cost to import (US$ per container)	1,795

Enforcing contracts (rank)	81
Procedures (number)	29
Time (days)	600
Cost (% of claim)	33.2

✔ Resolving insolvency (rank)	77
Time (years)	2.0
Cost (% of estate)	18
Recovery rate (cents on the dollar)	35.2

SPAIN

Ease of doing business (rank)	44	OECD high income High income		GNI per capita (US$) Population (m)	31,650 46.2

✔ Starting a business (rank)	133
Procedures (number)	10
Time (days)	28
Cost (% of income per capita)	4.7
Minimum capital (% of income per capita)	13.2

Dealing with construction permits (rank)	38
Procedures (number)	8
Time (days)	182
Cost (% of income per capita)	51.8

Getting electricity (rank)	69
Procedures (number)	5
Time (days)	101
Cost (% of income per capita)	231.9

Registering property (rank)	56
Procedures (number)	5
Time (days)	13
Cost (% of property value)	7.1

Getting credit (rank)	48
Strength of legal rights index (0-10)	6
Depth of credit information index (0-6)	5
Public registry coverage (% of adults)	54.7
Private bureau coverage (% of adults)	11.4

Protecting investors (rank)	97
Extent of disclosure index (0-10)	5
Extent of director liability index (0-10)	6
Ease of shareholder suits index (0-10)	4
Strength of investor protection index (0-10)	5.0

Paying taxes (rank)	48
Payments (number per year)	8
Time (hours per year)	187
Total tax rate (% of profit)	38.7

Trading across borders (rank)	55
Documents to export (number)	6
Time to export (days)	9
Cost to export (US$ per container)	1,221
Documents to import (number)	7
Time to import (days)	10
Cost to import (US$ per container)	1,221

Enforcing contracts (rank)	54
Procedures (number)	39
Time (days)	515
Cost (% of claim)	17.2

Resolving insolvency (rank)	20
Time (years)	1.5
Cost (% of estate)	11
Recovery rate (cents on the dollar)	75.6

Note: Most indicator sets refer to a case scenario in the largest business city of each economy. For more details, see the data notes.

✔ Reform making it easier to do business ✘ Reform making it more difficult to do business

SRI LANKA

Ease of doing business (rank)	89	South Asia Lower middle income		GNI per capita (US$) Population (m)		2,290 20.5
Starting a business (rank)	38	**Registering property** (rank)	161	**Trading across borders** (rank)		53
Procedures (number)	4	Procedures (number)	8	Documents to export (number)		6
Time (days)	35	Time (days)	83	Time to export (days)		21
Cost (% of income per capita)	4.7	Cost (% of property value)	5.1	Cost to export (US$ per container)		715
Minimum capital (% of income per capita)	0.0			Documents to import (number)		6
		Getting credit (rank)	78	Time to import (days)		19
		Strength of legal rights index (0-10)	4	Cost to import (US$ per container)		745
Dealing with construction permits (rank)	111	Depth of credit information index (0-6)	5			
Procedures (number)	18	Public registry coverage (% of adults)	0.0	**Enforcing contracts** (rank)		136
Time (days)	217	Private bureau coverage (% of adults)	29.4	Procedures (number)		40
Cost (% of income per capita)	40.6			Time (days)		1,318
		✔ **Protecting investors** (rank)	46	Cost (% of claim)		22.8
Getting electricity (rank)	95	Extent of disclosure index (0-10)	6			
Procedures (number)	4	Extent of director liability index (0-10)	5	**Resolving insolvency** (rank)		42
Time (days)	132	Ease of shareholder suits index (0-10)	7	Time (years)		1.7
Cost (% of income per capita)	1,191.8	Strength of investor protection index (0-10)	6.0	Cost (% of estate)		5
				Recovery rate (cents on the dollar)		48.3
		✔ **Paying taxes** (rank)	173			
		Payments (number per year)	71			
		Time (hours per year)	256			
		Total tax rate (% of profit)	105.2			

ST. KITTS AND NEVIS

Ease of doing business (rank)	95	Latin America & Caribbean Upper middle income		GNI per capita (US$) Population (m)		9,980 0.05
Starting a business (rank)	64	**Registering property** (rank)	164	**Trading across borders** (rank)		44
Procedures (number)	7	Procedures (number)	6	Documents to export (number)		5
Time (days)	19	Time (days)	81	Time to export (days)		11
Cost (% of income per capita)	11.5	Cost (% of property value)	13.3	Cost to export (US$ per container)		850
Minimum capital (% of income per capita)	0.0			Documents to import (number)		5
		Getting credit (rank)	126	Time to import (days)		12
		Strength of legal rights index (0-10)	7	Cost to import (US$ per container)		2,138
Dealing with construction permits (rank)	16	Depth of credit information index (0-6)	0			
Procedures (number)	11	Public registry coverage (% of adults)	0.0	**Enforcing contracts** (rank)		114
Time (days)	139	Private bureau coverage (% of adults)	0.0	Procedures (number)		47
Cost (% of income per capita)	6.8			Time (days)		578
		Protecting investors (rank)	29	Cost (% of claim)		20.5
Getting electricity (rank)	33	Extent of disclosure index (0-10)	4			
Procedures (number)	5	Extent of director liability index (0-10)	8	**Resolving insolvency** (rank)		183
Time (days)	18	Ease of shareholder suits index (0-10)	7	Time (years)		NO PRACTICE
Cost (% of income per capita)	383.5	Strength of investor protection index (0-10)	6.3	Cost (% of estate)		NO PRACTICE
				Recovery rate (cents on the dollar)		0.0
		✔ **Paying taxes** (rank)	133			
		Payments (number per year)	36			
		Time (hours per year)	203			
		Total tax rate (% of profit)	52.7			

ST. LUCIA

Ease of doing business (rank)	52	Latin America & Caribbean Upper middle income		GNI per capita (US$) Population (m)		4,970 0.2
Starting a business (rank)	53	**Registering property** (rank)	115	**Trading across borders** (rank)		110
Procedures (number)	5	Procedures (number)	8	Documents to export (number)		5
Time (days)	15	Time (days)	17	Time to export (days)		14
Cost (% of income per capita)	24.4	Cost (% of property value)	7.4	Cost to export (US$ per container)		1,700
Minimum capital (% of income per capita)	0.0			Documents to import (number)		8
		Getting credit (rank)	98	Time to import (days)		18
		Strength of legal rights index (0-10)	8	Cost to import (US$ per container)		2,745
Dealing with construction permits (rank)	13	Depth of credit information index (0-6)	0			
Procedures (number)	7	Public registry coverage (% of adults)	0.0	**Enforcing contracts** (rank)		165
Time (days)	125	Private bureau coverage (% of adults)	0.0	Procedures (number)		47
Cost (% of income per capita)	31.6			Time (days)		635
		Protecting investors (rank)	29	Cost (% of claim)		37.3
Getting electricity (rank)	13	Extent of disclosure index (0-10)	4			
Procedures (number)	4	Extent of director liability index (0-10)	8	**Resolving insolvency** (rank)		58
Time (days)	25	Ease of shareholder suits index (0-10)	7	Time (years)		2.0
Cost (% of income per capita)	241.0	Strength of investor protection index (0-10)	6.3	Cost (% of estate)		9
				Recovery rate (cents on the dollar)		41.7
		Paying taxes (rank)	52			
		Payments (number per year)	32			
		Time (hours per year)	92			
		Total tax rate (% of profit)	34.4			

Note: Most indicator sets refer to a case scenario in the largest business city of each economy. For more details, see the data notes.

✔ Reform making it easier to do business ✘ Reform making it more difficult to do business

ST. VINCENT AND THE GRENADINES

| | | Latin America & Caribbean | | GNI per capita (US$) | 4,850 |
| Ease of doing business (rank) | 75 | Upper middle income | | Population (m) | 0.1 |

Starting a business (rank)	58	**Registering property** (rank)	141	**Trading across borders** (rank)	38
Procedures (number)	7	Procedures (number)	7	Documents to export (number)	5
Time (days)	10	Time (days)	38	Time to export (days)	12
Cost (% of income per capita)	22.3	Cost (% of property value)	11.9	Cost to export (US$ per container)	1,075
Minimum capital (% of income per capita)	0.0			Documents to import (number)	4
		Getting credit (rank)	126	Time to import (days)	12
Dealing with construction permits (rank)	6	Strength of legal rights index (0-10)	7	Cost to import (US$ per container)	1,605
Procedures (number)	8	Depth of credit information index (0-6)	0		
Time (days)	112	Public registry coverage (% of adults)	0.0	**Enforcing contracts** (rank)	101
Cost (% of income per capita)	12.2	Private bureau coverage (% of adults)	0.0	Procedures (number)	45
				Time (days)	394
Getting electricity (rank)	21	**Protecting investors** (rank)	29	Cost (% of claim)	30.3
Procedures (number)	3	Extent of disclosure index (0-10)	4		
Time (days)	52	Extent of director liability index (0-10)	8	**Resolving insolvency** (rank)	183
Cost (% of income per capita)	307.9	Ease of shareholder suits index (0-10)	7	Time (years)	NO PRACTICE
		Strength of investor protection index (0-10)	6.3	Cost (% of estate)	NO PRACTICE
				Recovery rate (cents on the dollar)	0.0
		Paying taxes (rank)	73		
		Payments (number per year)	36		
		Time (hours per year)	111		
		Total tax rate (% of profit)	38.7		

SUDAN

| | | Sub-Saharan Africa | | GNI per capita (US$) | 1,270 |
| Ease of doing business (rank) | 135 | Lower middle income | | Population (m) | 43.6 |

Starting a business (rank)	126	**Registering property** (rank)	41	**Trading across borders** (rank)	151
Procedures (number)	10	Procedures (number)	6	Documents to export (number)	7
Time (days)	36	Time (days)	9	Time to export (days)	32
Cost (% of income per capita)	31.4	Cost (% of property value)	3.0	Cost to export (US$ per container)	2,050
Minimum capital (% of income per capita)	0.0			Documents to import (number)	7
		Getting credit (rank)	166	Time to import (days)	46
Dealing with construction permits (rank)	130	Strength of legal rights index (0-10)	4	Cost to import (US$ per container)	2,900
Procedures (number)	16	Depth of credit information index (0-6)	0		
Time (days)	270	Public registry coverage (% of adults)	0.0	**Enforcing contracts** (rank)	148
Cost (% of income per capita)	88.0	Private bureau coverage (% of adults)	0.0	Procedures (number)	53
				Time (days)	810
Getting electricity (rank)	107	**Protecting investors** (rank)	155	Cost (% of claim)	19.8
Procedures (number)	5	Extent of disclosure index (0-10)	0		
Time (days)	70	Extent of director liability index (0-10)	6	**Resolving insolvency** (rank)	84
Cost (% of income per capita)	3,949.3	Ease of shareholder suits index (0-10)	4	Time (years)	2.0
		Strength of investor protection index (0-10)	3.3	Cost (% of estate)	20
				Recovery rate (cents on the dollar)	33.2
		Paying taxes (rank)	103		
		Payments (number per year)	42		
		Time (hours per year)	180		
		Total tax rate (% of profit)	36.1		

SURINAME

| | | Latin America & Caribbean | | GNI per capita (US$) | 6,975 |
| Ease of doing business (rank) | 158 | Upper middle income | | Population (m) | 0.5 |

Starting a business (rank)	173	**Registering property** (rank)	170	**Trading across borders** (rank)	105
Procedures (number)	13	Procedures (number)	6	Documents to export (number)	8
Time (days)	694	Time (days)	197	Time to export (days)	25
Cost (% of income per capita)	115.0	Cost (% of property value)	13.8	Cost to export (US$ per container)	995
Minimum capital (% of income per capita)	0.5			Documents to import (number)	6
		Getting credit (rank)	159	Time to import (days)	25
Dealing with construction permits (rank)	98	Strength of legal rights index (0-10)	5	Cost to import (US$ per container)	1,065
Procedures (number)	11	Depth of credit information index (0-6)	0		
Time (days)	461	Public registry coverage (% of adults)	0.0	**Enforcing contracts** (rank)	178
Cost (% of income per capita)	72.0	Private bureau coverage (% of adults)	0.0	Procedures (number)	44
				Time (days)	1,715
Getting electricity (rank)	38	**Protecting investors** (rank)	181	Cost (% of claim)	37.1
Procedures (number)	4	Extent of disclosure index (0-10)	1		
Time (days)	58	Extent of director liability index (0-10)	0	**Resolving insolvency** (rank)	157
Cost (% of income per capita)	647.1	Ease of shareholder suits index (0-10)	5	Time (years)	5.0
		Strength of investor protection index (0-10)	2.0	Cost (% of estate)	30
				Recovery rate (cents on the dollar)	8.6
		Paying taxes (rank)	34		
		Payments (number per year)	17		
		Time (hours per year)	199		
		Total tax rate (% of profit)	27.9		

Note: Most indicator sets refer to a case scenario in the largest business city of each economy. For more details, see the data notes.

✔ Reform making it easier to do business ✘ Reform making it more difficult to do business

SWAZILAND

		Sub-Saharan Africa		GNI per capita (US$)	2,600
Ease of doing business (rank)	124	Lower middle income		Population (m)	1.2
Starting a business (rank)	161	✔ **Registering property** (rank)	128	**Trading across borders** (rank)	148
Procedures (number)	12	Procedures (number)	9	Documents to export (number)	9
Time (days)	56	Time (days)	21	Time to export (days)	18
Cost (% of income per capita)	29.2	Cost (% of property value)	7.1	Cost to export (US$ per container)	1,855
Minimum capital (% of income per capita)	0.5			Documents to import (number)	9
				Time to import (days)	27
		Getting credit (rank)	48	Cost to import (US$ per container)	2,030
Dealing with construction permits (rank)	47	Strength of legal rights index (0-10)	6		
Procedures (number)	13	Depth of credit information index (0-6)	5		
Time (days)	95	Public registry coverage (% of adults)	0.0	**Enforcing contracts** (rank)	171
Cost (% of income per capita)	115.2	Private bureau coverage (% of adults)	43.2	Procedures (number)	40
				Time (days)	972
				Cost (% of claim)	56.1
Getting electricity (rank)	158	**Protecting investors** (rank)	122		
Procedures (number)	6	Extent of disclosure index (0-10)	2		
Time (days)	137	Extent of director liability index (0-10)	5	**Resolving insolvency** (rank)	69
Cost (% of income per capita)	1,302.0	Ease of shareholder suits index (0-10)	6	Time (years)	2.0
		Strength of investor protection index (0-10)	4.3	Cost (% of estate)	15
				Recovery rate (cents on the dollar)	38.2
		Paying taxes (rank)	60		
		Payments (number per year)	33		
		Time (hours per year)	104		
		Total tax rate (% of profit)	36.8		

SWEDEN

		OECD high income		GNI per capita (US$)	49,930
Ease of doing business (rank)	14	High income		Population (m)	9.4
Starting a business (rank)	46	✘ **Registering property** (rank)	19	**Trading across borders** (rank)	8
Procedures (number)	3	Procedures (number)	1	Documents to export (number)	3
Time (days)	15	Time (days)	7	Time to export (days)	8
Cost (% of income per capita)	0.6	Cost (% of property value)	4.3	Cost to export (US$ per container)	697
Minimum capital (% of income per capita)	14.0			Documents to import (number)	3
		Getting credit (rank)	48	Time to import (days)	6
Dealing with construction permits (rank)	23	Strength of legal rights index (0-10)	7	Cost to import (US$ per container)	735
Procedures (number)	7	Depth of credit information index (0-6)	4		
Time (days)	116	Public registry coverage (% of adults)	0.0	**Enforcing contracts** (rank)	54
Cost (% of income per capita)	81.6	Private bureau coverage (% of adults)	100.0	Procedures (number)	30
				Time (days)	508
Getting electricity (rank)	8	**Protecting investors** (rank)	29	Cost (% of claim)	31.2
Procedures (number)	3	Extent of disclosure index (0-10)	8		
Time (days)	52	Extent of director liability index (0-10)	4	**Resolving insolvency** (rank)	19
Cost (% of income per capita)	20.7	Ease of shareholder suits index (0-10)	7	Time (years)	2.0
		Strength of investor protection index (0-10)	6.3	Cost (% of estate)	9
				Recovery rate (cents on the dollar)	75.8
		Paying taxes (rank)	50		
		Payments (number per year)	4		
		Time (hours per year)	122		
		Total tax rate (% of profit)	52.8		

SWITZERLAND

		OECD high income		GNI per capita (US$)	70,350
Ease of doing business (rank)	26	High income		Population (m)	7.8
Starting a business (rank)	85	**Registering property** (rank)	14	**Trading across borders** (rank)	41
Procedures (number)	6	Procedures (number)	4	Documents to export (number)	4
Time (days)	18	Time (days)	16	Time to export (days)	8
Cost (% of income per capita)	2.1	Cost (% of property value)	0.4	Cost to export (US$ per container)	1,537
Minimum capital (% of income per capita)	26.9			Documents to import (number)	5
		Getting credit (rank)	24	Time to import (days)	9
Dealing with construction permits (rank)	46	Strength of legal rights index (0-10)	8	Cost to import (US$ per container)	1,540
Procedures (number)	13	Depth of credit information index (0-6)	5		
Time (days)	154	Public registry coverage (% of adults)	0.0	**Enforcing contracts** (rank)	23
Cost (% of income per capita)	40.1	Private bureau coverage (% of adults)	27.3	Procedures (number)	32
				Time (days)	390
✔ **Getting electricity** (rank)	6	**Protecting investors** (rank)	166	Cost (% of claim)	24.0
Procedures (number)	3	Extent of disclosure index (0-10)	0		
Time (days)	39	Extent of director liability index (0-10)	5	✔ **Resolving insolvency** (rank)	43
Cost (% of income per capita)	62.7	Ease of shareholder suits index (0-10)	4	Time (years)	3.0
		Strength of investor protection index (0-10)	3.0	Cost (% of estate)	4
				Recovery rate (cents on the dollar)	47.5
		Paying taxes (rank)	12		
		Payments (number per year)	19		
		Time (hours per year)	63		
		Total tax rate (% of profit)	30.1		

Note: Most indicator sets refer to a case scenario in the largest business city of each economy. For more details, see the data notes.

✔ Reform making it easier to do business ✘ Reform making it more difficult to do business

SYRIAN ARAB REPUBLIC

Ease of doing business (rank)	134	Middle East & North Africa Lower middle income		GNI per capita (US$)	2,640
				Population (m)	21.6
✔ **Starting a business** (rank)	129	**Registering property** (rank)	82	**Trading across borders** (rank)	122
Procedures (number)	7	Procedures (number)	4	Documents to export (number)	8
Time (days)	13	Time (days)	19	Time to export (days)	15
Cost (% of income per capita)	17.1	Cost (% of property value)	27.9	Cost to export (US$ per container)	1,190
Minimum capital (% of income per capita)	127.7			Documents to import (number)	9
		Getting credit (rank)	174	Time to import (days)	21
Dealing with construction permits (rank)	133	Strength of legal rights index (0-10)	1	Cost to import (US$ per container)	1,625
Procedures (number)	23	Depth of credit information index (0-6)	2		
Time (days)	104	Public registry coverage (% of adults)	3.7	**Enforcing contracts** (rank)	175
Cost (% of income per capita)	504.1	Private bureau coverage (% of adults)	0.0	Procedures (number)	55
				Time (days)	872
Getting electricity (rank)	83	**Protecting investors** (rank)	111	Cost (% of claim)	29.3
Procedures (number)	5	Extent of disclosure index (0-10)	7		
Time (days)	71	Extent of director liability index (0-10)	5	**Resolving insolvency** (rank)	102
Cost (% of income per capita)	940.4	Ease of shareholder suits index (0-10)	2	Time (years)	4.1
		Strength of investor protection index (0-10)	4.7	Cost (% of estate)	9
				Recovery rate (cents on the dollar)	27.5
		Paying taxes (rank)	111		
		Payments (number per year)	19		
		Time (hours per year)	336		
		Total tax rate (% of profit)	39.7		

TAIWAN, CHINA

Ease of doing business (rank)	25	East Asia & Pacific High income		GNI per capita (US$)	18,458
				Population (m)	23.2
✔ **Starting a business** (rank)	16	**Registering property** (rank)	33	**Trading across borders** (rank)	23
Procedures (number)	3	Procedures (number)	3	Documents to export (number)	6
Time (days)	10	Time (days)	5	Time to export (days)	12
Cost (% of income per capita)	2.5	Cost (% of property value)	6.2	Cost to export (US$ per container)	655
Minimum capital (% of income per capita)	0.0			Documents to import (number)	6
		Getting credit (rank)	67	Time to import (days)	12
✔ **Dealing with construction permits** (rank)	87	Strength of legal rights index (0-10)	5	Cost to import (US$ per container)	720
Procedures (number)	25	Depth of credit information index (0-6)	5		
Time (days)	125	Public registry coverage (% of adults)	0.0	**Enforcing contracts** (rank)	88
Cost (% of income per capita)	41.9	Private bureau coverage (% of adults)	90.9	Procedures (number)	45
				Time (days)	510
Getting electricity (rank)	3	**Protecting investors** (rank)	79	Cost (% of claim)	17.7
Procedures (number)	4	Extent of disclosure index (0-10)	7		
Time (days)	23	Extent of director liability index (0-10)	4	**Resolving insolvency** (rank)	14
Cost (% of income per capita)	52.4	Ease of shareholder suits index (0-10)	5	Time (years)	1.9
		Strength of investor protection index (0-10)	5.3	Cost (% of estate)	4
				Recovery rate (cents on the dollar)	82.1
		Paying taxes (rank)	71		
		Payments (number per year)	15		
		Time (hours per year)	245		
		Total tax rate (% of profit)	35.6		

TAJIKISTAN

Ease of doing business (rank)	147	Eastern Europe & Central Asia Low income		GNI per capita (US$)	780
				Population (m)	7.1
✔ **Starting a business** (rank)	70	**Registering property** (rank)	90	**Trading across borders** (rank)	177
Procedures (number)	5	Procedures (number)	6	Documents to export (number)	11
Time (days)	24	Time (days)	37	Time to export (days)	82
Cost (% of income per capita)	33.3	Cost (% of property value)	5.3	Cost to export (US$ per container)	3,850
Minimum capital (% of income per capita)	0.0			Documents to import (number)	9
		✘ **Getting credit** (rank)	177	Time to import (days)	83
Dealing with construction permits (rank)	177	Strength of legal rights index (0-10)	2	Cost to import (US$ per container)	4,550
Procedures (number)	26	Depth of credit information index (0-6)	0		
Time (days)	228	Public registry coverage (% of adults)	0.0	**Enforcing contracts** (rank)	42
Cost (% of income per capita)	849.9	Private bureau coverage (% of adults)	0.0	Procedures (number)	35
				Time (days)	430
Getting electricity (rank)	178	**Protecting investors** (rank)	65	Cost (% of claim)	25.5
Procedures (number)	9	Extent of disclosure index (0-10)	8		
Time (days)	238	Extent of director liability index (0-10)	3	**Resolving insolvency** (rank)	68
Cost (% of income per capita)	1,297.9	Ease of shareholder suits index (0-10)	6	Time (years)	1.7
		Strength of investor protection index (0-10)	5.7	Cost (% of estate)	9
				Recovery rate (cents on the dollar)	38.2
		Paying taxes (rank)	168		
		Payments (number per year)	69		
		Time (hours per year)	224		
		Total tax rate (% of profit)	84.5		

Note: Most indicator sets refer to a case scenario in the largest business city of each economy. For more details, see the data notes.

✔ Reform making it easier to do business ✘ Reform making it more difficult to do business

TANZANIA

		Sub-Saharan Africa		GNI per capita (US$)	530
Ease of doing business (rank)	127	Low income		Population (m)	45.0

Starting a business (rank)	123	**Registering property** (rank)	158	✔ **Trading across borders** (rank)	92
Procedures (number)	12	Procedures (number)	9	Documents to export (number)	6
Time (days)	29	Time (days)	73	Time to export (days)	18
Cost (% of income per capita)	28.8	Cost (% of property value)	4.4	Cost to export (US$ per container)	1,255
Minimum capital (% of income per capita)	0.0			Documents to import (number)	6
		Getting credit (rank)	98	Time to import (days)	24
Dealing with construction permits (rank)	176	Strength of legal rights index (0-10)	8	Cost to import (US$ per container)	1,430
Procedures (number)	19	Depth of credit information index (0-6)	0		
Time (days)	303	Public registry coverage (% of adults)	0.0	**Enforcing contracts** (rank)	36
Cost (% of income per capita)	1,170.1	Private bureau coverage (% of adults)	0.0	Procedures (number)	38
				Time (days)	462
Getting electricity (rank)	78	**Protecting investors** (rank)	97	Cost (% of claim)	14.3
Procedures (number)	4	Extent of disclosure index (0-10)	3		
Time (days)	109	Extent of director liability index (0-10)	4	**Resolving insolvency** (rank)	122
Cost (% of income per capita)	1,040.5	Ease of shareholder suits index (0-10)	8	Time (years)	3.0
		Strength of investor protection index (0-10)	5.0	Cost (% of estate)	22
				Recovery rate (cents on the dollar)	22.0
		Paying taxes (rank)	129		
		Payments (number per year)	48		
		Time (hours per year)	172		
		Total tax rate (% of profit)	45.5		

THAILAND

		East Asia & Pacific		GNI per capita (US$)	4,210
Ease of doing business (rank)	17	Upper middle income		Population (m)	68.1

✔ **Starting a business** (rank)	78	✘ **Registering property** (rank)	28	**Trading across borders** (rank)	17
Procedures (number)	5	Procedures (number)	2	Documents to export (number)	5
Time (days)	29	Time (days)	2	Time to export (days)	14
Cost (% of income per capita)	6.2	Cost (% of property value)	6.3	Cost to export (US$ per container)	625
Minimum capital (% of income per capita)	0.0			Documents to import (number)	5
		Getting credit (rank)	67	Time to import (days)	13
Dealing with construction permits (rank)	14	Strength of legal rights index (0-10)	5	Cost to import (US$ per container)	750
Procedures (number)	8	Depth of credit information index (0-6)	5		
Time (days)	157	Public registry coverage (% of adults)	0.0	**Enforcing contracts** (rank)	24
Cost (% of income per capita)	9.5	Private bureau coverage (% of adults)	41.7	Procedures (number)	36
				Time (days)	479
Getting electricity (rank)	9	**Protecting investors** (rank)	13	Cost (% of claim)	12.3
Procedures (number)	4	Extent of disclosure index (0-10)	10		
Time (days)	35	Extent of director liability index (0-10)	7	**Resolving insolvency** (rank)	51
Cost (% of income per capita)	77.6	Ease of shareholder suits index (0-10)	6	Time (years)	2.7
		Strength of investor protection index (0-10)	7.7	Cost (% of estate)	36
				Recovery rate (cents on the dollar)	43.3
		Paying taxes (rank)	100		
		Payments (number per year)	23		
		Time (hours per year)	264		
		Total tax rate (% of profit)	37.5		

TIMOR-LESTE

		East Asia & Pacific		GNI per capita (US$)	2,200
Ease of doing business (rank)	168	Lower middle income		Population (m)	1.2

✔ **Starting a business** (rank)	157	**Registering property** (rank)	183	**Trading across borders** (rank)	89
Procedures (number)	10	Procedures (number)	NO PRACTICE	Documents to export (number)	6
Time (days)	103	Time (days)	NO PRACTICE	Time to export (days)	25
Cost (% of income per capita)	4.5	Cost (% of property value)	NO PRACTICE	Cost to export (US$ per container)	1,010
Minimum capital (% of income per capita)	227.3			Documents to import (number)	7
		✔ **Getting credit** (rank)	159	Time to import (days)	26
Dealing with construction permits (rank)	114	Strength of legal rights index (0-10)	2	Cost to import (US$ per container)	1,015
Procedures (number)	19	Depth of credit information index (0-6)	3		
Time (days)	238	Public registry coverage (% of adults)	1.8	**Enforcing contracts** (rank)	183
Cost (% of income per capita)	25.0	Private bureau coverage (% of adults)	0.0	Procedures (number)	51
				Time (days)	1,285
Getting electricity (rank)	55	**Protecting investors** (rank)	133	Cost (% of claim)	163.2
Procedures (number)	3	Extent of disclosure index (0-10)	3		
Time (days)	63	Extent of director liability index (0-10)	4	**Resolving insolvency** (rank)	183
Cost (% of income per capita)	1,818.2	Ease of shareholder suits index (0-10)	5	Time (years)	NO PRACTICE
		Strength of investor protection index (0-10)	4.0	Cost (% of estate)	NO PRACTICE
				Recovery rate (cents on the dollar)	0.0
		Paying taxes (rank)	31		
		Payments (number per year)	6		
		Time (hours per year)	276		
		Total tax rate (% of profit)	0.2		

Note: Most indicator sets refer to a case scenario in the largest business city of each economy. For more details, see the data notes.

✔ Reform making it easier to do business ✘ Reform making it more difficult to do business

TOGO

		Sub-Saharan Africa		GNI per capita (US$)	440
Ease of doing business (rank)	162	Low income		Population (m)	6.8
Starting a business (rank)	174	**Registering property** (rank)	162	**Trading across borders** (rank)	98
Procedures (number)	7	Procedures (number)	5	Documents to export (number)	6
Time (days)	84	Time (days)	295	Time to export (days)	24
Cost (% of income per capita)	177.2	Cost (% of property value)	13.0	Cost to export (US$ per container)	940
Minimum capital (% of income per capita)	484.5			Documents to import (number)	8
		✔ **Getting credit** (rank)	126	Time to import (days)	28
Dealing with construction permits (rank)	146	Strength of legal rights index (0-10)	6	Cost to import (US$ per container)	1,109
Procedures (number)	12	Depth of credit information index (0-6)	1		
Time (days)	309	Public registry coverage (% of adults)	2.5	**Enforcing contracts** (rank)	151
Cost (% of income per capita)	994.0	Private bureau coverage (% of adults)	0.0	Procedures (number)	41
				Time (days)	588
Getting electricity (rank)	92	**Protecting investors** (rank)	147	Cost (% of claim)	47.5
Procedures (number)	4	Extent of disclosure index (0-10)	6		
Time (days)	74	Extent of director liability index (0-10)	1	**Resolving insolvency** (rank)	93
Cost (% of income per capita)	6,023.2	Ease of shareholder suits index (0-10)	4	Time (years)	3.0
		Strength of investor protection index (0-10)	3.7	Cost (% of estate)	15
				Recovery rate (cents on the dollar)	30.5
		✔ **Paying taxes** (rank)	161		
		Payments (number per year)	53		
		Time (hours per year)	270		
		Total tax rate (% of profit)	49.5		

TONGA

		East Asia & Pacific		GNI per capita (US$)	3,380
Ease of doing business (rank)	58	Lower middle income		Population (m)	0.1
✔ **Starting a business** (rank)	33	✘ **Registering property** (rank)	141	**Trading across borders** (rank)	77
Procedures (number)	4	Procedures (number)	4	Documents to export (number)	7
Time (days)	16	Time (days)	108	Time to export (days)	20
Cost (% of income per capita)	10.3	Cost (% of property value)	15.2	Cost to export (US$ per container)	775
Minimum capital (% of income per capita)	0.0			Documents to import (number)	6
		✔ **Getting credit** (rank)	78	Time to import (days)	24
Dealing with construction permits (rank)	32	Strength of legal rights index (0-10)	9	Cost to import (US$ per container)	775
Procedures (number)	9	Depth of credit information index (0-6)	0		
Time (days)	69	Public registry coverage (% of adults)	0.0	**Enforcing contracts** (rank)	53
Cost (% of income per capita)	251.5	Private bureau coverage (% of adults)	0.0	Procedures (number)	37
				Time (days)	350
✔ **Getting electricity** (rank)	29	**Protecting investors** (rank)	111	Cost (% of claim)	30.5
Procedures (number)	5	Extent of disclosure index (0-10)	3		
Time (days)	42	Extent of director liability index (0-10)	3	**Resolving insolvency** (rank)	108
Cost (% of income per capita)	111.3	Ease of shareholder suits index (0-10)	8	Time (years)	2.7
		Strength of investor protection index (0-10)	4.7	Cost (% of estate)	22
				Recovery rate (cents on the dollar)	25.6
		Paying taxes (rank)	29		
		Payments (number per year)	20		
		Time (hours per year)	164		
		Total tax rate (% of profit)	25.7		

TRINIDAD AND TOBAGO

		Latin America & Caribbean		GNI per capita (US$)	15,380
Ease of doing business (rank)	68	High income		Population (m)	1.3
Starting a business (rank)	74	**Registering property** (rank)	175	**Trading across borders** (rank)	52
Procedures (number)	9	Procedures (number)	8	Documents to export (number)	5
Time (days)	43	Time (days)	162	Time to export (days)	14
Cost (% of income per capita)	0.9	Cost (% of property value)	7.0	Cost to export (US$ per container)	843
Minimum capital (% of income per capita)	0.0			Documents to import (number)	6
		Getting credit (rank)	40	Time to import (days)	19
✘ **Dealing with construction permits** (rank)	93	Strength of legal rights index (0-10)	8	Cost to import (US$ per container)	1,260
Procedures (number)	17	Depth of credit information index (0-6)	4		
Time (days)	297	Public registry coverage (% of adults)	0.0	**Enforcing contracts** (rank)	169
Cost (% of income per capita)	6.0	Private bureau coverage (% of adults)	46.0	Procedures (number)	42
				Time (days)	1,340
Getting electricity (rank)	24	**Protecting investors** (rank)	24	Cost (% of claim)	33.5
Procedures (number)	5	Extent of disclosure index (0-10)	4		
Time (days)	61	Extent of director liability index (0-10)	9	**Resolving insolvency** (rank)	133
Cost (% of income per capita)	7.9	Ease of shareholder suits index (0-10)	7	Time (years)	4.0
		Strength of investor protection index (0-10)	6.7	Cost (% of estate)	25
				Recovery rate (cents on the dollar)	17.9
		Paying taxes (rank)	65		
		Payments (number per year)	39		
		Time (hours per year)	210		
		Total tax rate (% of profit)	29.1		

Note: Most indicator sets refer to a case scenario in the largest business city of each economy. For more details, see the data notes.

✔ Reform making it easier to do business ✘ Reform making it more difficult to do business

TUNISIA

Ease of doing business (rank)	46	Middle East & North Africa Upper middle income		GNI per capita (US$) Population (m)		4,070 10.5
Starting a business (rank)	56	**Registering property** (rank)	65	**Trading across borders** (rank)		32
Procedures (number)	10	Procedures (number)	4	Documents to export (number)		4
Time (days)	11	Time (days)	39	Time to export (days)		13
Cost (% of income per capita)	4.2	Cost (% of property value)	6.1	Cost to export (US$ per container)		773
Minimum capital (% of income per capita)	0.0			Documents to import (number)		7
		Getting credit (rank)	98	Time to import (days)		17
Dealing with construction permits (rank)	86	Strength of legal rights index (0-10)	3	Cost to import (US$ per container)		858
Procedures (number)	17	Depth of credit information index (0-6)	5			
Time (days)	88	Public registry coverage (% of adults)	27.3	**Enforcing contracts** (rank)		76
Cost (% of income per capita)	260.6	Private bureau coverage (% of adults)	0.0	Procedures (number)		39
				Time (days)		565
Getting electricity (rank)	45	**Protecting investors** (rank)	46	Cost (% of claim)		21.8
Procedures (number)	4	Extent of disclosure index (0-10)	5			
Time (days)	65	Extent of director liability index (0-10)	7	**Resolving insolvency** (rank)		38
Cost (% of income per capita)	894.1	Ease of shareholder suits index (0-10)	6	Time (years)		1.3
		Strength of investor protection index (0-10)	6.0	Cost (% of estate)		7
				Recovery rate (cents on the dollar)		52.2
		Paying taxes (rank)	64			
		Payments (number per year)	8			
		Time (hours per year)	144			
		Total tax rate (% of profit)	62.9			

TURKEY

Ease of doing business (rank)	71	Eastern Europe & Central Asia Upper middle income		GNI per capita (US$) Population (m)		9,500 75.7
✔ **Starting a business** (rank)	61	**Registering property** (rank)	44	**Trading across borders** (rank)		80
Procedures (number)	6	Procedures (number)	6	Documents to export (number)		7
Time (days)	6	Time (days)	6	Time to export (days)		14
Cost (% of income per capita)	11.2	Cost (% of property value)	3.3	Cost to export (US$ per container)		990
Minimum capital (% of income per capita)	8.7			Documents to import (number)		8
		Getting credit (rank)	78	Time to import (days)		15
Dealing with construction permits (rank)	155	Strength of legal rights index (0-10)	4	Cost to import (US$ per container)		1,063
Procedures (number)	24	Depth of credit information index (0-6)	5			
Time (days)	189	Public registry coverage (% of adults)	23.8	**Enforcing contracts** (rank)		51
Cost (% of income per capita)	197.7	Private bureau coverage (% of adults)	60.5	Procedures (number)		36
				Time (days)		420
Getting electricity (rank)	72	**Protecting investors** (rank)	65	Cost (% of claim)		27.9
Procedures (number)	5	Extent of disclosure index (0-10)	9			
Time (days)	70	Extent of director liability index (0-10)	4	**Resolving insolvency** (rank)		120
Cost (% of income per capita)	624.4	Ease of shareholder suits index (0-10)	4	Time (years)		3.3
		Strength of investor protection index (0-10)	5.7	Cost (% of estate)		15
				Recovery rate (cents on the dollar)		22.3
		✔ **Paying taxes** (rank)	79			
		Payments (number per year)	15			
		Time (hours per year)	223			
		Total tax rate (% of profit)	41.1			

UGANDA

Ease of doing business (rank)	123	Sub-Saharan Africa Low income		GNI per capita (US$) Population (m)		490 33.8
✘ **Starting a business** (rank)	143	✔ **Registering property** (rank)	127	**Trading across borders** (rank)		158
Procedures (number)	16	Procedures (number)	13	Documents to export (number)		7
Time (days)	34	Time (days)	48	Time to export (days)		37
Cost (% of income per capita)	84.5	Cost (% of property value)	2.9	Cost to export (US$ per container)		2,880
Minimum capital (% of income per capita)	0.0			Documents to import (number)		9
		Getting credit (rank)	48	Time to import (days)		34
Dealing with construction permits (rank)	109	Strength of legal rights index (0-10)	7	Cost to import (US$ per container)		3,015
Procedures (number)	15	Depth of credit information index (0-6)	4			
Time (days)	125	Public registry coverage (% of adults)	0.0	**Enforcing contracts** (rank)		116
Cost (% of income per capita)	946.8	Private bureau coverage (% of adults)	3.0	Procedures (number)		38
				Time (days)		490
Getting electricity (rank)	129	**Protecting investors** (rank)	133	Cost (% of claim)		44.9
Procedures (number)	5	Extent of disclosure index (0-10)	2			
Time (days)	91	Extent of director liability index (0-10)	5	**Resolving insolvency** (rank)		63
Cost (% of income per capita)	5,130.1	Ease of shareholder suits index (0-10)	5	Time (years)		2.2
		Strength of investor protection index (0-10)	4.0	Cost (% of estate)		30
				Recovery rate (cents on the dollar)		40.2
		Paying taxes (rank)	93			
		Payments (number per year)	32			
		Time (hours per year)	213			
		Total tax rate (% of profit)	35.7			

Note: Most indicator sets refer to a case scenario in the largest business city of each economy. For more details, see the data notes.

✔ Reform making it easier to do business ✘ Reform making it more difficult to do business

UKRAINE

		Eastern Europe & Central Asia		GNI per capita (US$)	3,010
Ease of doing business (rank)	152	Lower middle income		Population (m)	45.8
✔ **Starting a business** (rank)	112	**Registering property** (rank)	166	✘ **Trading across borders** (rank)	140
Procedures (number)	9	Procedures (number)	10	Documents to export (number)	6
Time (days)	24	Time (days)	117	Time to export (days)	30
Cost (% of income per capita)	4.4	Cost (% of property value)	3.9	Cost to export (US$ per container)	1,865
Minimum capital (% of income per capita)	1.8			Documents to import (number)	8
		Getting credit (rank)	24	Time to import (days)	33
Dealing with construction permits (rank)	180	Strength of legal rights index (0-10)	9	Cost to import (US$ per container)	2,155
Procedures (number)	21	Depth of credit information index (0-6)	4		
Time (days)	375	Public registry coverage (% of adults)	0.0	✔ **Enforcing contracts** (rank)	44
Cost (% of income per capita)	1,462.3	Private bureau coverage (% of adults)	17.0	Procedures (number)	30
				Time (days)	343
Getting electricity (rank)	169	**Protecting investors** (rank)	111	Cost (% of claim)	41.5
Procedures (number)	11	Extent of disclosure index (0-10)	5		
Time (days)	274	Extent of director liability index (0-10)	2	✔ **Resolving insolvency** (rank)	156
Cost (% of income per capita)	229.2	Ease of shareholder suits index (0-10)	7	Time (years)	2.9
		Strength of investor protection index (0-10)	4.7	Cost (% of estate)	42
				Recovery rate (cents on the dollar)	8.9
		✔ **Paying taxes** (rank)	181		
		Payments (number per year)	135		
		Time (hours per year)	657		
		Total tax rate (% of profit)	57.1		

UNITED ARAB EMIRATES

		Middle East & North Africa		GNI per capita (US$)	59,717
Ease of doing business (rank)	33	High income		Population (m)	4.7
✔ **Starting a business** (rank)	42	**Registering property** (rank)	6	**Trading across borders** (rank)	5
Procedures (number)	7	Procedures (number)	1	Documents to export (number)	4
Time (days)	13	Time (days)	2	Time to export (days)	7
Cost (% of income per capita)	5.6	Cost (% of property value)	2.0	Cost to export (US$ per container)	630
Minimum capital (% of income per capita)	0.0			Documents to import (number)	5
		✔ **Getting credit** (rank)	78	Time to import (days)	7
Dealing with construction permits (rank)	12	Strength of legal rights index (0-10)	4	Cost to import (US$ per container)	635
Procedures (number)	14	Depth of credit information index (0-6)	5		
Time (days)	46	Public registry coverage (% of adults)	9.0	**Enforcing contracts** (rank)	134
Cost (% of income per capita)	5.2	Private bureau coverage (% of adults)	29.2	Procedures (number)	49
				Time (days)	537
Getting electricity (rank)	10	**Protecting investors** (rank)	122	Cost (% of claim)	26.2
Procedures (number)	4	Extent of disclosure index (0-10)	4		
Time (days)	55	Extent of director liability index (0-10)	7	**Resolving insolvency** (rank)	151
Cost (% of income per capita)	14.6	Ease of shareholder suits index (0-10)	2	Time (years)	5.1
		Strength of investor protection index (0-10)	4.3	Cost (% of estate)	30
				Recovery rate (cents on the dollar)	11.0
		Paying taxes (rank)	7		
		Payments (number per year)	14		
		Time (hours per year)	12		
		Total tax rate (% of profit)	14.1		

UNITED KINGDOM

		OECD high income		GNI per capita (US$)	38,540
Ease of doing business (rank)	7	High income		Population (m)	62.2
Starting a business (rank)	19	**Registering property** (rank)	68	**Trading across borders** (rank)	13
Procedures (number)	6	Procedures (number)	6	Documents to export (number)	4
Time (days)	13	Time (days)	29	Time to export (days)	7
Cost (% of income per capita)	0.7	Cost (% of property value)	4.7	Cost to export (US$ per container)	950
Minimum capital (% of income per capita)	0.0			Documents to import (number)	4
		Getting credit (rank)	1	Time to import (days)	6
✔ **Dealing with construction permits** (rank)	22	Strength of legal rights index (0-10)	10	Cost to import (US$ per container)	1,045
Procedures (number)	9	Depth of credit information index (0-6)	6		
Time (days)	99	Public registry coverage (% of adults)	0.0	**Enforcing contracts** (rank)	21
Cost (% of income per capita)	63.8	Private bureau coverage (% of adults)	100.0	Procedures (number)	28
				Time (days)	399
Getting electricity (rank)	60	**Protecting investors** (rank)	10	Cost (% of claim)	24.8
Procedures (number)	5	Extent of disclosure index (0-10)	10		
Time (days)	109	Extent of director liability index (0-10)	7	**Resolving insolvency** (rank)	6
Cost (% of income per capita)	72.3	Ease of shareholder suits index (0-10)	7	Time (years)	1.0
		Strength of investor protection index (0-10)	8.0	Cost (% of estate)	6
				Recovery rate (cents on the dollar)	88.6
		Paying taxes (rank)	24		
		Payments (number per year)	8		
		Time (hours per year)	110		
		Total tax rate (% of profit)	37.3		

Note: Most indicator sets refer to a case scenario in the largest business city of each economy. For more details, see the data notes.

✔ Reform making it easier to do business ✘ Reform making it more difficult to do business

UNITED STATES

Ease of doing business (rank)	4	OECD high income High income		GNI per capita (US$) Population (m)		47,140 309.7
Starting a business (rank)	13	**Registering property** (rank)	16	**Trading across borders** (rank)		20
Procedures (number)	6	Procedures (number)	4	Documents to export (number)		4
Time (days)	6	Time (days)	12	Time to export (days)		6
Cost (% of income per capita)	1.4	Cost (% of property value)	0.8	Cost to export (US$ per container)		1,050
Minimum capital (% of income per capita)	0.0			Documents to import (number)		5
		Getting credit (rank)	4	Time to import (days)		5
Dealing with construction permits (rank)	17	Strength of legal rights index (0-10)	9	Cost to import (US$ per container)		1,315
Procedures (number)	15	Depth of credit information index (0-6)	6			
Time (days)	26	Public registry coverage (% of adults)	0.0	**Enforcing contracts** (rank)		7
Cost (% of income per capita)	12.8	Private bureau coverage (% of adults)	100.0	Procedures (number)		32
				Time (days)		300
Getting electricity (rank)	17	**Protecting investors** (rank)	5	Cost (% of claim)		14.4
Procedures (number)	4	Extent of disclosure index (0-10)	7			
Time (days)	68	Extent of director liability index (0-10)	9	**Resolving insolvency** (rank)		15
Cost (% of income per capita)	16.8	Ease of shareholder suits index (0-10)	9	Time (years)		1.5
		Strength of investor protection index (0-10)	8.3	Cost (% of estate)		7
				Recovery rate (cents on the dollar)		81.5
		Paying taxes (rank)	72			
		Payments (number per year)	11			
		Time (hours per year)	187			
		Total tax rate (% of profit)	46.7			

URUGUAY

Ease of doing business (rank)	90	Latin America & Caribbean Upper middle income		GNI per capita (US$) Population (m)		10,590 3.4
✔ **Starting a business** (rank)	32	**Registering property** (rank)	165	**Trading across borders** (rank)		125
Procedures (number)	5	Procedures (number)	8	Documents to export (number)		9
Time (days)	7	Time (days)	66	Time to export (days)		17
Cost (% of income per capita)	24.9	Cost (% of property value)	7.1	Cost to export (US$ per container)		1,100
Minimum capital (% of income per capita)	0.0			Documents to import (number)		9
		✔ **Getting credit** (rank)	67	Time to import (days)		22
Dealing with construction permits (rank)	153	Strength of legal rights index (0-10)	4	Cost to import (US$ per container)		1,330
Procedures (number)	27	Depth of credit information index (0-6)	6			
Time (days)	234	Public registry coverage (% of adults)	28.6	**Enforcing contracts** (rank)		103
Cost (% of income per capita)	74.4	Private bureau coverage (% of adults)	100.0	Procedures (number)		41
				Time (days)		720
Getting electricity (rank)	7	**Protecting investors** (rank)	97	Cost (% of claim)		19.0
Procedures (number)	4	Extent of disclosure index (0-10)	3			
Time (days)	48	Extent of director liability index (0-10)	4	**Resolving insolvency** (rank)		50
Cost (% of income per capita)	15.9	Ease of shareholder suits index (0-10)	8	Time (years)		2.1
		Strength of investor protection index (0-10)	5.0	Cost (% of estate)		7
				Recovery rate (cents on the dollar)		43.4
		Paying taxes (rank)	160			
		Payments (number per year)	53			
		Time (hours per year)	336			
		Total tax rate (% of profit)	42.0			

UZBEKISTAN

Ease of doing business (rank)	166	Eastern Europe & Central Asia Lower middle income		GNI per capita (US$) Population (m)		1,280 28.2
✔ **Starting a business** (rank)	96	**Registering property** (rank)	136	**Trading across borders** (rank)		183
Procedures (number)	6	Procedures (number)	12	Documents to export (number)		10
Time (days)	14	Time (days)	78	Time to export (days)		71
Cost (% of income per capita)	6.4	Cost (% of property value)	0.9	Cost to export (US$ per container)		3,150
Minimum capital (% of income per capita)	27.2			Documents to import (number)		11
		Getting credit (rank)	159	Time to import (days)		92
Dealing with construction permits (rank)	145	Strength of legal rights index (0-10)	2	Cost to import (US$ per container)		4,650
Procedures (number)	25	Depth of credit information index (0-6)	3			
Time (days)	243	Public registry coverage (% of adults)	5.0	**Enforcing contracts** (rank)		43
Cost (% of income per capita)	57.0	Private bureau coverage (% of adults)	3.6	Procedures (number)		42
				Time (days)		195
Getting electricity (rank)	170	**Protecting investors** (rank)	133	Cost (% of claim)		22.2
Procedures (number)	9	Extent of disclosure index (0-10)	4			
Time (days)	117	Extent of director liability index (0-10)	1	**Resolving insolvency** (rank)		117
Cost (% of income per capita)	1,783.3	Ease of shareholder suits index (0-10)	7	Time (years)		4.0
		Strength of investor protection index (0-10)	4.0	Cost (% of estate)		10
				Recovery rate (cents on the dollar)		23.7
		Paying taxes (rank)	157			
		Payments (number per year)	41			
		Time (hours per year)	205			
		Total tax rate (% of profit)	97.5			

Note: Most indicator sets refer to a case scenario in the largest business city of each economy. For more details, see the data notes.

✔ Reform making it easier to do business ✘ Reform making it more difficult to do business

VANUATU

East Asia & Pacific
Lower middle income

Ease of doing business (rank)	76			GNI per capita (US$)	2,760	
				Population (m)	0.2	

✔ **Starting a business** (rank)	114	✔ **Registering property** (rank)	111	✔ **Trading across borders** (rank)	128
Procedures (number)	8	Procedures (number)	4	Documents to export (number)	7
Time (days)	35	Time (days)	118	Time to export (days)	21
Cost (% of income per capita)	47.1	Cost (% of property value)	7.0	Cost to export (US$ per container)	1,690
Minimum capital (% of income per capita)	0.0			Documents to import (number)	8
		Getting credit (rank)	78	Time to import (days)	20
✘ **Dealing with construction permits** (rank)	40	Strength of legal rights index (0-10)	9	Cost to import (US$ per container)	1,690
Procedures (number)	11	Depth of credit information index (0-6)	0		
Time (days)	39	Public registry coverage (% of adults)	0.0	**Enforcing contracts** (rank)	71
Cost (% of income per capita)	341.7	Private bureau coverage (% of adults)	0.0	Procedures (number)	30
				Time (days)	430
Getting electricity (rank)	147	**Protecting investors** (rank)	79	Cost (% of claim)	56.0
Procedures (number)	5	Extent of disclosure index (0-10)	5		
Time (days)	257	Extent of director liability index (0-10)	6	**Resolving insolvency** (rank)	53
Cost (% of income per capita)	1,171.3	Ease of shareholder suits index (0-10)	5	Time (years)	2.6
		Strength of investor protection index (0-10)	5.3	Cost (% of estate)	38
				Recovery rate (cents on the dollar)	42.7
		Paying taxes (rank)	32		
		Payments (number per year)	31		
		Time (hours per year)	120		
		Total tax rate (% of profit)	8.4		

VENEZUELA, RB

Latin America & Caribbean
Upper middle income

Ease of doing business (rank)	177			GNI per capita (US$)	11,590
				Population (m)	28.8

Starting a business (rank)	147	**Registering property** (rank)	91	**Trading across borders** (rank)	166
Procedures (number)	17	Procedures (number)	8	Documents to export (number)	8
Time (days)	141	Time (days)	38	Time to export (days)	49
Cost (% of income per capita)	26.1	Cost (% of property value)	2.5	Cost to export (US$ per container)	2,590
Minimum capital (% of income per capita)	0.0			Documents to import (number)	9
		Getting credit (rank)	182	Time to import (days)	71
Dealing with construction permits (rank)	109	Strength of legal rights index (0-10)	1	Cost to import (US$ per container)	2,868
Procedures (number)	10	Depth of credit information index (0-6)	0		
Time (days)	381	Public registry coverage (% of adults)	0.0	**Enforcing contracts** (rank)	77
Cost (% of income per capita)	161.9	Private bureau coverage (% of adults)	0.0	Procedures (number)	30
				Time (days)	510
Getting electricity (rank)	155	**Protecting investors** (rank)	179	Cost (% of claim)	43.7
Procedures (number)	6	Extent of disclosure index (0-10)	3		
Time (days)	125	Extent of director liability index (0-10)	2	**Resolving insolvency** (rank)	161
Cost (% of income per capita)	1,341.1	Ease of shareholder suits index (0-10)	2	Time (years)	4.0
		Strength of investor protection index (0-10)	2.3	Cost (% of estate)	38
				Recovery rate (cents on the dollar)	6.2
		✘ **Paying taxes** (rank)	183		
		Payments (number per year)	70		
		Time (hours per year)	864		
		Total tax rate (% of profit)	63.5		

VIETNAM

East Asia & Pacific
Lower middle income

Ease of doing business (rank)	98			GNI per capita (US$)	1,100
				Population (m)	88.4

Starting a business (rank)	103	**Registering property** (rank)	47	**Trading across borders** (rank)	68
Procedures (number)	9	Procedures (number)	4	Documents to export (number)	6
Time (days)	44	Time (days)	57	Time to export (days)	22
Cost (% of income per capita)	10.6	Cost (% of property value)	0.6	Cost to export (US$ per container)	580
Minimum capital (% of income per capita)	0.0			Documents to import (number)	8
		Getting credit (rank)	24	Time to import (days)	21
Dealing with construction permits (rank)	67	Strength of legal rights index (0-10)	8	Cost to import (US$ per container)	670
Procedures (number)	10	Depth of credit information index (0-6)	5		
Time (days)	200	Public registry coverage (% of adults)	29.8	**Enforcing contracts** (rank)	30
Cost (% of income per capita)	109.0	Private bureau coverage (% of adults)	0.0	Procedures (number)	34
				Time (days)	295
Getting electricity (rank)	135	✔ **Protecting investors** (rank)	166	Cost (% of claim)	28.5
Procedures (number)	5	Extent of disclosure index (0-10)	6		
Time (days)	142	Extent of director liability index (0-10)	1	**Resolving insolvency** (rank)	142
Cost (% of income per capita)	1,343.0	Ease of shareholder suits index (0-10)	2	Time (years)	5.0
		Strength of investor protection index (0-10)	3.0	Cost (% of estate)	15
				Recovery rate (cents on the dollar)	16.5
		Paying taxes (rank)	151		
		Payments (number per year)	32		
		Time (hours per year)	941		
		Total tax rate (% of profit)	40.1		

Note: Most indicator sets refer to a case scenario in the largest business city of each economy. For more details, see the data notes.

✔ Reform making it easier to do business ✘ Reform making it more difficult to do business

WEST BANK AND GAZA

Ease of doing business (rank)	131	Middle East & North Africa Lower middle income		GNI per capita (US$) Population (m)	1,523 4.2
Starting a business (rank)	177	**Registering property** (rank)	78	**Trading across borders** (rank)	114
Procedures (number)	11	Procedures (number)	7	Documents to export (number)	6
Time (days)	49	Time (days)	47	Time to export (days)	23
Cost (% of income per capita)	96.0	Cost (% of property value)	0.8	Cost to export (US$ per container)	1,310
Minimum capital (% of income per capita)	218.8			Documents to import (number)	6
		Getting credit (rank)	166	Time to import (days)	40
Dealing with construction permits (rank)	129	Strength of legal rights index (0-10)	1	Cost to import (US$ per container)	1,295
Procedures (number)	18	Depth of credit information index (0-6)	3		
Time (days)	119	Public registry coverage (% of adults)	5.5	**Enforcing contracts** (rank)	93
Cost (% of income per capita)	1,000.5	Private bureau coverage (% of adults)	0.0	Procedures (number)	44
				Time (days)	540
Getting electricity (rank)	85	**Protecting investors** (rank)	46	Cost (% of claim)	21.2
Procedures (number)	5	Extent of disclosure index (0-10)	6		
Time (days)	63	Extent of director liability index (0-10)	5	**Resolving insolvency** (rank)	183
Cost (% of income per capita)	1,627.8	Ease of shareholder suits index (0-10)	7	Time (years)	NO PRACTICE
		Strength of investor protection index (0-10)	6.0	Cost (% of estate)	NO PRACTICE
				Recovery rate (cents on the dollar)	0.0
		Paying taxes (rank)	39		
		Payments (number per year)	27		
		Time (hours per year)	154		
		Total tax rate (% of profit)	16.8		

YEMEN, REP.

Ease of doing business (rank)	99	Middle East & North Africa Lower middle income		GNI per capita (US$) Population (m)	1,060 24.3
Starting a business (rank)	66	**Registering property** (rank)	55	**Trading across borders** (rank)	118
Procedures (number)	6	Procedures (number)	6	Documents to export (number)	6
Time (days)	12	Time (days)	19	Time to export (days)	27
Cost (% of income per capita)	83.8	Cost (% of property value)	3.8	Cost to export (US$ per container)	890
Minimum capital (% of income per capita)	0.0			Documents to import (number)	9
		Getting credit (rank)	159	Time to import (days)	25
Dealing with construction permits (rank)	35	Strength of legal rights index (0-10)	3	Cost to import (US$ per container)	1,475
Procedures (number)	12	Depth of credit information index (0-6)	2		
Time (days)	116	Public registry coverage (% of adults)	0.7	**Enforcing contracts** (rank)	38
Cost (% of income per capita)	61.1	Private bureau coverage (% of adults)	0.0	Procedures (number)	36
				Time (days)	520
Getting electricity (rank)	52	**Protecting investors** (rank)	133	Cost (% of claim)	16.5
Procedures (number)	4	Extent of disclosure index (0-10)	6		
Time (days)	35	Extent of director liability index (0-10)	4	**Resolving insolvency** (rank)	114
Cost (% of income per capita)	4,569.8	Ease of shareholder suits index (0-10)	2	Time (years)	3.0
		Strength of investor protection index (0-10)	4.0	Cost (% of estate)	8
				Recovery rate (cents on the dollar)	24.1
		✔ **Paying taxes** (rank)	116		
		Payments (number per year)	44		
		Time (hours per year)	248		
		Total tax rate (% of profit)	32.9		

ZAMBIA

Ease of doing business (rank)	84	Sub-Saharan Africa Lower middle income		GNI per capita (US$) Population (m)	1,070 12.9
Starting a business (rank)	69	✘ **Registering property** (rank)	96	**Trading across borders** (rank)	153
Procedures (number)	6	Procedures (number)	5	Documents to export (number)	6
Time (days)	18	Time (days)	40	Time to export (days)	44
Cost (% of income per capita)	27.4	Cost (% of property value)	8.3	Cost to export (US$ per container)	2,678
Minimum capital (% of income per capita)	0.0			Documents to import (number)	8
		Getting credit (rank)	8	Time to import (days)	56
Dealing with construction permits (rank)	148	Strength of legal rights index (0-10)	9	Cost to import (US$ per container)	3,315
Procedures (number)	14	Depth of credit information index (0-6)	5		
Time (days)	196	Public registry coverage (% of adults)	0.0	**Enforcing contracts** (rank)	85
Cost (% of income per capita)	2,015.2	Private bureau coverage (% of adults)	4.3	Procedures (number)	35
				Time (days)	471
Getting electricity (rank)	118	**Protecting investors** (rank)	79	Cost (% of claim)	38.7
Procedures (number)	5	Extent of disclosure index (0-10)	3		
Time (days)	117	Extent of director liability index (0-10)	6	**Resolving insolvency** (rank)	96
Cost (% of income per capita)	1,317.9	Ease of shareholder suits index (0-10)	7	Time (years)	2.7
		Strength of investor protection index (0-10)	5.3	Cost (% of estate)	9
				Recovery rate (cents on the dollar)	29.3
		Paying taxes (rank)	47		
		Payments (number per year)	37		
		Time (hours per year)	132		
		Total tax rate (% of profit)	14.5		

Note: Most indicator sets refer to a case scenario in the largest business city of each economy. For more details, see the data notes.

✔ Reform making it easier to do business ✘ Reform making it more difficult to do business

ZIMBABWE

Ease of doing business (rank)	171	Sub-Saharan Africa Low income		GNI per capita (US$)	460		
				Population (m)	12.6		

Starting a business (rank)	144	**Registering property** (rank)	85	**Trading across borders** (rank)	172
Procedures (number)	9	Procedures (number)	5	Documents to export (number)	8
Time (days)	90	Time (days)	31	Time to export (days)	53
Cost (% of income per capita)	148.9	Cost (% of property value)	8.0	Cost to export (US$ per container)	3,280
Minimum capital (% of income per capita)	0.0			Documents to import (number)	9
		Getting credit (rank)	126	Time to import (days)	73
Dealing with construction permits (rank)	166	Strength of legal rights index (0-10)	7	Cost to import (US$ per container)	5,101
Procedures (number)	12	Depth of credit information index (0-6)	0		
Time (days)	614	Public registry coverage (% of adults)	0.0	**Enforcing contracts** (rank)	112
Cost (% of income per capita)	6,154.3	Private bureau coverage (% of adults)	0.0	Procedures (number)	38
				Time (days)	410
Getting electricity (rank)	167	**Protecting investors** (rank)	122	Cost (% of claim)	113.1
Procedures (number)	6	Extent of disclosure index (0-10)	8		
Time (days)	125	Extent of director liability index (0-10)	1	**Resolving insolvency** (rank)	153
Cost (% of income per capita)	5,305.5	Ease of shareholder suits index (0-10)	4	Time (years)	3.3
		Strength of investor protection index (0-10)	4.3	Cost (% of estate)	22
				Recovery rate (cents on the dollar)	10.0
		Paying taxes (rank)	127		
		Payments (number per year)	49		
		Time (hours per year)	242		
		Total tax rate (% of profit)	35.6		

Note: Most indicator sets refer to a case scenario in the largest business city of each economy. For more details, see the data notes.

This page intentionally left blank.

Employing workers data

Employing workers data

Economy	Fixed-term contracts prohibited for permanent tasks?	Maximum length of fixed-term contracts (months)[a]	Minimum wage for a 19-year-old worker or an apprentice (US$/month)[b]	Ratio of minimum wage to value added per worker	50-hour workweek allowed?[c]	Maximum working days per week	Premium for night work (% of hourly pay)[d]	Premium for work on weekly rest day (% of hourly pay)[d]	Major restrictions on night work?[d]	Major restrictions on weekly holiday work?[d]	Paid annual leave (working days)[e]	Dismissal due to redundancy allowed by law?	Third-party notification if 1 worker is dismissed?	Third-party approval if 1 worker is dismissed?	Third-party notification if 9 workers are dismissed?	Third-party approval if 9 workers are dismissed?	Retraining or reassignment?[f]	Priority rules for redundancies?	Priority rules for reemployment?	Notice period for redundancy dismissal (weeks of salary)[e]	Severance pay for redundancy dismissal (weeks of salary)[e]
Afghanistan	No	No limit	0.0	0.00	Yes	6	25	50	No	No	20.0	Yes	Yes	Yes	Yes	Yes	No	Yes	Yes	4.3	17.3
Albania	Yes	No limit	198.4	0.40	Yes	6	50	25	Yes	No	20.0	Yes	No	No	No	No	No	No	No	10.1	10.7
Algeria	Yes	No limit	204.8	0.38	Yes	6	0	100	Yes	No	22.0	Yes	No	No	Yes	No	Yes	No	Yes	4.3	13.0
Angola	Yes	12	126.9	0.20	Yes	6	0	0	No	No	22.0	Yes	Yes	No	Yes	No	Yes	Yes	No	4.3	11.6
Antigua and Barbuda	No	No limit	572.5	0.41	No	6	25	50	No	No	12.0	Yes	No	No	No	No	No	No	No	3.4	12.8
Argentina	Yes	60	456.9	0.42	Yes	6	13	100	No	No	18.0	Yes	No	No	No	No	No	No	No	7.2	23.1
Armenia	Yes	No limit	88.1	0.23	Yes	6	30	50	No	No	20.0	Yes	No	No	No	No	Yes	No	No	6.0	5.0
Australia	No	No limit	1,597.1	0.30	Yes	7	0	0	No	No	20.0	Yes	No	No	Yes	Yes	Yes	No	No	3.0	8.7
Austria	No	No limit	715.5	0.12	Yes	5.5	17	0	No	No	25.0	Yes	Yes	No	Yes	No	Yes	Yes	Yes	2.0	0.0
Azerbaijan	No	60	103.9	0.17	Yes	6	40	150	Yes	No	17.0	Yes	No	No	No	No	No	Yes	No	8.7	10.7
Bahamas, The	No	No limit	695.8	0.26	Yes	5.5	0	0	No	No	11.7	Yes	No	No	No	No	No	No	Yes	2.0	13.0
Bahrain	No	No limit	0.0	0.00	Yes	6	0	150	No	No	18.3	Yes	Yes	Yes	Yes	Yes	No	No	No	4.3	26.7
Bangladesh	Yes	No limit	23.1	0.28	Yes	6	0	100	No	No	18.0	Yes	Yes	No	Yes	No	No	Yes	Yes	4.3	13.0
Belarus	No	No limit	163.3	0.23	Yes	6	20	100	No	No	17.0	Yes	Yes	No	Yes	No	Yes	Yes	No	8.7	0.0
Belgium	No	No limit	1,725.4	0.30	Yes	6	4	100	No	Yes	20.0	Yes	No	No	No	No	No	No	No	6.3	0.0
Belize	No	No limit	289.5	0.56	Yes	6	0	50	No	No	10.0	Yes	No	No	No	No	No	No	Yes	3.3	5.0
Benin	No	48	66.5	0.57	Yes	6	0	0	No	No	24.0	Yes	Yes	No	Yes	No	No	Yes	Yes	4.3	7.3
Bhutan	No	No limit	0.0	0.00	Yes	6	0	0	No	No	15.0	Yes	No	No	No	No	No	No	No	8.3	0.0
Bolivia[g]	Yes	24	110.2	0.44	Yes	6	30	100	Yes	No	21.7	No	n.a.	n.a.	n.a.	n.a.	n.a.	n.a.	n.a.	n.a.	n.a.
Bosnia and Herzegovina	No	24	520.1	0.92	Yes	6	30	20	No	No	18.0	Yes	No	No	Yes	No	No	No	Yes	2.0	7.2
Botswana	No	No limit	100.6	0.11	Yes	6	0	100	Yes	No	15.0	Yes	No	No	Yes	No	No	Yes	No	4.9	16.8
Brazil	Yes	24	299.6	0.26	Yes	6	20	100	Yes	No	26.0	Yes	No	No	No	No	No	No	No	4.3	0.0
Brunei Darussalam	No	No limit	0.0	0.00	Yes	6	0	50	No	No	13.3	Yes	No	No	No	No	No	No	No	3.0	0.0
Bulgaria	No	36	167.2	0.22	Yes	6	10	0	Yes	No	20.0	Yes	No	No	No	No	Yes	No	No	4.3	3.2
Burkina Faso	No	No limit	63.0	0.71	Yes	6	0	0	No	Yes	22.0	Yes	No	No	Yes	No	No	Yes	Yes	4.3	6.1
Burundi	No	No limit	3.0	0.13	Yes	6	30	0	No	Yes	21.0	Yes	No	No	Yes	No	No	Yes	Yes	8.7	7.2
Cambodia	No	24	43.0	0.43	Yes	6	30	100	No	No	19.3	Yes	No	No	Yes	No	No	Yes	Yes	7.9	11.4

Employing workers data	Fixed-term contracts prohibited for permanent tasks?	Maximum length of fixed-term contracts (months) [a]	Minimum wage for a 19-year-old worker or an apprentice (US$/month) [b]	Ratio of minimum wage to value added per worker	50-hour workweek allowed? [c]	Maximum working days per week	Premium for night work (% of hourly pay) [d]	Premium for work on weekly rest day (% of hourly pay) [d]	Major restrictions on night work? [d]	Major restrictions on weekly holiday work? [d]	Paid annual leave (working days) [e]	Dismissal due to redundancy allowed by law?	Third-party notification if 1 worker is dismissed?	Third-party approval if 1 worker is dismissed?	Third-party notification if 9 workers are dismissed?	Third-party approval if 9 workers are dismissed?	Retraining or reassignment? [f]	Priority rules for redundancies?	Priority rules for reemployment?	Notice period for redundancy dismissal (weeks of salary) [e]	Severance pay for redundancy dismissal (weeks of salary) [e]
Cameroon	No	48	59.9	0.34	Yes	6	50	0	No	No	26.0	Yes	No	No	No	No	No	No	No	6.1	8.1
Canada	No	No limit	1,903.5	0.34	Yes	6	0	0	No	No	10.0	Yes	No	No	No	No	No	No	No	5.0	5.0
Cape Verde	Yes	60	0.0	0.00	Yes	6	25	100	No	No	22.0	Yes	No	No	No	No	No	No	No	6.4	23.1
Central African Republic	Yes	48	39.3	0.57	Yes	5	0	50	No	Yes	25.3	Yes	Yes	Yes	Yes	Yes	Yes	Yes	Yes	4.3	17.3
Chad	No	48	124.2	1.28	Yes	6	0	100	No	No	24.7	Yes	No	No	No	No	No	No	Yes	7.2	5.8
Chile	No	24	0.0	0.00	Yes	6	0	0	No	No	15.0	Yes	No	No	No	No	No	Yes	No	4.3	12.0
China	No	No limit	182.5	0.37	Yes	6	39	100	No	Yes	6.7	Yes	Yes	No	Yes	No	Yes	Yes	Yes	4.3	23.1
Colombia	No	No limit	260.8	0.37	Yes	6	35	75	No	No	15.0	Yes	No	No	No	No	No	No	No	0.0	16.7
Comoros	No	36	60.8	0.52	Yes	6	0	0	No	No	15.0	Yes	Yes	No	Yes	No	No	No	No	13.0	23.1
Congo, Dem. Rep.	Yes	48	65.0	2.20	No	5	25	0	No	No	13.0	Yes	Yes	Yes	Yes	Yes	No	Yes	No	10.3	0.0
Congo, Rep.	Yes	24	102.5	0.30	Yes	6	0	50	No	No	29.0	Yes	Yes	Yes	Yes	Yes	No	Yes	Yes	4.3	6.5
Costa Rica	Yes	12	387.7	0.48	Yes	6	0	100	No	No	12.0	Yes	Yes	No	Yes	No	No	No	Yes	4.3	14.4
Côte d'Ivoire	No	24	0.00	0.00	No	6	38	0	No	No	27.4	Yes	No	No	No	No	No	No	Yes	5.8	7.3
Croatia	Yes	36	534.2	0.32	Yes	6	10	35	No	Yes	20.0	Yes	No	No	Yes	No	Yes	Yes	Yes	7.9	7.2
Cyprus	No	30	0.0	0.00	Yes	6	0	0	No	No	20.0	Yes	No	No	No	No	No	No	Yes	5.7	0.0
Czech Republic	No	24	439.2	0.21	Yes	6	10	10	No	Yes	20.0	Yes	No	No	No	No	No	Yes	No	8.7	13.0
Denmark	No	No limit	0.0	0.00	Yes	6	0	0	No	No	25.0	Yes	No	No	No	No	No	No	No	0.0	0.0
Djibouti	Yes	24	0.0	0.00	Yes	6	10	10	No	No	30.0	Yes	No	No	No	No	No	No	No	4.3	0.0
Dominica	No	No limit	290.9	0.45	Yes	6	0	0	No	No	15.0	Yes	No	No	No	No	No	No	Yes	4.3	13.0
Dominican Republic	Yes	No limit	215.8	0.33	Yes	6	0	100	No	No	14.0	Yes	No	No	No	No	No	Yes	Yes	4.0	9.3
Ecuador	No	24	253.6	0.42	Yes	6	25	100	No	No	12.3	Yes	No	Yes	No	Yes	No	Yes	No	4.3	22.2
Egypt, Arab Rep.	No	No limit	31.8	0.10	Yes	6	0	100	No	No	24.0	Yes	No	Yes	Yes	Yes	No	Yes	No	10.1	26.7
El Salvador	Yes	No limit	80.8	0.17	Yes	6	25	0	Yes	No	11.0	Yes	No	No	No	No	No	No	No	0.0	22.9
Equatorial Guinea	Yes	24	236.0	0.11	Yes	6	25	50	No	Yes	22.0	Yes	Yes	Yes	Yes	Yes	No	Yes	Yes	4.3	34.3
Eritrea	Yes	No limit	0.0	0.00	Yes	6	0	0	No	No	19.0	Yes	No	No	No	No	No	No	Yes	3.1	12.3
Estonia	Yes	120	389.9	0.22	Yes	5	25	0	No	No	24.0	Yes	No	No	No	No	No	Yes	No	8.6	4.3
Ethiopia	Yes	No limit	0.0	0.00	Yes	6	0	0	No	No	18.3	Yes	No	No	Yes	No	Yes	Yes	No	10.1	10.5

Employing workers data

	Difficulty of hiring index				Rigidity of hours index							Difficulty of redundancy index								Redundancy cost	
	Fixed-term contracts prohibited for permanent tasks?	Maximum length of fixed-term contracts (months) [a]	Minimum wage for a 19-year-old worker or an apprentice (US$/month) [b]	Ratio of minimum wage to value added per worker	50-hour workweek allowed? [c]	Maximum working days per week	Premium for night work (% of hourly pay) [d]	Premium for work on weekly rest day (% of hourly pay) [d]	Major restrictions on night work? [d]	Major restrictions on weekly holiday work? [d]	Paid annual leave (working days) [e]	Dismissal due to redundancy allowed by law?	Third-party notification if 1 worker is dismissed?	Third-party approval if 1 worker is dismissed?	Third-party notification if 9 workers are dismissed?	Third-party approval if 9 workers are dismissed?	Retraining or reassignment? [f]	Priority rules for redundancies?	Priority rules for reemployment?	Notice period for redundancy dismissal (weeks of salary) [e]	Severance pay for redundancy dismissal (weeks of salary) [e]
Fiji	No	No Limit	336.5	0.71	Yes	6	3	100	No	No	10.0	Yes	No	No	No	No	No	No	No	4.3	5.3
Finland	Yes	60	1,989.5	0.34	Yes	6	8	100	No	Yes	30.0	Yes	Yes	No	Yes	No	Yes	Yes	Yes	10.1	0.0
France	Yes	18	782.0	0.14	No	6	0	0	No	Yes	30.0	Yes	No	No	Yes	No	Yes	Yes	Yes	7.2	7.2
Gabon	No	48	41.0	0.04	Yes	6	50	100	No	Yes	24.0	Yes	Yes	Yes	Yes	Yes	No	Yes	No	10.4	4.6
Gambia, The	No	No limit	0.0	0.00	Yes	5	0	0	No	No	21.0	Yes	Yes	No	Yes	No	No	No	No	26.0	0.0
Georgia	No	No limit	23.4	0.07	Yes	7	0	0	No	No	24.0	Yes	No	No	No	No	No	No	No	4.3	4.3
Germany	No	24	1,145.5	0.21	Yes	6	13	100	No	No	24.0	Yes	Yes	No	Yes	No	Yes	Yes	No	10.0	11.6
Ghana	No	No limit	27.6	0.15	Yes	5	0	0	No	No	15.0	Yes	No	No	No	No	No	No	No	3.6	46.2
Greece	Yes	No limit	986.9	0.29	Yes	5	25	20	No	No	22.3	Yes	No	No	Yes	No	No	No	No	11.6	7.9
Grenada	Yes	No limit	223.5	0.31	Yes	6	0	0	No	No	13.3	Yes	No	No	No	No	No	No	No	7.2	5.3
Guatemala	Yes	No limit	185.5	0.44	Yes	6	0	50	No	No	15.0	Yes	Yes	No	Yes	No	No	No	No	0.0	27.0
Guinea	No	24	0.0	0.00	Yes	6	20	45	No	No	30.0	Yes	No	Yes	No	Yes	No	Yes	No	2.1	5.8
Guinea-Bissau	Yes	12	0.0	0.00	Yes	6	25	50	No	No	21.0	Yes	No	Yes	No	Yes	No	Yes	Yes	0.0	26.0
Guyana	No	No limit	0.0	0.00	Yes	7	0	100	No	No	12.0	Yes	No	No	No	No	No	No	No	4.3	12.3
Haiti	No	No Limit	125.6	1.38	Yes	6	50	50	No	No	13.0	Yes	No	No	No	No	No	No	No	10.1	0.0
Honduras	Yes	24	279.3	1.04	Yes	6	25	100	No	No	16.7	Yes	Yes	No	Yes	No	No	No	No	7.2	23.1
Hong Kong SAR, China	No	No limit	0.0	0.00	Yes	6	0	0	No	No	10.3	Yes	No	No	No	No	No	No	No	4.3	1.5
Hungary	No	60	394.0	0.25	Yes	5	40	100	No	No	21.3	Yes	No	No	Yes	No	No	No	No	6.2	7.2
Iceland	No	24	1,406.7	0.34	Yes	6	80	80	No	No	24.0	Yes	No	No	No	No	No	No	No	10.1	0.0
India	No	No limit	29.9	0.17	Yes	6	0	0	Yes	Yes	15.0	Yes	No	Yes	No	Yes	Yes	Yes	Yes	4.3	11.4
Indonesia	Yes	36	132.7	0.41	Yes	6	0	0	No	Yes	12.0	Yes	Yes	Yes	Yes	Yes	Yes	No	No	0.0	57.8
Iran, Islamic Rep.	No	No limit	318.3	0.57	Yes	6	23	40	No	Yes	24.0	Yes	No	Yes	No	Yes	No	No	No	0.0	23.1
Iraq	Yes	No limit	98.7	0.28	Yes	5	100	50	No	No	22.0	Yes	No	No	No	No	No	No	No	0.0	0.0
Ireland	No	No limit	1,536.1	0.31	Yes	6	0	0	No	No	20.0	Yes	No	No	Yes	No	No	Yes	Yes	4.0	2.8
Israel	No	No limit	1,014.0	0.28	Yes	5.5	15	50	No	No	18.0	Yes	No	No	No	No	No	No	No	4.3	23.1
Italy	Yes	44	1,641.4	0.37	Yes	6	0	0	No	No	20.3	Yes	No	No	Yes	No	No	No	No	7.2	0.0
Jamaica	No	No limit	215.0	0.34	Yes	6	0	100	No	No	11.7	Yes	No	No	No	No	No	No	No	4.0	10.0
Japan	No	No limit	1,547.6	0.29	Yes	6	25	35	No	No	15.3	Yes	Yes	No	Yes	No	Yes	No	No	4.3	0.0

Employing workers data

Economy	Fixed-term contracts prohibited for permanent tasks?	Maximum length of fixed-term contracts (months) [a]	Minimum wage for a 19-year-old worker or an apprentice (US$/month) [b]	Ratio of minimum wage to value added per worker	50-hour workweek allowed? [c]	Maximum working days per week	Premium for night work (% of hourly pay) [d]	Premium for work on weekly rest day (% of hourly pay) [d]	Major restrictions on night work? [d]	Major restrictions on weekly holiday work? [d]	Paid annual leave (working days) [e]	Dismissal due to redundancy allowed by law?	Third-party notification if 1 worker is dismissed?	Third-party approval if 1 worker is dismissed?	Third-party notification if 9 workers are dismissed?	Third-party approval if 9 workers are dismissed?	Retraining or reassignment? [f]	Priority rules for redundancies?	Priority rules for reemployment?	Notice period for redundancy dismissal (weeks of salary) [e]	Severance pay for redundancy dismissal (weeks of salary) [e]
																				Difficulty of hiring index → Rigidity of hours index → Difficulty of redundancy index → Redundancy cost	
Jordan	No	No limit	199.9	0.34	Yes	6	0	150	No	No	18.7	Yes	Yes	Yes	Yes	Yes	No	No	Yes	4.3	0.0
Kazakhstan	No	No limit	0.1	0.00	Yes	6	50	100	No	No	18.0	Yes	No	No	Yes	No	No	No	No	4.3	4.3
Kenya	No	No limit	78.9	0.66	Yes	6	0	0	No	No	21.0	Yes	No	No	Yes	No	No	No	No	4.3	11.4
Kiribati	No	No limit	0.0	0.00	Yes	7	0	0	No	No	0.0	Yes	No	No	No	No	No	No	No	0.0	0.0
Korea, Rep.	No	24	558.5	0.24	Yes	6	50	50	Yes	No	17.0	Yes	Yes	No	Yes	No	Yes	No	Yes	4.3	23.1
Kosovo	No	No limit	0.0	0.00	No	6	30	0	No	No	0.0	Yes	Yes	No	Yes	No	No	No	No	4.3	7.2
Kuwait	No	No limit	166.2	0.04	No	6	0	50	No	No	26.0	Yes	No	No	No	No	No	No	Yes	13.0	15.1
Kyrgyz Republic	Yes	60	11.5	0.10	Yes	6	50	100	No	No	20.0	Yes	Yes	No	Yes	Yes	No	No	No	4.3	13.0
Lao PDR	No	No limit	63.7	0.44	Yes	6	15	150	No	No	15.0	Yes	Yes	Yes	Yes	Yes	No	No	No	6.4	40.7
Latvia	Yes	36	408.2	0.29	Yes	5.5	50	0	Yes	No	20.0	Yes	Yes	No	Yes	No	No	No	No	1.0	8.7
Lebanon	No	24	318.0	0.29	Yes	6	0	50	No	No	15.0	Yes	No	No	Yes	No	No	No	No	8.7	0.0
Lesotho	No	No limit	93.7	0.59	Yes	6	0	100	No	Yes	12.0	Yes	Yes	No	Yes	Yes	No	Yes	Yes	4.3	10.7
Liberia	No	No Limit	52.0	1.78	Yes	6	50	50	No	No	16.0	Yes	Yes	No	Yes	No	No	Yes	No	4.3	21.3
Lithuania	No	60	325.4	0.24	No	5.5	50	100	No	No	20.7	Yes	Yes	No	Yes	Yes	No	Yes	Yes	8.7	15.9
Luxembourg	Yes	24	2,389.3	0.25	No	5.5	15	70	No	No	25.0	Yes	Yes	No	Yes	Yes	No	Yes	Yes	17.3	4.3
Macedonia, FYR	No	60	167.5	0.31	Yes	6	35	50	Yes	No	20.0	Yes	Yes	No	Yes	No	No	Yes	No	4.3	8.7
Madagascar	Yes	24	37.9	0.56	Yes	6	30	40	No	No	24.0	Yes	Yes	No	Yes	Yes	No	Yes	Yes	3.4	8.9
Malawi	Yes	No Limit	30.4	0.56	Yes	6	0	100	No	No	15.0	Yes	No	No	No	No	No	No	No	4.3	12.3
Malaysia	No	No limit	0.0	0.00	Yes	6	0	0	No	No	13.3	Yes	No	No	Yes	No	No	No	No	4.3	13.3
Maldives	No	24	0.0	0.00	Yes	6	0	50	No	No	30.0	Yes	No	No	No	No	No	No	No	5.8	0.0
Mali	Yes	72	14.9	0.16	Yes	6	0	0	No	No	22.0	Yes	Yes	No	Yes	No	No	Yes	No	4.3	9.3
Marshall Islands	No	No limit	0.0	0.00	Yes	7	0	0	No	No	0.0	Yes	No	No	No	No	No	No	No	0.0	0.0
Mauritania	No	24	74.5	0.49	Yes	6	0	50	No	No	18.0	Yes	Yes	No	Yes	No	No	Yes	No	4.3	6.1
Mauritius	No	No limit	170.5	0.19	Yes	6	0	100	No	Yes	22.0	Yes	Yes	No	Yes	Yes	No	Yes	Yes	4.3	6.3
Mexico	Yes	No limit	121.6	0.10	Yes	6	0	25	No	No	12.0	Yes	No	No	No	Yes	Yes	No	Yes	0.0	22.0
Micronesia, Fed. Sts.	No	No limit	227.3	0.60	Yes	7	0	0	No	No	0.0	Yes	No	Yes	No	Yes	No	No	No	0.0	0.0
Moldova	Yes	No limit	91.3	0.44	Yes	6	50	100	Yes	Yes	20.0	Yes	Yes	No	Yes	No	Yes	Yes	No	8.7	13.9
Mongolia	No	No limit	95.6	0.42	Yes	5	0	50	No	No	16.0	Yes	No	No	No	No	No	No	No	4.3	4.3

Employing workers data	Fixed-term contracts prohibited for permanent tasks?	Maximum length of fixed-term contracts (months) [a]	Minimum wage for a 19-year-old worker or an apprentice (US$/month) [b]	Ratio of minimum wage to value added per worker	50-hour workweek allowed? [c]	Maximum working days per week	Premium for night work (% of hourly pay) [d]	Premium for work on weekly rest day (% of hourly pay) [d]	Major restrictions on night work? [d]	Major restrictions on weekly holiday work? [d]	Paid annual leave (working days) [e]	Dismissal due to redundancy allowed by law?	Third-party notification if 1 worker is dismissed?	Third-party approval if 1 worker is dismissed?	Third-party notification if 9 workers are dismissed?	Third-party approval if 9 workers are dismissed?	Retraining or reassignment? [f]	Priority rules for redundancies?	Priority rules for reemployment?	Notice period for redundancy dismissal (weeks of salary) [e]	Severance pay for redundancy dismissal (weeks of salary) [e]
	Difficulty of hiring index				Rigidity of hours index							Difficulty of redundancy index								Redundancy cost	
Montenegro	No	No limit	303.9	0.37	Yes	6	40	0	No	No	19.0	Yes	No	No	No	No	Yes	No	No	2.1	26.0
Morocco	Yes	12	246.5	0.69	Yes	6	0	100	No	No	19.5	Yes	Yes	No	Yes	No	Yes	No	No	7.2	13.5
Mozambique	Yes	72	80.5	1.16	Yes	6	0	100	No	No	21.3	Yes	Yes	No	Yes	No	No	No	No	4.3	36.8
Namibia	No	No limit	0.0	0.00	Yes	6	6	100	No	No	20.0	Yes	No	No	Yes	No	No	No	No	4.3	5.3
Nepal	Yes	No limit	57.0	0.83	Yes	6	6	50	No	No	18.0	Yes	No	No	Yes	No	No	Yes	No	4.3	22.9
Netherlands	No	36	1,041.5	0.17	Yes	5.5	0	0	No	No	20.0	Yes	Yes	Yes	Yes	Yes	Yes	Yes	No	8.7	0.0
New Zealand	Yes	No limit	1,379.3	0.41	Yes	7	0	0	No	No	20.0	Yes	No	No	No	No	No	No	No	0.0	0.0
Nicaragua	No	No limit	132.8	0.89	Yes	6	0	100	No	No	30.0	Yes	Yes	No	Yes	No	No	No	No	0.0	14.9
Niger	Yes	24	59.6	0.96	No	6	38	0	No	No	22.0	Yes	Yes	No	Yes	Yes	Yes	Yes	Yes	4.3	5.8
Nigeria	No	No limit	126.5	0.70	Yes	6	0	0	No	No	22.0	Yes	No	No	No	No	No	No	No	4.0	12.2
Norway	Yes	48	3,608.9	0.34	Yes	6	0	0	Yes	Yes	21.0	Yes	Yes	No	Yes	No	Yes	Yes	No	8.7	0.0
Oman	No	No Limit	506.9	0.21	Yes	6	50	0	Yes	No	20.0	Yes	No	No	No	No	No	Yes	Yes	4.3	0.0
Pakistan	Yes	9	41.8	0.28	Yes	6	0	100	No	Yes	14.0	Yes	No	No	Yes	Yes	No	Yes	Yes	4.3	22.9
Palau	No	No Limit	474.5	0.56	Yes	7	0	0	No	No	0.0	Yes	No	No	No	No	No	No	No	0.0	0.0
Panama	Yes	12	370.6	0.41	Yes	6	0	50	No	Yes	22.0	Yes	Yes	Yes	Yes	Yes	No	No	Yes	0.0	19.0
Papua New Guinea	No	No Limit	116.4	0.62	Yes	6	0	0	No	No	11.0	Yes	No	No	No	No	No	No	No	3.3	9.2
Paraguay	Yes	No Limit	191.9	0.48	Yes	6	30	100	Yes	No	20.0	Yes	Yes	No	Yes	No	No	Yes	No	7.5	18.6
Peru	Yes	60	200.3	0.33	Yes	6	35	100	No	No	13.0	Yes	Yes	No	Yes	Yes	No	Yes	Yes	0.0	11.4
Philippines	Yes	No limit	181.6	0.66	Yes	6	10	30	No	No	5.0	Yes	Yes	No	Yes	No	No	No	No	4.3	23.1
Poland	No	24	386.2	0.27	Yes	6	20	100	No	No	22.0	Yes	Yes	No	Yes	No	Yes	Yes	Yes	10.1	0.0
Portugal	Yes	36	789.6	0.29	Yes	6	25	100	No	No	22.0	Yes	Yes	No	Yes	No	Yes	Yes	No	7.9	26.0
Puerto Rico (U.S.)	No	No Limit	1,256.7	0.58	Yes	7	0	100	No	No	15.0	Yes	No	No	No	No	No	No	No	0.0	0.0
Qatar	No	No limit	0.0	0.00	Yes	6	0	0	No	No	22.0	Yes	No	No	No	No	No	No	No	7.2	16.0
Romania	Yes	36	222.9	0.24	Yes	5	25	100	No	No	20.0	Yes	Yes	No	Yes	No	No	Yes	No	4.0	4.3
Russian Federation	Yes	60	139.0	0.12	Yes	6	20	0	No	No	22.0	Yes	Yes	No	Yes	No	Yes	Yes	No	8.7	4.3
Rwanda	No	No limit	18.5	0.23	Yes	6	0	0	No	No	19.3	Yes	No	No	No	No	Yes	Yes	No	4.3	8.7
Samoa	No	No Limit	131.7	0.30	Yes	6	0	100	No	No	10.0	Yes	No	No	No	No	No	No	No	5.8	0.0
São Tomé and Príncipe	Yes	36	0.0	0.00	No	6	25	100	No	Yes	26.0	Yes	Yes	Yes	Yes	Yes	No	No	Yes	4.3	26.0

Employing worker's data

Economy	Fixed-term contracts prohibited for permanent tasks?	Maximum length of fixed-term contracts (months)[a]	Minimum wage for a 19-year-old worker or an apprentice (US$/month)[b]	Ratio of minimum wage to value added per worker	50-hour workweek allowed?[c]	Maximum working days per week	Premium for night work (% of hourly pay)[d]	Premium for work on weekly rest day (% of hourly pay)[d]	Major restrictions on night work?[d]	Major restrictions on weekly holiday work?[d]	Paid annual leave (working days)[e]	Dismissal due to redundancy allowed by law?	Third-party notification if 1 worker is dismissed?	Third-party approval if 1 worker is dismissed?	Third-party notification if 9 workers are dismissed?	Third-party approval if 9 workers are dismissed?	Retraining or reassignment?[f]	Priority rules for redundancies?	Priority rules for reemployment?	Notice period for redundancy dismissal (weeks of salary)[e]	Severance pay for redundancy dismissal (weeks of salary)[e]
Saudi Arabia	No	No limit	0.0	0.00	Yes	6	0	0	No	No	20.7	Yes	No	No	No	No	No	No	No	4.3	15.2
Senegal	Yes	48	77.3	0.48	Yes	6	38	0	No	No	24.3	Yes	No	No	Yes	No	No	Yes	Yes	3.2	10.5
Serbia	Yes	12	188.0	0.26	Yes	6	26	26	No	No	20.0	Yes	No	No	Yes	No	Yes	No	No	0.0	7.7
Seychelles	Yes	No limit	337.2	0.27	Yes	6	0	100	No	No	21.0	Yes	No	No	Yes	No	Yes	Yes	Yes	4.3	9.1
Sierra Leone	Yes	No limit	10.7	0.21	Yes	5	15	0	No	No	21.7	Yes	No	No	Yes	No	No	Yes	No	8.7	34.8
Singapore	No	No limit	0.0	0.00	Yes	6	0	100	No	No	10.7	Yes	No	No	No	No	No	No	No	0.0	0.0
Slovak Republic	No	24	429.2	0.23	Yes	6	20	100	No	No	25.0	Yes	No	No	Yes	No	Yes	No	Yes	3.0	11.6
Slovenia	Yes	24	1,038.0	0.37	Yes	6	30	50	No	No	21.0	Yes	Yes	No	Yes	No	Yes	Yes	Yes	11.6	5.7
Solomon Islands	No	No limit	96.2	0.65	Yes	6	0	0	No	No	15.0	Yes	Yes	No	Yes	No	No	No	No	3.0	11.6
South Africa	Yes	No limit	543.1	0.69	Yes	6	0	100	No	No	15.0	Yes	Yes	No	Yes	No	Yes	No	No	4.3	5.7
Spain	Yes	12	1,044.0	0.27	Yes	5.5	25	0	Yes	No	22.0	Yes	Yes	No	Yes	No	No	No	Yes	4.0	5.3
Sri Lanka	No	No limit	35.6	0.13	Yes	5.5	0	50	Yes	Yes	14.0	Yes	Yes	Yes	Yes	Yes	No	No	No	2.1	15.2
St. Kitts and Nevis	No	No limit	505.1	0.39	Yes	7	0	0	No	No	14.0	Yes	No	No	Yes	No	No	No	No	8.7	54.2
St. Lucia	No	No limit	0.0	0.00	Yes	6	0	150	No	No	21.0	Yes	No	No	Yes	No	No	No	No	3.7	9.3
St. Vincent and the Grenadines	No	No Limit	173.5	0.28	Yes	6	0	0	No	No	19.3	Yes	No	No	Yes	No	No	No	Yes	4.0	10.0
Sudan	No	48	79.4	0.43	Yes	6	0	0	No	No	23.3	Yes	Yes	Yes	Yes	Yes	No	No	No	4.3	21.7
Suriname	No	No limit	0.0	0.00	Yes	6	0	100	No	No	16.0	Yes	Yes	Yes	Yes	Yes	No	No	No	0.0	8.8
Swaziland	No	No limit	83.7	0.22	Yes	5.5	0	0	No	No	11.0	Yes	No	No	Yes	No	Yes	No	No	5.9	8.7
Sweden	No	24	0.0	0.00	Yes	5.5	0	0	No	Yes	25.0	Yes	Yes	No	Yes	No	Yes	Yes	Yes	14.4	0.0
Switzerland	No	120	0.0	0.00	Yes	6	0	0	No	Yes	20.0	Yes	No	No	Yes	No	No	No	No	10.1	0.0
Syrian Arab Republic	No	60	205.8	0.58	Yes	6	0	100	No	No	21.7	Yes	Yes	No	Yes	No	No	No	No	8.7	21.7
Taiwan, China	Yes	12	561.2	0.26	No	6	0	100	Yes	No	12.0	Yes	Yes	No	Yes	No	Yes	No	Yes	3.8	18.8
Tajikistan	Yes	No limit	18.1	0.17	Yes	6	5	100	No	No	23.3	Yes	Yes	No	Yes	No	No	Yes	No	8.7	6.9
Tanzania	Yes	0	58.9	0.70	Yes	6	0	0	No	No	20.0	Yes	No	No	Yes	No	No	No	No	4.0	5.3
Thailand	Yes	No limit	79.5	0.16	Yes	6	0	100	No	No	6.0	Yes	No	No	Yes	No	No	No	No	4.3	31.7
Timor-Leste	Yes	No limit	0.0	0.00	Yes	6	0	100	No	No	12.0	Yes	Yes	No	Yes	No	No	No	No	4.3	0.0
Togo	Yes	48	59.7	0.92	Yes	6	38	60	No	No	30.0	Yes	Yes	No	Yes	No	No	Yes	Yes	4.3	7.3

Employing workers data

	Difficulty of hiring index				Rigidity of hours index							Difficulty of redundancy index								Redundancy cost	
	Fixed-term contracts prohibited for permanent tasks?	Maximum length of fixed-term contracts (months) [a]	Minimum wage for a 19-year-old worker or an apprentice (US$/month) [b]	Ratio of minimum wage to value added per worker	50-hour workweek allowed? [c]	Maximum working days per week	Premium for night work (% of hourly pay) [d]	Premium for work on weekly rest day (% of hourly pay) [d]	Major restrictions on night work? [d]	Major restrictions on weekly holiday work? [d]	Paid annual leave (working days) [e]	Dismissal due to redundancy allowed by law?	Third-party notification if 1 worker is dismissed?	Third-party approval if 1 worker is dismissed?	Third-party notification if 9 workers are dismissed?	Third-party approval if 9 workers are dismissed?	Retraining or reassignment? [f]	Priority rules for redundancies?	Priority rules for reemployment?	Notice period for redundancy dismissal (weeks of salary) [e]	Severance pay for redundancy dismissal (weeks of salary) [e]
Tonga	No	No limit	0.0	0.00	Yes	6	0	0	No	Yes	0.0	Yes	No	No	No	No	No	No	No	0.0	0.0
Trinidad and Tobago	No	No limit	0.0	0.00	Yes	6	0	0	No	No	10.0	Yes	No	No	No	No	No	Yes	No	6.4	14.1
Tunisia	No	48	115.9	0.24	Yes	6	0	100	Yes	No	13.0	Yes	Yes	Yes	Yes	Yes	No	No	No	4.3	7.8
Turkey	Yes	No limit	550.6	0.47	Yes	6	0	100	Yes	Yes	18.0	Yes	No	No	Yes	Yes	Yes	Yes	No	6.7	23.1
Uganda	No	No limit	2.9	0.03	Yes	6	0	0	No	No	21.0	Yes	No	No	No	No	No	Yes	Yes	8.7	0.0
Ukraine	Yes	No limit	122.5	0.34	No	5.5	20	100	No	No	18.0	Yes	Yes	Yes	Yes	Yes	Yes	Yes	Yes	8.7	4.3
United Arab Emirates	No	No limit	0.0	0.00	Yes	6	0	50	No	No	26.0	Yes	No	No	No	No	No	No	No	4.3	0.0
United Kingdom	No	No limit	1,655.0	0.34	Yes	6	0	0	No	No	28.0	Yes	No	No	Yes	No	No	No	No	5.3	2.7
United States	No	No limit	1,242.6	0.21	Yes	6	0	0	No	No	0.0	Yes	No	No	No	No	No	No	No	0.0	0.0
Uruguay	No	No limit	294.1	0.21	Yes	6	0	100	No	No	21.0	Yes	No	No	No	No	No	No	No	0.0	20.8
Uzbekistan	Yes	60	29.0	0.18	Yes	6	50	100	Yes	No	15.0	Yes	Yes	No	Yes	No	Yes	Yes	No	8.7	13.0
Vanuatu	No	No limit	254.0	0.64	Yes	6	75	50	No	No	15.0	Yes	No	No	No	No	No	No	No	9.3	23.1
Venezuela, RB [g]	Yes	24	303.5	0.20	Yes	6	30	50	Yes	Yes	19.3	No	n.a.	n.a.	n.a.	n.a.	n.a.	n.a.	n.a.	n.a.	n.a.
Vietnam	No	72	49.9	0.37	Yes	6	30	100	No	No	13.0	Yes	Yes	No	Yes	Yes	Yes	Yes	Yes	0.0	23.1
West Bank and Gaza	No	24	0.0	0.00	Yes	6	0	150	Yes	Yes	18.0	Yes	Yes	No	Yes	No	No	No	No	4.3	23.1
Yemen, Rep.	No	No limit	74.9	0.46	Yes	6	15	100	No	No	30.0	Yes	Yes	No	Yes	No	No	No	Yes	4.3	23.1
Zambia	No	No limit	91.5	0.52	Yes	5.5	4	100	No	No	24.0	Yes	Yes	No	Yes	No	No	No	No	4.3	46.2
Zimbabwe	No	No limit	74.9	1.09	Yes	6	0	0	No	No	22.0	Yes	Yes	Yes	Yes	Yes	Yes	No	No	13.0	69.3

a. Including renewals.
b. Economies for which 0.0 is shown have no minimum wage.
c. For 2 months a year in case of a seasonal increase in production.
d. In case of continuous operations.
e. Average for workers with 1, 5 and 10 years of tenure.
f. Whether compulsory before redundancy.
g. Some questions are not applicable ("n.a.") for economies where dismissal due to redundancy is not allowed.
Source: Doing Business database.

Acknowledgments

Contact details for local partners are available on the *Doing Business* website at http://www.doingbusiness.org

Doing Business would not be possible without the expertise and generous input of a network of more than 9,000 local partners, including legal experts, business consultants, accountants, freight forwarders, government officials and other professionals routinely administering or advising on the relevant legal and regulatory requirements in the 183 economies covered. Contact details for local partners are available on the *Doing Business* website at http://www.doingbusiness.org.

Doing Business 2012 was prepared by a team led by Sylvia Solf, Neil Gregory (through March 2011) and Augusto Lopez Claros (from April 2011) under the general direction of Janamitra Devan. The team comprised Beatriz Mejia Asserias, Andres Baquero Franco, Karim O. Belayachi, Iryna Bilotserkivska, Mariana Carvalho, Maya Choueiri, Santiago Croci, Fernando Dancausa Diaz, Marie-Lily Delion, Raian Divanbeigi, Alejandro Espinosa-Wang, Margherita Fabbri, Caroline Frontigny, Carolin Geginat, Cemile Hacibeyoglu, Jamal Haidar, Betina Hennig, Sabine Hertveldt, Hussam Hussein, Joyce Ibrahim, Fakhriyar Jabbarov, Ludmila Jantuan, Nan Jiang, Hervé Kaddoura, Nadezhda Lissogor, Jean Michel Lobet, Jean-Philippe Lodugnon-Harding, Valerie Erica Marechal, Frédéric Meunier, Robert Murillo, Joanna Nasr, Nuria de Oca, Mikiko Imai Ollison, Pilar Salgado-Otónel, Valentina Saltane, Lucas Seabra, Paula Garcia Serna, Anastasia Shegay, Jayashree Srinivasan, Susanne Szymanski, Tea Trumbic, Marina Turlakova, Julien Vilquin and Yasmin Zand. Donny Eryastha, Rong Li, Justin Liang, Chang Liu, Yukihiro Nakamura, Alexandre Revia, Fang Xia and Beijing Zhu assisted in the months before publication.

The online service of the *Doing Business* database is managed by Preeti Endlaw, Graeme Littler, Kunal H. Patel, Vinod Thottikkatu and Hashim Zia. The *Doing Business 2012* report media and marketing strategy is managed by Nadine Ghannam. The events and roadshow strategy is managed by Jamile Ramadan.

The team is grateful for valuable comments provided by colleagues across the World Bank Group and for the guidance of World Bank Group Executive Directors. It would especially like to acknowledge the comments and guidance of Aart C. Kraay. Comments were also received from Alejandro Alvarez de la Campa, Sudeshna Ghosh Banerjee, Alexander Berg, Lada Busevac, Dobromir Christow, Fabrizio Fraboni, Jose Maria Garrido, Heike Gramkow, Akvile Gropper, Olivier Hartmann, Neville Howlett, Dahlia Khalifa, Arvo Kuddo, Charles Kunaka, Oscar Madeddu, Andres Federico Martinez, Tadatsugu Matsudaira, Gerard McLinden, Andrei Mikhnev, Nina Mocheva, Riz Mokal, Fredesvinda Fatima Montes Herraiz, Thomas Moullier, Monica Alina Mustra, Jean Denis Pesme, Maria Teresa Goodman Pincetich, Colin Ewell Wesley Raymond, Francesca Recanatini, Shalini Sankaranarayanan, Raha Shahidsaless, Peter Douglas Sheerin, Victoria Stanley, Susan Symons, Ignacio Jose Tirado, Mahesh Uttamchandani, Barry Raymond Walsh and Ulrich Matthias Zeisluft.

Oliver Hart and Andrei Shleifer provided academic advice on the project. The paying taxes project was conducted in collaboration with PwC, led by Robert Morris. The development of the getting electricity indicators was financed by the Norwegian Trust Fund. The governments of Korea, FYR Macedonia, Mexico and the United Kingdom commented on the economy case studies.

Alison Strong copyedited the manuscript. Corporate Vision, Inc. designed the report and the graphs.

Quotations in this report are from *Doing Business* local partners unless otherwise indicated. The names of those wishing to be acknowledged individually are listed below. The global and regional contributors listed are firms that have completed multiple surveys in their various offices around the world.

GLOBAL CONTRIBUTORS

Allen & Overy LLP

Baker & McKenzie

Cleary Gottlieb Steen & Hamilton LLP

Ernst & Young

Ius Laboris, Alliance of Labor, Employment, Benefits and Pensions Law Firms

KPMG

Law Society of England and Wales

Lex Mundi, Association of Independent Law Firms

Panalpina

PwC

Raposo Bernardo & Associados

Russell Bedford International

SDV International Logistics

Toboc Inc.

REGIONAL CONTRIBUTORS

A.P. Moller-Maersk Group

East Africa Law Society

García & Bodán

Globalink Transportation & Logistics Worldwide LLP

Grata Law Firm

IKRP Rokas & Partners

Private Investors for Africa (PIA)

Salans International Law Firm

Talal Abu Ghazaleh Legal (TAG-Legal)

Transunion International

Wolf Theiss

AFGHANISTAN

Taqi Ahmad
A.F. Fergusons & Co.

Naseem Akbar
Afghanistan Investment Support Agency

Mohammad Zarif Alam Stanikzai
Afghan Bar Association

Mirwais Alami
Da Afghanistan Breshna Sherkat

Ziaullah Astana
Afghan Land Consulting Organization (ALCO)

Tor Bahdrey
Property Consulting Afghanistan

Katherine Blanchette
Deloitte Consulting LLP

Jay Doeden
Dfloitte Consulting LLP

Abdullah Dowrani
Financial Disputes Resolution Commission (FDRC)

Khan Hadawal
Bank Mille Afghan

Zabiullah Hamdard
Ahmad Javed

Abdul Hanan
Afghan Land Consulting Organization (ALCO)

Abdul Wassay Haqiqi
Haqiqi Auditing & Consulting Co.

Saduddin Haziq
Afghan United Bank

Rashid Ibrahim
A.F. Fergusons & Co.

Sanzar Kakar
Afghanistan Financial Services, LLC

Maryam Kargar
USAID Economic Growth and Governance Initiative

Mohammed Masood Khwaja
Da Afghanistan Breshna Sherkat

Gulya Kolakova
Arrow General Supplies Company

Prakash LB
USAID

Zahoor Malla
Globalink Logistics Group

Immamudin Masaheb
Masaheb Barrister Office

Zabihullah Modaser
USAID Economic Growth and Governance Initiative

Tali Mohammed
Afghanistan Investment Support Agency

Shekeeb Nessar
Da Afghanistan Breshna Sherkat

Gul Pacha
Afghanistan Investment Support Agency

Hussairi Rahmani
ARAZI

Tamsil Rashid
Afghanistan International Bank

Mudassir Rizwan
A.F. Fergusons & Co.

Abdul Sami Saber
Da Afghanistan Bank

Ahmad Javed Sadeqi
Deloitte Consulting LLP

Zakaria Sahibzada
Arrow General Supplies Company

Abdul Saleem
USAID Economic Growth and Governance Initiative

Richard Scarth
Property Consulting Afghanistan

Shafiqullah Seddiqi

Khalil Sediq
Afghanistan International Bank

Sharifullah Shirzad
Da Afghanistan Bank

Farah Siddiq
Maverick Entreprises

Qasem Toddaye
USAID Economic Growth and Governance Initiative

Gulrahman Totakhail
USAID Economic Growth and Governance Initiative

Shah Wali Wardak
Barrister Office

Najibullah Wardak
LARA

Abdul Fatah Waziry
Civil Engineer

Mohammadi Khan Yaqoobi
Da Afghanistan Bank

Badruddin Yasini
Da Afghanistan Bank

Abdul Salam Zahed
Afghanistan Investment Support Agency

Mir Nasiruddin Ziwari
Appeal Court of Kabul

ALBANIA

Kuehne + Nagel Ltd.

ManeTCI (Mane Trading Construction & Investment)

Iris Ago
A&B Business Consulting

Artur Asllani
Tonucci & Partners

Sabina Baboci
Kalo & Associates

Redjan Basha
A&B Business Consulting

Ledia Beçi
Hoxha, Memi & Hoxha

Alban Bello
KPMG Albania shpk

Jona Bica
Kalo & Associates

Artan Bozo
Bozo & Associates Law Firm

Ilir Daci
OPTIMA Legal and Financial

Sajmir Dautaj
Tonucci & Partners

Dael Dervishi
OPTIMA Legal and Financial

Erinda Duraj
Bozo & Associates Law Firm

Sokol Elmazaj
Boga & Associates

Alba Fagu
Bank of Albania

Lorena Gega
PwC Albania

Irsida Gjino
Kalo & Associates

Aurela Gjokutaj
Al-Tax Studio

Eduart Gjokutaj
Al-Tax Studio

Valbona Gjonçari
Boga & Associates

Emel Haxhillari
Kalo & Associates

Eljon Hila
Bozo & Associates Law Firm

Blerina Hilaj
A&B Business Consulting

Shpati Hoxha
Hoxha, Memi & Hoxha

Elona Hoxhaj
Boga & Associates

Ilir Johollari
Hoxha, Memi & Hoxha

Neritan Kallfa
Tonucci & Partners

Erlind Kodhelaj
Boga & Associates

Sabina Lalaj
Boga & Associates

Fatos Lazimi
Kalo & Associates

Renata Leka
Boga & Associates

Petrit Malaj
P.B.M. Ltd., member of Russell Bedford International

Dorjana Maliqi
A&B Business Consulting

Evis Melonashi (Zaja)
OPTIMA Legal and Financial

Andi Memi
Hoxha, Memi & Hoxha

Dairida Metalia
PwC Albania

Aigest Milo
Kalo & Associates

Blerta Nesho
Wolf Theiss

Loreta Peci
PwC Albania

Florian Piperi
OPTIMA Legal and Financial

Laura Qorlaze
Avanntive Consulting sh.p.k.

Artila Rama
Boga & Associates

Loriana Robo
Kalo & Associates

Anisa Rrumbullaku
Kalo & Associates

Ergis Sefa
ERG, LLC

Enkelejd Seitllari
Kalo & Associates

Ardjana Shehi
Kalo & Associates

Gentian Sinani
A&B Business Consulting

Majlinda Sulstarova
Tonucci & Partners

Besa Tauzi
Boga & Associates

Paul Tobin
PwC Bulgaria

Ketrin Topçiu
Bozo & Associates Law Firm

Ened Topi
Boga & Associates

Fioralba Trebicka
Hoxha, Memi & Hoxha

Alketa Uruçi
Boga & Associates

Gerhard Velaj
Boga & Associates

Silva Velaj
Boga & Associates

Aspasi Xhori
CEZ Shperndarje sh.a

Selena Ymeri
Hoxha, Memi & Hoxha

Enida Zeneli
Bozo & Associates Law Firm

ALGERIA

Chafika Abdat
Cabinet d'Avocats Samir Hamouda

Branka Achari-Djokic
Banque d'Algérie

Samina Allam
Notary Bouchali

Mohamed Atbi
Etude notariale Mohamed Atbi

Djamila Azzouz
Cabinet d'Audit Azzouz, Correspondent of Russell Bedford International

Mohammed Salim Azzouz
Cabinet d'Audit Azzouz, Correspondent of Russell Bedford International

Khodja Bachir
SNC Khodja & Co.

Hassan Djamel Belloula
Cabinet Belloula

Nabil Belloula
Cabinet Belloula

Tayeb Belloula
Cabinet Belloula

Adnane Bouchaib
Bouchaib Law Firm

Bouchali
Notary Bouchali

Amine Bouhaddi
Entreprise Bouhaddi

Said Dib
Banque d'Algérie

Arezki Djadour
Gide Loyrette Nouel, member of Lex Mundi

Brahim Embouazza
MCDConsulting

Halim Faidi
Studio A

Nicolas Granier
Landwell & Associés

Mohamed El-Amine Haddad
Cabinet Avocat Amine Haddad

Sakina Haddad
Crédit Populaire d'Algerie

Samir Hamouda
Cabinet d'Avocats Samir Hamouda

Imendassen
Notary Imendassen

Nabila Kerri
Palatine International Services

Goussanem Khaled
Law Firm Goussanem & Aloui

Samy Laghouati
Gide Loyrette Nouel, member of Lex Mundi

Mohamed Lanouar
Lefèvre Pelletier & Associés

Karine Lasne
Landwell & Associés

Vincent Lunel
Lefèvre Pelletier & Associés

Ahmed Mekerba
Ghellal & Mekerba

Tahar Melakhessou
Notaire Melakhessou

Narimane Naas
Gide Loyrette Nouel, member of Lex Mundi

Hassane Nait Ibrahim
Universal Transit

Fares Ouzegdouh
Béjaia Mediterranean Terminal

Aloui Salima
Law Firm Goussanem & Aloui

Mourad Seghir
Ghellal & Mekerba

Benabid Mohammed Tahar
Cabinet Mohammed Tahar Benabid

Nabiha Zerigui
Cabinet d'Avocats Samir Hamouda

ANGOLA

Banco Nacional de Angola

EDEL-EP

F. Castelo Branco & Associados

José Rodrigues Alentejo
Câmara de Comércio e Indústria de Angola

Sika Awoonor
Global Choice Services LLC

Fernando Barros
PwC Angola

Alain Brachet
SDV Logistics

Pedro Calixto
PwC Angola

Anacleta Cipriano
FBL Advogados

Patricia Dias
AVM Advogados

Lourdes Caposso Fernandes
Lourdes Caposso Fernandes & Associados

Sónia Neto Foreid
AVM Advogados

Victor Leonel
Ordem dos Arquitectos

Paulette Lopes
FBL Advogados

Teresinha Lopes
FBL Advogados

Joaquim Mahando
AVM Advogados

Manuel Malufuene
Ordem dos Arquitectos

Vítor Marques da Cruz
FCB&A in association with Eduardo Vera-Cruz Advogados

Luis Miguel Nunes
AVM Advogados

Sofia Oliveira
FBL Advogados

Eduardo Paiva
PwC Angola

Laurinda Prazeres Cardoso
FBL Advogados

Elisa Rangel Nunes
ERN Advogados

Cristina Teixeira
PwC Angola

N'Gunu Tiny
CFRA Advogados Associados

António Vicente Marques
AVM Advogados

Filomena Victor
ERN Advogados

ANTIGUA AND BARBUDA

Clarke & Clarke

Vernon Bird
Survey Department (Ministry of Agriculture, Lands, Housing & the Environment)

Ricki Camacho
Antigua & Barbuda Intellectual Property & Commerce (ABIPCO)

Neil Coates
PwC Antigua

Nicolette Doherty
Nicolette M. Doherty Attorney at Law and Notary Public

Terence Dornellas
Consolidated Maritime Services

Brian D'Ornellas
OBM International, Antigua Ltd.

Joy Dublin
James & Associates

Vernon Edwards Jr.
Freight Forwarding & Deconsolidating

Gilbert Findlay
KPMG

Ann Henry
Henry & Burnette

Cecile Hill
Land Registry

Sherelyn Hughes Thomas
Antigua and Barbuda Investment Authority

Alfred McKelly James
James & Associates

Lisa M. John Weste
Thomas, John & Co.

Hugh C. Marshall
Marshall & Co.

Girvan Pigott
Antigua Public Utility Authority

Marsha Prince-Thomas
PwC Antigua

Septimus A. Rhudd
Rhudd & Associates

Andrea Roberts
Roberts & Co.

Lesroy Samuel
Internal Revenue Department

Lestroy Samuel
Antigua and Barbuda Investment Authority

Cathrona Samuel
Antigua Public Utility Authority

Sharon Simmons
Land Registry

Patricia Simon-Forde
Chambers Patricia Simon-Forde

Denzil Solomon
Development Control Authority

Arthur Thomas
Thomas, John & Co.

Cherissa Thomas
Antigua & Barbuda Bar Association

Charles Walwyn
PwC Antigua

ARGENTINA

María Victoria Abudara
M. & M. Bomchil

Fernando Aguinaga
Zang, Bergel & Viñes Abogados

Dolores Aispuru
PricewaterhouseCoopers Jurídico Fiscal S.R.L

Lisandro A. Allende
Brons & Salas Abogados

María Florencia Angélico
Canosa Abogados

Natalia Artmann
Alfaro Abogados

Vanesa Balda
Vitale, Manoff & Feilbogen

Federico Martín Basile
M. & M. Bomchil

Néstor J. Belgrano
M. & M. Bomchil

Nicolás Belgrano
M. & M. Bomchil

Gabriela Bindi
Zang, Bergel & Viñes Abogados

Sebastián Bittner
Jebsen & Co.

Pilar Etcheverry Boneo
Marval, O'Farrell & Mairal, member of Lex Mundi

Ignacio Fernández Borzese
Luna Requena & Fernández Borzese Tax Law Firm

Mariano Bourdieu
Severgnini Robiola Grinberg & Larrechea

Nicolás Bühler
Hope, Duggan & Silva

Luis Bullrich
Nicholson y Cano Abogados

Iván Burín
Zang, Bergel & Viñes Abogados

Adriana Estefanía Camaño
Canosa Abogados

Javier Canosa
Canosa Abogados

Federico Carenzo
Leonhardt, Dietl, Graf & von der Fecht

Mariano E. Carricart
Fornieles Law Firm

Gustavo Casir
Quattrini, Laprida & Asociados

Agustín Castro Bravo
Estudio Beccar Varela

Luciano Cativa
Luna Requena & Fernández Borzese Tax Law Firm

Pablo L. Cavallaro
Estudio Cavallaro Abogados

Celeste Cicania
Allonca Esquivel Abogados. Legal & Business Consulting

Guadalupe Cores
Quattrini, Laprida & Asociados

Roberto H. Crouzel
Estudio Beccar Varela

Valeria D'Alessandro
Marval, O'Farrell & Mairal, member of Lex Mundi

Nicolás de Ezcurra
Estudio Beccar Varela

Ángeles del Prado
Zang, Bergel & Viñes Abogados

Carola Del Rio
Severgnini Robiola Grinberg & Larrechea

Oscar Alberto del Río
Central Bank of Argentina

Leonardo Damián Diaz
PricewaterhouseCoopers Jurídico Fiscal S.R.L

Andrés Edelstein
PwC Argentina

Joaquín Eppens
Murray y d'André & Sirito de Zavalía

Juan M. Espeso
Jebsen & Co.

Diego Etchepare
PwC Argentina

Domingo Fernandez y Rajo
Fernandez y Rajo y Asociados

Diego M. Fissore
G. Breuer

Alejandro D. Fiuza
Marval, O'Farrell & Mairal, member of Lex Mundi

Nicolás Fossatti
Severgnini Robiola Grinberg & Larrechea

Victoria Funes
M. & M. Bomchil

Ignacio Funes de Rioja
Funes de Rioja & Asociados, member of Ius Laboris

Martín Gastaldi
Estudio Beccar Varela

Javier M. Gattó Bicain
Candioti Gatto Bicain & Ocantos

María Soledad Gonzalez
Marval, O'Farrell & Mairal, member of Lex Mundi

Laura González
Quattrini, Laprida & Asociados

Matías Grinberg
Severgnini Robiola Grinberg & Larrechea

Eduardo Guglielmini

Sandra S. Guillan
De Dios & Goyena Abogados Consultores

Daniel Intile
Daniel Intile & Assoc., member of Russell Bedford International

Martín Jebsen
Jebsen & Co.

Santiago Laclau
Marval, O'Farrell & Mairal, member of Lex Mundi

Ernesto Leconte
Marval, O'Farrell & Mairal, member of Lex Mundi

Bastiana Locurscio
Rattagan, Macchiavello Arocena & Peña Robirosa Abogados

Alvaro Luna Requena
Luna Requena & Fernández Borzese Tax Law Firm

Dolores Madueño
Jebsen & Co.

Rodrigo Marchan
MetA

Patricio Martin
M. & M. Bomchil

Pablo Mastromarino
Estudio Beccar Varela

Soledad Matteozzi
Alfaro Abogados

Pedro Mazer
Alfaro Abogados

Julian Melis
Candioti Gatto Bicain & Ocantos

José Oscar Mira
Central Bank of Argentina

Jorge Miranda
Clippers S.A.

Enrique Monsegur
Clippers S.A.

Mariana Morelli
Alfaro Abogados

Natalia Virginia Muller
De Dios & Goyena Abogados Consultores

Pablo Murray
Fiorito Murray & Diaz Cordero

Miguel P. Murray
Murray, d'André & Sirito de Zavalía

Isabel Muscolo
Quattrini, Laprida & Asociados

Damián Mauricio Najenson
Estudio Spota

Ingrid Nardelli
Allonca Esquivel Abogados. Legal & Business Consulting

Alfredo Miguel O'Farrell
Marval, O'Farrell & Mairal, member of Lex Mundi

Gonzalo Oliva Beltran
Rattagan, Macchiavello Arocena & Peña Robirosa Abogados

Guillermo Pavan
Brons & Salas Abogados

Angel Pereira
Marval, O'Farrell & Mairal, member of Lex Mundi

Javier Martín Petrantonio
M. & M. Bomchil

Juan Pedro Pomes
Hope, Duggan & Silva

Luis Ponsati
J.P. O'Farrell Abogados

José Miguel Puccinelli
Estudio Beccar Varela

Julio Alberto Pueyrredón
PricewaterhouseCoopers Jurídico Fiscal S.R.I.

Juan Manuel Quintana
Zang, Bergel & Viñes Abogados

Federico José Reibestein
Reibestein Asociados

Flavia Ríos
J.P. O'Farrell Abogados

Sebastián Rodrigo
Alfaro Abogados

Ignacio Rodriguez
PwC Argentina

Mariana Sanchez
Quattrini, Laprida & Asociados

Jorge Sanchez Diaz
Ecobamboo S.A.

Esteban Aguirre Saravia
Luna Requena & Fernández Borzese Tax Law Firm

Rodrigo Solá Torino
Marval, O'Farrell & Mairal, member of Lex Mundi

Pablo Staszewski
Staszewski & Asoc.

Maria Alejandra Stefanich
Marval, O'Farrell & Mairal, member of Lex Mundi

Javier Tarasido
Severgnini Robiola Grinberg & Larrechea

Adolfo Tombolini
Daniel Intile & Assoc., member of Russell Bedford International

Martín Torres Girotti
M. & M. Bomchil

Marcelo Torterola
Quattrini, Laprida & Asociados

María Paola Trigiani
Alfaro Abogados

Susana Urresti
Edesur Electricidad Distribuidora Sur S.A.

Emilio Beccar Varela
Estudio Beccar Varela

Gustavo Vayo
Hope, Duggan & Silva

Hernan Verly
Alfaro Abogados

Paz Villamil
Rattagan, Macchiavello Arocena & Peña Robirosa Abogados

Eduardo J. Viñales
Funes de Rioja & Asociados, member of Ius Laboris

Silvana Wasersztrom
Zang, Bergel & Viñes Abogados

Saúl Zang
Zang, Bergel & Viñes Abogados

Joaquín Emilio Zappa
J.P. O'Farrell Abogados

Carlos Zima
PwC Argentina

ARMENIA

CENTRAL BANK OF ARMENIA

ELECTRIC NETWORKS OF ARMENIA

PUBLIC SERVICES REGULATORY COMMISSION OF ARMENIA

Mher Abrahamyan
CENTRAL BANK OF ARMENIA

Armen Alaverdyan
STATE REVENUE COMMITTEE OF THE GOVERNMENT OF THE REPUBLIC OF ARMENIA

Sevak Alexanian
INVESTMENT LAW GROUP LLC

Artak Arzoyan
ACRA CREDIT BUREAU

Sedrak Asatryan
CONCERN-DIALOG LAW FIRM

Musayan Ashot
STATE COMMITTEE OF THE REAL PROPERTY CADASTRE

Eduard Avetisyan
KPMG

Inessa Avzhiyan
GLOBAL SPC

Sayad S. Badalyan
INVESTMENT LAW GROUP LLC

Karapet Badalyan
PRUDENCE LEGAL

Seda Baghdasaryan
GLOBAL SPC

Anna Baghdasaryan
TER-TACHATYAN LEGAL AND BUSINESS CONSULTING

Vardan Bezhanyan
LAW FACULTY, YEREVAN STATE UNIVERSITY

Hovhannes Burmanyan
CORPORATE INTEGRAL SOLUTIONS LLC

Peter Burnie
PwC KAZAKHSTAN

Vahe Chibukhchyan
MINISTRY OF ECONOMY OF ARMENIA

Andrew Coxshall
KPMG

Vahe Danielyan
MINISTRY OF ECONOMY OF ARMENIA

Kristina Dudukhchyan
KPMG

Aikanush Edigaryan
TRANS-ALLIANCE

Shoghik Gharibyan
KPMG

Vahe Ghavalyan
PARADIGMA ARMENIA CJSC

Hayk Ghazazyan
KPMG

Suren Gomtsyan
CONCERN-DIALOG LAW FIRM

Tigran Grigoryan
AMERIA CJSC

Andranik Grigoryan
CENTRAL BANK OF ARMENIA

Sargis Grigoryan
GPARTNERS

Armine Grigoryan
STATE COMMITTEE OF THE REAL PROPERTY CADASTRE

Narek Grigoryan
STATE COMMITTEE OF THE REAL PROPERTY CADASTRE

Sargis H. Martirosyan
TRANS-ALLIANCE

Armine Hakobyan
GLOBAL SPC

Monica Harutyunyan
HSBC BANK

Hasmik Harutyunyan
PARADIGMA ARMENIA CJSC

Davit Harutyunyan
PwC ARMENIA

Isabella Hovhannisyan
INVESTMENT LAW GROUP LLC

Davit Iskandarian
HSBC BANK

Paruyr Jangulyan
MINISTRY OF ECONOMY OF ARMENIA

Artashes F. Kakoyan
INVESTMENT LAW GROUP LLC

Vahe G. Kakoyan
INVESTMENT LAW GROUP LLC

Arshak Karapetyan
INVESTMENT LAW GROUP LLC

Karen Khachaturyan
STATE COMMITTEE OF THE REAL PROPERTY CADASTRE

Karen Martirosyan
AMERIA CJSC

Lilit Martirosyan
HOVNANIAN INTERNATIONAL LTD.

Lilit Matevosya
PwC ARMENIA

Armen Melkumyan
PRUDENCE LEGAL

Gurgen Migranovich Minasyan
UNION OF BUILDERS OF ARMENIA

Armen Mkoyan
ELITE GROUP

Edward Mouradian
PRUDENCE CJSC

Vahe Movsisyan
INVESTMENT LAW GROUP LLC

Rajiv Nagri
GLOBALINK LOGISTICS GROUP

Nerses Nersisyan
PwC ARMENIA

Marianna Nikoghosyan
GLOBAL SPC

Karen Petrosyan
INVESTMENT LAW GROUP LLC

Vahe Petrosyan
LOGICON DEVELOPMENT LLC

Anahit Petrosyan
PARADIGMA ARMENIA CJSC

Naira Petrosyan
PARADIGMA ARMENIA CJSC

Apetnak Poghosyan
CORPORATE INTEGRAL SOLUTIONS LLC

Aram Poghosyan
GRANT THORNTON LLP

Artak Poghosyan
MINISTRY OF ECONOMY OF ARMENIA

Arman Porsughyan
AMERIA CJSC

Gagik Sahakyan
AMERIA CJSC

David Sargsyan
AMERIA CJSC

Ruben Shahmuradyan
R&V COMFORT

Nelly Stepanyan
PARADIGMA ARMENIA CJSC

Aleqsey Suqoyan
COURT OF FIRST INSTANCE

Hakob Tadevosyan
GRANT THORNTON LLP

Altaf Tapia
PwC GEORGIA

Arsen Tavadyan
TER-TACHATYAN LEGAL AND BUSINESS CONSULTING

Armen Ter-Tachatyan
TER-TACHATYAN LEGAL AND BUSINESS CONSULTING

Lilit Tunyan
"FINCA" UNIVERSAL CREDIT ORGANIZATION CJSC

Artur Tunyan
JUDICIAL REFORM PROJECT

Araik Vardanyan
CHAMBER OF COMMERCE AND INDUSTRY OF THE REPUBLIC OF ARMENIA

Tserun Voskanyan
ELECTRIC NETWORKS OF ARMENIA

Liana Yordanyan
TER-TACHATYAN LEGAL AND BUSINESS CONSULTING

Anush Zadoyan
GLOBAL SPC

Samuel Zakarian
GLOBAL SPC

Karen Zakaryan
THE NASDAQ OMX GROUP ARMENIA

Robert Zakharyan
TER-TACHATYAN LEGAL AND BUSINESS CONSULTING

Arman Zargaryan
STATE REVENUE COMMITTEE OF THE GOVERNMENT OF THE REPUBLIC OF ARMENIA

AUSTRALIA

ALLEN & OVERY

FAYMAN INTERNATIONAL PTY. LTD.

Zeallie Ainsworth
CHANG, PISTILLI & SIMMONS

Matthew Allison
VEDA ADVANTAGE

Ameet Awasthi
AMERINDE CONSOLIDATED, INC.

Rasa Baranauskaite
AMERINDE CONSOLIDATED, INC.

Lynda Brumm
PwC AUSTRALIA

David Buda
RBHM COMMERCIAL LAWYERS

Joe Catanzariti
CLAYTON UTZ, member of LEX MUNDI

Fiona Chung
ALLENS ARTHUR ROBINSON

Gaibrielle Cleary
GOULD RALPH PTY. LTD., member of RUSSELL BEDFORD INTERNATIONAL

Vanessa Coffey
MALLESONS STEPHEN JACQUES

Rachel Cornes
BLAKE DAWSON

Tim Cox
PwC AUSTRALIA

Mark Dalby
OFFICE OF STATE REVENUE, NSW TREASURY

Anne Davis
CLAYTON UTZ, member of LEX MUNDI

Jenny Davis
ENERGYAUSTRALIA

Ian Farmer
PwC AUSTRALIA

Joan Fitzhenry
BAKER & McKENZIE

Helen Foy
MARQUE LAWYERS

Mike Gooley
McKENZIE GROUP

Owen Hayford
CLAYTON UTZ, member of LEX MUNDI

Jason Henniker
ENERGYAUSTRALIA

Erica Henshilwood
MARQUE LAWYERS

Eva Hucker
BAKER & McKENZIE

Ian Humphreys
BLAKE DAWSON

Stephen Jauncey
HENRY DAVIS YORK

Doug Jones
CLAYTON UTZ, member of LEX MUNDI

Morgan Kelly
FERRIER HODGSON LIMITED

Sanjay Kinger
AMERINDE CONSOLIDATED, INC.

Przemek Kucharski
ALLENS ARTHUR ROBINSON

Peter Leonard
GILBERT TOBIN

John Lobban
BLAKE DAWSON

John Martin
THOMSON PLAYFORD

Mitchell Mathas

Nathan Mattock
MARQUE LAWYERS

Kylie McPherson
MARQUE LAWYERS

Stephanie Newton
PwC AUSTRALIA

Maria Nicolof
GILBERT TOBIN

Kylie Parker
LOGICCA CHARTERED ACCOUNTANTS

Meredith Paynter
MALLESONS STEPHEN JACQUES

Mark Pistilli
CHANG, PISTILLI & SIMMONS

Michael Quinlan
ALLENS ARTHUR ROBINSON

John Reid
OFFICE OF STATE REVENUE, NSW TREASURY

Mitch Riley
ALLENS ARTHUR ROBINSON

Louise Rumble
MARQUE LAWYERS

Tim Short
GILBERT TOBIN

Mattew Speirs
PwC AUSTRALIA

Amy Spira
ALLENS ARTHUR ROBINSON

Damian Sturzaker
MARQUE LAWYERS

Nick Thomas
CLAYTON UTZ, member of LEX MUNDI

Simon Truskett
CLAYTON UTZ, member of LEX MUNDI

David Twigg
ENERGYAUSTRALIA

Craig Weston
W. T. EXPORTERS

Andrew Wheeler
PwC AUSTRALIA

Katarina Zlatar
GILBERT TOBIN

AUSTRIA

AUSTRIAN REGULATORY AUTHORITY

Clemens Baerenthaler
DLA PIPER WEISS-TESSBACH RECHTSANWÄLTE GMBH

Georg Brandstetter
BRANDSTETTER PRITZ & PARTNER

Alexander Brezman
BINDER GRÖSSWANG RECHTSANWÄLTE GMBH

Doris Buxbaum
HEGER & PARTNER

Werner Christlbauer
COLUMBUS CARGO INTERNATIONAL SPEDITION GMBH

Martin Eckel
E|N|W|C NATLACEN WALDERDORFF CANCOLA RECHTSANWÄLTE GMBH

Agnes Eigner
BRANDSTETTER PRITZ & PARTNER

Tibor Fabian
BINDER GRÖSSWANG RECHTSANWÄLTE GMBH

Julian Feichtinger
CHSH CERHA HEMPEL SPIEGELFELD HLAWATI

Ferdinand Graf
GRAF & PITKOWITZ RECHTSANWÄLTE GMBH

Herbert Greinecker
PwC AUSTRIA

Andreas Hable
BINDER GRÖSSWANG RECHTSANWÄLTE GMBH

Friedrich Helml
SAXINGER, CHALUPSKY, WEBER & PARTNERS

Herbert Herzig
AUSTRIAN CHAMBER OF COMMERCE

Meinrad Meinrad Höfferer
CHAMBER OF COMMERCE OF CARINTHIA

Alexander Hofmann
RA DR. ALEXANDER HOFMANN, LL.M.

Alexander Isola
GRAF & PITKOWITZ RECHTSANWÄLTE GMBH

Rudolf Kaindl
KOEHLER, KAINDL, DUERR & PARTNER, CIVIL LAW NOTARIES

Susanne Kappel
KUNZ SCHIMA WALLENTIN RECHTSANWÄLTE OG, member of IUS LABORIS

Alexander Klauser
BRAUNEIS KLAUSER PRÄNDL RECHTSANWÄLTE GMBH

Ulrike Koller
PwC AUSTRIA

Rudolf Krickl
PwC AUSTRIA

Peter Madl
SCHOENHERR

Patrick Mandl
bpv HÜGEL RECHTSANWÄLTE OG

Elena Martino
LIMAR CONSULTING GMBH

Tanja Melber
GRAF & PITKOWITZ RECHTSANWÄLTE GMBH

Wolfgang Messeritsch
NATIONAL BANK OF AUSTRIA

Elke Napokoj
bpv HÜGEL RECHTSANWÄLTE OG

Michael Podesser
PwC AUSTRIA

Barbara Pogacar

Martina Raczova
GRAF & PITKOWITZ RECHTSANWÄLTE GMBH

Gottfried Schellmann
BRAUNEIS KLAUSER PRÄNDL RECHTSANWÄLTE GMBH

Georg Schima
KUNZ SCHIMA WALLENTIN RECHTSANWÄLTE OG, member of IUS LABORIS

Stephan Schmalzl
Graf & Pitkowitz Rechtsanwälte GmbH

Ernst Schmidt
Halpern & Prinz

Christian Schuppich
CHSH Cerha Hempel Spiegelfeld Hlawati

Franz Schwarzinger
Revisionstreuhand, member of Russell Bedford International

Benedikt Spiegelfeld
CHSH Cerha Hempel Spiegelfeld Hlawati

Felix Steinlechner
Technisches Büro Filos

Alexander Teutsch
Graf & Pitkowitz Rechtsanwälte GmbH

Wolfgang Tichy
Schoenherr

Thomas Trettnak
CHSH Cerha Hempel Spiegelfeld Hlawati

Christoph Twaroch
Technical University Vienna

Alexandra Vacek
KSV 1870

Birgit Vogt-Majarek
Kunz Schima Wallentin Rechtsanwälte OG, member of Ius Laboris

Gerhard Wagner
KSV 1870

Anton Zeilinger
Ministry of Finance

AZERBAIJAN

Ernst & Young

Sabit Abdullayev
OMNI Law Firm

Aliagha Akhundov
Baker & McKenzie - CIS, Limited

Rashid Aliyev
Baker & McKenzie - CIS, Limited

Elnur Aliyev
BHM Baku Law Centre LLC

Aykhan Asadov
Baker & McKenzie - CIS, Limited

Anar Baghirov
BHM Baku Law Centre LLC

Samir Balayev
Unibank

Johanna Cronin
BHM Baku Law Centre LLC

Zaur Fatizadeh
Ministry of Taxes

Rashad Gafarov
Panalpina Central Asia EC Black and Caspian Sea Area

Sevil Gasimova
Baker & McKenzie - CIS, Limited

Fidan Gayibova
BM International LLC

Rizvan Gubiyev
PwC Azerbaijan

Abbas Guliyev
Baker & McKenzie - CIS, Limited

Arif Guliyev
PwC Azerbaijan

Gulnar Gurbanova
BHM Baku Law Centre LLC

Elchin Habibov
National Bank of Azerbaijan

Samir Hadjiyev
Michael Wilson & Partners Ltd.

Nigar Hajiyeva
Baker & McKenzie - CIS, Limited

Faig Huseynov
Unibank

Ruhiyya Isayeva
Salans

Delara Israfilova
BM International LLC

Vagif Karimli
Baker & McKenzie - CIS, Limited

Gunduz Karimov
Baker & McKenzie - CIS, Limited

Natik Mamedov
Baker & McKenzie

Kamal Mamedzade
Salans

Javanshir Mammadov
Grata Law Firm

Kamil Mammadov
Mammadov & Partners Law Firm

Faiq S. Manafov
Unibank

Daniel Matthews
Baker & McKenzie - CIS, Limited

Aysu Memmedova
Ministry of Taxes

Farhad Mirzayev
BM International LLC

Ruslan Mukhtarov
BM International LLC

Rauf Namazov
Ministry of Taxes

Movlan Pashayev
PwC Azerbaijan

Naida Sadigova
Salans

Leyla Safarova
Baker & McKenzie - CIS, Limited

Mustafa Salamov
BM International LLC

Vakhid Saparov
Grata Law Firm

Emma Silyayeva
Salans

Yekaterina V. Kim
Michael Wilson & Partners Ltd.

Matlab Valiyev
PwC Azerbaijan

Kamil Valiyev
State Oil Company of Azerbaijan Republic

Ilkin Veliyev
Ministry of Taxes

Murad Yahyayev
Unibank

Mahmud Yusifli
Baker & McKenzie - CIS, Limited

Ulvia Zeynalova-Bockin
Salans

Nazim Ziyadov
OMNI Law Firm

BAHAMAS, THE

Graham, Thompson & Co.

Supreme Court of Freeport

David F. Allen
Bahamas Law Chambers

Kevin Basden
Bahamas Electricity Corporation

Lisa Bostwick
Bostwick and Bostwick

Rodney W. Braynen
Design Häus

Jilian Chase-Johnson
Higgs & Johnson

Tara Cooper Burnside
Higgs & Johnson

Erica Culmer-Curry
PwC Bahamas

Makeba Darville
Lennox Paton

Surinder Deal
Higgs & Johnson

Craig G. Delancy
The Commonwealth of the Bahamas, Ministry of Works & Transport

John Delaney
Higgs & Johnson

Amos J. Ferguson Jr.
Ferguson Associates & Planners

Wendy Forsythe
Import Export Brokers Ltd.

Vann P. Gaitor
Higgs & Johnson

Audley Hanna, Jr
Higgs & Johnson

Portia Nicholson
Higgs & Johnson

Michael L. Paton
Lennox Paton

Castino D. Sands
Lennox Paton

Kevin Seymour
PwC Bahamas

Everette B. Sweeting
Bahamas Electricity Corporation

Debi Williams
Williams Law Chambers

BAHRAIN

Agility Logistics

Electricity & Water Authority

Ernst & Young

Noora Abdulla
Qays H. Zu'bi Attorneys & Legal Consultants

Najma AbdulRedha Hassan
Ministry of Municipalities & Agriculture Affairs. Municipal One Stop Shop

Amel Al Aseeri
Zeenat Al Mansoori & Associates

Faten Al Haddad
Talal Abu-Ghazaleh Legal (TAG-Legal)

Zeenat Al Mansoori
Zeenat Al Mansoori & Associates

Reem Al Rayes
Zeenat Al Mansoori & Associates

Raju Alagarsamy
Hassan Radhi & Associates

Ebtihal Al-Hashimi
Ministry of Municipalities & Agriculture Affairs. Municipal One Stop Shop

Haider Alnoaimi
Mohamed Salahuddin Consulting Engineering Bureau

Shaji Alukkal
Panalpina World Transport LLP

Michael Durgavich
ASAR – Al Ruwayeh & Partners

Simon Green
Norton Rose

Qays H. Zu'bi
Qays H. Zu'bi Attorneys & Legal Consultants

Hessa Hussain
The Benefit Company

Seema Isa Al-Thawadi
Ministry of Municipalities & Agriculture Affairs. Municipal One Stop Shop

Jawad Habib Jawad
BDO Jawad Habib

Ebrahim Karolia
PwC Bahrain

Ming Huey Lim
PwC Bahrain

Saifuddin Mahmood
Hassan Radhi & Associates

Mohammed Mirza Abdul Hussain
Ministry of Municipalities & Agriculture Affairs. Municipal One Stop Shop

Eman Omar
Qays H. Zu'bi Attorneys & Legal Consultants

Hassan Ali Radhi
Hassan Radhi & Associates

Najib Saade
ASAR – Al Ruwayeh & Partners

Mohamed Salahuddin
Mohamed Salahuddin Consulting Engineering Bureau

Thamer Salahuddin
Mohamed Salahuddin Consulting Engineering Bureau

Hamza Saleem
Qays H. Zu'bi Attorneys & Legal Consultants

Ali Asghar Sheikh
ASAR – Al Ruwayeh & Partners

Judith Tosh
Norton Rose

Hatim S. Zu'bi
Hatim S. Zu'bi & Partners

BANGLADESH

Multi Trade

Md. Abdul Maleque Mian Abdullah
Bank of Bangladesh

Zainul Abedin
A. Qasem & Co.

Ishrat Ahmed
Amir & Amir Law Associates, member of Lex Mundi

Sahahuddin Ahmed
Dr. Kamal Hossain & Associates

Afrin Akhter
A. Qasem & Co.

Sharmin Akter
Amir & Amir Law Associates, member of Lex Mundi

Tanjib-ul Alam
Dr. Kamal Hossain & Associates

Md. Shafiul Alam
The Hongkong and Shanghai Banking Corporation Ltd.

MD. Nurul Amin
Development Constructions Ltd.

Mehedy Amin
Development Constructions Ltd.

Saady Amin
Development Constructions Ltd.

Jennifer Ashraf
FM Associates

Noorul Azhar
Azhar & Associates

Sharif Bhuiyan
Dr. Kamal Hossain & Associates

Badrud Doulah
Doulah & Doulah Advocates

Nasirud Doulah
Doulah & Doulah Advocates

Shamsud Doulah
Doulah & Doulah Advocates

Moin Ghani
Dr. Kamal Hossain & Associates

K M A Halim
Upright Textile Supports

Aneek Haque
Haque & Associates

Kamal Hossain

Abdul Hye
Bank of Bangladesh

Arif Imtiaz
FM Associates

Amir-Ul Islam
Amir & Amir Law Associates, member of Lex Mundi

Seema Karim
Amir & Amir Law Associates, member of Lex Mundi

Sohel Kasem
A. Qasem & Co.

Asif Khan
A. Qasem & Co.

Amina Khatoon
Doulah & Doulah Advocates

Shahjahan Mia
Dhaka Electricity Supply Company Ltd. (DESCO)

Nahid Monjur
Amir & Amir Law Associates, member of Lex Mundi

Eva Quasem
Amir & Amir Law Associates, member of Lex Mundi

Ahmedur Rahim
Registrar, Joint Stock Companies & Firms

Al Amin Rahman
FM Associates

Habibur Rahman
The Law Counsel

Nazmul Hasan Serneabat
Protex International

Imran Siddiq
The Law Counsel

Shahriar Syeed
V-Teac Fashion Pvt Ltd.

Sabrina Zarin
Al Amin Sabrina & Associates

BELARUS

Minsk Cable (Electrical) Network

Nadeznyi Kontakt

Tatiana Aleksnina
CHSH Cerha Hempel Spiegelfeld Hlawati

Alexey Anischenko
Sorainen & Partners FLLC

Aleksandr Anisovitch
Promaudit

Aleksander V. Antushevich
National Bank of the Republic of Belarus

Kiryl Apanasevich
Vlasova Mikhel & Partners

Dmitry Arkhipenko
Revera Consulting Group

Vladimir G. Biruk
Capital Group

Denis Bogdanov
Revera Consulting Group

Dmitry Bokhan
Businessconsult Law Firm

Elena Bortnovskaya
Revera Consulting Group

Alexander Botian
Borovtsov & Salei Law Offices

Alexey Daryin
Revera Consulting Group

Sergey Dubovik
National Bank of the Republic of Belarus

Marina Dymovich
Borovtsov & Salei Law Offices

Andrej Ermolenko
Vlasova Mikhel & Partners

Kirill Golovko
Revera Consulting Group

Oleg Gvozd
PwC Belarus

Elena Hmeleva
Businessconsult Law Firm

Antonina Ivanova
Law firm DICSA

Elena Kagarlitskaya
Law Firm Sherstnev and Partners Ltd.

Marina Kalinovskaya
Jurznak Law Firm LLC

Uljana Karpekina
Revera Consulting Group

Michael Karpuk
Revera Consulting Group

Dmitry Khalimonchyk
Jurznak Law Firm LLC

Maria Khomenko
PwC Belarus

Alexander Khrapoutski
Stepanovski, Papakul and Partners Ltd.

Alexander Kirilenko
Agency of Ternaround Technologies

Nina Knyazeva
Businessconsult Law Firm

Irina Koikova
Law firm DICSA

Oksana Kotel
Revera Consulting Group

Dmitry Kovalchik
Stepanovski, Papakul and Partners Ltd.

Mikhail Kozlov
AsstrA Weissrussland Ltd.

Kristina Kriščiūnaitė
PwC Lithuania

Ronaldas Kubilius
PwC Lithuania

Olga Kuchinskaya
Vlasova Mikhel & Partners

Vladimir Kukuruzin
CHSH Cerha Hempel Spiegelfeld Hlawati

Elena Kulchitskaya
AsstrA Weissrussland Ltd.

Egidijus Kundelis
PwC Lithuania

Tatsiana Kuushynava
Revera Consulting Group

Sergei Makarchuk
CHSH Cerha Hempel Spiegelfeld Hlawati

Olga Mankevich
Jurznak Law Firm LLC

Mikalai Markounik
Vlasova Mikhel & Partners

Dmitry Matveyev
Law Group Argument

Konstantin Mikhel
Vlasova Mikhel & Partners

Aleksandr Mironichenko
Ministry of Economy of Republic of Belarus

Dmitry Montik
Individual Entrepreneur

Helen Mourashko
Revera Consulting Group

Valiantsina Neizvestnaya
Audit and Consulting Ltd., Belarus

Sergei Oditsov
PwC Belarus

Yulia Ovseichyk
Revera Consulting Group

Sergey Pinchuk
Lawyer

Antonina Raduk
Jurznak Law Firm LLC

Maksim Salahub
Vlasova Mikhel & Partners

Vassili I. Salei
Borovtsov & Salei Law Offices

Yury Samkov
Borovtsov & Salei Law Offices

Katerina Sereda
Law Firm Sherstnev and Partners Ltd.

Denis Sherstnev
Law Firm Sherstnev and Partners Ltd.

Kristina Shibeko
Revera Consulting Group

Dmitry Skorodulin
Belarus State University

Anna Skorodulina
Jurznak Law Firm LLC

Vyacheslav Slabodnik
Univest-M

Sergey Strelchik
Valex Consult

Andrey Sviridov
Slonim Trade Center

Natalia Talai
Vlasova Mikhel & Partners

Pavel Tsarev
Revera Consulting Group

Alesia Tsekhanava
Law firm DICSA

Natalia Ulasevich
Glimstedt

Eugenia Urodnich
Glimstedt

Sviatlana Valuyeva
Stepanovski, Papakul and Partners Ltd.

Alexander Vasilevsky
Valex Consult

Igor Verkhovodko
Businessconsult Law Firm

Maria Yurieva
Sorainen & Partners FLLC

Pavel S. Yurkevich
The Supreme Economic Court of the Republic of Belarus

Ekaterina Zabello
Vlasova Mikhel & Partners

Darya Zhuk
Glimstedt

Maxim Znak
Jurznak Law Firm LLC

Nadezhda Znak
Jurznak Law Firm LLC

BELGIUM

Cour de Cassation

HVG Advocaten / Avocats, with the support of Ernst & Young

Sibelga

Hubert André-Dumont
McGuire Woods LLP

Géraldine Blairvacq
SPF Finances - AGDP

Erik Bomans
Deminor International SCRL

Hakim Boularbah
Liedekerke Wolters Waelbroeck Kirkpatrick, member of Lex Mundi

Charlotte Boumal
Altius

Yves Brosens
DLA Piper UK LLP

Tim Carnewal
Notaires Associés CVBA/SCRL

Adriaan Dauwe
Altius

Arnaud Dawans
Lucid - Lab for User Cognition and Innovative Design

Kris De Schutter
Loyens & Loeff

Didier De Vliegher
NautaDutilh

Olivier Debray
Claeys & Engels, member of Ius Laboris

Jean-Michel Detry
DLA Piper UK LLP

Frank Dierckx
PwC Belgium

Camille Dümm
National Bank of Belgium

David DuPont
Ashurst

Jürgen Egger
Laga

Aline Etienne
NautaDutilh

Pierrette Fraisse
SPF Finances - AGDP

Alain François
Eubelius Attorneys

Christel Godfroid
HVG Advocaten/Avocats, with the support of Ernst & Young

Conny Grenson
Eubelius Attorneys

Kurt Grillet
Altius

Sandrine Hirsch
Simont Braun

Thibaut Hollanders de Ouderaen
DLA Piper UK LLP

An Jacobs
Liedekerke Wolters Waelbroeck Kirkpatrick, member of Lex Mundi

Erika Leenknecht
Eubelius Attorneys

Stephan Legein
Federal Public Service Finance

Luc Legon
PwC Belgium

Axel Maeterlinck
Simont Braun

Sabine Martin
CREG

Dominique Mougenot
Commercial Court Mons

Sabrina Otten
PwC Belgium

Stéphane Robyns
DLA Piper UK LLP

Peter Rooryck
Monard-D'Hulst

Julien Sad
McGuire Woods LLP

Frédéric Souchon
PwC Belgium

Nicolas Stoffels
PwC Belgium

William Timmermans
Altius

Jan Van Celst
DLA Piper UK LLP

Peter Van Melkebeke
Notaires Berquin

Bart Van Rossum
B.T.V.

Sibylle Vandenberghe
PwC Belgium

Grégory Vandenbussche
Aren Architects and Engineers sprl

Marie-Noëlle Vanderhoven
PwC Belgium

Tom Vantroyen
Altius

Isabel Vergooghe
Ashurst

Katrien Vorlat
Stibbe

Bram Vuylsteke
Notary Bram VUYLSTEKE

Herman De Wilde
HVG Advocaten/Avocats, with the support of Ernst & Young

Christian Willems
Loyens & Loeff

Dirk Wouters
Wouters, Van Merode & Co. Bedrijfsrevisoren B.V.B.A, member of Russell Bedford International

BELIZE

Navid Ahmadiyeh
Belize Electricity Ltd.

Emil Arguelles
Arguelles & Company LLC

John Avery
Public Utilities Commission

José A. Bautista
PKF International

Emory K. Bennett
Young's Engineering Consultancy Ltd.

Claude Burrell
Castillo Sanchez & Burrell, LLP.

Christopher Coye
Courtenay Coye LLP

Sherman Ferguson
Belize Electricity Ltd.

Gian C. Gandhi
International Financial Services Commission

Glenn D Godfrey S.C.
Glenn D. Godfrey & Co. LLP

Rodolfo Gutierrez
Belize Electricity Ltd.

Mirna Lara
Eurocaribe Shipping Services, Ltd.

Russell Longsworth
Caribbean Shipping Agencies Ltd.

Frod Lumor
Fred Lumor & Co.

Reynaldo F. Magana
RFMagana & Associates

Andrew Marshalleck
Barrow & Co., Attorneys-at-Law

Tania Moody
Barrow & Williams

Jose Moreno
Belize Electricity Ltd.

Patricia Rodriguez
Belize Companies and Corporate Affairs Registry

Oscar Sabido S.C.
Sabido & Company

Dawn Sampson
Belize Electricity Ltd.

Giacomo Sanchez
Castillo Sanchez & Burrell, LLP.

Janelle Tillett
Eurocaribe Shipping Services, Ltd.

Robert Tillett
Public Utilities Commission

Saidi Vaccaro
Arguelles & Company LLC

C. Phillip Waight
Waight & Associates

Ryan Wrobel
Wrobel & Co., Attorneys-at-Law

Carlton Young
Young's Engineering Consultancy Ltd.

BENIN

Safia Abdoulaye
Cabinet d'Avocats

Diaby Aboubakar
BCEAO

Ganiou Adechy
Etude de Me Ganiou Adechy

Isbatou Adjaho Maliki
Cabinet de Me Isbatou Adjaho Maliki

A. Abdou Kabir Adoumbou
Cabinet Maître Rafikou Alabi

Agathe Affougnon Ago
Cabinet Agathe Affougnon Ago

Saïdou Agbantou
Cabinet d'Avocats

Rodolphe Kadoukpe Akoto
Coman S.A.

Sybel Akuesson
Cabinet Fiduciaire d'Afrique

Rafikou Agnila Alabi
Cabinet Maître Rafikou Alabi

Jacques Moïse Atchade
Cabinet de Me Atchade

Godefroy Chekete
Societe Beninoise D'Energie Electrique (SBEE)

Alice Codjia-Sohouenou
Cabinet d'Avocats Me Alice Codjia Sohouénou

Michel Djossouvi
Cabinet de Maître Michel Djossouvi

Henri Fadonougbo
Tribunal de Première Instance de Cotonou

Jean Claude Gnamien
PwC Côte d'Ivoire

Marcel Sègbégnon Hounnou
Cabinet d'Avocats

Camille Kpogbemabou
Societe Beninoise D'Energie Electrique (SBEE)

Loukmanou Ladany
Cabinet de Me Loukmanou Ladany

Taoïdi Osseni
Societe Beninoise D'Energie Electrique (SBEE)

Olagnika Salam
Office Notarial Olagnika

Adegbindin Saliou
Cabinet des Experts Associés - CEA Sarl

Ousmane Samba Mamadou
BCEAO

Zakari Djibril Sambaou

Didier Sterlingot
SDV Logistics

Nelly Tagnon Gambor
Cabinet Fiduciaire d'Afrique

Dominique Taty
PwC Côte d'Ivoire

Jean-Bosco Todjinou
ECOPLAN sarl

José Tonato
IMPACT Consultants

Emmanuel Yehouessi
BCEAO

Wassi Yessoufou
Societe Beninoise D'Energie Electrique (SBEE)

BHUTAN

Loknath Chapagai
Ministry of Economic Affairs

Tashi Chenzom
Ministry of Labour and Human Resources

Dawa Dakpa
Royal Securities Exchange of Bhutan Ltd.

Tashi Delek
Office of Legal Affairs

Eden Dema
Royal Monetary Authority of Bhutan

Ugyen Dhendup
Bhutan Development Finance Corporation Ltd.

Bhim L. Dhungel
Zorig Consultancy

Tashi Dorji
District Court of Thimphu

Lhundub Dorji
East - West Construction

Kencho Dorji
Leko Packers

Sonam Tobgay Dorji
Nima Construction Company

Tashi Dorji
Tashi Logistics Services

Chheku Dukpa
Construction Association of Bhutan

N. B. Gurung
Global Logistics

Rebecca Gurung
Zorig Consultancy

Sonam Gyeltshen
Bhutan Power Corporation Ltd.

Sonam Letho
Bhutan Development Finance Corporation Ltd.

Shera Lhendup
Sayang Law Chambers

Sonam Lhundrup
Druk Holding and Investments

Jigme Thinlye Namgyal
G-C Project

Tashi Pem
Ministry of Finance

Sonam Pema
Thimphu City Corporation

Dorji Phuntsho
Royal Securities Exchange of Bhutan Ltd.

T. B. Rai
Zorig Consultancy

Pelzore Rumba
Bhutan National Bank

Yeshey Selden
Ministry of Economic Affairs

Lalit Singhal
Bhutan Electric Company

Sonam Tobgay
Bhutan National Bank

Dorji Tshering
Bhutan Power Corporation Ltd.

Gem Tshering
Bhutan Power Corporation Ltd.

Sonam Tshering
Ministry of Finance

Sonam P. Wangdi
Ministry of Economic Affairs

Reezang Wangdi
Thimphu City Corporation

Deki Wangmo
Bhutan National Bank

Karma Yeshey
Ministry of Economic Affairs

Tashi Yezer
Royal Securities Exchange of Bhutan Ltd.

Yishay Wangdi Yontan
Nima Construction Company

Tshering Zam
National Land Commission Secretariat

BOLIVIA

Fernando Aguirre
Bufete Aguirre Soc. Civ.

Ignacio Aguirre
Bufete Aguirre Soc. Civ.

Carolina Aguirre Urioste
Bufete Aguirre Soc. Civ.

David Alcózer
Criales, Urcullo & Antezana

Christian Amestegui
Asesores Legales CP

Daniela Aragones Cortez
Sanjinés & Asociados Soc. Civ. Abogados

Eduardo Aramayo
PwC Bolivia

Miguel Arduz
Electropaz S.A.

Johnny Arteaga

Carola Ayaroa Mantilla

Raúl A. Baldivia
Baldivia Unzaga & Asociados

Maria del Carmen Ballivián
C.R. & F. Rojas, member of Lex Mundi

Adrián Barrenechea
Criales, Urcullo & Antezana

Armando Berdecio DeMartini
Vanguard Muebles

Hugo Berthin
BDO Berthin Amengual & Asociados

Marco Blaker

Mariela Castro
Superintendencia De Bancos y Entidades Financieras

Mauricio Costa du Rels
Würth Kim Costa du Rels

Dorian de Rojas
Gava Bolivia

Jose Luis Diaz Romero
Servicios Generales en Electricidad y Construcción (SGEC)

Ewaldo Fischer
Würth Kim Costa du Rels

Roberto Gomez-Justiniano
Salazar, Salazar & Asociados, Soc. Civ.

Primitivo Gutiérrez
Guevara & Gutiérrez S.C.

Ana Carola Guzman Gonzales
Salazar, Salazar & Asociados, Soc. Civ.

Rachel Hardcastle
Würth Kim Costa du Rels

Marcelo Hurtado-Sandoval
Salazar, Salazar & Asociados, Soc. Civ.

Jorge Luis Inchauste
Guevara & Gutiérrez S.C.

Jaime M. Jiménez Alvarez
Colegio de Ingenieros Electricistas y Electrónicos La Paz

Rodrigo Jimenez-Cusicanqui
Salazar, Salazar & Asociados, Soc. Civ.

Paola Justiniano Arias
Sanjinés & Asociados Soc. Civ. Abogados

Mario Kempff
C.R. & F. Rojas, member of Lex Mundi

Maria Kim
Shin Würth Kim Costa du Rels

Julio César Landívar Castro
Guévara & Gutiérrez S.C.

Sandra Leiton
Superintendencia De Bancos y Entidades Financieras

Alex Linares Cabrera
Sanjinés & Asociados Soc. Civ. Abogados

César Lora Moretto
PwC Bolivia

Daniel Mariaca
Criales, Urcullo & Antezana

Gonzalo Mendieta Romero
Estudio de Abogados Mendieta Romero & Asociados

Ariel Morales Vasquez
C.R. & F. Rojas, member of Lex Mundi

Ana Carola Muñoz
Würth Kim Costa du Rels

Jaime Muñoz-Reyes G.
Corporative Law Bolivia Consultores Asociados

Daniela Murialdo Lopez
Estudio de Abogados Mendieta Romero & Asociados

Orlando Pérez
Electropaz S.A.

Oscar Antonio Plaza Ponte
Entidad De Servicios De Información Enserbic S.A.

Julio Quintanilla Quiroga
Quintanilla, Soria & Nishizawa Soc. Civ

Diego Rojas
C.R. & F. Rojas, member of Lex Mundi

Patricio Rojas
C.R. & F. Rojas, member of Lex Mundi

Mariela Rojas
Entidad De Servicios De Información Enserbic S.A.

Pilar Salasar
Bufete Aguirre Soc. Civ.

Esteban Salazar-Machicado
Salazar, Salazar & Asociados, Soc. Civ.

Sergio Salazar-Machicado
Salazar, Salazar & Asociados, Soc. Civ.

Fernando Salazar-Paredes
Salazar, Salazar & Asociados, Soc. Civ.

Sandra Salinas
C.R. & F. Rojas, member of Lex Mundi

Rodolfo Raúl Sanjinés Elizagoyen
Sanjinés & Asociados Soc. Civ. Abogados

Claudio Sejas
Beraters

Jorge Nelson Serrate
Würth Kim Costa du Rels

A. Mauricio Torrico Galindo
Quintanilla, Soria & Nishizawa Soc. Civ

Javier Urcullo
Criales, Urcullo & Antezana

Lenny Valdivia
Superintendencia De Bancos y Entidades Financieras

Lizet Vanessa Villarroel
Baldivia Unzaga & Asociados

Roberto Viscafé Ureña
PwC Bolivia

Karla Würth
Würth Kim Costa du Rels

Mauricio Zambrana Cuéllar
Infocred - Servicio de Informacion Crediticia BIC S.A.

BOSNIA AND HERZEGOVINA

DERK (State Electricity Regulatory Commission)

FERK (Regulatory Commission for Electricity in the Federation of Bosnia and Herzegovina)

KN Karanović & Nikolić

Aida Ajanović
IKRP Rokas & Partners

Dunja Arnaut
Law Office Spaho

Ankush Bahl
Interliner Agencies d.o.o.

Amar Bajramović
Law Office Miljković

Samir Bajrović
Law Office Femil Curt (part of DLA Piper Group)

Dario Biščević
DB Schenker

Petar Bosnić
USAID Tax and Fiscal Project in BiH (TAF)

Mubera Brković
PwC Bosnia and Herzegovina

Zlatko Čengić
Unioninvest d.d

Višnja Dizdarević
Marić & Co. Law Firm

Ozren Dolic
FedEx Express

Dula Dukić
Federal Ministry of Trade

Feđa Dupovac
Law Office Spaho

Dina Duraković Morankić
Law Office Durakovic

Almir Gagula
Advokatski ured Mujaric & Gagula

Jasmina Gabela
Unioninvest d.d

Igor Gavran
Foreign Trade Chamber of Bosnia and Herzegovina International Freight Forwarders Association

Alen Glinac
Širbegović Group

Dzemila Gavrankapetanovic
Gavrankapetanovic Koldzo

Emin Hadžić
Marić & Co. Law Firm

Edin Hatibović
Interliner Agencies d.o.o.

Senada Havić Hrenovica
LRC Credit Bureau

Munevera Hodzic
Municipality of Centar

Ismeta Huremović
Land Registry Office of the Sarajevo Municipal Court

Amra Isic
Marić & Co. Law Firm

Arela Jusufbasić-Goloman
Lawyers' office Bojana Tkalcic - Djulic, Olodar Prebanic, Adela Rizvic & Arela Jusufbasic - Goloman

Lejla Kaknjo
PKF International

Nedžada Kapidžić
Notary

Kerim Karabdić
Advokat Karabdic Kerim

Almedina Karšić
Law Office of Emir Kovačević

Muhidin Karšić
Law Office of Emir Kovačević

Damir Koldžo
Gavrankapetanovic Koldzo

Damir Konjičanin
Municipality of Centar

Emir Kovačević
Law Office of Emir Kovačević

Fariz Kulenović
Triland Developement

Krzysztof Lipka
PwC Serbia

Anja Margetić
Central Bank of Bosnia and Herzegovina

Branko Marić
Marić & Co. Law Firm

Zoran Mićević
Architect

Sead Miljković
Wolf Theiss d.o.o.

Džemaludin Mutapčić
Notary

Mehmed Omeragic
Covjek i prostor

Ermin Omeragic
FedEx Express

Indir Osmic
CMS Reich-Rohrwig Hainz d.o.o.

Mirsad Pitić
Municipality of Novo Sarajevo

Edin Praso
N.P. Projekt d.o.o. Mostar

Đorđe Racković
Central Bank of Bosnia and Herzegovina

Alma Ramezić
PwC Bosnia and Herzegovina

Faruk Sahinagic
FedEx Express

Goran Salihovic
Sarajevo Municipal Court

Nedžida Salihović-Whalen
CMS Reich-Rohrwig Hainz d.o.o.

Hasib Salkić
Jump Logistics d.o.o.

Arijana Selimic
JP Elektroprivreda BiH Podružnica "Elektrodistribucija" Sarajevo

Maja Šimunac
Wolf Theiss d.o.o.

Berna Šljokić
PKF International

Džana Smailagić-Hromić
Marić & Co. Law Firm

Emir Spaho
Law Office Spaho

Mehmed Spaho
Law Office Spaho

Selma Spaho
Law Office Spaho

Anisa Strujić
Marić & Co. Law Firm

Bojana Tkalčić-Djulić
Lawyers' office Bojana Tkalcic - Djulic, Olodar Prebanic, Adela Rizvic & Arela Jusufbasic - Goloman

Vildana Uščuplić
Wolf Theiss d.o.o.

Sabina Viteskic
Municipality of Ilidza

BOTSWANA
Collins Newman & Co.

Jeffrey Bookbinder
Bookbinder Business Law

John Carr-Hartley
Armstrongs Attorneys

Ofentse Chifedi
Hoya Removals & Freight

Tatenda Dumba
Armstrongs Attorneys

Edward W. Fasholé-Luke II
Luke & Associates

Akheel Jinabhai
Akheel Jinabhai & Associates

Pauline Mabelebele
Armstrongs Attorneys

Finola McMahon
Osei-Ofei Swabi & Co.

Tsemetse Mmolai
Botswana Stock Exchange

Neo Thelma Moathlodi

Moilwa
Zismo Engineering (Pty) Ltd.

Claude A. Mojafi
Ministry of Labour and Home Affairs

Mmatshipi Motsepe
Manica Africa Pty. Ltd.

Jack Allan Mutua
Tectura International Botswana

Rajesh Narasimhan
Grant Thornton LLP

Buhlebenkosi Ncube
Luke & Associates

Milikani Ndaba
Armstrongs Attorneys

Kwadwo Osei-Ofei
Osei-Ofei Swabi & Co.

Chabo Peo
Bookbinder Business Law

Butler Phirie
PwC Botswana

Claudio Rossi
Sharps Electrical (Pty) Ltd.

Daniel Swabi
Osei-Ofei Swabi & Co.

Moemedi J. Tafa
Armstrongs Attorneys

Onkemetse Thomas
Botswana Stock Exchange

Dilini Waidyanatha
PwC Botswana

Frederick Webb
Armstrongs Attorneys

Sipho Ziga
Armstrongs Attorneys

BRAZIL
Ulhôa Canto, Rezende e Guerra-Advogados

Antonio Aires
Demarest e Almeida Advogados

Carlos Alberto Alvares Vono
Adccont

Julio Cesar Alves
Noronha Advogados

Antonio Amendola
Felsberg, Pedretti, Mannrich e Aidar Advogados e Consultores Legais

Marco Antonio Sabino
KLA-Koury Lopes Advogados

Mariana Aranha
Machado Meyer Sendacz e Opice Advogados

Pedro Vitor Araujo da Costa
Vitor Costa Advogados

Fernanda Azevedo
Rayes, Fagundes & Oliveira Ramos Advogados

Bruno Balduccini
Pinheiro Neto Advogados

Priscyla Barbosa
Veirano Advogados

Valmir Souza Barbosa
Adccont

Julio Henrique Batista
Guerra e Batista Advogados

Celina Bernardes
18o Oficio de Notas

Guilherme Bertolini Fernandes dos Santos
Fleury Malheiros, Gasparini, De Cresci e Nogueira de Lima Advogados

Bernardo Bessa
Felsberg, Pedretti, Mannrich e Aidar Advogados e Consultores Legais

Camila Biral
Demarest e Almeida Advogados

Richard Blanchet
Loeser e Portela Advogados

Adriano Boni De Souza
Noronha Advogados

Adriano Borges
De Vivo, Whitaker, Castro e Gonçalves Advogados

Altimiro Boscoli
Demarest e Almeida Advogados

Sergio Bronstein
Veirano Advogados

Joao Henrique Brum
Dominges E Pinho Contadores

Clarissa Abrahão Bruzzi
Noronha Advogados

Júlio César Bueno
Pinheiro Neto Advogados

Gisela Velloso Cafe
C. Barreto Avogados Associados

Ronaldo Camargo
Prefeitura do Municipio de Sao Paulo

Paulo Campana
Felsberg, Pedretti, Mannrich e Aidar Advogados e Consultores Legais

Renato Canizares
Demarest e Almeida Advogados

Paulo Henrique Carvalho Pinto
Machado Meyer Sendacz e Opice Advogados

Debora Casseb
Felsberg, Pedretti, Mannrich e Aidar Advogados e Consultores Legais

Marina Castro Aranha
Souza, Cescon, Barrieu & Flesch Advogados

Veridiana Celestino
Veirano Advogados

Fernanda Cirne Montorfano
Gouvêa Vieira Advogados

Ricardo E. Vieira Coelho
Pinheiro Neto Advogados

Gilberto Deon Corrêa Jr.
Veirano Advogados

Tiago Cortez
KLA-Koury Lopes Advogados

Gladztone Oliveira da Silva
AGS Brazil

Jose Lusiano da Silva
Governo do Estado do Rio de Janeiro

Adriana Daiuto
Demarest e Almeida Advogados

Cleber Dal Rovere Peluzo
Cunha Oricchio Ricca Lopes Advogados

Bruno Henrique de Aguiar
Rayes, Fagundes & Oliveira Ramos Advogados

Joao Luis Ribeiro de Almeida
Demarest e Almeida Advogados

Flavio Coelho de Almeida
Pinheiro Neto Advogados

Jose Constantino de Bastos Jr.
Governo do Estado de Sao Paulo

Rafael De Conti
De Conti Law Office

Aldo de Cresci Neto
Fleury Malheiros, Gasparini, De Cresci e Nogueira de Lima Advogados

Ingrid E. T. Schwartz de Mendonca
Noronha Advogados

Beatriz Gross Bueno de Moraes Visnevski
De Vivo, Whitaker, Castro e Gonçalves Advogados

Marcelo Viveiros de Moura
Pinheiro Neto Advogados

Flavia Soeiro de Nascimento
Demarest e Almeida Advogados

Paulo Marcelo de Oliveira Bento
Souza, Cescon, Barrieu & Flesch Advogados

Andreza de Souza Ribeiro
Souza, Cescon, Barrieu & Flesch Advogados

Nadia Demoliner Lacerda
Mesquita Barros Advogados, member of Ius Laboris

Eduardo Depassier
Loeser e Portela Advogados

Ubajara Arcas Dias
Fleury Malheiros, Gasparini, De Cresci e Nogueira de Lima Advogados

Alexandre Augusto Dias Ramos Huffell Viola
Fleury Malheiros, Gasparini, De Cresci e Nogueira de Lima Advogados

Antonio Donizetti
DAS Consultoria

José Ricardo dos Santos Luz Júnior
Duarte Garcia, Caselli Guimarães e Terra Advogados

Brigida Melo e Cruz
Pinheiro Neto Advogados

Joao Paulo F.A. Fagundes
Rayes, Fagundes & Oliveira Ramos Advogados

Vanessa Felício
Veirano Advogados

Thomas Benes Felsberg
Felsberg, Pedretti, Mannrich e Aidar Advogados e Consultores Legais

Alexsander Fernandes de Andrade
Duarte Garcia, Caselli Guimarães e Terra Advogados

Glaucia Ferreira
Demarest e Almeida Advogados

Silvia Rajsfeld Fiszman
Machado Meyer Sendacz e Opice Advogados

Álvaro Luis Fleury Malheiros
Fleury Malheiros, Gasparini, De Cresci e Nogueira de Lima Advogados

Gabriella Florence Victorino Read
Souza, Cescon, Barrieu & Flesch Advogados

Clarissa Freitas
Machado Meyer Sendacz e Opice Advogados

Fernando Frugiuele Pascowitch
Souza, Cescon, Barrieu & Flesch Advogados

Rafael Gagliardi
Demarest e Almeida Advogados

Alessandra Ganz
Veirano Advogados

Thelma Eliza Gatuzzo
Loeser e Portela Advogados

Thiago Giantomassi Medeiros
Demarest e Almeida Advogados

Michelle Giraldi Lacerda
PwC Brazil

Claudio R. F. Golgo
Golgo Advogados

Rodrigo Gomes Maia
Noronha Advogados

Agildo Goncalves
A. Goncalves Assessoria & Contabilidade Ltda.

Jorge Eduardo Gouvêa Vieira
Gouvêa Vieira Advogados

Vanessa Grosso da Silveria Lardosa
Gouvêa Vieira Advogados

Eduardo Ferraz Guerra
Guerra e Batista Advogados

Luis Guidetti
TMF Group - Brazil

Enrique Hadad
Loeser e Portela Advogados

Daniel Henrique Calvoso Alvarenga
Noronha Advogados

Ricardo Higashitani
KLA-Koury Lopes Advogados

Luiz Felipe Horta Maia
Rayes, Fagundes & Oliveira Ramos Advogados

Carlos Alberto Iacia
PwC Brazil

Marcelo Inglez de Souza
Demarest e Almeida Advogados

Maria Cristina Junqueira
KLA-Koury Lopes Advogados

Eduardo Takemi Kataoka
Castro, Barros, Sobral, Gomes Advogados

Fernando Koury Lopes
KLA-Koury Lopes Advogados

Miguel Kreling
Pinheiro Neto Advogados

Leonardo Kriuger
AGS Brazil

Everaldo Lacerda
Cartorio Maritimo

José Paulo Lago Alves Pequeno
Noronha Advogados

Flavio Lantelme
Prefeitura da Cidade de Sao Paulo

Jose Augusto Leal
Castro, Barros, Sobral, Gomes Advogados

Fernando Loeser
Loeser e Portela Advogados

Ricardo Loureiro
Serasa S.A.

Marina Maccabelli
Demarest e Almeida Advogados

Pedro Maciel
Veirano Advogados

Joao Gabriel A. L. Clark Magon
Demarest e Almeida Advogados

André Marques
Pinheiro Neto Advogados

Ana Paula Martins Quintão
Prefeitura do Municipio do Rio De Janerio

Renata Martins de Oliveira
Machado Meyer Sendacz e Opice Advogados

Laura Massetto Meyer
Pinheiro Guimarães Advogados

Felipe Oliveira Mavignier
Fleury Malheiros, Gasparini, De Cresci e Nogueira de Lima Advogados

Thiago Medaglia
Felsberg, Pedretti, Mannrich e Aidar Advogados e Consultores Legais

Marianne Mendes Webber
Souza, Cescon, Barrieu & Flesch Advogados

Cássio Mesquita Barros
Mesquita Barros Advogados, member of Ius Laboris

Sarah Mila Barbassa
Souza, Cescon, Barrieu & Flesch Advogados

Gustavo Morel
Veirano Advogados

Cassio S. Namur
Souza, Cescon, Barrieu & Flesch Advogados

Diogo Nebias
Souza, Cescon, Barrieu & Flesch Advogados

Jorge Nemr
Leite, Tosto e Barros

Fernando Nieto
Souza, Cescon, Barrieu & Flesch Advogados

Walter Nimir
De Vivo, Whitaker, Castro e Gonçalves Advogados

Alexandre Nogueira
TMF Group - Brazil

João Paulo Nogueira Barros
Gouvêa Vieira Advogados

Danilo Nogueira de Almeida
Fleury Malheiros, Gasparini, De Cresci e Nogueira de Lima Advogados

Flavio Pinto Nunes
ThyssenKrupp CSA Siderurgica do Atlantico

Ricardo Oliva
Souza, Cescon, Barrieu & Flesch Advogados

Evany Oliveira
PwC Brazil

Daniel Oliveira
Souza, Cescon, Barrieu & Flesch Advogados

João Otávio Pinheiro Olivério
Campos Mello Advogados, in cooperation with DLA Piper

Andrea Oricchio Kirsh
Cunha Oricchio Ricca Lopes Advogados

Simone Orlandini
Light Servicos de Eletricidade S.A.

Priscilla Palazzo
De Vivo, Whitaker, Castro e Gonçalves Advogados

Gyedre Palma Carneiro de Oliveira
Souza, Cescon, Barrieu & Flesch Advogados

Rogerio Rabelo Peixoto
Banco Central do Brasil

Luiz Eduardo Pereira Paz
Light Servicos de Eletricidade S.A.

Monica Pinheiro dos Anjos
Planeta Brasil Consultancy

Laércio Pinto
Serasa S.A.

Andréa Pitthan Françolin
De Vivo, Whitaker, Castro e Gonçalves Advogados

Raphael Polito
RAYES, FAGUNDES & OLIVEIRA RAMOS ADVOGADOS

Durval Portela
LOESER E PORTELA ADVOGADOS

José Ribeiro do Prado Junior
MACHADO MEYER SENDACZ E OPICE ADVOGADOS

Rodrigo Eduardo Pricoli
RAYES, FAGUNDES & OLIVEIRA RAMOS ADVOGADOS

Daniela Prieto
VEIRANO ADVOGADOS

Ana Paula Martins Quintao
RIO PREFEITURA

Dario Rabay
SOUZA, CESCON, BARRIEU & FLESCH ADVOGADOS

Fernanda Rabelo
PINHEIRO GUIMARÃES ADVOGADOS

Ronaldo Rayes
RAYES, FAGUNDES & OLIVEIRA RAMOS ADVOGADOS

Domingos Fernando Refinetti
MACHADO MEYER SENDACZ E OPICE ADVOGADOS

Eliane Ribeiro Gago
DUARTE GARCIA, CASELLI GUIMARÃES E TERRA ADVOGADOS

Laura Ribeiro Vissotto
1º CARTÓRIO DE NOTAS DE SÃO JOSÉ DOS CAMPOS

Viviane Rodrigues
SOUZA, CESCON, BARRIEU & FLESCH ADVOGADOS

Ana Carolina Rua Rodriguez Rochedo
NORONHA ADVOGADOS

Cezar Roedel
HALLEY DO BRASIL

Raphael Roque
CASTRO, BARROS, SOBRAL, GOMES ADVOGADOS

Tulio Fernandes Rosa
AGS BRAZIL

Andrea Giamondo Massei Rossi
MACHADO MEYER SENDACZ E OPICE ADVOGADOS

Lia Roston
RAYES, FAGUNDES & OLIVEIRA RAMOS ADVOGADOS

Marcos Sader
ULHÔA CANTO, REZENDE E GUERRA-ADVOGADOS

José Samurai Saiani
MACHADO MEYER SENDACZ E OPICE ADVOGADOS

Bruno Sanchez Belo
NORONHA ADVOGADOS

Sérgio Savi
CASTRO, BARROS, SOBRAL, GOMES ADVOGADOS

Joana Scarpa
VEIRANO ADVOGADOS

Gabriel Seijo Leal de Figueiredo
SOUZA, CESCON, BARRIEU & FLESCH ADVOGADOS

Robson Silva Campos
AGRURAL

Raissa Simões Tavares de Melo
DEMAREST E ALMEIDA ADVOGADOS

Sydney Simonaggio
AES ELETROPAULO

Keila Fonseca Soares
NORONHA ADVOGADOS

Beatriz Souza
SOUZA, CESCON, BARRIEU & FLESCH ADVOGADOS

Renato Souza Coelho
SOUZA, CESCON, BARRIEU & FLESCH ADVOGADOS

Walter Stuber
WALTER STUBER CONSULTORIA JURÍDICA

Milena Tesser
RAYES, FAGUNDES & OLIVEIRA RAMOS ADVOGADOS

Heloisa Tourinho
C. BARRETO AVOGADOS ASSOCIADOS

Ivandro Trevelim
SOUZA, CESCON, BARRIEU & FLESCH ADVOGADOS

Suslei Tufaniuk
AES ELETROPAULO

Luiz Fernando Valente De Paiva
PINHEIRO NETO ADVOGADOS

Vitor Hugo Erlich Varella
DEMAREST E ALMEIDA ADVOGADOS

Ronaldo C. Veirano
VEIRANO ADVOGADOS

Pedro Vieira
CASTRO, BARROS, SOBRAL, GOMES ADVOGADOS

José Carlos Wahle
VEIRANO ADVOGADOS

Eduardo Guimarães Wanderley
VEIRANO ADVOGADOS

Thiago Wscieklica
SOUZA, CESCON, BARRIEU & FLESCH ADVOGADOS

Celso Xavier
DEMAREST E ALMEIDA ADVOGADOS

Karin Yamauti Hatanaka
SOUZA, CESCON, BARRIEU & FLESCH ADVOGADOS

Alessandra Zequi Salybe de Moura
SOUZA, CESCON, BARRIEU & FLESCH ADVOGADOS

BRUNEI DARUSSALAM

ERNST & YOUNG

HSE ENGINEERING SDN BHD

Danny Chua
BRUNEI TRANSPORTING COMPANY

Nur al-Ain Haji Abdullah
ATTORNEY GENERAL'S CHAMBERS

Amiriah Haji Ali
ATTORNEY GENERAL'S CHAMBERS

Haji Abidin Haji Saidin
ABCi

Ridzlan Ibrahim
RIDZLAN & CO. ADVOCATES AND SOLICITORS

Cynthia Kong
WIDDOWS KONG & ASSOCIATES

Nancy Lai
LEE CORPORATEHOUSE ASSOCIATES

Kin Chee Lee
LEE CORPORATEHOUSE ASSOCIATES

Lennon Lee
PwC SINGAPORE

Yew Choh Lee
Y.C. LEE & LEE ADVOCATES & SOLICITORS

Kelvin Lim
K. LIM & CO.

Siew Yen Lim
THE JUDICIAL DEPARTMENT

Chris Loh
PwC SINGAPORE

Naimah Md Ali
ATTORNEY GENERAL'S CHAMBERS

Yong Muhd. Robin
ABCi

Colin Ong
DR. COLIN ONG LEGAL SERVICES

Rostaina Pg Hj Duraman
THE JUDICIAL DEPARTMENT

See Tiat Quek
PwC SINGAPORE

Alan Ross
PwC SINGAPORE

Martin Sinnung Jr.
BRUNEI TRANSPORTING COMPANY

Shazali Sulaiman
KPMG

Cecilia Wong
TRICOR

Soon Teck Yu
PETAR PERUNDING SDN BHD

Joanita Zain
THE BRUNEI ECONOMIC DEVELOPMENT BOARD

BULGARIA

EXPERIAN BULGARIA EAD

Svetlin Adrianov
PENKOV, MARKOV & PARTNERS

Anton Andreev
SCHOENHERR

Stefan Angelov
V CONSULTING BULGARIA

Rusalena Angelova
DJINGOV, GOUGINSKI, KYUTCHUKOV & VELICHKOV

Iva Baeva
LEGALEX

Plamen Borissov
BORISSOV & PARTNERS

Christopher Christov
PENEV LLP

Maria Danailova
WOLF THEISS

George Dimitrov
DIMITROV, PETROV & CO.

Yana Dimitrova
PENEV LLP

Kristina Dimitrova
TSVETKOVA, BEBOV AND PARTNERS

Elina Dimova
PENKOV, MARKOV & PARTNERS

Alexandra Doytchinova
SCHOENHERR

Silvia Dulevska
BULGARIAN NATIONAL BANK

Alexander Georgiev
DOBREV, KINKIN & LYUTSKANOV

Plamen Georgiev
ECONOMOU INTERNATIONAL SHIPPING AGENCY LIMITED

Atanas Georgiev
UCONOMICS

Velislava Georgieva
ECONOMOU INTERNATIONAL SHIPPING AGENCY LIMITED

Marieta Getcheva
PwC BULGARIA

Matea Gospodinova
DJINGOV, GOUGINSKI, KYUTCHUKOV & VELICHKOV

Ralitsa Gougleva
DJINGOV, GOUGINSKI, KYUTCHUKOV & VELICHKOV

Katerina Gramatikova
DOBREV, KINKIN & LYUTSKANOV

Stefan Gugushev
GUGUSHEV & PARTNERS

Iassen Hristev
DOBREV, KINKIN & LYUTSKANOV

Tatyana Hristova
LEGALEX

Katerina Ilcheva
ECONOMOU INTERNATIONAL SHIPPING AGENCY LIMITED

Ginka Iskrova
PwC BULGARIA

Vesela Kabatliyska
DINOVA RUSEV & PARTNERS

Angel Kalaidjiev
KALAIDJIEV, GEORGIEV & MINCHEV

Yavor Kambourov
KAMBOUROV & PARTNERS

Irena Karpe
KAMBOUROV & PARTNERS

Hristina Kirilova
KAMBOUROV & PARTNERS

Nikolay Kolev
BORISLAV BOYANOV & CO.

Donko Kolev

Ilya Komarevski
TSVETKOVA, BEBOV AND PARTNERS

Boika Komsulova
PwC BULGARIA

Tsvetan Krumov
SCHOENHERR

Stephan Kyutchukov
DJINGOV, GOUGINSKI, KYUTCHUKOV & VELICHKOV

Jordan Manahilov
BULGARIAN NATIONAL BANK

Ivan Markov
PENKOV, MARKOV & PARTNERS

Slavi Mikinski
LEGALEX

Blagomir Minov
TSVETKOVA, BEBOV AND PARTNERS

Tzvetoslav Mitev
GEORGIEV, TODOROV & CO.

Vladimir Natchev
ARSOV NATCHEV GANEVA

Yordan Naydenov
BORISLAV BOYANOV & CO.

Neli Nedkova
WOLF THEISS

Violeta Nikolova
REGISTRY AGENCY OF BULGARIA

Yulia Peeva
REX CONSULTING LTD., MEMBER OF RUSSELL BEDFORD INTERNATIONAL

Sergey Penev
PENEV LLP

Veselka Petrova
TSVETKOVA, BEBOV AND PARTNERS

Martin Plamenov Stanchev
DOBREV, KINKIN & LYUTSKANOV

Gergana Popova
GEORGIEV, TODOROV & CO.

Svilena Ralcheva
PENEV LLP

Alexander Rangelov
PwC BULGARIA

Milen Rusev
DINOVA RUSEV & PARTNERS

Anna Saeva
BORISLAV BOYANOV & CO.

Roman Stoyanov
PENKOV, MARKOV & PARTNERS

Margarita Stoyanova
KAMBOUROV & PARTNERS

Kalina Tchakarova
DJINGOV, GOUGINSKI, KYUTCHUKOV & VELICHKOV

Vessela Tcherneva Yankova
V CONSULTING BULGARIA

Yordan Terziev
ARSOV NATCHEV GANEVA

Svilen Todorov
TODOROV & DOYKOVA LAW FIRM

Kaloyan Todorov
WOLF THEISS

Lily Trifonova
REX CONSULTING LTD., MEMBER OF RUSSELL BEDFORD INTERNATIONAL

Irina Tsvetkova
TSVETKOVA, BEBOV AND PARTNERS

Stefan Tzakov
KAMBOUROV & PARTNERS

Georgi Tzvetkov
DJINGOV, GOUGINSKI, KYUTCHUKOV & VELICHKOV

Maria Urmanova
TSVETKOVA, BEBOV AND PARTNERS

Kamena Valcheva
TSVETKOVA, BEBOV AND PARTNERS

Atanas Valov
PENKOV, MARKOV & PARTNERS

Miroslav Varnaliev
UNIMASTERS LOGISTICS PLC.

Venzi Vassilev
REX CONSULTING LTD., MEMBER OF RUSSELL BEDFORD INTERNATIONAL

BURKINA FASO

BOLLORÉ AFRICA LOGISTICS

JFA AFRIQUE

Diaby Aboubakar
BCEAO

Antoine Apiou
KOMBOÏGO & ASSOCIÉS

Joséphine Bassolet
SONABEL

Fortune Bicaba
ETUDE DE MAÎTRE FORTUNE BICABA

Flora Josiane Bila
SCPA YAGUIBOU & YANOGO

Aimé Bonkoungou
SONABEL

B. Thierry Compaoré
INGENIERIE-DESIGN-ARCHITECTURE

Bobson Coulibaly
CABINET D'AVOCATS BARTHÉLEMY KERE

Denis Dawende
OFFICE NOTARIAL ME JEAN CELESTIN ZOURE

Seydou Diarra
BANQUE COMMERCIALE DU BURKINA

Ambroise Farama

Jean Claude Gnamien
PwC CÔTE D'IVOIRE

Sibi Desire Gouba
OFFICE NOTARIAL ME JEAN CELESTIN ZOURE

Jean Bedel Gouba
SONABEL

Fulgence Habiyaremye
CABINET D'AVOCATS BARTHÉLEMY KERE

Issaka Kargougou
MAISON DE L'ENTREPRISE DU BURKINA FASO

Barthélémy Kere
CABINET D'AVOCATS BARTHÉLEMY KERE

Gilbert Kibtonre
CEFAC

Clarisse Kienou
MAISON DE L'ENTREPRISE DU BURKINA FASO

Eddie Komboïgo
KOMBOÏGO & ASSOCIÉS

Moumouny Kopiho
CABINET D'AVOCATS MOUMOUNY KOPIHO

Raphaël Kouraogo
SONABEL

Frédéric O. Lompo
ETUDE MAÎTRE LOMPO

Adeline Messou
PwC Côte d'Ivoire

Ange Laure M'Pow
SCPA Yaguibou & Yanogo

S. Al Nadia
Cabinet d'Avocats Moumouny Kopiho

Marie Ouedraogo
Barreau du Burkina Faso

Pascal Ouedraogo
Cabinet d'Avocats Barthélemy Kere

Oumarou Ouedraogo
Cabinet Ouedraogo

Thierry Ismael Ouedraogo
Direction Générale du Trésor et de la Comptabilité Publique

Denise Ouedraogo
Etude de Maître Ouedraogo

Ousmane Honore Ouedraogo
Maison de l'entreprise du Burkina Faso

Moussa Ouedraogo
SCPA Yaguibou & Yanogo

François de Salle Ouedraogo
SONABEL

Martin Ouedraogo
Union Internationale de Notariat Latin

Roger Omer Ouédraogo
Association Professionnelle des Transitaires & Commissionnaires en Douane Agréés

Alain Serge Paré
Cabinet Yaguibou & Yanogo

Sawadogo W. Pulchérie
Tribunal d'Instance de Ouagadougou

Ousmane Samba Mamadou
BCEAO

Bénéwendé S. Sankara
Cabinet Maître Sankara

Hermann Lambert Sanon
Groupe Hage

Dieudonné Sawadogo
Cabinet d'Avocats Moumouny Kopiho

Moussa Ousmane Sawadogo
Direction Générale des Impôts

Noël Soumnere
SONABEL

Olga Tamini
SCPA Yaguibou & Yanogo

Hyppolite Tapsoba
Tribunal d'Instance de Ouagadougou

Dominique Taty
PwC Côte d'Ivoire

Kassoum Traore
Direction Générale des Impôts

Moussa Traore
Direction Générale des Impôts

Moussa Traore
Maison de l'entreprise du Burkina Faso

Emmanuel Yehouessi
BCEAO

K. Cyrille Zangre
Cabinet d'Avocats Moumouny Kopiho

Bassinaly Zerbo
SONABEL

Ousmane Prosper Zoungrana
Tribunal de Grande Instance de Ouagadougou

Jean Celéstin Zoure
Office Notarial Me Jean Celestin Zoure

Théophane Noël Zoure
Office Notarial Me Jean Celestin Zoure

BURUNDI

REGIDESO-Burundi

Joseph Bahizi
Banque de la République du Burundi

Sylvestre Banzubaze
Avocat au barreau du Burundi

Cyprien Bigirimana
Tribunal de Grande Instance de Gitega

Mélance Bukera
Intercontact Services, S.A.

Ange Gakundwakazi
Deloitte LLP

Gerard Handika
Deloitte LLP

René Claude Madebari
Mkono & Co. Advocates

Kelly Mategeko
Le Genie Civil, SPRL

Ildephonse Nahimana
Banque de la République du Burundi

Patrick Ndayishimiye

Bonaventure Nicimpaye
Intercontact Services, S.A.

Lambert Nigarura
Mkono & Co. Advocates

Claver Nigarura
Rubeya & Co. - Advocates

Charles Nihangaza

Gustave Niyonzima
Mkono & Co. Advocates

Prosper Niyoyankana

Jocelyne Ntibangana
Cabinet de Me Ntibangana

Antoine Ntisigana
SODETRA Ltd.

Happy Ntwari
Mkono & Co. Advocates

François Nyamoya
Avocat à la Cour

Gilbert L.P. Nyatanyi
Mkono & Co. Advocates

Déogratias Nzemba
Attorney-at-Law

Prosper Ringuyeneza
Le Genie Civil, SPRL

Willy Rubeya
Rubeya & Co. - Advocates

Benjamin Rufagari
Deloitte LLP

Thierry Rujerwaka
Laboratoire National du Bâtiment et des Travaux Publics (LNBTP) Burundi

Fabien Segatwa
Etude Me Segatwa

Gabriel Sinarinzi
Cabinet Me Gabriel Sinarinzi

Egide Uwimana
Tribunal du Travail de Bujumbura

CAMBODIA

Acleda Bank Plc.

Ernst & Young

Kearath Chan
Linehaul Express (Cambodia) Co., Ltd.

Phanin Cheam
Municipality of Phnom Penh Bureau of Urban Affairs

Rithy Chey
BNG Legal

Susanna Coghlan
AAA Cambodia Ltd.

Antoine Fontaine
Bun & Associates

Leanghor Hak
Linehaul Express (Cambodia) Co., Ltd.

Hour Naryth Hem
BNG Legal

Sokpheaneath Huon
Cambodian Federation of Employers and Business Associations

Phalla Im
Sciaroni & Associates

Sophealeak Ing
Bun & Associates

Visal Iv
Electricite du Cambodge

Phoung Wattey Kemnay
BNG Legal

Chhorpornpisey Keo
Acleda Bank Plc.

Sonya Kim
Arbitration Council Foundation

Vicheka Lay

Michael Liam Garvey
BNG Legal

Long Mom
RAF International Forwarding (Cambodia) Inc.

Vichhra Mouyly
Arbitration Council Foundation

Sokvirak Peang
PwC Cambodia

Thea Pheng
BNG Legal

Sotheaphal Pho
Sciaroni & Associates

Muny Samreth
PwC Cambodia

Chanthy Sin
Linehaul Express (Cambodia) Co., Ltd.

Chea Sinhel
Electricite du Cambodge

Lor Sok
Arbitration Council Foundation

Chamnan Som
Cambodian Federation of Employers and Business Associations

Ny Som
SDV Logistics

Vannaroth Sovann
BNG Legal

Ousaphea Suos
Acleda Bank Plc.

Bridie Sweetman
BNG Legal

Michael Tan
RAF International Forwarding (Cambodia) Inc.

Chesda Teng
Arbitration Council Foundation

Rathvisal Thara
BNG Legal

Heng Thy
PwC Cambodia

Janvibol Tip
Tip & Partners

Sokhan Uch
Acleda Bank Plc.

Bun Youdy
Bun & Associates

Potim Yun
DFDL Mekong Law Group

CAMEROON

La Banque des Etats de l'Afrique Centrale

Roland Abeng
The Abeng Law Firm

Pierre Aloma
Guichet Unique des Operations du Commerce Exterieur-Gie

Daniel Ambassa Kedy
Lafarge

Gilbert Awah Bongam
Achu and Fon-Ndikum Law Firm

Thomas Didier Remy Batoumbouck
Cadire

Mohaman Bello
Lafarge

Pierre Bertin Simbafo
BICEC

Isidore Biyiha
Guichet Unique des Operations du Commerce Exterieur-Gié

Hiol Bonheur
FIDUCIAIRE RATIO

Miafo Bonny Bonn
Bonny Bonn Enterprises

David Boyo
Boyo & Patimark LLP

Bernard Burinyuy Ngaibe
The Abeng Law Firm

Anne Marie Diboundje Njocke
Cabinet Ekobo

Paul Marie Djamen
Mobile Telephone Networks Cameroon (MTN)

Aurelien Djengue Kotte
Cabinet Ekobo

Joseph Djeuga
Lafarge

Etienne Donfack
GIEA

Laurent Dongmo
Jing & Partners

Régine Dooh Collins
Etude Me Régine Dooh Collins

William Douandji
Lafarge

Lisette Catherine Elobo
Ministry of Small and Medium-Sized Enterprises, Social Economy and Handicrafts

Marie Marceline Enganalim
Etude Me Enganalim Marceline

Pascal Enpe

Mboule Reagan Esone
Cabinet d'Avocats Henri Job

Lucas Florent Essomba
Cabinet Essomba & Associés

Joël Etoke
Etude Me Etoke

Marie-Claude Etoke
Etude Me Etoke

Hyacinthe Clément Fansi Ngamou
Ngassamnjike & Associés

Oréol Marcel Fetue
Nimba Conseil SARL

Atsishi Fon Ndikum
Achu and Fon-Ndikum Law Firm

Georges Fopa
GIEA

Bertrand Gieangnitchoke
GIEA

Kingue Godor Dummas
Legal Power Law Firm

Samuel Iyug Iyug
Groupement des Entreprises de Fret et Messagerie du Cameroun (GEFMCAM)

Henri Pierre Job
Cabinet d'Avocats Henri Job

Serge Jokung
Cabinet Maître Marie Andrée Ngwe

Eugene Romeo Kengne Sikadi
Nimba Conseil SARL

Julienne Kengue Piam
Nimba Conseil SARL

Jean Aime Kounga
Cabinet d'Avocats Abeng Roland

Kéedji à Moudji Mathurin
CAGES

Alain Serges Mbebi
Cadire

Jean Michel Mbock Biumla
M&N Law Firm

Patrick Menyeng Manga
The Abeng Law Firm

Jules Minamo
Karvan Finance

A.D. Monkam
Etude de notaire Wo'o

Jacqueline Moussinga Bapes

Jean Jacques Mpanjo Lobe
MCA Audit & Conseil

Marie Agathe Ndeme
Cadire

Marcelin Yoyo Ndoum
Etude de notaire Wo'o

Simon Pierre Nemba
Cabinet Maître Marie Andrée Ngwe

Pierre Roger Ngangwou
PwC Cameroon

Virgile Ngassam Njiké
Ngassamnjike & Associés

Julius Ngu Tabe Achu
Achu and Fon-Ndikum Law Firm

Marie-Andrée Ngwe
Cabinet Maître Marie Andrée Ngwe

Mosely Njebayi
CSE

Eugénie Carolle Njignou Mdojang
Nimba Conseil SARL

Noupoue Ngaffa Richard
Legal Power Law Firm

Ndie Tadmi
Legal Power Law Firm

Joseph Mbi Tanyi
Tanyi Mbi & Partners

Dominique Taty
PwC Côte d'Ivoire

Pierre Morgant Tchuikwa
Cadire

Nadine Tinen
PricewaterhouseCoopers Tax & Legal SARL

Chrétien Toudjui
Afrique Audit Conseil Baker Tilly

Tamfu Ngarka Tristel Richard
Legal Power Law Firm

Jean Vincent Whassom
Lafarge

Eliane Yomsi
Karvan Finance

Philippe Zouna
PwC Cameroon

CANADA

SDV Logistics (Canada) Inc.

Saad Ahmad
Blake, Cassels & Graydon, member of Lex Mundi

Marlon Alfred
PwC Canada

David Bish
Torys LLP

Ann Borooah
Toronto City Hall

Colin L. Campbell
Superior Court of Justice of Ontario

Allan Coleman
Osler, Hoskin & Harcourt LLP

John Craig
Heenan Blaikie LLP, member of Ius Laboris

Aaron Dovell
Berris Mangan, member of Russell Bedford International

Abe Dube
Amerinde Law Group

David G. Ellis
Oxford properties

Diedier Eric

Isabelle Foley
Corporations Canada

Jeremy Fraiberg
Osler, Hoskin & Harcourt LLP

Kelly Francis
McMillan LLP

Paul Gasparatto
Ontario Energy Board

Marlow Gereluk
Macleod Dixon

Anne Glover
Blake, Cassels & Graydon, member of Lex Mundi

Yoine Goldstein
McMillan LLP

Karen Grant
TransUnion

Pamela S. Hughes
Blake, Cassels & Graydon, member of Lex Mundi

Robert Hughes
Osler, Hoskin & Harcourt LLP

Dino Infanti
Berris Mangan, member of Russell Bedford International

Andrew Kent
McMillan LLP

Matthew Kindree
Baker & McKenzie

Joshua Kochath
Comage Container Lines

Susan Leslie
First Canadian Title

Craig Lockwood
Osler, Hoskin & Harcourt LLP

Rebecca Ma
Baker & McKenzie

Patrick Mangan
Berris Mangan, member of Russell Bedford International

Terry McCann
MLG Enterprises Ltd.

William McCarthy
First Canadian Title

Dave McKechnie
McMillan LLP

Patricia Meehan
PwC Canada

Michael Nowina
Baker & McKenzie

Eric Paton
PwC Canada

Saul Plener
PwC Canada

Martin Post
Electrical Safety Authority

Antonin Pribetic
Steinberg Morton Hope & Israel LLP

Christopher Richter
Woods LLP

Damian Rigolo
Osler, Hoskin & Harcourt LLP

Jenifer Robertson
Electrical Safety Authority

Harris M. Rosen
Fogler Rubinoff

Paul Schabas
Blake, Cassels & Graydon, member of Lex Mundi

Nicholas Scheib
McMillan LLP

Lincoln Schreiner
PwC Canada

Shane Todd
Heenan Blaikie LLP, member of Ius Laboris

Dmitry Uduman
PwC Canada

Randal S. Van de Mosselaer
Macleod Dixon

Sharon Vogel
Borden Ladner Gervais LLP

George Waggot
McMillan LLP

CAPE VERDE

Empresa de Electricidade e Agua (Electra)

Hermínio Afonso
PwC Cape Verde

Ana Cristina Almada
D. Hopffer Almada & Associados

Bruno Andrade Alves
PwC Portugal

José Manuel Andrade
Núcleo Operacional da Sociedade de Informação

Susana Caetano
PwC Portugal

Liver Canuto
PwC Portugal

Ana Catarina Carnaz
PwC Portugal

Ana Raquel Costa
PwC Portugal

Ilidio Cruz
Ilidio Cruz & Associados-Sociedade de Advogados RL

Jorge Lima Delgado Lopes
Núcleo Operacional da Sociedade de Informação

John Duggan
PwC Portugal

Florentino Jorge Fonseca Jesus
Municipality of Praia

João Gomes
D. Hopffer Almada & Associados

Julio Martins Jr.
Raposo Bernardo & Associados

João Medina
Neville de Rougemont & Associados

Francisco Guimarães Melo
PwC Portugal

Fernando Aguiar Monteiro
Advogados Associados

Ana Pinto Morais
PwC Portugal

Catarina Nunes
PwC Portugal

Ana Rita Reis
Neville de Rougemont & Associados

Armando J.F. Rodrigues
PwC Cape Verde

Henrique Semedo Borges
Law Firm Semedo Borges

Zilmar D. Silva Lopes
Amado & Medina Advogadas

Luís Filipe Sousa
PwC Portugal

Jose Spinola
FPS

Frantz Tavares
INOVE - Consultores Empresariais

João Carlos Tavares Fidalgo
Banco Central de Cabo Verde

Liza Helena Vaz
PwC Portugal

Leendert Verschoor
PwC Portugal

CENTRAL AFRICAN REPUBLIC

La Banque des Etats de l'Afrique Centrale

Blaise Banguitoumba
ENERCA (Energie Centrafricaine)

Thierry Chaou
Cabinet G.E.C. SA Fiduciaire

Maurice Dibert-Dollet
Ministère de la Justice

Christiane Doraz-Serefessenet
Cabinet Notaire Doraz-Serefessenet

Emile Doraz-Serefessenet
Cabinet Notaire Doraz-Serefessenet

Dolly Gotilogue
Avocat à la Cour

Théodore Lawson
Cabinet Lawson & Associés

Jean Paul Maradas Nado
Ministère de l'Urbanisme

Timothee M'beto
TTCI

Serge Médard Missamou
Club OHADA République Centrafricaine

Yves Namkomokoina
Tribunal de Commerce de Bangui

Jacob Ngaya
Ministère des Finances - Direction Générale des Impôts et des Domaines

Marcelin Ngondang
Ministère des Finances - Direction Générale des Impôts et des Domaines

Gina Roosalem
Chambre des Notaires de Centrafrique

François Sabegala
Guichet Unique de Formalités des Entreprises (GUFE)

Ghislain Samba Mokamanede
BAMELEC

Bandiba Max Symphorien
Club OHADA République Centrafricaine

Nicolas Tiangaye
Nicolas Tiangaye Law Firm

Marcial Zoba
Ministère des Finances - Direction Générale des Impôts et des Domaines

CHAD

La Banque des Etats de l'Afrique Centrale

Mahamat Hassan Abakar
Cabinet Me Mahamat Hassan Abakar

Dana Abdelkader Waya
Cabinet Notarial Bongoro

Adoum Daoud Adoum Haroun
S.C.G.A.D.A. et Fils

Abdelkerim Ahmat
SDV Logistics

Atadet Azarak Mogro
Société Tchadienne d'Eau et d'Electricité (STEE)

Theophile B. Bongoro
Cabinet Notarial Bongoro

Oscar D'estaing Deffosso
PricewaterhouseCoopers Tax & Legal SARL

Thomas Dingamgoto
Cabinet Thomas Dingamgoto

Mahamat Ousman Djidda
Cabinet d'Architecture & Urbanisme

N'Doningar Djimasna
Faculté de Droit, Université de N'Djamena

Mahamat Nour Idriss Haggar
Société Tchadienne d'Eau et d'Electricité (STEE)

Delphine K. Djiraibe
Avocate à la Cour

Francis Kadjilembaye
Cabinet Thomas Dingamgoto

Gérard Leclaire
Cabinet d'Architecture & Urbanisme

Béchir Madet
Office Notarial

Athanase Mbaigangnon
Cabinet Notarial Bongoro

Issa Ngarmbassa
Etude Me Issa Ngar mbassa

Tchouafiene Pandare
Cabinet Notarial Bongoro

Nissaouabé Passang
Etude Me Passang

Nastasja Schnorfeil-Pauthe
PricewaterhouseCoopers Tax & Legal SARL

Gilles Schwarz
SDV Logistics

Senoussi Ahmat Senoussi
Cabinet d'Architecture & Urbanisme

Amos D. Tatoloum Onde
Societe Africaine d'Architecture et d'Ingénierie

Dominique Taty
PwC Côte d'Ivoire

Nadine Tinen
PricewaterhouseCoopers Tax & Legal SARL

Masrangue Trahogra
Cabinet d'Avocats Associés

Issouf Traore
Imperial Tobacco

Sobdibé Zoua
Cabinet Sobdibe Zoua

Patedjore Zoukalne
Direction de l'enregistrement des Domaines, du Timbre et de la Conservation Foncière

CHILE

Boletin Comercial

Leticia Acosta Aguirre
Redlines Group

Tania Almuna
Cruz & Cia. Abogados

Luis Avello
PwC Chile

Angeles Barría
Philippi, Yrarrazaval, Pulido & Brunner, Abogados Ltda.

José Benitez
PwC Chile

Enrique Benitez Urrutia
Urrutia & Cía

Jorge Benitez Urrutia
Urrutia & Cía

Mario Bezanilla
Alcaíno, Rodríguez & Sahli Limitada

Manuel Brunet Bofill
Cámara Chilena de la Construcción

Rodrigo Cabrera Ortiz
Chilectra

Josefina Campos
Claro & Ciá., Abogados, member of Lex Mundi

Miguel Capo Valdes
Besalco S.A.

Javier Carrasco
Núñez Muñoz & Cía Ltda. Abogados

Héctor Carrasco
Superintendencia de Bancos y Instituciones Financieras Chile

Andrés Chirgwin
Chirgwin Recart Abogados SpA

Cristobal Correa Echavarria
Guerrero, Olivos, Novoa & Errázuriz Abogados

Sergio Cruz
Cruz & Cia. Abogados

Bernardita Dittus
Alessandri & Compañía

Fernando Echeverria
Cámara Chilena de la Construcción

Alejandro Eliash
Cámara Chilena de la Construcción

Claudia Paz Escobar
Chirgwin Recart Abogados SpA

Jaime Espina
PwC Chile

Cristián S. Eyzaguirre
Eyzaguirre & Cía.

Maria Teresa Fernandez
Bahamondez, Alvarez & Zegers

Benjamín Ferrada
Guerrero, Olivos, Novoa & Errázuriz Abogados

Pamela Flores
PwC Chile

Rodrigo Galleguillos
Núñez Muñoz & Cía Ltda. Abogados

Nicolás García
Núñez Muñoz & Cía Ltda. Abogados

Gianfranco Gazzana
Guerrero, Olivos, Novoa & Errázuriz Abogados

Andrés González
Núñez Muñoz & Cía Ltda. Abogados

Mauricio Hederra
Cruz & Cia. Abogados

Christian Hermansen Rebolledo
ACTIC Consultores

Manuel Hinojosa
Núñez Muñoz & Cía Ltda. Abogados

Javier Hurtado
Cámara Chilena de la Construcción

Fernando Jamarne
Alessandri & Compañía

Andrés Jara
Guerrero, Olivos, Novoa & Errázuriz Abogados

José Ignacio Jiménez
Guerrero, Olivos, Novoa & Errázuriz Abogados

Pedro Lagos
Yrarrázaval, Ruiz-Tagle, Goldenberg, Lagos & Silva

Jose Luis Letelier
Cariola Diez Perez-Copatos & Cia

Gianfranco Lotito
Claro & Ciá., Abogados, member of Lex Mundi

Luis Maldonado Croquevielle
Conservador de Bienes Raíces y Comercio de Santiago

Juan Ignacio Marín
GUERRERO, OLIVOS, NOVOA & ERRÁZURIZ ABOGADOS

Nicolas Maturana
CHIRGWIN RECART ABOGADOS SPA

Consuelo Maze
NÚÑEZ MUÑOZ & CÍA LTDA. ABOGADOS

Enrique Munita
PHILIPPI, YRARRAZAVAL, PULIDO & BRUNNER, ABOGADOS LTDA.

Rodrigo Muñoz
NÚÑEZ MUÑOZ & CÍA LTDA. ABOGADOS

Alberto Oltra
DHL GLOBAL FORWARDING

Felipe Ossa
CLARO & CÍA., ABOGADOS, MEMBER OF LEX MUNDI

Gerardo Ovalle Mahns
YRARRÁZAVAL, RUIZ-TAGLE, GOLDENBERG, LAGOS & SILVA

Luis Parada Hoyl
BAHAMONDEZ, ALVAREZ & ZEGERS

Miguel Pavez
RUSSELL BEDFORD CHILE, MEMBER OF RUSSELL BEDFORD INTERNATIONAL

Carmen Paz Cruz Lozano
CÁMARA CHILENA DE LA CONSTRUCCIÓN

Alberto Pulido A.
PHILIPPI, YRARRAZAVAL, PULIDO & BRUNNER, ABOGADOS LTDA.

Alfonso Reymond Larrain
CHADWICK & ALDUNATE ABOGADOS

Sebastián Riesco
EYZAGUIRRE & CÍA.

Ricardo Riesco
PHILIPPI, YRARRAZAVAL, PULIDO & BRUNNER, ABOGADOS LTDA.

Constanza Rodriguez
PHILIPPI, YRARRAZAVAL, PULIDO & BRUNNER, ABOGADOS LTDA.

Edmundo Rojas García
CONSERVADOR DE BIENES RAÍCES Y COMERCIO DE SANTIAGO

Pamela Rubio
NÚÑEZ MUÑOZ & CÍA LTDA. ABOGADOS

Carlos Saavedra
CRUZ & CÍA. ABOGADOS

Bernardita Saez
ALESSANDRI & COMPAÑÍA

Marco Salgado
ALCAÍNO, RODRÍGUEZ & SAHLI LIMITADA

Adriana Salias
REDLINES GROUP

Hugo Salinas
PWC CHILE

Andrés Sanfuentes
PHILIPPI, YRARRAZAVAL, PULIDO & BRUNNER, ABOGADOS LTDA.

Martín Santa María O.
GUERRERO, OLIVOS, NOVOA & ERRÁZURIZ ABOGADOS

Francisco Selamé
PWC CHILE

Marcela Silva
PHILIPPI, YRARRAZAVAL, PULIDO & BRUNNER, ABOGADOS LTDA.

Luis Fernando Silva Ibañez
YRARRÁZAVAL, RUIZ-TAGLE, GOLDENBERG, LAGOS & SILVA

Alan Smith
AGENCIA DE ADUANA SMITH Y CÍA. LTDA.

Cristobal Smythe
BAHAMONDEZ, ALVAREZ & ZEGERS

Alan Spencer
ALESSANDRI & COMPAÑÍA

Victor Tavera
CHILECTRA

Ricardo Tisi L.
CARIOLA DIEZ PEREZ-COPATOS & CIA

Esteban Tomic Errázuriz
CRUZ & CIA. ABOGADOS

Carlos Torres
REDLINES GROUP

Sebastián Valdivieso
YRARRÁZAVAL, RUIZ-TAGLE, GOLDENBERG, LAGOS & SILVA

Matias Valenzuela
ALESSANDRI & COMPAÑÍA

Luis Felipe Vergara
CONSERVADOR DE BIENES RAÍCES Y COMERCIO DE SANTIAGO

Arturo Yrarrázaval Covarrubias
YRARRÁZAVAL, RUIZ-TAGLE, GOLDENBERG, LAGOS & SILVA

Jean Paul Zalaquett
CHILECTRA

Matías Zegers
BAHAMONDEZ, ALVAREZ & ZEGERS

CHINA

ALLEN & OVERY LLP

BYZ DIGITAL TECHNOLOGY

Russell Brown
LEHMANBROWN

Rico Chan
BAKER & MCKENZIE

Rex Chan
PWC CHINA

Jie Chen
JUN HE LAW OFFICE, MEMBER OF LEX MUNDI

Elliott Youchun Chen
JUN ZE JUN LAW OFFICES

Donald Chen
NINGBO SUNSEA APPAREL

Grace Cheng
CAPITAL LAW & PARTNERS

Ke Deng
AG LOGISTICS

Robert Du
HKS

Yu Du
MMLC GROUP

Xi Jun Duan
AG LOGISTICS

Hongtao Fan
JOINWAY LAWFIRM

Elwin Feng
QINGHE COUNTY BAOSHIDA AUTOMOBILE PARTS CO. LTD.

Wei Gao

Lawrence Linjun Guo
JADE & FOUNTAIN PRC LAWYERS

Joanna Guo
ZHONG LUN LAW FIRM

Jennifer He
LEHMANBROWN

Kian Heong Hew
PINSENT MASONS

Vivian Ho
BAKER & MCKENZIE

Sheng Ho
SHANGHAI TRICO BARIUM SALTS BUSINESS DEPARTMENT

Jinquan Hu
KING & WOOD PRC LAWYERS

Felix Hu
SHENZHEN EONVER CO. LTD.

Marvin Jiang
TELOON CHEMICALS

Liu Jing
BEIJING HUANZHONG & PARTNERS

Edward E. Lehman
LEHMAN, LEE & XU

Ian Lewis
MAYER BROWN JSM

Qing Li
JUN HE LAW OFFICE, MEMBER OF LEX MUNDI

Jane Li
NORONHA ADVOGADOS

Audry Li
ZHONG LUN LAW FIRM

Mark Li
ZHONG LUN LAW FIRM

Frankie Lin
ZHECHEM

Grace Liu
HUA-ANDER CPAS, MEMBER OF RUSSELL BEDFORD INTERNATIONAL

Li Liu
JINGJIANG TAIGOO IMPORT & EXPORT TRADING COMPANY

Jingtao Liu
JONES LANG LASALLE

Zhiqiang Liu
KING & WOOD PRC LAWYERS

Lucy Lu
KING & WOOD PRC LAWYERS

Hongli Ma
JUN HE LAW OFFICE, MEMBER OF LEX MUNDI

Natalie Ma
PWC CHINA

Mark Ma
YANTAI I.G. PRODUCE CO., LTD.

Thomas Man

Matthew Murphy
MMLC GROUP

Stephen Rynhart
JONES LANG LASALLE

Han Shen
DAVIS POLK & WARDWELL

Tina Shi
MAYER BROWN JSM

Jack Sun
HOGAN LOVELLS

Jessie Tang
GLOBAL STAR LOGISTICS CO. LTD.

Terence Tung
MAYER BROWN JSM

Felicity Wang
AG LOGISTICS

Xuehua Wang
BEIJING HUANZHONG & PARTNERS

Fenghe Wang
DACHENG LAW OFFICES

Guoqi Wang
HUA-ANDER CPAS, MEMBER OF RUSSELL BEDFORD INTERNATIONAL

George Wang
JUN HE LAW OFFICE, MEMBER OF LEX MUNDI

Xin Wang
PINSENT MASONS

Celia Wang
PWC CHINA

William Wang
PWC CHINA

Max Wong
JONES LANG LASALLE

Chris Wong
LEHMANBROWN

Anthea Wong
PWC CHINA

Cassie Wong
PWC CHINA

Kent Woo
GUANGDA LAW FIRM

Christina Wu
CAPITAL LAW & PARTNERS

Bruce Wu
JIANGSU HONGTENG FOOD CO., LTD.

Elisa Xiao
HUA-ANDER CPAS, MEMBER OF RUSSELL BEDFORD INTERNATIONAL

Wang Xiaolei
PEOPLE'S BANK OF CHINA

Emily Xiong
SHENZHEN QIFENG STONE MATERIAL CO. LTD.

Hua Xuan
MMLC GROUP

Maggie Yan
HUA-ANDER CPAS, MEMBER OF RUSSELL BEDFORD INTERNATIONAL

Frank Yang
MAYER BROWN JSM

Queenie Yip
EXPORT/IMPORT

Ricky Yiu
BAKER & MCKENZIE

Hai Yong
BAKER & MCKENZIE

Tian Yongsheng
Y-AXIS INTERNATIONAL TRADING CO.

Eugenia Yu
HKS

Xia Yu
MMLC GROUP

Natalie Yu
SHU JIN LAW FIRM

Yvonne Zeng
LEHMANBROWN

Honglei Zhang
BEIJING HUANZHONG & PARTNERS

Sarah Zhang
HOGAN LOVELLS

Yi Zhang
KING & WOOD PRC LAWYERS

Sheng Hui Zhao
BEIJING HUANZHONG & PARTNERS

Zoe Zhu
JOINWAY LAWFIRM

Judy Zhu
MAYER BROWN JSM

Alina Zhu
ZHONG LUN LAW FIRM

COLOMBIA

EINCE LTDA.

LEWIN & WILLS, ABOGADOS

Julio César Acosta
DHL GLOBAL FORWARDING

Enrique Alvarez
JOSE LLOREDA CAMACHO & CO.

Jaime Mauricio Angulo Sanchez
COMPUTEC - DATACRÉDITO

Lorena Arambula
CÁRDENAS & CÁRDENAS

Alexandra Arbeláez Cardona
RUSSELL BEDFORD COLOMBIA, MEMBER OF RUSSELL BEDFORD INTERNATIONAL

Jorge Mauricio Arenas Sanchez
CODENSA S.A. ESP

Manuela Arizmendi
POSSE HERRERA & RUIZ

Patricia Arrázola-Bustillo
GÓMEZ-PINZÓN ZULETA ABOGADOS S.A.

Bernardo Avila
PARRA RODRIGUEZ & CAVELIER

María Camila Bagés
BRIGARD & URRUTIA, MEMBER OF LEX MUNDI

Luis Alfredo Barragán
BRIGARD & URRUTIA, MEMBER OF LEX MUNDI

Daniel Bayona
MUÑOZ TAMAYO & ASOCIADOS

Fernando Bermúdez Durana
MUÑOZ TAMAYO & ASOCIADOS

Joe Ignacio Bonilla Gálvez
MUÑOZ TAMAYO & ASOCIADOS

Carolina Camacho
POSSE HERRERA & RUIZ

Claudia Marcela Camargo
PWC COLOMBIA

Pablo Cárdenas
BRIGARD & URRUTIA, MEMBER OF LEX MUNDI

Darío Cárdenas
CÁRDENAS & CÁRDENAS

Daniel Cardoso
PWC COLOMBIA

Carlos Carvajal
JOSE LLOREDA CAMACHO & CO.

Felipe Cuberos
PRIETO & CARRIZOSA S.A.

Maria Cristina Cuestas
DHL GLOBAL FORWARDING

Andrés de la Rosa
CAVELIER ABOGADOS

Lorena Diaz
JOSE LLOREDA CAMACHO & CO.

María Helena Díaz Méndez
PWC COLOMBIA

Paula Duarte
NIETO & CHALELA

Karla Sofia Escobar Arango
POSSE HERRERA & RUIZ

Jairo Flechas
GENELEC LTDA.

Carlos Fradique-Méndez
BRIGARD & URRUTIA, MEMBER OF LEX MUNDI

Luis Hernando Gallo Medina
GALLO MEDINA ABOGADOS ASOCIADOS

Hermes García
CAVELIER ABOGADOS

Yamile Andrea Gómez
PRODUCTOS STAHL DE COLOMBIA S.A.

Santiago Gutiérrez
JOSE LLOREDA CAMACHO & CO.

Natalia Gutierrez de Larrauri
BRIGARD & URRUTIA, MEMBER OF LEX MUNDI

Monica Hernandez
ARRIETA BUSTAMANTE

Laura Villaveces Hollman
BRIGARD & URRUTIA, MEMBER OF LEX MUNDI

Jorge Lara-Urbaneja
LARA CONSULTORES

Ernesto López
CÁRDENAS & CÁRDENAS

Adriana Lopez Moncayo
CURADURIA URBANA 3

Carlos Mantilla
MUÑOZ TAMAYO & ASOCIADOS

Luis Mendoza
JOSE LLOREDA CAMACHO & CO.

Maria Montejo
GÓMEZ-PINZÓN ZULETA ABOGADOS S.A.

Luis Gabriel Morcillo-Méndez
BRIGARD & URRUTIA, MEMBER OF LEX MUNDI

Sandra Marcela Murcia Mora
CIBERGESTION COLOMBIA S.A.S.

Diana Navas
JOSE LLOREDA CAMACHO & CO.

Luis Carlos Neira Mejía
HOLGUÍN, NEIRA & POMBO ABOGADOS

María Neira Tobón
HOLGUÍN, NEIRA & POMBO ABOGADOS

Luis E. Nieto
NIETO & CHALELA

Adriana Carolina Ospina Jiménez
BRIGARD & URRUTIA, MEMBER OF LEX MUNDI

Felipe Payan
CAVELIER ABOGADOS

Mónica Pedroza Garcés
CORPORACIÓN EXCELENCIA EN LA JUSTICIA

Carolina Posada
POSSE HERRERA & RUIZ

Raul Quevedo
JOSE LLOREDA CAMACHO & CO.

Daniel Reyes
CURADURIA URBANA 3

Catalina Reyes
JOSE LLOREDA CAMACHO & CO.

Irma Rivera
BRIGARD & URRUTIA, MEMBER OF LEX MUNDI

Luis Carlos Robayo Higuera
RUSSELL BEDFORD COLOMBIA, MEMBER OF RUSSELL BEDFORD INTERNATIONAL

Jaime Rodriguez
NOTARIA 13 DE BOGOTÁ

Bernardo Rodriguez
PARRA RODRIGUEZ & CAVELIER

Maria Isabel Rodriguez
POSSE HERRERA & RUIZ

Sonia Elizabeth Rojas Izaquita
GALLO MEDINA ABOGADOS ASOCIADOS

Carolina Romero
GÓMEZ-PINZÓN ZULETA ABOGADOS S.A.

Juan Carlos Ruiz
JOSE LLOREDA CAMACHO & CO.

Angela Salazar Blanco
JOSE LLOREDA CAMACHO & CO.

Paola Spada
CORPORACIÓN EXCELENCIA EN LA JUSTICIA

Raúl Alberto Suárez Arcila

Gustavo Tamayo Arango
JOSE LLOREDA CAMACHO & CO.

Marcel Tangarife
PARRA RODRIGUEZ & CAVELIER

Jose Alejandro Torres
POSSE HERRERA & RUIZ

Carolina Villadiego Burbano
CORPORACIÓN EXCELENCIA EN LA JUSTICIA

Alberto Zuleta
CÁRDENAS & CÁRDENAS

Diana Zuleta
PARRA RODRIGUEZ & CAVELIER

COMOROS

Chabani Abdallah Halifa
GROUPE HASSANATI SOILIHI - GROUPE HASOIL

Mohamed Abdallah Halifa
GROUPE HASSANATI SOILIHI - GROUPE HASOIL

Issiaka Abdourazak
ETUDE MAÎTRE ABDOURAZAK

Hilmy Aboudsaid
COMORES CARGO INTERNATIONAL

Yassian Ahamed
DIRECTION DE L'ENERGIE

Mouzaoui Amroine
ORGANISATION PATRONALE DES COMORES

Said Ali Said Athouman
UNION OF THE CHAMBER OF COMMERCE

Mohamed Ahamada Baco
LAWYER

Ali Mohamed Choibou
ETUDE MAÎTRE CHOIBOU

Ali Abdou Elaniou
CABINET ELANIOU

Remy Grondin
VITOGAZ COMORES

Adill Hassani
ELECTRICITÉ ET EAU DES COMORES

Youssouf Ismael
DIRECTION GÉNÉRALE DES IMPÔTS

Madiane Mohamed Issa
LAWYER

Faouzi Mohamed Lakj
TRIBUNAL DE COMMERCE COMOROS

Abdoulabastoi Moudjahid
CLUB OHADA COMORES

Said Mohamed Nassur
ENERGIE COMORES

Siti-Kalathoumi Soidri
AVOCAT À LA COUR

Daoud Saidali Toihiri
MINISTRY OF PROMOTION AND EMPLOYMENT

Mohamed Youssouf
ETUDE MAÎTRE ABDOURAZAK

CONGO, DEM. REP.

Louise Abonzore Alebam
MINISTÈRE DE L'URBANISME ET DE L'HABITAT

Alphin Babala Mangala
GTS EXPRESS

Romain Battajon
CABINET BATTAJON

Prince Bintene
CABINET MASAMBA

Patrick Bondonga Lesambo
CABINET EMERY MUKENDI WAFWANA & ASSOCIÉS

Deo Bukayafwa
MBM CONSEIL

Edmond Cibamba Diata
CABINET EMERY MUKENDI WAFWANA & ASSOCIÉS

Claudine Dipo
MINISTÈRE DE L'URBANISME ET DE L'HABITAT

Prosper Djuma Bilali
CABINET MASAMBA

Irénée Falanka
CABINET IRÉNÉE FALANKA

Patrick Gérenthon
SDV LOGISTICS

Ngalamulume Kalala Emmanuel
BARREAU DE KINSHASA/MATETE

Robert Katambu
CABINET ROBERT KATAMBU & ASSOCIÉS

Pierrot Kazadi Tshibanda
CABINET MASAMBA

Kamba Kitabi Clovis
CABINET ROBERT KATAMBU & ASSOCIÉS

Jean-Délphin Lokonde Mvulukunda
CABINET MASAMBA

Francis Lugunda Lubamba
CABINET LUGUNDA LUBAMBA

Serge Mwankana Lulu
AVOCAT

Aubin Mabanza
KLAM & PARTNERS AVOCATS

Béatrice Mabanza
KLAM & PARTNERS AVOCATS

Andre Malangu Muabila
CABINET FAMILLE

Antoine Mandemvo
SOCIÉTÉ NATIONALE D'ELECTRICITÉ (SNEL)

Roger Masamba Makela
CABINET MASAMBA

Jean Claude Mbaki Siluzaku
CABINET MBAKI ET ASSOCIÉS

Didier Mopiti
MBM CONSEIL

Gérard Mosolo
MBM CONSEIL

Louman Mpoy
MPOY LOUMAN & ASSOCIÉS

Emery Mukendi Wafwana
CABINET EMERY MUKENDI WAFWANA & ASSOCIÉS

Hilaire Mumvudi Mulangi
MINISTÈRE DE L'URBANISME ET DE L'HABITAT

Eric Mumwena Kasonga Bassu
CABINET EMERY MUKENDI WAFWANA & ASSOCIÉS

Jacques Munday
CABINET NTOTO ET NSWAL

Jean Pierre Muyaya
CABINET EMERY MUKENDI WAFWANA & ASSOCIÉS

Ilunga Israel Ndambi
S.I.E.C. SPRL

Victorine Bibiche Nsimba Kilembe
BARREAU DE KINSHASA/MATETE

Adam Ntumba
ANAPI

Laurent Okitonembo
CABINET DJUNGA & RISASI

Otton Oligo Mbelia Kanalia
ANAPI

R. Rigo

Pierre Risasi
CABINET DJUNGA & RISASI

Dominique Taty
PwC CÔTE D'IVOIRE

Antoine Tshibuabua Mbuyi
SOCIÉTÉ NATIONALE D'ELECTRICITÉ (SNEL)

CONGO, REP.

LA BANQUE DES ETATS DE L'AFRIQUE CENTRALE

SOCIÉTÉ NATIONALE D'ELECTRICITÉ (SNEL)

Jean Roger Bakoulou
LA BANQUE DES ETATS DE L'AFRIQUE CENTRALE

Prosper Bizitou
PwC CONGO (DEMOCRATIC REPUBLIC OF)

Claude Coelho
CABINET D'AVOCATS CLAUDE COELHO

Mohammad Daoudou
PwC CONGO (DEMOCRATIC REPUBLIC OF)

Mathias Esserebe
CABINET D'AVOCATS CLAUDE COELHO

Henriette Lucie Arlette Galiba
OFFICE NOTARIAL ME GALIBA

Gaston Gapo
ATELIER D'ARCHITECTURE ET D'URBANISME

Moise Kokolo
PwC CONGO (DEMOCRATIC REPUBLIC OF)

Karelle Koubatika
OFFICE 2K ARCHITECTURE & DESIGN

Christian Eric Locko
BRUDEY, ONDZIEL GNELENGA, LOCKO CABINET D'AVOCATS

Salomon Louboula
SCP SENGHOR & SARR, NOTAIRES ASSOCIÉS

Jean Prosper Mabassi
ORDRE NATIONAL DES AVOCATS DU CONGO BARREAU DE BRAZZAVILLE

Ado Patricia Marlene Matissa
CABINET NOTARIAL MATISSA

François Ngaka
LA BANQUE DES ETATS DE L'AFRIQUE CENTRALE

Regina Nicole Okandza Yoka
DIRECTION GÉNÉRALE DES IMPÔTS

Armand Robert Okoko
CABINET ARMAND ROBERT OKOKO

Jean Petro
CABINET D'AVOCATS JEAN PETRO

Chimène Prisca Nina Pongui
ETUDE DE ME CHIMÈNE PRISCA NINA PONGUI

Andre Francois Quenum
CABINET ANDRE FRANCOIS QUENUM

COSTA RICA

AUTORIDAD REGULADORA DE LOS SERVICIOS PUBLICOS (ARESEP)

FACIO & CAÑAS, MEMBER OF LEX MUNDI

Aisha Acuña
ANDRÉ TINOCO ABOGADOS

Arnoldo André
ANDRÉ TINOCO ABOGADOS

Alejandro Antillon
PACHECO COTO

Carlos Araya
QUIROS ABOGADOS CENTRAL LAW

Alvaro Barrantes
AUTORIDAD REGULADORA DE LOS SERVICIOS PUBLICOS (ARESEP)

Carlos Barrantes
PwC COSTA RICA

Ignacio Beirute
QUIROS ABOGADOS CENTRAL LAW

Alejandro Bettoni Traube
DONINELLI & DONINELLI - ASESORES JURÍDICOS ASOCIADOS

Gerardo Bogantes
BLP ABOGADOS

Eduardo Calderón-Odio
BLP ABOGADOS

Bernardo Calvo M.
GRUPO MEGA DE COSTA RICA BR, S.A

Juan José Carreras
BLP ABOGADOS

Adriana Castro
BLP ABOGADOS

Juan Jose Castro
EDIFICAR S.A.

Leonardo Castro
OLLER ABOGADOS

Silvia Chacon
ALFREDO FOURNIER & ASOCIADOS

Daniel Chaves
CINDE

Luis Fernando Escalante J.
GRUPO MEGA DE COSTA RICA BR, S.A

Roberto Esquivel
OLLER ABOGADOS

Freddy Fachler
PACHECO COTO

Elizabeth Fallas
QUIROS ABOGADOS CENTRAL LAW

Irene Fernández
LEX COUNSEL

Alejandro Fernández de Castro
PwC DOMINICAN REPUBLIC

Octavio Fournier
ALFREDO FOURNIER & ASOCIADOS

Alfredo Fournier-Beeche
ALFREDO FOURNIER & ASOCIADOS

V. Andrés Gómez
PwC COSTA RICA

Andrea González
BLP ABOGADOS

Randall González
BLP ABOGADOS

David Gutierrez
BLP ABOGADOS

Paola Gutiérrez Mora
LEX COUNSEL

Mario Gutiérrez Quintero
LEX COUNSEL

Jorge Guzmán
LEX COUNSEL

Roy Guzman Ramirez
COMPAÑÍA NACIONAL DE FUERZA Y LUZ

Randall Zamora Hidalgo
COSTA RICA ABC

Milena Hidalgo
TELETEC S.A.

Anneth Jimenez
BLP ABOGADOS

Vivian Jiménez
OLLER ABOGADOS

Elvis Eduardo Jiménez Gutiérrez
SUPERINTENDENCIA GENERAL DE ENTIDADES FINANCIERAS

Ivannia Méndez Rodríguez
OLLER ABOGADOS

Andres Mercado
OLLER ABOGADOS

Gabriela Miranda
OLLER ABOGADOS

Jaime Molina
PROYECTOS ICC S.A.

Jorge Montenegro
SCGMT ARQUITECTURA Y DISEÑO

Eduardo Montoya Solano
SUPERINTENDENCIA GENERAL DE ENTIDADES FINANCIERAS

Freddy Morales
JAPDEVA CARIBBEAN PORT AUTHORITY

Cecilia Naranjo
LEX COUNSEL

Pedro Oller
OLLER ABOGADOS

Ramón Ortega
PwC DOMINICAN REPUBLIC

Andrea Paniagua
PwC DOMINICAN REPUBLIC

Felix Pecou Johnson
JAPDEVA CARIBBEAN PORT AUTHORITY

Laura Perez
CINDE

Sergio Pérez
ANDRÉ TINOCO ABOGADOS

Mainor Quesada
TELETEC S.A.

Alvaro Quesada Loría
AGUILAR CASTILLO LOVE

Mauricio Quiros
QUIROS ABOGADOS CENTRAL LAW

Rafael Quiros
QUIROS ABOGADOS CENTRAL LAW

Ana Quiros Vaglio
TransUnion

Manrique Rojas
ANDRÉ TINOCO ABOGADOS

Miguel Ruiz Herrera
LEX COUNSEL

Mauricio Salas
BLP ABOGADOS

Jose Luis Salinas
SCGMT ARQUITECTURA Y DISEÑO

Walter Anderson Salomons
JAPDEVA CARIBBEAN PORT AUTHORITY

Fernando Sanchez Castillo
Russell Bedford Costa Rica, ABBQ Consultores, S.A, member of Russell Bedford International

Luis Sibaja
LEX Counsel

Dagoberto Sibaja Morales
Registro Nacional de Costa Rica

Alonso Vargas
André Tinoco Abogados

Marianela Vargas
PwC Costa Rica

Rocio Vega
Grupo Mega de Costa Rica BR, S.A.

Jafet Zúñiga Salas
Superintendencia General de Entidades Financieras

CÔTE D'IVOIRE
Cabinet Raux, Amien & Associés

Etude de Maître Kone Mahoua

Diaby Aboubakar
BCEAO

César Asman
Cabinet N'Goan, Asman & Associés

Binta Nany Bakayoko
CLK Avocats

Kizito Brizoua-Bi
Bile-Aka, Brizoua-Bi & Associés

Michel Brizoua-Bi
Bile-Aka, Brizoua-Bi & Associés

Lassiney Kathann Camara
CLK Avocats

Aminata Cone
SCPA Dogué-Abbé Yao & Associés

Dorothée K. Dreesen
Etude Maître Dreesen

Olivier Germanos
Bolloré Africa LogisticsCI

Barnabe Kabore
NOVELEC Sarl

Fatoumata Konate Toure-B.
Etude de Me Konate Toure-B. Fatoumata

Dogbémin Gérard Kone
SCPA Nambeya-Dogbemin & Associes

Arsène Dablé Kouassi
SCPA Dogué-Abbé Yao & Associés

Charlotte-Yolande Mangoua
Etude de Maître Mangoua

Adeline Messou
PwC Côte d'Ivoire

André Monso
PwC Côte d'Ivoire

Georges N'Goan
Cabinet N'Goan, Asman & Associés

Ousmane Samba Mamadou
BCEAO

Simon Dognima Silué
Bile-Aka, Brizoua-Bi & Associés

Dominique Taty
PwC Côte d'Ivoire

Fousséni Traoré
PwC Côte d'Ivoire

Jean Christian Turkson
CIE

Koffi Noël Yao
Cabinet YZAS Baker Tilly

Emmanuel Yehouessi
BCEAO

Seydou Zerbo
SCPA Dogué-Abbé Yao & Associés

CROATIA
Ernst & Young

Andrea August
Financial agency - Centre for HITRO.HR

Zoran Avramović
Ministry of Justice

Emir Bahtijarević
Divjak, Topić & Bahtijarević

Ivana Bandov
Juric and Partners Attorneys at Law

Hrvoje Bardek
CMS Legal

Ivo Bijelic
PwC Croatia

Marko Borsky
Divjak, Topić & Bahtijarević

Marijana Božić
Divjak, Topić & Bahtijarević

Linda Brcic
Divjak, Topić & Bahtijarević

Lana Brlek
PwC Croatia

Nana Bulat
Čačić & Partners

Belinda Čačić
Čačić & Partners

Ivan Čuk
Vukmir & Asociates Law Firm

Stefanija Čukman
Juric and Partners Attorneys at Law

Saša Divjak
Divjak, Topić & Bahtijarević

Anela Dizdarević
Sihtar Attorneys at Law

Ronald Given
Wolf Theiss

Tonka Gjoić
Glinska & Mišković Ltd.

Ivan Gjurgjan
Gjurgjan & Šribar Radić Law Firm

Kresimir Golubić
Golmax d.o.o.

Tom Hadzija
Korper & Partneri Law Firm

Lidija Hanžek
HROK d.o.o.

Jana Hitrec
Čačić & Partners

Branimir Iveković
Iveković Law Office

Irina Jelčić
Hanžeković & Partners Ltd., member of Lex Mundi

Ivica Jelovcic
Damco

Saša Jovičić
Wolf Theiss

Sanja Jurkovic
PwC Croatia

Anela Kedić
Wolf Theiss

Branko Kirin
Čačić & Partners

Ozren Kobsa
Divjak, Topić & Bahtijarević

Dina Korper
Korper & Partneri Law Firm

Marija Krizanec
Juric and Partners Attorneys at Law

Anita Krizmanić
Mačešić & Partners, Odvjetnicko drustvo

Dubravka Lacković
CMS Legal

Krešimir Ljubić
Leko i Partneri Attorneys at Law

Andrea Loncar
Glinska & Mišković Ltd.

Marko Lovrić
Divjak, Topić & Bahtijarević

Miroljub Mačešić
Mačešić & Partners, Odvjetnicko drustvo

Josip Marohnić
Glinska & Mišković Ltd.

Andrej Matijevich
Matijevich Law Office

Jan Mokos
Korper & Partneri Law Firm

Marija Mušec
CMS Legal

Tatjana Pahljina
Transadria

Tomislav Pedišić
Vukmir & Asociates Law Firm

Miroslav Plašćar
Žurić I Partneri

Marko Praljak
Attorney Partnership

Branimir Puskaric
Korper & Partneri Law Firm

Hrvoje Radić
Gjurgjan & Šribar Radić Law Firm

Kristina Rihtar
Iveković Law Office

Gordan Rotkvić
PwC Croatia

Davor Rukonić
Divjak, Topić & Bahtijarević

Boris Sarovic
Šavorić & Partners

Ana Sihtar
Sihtar Attorneys at Law

Andrej Skočić
MERVIS d.o.o., member of Russell Bedford International

Vladimir Skočić
MERVIS d.o.o., member of Russell Bedford International

Toni Smrcek
Šavorić & Partners

Manuela Špoljarić
Leko i Partneri Attorneys at Law

Irena Šribar Radić
Gjurgjan & Šribar Radić Law Firm

Tihana Svetek
Leko i Partneri Attorneys at Law

Marin Svić
Praljak & Svić

Tena Tomek
Divjak, Topić & Bahtijarević

Branka Tutek
Juric and Partners Attorneys at Law

Ivana Urem
Assono Ltd. Croatia

Hrvoje Vidan
Iveković Law Office

Zeljko Vrban
HEP Distribution System Operator Ltd.

Zrinka Vrtaric
CMS Legal

Mario Vukelić
High Commercial Court of the Republic of Croatia

Marin Vukovic
Divjak, Topić & Bahtijarević

Gorana Vukušić
Leko i Partneri Attorneys at Law

Eugen Zadravec
Eugen Zadravec Law Firm

CYPRUS
Ernst & Young

RAS Restructuring Advisory Services Ltd.

Olga Adamidou
Antis Triantafyllides & Sons LLC

Alexandros Alexandrou
Tornaritis Law Firm

Irene Anastassiou
Dr. K. Chrysostomides & Co. LLC

Andreas Andreou
Cyprus Global Logistics

Pavlos Aristodemou
Aristodemou Loizides Yiolitis LLC

Anja Arsalides
Cyprus Investment Promotion Agency

Anita Boyadjian
Info Credit Group

Amanda Cacoyanni
Chrysses Demetriades & Co.

Antonis Christodoulides
PwC Cyprus

Thomas Christodoulou
Chrysses Demetriades & Co.

Christakis Christou
PwC Cyprus

Kypros Chrysostomides
Dr. K. Chrysostomides & Co. LLC

Alexandros Economou
Chrysses Demetriades & Co.

Lefteris S. Eleftheriou
Cyprus Investment Promotion Agency

Marios Eliades
M.Eliades & Partners LLC

Panicos Florides
P.G. Economides & Co. Limited, member of Russell Bedford International

Angela T. Frangou
Cyprus Stock Exchange

Elena Frixou
Artemis Bank Information Systems Ltd.

Olga Gaponova
Deloitte LLP

Elvira Georgiou
Antis Triantafyllides & Sons LLC

Marios Hadjigavriel
Antis Triantafyllides & Sons LLC

Iacovos Hadjivarnavas
Cyprus General Bonded and Transit Stores Association

Samantha G. Hellicar
Antis Triantafyllides & Sons LLC

Marina Ierokipiotou
Antis Triantafyllides & Sons LLC

Christina Ioannidou
Ioannides Demetriou LLC

Demetra Kalogerou
Cyprus Stock Exchange

George Karakannas
CH.P. Karakannas Electrical Ltd.

Melina Karaolia
M.Eliades & Partners LLC

Thomas Keane
Chrysses Demetriades & Co.

Harris Kleanthous
Deloitte LLP

Spyros G. Kokkinos
Department of Registrar of Companies and Official Receiver

Christina Koronis
PwC Cyprus

Christina Kotsapa
Antis Triantafyllides & Sons LLC

Theodoros Kringou
First Cyprus Credit Bureau

Nicholas Ktenas
Andreas Neocleous & Co. Legal Consultants

Olga Lambrou
Mouaimis & Mouaimis Advocates

Pieris M. Markou
Deloitte LLP

Christos Mavrellis
Chrysses Demetriades & Co.

Demosthenes Mavrellis
Chrysses Demetriades & Co.

Phivos Michaelides
Ioannides Demetriou LLC

Panayotis Mouaimis
Mouaimis & Mouaimis Advocates

Alexia Mouskou
Ioannides Demetriou LLC

Demetris Nicolaou
Aristodemou Loizides Yiolitis LLC

Themis Panayi
Cyprus Stock Exchange

Marios Panayiotou
Tornaritis Law Firm

Georgios Papadopoulos
M.Eliades & Partners LLC

Stella Papadopoulou
Ministry of Interior of Cyprus

Marios Pelekanos
Mesaritis Pelekanos Architects - Engineers

Chrysilios Pelekanos
PwC Cyprus

Maria Pilikou
Dr. K. Chrysostomides & Co. LLC

Yiannos Pipis
Nice Day Developers

Petros Rialas
P.G. Economides & Co. Limited, member of Russell Bedford International

Criton Tornaritis
Tornaritis Law Firm

Nikos Tripatsas
Cyprus Stock Exchange

Panikos Tsiailis
PwC Cyprus

James West
Antis Triantafyllides & Sons LLC

Xenios Xenopoulos
Lawyer

CZECH REPUBLIC
Allen & Overy (Czech Republic) LLP, organizační složka

Maurice Ward & Co. sro

PREDistribuce

Vladimír Ambruz
Ambruz & Dark Law Firm

Tomas Babacek
Ambruz & Dark Law Firm

Michaela Baranyková
Euro-Trend, s. r. o., member of Russell Bedford International

Libor Basl
Baker & McKenzie

Stanislav Bednár
Peterka & Partners

Tomáš Běhounek
BNT - pravda & partner, s.r.o.

Stanislav Beran
Peterka & Partners

Jan Beres
Kocian Solc Balastik

Martin Bohuslav
AMBRUZ & DARK LAW FIRM

Jiří Černý
PETERKA & PARTNERS

Ivan Chalupa
*SQUIRE, SANDERS & DEMPSEY, V.O.S.
ADVOKÁTNÍ KANCELÁŘ*

Peter Chrenko
PwC CZECH REPUBLIC

Pavel Cirek
*ENERGY REGULATOR OFFICE CZECH
REPUBLIC*

Martin Dančišin
GLATZOVÁ & CO.

Matěj Daněk
*PRK PARTNERS S.R.O. ADVOKÁTNÍ
KANCELÁŘ*

Dagmar Dubecka
KOCIAN SOLC BALASTIK

Tomáš Elbert
WHITE & CASE

Tereza Erényi
*PRK PARTNERS S.R.O. ADVOKÁTNÍ
KANCELÁŘ*

Pavel Ficek
PANALPINA CZECH S.R.O.

Michal Forýtek
KINSTELLAR

Jakub Hajek
AMBRUZ & DARK LAW FIRM

Michal Hanko
BUBNIK, MYSLIL & PARTNERS

Jarmila Hanzalova
*PRK PARTNERS S.R.O. ADVOKÁTNÍ
KANCELÁŘ*

Jitka Hlavova
*PRK PARTNERS S.R.O. ADVOKÁTNÍ
KANCELÁŘ*

Vít Horáček
GLATZOVÁ & CO.

Radek Horký
NOTARY CHAMBER, CZECH REPUBLIC

Michal Hrnčíř
AMBRUZ & DARK LAW FIRM

Pavel Jakab
PETERKA & PARTNERS

Kateřina Jarolímková
NOTÁŘSKÁ KOMORA ČESKÉ REPUBLIKY

Ludvik Juřička
AMBRUZ & DARK LAW FIRM

Jitka Korejzova
*PRK PARTNERS S.R.O. ADVOKÁTNÍ
KANCELÁŘ*

Adela Krbcová
PETERKA & PARTNERS

Martin Krechler
GLATZOVÁ & CO.

Tomáš Kren
WHITE & CASE

Aleš Kubáč
AMBRUZ & DARK LAW FIRM

Petr Kucera
CCB - CZECH CREDIT BUREAU

Petr Kuhn
WHITE & CASE

Bohumil Kunc
NOTARY CHAMBER, CZECH REPUBLIC

Irena Lazurova
LAW OFFICE IRENA LAZUROVA

Zuzana Luklova
AMBRUZ & DARK LAW FIRM

Ondřej Mánek
WOLF THEISS

Jiří Markvart
AMBRUZ & DARK LAW FIRM

Peter Maysenhölder
BNT - PRAVDA & PARTNER, S.R.O.

Petr Měšťánek
KINSTELLAR

Veronika Mistova
*PRK PARTNERS S.R.O. ADVOKÁTNÍ
KANCELÁŘ*

Pavlína Mišutová
WHITE & CASE

Marie Mrázková
PETERKA & PARTNERS

Lenka Mrazova
PwC CZECH REPUBLIC

David Musil
PwC CZECH REPUBLIC

Jarmila Musilova
CZECH NATIONAL BANK

Lenka Navrátilová
AMBRUZ & DARK LAW FIRM

Robert Nemec
*PRK PARTNERS S.R.O. ADVOKÁTNÍ
KANCELÁŘ*

Martina Pavelkova
PANALPINA CZECH S.R.O.

Marketa Penazova
AMBRUZ & DARK LAW FIRM

Veronika Plešková
*HAVEL, HOLÁSEK & PARTNERS S.R.O.,
ADVOKÁTNÍ KANCELÁŘ*

Jan Procházka
AMBRUZ & DARK LAW FIRM

Markéta Protivankova
VEJMELKA & WÜNSCH, S.R.O.

Zdenek Rosicky
*SQUIRE, SANDERS & DEMPSEY, V.O.S.
ADVOKÁTNÍ KANCELÁŘ*

Petra Schneiderova
AMBRUZ & DARK LAW FIRM

Paul Sestak
WOLF THEISS

Leona Ševčíková
PANALPINA CZECH S.R.O.

Robert Sgariboldi
PANALPINA CZECH S.R.O.

Dana Sládečková
CZECH NATIONAL BANK

Ladislav Smejkal
WHITE & CASE

Petra Sochorova
*HAVEL, HOLÁSEK & PARTNERS S.R.O.,
ADVOKÁTNÍ KANCELÁŘ*

Erik Steger
WOLF THEISS

Martin Štěpaník
PETERKA & PARTNERS

Paul Stewart
PwC CZECH REPUBLIC

Stanislav Travnicek
*ENERGY REGULATOR OFFICE CZECH
REPUBLIC*

Růžena Trojánková
KINSTELLAR

Klara Valentova
AMBRUZ & DARK LAW FIRM

Ludek Vrána
VRÁNA & PELIKÁN

Vaclav Zaloudek
WHITE & CASE

DENMARK

Elsebeth Aaes-Jørgensen
*NORRBOM VINDING, MEMBER OF IUS
LABORIS*

Niels Bang
GORRISSEN FEDERSPIEL

Thomas Bang
LETT LAW FIRM

Peter Bang
PLESNER

Ole Borch
BECH-BRUUN LAW FIRM

Frants Dalgaard-Knudsen
PLESNER

Mogens Ebeling
BRUUN & HJEJLE

Alice Folker
GORRISSEN FEDERSPIEL

Anne Birgitte Gammeljord
GORRISSEN FEDERSPIEL

Ata Ghilassi
*KROMANN REUMERT, MEMBER OF LEX
MUNDI*

Anne Louise Haack Andersen
LETT LAW FIRM

Lita Misozi Hansen
PwC DENMARK

Annette Hastrup
MAGNUSSON

Anders Hjortsholm
*KROMANN REUMERT, MEMBER OF LEX
MUNDI*

Jens Hjortskov
PHILIP LAW FIRM

Heidi Hoelgaard
EXPERIAN NORTHERN EUROPE

Peter Honoré
*KROMANN REUMERT, MEMBER OF LEX
MUNDI*

Jens Steen Jensen
*KROMANN REUMERT, MEMBER OF LEX
MUNDI*

Poul Jespersen

Camilla Jørgensen
PHILIP LAW FIRM

Lars Kjaer
BECH-BRUUN LAW FIRM

Alexander Troeltzsch Larsen
BECH-BRUUN LAW FIRM

Mikkel Stig Larsen
*KROMANN REUMERT, MEMBER OF LEX
MUNDI*

Susanne Schjølin Larsen
*KROMANN REUMERT, MEMBER OF LEX
MUNDI*

Morten Bang Mikkelsen
PwC DENMARK

Andreas Nielsen
BRUUN & HJEJLE

Susanne Nørgaard
PwC DENMARK

Jim Øksnebjerg
ADVOKATAKTIESELSKABET HORTEN

Carsten Pedersen
BECH-BRUUN LAW FIRM

Lars Lindencrone Petersen
BECH-BRUUN LAW FIRM

Jette H. Rønøe
BECH-BRUUN LAW FIRM

Kim Sejberg

Louise Krarup Simonsen
*KROMANN REUMERT, MEMBER OF LEX
MUNDI*

Martin Sørensen
2M EL-INSTALLATION A/S

Christel Tegler
*KROMANN REUMERT, MEMBER OF LEX
MUNDI*

Anette Thorburn

Henrik Thuesen

Kim Trenskow
*KROMANN REUMERT, MEMBER OF LEX
MUNDI*

Knud Villemoes Hansen
NATIONAL SURVEY AND CADASTRE

Anders Worsøe
MAGNUSSON

DJIBOUTI

ELECTRICITÉ DE DJIBOUTI

Souleiman Idriss Abdi
MSC DJIBOUTI

Fatouma Ahmed
SERVICE DES DOMAINES, DJIBOUTI

Houmed Abdallah Bourhan
CONSERVATION FONCIERE, DJIBOUTI

Wabat Daoud
AVOCAT À LA COUR

Bruno Detroyat
SOCIÉTÉ MARITIME L. SAVON & RIES

Daniel Dubois
ATELIER D'ARCHITECTURE

Hassam Mohamed Egaeh
*DIRECTION LEGISLATION & CONTENTIEUX
DE LA DIRECTIONS DES IMPOTS*

Félix Emok N'Dolo
CHD GROUP

Mourad Farah

Malik Garad
BANQUE CENTRALE DE DJIBOUTI

Habib Ibrahim Mohamed
*DIRECTION DE L'HABITAT ET DE
L'URBANISME*

Ismael Mahamoud
UNIVERSITE DE DJIBOUTI

Fatouma Mahamoud Hassan

Alain Martinet
*CABINET D'AVOCATS MARTINET &
MARTINET*

Marie-Paule Martinet
*CABINET D'AVOCATS MARTINET &
MARTINET*

Mayank Metha
SOCIÉTÉ MARITIME L. SAVON & RIES

Ibrahim Mohamed Omar
CABINET CECA

Abdallah Mohammed Kamil
ETUDE NOTARIALE

Mohamed Omar Mohamed

Ahmed Osman
BANQUE CENTRALE DE DJIBOUTI

Lantosoa Hurfin Ralaiarinosy
GROUPEMENT COSMEZZ DJIBOUTI S.A.

Harilalao Ravalison
*CABINET D'AVOCATS MARTINET
& MARTINET*

Aicha Youssouf Abdi
CABINET CECA

DOMINICA

Joelle A.V. Harris
HARRIS & HARRIS

Jerry Brisbane
O.D. BRISBANE & SONS

Marvlyn Estrado
KPB CHARTERED ACCOUNTANTS

F. Adler Hamlet
REALCO COMPANY LIMITED

Sandra Julien
*COMPANIES AND INTELLECTUAL PROPERTY
OFFICE*

Charlene Mae Magnaye
PwC ST. LUCIA

Severin McKenzie
*MCKENZIE ARCHITECTURAL &
CONSTRUCTION SERVICES INC.*

Richard Peterkin
PwC ST. LUCIA

Joan K.R. Prevost
PREVOST & ROBERTS

Eugene G. Royer
EUGENE G. ROYER CHARTERED ARCHITECT

Duncan G. Stowe
STOWE & CO.

Dawn Yearwood
YEARWOOD CHAMBERS

DOMINICAN REPUBLIC

Rhadys Abreu de Polanco
*UNION INTERNACIONAL DEL NOTARIADO
LATINO*

Cristian Alvarez
*RC ADVISORS, MEMBER OF RUSSELL
BEDFORD INTERNATIONAL*

Odalys Burgos
PwC DOMINICAN REPUBLIC

Ana Isabel Caceres
TRONCOSO Y CACERES

Giselle Castillo
SUPERINTENDENCIA DE BANCOS

Ramon Ceballos
*CEBALLOS & SÁNCHEZ, INGENIERÍA Y
ENERGÍA, C. POR A.*

Laureana Corral
DANNA CONSULTING

Mariano Corral
DANNA CONSULTING

Leandro Corral
ESTRELLA & TUPETE

José Cruz Campillo
JIMÉNEZ CRUZ PEÑA

Robinson Cuello Shanlatte
*PROGRAMA DE CONSOLIDACION DE
LA JURISDICCION INMOBILIARIA PODER
JUDICIAL*

Richard De la Cruz
*RC ADVISORS, MEMBER OF RUSSELL
BEDFORD INTERNATIONAL*

Marcos de Leon
SUPERINTENDENCIA DE BANCOS

Sarah de León Perelló
HEADRICK RIZIK ALVAREZ & FERNÁNDEZ

Raúl De Moya
ARQUITECTURA & PLANIFICACIÓN

Juan Carlos De Moya
GONZÁLEZ & COISCOU

Rosa Díaz
JIMÉNEZ CRUZ PEÑA

Ana Esther Dominguez
BIAGGI & MESSINA

Joaquín Guillermo Estrella Ramia
ESTRELLA & TUPETE

Alejandro Fernández de Castro
PwC DOMINICAN REPUBLIC

Mary Fernández Rodríguez
HEADRICK RIZIK ALVAREZ & FERNÁNDEZ

Jose Ernesto Garcia A.
TRANSGLOBAL LOGISTIC

Gloria Gasso
HEADRICK RIZIK ALVAREZ & FERNÁNDEZ

Jetti Gomez
BIAGGI & MESSINA

Pablo Gonzalez Tapia
GONZÁLEZ & COISCOU

Ralvin Gross
HEADRICK RIZIK ALVAREZ & FERNÁNDEZ

Luis Heredia Bonetti
RUSSIN & VECCHI, LLC.

María Elisa Holguín López
RUSSIN & VECCHI, LLC.

José Antonio Logroño Morales
ADAMS GUZMAN & LOGROÑO

José Ramón Logroño Morales
ADAMS GUZMAN & LOGROÑO

Annie Luna
*PELLERANO & HERRERA, MEMBER OF LEX
MUNDI*

Fernando Marranzini
HEADRICK RIZIK ALVAREZ & FERNÁNDEZ

Carlos Marte
AGENCIA DE COMERCIO EXTERIOR CM

Jesús Geraldo Martínez
SUPERINTENDENCIA DE BANCOS

Laura Medina
JIMÉNEZ CRUZ PEÑA

Fabiola Medina
MEDINA & RIZEK, ABOGADOS

Doris Miranda
GONZÁLEZ & COISCOU

Natia Núñez
HEADRICK RIZIK ALVAREZ & FERNÁNDEZ

Ramón Ortega
PwC DOMINICAN REPUBLIC

Andrea Paniagua
PwC DOMINICAN REPUBLIC

Luis R. Pellerano
PELLERANO & HERRERA, MEMBER OF LEX MUNDI

Carolina Pichardo
BIAGGI & MESSINA

Edward Piña Fernandez
BIAGGI & MESSINA

Julio Pinedo
PwC DOMINICAN REPUBLIC

Maria Portes
CASTILLO Y CASTILLO

Alejandro Miguel Ramirez Suzaña
RAMIREZ SUZAÑA & ASOC.

Nelson Rodriguez
GAMEI

Wendy Sánchez
TransUnion

Carolina Silié
HEADRICK RIZIK ALVAREZ & FERNÁNDEZ

Maricell Silvestre Rodriguez
JIMÉNEZ CRUZ PEÑA

Juan Tejada
PwC DOMINICAN REPUBLIC

Vilma Verras Terrero
JIMÉNEZ CRUZ PEÑA

Nathalie Vidal
GONZÁLEZ & COISCOU

Chery Zacarías
MEDINA & RIZEK, ABOGADOS

ECUADOR
ACREDITA BURÓ DE INFORMACIÓN CREDITICIA S.A.

EMPRESA ELÉCTRICA "QUITO" S.A.

Pablo Aguirre
PwC ECUADOR

Gerardo Aguirre
VIVANCO & VIVANCO

Natalia Almeida
PÉREZ, BUSTAMANTE Y PONCE, MEMBER OF LEX MUNDI

Xavier Bravo
SUPERINTENDENCIA DE BANCOS Y SEGUROS

Xavier Andrade Cadena
ANDRADE VELOZ & ASOCIADOS

Patricio Carrion

Pablo Chiriboga Dechiara
PUENTE REYES & GALARZA ATTORNEYS AT LAW CIA. LTDA.

Fernando Coral
PANALPINA WORLD TRANSPORT LLP

Lucía Cordero Ledergerber
FALCONI PUIG ABOGADOS

Renato Coronel
PINTO & GARCES ASOC. CIA LTDA, MEMBER OF RUSSELL BEDFORD INTERNATIONAL

Fernando Del Pozo Contreras
GALLEGOS, VALAREZO & NEIRA

Miguel Falconi-Puig
FALCONI PUIG ABOGADOS

Martin Galarza Lanas
PUENTE REYES & GALARZA ATTORNEYS AT LAW CIA. LTDA.

Leopoldo González R.
PAZ HOROWITZ ABOGADOS

Alvaro Jarrín
SUPERINTENDENCIA DE BANCOS Y SEGUROS

María Isabel Machado Tovar
FALCONI PUIG ABOGADOS

Juan Manuel Marchán
PÉREZ, BUSTAMANTE Y PONCE, MEMBER OF LEX MUNDI

Luis Marin-Tobar
PÉREZ, BUSTAMANTE Y PONCE, MEMBER OF LEX MUNDI

Sansone Massimiliano

Romina Meuti
PwC ECUADOR

Francisco Javier Naranjo Grijalva
PAZ HOROWITZ ABOGADOS

María Dolores Orbe
VIVANCO & VIVANCO

Esteban Ortiz
PÉREZ, BUSTAMANTE Y PONCE, MEMBER OF LEX MUNDI

Pablo Padilla Muirragui
ECUADOR CARGO SYSTEM

Jorge Paz Durini
PAZ HOROWITZ ABOGADOS

Bruno Pineda-Cordero
PÉREZ, BUSTAMANTE Y PONCE, MEMBER OF LEX MUNDI

Patricia Ponce Arteta
BUSTAMANTE & BUSTAMANTE

Juan Carlos Proaño
PANALPINA WORLD TRANSPORT LLP

Angel Alfonso Puente Reyes
PUENTE REYES & GALARZA ATTORNEYS AT LAW CIA. LTDA.

Juan Jose Puente Reyes
PUENTE REYES & GALARZA ATTORNEYS AT LAW CIA. LTDA.

Falconi Puig
FALCONI PUIG ABOGADOS

Sandra Reed
PÉREZ, BUSTAMANTE Y PONCE, MEMBER OF LEX MUNDI

Gustavo Romero
ROMERO ARTETA PONCE

Montserrat Sánchez
CORONEL Y PÉREZ

Michelle Semanate
FALCONI PUIG ABOGADOS

Leonardo Sempértegui
SEMPÉRTEGUI ONTANEDA

Esteban Alejandro Torres Valencia
PUENTE REYES & GALARZA ATTORNEYS AT LAW CIA. LTDA.

Ruth Urbano
SEMPÉRTEGUI ONTANEDA

EGYPT, ARAB REP.
TALAL ABU GHAZALEH LEGAL (TAG-LEGAL)

Abdel Aal Aly
AFIFI WORLD TRANSPORT ALEXANDRIA

Naguib Abadir
NACITA CORPORATION

Ghada Abdel Aziz
IBRACHY & DERMARKAR LAW FIRM

Sara Abdel Gabbar
NOUR LAW OFFICE, MANAGED BY TROWERS & HAMLINS

Ibrahim Mustafa Ibrahim Abdel Khalek
GENERAL AUTHORITY FOR INVESTMENT GAFI

Sayed Abuelkomsan
MINISTRY OF INDUSTRY AND FOREIGN TRADE

Nermine Abulata
MINISTRY OF INDUSTRY AND FOREIGN TRADE

Ghada Adel
PwC EGYPT

Shaimaa Ali
MINISTRY OF INDUSTRY AND FOREIGN TRADE

Osama Abd Al-Monem
MINISTRY OF INDUSTRY AND FOREIGN TRADE

Abdoul Karim Alpha Gado
GEREC-AFRIKIYA

Abd El Wahab Aly Ibrahim
ABD EL WAHAB SONS

Sarah Ammar
AL KAMEL LAW OFFICE

Sayed Ammar
AL KAMEL LAW OFFICE

Tim Armsby
NOUR LAW OFFICE, MANAGED BY TROWERS & HAMLINS

Khaled Balbaa
KPMG

Karim Dabbous
SHERIF DABBOUS, AUDITORS & FINANCIAL CONSULTANCIES, MEMBER OF RUSSELL BEDFORD INTERNATIONAL

Sherif Dabbous
SHERIF DABBOUS, AUDITORS & FINANCIAL CONSULTANCIES, MEMBER OF RUSSELL BEDFORD INTERNATIONAL

Sameh Dahroug
IBRACHY & DERMARKAR LAW FIRM

Abdallah El Adly
PwC EGYPT

Amany El Bagoury
AL KAMEL LAW OFFICE

Cherine El Dib
SHALAKANY LAW OFFICE, MEMBER OF LEX MUNDI

Ahmed El Gammal
SHALAKANY LAW OFFICE, MEMBER OF LEX MUNDI

Mohamed Refaat El Houshy
THE EGYPTIAN CREDIT BUREAU I-SCORE

Hassan El Maraashly
AAW CONSULTING ENGINEERS

Zienab El Oraby
SHALAKANY LAW OFFICE, MEMBER OF LEX MUNDI

Emad El Shalakany
SHALAKANY LAW OFFICE, MEMBER OF LEX MUNDI

Khaled El Shalakany
SHALAKANY LAW OFFICE, MEMBER OF LEX MUNDI

Sally El Shalakany
SHALAKANY LAW OFFICE, MEMBER OF LEX MUNDI

Passant El Tabei
PwC EGYPT

Soheir Elbanna
IBRACHY LAW FIRM

Samir El-Gammal
MINISTRY OF INDUSTRY AND FOREIGN TRADE

Ashraf Elibrachy
IBRACHY LAW FIRM

Sara Elmatbouly
NOUR LAW OFFICE, MANAGED BY TROWERS & HAMLINS

Rana Elnahal
IBRACHY LAW FIRM

Mostafa Elshafei
IBRACHY LAW FIRM

Amany Elwessal
MINISTRY OF INDUSTRY AND FOREIGN TRADE

Hassan Fahmy
MINISTRY OF INVESTMENT

Mariam Fahmy
SHALAKANY LAW OFFICE, MEMBER OF LEX MUNDI

Ghada Farouk
SHALAKANY LAW OFFICE, MEMBER OF LEX MUNDI

Tarek Gadallah
IBRACHY LAW FIRM

Ashraf Gamal El-Din
EGYPTIAN INSTITUTE OF DIRECTORS

Mahmoud Gamal El-Din
MINISTRY OF INDUSTRY AND FOREIGN TRADE

Dena Ghobashy
DLA MATOUK BASSIOUNY (PART OF DLA PIPER GROUP)

Zeinab Saieed Gohar
CENTRAL BANK OF EGYPT

Mohamed Gomaa Ali
MINISTRY OF INDUSTRY AND FOREIGN TRADE

Farah Ahmed Haggag
MINISTRY OF INDUSTRY AND FOREIGN TRADE

Mohamed Hashish
TELELAWS

Maha Hassan
AFIFI WORLD TRANSPORT ALEXANDRIA

Emad Hassan
MINISTRY OF STATE FOR ADMINISTRATIVE DEVELOPMENT

Tarek Hassib
AL KAMEL LAW OFFICE

Omneia Helmy
EGYPTIAN CENTER FOR ECONOMIC STUDIES

Mohamed Hisham Hassan
MINISTRY OF INVESTMENT

Mohamed Ibrahim
DLA MATOUK BASSIOUNY (PART OF DLA PIPER GROUP)

Badawi Ibrahim
MINISTRY OF INDUSTRY AND FOREIGN TRADE

Ahmed Ibrahim
NOUR LAW OFFICE, MANAGED BY TROWERS & HAMLINS

Stephan Jäger
AMERELLER RECHTSANWÄLTE

Mohamed Kamal
SHALAKANY LAW OFFICE, MEMBER OF LEX MUNDI

Mohamed Kamel
AL KAMEL LAW OFFICE

Shahira Khaled
AL KAMEL LAW OFFICE

Mohanad Khaled
BDO, KHALED & CO.

Taha Khaled
BDO, KHALED & CO.

Minas Khatchadourian
EGYPT LEGAL DESK

Adel Kheir
ADEL KHEIR LAW OFFICE

Mustafa Makram
BDO, KHALED & CO.

John Matouk
DLA MATOUK BASSIOUNY (PART OF DLA PIPER GROUP)

Mostafa Mostafa
AL KAMEL LAW OFFICE

Mostafa Mohamed Mostafa
AL KAMEL LAW OFFICE

Marwa Omara
TELELAWS

Alya Rady
MINISTRY OF INDUSTRY AND FOREIGN TRADE

Mohamed Ramadan
DLA MATOUK BASSIOUNY (PART OF DLA PIPER GROUP)

Ingy Rasekh
MENA ASSOCIATES, MEMBER OF AMERELLER RECHTSANWÄLTE

Menha Samy
IBRACHY & DERMARKAR LAW FIRM

Mohamed Serry
SERRY LAW OFFICE

Mohamed Shafik
MINISTRY OF INDUSTRY AND FOREIGN TRADE

Abdallah Shalash
ABDALLAH SHALASH & CO. (CHARTERED ACCOUNTANTS - TAX CONSULTANTS - BUSINESS ADVISORS)

Ramy Shalash
ABDALLAH SHALASH & CO. (CHARTERED ACCOUNTANTS - TAX CONSULTANTS - BUSINESS ADVISORS)

Abdelrahman Sherif
MENA ASSOCIATES, MEMBER OF AMERELLER RECHTSANWÄLTE

Omar Sherif
SHALAKANY LAW OFFICE, MEMBER OF LEX MUNDI

Adham Shetehy
AASTMT

Sharif Shihata
SHALAKANY LAW OFFICE, MEMBER OF LEX MUNDI

Frédéric Soliman
TELELAWS

Emile Tadros
TADROS & KHATCHADOURIAN LAW FIRM

Amira Thabet
SHERIF DABBOUS, AUDITORS & FINANCIAL CONSULTANCIES, MEMBER OF RUSSELL BEDFORD INTERNATIONAL

Randa Tharwat
NACITA CORPORATION

Tarek Zahran
AL KAMEL LAW OFFICE

Mona Zobaa
MINISTRY OF INVESTMENT

EL SALVADOR
Miguel Angel
ALE CARGO S.A. DE C.V.

Ana Margoth Arévalo
SUPERINTENDENCIA DEL SISTEMA FINANCIERO

Francisco Armando Arias Rivera
ARIAS & MUÑOZ

Irene Arrieta de Díaz Nuila
ARRIETA BUSTAMANTE

Francisco José Barrientos
AGUILAR CASTILLO LOVE

Abraham Bichara
AES EL SALVADOR

Carlos Roberto Alfaro Castillo
AGUILAR CASTILLO LOVE

Francesca Cedrola
PwC EL SALVADOR

Ricardo Cevallos
Consortium Centro América Abogados

Walter Chávez
Gold Service

David Claros
García & Bodán

Porfirio Diaz Fuentes
DLM, Abogados, Notarios & Consultores

Gabriel Dominguez
Rusconi, Medina & Asociados

Roberta Gallardo de Cromeyer
Arias & Muñoz

Carlos Hernán Gil
Lexincorp

Karla Guzmán Martinez
Arrieta Bustamante

Erwin Alexander Haas Quinteros
Rusconi, Medina & Asociados

Carlos Henriquez
Gold Service

America Hernandez
Ale Cargo S.A. de C.V.

Luis Lievano
Associacion de Ingenieros y Arquitectos

Thelma Dinora Lizama de Osorio
Superintendencia del Sistema Financiero

Jerson Lopez
Gold Service

Mario Lozano
Arias & Muñoz

Mónica Pineda Machuca

Fidel Márquez
Arias & Muñoz

Luis Alonso Medina Lopez
Rusconi, Medina & Asociados

Astrud María Meléndez
Asociación Protectora de Créditos de El Salvador (PROCREDITO)

Mauricio Melhado
Gold Service

Camilo Mena
Gold Service

Antonio R. Mendez Llort
Romero Pineda & Asociados, member of Lex Mundi

Edgar Mendoza
PwC Guatemala

Miriam Eleana Mixco Reyna
Gold Service

Jocelyn Mónico
Aguilar Castillo Love

Fernando Montano
Arias & Muñoz

Ramón Ortega
PwC Dominican Republic

Andrea Paniagua
PwC Dominican Republic

Jessica Margarita Pineda Machuca
ACZALAW

Jose Antonio Polanco
Lexincorp

Ana Patricia Portillo Reyes
Guandique Segovia Quintanilla

Hector Rios
Consortium Centro América Abogados

Emilio Rivera
PwC El Salvador

Flor de Maria Rodriguez
Arias & Muñoz

Roxana Romero
Romero Pineda & Asociados, member of Lex Mundi

Kelly Beatriz Romero
Rusconi, Medina & Asociados

Mario Enrique Sáenz
Sáenz & Asociados

Ana Guadalupe Sáenz Padilla
Sáenz & Asociados

Oscar Samour
Consortium Centro América Abogados

Alonso V. Saravia
Asociación Salvadoreña de Ingenieros y Arquitectos (ASIA)

Manuel Telles Suvillaga
Lexincorp

Oscar Torres
García & Bodán

María Alejandra Tulipano
Consortium Centro América Abogados

Mauricio Antonio Urrutia
Superintendencia del Sistema Financiero

Julio Vargas
García & Bodán

Juan Vásquez
Gold Service

Rene Velasquez
Arias & Muñoz

Luis Mario Villalta
Consortium Centro América Abogados

Ligia Villeda
Arrieta Bustamante

EQUATORIAL GUINEA

La Banque des Etats de l'Afrique Centrale

SEGESA (Sociedad de Electricidad de Guinea Ecuatorial)

Angel Mba Abeso
Centurion LLP

Gabriel Amugu
Interactivos GE

N.J. Ayuk
Centurion LLP

Eddy Garrigo
PricewaterhouseCoopers Tax & Legal SARL

Sébastien Lechêne
PricewaterhouseCoopers Tax & Legal SARL

Paulino Mbo Obama
Oficina de estudios - ATEG

François Münzer
PricewaterhouseCoopers Tax & Legal SARL

Maria Nchana
Centurion LLP

Gustavo Ndong Edu
Afri Logistics

Jacinto Ona
Centurion LLP

ERITREA

Berhane Woldu, with the support of *Ernst & Young*

Rahel Abera
Berhane Gila-Michael Law Firm

Senai Andemariam
University of Asmara

Tadesse Beraki

Biniam Fessehazion Ghebremichael
Eritrean Airlines

Tesfai Ghebrehiwet
Department of Energy

Berhane Gila-Michael
Berhane Gila-Michael Law Firm

Fessahaie Habte
Attorney-at-Law and Legal Consultant

Mulgheta Hailu
Teferi Berhane & Mulgheta Hailu Law Firm

Tekeste Mesghenna
MTD Enterprises PLC

Akberom Tedla
Chamber of Commerce

Isac Tesfazion

ESTONIA

Estonian Logistics and Freight Forwarding Association

Ott Aava
Attorneys at Law BORENIUS

Katrin Altmets
Law firm SORAINEN

Aet Bergmann
Law Office Bergmann

Mark Butzmann
BNT Klauberg Krauklis Advokaadibüroo

Jane Eespõld
Law firm SORAINEN

Indrek Ergma
Law Office Bergmann

Alger Ers
AE Projekti Insener

Diana Freivald
Ministry of Justice

Helen Ginter
Law firm SORAINEN

Heili Haabu
Attorneys at Law BORENIUS

Kristjan Hänni
Kawe Kapital

Pirkko-Liis Harkmaa
LAWIN

Triinu Hiob
LAWIN

Risto Hübner
Law Office Tark Grunte Sutkiene

Annika Jaanson
Attorneys at Law BORENIUS

Andres Juss
Estonian Land Board

Riina Käämer
Law Office Vares & Partnerid

Erica Kaldre
Hough, Hutt & Partners OU

Helerin Kaldvee
Raidla Lejins & Norcous

Aidi Kallavus
KPMG

Meelis Kaps
Eesti Energia Jaotusvõrk OÜ (Distribution Grid)

Kadri-Catre Kasak
Ministry of Justice

Kersti Kerstna-Vaks
Tartu County Court

Kilvar Kessler
Law Office Tark Grunte Sutkiene

Gerli Kilusk
LAWIN

Igor Kostjuk
Hough, Hutt & Partners OU

Villu Kõve
Estonian Supreme Court

Ksenia Kravtshenko
Law Office Vares & Partnerid

Tanja Kriisa
PwC Estonia

Paul Künnap
Law firm SORAINEN

Timo Kullerkupp
MAQS Law Firm

Piia Kulm
Lextal Law Office

Peeter Kutman
Attorneys at Law BORENIUS

Priit Lepasepp
Law firm SORAINEN

Erik Lepik
LAWIN

Gerda Liik
Raidla Lejins & Norcous

Liina Linsi
LAWIN

Karin Madisson
Law firm SORAINEN

Mart Maidla
Eesti Energia Jaotusvõrk OÜ (Distribution Grid)

Olger Marjak
Law Office Tark Grunte Sutkiene

Marko Mehilane
LAWIN

Veiko Meos
Krediidiinfo A.S.

Jaanus Mody
Attorneys at Law BORENIUS

Margus Mugu
Attorneys at Law BORENIUS

Arne Ots
Raidla Lejins & Norcous

Karina Paatsi
Attorneys at Law BORENIUS

Priit Pahapill
Attorneys at Law BORENIUS

Sven Papp
Raidla Lejins & Norcous

Evelin Pärn-Lee
MAQS Law Firm

Kirsti Pent
Law Office Tark Grunte Sutkiene

Leho Pihkva
Law firm SORAINEN

Tiina Pukk
Lextal Law Office

Kristiina Puuste
KPMG

Kaidi Reiljan-Sihvart
LAWIN

Dmitri Rozenblat
LAWIN

Merle Saaliste
Law firm SORAINEN

Piret Saartee

Katrin Sarap
MAQS Law Firm

Martin Simovart
LAWIN

Monika Tamm
LAWIN

Tarvi Thomberg
Eesti Energia Jaotusvõrk OÜ (Distribution Grid)

Holger Tilk
LAWIN

Villi Tõntson
PwC Estonia

Triin Toomemets
Law firm SORAINEN

Veiko Toomere
MAQS Law Firm

Karolina Ullmann
MAQS Law Firm

Neve Uudelt
Raidla Lejins & Norcous

Ingmar Vali
Registrite ja infosüsteemide Keskus

Aleksander Vares
Law Office Vares & Partnerid

Mirjam Vili
BNT Klauberg Krauklis Advokaadibüroo

Ago Vilu
PwC Estonia

Vesse Võhma
LAWIN

Urmas Volens
Law firm SORAINEN

Joel Zernask
KPMG

ETHIOPIA

Ernst & Young

Woubishet Amanuel
Bete Sam PLC

Nassir Jemal Amdehun
Amdehun General Trading

Bekure Assefa
Bekure Assefa Law Office

Teshome Gabre-Mariam Bokan
Teshome Gabre-Mariam Law Firm

Tesfaye Dagnachew
Dagnachew Tesfaye Law Office

Teferra Demiss
Legal and Insurance Consultant and Attorney

Solomon Desta
National Bank of Ethiopia

Berhane Ghebray
Berhane Ghebray & Associates

Zekarias Keneaa
Addis Ababa University

Taddesse Lencho
Addis Ababa University

Molla Mengistu
Addis Ababa University

Belachew Moges
EEPCo.

Hailye Sahle Seifu
Attorney-at-Law

Eyasu Tequame
Jehoiachin Techno Pvt. Ltd. Co.

Elias Tesfaye
National Bank of Ethiopia

Amanuel Teshome
Aman & Partners

Meheret Tewodros
Addis Ababa University

Shimelis Tilahun
Net Consult

Abuye Tsehay
University of Trento

Merga Wakweya
National Bank of Ethiopia

FIJI

Ernst & Young

David Aidney
Williams & Gosling Ltd.

Caroll Sela Ali
Cromptons Solicitors

Eddielin Almonte
PwC Fiji

Lisa Apted
KPMG

Jon Apted
Munro Leys

Nehla Basawaiya
Munro Leys

Mahendra Chand
Munro Leys

Jeremy Chang
Suva City Council

William Wylie Clarke
Howards Lawyers

Delores Elliott

Isireli Fa
The Fiji Law Society / FA & Company Barristers & Solicitors

Vamarasi Faktaufon
Q. B. Bale & Associates

Florence Fenton
Munro Leys

Dilip Jamnadas
Jamnadas and Associates

Jerome Kado
PwC Fiji

Viren Kapadia
Sherani & Co.

Releshni Karan
Mishra Prakash & Associates

Usenia Losalini
Ministry of Justice

Paul McDonnell
Cromptons Solicitors

Richard Naidu
Munro Leys

Anuleshni Neelum Neelta
Neelta Law

Jon Orton
Orton Architects

Pradeep Patel
PKF International

Ramesh Prakash
Mishra Prakash & Associates

Ramesh Prasad Lal
Carpenters Shipping

Colin Radford
Larsen Holten Maybin & Company Ltd.

Abhi Ram
Companies Registrar

Varun Shandil
Munro Leys

Shelvin Singh
Parshotam & Co.

James Sloan
Siwatibau & Sloan

Narotam Solanki
PwC Fiji

Shayne Sorby
Munro Leys

Mark Swamy
Larsen Holten Maybin & Company Ltd.

Eparama Tawake
FEA (Fiji electricity authority)

Vulisere Tukama
Suva City Council

Chirk Yam
PwC Fiji

Eddie Yuen
Williams & Gosling Ltd.

FINLAND

Markku Aaltonen
Confederation of Finnish Construction Industries

Ville Ahtola
Castrén & Snellman Attorneys Ltd.

Mikko Äijälä
Krogerus Attorneys Ltd.

Manne Airaksinen
Roschier Attorneys Ltd., member of Lex Mundi

Tuomo Åvall
Wabuco Oy, member of Russell Bedford International

Kasper Björkstén
Helen Sähköverkko Oy

Claudio Busi
Castrén & Snellman Attorneys Ltd.

Marja Eskola
PwC Finland

Johannes Frände
Roschier Attorneys Ltd., member of Lex Mundi

Esa Halmari
Hedman Partners

Pekka Halme

Johanna Haltia-Tapio
Hannes Snellman LLC

Joni Hatanmaa
Hedman Partners

Berndt Heikel
Hannes Snellman LLC

Leenamaija Heinonen
Roschier Attorneys Ltd., member of Lex Mundi

Harri Hirvonen
PwC Finland

Jani Hovila
Hannes Snellman LLC

Mia Hukkinen
Roschier Attorneys Ltd., member of Lex Mundi

Nina Isokorpi
Roschier Attorneys Ltd., member of Lex Mundi

Pekka Jaatinen
Castrén & Snellman Attorneys Ltd.

Nina Järvinen
Cargoworld Ab/Oy

Juuso Jokela
Suomen Asiakastieto Oy

Tanja Jussila
Waselius & Wist

Sakari Kauppinen
National Board of Patents & Registration

Aki Kauppinen
Roschier Attorneys Ltd., member of Lex Mundi

Antti Kivipuro
Energy Market Authority

Gisela Knuts
Roschier Attorneys Ltd., member of Lex Mundi

Markku Korvenmaa
HH Partners, Attorneys-at-law Ltd.

Arto Kukkonen
HH Partners, Attorneys-at-law Ltd.

Jouni Lehtinen
Helen Sähköverkko Oy

Tiina Leppälahti
Helen Sähköverkko Oy

Jan Lilius
Hannes Snellman LLC

Patrik Lindfors
Lindfors & Co., Attorneys-at-Law Ltd.

Risto Löf
PwC Finland

Tuomas Lukkarinen
National Land Survey of Finland

Anna Lumijärvi
Krogerus Attorneys Ltd.

Jyri Makela
Confederation of Finnish Construction Industries

Kimmo Mettälä
Krogerus Attorneys Ltd.

Ville Mykkänen
Wabuco Oy, member of Russell Bedford International

Emma Niemistö
Castrén & Snellman Attorneys Ltd.

Linda Nyman
Waselius & Wist

Ilona Paakkala
PwC Finland

Laura Peltonen
PwC Finland

Elina Pesonen
Castrén & Snellman Attorneys Ltd.

Ilkka Pesonen
Wabuco Oy, member of Russell Bedford International

Markku Pulkkinen
Hedman Partners

Mikko Reinikainen
PwC Finland

Veli-Pekka Saajo
Energy Market Authority

Petri Taivalkoski
Roschier Attorneys Ltd., member of Lex Mundi

Seija Vartiainen
PwC Finland

Helena Viita
Roschier Attorneys Ltd., member of Lex Mundi

Anna Vuori
Hedman Partners

Marko Vuori
Krogerus Attorneys Ltd.

Christoffer Waselius
Waselius & Wist

Gunnar Westerlund
Roschier Attorneys Ltd., member of Lex Mundi

Kai Wist
PwC Finland

FRANCE
Allen & Overy LLP

Brémond & Associés

Anne Antoni
Gide Loyrette Nouel A.A.R.P.I., member of Lex Mundi

Nicolas Barberis
Ashurst

Andrew Booth
Andrew Booth Architect

Guillaume Bordier
Capstan

Franck Buffaud
Delsol Avocats

Stèphanie Chatelon
Taj, member of Deloitte Touche Tohmatsu Limited

Frédérique Chifflot Bourgeois
Lawyer at the Bar of Paris

Michel Combe
Landwell & Associés

Raphaëlle de Ruffi de Pontevès
Landwell & Associés

Nicolas Deshayes
AJAssociés

Olivier Everaere
Agence Epure SARL

Benoit Fauvelet
Banque de France

Ingrid Fauvelière
Gide Loyrette Nouel A.A.R.P.I., member of Lex Mundi

Sylvie Ghesquiere
Banque de France

Kevin Grossmann
Mayer Brown

Philippe Guibert
FIEEC

Sabrina Henocq
Delsol Avocats

Marc Jobert
Jobert & Associés

Carol Khoury
Jones Day

Daniel Arthur Laprès
Cabinet d'Avocats

Julien Maire du Poset
Smith Violet

Jean-Louis Martin
Jones Day

Nathalie Morel
Mayer Brown

Jerome Orsel
Schenker

Arnaud Pèdron
Taj, member of Deloitte Touche Tohmatsu Limited

Arnaud Pelpel
Pelpel Avocats

Caroline Poncelet
Mayer Brown

Hugues Roux
Banque de France

Carole Sabbah
Mayer Brown

Pierre-Nicolas Sanzey
Herbert Smith Paris LLP

Isabelle Smith Monnerville
Smith Violet

Agnes Soizic
Ashurst

Camille Sparfel
Capstan

Caroline Stéphane
Delsol Avocats

Jean Luc Vallens
Cour d'appel de Colmar

Philippe Xavier-Bender
Gide Loyrette Nouel A.A.R.P.I., member of Lex Mundi

Claire Zuliani
Transparence, a member of Russell Bedford International

GABON
La Banque des Etats de l'Afrique Centrale

Notary

Marcellin Massila Akendengue
SEEG, Société d'Energie et d'Eau du Gabon

Gianni Ardizzone
SATRAM

Marie Carmel Ketty Ayimambenwe
Banque Internationale pour le Commerce et l'Industrie du Gabon

Albert Bikalou
Etude Bikalou

Benoît Boulikou
SEEG, Société d'Energie et d'Eau du Gabon

Daniel Chevallon
Matelec

Gilbert Erangah
Etude Maître Erangah

Augustin Fang

Michael Jeannot
Matelec

Pélagie Massamba Mouckocko
PricewaterhouseCoopers Tax & Legal SA

Jean Mbagou
Banque Internationale pour le Commerce et l'Industrie du Gabon

Jean-Joel Mebaley
Destiny Executives Architects - Agence du Bord de Mer

Célestin Ndelia
Etude Maître Ndelia Célestin

Ruben Mindonga Ndongo
Cabinet Me Anguiler

Thierry Ngomo
ArchiPro International

Lubin Ntoutoume
Avocat

Josette Cadie Olendo

Marie-Jose Ongo Mendou
Business Consulting

Laurent Pommera
PricewaterhouseCoopers Tax & Legal SA

Christophe A. Relongoué
PricewaterhouseCoopers Tax & Legal SA

Yala Tchimbakala
Etude Bikalou

GAMBIA, THE

Gideon Ayi-Owoo
PwC Ghana

Christiana Baah
PwC Ghana

Alpha Amadou Barry
DT Associates, Independent Correspondence Firm of Deloitte Touche Tohmatsu Limited

Amie N.D. Bensouda
Amie Bensouda & Co.

Abdul Aziz Bensouda

Bakary Demba
Gambia Shipping Agencies

Ida Denise Drameh
Ida D. Drameh & Associates

Abdul Aleem Faye
Gambia Shipping Agencies

Jon Goldy
Amie Bensouda & Co.

Cherno Alieu Jallow
DT Associates, Independent Correspondence Firm of Deloitte Touche Tohmatsu Limited

Alhaji Jallow
National Water and Electricity Company Ltd.

Lamin S. Jatta
DT Associates, Independent Correspondence Firm of Deloitte Touche Tohmatsu Limited

Sulayman M. Joof
S.M. Joof Agency

Nani Juwara
National Water and Electricity Company Ltd.

Lamin Keita
Msita Enterprise

Mary Kwarteng
PwC Ghana

George Kwatia
PwC Ghana

Prossie Namakula
PwC Ghana

Omar Njie
Law Firm Omar Njie

Miriam Nortey
PwC Ghana

Mary Abdoulie Samba-Christensen
LEGAL PRACTITIONER

Hawa Sisay-Sabally
LAWYER

Salieu Taal
TEMPLE LEGAL PRACTITIONERS

Darcy White
PwC GHANA

GEORGIA

Mushfig Aliyev
PwC AZERBAIJAN

Natalia Babakishvili
MGALOBLISHVILI, KIPIANI, DZIDZIGURI (MKD) LAW FIRM

Niko Bakashvilli
AUDITORIAL FIRM BAKASHVILI & CO.

Zaza Bibilashvili
BGI LEGAL

Temur Bolotashvili
USAID ECONOMIC PROSPERITY INITIATIVE

Kakha Damenia
GDC SOLUTIONS

Lasha Gogiberidze
BGI LEGAL

Mamuka Gordeziani
ITM GLOBAL LOGISTICS

Bela Gutidze
GDC SOLUTIONS

Irakli Gvilia
ALLIANCE GROUP HOLDING

Gia Jandieri
NEW ECONOMIC SCHOOL - GEORGIA

Revaz Javelidze
GRATA GEORGIA LLC

Aleksandre Kacharava
CHANCELLERY OF THE GOVERNMENT OF GEORGIA

David Kakabadze

Grigol Kakauridze
MINISTRY OF ECONOMIC DEVELOPMENT GEORGIA

Mari Khardziani
NATIONAL AGENCY OF PUBLIC REGISTRY

Victor Kipiani
MGALOBLISHVILI, KIPIANI, DZIDZIGURI (MKD) LAW FIRM

Anastasia Kipiani
PwC GEORGIA

Koba Koakhidze
JSC CREDIT INFO GEORGIA

Sergi Kobakhidze
PwC GEORGIA

Aieti Kukava
ALLIANCE GROUP HOLDING

Vakhtang Lejava
CHANCELLERY OF THE GOVERNMENT OF GEORGIA

Nino Lortkipanidze
PwC GEORGIA

Vano Mechurchishvili
GEORGIA NATIONAL ENERGY AND WATER SUPPLY REGULATORY COMMISSION

Ekaterina Meskhidze
NATIONAL AGENCY OF PUBLIC REGISTRY

Kakhaber Nariashvili

Merab Narmania
CHANCELLERY OF THE GOVERNMENT OF GEORGIA

Vachtang Okreshidze
GEORGIA NATIONAL ENERGY AND WATER SUPPLY REGULATORY COMMISSION

Maia Okruashvili
GEORGIAN LEGAL PARTNERSHIP

Vakhtang Paresishvili
DLA PIPER GEORGIA LP

Tinatin Petriashvili
MGALOBLISHVILI, KIPIANI, DZIDZIGURI (MKD) LAW FIRM

Irakli Pipia
DLA PIPER GEORGIA LP

Joseph Salukvadze
TBILISI STATE UNIVERSITY

Natia Samushia
CHANCELLERY OF THE GOVERNMENT OF GEORGIA

Manzoor Shah
GLOBALINK LOGISTICS GROUP

Vakhtang Shevardnadze
MGALOBLISHVILI, KIPIANI, DZIDZIGURI (MKD) LAW FIRM

Manana Shurghulaia
AGENCY FOR FREE TRADE AND COMPETITION

Eka Siradze
GRATA GEORGIA LLC

Rusa Sreseli
GDC SOLUTIONS

Avto Svanidze
DLA PIPER GEORGIA LP

Anna Tabidze
MGALOBLISHVILI, KIPIANI, DZIDZIGURI (MKD) LAW FIRM

Altaf Tapia
PwC GEORGIA

Tamara Tevdoradze
BGI LEGAL

Tato Urjumelashvili
STATE PROCUREMENT AGENCY

GERMANY

SENATSVERWALTUNG FÜR STADTENTWICKLUNG BERLIN

Bassem Al Abed
GRAF VON WESTPHALEN INSOLVENZVERWALTUNG UND SANIERUNG

Friedhold E. Andreas
FREILING, ANDREAS & PARTNER

Stephan Bank
CLEARY GOTTLIEB STEEN & HAMILTON LLP

Henning Berger
WHITE & CASE

Jennifer Bierly
GSK STOCKMANN + KOLLEGEN

Joerg Boehmer

Arnd Böken
GRAF VON WESTPHALEN INSOLVENZVERWALTUNG UND SANIERUNG

Cord-Henning Brandes
GRAF VON WESTPHALEN INSOLVENZVERWALTUNG UND SANIERUNG

Thomas Büssow
PwC GERMANY

Lorenz Czajka
GRAF VON WESTPHALEN INSOLVENZVERWALTUNG UND SANIERUNG

Helge Dammann
PRICEWATERHOUSECOOPERS LEGAL AKTIENGESELLSCHAFT RECHTSANWALTSGESELLSCHAFT

Stefan Ditsch
PwC GERMANY

Dieter Endres
PwC GERMANY

Shahzadi Firdous
GRAF VON WESTPHALEN INSOLVENZVERWALTUNG UND SANIERUNG

Peter Fissenewert
BUSE HEBERER FROMM

Alexander Freiherr von Aretin
GRAF VON WESTPHALEN INSOLVENZVERWALTUNG UND SANIERUNG

Björn Gaul
CMS HASCHE SIGLE

Markus J. Goetzmann
C·B·H RECHTSANWÄLTE

Andrea Gruss
MERGET + PARTNER

Klaus Günther
OPPENHOFF & PARTNER

Henrich C. Heggemann
GRAF VON WESTPHALEN INSOLVENZVERWALTUNG UND SANIERUNG

Ilka Heinemeyer
SJ BERWIN LLP

Manfred Heinrich
DEUTSCHE BUNDESBANK

Silvanne Helle
OPPENHOFF & PARTNER

Götz-Sebastian Hök
DR. HÖK STIEGLMEIER & PARTNER

Peter Holzhäuser
PRICEWATERHOUSECOOPERS LEGAL AKTIENGESELLSCHAFT RECHTSANWALTSGESELLSCHAFT

Markus Jakoby
JAKOBY RECHTSANWÄLTE

Christof Kautzsch
SALANS

Henrik Kirchhoff
LATHAM & WATKINS LLP

Britta Klatte
SCHUFA HOLDING AG

Johann Klein
BEEH & HAPPICH GMBH WIRTSCHAFTSPRÜFUNGSGESELLSCHAFT STEUERBERATUNGSGESELLSCHAFT, MEMBER OF RUSSELL BEDFORD INTERNATIONAL

Jörg Kraffel
WHITE & CASE

Holger Kühl
GRAF VON WESTPHALEN INSOLVENZVERWALTUNG UND SANIERUNG

Carsten Liersch
GRAF VON WESTPHALEN INSOLVENZVERWALTUNG UND SANIERUNG

Peter Limmer
NOTARE DR. LIMMER & DR. FRIEDERICH

Frank Lohrmann
CLEARY GOTTLIEB STEEN & HAMILTON LLP

Cornelia Marquardt
NORTON ROSE

Jan Geert Meents
DLA PIPER UK LLP

Dirk Meyer-Claassen
SENATSVERWALTUNG FÜR STADTENTWICKLUNG BERLIN

Thomas Miller
KROHN RECHTSANWÄLTE

Peter Mussaeus
PRICEWATERHOUSECOOPERS LEGAL AKTIENGESELLSCHAFT RECHTSANWALTSGESELLSCHAFT

Eike Najork
C·B·H RECHTSANWÄLTE

Wolfgang Nardi
KIRKLAND & ELLIS LLP GERMANY MUNICH

Dirk Otto
NORTON ROSE LLP

Laura Pfirrmann
CLEARY GOTTLIEB STEEN & HAMILTON LLP

Peter Polke
CLEARY GOTTLIEB STEEN & HAMILTON LLP

Sebastian Prügel
WHITE & CASE

Jörn Radloff
PRICEWATERHOUSECOOPERS LEGAL AKTIENGESELLSCHAFT RECHTSANWALTSGESELLSCHAFT

Michael Rinas
PRICEWATERHOUSECOOPERS LEGAL AKTIENGESELLSCHAFT RECHTSANWALTSGESELLSCHAFT

Michael Roemer
VATTENFALL EUROPE DISTRIBUTION HAMBURG GMBH

Christoph Schauenburg
CLEARY GOTTLIEB STEEN & HAMILTON LLP

Ulrich Schroeder
GRAF VON WESTPHALEN INSOLVENZVERWALTUNG UND SANIERUNG

Thomas Schulz
NÖRR STIEFENHOFER LUTZ, MEMBER OF LEX MUNDI

Kirstin Schwedt
LINKLATERS LLP

Ingrid Seitz
DEUTSCHE BUNDESBANK

Hyeon-Won Song
PwC GERMANY

Kai Sebastian Staak
PRICEWATERHOUSECOOPERS LEGAL AKTIENGESELLSCHAFT RECHTSANWALTSGESELLSCHAFT

Susanne Stellbrink
PwC GERMANY

Dirk Stiller
PRICEWATERHOUSECOOPERS LEGAL AKTIENGESELLSCHAFT RECHTSANWALTSGESELLSCHAFT

Dieter Straub

Tobias Taetzner
PwC GERMANY

Nora Thies
GRAF VON WESTPHALEN INSOLVENZVERWALTUNG UND SANIERUNG

Holger Thomas
SJ BERWIN LLP

Matthias Thorns
BDA | CONFEDERATION OF GERMAN EMPLOYERS

Arne Vogel
PRICEWATERHOUSECOOPERS LEGAL AKTIENGESELLSCHAFT RECHTSANWALTSGESELLSCHAFT

Heiko Vogt
PANALPINA WELTTRANSPORT GMBH

Annekatren Werthmann-Feldhues
PRICEWATERHOUSECOOPERS LEGAL AKTIENGESELLSCHAFT RECHTSANWALTSGESELLSCHAFT

Gerlind Wisskirchen
CMS HASCHE SIGLE

Uwe Witt
PRICEWATERHOUSECOOPERS LEGAL AKTIENGESELLSCHAFT RECHTSANWALTSGESELLSCHAFT

Christian Zeissler
C·B·H RECHTSANWÄLTE

GHANA

Samuel Abbiaw
ANDAH AND ANDAH CHARTERED ACCOUNTANTS

George K. Acquah
LARYEA, LARYEA & CO. P.C.

Larry Adjetey
LAW TRUST COMPANY

Stephen N. Adu
PUBLIC UTILITIES REGULATORY COMMISSION OF GHANA

George Ahiafor
XDSDATA GHANA LTD.

Brigitte Ainuson
AB LEXMALL & ASSOCIATES

Kwesi Ainuson
KGA EXCELLENCE CONSULT

Kweku Ainuson
MISSISSIPPI STATE UNIVERSITY

Godwin Prince Amartey
ANDAH AND ANDAH CHARTERED ACCOUNTANTS

Nene Amegatcher
SAM OKUDZETO & ASSOCIATES

Kennedy Paschal Anaba
LAWFIELDS CONSULTING

Kweku Brebu Andah
ANDAH AND ANDAH CHARTERED ACCOUNTANTS

Wilfred Kwabena Anim-Odame
LAND COMMISSION

Adwoa S. Asamoah-Addo
LAWFIELDS CONSULTING

Fred Asiamah-Koranteng
BANK OF GHANA

Elsie A. Awadzi
LAWFIELDS CONSULTING

Gideon Ayi-Owoo
PwC GHANA

Christiana Baah
PwC GHANA

Rachel Baddoo
LARYEA, LARYEA & CO. P.C.

Ellen Bannerman
BRUCE-LYLE BANNERMAN & ASSOCIATES

Reginald Bannerman
BRUCE-LYLE BANNERMAN & ASSOCIATES

Kojo Bentsi-Enchill
BENTSI-ENCHILL, LETSA & ANKOMAH, MEMBER OF LEX MUNDI

Joe Biney
BAJ FREIGHT & LOGISTICS

Binditi Chitor
AB LEXMALL & ASSOCIATES

Nana Ato Dadzie
AB LEXMALL & ASSOCIATES

Ras Afful Davis
CLIMATE SHIPPING & TRADING

Appiah Densu
APDCONSULT GHANA LTD.

Emmanuel Dorsu
TOWN AND COUNTRY PLANNING DEPT

Clifford Gershon Fiadjoe
ANDAH AND ANDAH CHARTERED ACCOUNTANTS

Emmanuel Fiati
PUBLIC UTILITIES REGULATORY COMMISSION OF GHANA

Angela Gyasi
BENTSI-ENCHILL, LETSA & ANKOMAH, MEMBER OF LEX MUNDI

Adam Imoru-Ayarna
SAFMARINE CONTAINER LINES

Cynthia Jumu
BEYUO JUMU & CO.

Farida Karim
CROWN AGENTS LTD.

Dorothy Kingsley Nyinah
COMMERCIAL DIVISION, HIGH COURT

Emmanuel Kissi-Boateng
PUBLIC UTILITIES REGULATORY COMMISSION OF GHANA

Rosa Kudoadzi
BENTSI-ENCHILL, LETSA & ANKOMAH, MEMBER OF LEX MUNDI

Mary Kwarteng
PwC GHANA

Emmanuel Manu
LAW TRUST COMPANY

Prossie Namakula
PwC GHANA

Miriam Nortey
PwC GHANA

Woodsworth Odame Larbi
Lands Commission

Akosua Poku
Bentsi-Enchill, Letsa & Ankomah, member of Lex Mundi

Jacob Saah
Saah & Co.

Marc Tankam

Darcy White
PwC Ghana

GREECE

George Apostolakos
Apostolakos Architects

Ioanna Argyraki
Kyriakides Georgopoulos & Daniolos Issaias Law Firm

Antonis Bavas
Stephenson Harwood, Piraeus

Marilena Bellou
Drakopoulos Law Firm

Stefanos Charaktiniotis
Zepos & Yannopoulos Law Firm, member of Lex Mundi

Ira Charisiadou
Charisiadou Law Office

Alkistis - Marina Christofilou
IKRP Rokas & Partners

Sotiris Constantinou
Grant Thornton LLP

Theodora D. Karagiorgou
Koutalidis Law Firm

Nikos Daskalakis
Hellenic Confederation of Professionals, Craftsmen and Merchants

Eleni Dikonimaki
Teiresias S.A. Interbanking Information Systems

Panagiotis Drakopoulos
Drakopoulos Law Firm

Anastasia Dritsa
Kyriakides Georgopoulos & Daniolos Issaias Law Firm

Margarita Flerianou
Economou International Shipping Agencies

Sotiris Gioussios
Grant Thornton LLP

Yanos Gramatidis
Bahas, Gramatidis & Partners

Marinela Kampadelli

Vanessa Kapnoutzi
M & P Bernitsas Law Offices

Evangelos Karaindros
Evangelos Karaindros Law Firm

Artemis Karathanassi
PwC Greece

Constantine Karydis
PwC Greece

Nikos Klironomos
MaritimeSun

Alexandra Kondyli
Karatzas & Partners

Nicholas Kontizas
Zepos & Yannopoulos Law Firm, member of Lex Mundi

Panos Koromantzos
Bahas, Gramatidis & Partners

Olga Koromilia
PwC Greece

Yannis Kourniotis
M & P Bernitsas Law Offices

Dimitrios Kremalis L.L.M
Kremalis Law Firm, member of Ius Laboris

Christina Lampropoulou
PotamitisVekris

Vassiliki G. Lazarakou
Zepos & Yannopoulos Law Firm, member of Lex Mundi

Konstantinos Logaras
Zepos & Yannopoulos Law Firm, member of Lex Mundi

Evangelia Martinovits
IKRP Rokas & Partners

Panorea Mastora
Kremalis Law Firm, member of Ius Laboris

Emmanuel Mastromanolis
Zepos & Yannopoulos Law Firm, member of Lex Mundi

Margarita Matsi
Kelemenis & Co.

John Mazarakos
Elias Paraskevas Attorneys 1933

Makariou Panagiota
Grant Thornton LLP

Panayis Panagiotopoulos
Kremmydas-Doris & Associates Law Firm

Elena Papachristou
Zepos & Yannopoulos Law Firm, member of Lex Mundi

Eleftheria Papakanellou
Intersea Container Services

Dimitris E. Paraskevas
Elias Paraskevas Attorneys 1933

Michalis Pattakos
Zepos & Yannopoulos Law Firm, member of Lex Mundi

Katerina Politi
Kyriakides Georgopoulos & Daniolos Issaias Law Firm

Chryssiis Poulakou
Kyriakides Georgopoulos & Daniolos Issaias Law Firm

Mary Psylla
PwC Greece

Sofia Pyriochou
Kremalis Law Firm, member of Ius Laboris

Vasiliki Salaka
Karatzas & Partners

Constantine Sarantis
Zepos & Yannopoulos Law Firm, member of Lex Mundi

Anastasia Stamou
Athens Exchange SA

Nehtarios Stefanidis
Nehtarius

Alexia Stratou
Kremalis Law Firm, member of Ius Laboris

Fotini Trigazi
Notary

John Tripidakis
John M. Tripidakis and Associates

Antonios Tsavdaridis
IKRP Rokas & Partners

Ioannis Vekris
PotamitisVekris

Kalliopi Vlachopoulou
Kelemenis & Co.

Sofia Xanthoulea
John M. Tripidakis and Associates

Vicky Xourafa
Kyriakides Georgopoulos & Daniolos Issaias Law Firm

Fredy Yatracou
PwC Greece

GRENADA

Danny Williams & Co.

W.R. Agostini
Agostini W.R. Fcca

James Bristol
Henry, Henry & Bristol

Thaddus Charles
Inland Revenue Department

Christopher DeRiggs
Ministry of Finance, Planning, Economy, Energy, Foreign Trade & Co-operatives

Richard W. Duncan
Grenada Co-operative Bank Limited

Ruggles Ferguson
Ciboney Chambers

Keisha Greenidge
Grenada Co-operative Bank Limited

Annette Henry
Ministry of Legal Affairs

Winston Hosten
Hosten's (Electrical Services) Ltd

Kelvin Jacobs
Creative Design

Claudette Joseph
Amicus Attorneys

Henry Joseph
PKF International

Michell Julien
Ministry of Finance, Planning, Economy, Energy, Foreign Trade & Co-operatives

Kurt LaBarrie
Creative Design

Sonia Roden
Grenada Industrial Development Corporation

Ian H. Sandy
Amicus Attorneys

Valentino Sawney
Tradship International

David Sinclair
Sinclair Enterprises Limited

Trevor St. Bernard
Lewis & Renwick

Phinsley St. Louis
St. Louis Service

Lisa Telesford
Supreme Court Registry

GUATEMALA

Empresa Eléctrica de Guatemala, S. A.

Ernst & Young

Gabriella Aguirre
Consortium - RACSA

Pedro Aragón
Aragón & Aragón

Mario R. Archila Cruz
Consortium - RACSA

Oscar Arriaga
Comisión Nacional de Energía Eléctrica

Elias Arriaza
Consortium - RACSA

Ruby María Asturias Castillo
ACZALAW

María de los Angeles Barillas Buchhalter
Saravia & Muñoz

Amaury Barrera
DHV Consultants

Jorge Rolando Barrios
Bonilla, Montano, Toriello & Barrios

Julio Roberto Berduo
Palacios & Asociados

Mario Adolfo Búcaro Flores
Díaz-Durán & Asociados Central Law

Eva Cacacho González
Quiñones, Ibargüen, Luján & Mata, S.C.

Rodrigo Callejas Aquino
Carrillo & Asociados

José Alfredo Cándido Durón
Superintendencia de Bancos

Juan Pablo Carrasco de Groote
Díaz-Durán & Asociados Central Law

Francisco José Castillo Chacón
Castillo Love Abogados

Juan Carlos Castillo Chacón
Castillo Love Abogados

Paola van der Beek de Andrino
Cámara Guatemalteca de la Construcción

Fanny de Estrada
Asociación Guatemalteca de Exportadores

Karla de Mata
CPS Logistics

Cristóbal Fernández
Mayora & Mayora S.C.

Walter Figueroa
Cámara Guatemalteca de la Construcción

Hugo Daniel Figueroa Estrada
Superintendencia de Bancos

Lorena Flores Estrada
Díaz-Durán & Asociados Central Law

Rodolfo Fuentes
Protectora de Crédito Comercial

Rafael Garavito
Bufete Garavito

Wendy Garcia
Russell Bedford Guatemala García Sierra Y Asociados, S.C., member of Russell Bedford International

Oscar Ernesto Garcia Sierra
Russell Bedford Guatemala García Sierra Y Asociados, S.C., member of Russell Bedford International

Raúl Stuardo Juárez Leal
Superintendencia de Bancos

Christian Lanuza
Díaz-Durán & Asociados Central Law

María Isabel Luján Zilbermann
Quiñones, Ibargüen, Luján & Mata, S.C.

Víctor Manuel Mancilla Castro
Superintendencia de Bancos

Marco Antonio Martinez
CPS Logistics

Eduardo Mayora Alvarado
Mayora & Mayora S.C.

Guillermo Melgar
Cámara Guatemalteca de la Construcción

Edgar Mendoza
PwC Guatemala

Hugo Menes
Mayora & Mayora S.C.

Christian Michelangeli
Carrillo & Asociados

María José Morales Guillén
Castillo Love Abogados

Anajoyce Oliva
Municipalidad de Guatemala

Marco Antonio Palacios
Palacios & Asociados

Jose Enrique Pensabene
Palacios & Asociados

Rita Pérez
Aragón & Aragón

Melida Pineda
Carrillo & Asociados

Evelyn Rebuli
Quiñones, Ibargüen, Luján & Mata, S.C.

Edgar Alfredo Rodríguez
Registro General de la Propiedad de Guatemala

Alfredo Rodríguez Mahuad
Consortium - RACSA

Rodrigo Salguero
PwC Guatemala

Salvador A. Saravia Castillo

Salvador Augusto Saravia Castillo
Saravia & Muñoz

José Augusto Toledo Cruz
Arias & Muñoz

Allan F. Unfried
DHL Global Forwarding

Elmer Vargas
ACZALAW

Julio Zaldaña
Registro General de la Propiedad de Guatemala

GUINEA

Ernst & Young

Aminatou Bah
Nimba Conseil SARL

Aminata Bah Tall
Nimba Conseil SARL

Boubacar Barry
Jurifis Consult Guinee

Lousseny Cisse
Nimba Conseil SARL

Aïssata Diakite
Nimba Conseil SARL

Mohamed Kadialiou Diallo
Electricité de Guinée

Ahmadou Diallo

El Hajj Barry Djoudja
AICHFEET

Soukeina Fofana
Banque Centrale de Guinee - B.C.R.G.

Jean Baptiste Jocamey
Cabinet Koúmy

Lansana Kaba
CARIG

Abdel Aziz Kaba
Nimba Conseil SARL

Mariama Ciré Keita Diallo
Nimba Conseil SARL

Nounké Kourouma
Administration et Contrôle des Grands Projets

Mohamed Lahlou
PwC Guinea

Guy Piam
Nimba Conseil SARL

Raffi Raja
Cabinet Koúmy

Assiatou Sow
Ministère de la Construction, de l'Urbanisme et Habitat

Dominique Taty
PwC Côte d'Ivoire

Hakilas Paul Tchagna
PwC Côte d'Ivoire

Abdourahamane Tounkara
Guinée Consulting

Aboubacar Salimatou Toure
Nimba Conseil SARL

Yansane Fatoumata Yari Soumah
Office notarial

GUINEA-BISSAU

Electricidade e Aguas da Guine-Bissau

Diaby Aboubakar
BCEAO

José Alves Té
MINISTÉRIO DA JUSTIÇA

Emílio Ano Mendes
GB LEGAL - MIRANDA ALLIANCE

Abú Camará
MINISTÉRIO DAS INFRAESTRUTURAS

Humiliano Alves Cardoso
GABINETE ADVOCACIA

Adelaida Mesa D'Almeida
JURISCONTA SRL

Radu Krohne
INTEC

Octávio Lopes
GB LEGAL - MIRANDA ALLIANCE

Suzette Maria Lopes da Costa Graça
MINISTÉRIO DA JUSTIÇA

Jorge Mandinga
MANDINGA EMPREITEROS SA

Miguel Mango
AUDI - CONTA LDA

Vítor Marques da Cruz
FCB&A IN ASSOCIATION WITH ARMANDO MANGO & ASSOCIADOS

Joaozinho Mendes
MINISTERIO DA JUSTICA - DIRECCAO GERAL DE IDENTIFICACAO CIVIL, REGISTRO E NOTARIADO

Francisco Mendes
MINISTRY OF FOREIGN AFFAIRS

Ismael Mendes de Medina
GB LEGAL - MIRANDA ALLIANCE

Eduardo Pimentel
CENTRO DE FORMALIZAÇÃO DE EMPRESAS (C.F.E.)

Osiris Francisco Pina Ferreira
CONSELHO JUDICIAL DA MAGISTRADURA, REPÚBLICA DA GUINÉ - BISSAU

Armando Procel
REPÚBLICA DA GUINÉ-BISSAU

Augusto Regala

Rogério Reis
ROGÉRIO REIS DESPACHANTE

Ousmane Samba Mamadou
BCEAO

Suleimane Seide
MINISTRY OF FINANCE

Fernando Tavares
TRANSMAR SERVICES

Djunco Suleiman Ture
MUNICIPALITY OF BISSAU

Carlos Vamain
GOMES & VAMAIN ASSOCIADOS

Emmanuel Yehouessi
BCEAO

GUYANA

Faye Barker
HUGHES FIELDS & STOBY

Marcel Bobb
FRASER, HOUSTY & YEARWOOD ATTORNEYS-AT-LAW

Ashton Chase
LAW OFFICE OF ASHTON CHASE ASSOCIATES

Lucia Desir-John
D & J SHIPPING SERVICES

Orin Hinds
ORIN HINDS & ASSCOIATES ARCH. LTD.

Gary Holder
ORIN HINDS & ASSCOIATES ARCH. LTD.

Renford Homer
GUYANA POWER & LIGHT INC.

Teni Housty
FRASER, HOUSTY & YEARWOOD ATTORNEYS-AT-LAW

Rexford Jackson
SINGH, DOODNAUTH LAW FIRM

Cliffton Mortimer Llewelyn John
ATTORNEY-AT-LAW

Kalam Azad Juman-Yassin
GUYANA OLYMPIC ASSOCIATION

Kashir Khan

Rakesh Latchana
RAM & MCRAE

Alexis Monize
GUYANA OFFICE FOR INVESTMENT

Colin Murray
COASTAL CONSTRUCTION SERVICES

Harry Noel Narine
PKF INTERNATIONAL

Clarence Antony Nigel Hughes
HUGHES FIELDS & STOBY

Carolyn Paul
AMICE LEGAL CONSULTANTS INC.

R.N. Poonai
POONAI & POONAI

Christopher Ram
RAM & MCRAE

Vishwamint Ramnarine
PFK BARCELLOS, NARINE & CO.

Reginald Roach
R&D ENGINEERING SERVICES

Albert Rodrigues
RODRIGUES ARCHITECTS LTD.

Shaundell Stephenson
OFFICE OF THE PRIME MINISTER

Germene Stewart
CENTRAL HOUSING & PLANNING AUTHORITY

Gidel Thomside
NATIONAL SHIPPING CORPORATION LTD.

Josephine Whitehead
CAMERON & SHEPHERD

Troy Williams
RAM & MCRAE

Roger Yearwood
BRITTON, HAMILTON & ADAMS

HAITI

MÉROVÉ-PIERRE - CABINET D'EXPERTS-COMPTABLES

Claudette Belfont
CABINET PIERRE DELVA

Karine Jadotte Bouchereau
BENJAMIN-JADOTTE ARCHITECTE ET INGÉNIEURS ASSOCIÉS

Jean Baptiste Brown
BROWN LEGAL GROUP

Martin Camille Cangé
ELECTRICITÉ D'HAÏTI

Monique César Guillaume
PAGS - CABINET D'EXPERTS COMPATBLES

Robinson Charles
BANQUE DE LA RÉPUBLIQUE D'HAITI

Djacaman Charles
CABINET GASSANT

Karine Chenet

Martine Chevalier
CABINET LEBLANC & ASSOCIÉS

Diggan d'Adesky
D'ADESKY IMPORT EXPORT S.A.

Inelor Dorval

Jean Gerard Eveillard
CABINET EVEILLARD

Lucien Fresnel
CABINET GASSANT

Enerlio Gassant
CABINET GASSANT

Giordani Gilbert Emile
ETUDE BRISSON CASSAGNOL

Emile Giordani

Marc Hebert Ignace
BANQUE DE LA RÉPUBLIQUE D'HAITI

Lucliner Joseph
MAIRIE DE PETIONVILLE

Robert Laforest
CABINET LAFOREST

Camille Leblanc
CABINET LEBLANC & ASSOCIÉS

Wilhelm E. Lemke, Jr
ENMARCOLDA (D'ADESKY)

Louis Gary Lissade
CABINET LISSADE

Roberson Louis
CABINET GASSANT

Kathia Magloire
CABINET GASSANT

Alexandrine Nelson
CHATELAIN CARGO SERVICES

Joseph Paillant
BUCOFISC

Micosky Pompilus
CABINET D'AVOCATS CHALMERS

Jean Frederic Sales
CABINET SALES

Salim Succar
CABINET LISSADE

Antoine Turnier
FIRME TURNIER - COMPTABLE PROFESSIONNELS AGRÉÉS CONSEILS DE DIRECTION

HONDURAS

EMPRESA NACIONAL DE ENERGÍA ELÉCTRICA

José Antonio Abate
ABAS CONSULTORES

Juan José Alcerro Milla
AGUILAR CASTILLO LOVE

Jose Miguel Alvarez
CONSORTIUM CENTRO AMÉRICA ABOGADOS

José Simón Azcona
INMOBILIARIA ALIANZA SA

César Augusto Cabrera Zapata
TransUnion

Janeth Castañeda de Aquino
GRUPO CROPA PANALPINA

Graciela Cruz
GARCÍA & BODÁN

Ramón Discua
BATRES, DISCUA, MARTINEZ ABOGADOS

Gilda Espinal Veliz
ASJ - ASOCIACION PARA UNA SOCIEDAD MAS JUSTA

Alejandro Fernández de Castro
PwC DOMINICAN REPUBLIC

Lillizeth Garay
CNBS - COMISION NACIONAL DE BANCOS Y SEGUROS

Doris García
CONSORTIUM CENTRO AMÉRICA ABOGADOS

Oscar Armando Girón
ASOCIACIÓN HONDUREÑA DE COMPAÑÍAS Y REPRESENTANTES NAVIEROS (AHCORENA)

Jose Ramon Gonzales
CNBS - COMISION NACIONAL DE BANCOS Y SEGUROS

Jessica Handal
ARIAS & MUÑOZ

Jorge Hernandez
CNBS - COMISION NACIONAL DE BANCOS Y SEGUROS

Camilo Janania
AGUILAR CASTILLO LOVE

Carmen Jovel
PwC HONDURAS

Juan Diego Lacayo González
AGUILAR CASTILLO LOVE

Evangelina Lardizábal
ARIAS & MUÑOZ

German E. Leitzelar H.
DESPACHO LEGAL LEITZELAR Y ASOCIADOS

Dennis Matamoros Batson
ARIAS & MUÑOZ

Juan Carlos Mejía Cotto
INSTITUTO DE LA PROPIEDAD

Iván Alfredo Vigíl Molina
ABOGADO

Ricardo Montes
ARIAS & MUÑOZ

Ramón E. Morales
PwC HONDURAS

Vanessa Oquelí
GARCÍA & BODÁN

Ramón Ortega
PwC DOMINICAN REPUBLIC

Jose Ramon Paz
CONSORTIUM CENTRO AMÉRICA ABOGADOS

Jessica Ramos Guifarro
CONSORTIUM CENTRO AMÉRICA ABOGADOS

Daniel Rivera
PwC HONDURAS

José Rafael Rivera Ferrari
CONSORTIUM CENTRO AMÉRICA ABOGADOS

Enrique Rodriguez Burchard
AGUILAR CASTILLO LOVE

Fanny Rodríguez del Cid
ARIAS & MUÑOZ

René Serrano
ARIAS & MUÑOZ

Godofredo Siercke
GARCÍA & BODÁN

Cristian Stefan Handal
ZACARÍAS & ASOCIADOS

Gricelda Urquía
TransUnion

Roberto Manuel Zacarías Urrutia
ZACARÍAS & ASOCIADOS

Mario Rubén Zelaya
ENERGÍA INTEGRAL S. DE R.L. DE C.V.

HONG KONG SAR, CHINA

ALLEN & OVERY

David Bateson
MALLESONS STEPHEN JACQUES

Rico Chan
BAKER & MCKENZIE

WC Chan
HONG KONG FINANCIAL SECRETARY

Albert P.C. Chan
THE HONG KONG POLYTECHNIC UNIVERSITY

Vashi Ram Chandi
EXCELLENCE INTERNATIONAL

Deborah Y. Cheng
SQUIRE, SANDERS & DEMPSEY L.L.P.

Winnie Cheung
THE LAND REGISTRY OF HONG KONG

Robert Chu
ECONOMIC ANALYSIS AND BUSINESS FACILITATION UNIT, HONG KONG SAR GOVERNMENT

Anna Chu
MAYER BROWN JSM

Jimmy Chung
RUSSELL BEDFORD HONG KONG LIMITED, JAMES NGAI & PARTNERS CPA LIMITED, MEMBER OF RUSSELL BEDFORD INTERNATIONAL

Greta Gerazimaite
AMERINDE CONSOLIDATED, INC.

Vivian Ho
BAKER & MCKENZIE

Keith Man Kei Ho
WILKINSON & GRIST

Tam Yuen Hung
GUANGDONG AND HONG KONG FEEDER ASSOCIATION LTD.

Basil Hwang
DECHERT

Edita Jauniute
AMERINDE CONSOLIDATED, INC.

Salina Ko
APL

Howard Lam
LINKLATERS

Billy Lam
MAYER BROWN JSM

Cindy Lam
THE LAND REGISTRY OF HONG KONG

Lauren Lau
KLC KENNIC LUI & CO

Candas Lee
EDMUND W. H. CHOW & CO

Juliana Lee
MAYER BROWN JSM

Tommy Li
EDMUND W. H. CHOW & CO

Maurice Loo
HONG KONG ECONOMIC & TRADE OFFICE

Kennic L H Lui
KLC KENNIC LUI & CO

James Ngai
RUSSELL BEDFORD HONG KONG LIMITED, JAMES NGAI & PARTNERS CPA LIMITED, MEMBER OF RUSSELL BEDFORD INTERNATIONAL

Kok Leong Ngan
CLP POWER HONG KONG LIMITED

Kenneth Poon
THE LAND REGISTRY OF HONG KONG

Martinal Quan
METOPRO ASSOCIATES LIMITED

Ashish Sahi
TOP IMPETUS

Bassanio So
HONG KONG ECONOMIC & TRADE OFFICE

Derek Tsang
MAYER BROWN JSM

Anita Tsang
PwC HONG KONG

Laurence Tsong
TransUnion HONG KONG

Paul Tsui
HONG KONG ASSOCIATION OF FREIGHT FORWARDING & LOGISTICS LTD. (HAFFA)

Yuen-ho Wan
RUSSELL BEDFORD HONG KONG LIMITED, JAMES NGAI & PARTNERS CPA LIMITED, MEMBER OF RUSSELL BEDFORD INTERNATIONAL

Jackson Wong
HONG KONG ECONOMIC & TRADE OFFICE

James Wong
THE HONG KONG POLYTECHNIC UNIVERSITY

Patrick Wong
MAYER BROWN JSM

Fergus Wong
PwC HONG KONG

Ricky Yiu
BAKER & MCKENZIE

Hai Yong
Baker & McKenzie

Peter Yu
PwC Hong Kong

Frank Yuen
KLC Kennic Lui & Co.

Gordon Zhu
Amerinde Consolidated, Inc.

HUNGARY

Jones Lang LaSalle

Maltacourt Hungary

Morley Allen & Overy Iroda

Péter Bárdos
Law Firm Dr. Péter and Rita Bárdos

Marianna Bártfai
BDO Hungary

Sándor Békési
Partos & Noblet Hogan Lovells

Péter Berethalmi
Nagy és Trócsányi Law Office, member of Lex Mundi

Hedi Bozsonyik
Szecskay Attorneys at Law

Jan Burmeister
bnt Szabó Tom Burmeister Ügyvédi Iroda

Zsuzsanna Cseri
Bárd, Cseri & Partners Law Firm

András Elekes
Immobilia Real Estate Development kft

Gabriella Erdos
PwC Hungary

Ágnes Fábry
PRK Partners / Fábry Law Office

György Fehér
PRK Partners / Fábry Law Office

Ernő Garamvölgyi
Budapest IX District Municipality

Anna Gáspár
Build-Econ Ltd.

Zoltán Gerendy
BDO Hungary

Csaba Attila Hajdu
bnt Szabó Tom Burmeister Ügyvédi Iroda

Tamas Halmos
Partos & Noblet Hogan Lovells

Vilma Hasuly
PRK Partners / Fábry Law Office

Dóra Horváth
Reti, Antall and Partners Law Firm

Norbert Izer
PwC Hungary

David Kerpel
Szecskay Attorneys at Law

Dorottya Kovacsics
Partos & Noblet Hogan Lovells

Russell Lambert
PwC Hungary

Petra Lencs
Bárd, Cseri & Partners Law Firm

Andrea Májer
BDO Hungary

Dóra Máthé
PwC Hungary

László Mohai

Robert Nagy
BISZ Central Credit Information (PLC)

Sándor Németh
Szecskay Attorneys at Law

Christopher Noblet
Partos & Noblet Hogan Lovells

Tamás Pásztor
Nagy és Trócsányi Law Office, member of Lex Mundi

István Sándor
Kelemen, Meszaros, Sandor & Partners

Zsolt Sóki
BDO Hungary

Krisztina Stacho
bpv | Legal Jádi Németh

Tibor Szabó
Reti, Antall and Partners Law Firm

András Szecskay
Szecskay Attorneys at Law

Ágnes Szent-Ivány
Sándor Szegedi Szent-Ivány Komáromi Eversheds

Viktória Szilágyi
Nagy és Trócsányi Law Office, member of Lex Mundi

Gábor Varga
BISZ Central Credit Information (PLC)

Blanka Zombori
PwC Hungary

Antonia Zsigmon
bpv | Legal Jádi Németh

ICELAND

Halla Ýr Albertsdóttir
PricewaterhouseCoopers Legal ehf

Jón Gunnar Ásbjörnsson
BBA Legal

Arnar Bjarnason
Frakt.is

Þórður Búason
Reykjavik Construction Agency

Eymundur Einarsson
Endurskodun og rádgjöf ehf, member of Russell Bedford International

Ólafur Eiríksson
LOGOS, member of Lex Mundi

Skuli Th. Fjeldsted
Fjeldsted, Blöndal & Fjeldsted

Benedikt Geirsson
ISTAK

Gier Gestsson
Jonsson & Hall Law Firm

Erlendur Gíslason
LOGOS, member of Lex Mundi

Elísabet Guðbjörnsdóttir
PricewaterhouseCoopers Legal ehf

Sindri Gudjónsson
LOGOS, member of Lex Mundi

Guðrún Guðmundsdóttir
Jónar Transport

Hjördís Gulla Gylfadóttir
BBA Legal

Gisli Gudni Hall
Jonsson & Hall Law Firm

Ragnar Halldor Hall
Jonsson & Hall Law Firm

Reynir Haraldsson
Jónar Transport

Hordur Felix Hardarson
Jonsson & Hall Law Firm

Margrét Hauksdóttir
The Land Registry of Iceland

Thora Jónsdóttir
Juris Law office

Jóhanna Áskels Jónsdóttir
PricewaterhouseCoopers Legal ehf

Gestur Jonsson
Jonsson & Hall Law Firm

Gunnar Jonsson
Jonsson & Hall Law Firm

Lára V. Júlíusdóttir
Lögmenn Laugavegi 3 ehf.

Ásta Kristjánsdóttir
PwC Iceland

Jóhann Magnús Jóhannsson
LOGOS, member of Lex Mundi

Benedetto Nardini
BBA Legal

Dagbjört Oddsdóttir
BBA Legal

Dögg Pàksdóttir
Reykjavik University

Kristján Pálsson
Jónar Transport

Margrét Ragnarsdóttir
LOGOS, member of Lex Mundi

Fridgeir Sigurdsson
PwC Iceland

Eyvindur Sólnes
LVA-legal services

Jóhannes Stephensen
Creditinfo Iceland

Gunnar Sturluson
LOGOS, member of Lex Mundi

Rúnar Svavar Svavarsson
Orkuveita Reykjavíkur, Distribution-Electrical System

Stefán A. Svensson
Juris Law office

Einor Thor Sverisson
Jonsson & Hall Law Firm

INDIA

FoxMandal Little

G. D. International

Mahamuni Export Import

Transworld Ventures

Subramaniam A.
Subramaniam Importers

John Agana
Yuri-Enga Enga Enterprise

Amit Agarwal
PwC India

Bhavuk Agarwal
Singhania & Co. LLP

Fraser Alexander
Juris Corp

Clarence Anthony
Juris Corp

Mansij Arya
KNM & Partners, Law Offices

Pavithra B.
Maharani Laxmi Ammanni Centre for Social Science Research

Madhu Barisal
PwC India

Daksha Bara
Maharani Laxmi Ammanni Centre for Social Science Research

Meghalee Barthakur
PwC India

Sumant Batra
Kesar Dass B & Associates

Shruti Baya
Juris Corp

Abhishek Bhalla
Phoenix Legal

Pradeep Bhandari
Proteam Consulting Private Limited

Gopa Bhardwaz
International Law Affiliates

Sushil Bhasin
Bhasin International

Prabjot Bhullar
Khaitan & Co.

Ugen Bhutia
FoxMandal Little

Rewati Bobde
Juris Corp

Nidhi Bothra
Vinod Kothari & Co., Company Secretaries

Bharat Budholia
Juris Corp

Rajarshi Chakrabarti
Kochhar & Co.

Harshala Chandorkar
Credit Information Bureau Ltd.

Bidan Chandran
Singhania & Partners LLP Solicitors & Advocates

Prashant Chauhan
Advocate

Manjula Chawla
Phoenix Legal

Daizy Chawla
Singh & Associates Advocates and Solicitors

Jijo Cherian
Phoenix Legal

Ipsita Chowdhury
Trilegal

Sachin Chugh
Singhi Chugh & Kumar, Chartered Accountants

Manish Dadhania
Precision Sintered Products

Ketan Dalal
PwC India

Vishwang Desai
Desai & Diwanji

Devendra Deshmukh
Khaitan & Co.

Prashant Dharia
Anant Industries

Suruchi Dhavale
Juris Corp

Farida Dholkawala
Desai & Diwanji

Rajendran Dorai
Supriya Construction

Siddharth Dubey
Singhania & Partners LLP Solicitors & Advocates

Thambi Durai
T. Durai & Co.

Nehal Gandhi
A-1 Electricals

Vir Gandhi
Profound Outsourcing Solutions Pvt. Ltd.

Ritika Ganju
Phoenix Legal

Rahul Garg
PwC India

Tanushree Ghildiyal
KNM & Partners, Law Offices

Karanvir Gill
Khaitan & Co.

Vijay Goel
Singhania & Co. LLP

Chandrika Gogia
PwC India

Trupti Guha
Kochhar & Co.

Sameer Guha
Trilegal

Arun Gupta
Corporate Professionals

Deepak Gupta
PwC India

Nikhil Gupta
PwC India

Ruchira Gupta
The Juris Sociis

Atul Gupta
Trilegal

Adarsh Hathi
Hathi & Associates

Kabir Hathi
Hathi & Associates

Akil Hirani
Majmudar & Co.

Raina Jain
Amerinde Consolidated, Inc.

Ruchi Jain
PwC India

Vipin Jain
Shree Bhikshu Marble and Granites

Ashok Jain
Veeplus Industries Pvt., Ltd Runtai Industry Co., Ltd

Yogesh Jare
Suhasini Impex

Anil Jarial
Juris Corp

H. Jayesh
Juris Corp

Dharmendra Johari
Stonex Inc.

Rajat Joneja
KNM & Partners, Law Offices

Jayesh Karandikar
Kochhar & Co.

Rajas Kasbekar
Little & Co.

Mukund Kasture
Hitech Equipments

Charandeep Kaur
Trilegal

Mitalee Kaushal
KNM & Partners, Law Offices

Arun Kedia
VAV Life Sciences P. Ltd.

Amruta Kelkar
Juris Corp

Anup Khanna
Majmudar & Co.

Gautam Khattar
PwC India

Bhavna Kohli
PwC India

Ravinder Komaragiri
The Tata Power Company Limited

Vinod Kothari
Vinod Kothari & Co., Company Secretaries

Madan Krishna
Raytheon

Mukesh Kumar
KNM & Partners, Law Offices

Ra Kumar
Singhania & Partners LLP Solicitors & Advocates

Harsh Kumar
Singhi Chugh & Kumar, Chartered Accountants

Vikram Kumar
Supply Source India

Dilip Kumar Niranjan
Singh & Associates Advocates and Solicitors

Manoj Kumar Singh
Singh & Associates Advocates and Solicitors

Vijay Kumar Singh
Singh & Associates Advocates and Solicitors

Sumit Kumar Vij
FoxMandal Little

Sougata Kundu
PwC India

Shreedhar Kunte
Sharp and Tannan, member of Russell Bedford

Harjeet Lall
Axon Partners LLP

Chandni Lochan
Trilegal

Rajiv Luthra
Luthra & Luthra

Neha Madan
Kesar Dass B & Associates

Ravi Mahto
Trilegal

Shipra Makkar
Singh & Associates Advocates and Solicitors

Jignesh Makwana
SwiftIndiaInc Corporate Services Private Limited

Aditi Manchanda
Juris Corp

Som Mandal
FoxMandal Little

Vipender Mann
KNM & Partners, Law Offices

Rishabh G Mastaram
Naik Naik and Company

Preeti G. Mehta
Kanga & Co.

Dara Mehta
Little & Co.

Vikas Mehta
Pradeep Traders

Jitesh Mehta
Source India

Sharad Mishra
Neo Multimedian

Saurabh Misra
Saurabh Misra & Associates, Advocates

Atul Mittal
PwC India

Shyamal Mukherjee
PwC India

Sudip Mullick
Khaitan & Co.

Rajiv Mundhra
Crown Agents Ltd.

Ramaratnam Muralidharan
PwC India

Vidya Nashimath
TOBOC

Madhav Pande

Girija Shankar Pandey

Janak Pandya
Nishith Desai Associates

Tejas R. Parekh
Nishith Desai Associates

Amir Z. Singh Pasrich
International Law Affiliates

Swagateeka Patel
Kesar Dass B & Associates

Shreyas Patel
Majmudar & Co.

Sanjay Patil
BDH Industries Limited

Dhruv Paul
Trilegal

Francisca Philip
Singhania & Partners LLP Solicitors & Advocates

Bhadrinath Madhusudan Pogul
Kalki International

Madhavi Pogul
Kalki International

Madhusudan Venkatesh Pogul
Kalki International

M. Prabhakaran
Consulta Juris

Ajay Raghavan
Trilegal

Anil Raj
Phoenix Legal

Mohan Rajasekharan
Phoenix Legal

J.T. Rajasuriya
J.T.Rajasuriya & Associates

Ashok Ramgir
Harsh Impex

Harsh Ramgir
Harsh Impex

Ami Ranjan
Singhania & Partners LLP Solicitors & Advocates

Dipak Rao
Singhania & Partners LLP Solicitors & Advocates

Ragini Rastogi
PwC India

Prem Rath
Amerinde Consolidated, Inc.

Tanya Rath
Amerinde Consolidated, Inc.

Rahul Renavikar
PwC India

Sameer Sah
Majmudar & Co.

Richie Sancheti
Nishith Desai Associates

Aayushi Sehgal
Khaitan & Co.

Vandana Sekhri
Juris Corp

Ramani Seshadri

Manav Shah
Kochhar & Co.

Parag Shah
Parag G Shah and Associates

Prakash Shah
Parijat Marketing Services

Vikram Shroff
Nishith Desai Associates

Manjosh K Sidhu

Ankita Singh
FoxMandal Little

Praveen Singh
FoxMandal Little

Nirmal Singh
PwC India

Harsimran Singh
Singh & Associates Advocates and Solicitors

Kaviraj Singh
Trustman & Co

Mukesh Singhal
KNM & Partners, Law Offices

Ravinder Singhania
Singhania & Partners LLP Solicitors & Advocates

Ankit Singhi
Corporate Professionals

Arvind Sinha
RCS Pvt. Ltd. Business Advisors Group

Rajat Ratan Sinha
RCS Pvt. Ltd. Business Advisors Group

Vinay Sirohia
Axon Partners LLP

Veena Sivaramakrishnan
Juris Corp

Harshita Srivastava
Nishith Desai Associates

Prashant Suthar
Indian Artisanal

Niranjan Talati
Shreeji Marketing

Sandhya Tanwar
PwC India

Rajesh Tayal
KNM & Partners, Law Offices

Chetan Thakkar
Kanga & Co.

Piyush Thareja
Neeraj Bhagat & Co.

Richa Tiwari
PwC India

Praveen Kumar Tiwary
FoxMandal Little

Dhirajkumar Totala
Juris Corp

Suhas Tuljapurkar
Legasis Services Pvt. Ltd.

Rahul Tyagi
FoxMandal Little

Kanisshka Tyagi
Kesar Dass B & Associates

Harsh Vijayvargiya
FoxMandal Little

Ramesh Babu Vishwanathula
Vishwanath & Global Attorneys

Rajat Vohra
Trilegal

Saral Kumar Yadav
INFOSOL Information Solution Word

Aashii Yadav
Kesar Dass B & Associates

Amit Yadkikar
Desai & Diwanji

INDONESIA

CV. Fortune Enterprise

Nafis Adwani
Ali Budiardjo, Nugroho, Reksodiputro, member of Lex Mundi

Retno Anggraeni
Leks & Co.

Jhony Anugrah
PT Sentra Anugrah Motor

Hamud M. Balfas
Ali Budiardjo, Nugroho, Reksodiputro, member of Lex Mundi

Simon Barrie
KarimSyah Law Firm

Fabian Buddy Pascoal
Hanafiah Ponggawa & Partners

Ita Budhi
PwC Indonesia

Prianto Budi
PT Pratama Indomitra Konsultan, member of Russell Bedford International

Tony Budidjaja
Budidjaja & Associates Law Offices

Juni Dani
Budidjaja & Associates Law Offices

Utari Dyah Kusuma
Brigitta I. Rahayoe & Partners

Ira A. Eddymurthy
Soewito Suhardiman Eddymurthy Kardono

Sani Eka Duta
Bank Indonesia

Ayik Gunadi
Ali Budiardjo, Nugroho, Reksodiputro, member of Lex Mundi

Didik S. Hadiwidodo
PT. Nasio Karya Pratama

Dedet Hardiansyah
Budiman and Partners

Michael Hasian Giovanni
Brigitta I. Rahayoe & Partners

Ray Headifen
PwC Indonesia

Erwandi Hendarta
Hadiputranto, Hadinoto & Partners

Mohammad Kamal Hidayat
Furniture Fikamar

Rahayuningsih Hoed
Makarim & Taira S.

Alexander Hutauruk
Hadiputranto, Hadinoto & Partners

Brigitta Imam Rahayoe
Brigitta I. Rahayoe & Partners

Robert Buana Jaya
Budidjaja & Associates Law Offices

Timothy Jhansen
PT Post Cycle Global

Iswahjudi A. Karim
KarimSyah Law Firm

Mirza Karim
KarimSyah Law Firm

Herry N. Kurniawan
Ali Budiardjo, Nugroho, Reksodiputro, member of Lex Mundi

Rudy Kusmanto
Makarim & Taira S.

Winita E. Kusnandar
Kusnandar & Co.

Eddy M. Leks
Leks & Co.

Ferry P. Madian
Ali Budiardjo, Nugroho, Reksodiputro, member of Lex Mundi

Marshel Tristant Makaminan
Budidjaja & Associates Law Offices

Ella Melany
Hanafiah Ponggawa & Partners

Karen Mills
KarimSyah Law Firm

Norma Mutalib
Makarim & Taira S.

Julinus Omrie Napitupulu
Budidjaja & Associates Law Offices

Chandra Nataadmadja
Suria Nataadmadja & Associates

Suria Nataadmadja
Suria Nataadmadja & Associates

Mia Noni Yuniar
Brigitta I. Rahayoe & Partners

Doddy B. Pangaribuan
PT Perusahaan Listrik Negara

Meiske Panggabean
Bahar & Partners

Ilman Rakhmat
KarimSyah Law Firm

Sophia Rengganis
PwC Indonesia

Arno F. Rizaldi
Kusnandar & Co.

Kelvin Santoso
PwC Indonesia

Gatot Sanyoto
Kusnandar & Co.

Mahardikha K. Sardjana
Hadiputranto, Hadinoto & Partners

Nur Asyura Anggini Sari
Bank Indonesia

Marinza Savanthy
Widyawan & Partners

Natasha A. Sebayang
Soewito Suhardiman Eddymurthy Kardono

Indra Setiawan
Ali Budiardjo, Nugroho, Reksodiputro, member of Lex Mundi

Kevin Omar Sidharta
Ali Budiardjo, Nugroho, Reksodiputro, member of Lex Mundi

Ricardo Simanjuntak
Ricardo Simanjuntak & Partners

Terman Siregar
Jakarta Investment and Promotion Board

Dyah Sitawati
PwC Indonesia

Yukiko Lyla Usman Tambunan
Bank Indonesia

Yuliana Tjhai
Bahar & Partners

Hanum Ariana Tobing
Budidjaja & Associates Law Offices

Gatot Triprasetio
Widyawan & Partners

Heru Tumbelaka
Suria Nataadmadja & Associates

Pudji Wahjuni Purbo
Makarim & Taira S.

Sony Panji Wicaksono
Bank Indonesia

Fransiska Ade Kurnia Widodo
Budidjaja & Associates Law Offices

Aditya Kesha Wijayanto
Widyawan & Partners

IRAN, ISLAMIC REP.

Moradi Lawyer Company

Camellia Abdolsamad
International Law Office of Dr. Behrooz Akhlaghi & Associates

Hamid Reza Adabi

Allah Mohammad Aghaee
Iranian National Tax Administration

Ahmadi Ahmadi
Iran Credit Scoring

Nazem Ahmadian Nasrabadi
State Organization for Registration of Deeds & Properties of Islamic Republic of Iran

Behrooz Akhlaghi
International Law Office of Dr. Behrooz Akhlaghi & Associates

Ali Amani
Dayarayan Auditing & Financial Services

Mahdi Amouri
Iranian National Tax Administration

Abbas Arbabsoleimani
Iranian Association of Certified Public Accountants

Gholam Ali Asghari
Great Tehran Electricity Distribution Company (GTEDC)

Mir Rostam Assadollahzadeh Bali

Saeed Astaraki
Khaybar

Hassan Badamchi
HAMI Legal Services

Mohammad Badamchi
HAMI Legal Services

Behrooz Bagheri
Ehsagarane Danesh Afrooz

Peyman Barazandeh
Ghods Niroo Consulting Engineers

Mohammad Hossein Barkhordar
Mohammad Hossein

Gholamhossein Davani
Dayarayan Auditing & Financial Services

Morteza Dezfoulian
Morteza

Mahmoud Ebadi Tabrizi
M. Ebadi Tabrizi & Associates

Mona Ebrahimi
International Law Office of Dr. Behrooz Akhlaghi & Associates

Maryam Ebrahimi
Tehran Stock Exchange (TSE)

Mohammadali Eshaghi
The State Organization for Registration of Deeds and Properties

Sarah Eshaghi
The State Organization for Registration of Deeds and Properties

Mahmoud Eskandari
Iran Trade Promotion Organization

Shirzad Eslami

Hossein Fahimi
Securities and Exchange Organization of Iran

Zahra Farzaliyan
State Organization for Registration of Deeds & Properties of Islamic Republic of Iran

Hengameh Fazeli Daie Zangi
State Organization for Registration of Deeds & Properties of Islamic Republic of Iran

Nematollah Hajali
Tehran Insolvency Affairs Liquidation Office, General Directorate of Insolvency Affairs Liquidation, The Judiciary of Iran

Mahdiyar Hosseini
Notary Office No. 1286 of Tehran

Behboud Hosseinpour
Ports and Maritime Organization

Soraya Hosseinpour Kolli
Morteza

Mohammad Javad Hosseynzade
Tehran Insolvency Affairs Liquidation Office, General Directorate of Insolvency Affairs Liquidation, The Judiciary of Iran

Nassim Jahanbani
Great Tehran Electricity Distribution Company (GTEDC)

Mohammad Jalili
Iran Credit Scoring

Farid Kani
Atieh Associates

Kiumars Kermanshahi
Iran Trade Promotion Organization

Kheirollah Khadem
Iran Trade Promotion Organization

Fatemeh Khademi
Aftabe Edalat

Behnam Khatami
Atieh Associates

Amir Kheirollahy
HT Co, Ltd.

Masoud Kiumarthi
Central Bank of the Islamic Republic of Iran

Majid Mahallati
Mahallati & Co. Chartered Accountants

Amir Ahmad Mahdian Rad
Sohrab Sepehri

Shahrzad Majdameli
International Law Office of Dr. Behrooz Akhlaghi & Associates

Gholam Reza Malekshoar
Central Bank of the Islamic Republic of Iran

Seyed Ali Mirshafiei
Tehran Chamber of Commerce, Industry and Mines

Younes Gharbali Moghadam
Ports and Maritime Organization

Seyedeh Fatemeh Moghimi
Sadid Bar Int Transport

Seyed Iman Mohamadian
International Law Office of Dr. Behrooz Akhlaghi & Associates

Mozaffar Mohammadian
Teema Bar International Transport

Majid Mohebi
Great Tehran Electricity Distribution Company (GTEDC)

Mehrdad Mostaghimi
Ghods Niroo Consulting Engineers

Seyed Mohamad Sadegh Mousavianfar
Tehran Insolvency Affairs Liquidation Office, General Directorate of Insolvency Affairs Liquidation, The Judiciary of Iran

Babak Namazi
Atieh Associates

Rassoul Nowroozi
Iran Trade Promotion Organization

Ahmad Parkhideh
Iran Chamber of Commerce

Mohammad Reza Pasban
Allame Tabatabaei Un.- Iranian Central Bar Association

Farmand Pourkarim
Tehran Municipality

Yahya Rayegani
Farjam Law Office

Aria Roustapour
Ports and Maritime Organization

Encyeh Seyed Sadr
International Law Office of Dr. Behrooz Akhlaghi & Associates

Cyrus Shafizadeh
Atieh Associates

Ali Shahabi
International Law Office of Dr. Behrooz Akhlaghi & Associates

Abolfazl Shahrabadi
Tehran Stock Exchange (TSE)

Javad Bahar Shanjani
Farjam Law Office

Narges Shariati
International Law Office of Dr. Behrooz Akhlaghi & Associates

Alireza Shariaty Eivari

Rajat Ratan Sinha
RCS Pvt. Ltd. Business Advisors Group

Pedram Soltani
PERSOL Corporation

Mohammad Soltani
Securities and Exchange Organization of Iran

Abbas Taghipour
Central Bank of the Islamic Republic of Iran

Ebrahim Tavakoli
Tavakoli & Shahabi

Meghdad Torabi
Tavakoli & Shahabi

Vrej Torossian
Torossian, Avanessian & Associate

Abdolamir Yaghouti
Great Tehran Electricity Distribution Company (GTEDC)

Farhad Yazdi

Azadeh Zarei
Iran Trade Promotion Organization

IRAQ
Ernst & Young

Iraqi Association of Securities Dealers

Talal Abu Ghazaleh Legal (TAG-Legal)

Hadeel Salih Abboud Al-Janabi
Mena Associates, member of Amereller Rechtsanwälte

Ahmed Al-Jannabi
Mena Associates, member of Amereller Rechtsanwälte

Florian Amereller
Amereller Rechtsanwälte

Munther B. Hamoudi
Al Attar Real Estate Office

Ali Baker
Al-Furat for Legal and Business Consultancy LLC

Majed Butrous

Ahmed Dawood
Baet Al Hikma for Legal Services and Consultancy LLC

Ninos Hozaya
BCC Logistics

Stephan Jäger
Amereller Rechtsanwälte

Jamal Mehdi Shalal
Al Attar Real Estate Office

Mohammad Murad
Al Rafidain Brokers

Ibrahim Musa Qadori Ahmed
Al Rawdha Real-estate Office

Ammar Naji
Al-Furat for Legal and Business Consultancy LLC

Auday Najim Ali
Ashur International Bank

Oday Najim Ali
Ashur International Bank

Arin Pinto
Khudairi Group

Ahmed Salih Al-Janabi
Mena Associates, member of Amereller Rechtsanwälte

David Salman
Ashur International Bank

Abdelrahman Sherif
Mena Associates, member of Amereller Rechtsanwälte

Khaled Yaseen
Iraqi National Investment Commission

IRELAND
ESB Networks

Irish Credit Bureau

Margaret Austin
Eugene F. Collins Solicitors

Andrew Bates
Dillon Eustace

Roisin Bennett
Reddy Charlton McKnight

Michael Bergin
PwC Ireland

Finola Boyle
Eugene F. Collins Solicitors

Alan Browning
LK Shields Solicitors, member of Ius Laboris

John Comerford
Cooney Carey, member of Russell Bedford International

Eoin Cunneen
LK Shields Solicitors, member of Ius Laboris

Richard Curran
LK Shields Solicitors, member of Ius Laboris

Patrick Daly
Arthur Cox, member of Lex Mundi

Kiara Daly
Daniel Murphy Solicitors

Gavin Doherty
Eugene F. Collins Solicitors

John Doyle
Dillon Eustace

Ray Duffy
The Property Registration Authority

Bryan Dunne
Matheson Ormsby Prentice

Garret Farrelly
Matheson Ormsby Prentice

Frank Flanagan
Mason Hayes+Curran

Sarah Gallagher
Dillon Eustace

Micheál Grace
Mason Hayes+Curran

Sinéad Greene
LK Shields Solicitors, member of Ius Laboris

Darren Isaacson
Arthur Cox, member of Lex Mundi

Thomas Johnson
Irish Building Control Institute

William Johnston
Arthur Cox, member of Lex Mundi

Georgina Kabemba
Matheson Ormsby Prentice

Ian Lavelle
LK Shields Solicitors, member of Ius Laboris

Niamh Loughran
Dillon Eustace

Paul McCutcheon
L.K. Shields Solicitors

Elaine McGrath
Reddy Charlton McKnight

Kevin Meehan
Compass Maritime Ltd.

Gavan Neary
PwC Ireland

Michael O'Connor
Matheson Ormsby Prentice

Matt O'Keeffe
PwC Ireland

Deirdre O'Mahony
Arthur Cox, member of Lex Mundi

Feargal Orourke
PwC Ireland

Robert O'Shea
Matheson Ormsby Prentice

Maurice Phelan
Mason Hayes+Curran

Matthew Ryan
Dillon Eustace

Brendan Sharkey
Reddy Charlton McKnight

Gavin Simons
Daniel Murphy Solicitors

Caroline Sommers
Matheson Ormsby Prentice

Lorcan Tiernan
Dillon Eustace

Mark Traynor
A&L Goodbody

Colm Walsh
Irish International Freight Association

Barry Walsh
Mason Hayes+Curran

Maeve Walsh
Reddy Charlton McKnight

Emma Weld-Moore
Daniel Murphy Solicitors

ISRAEL
Public Utility Authority-Electricity

Ofer Bar-On
Shavit Bar-On Gal-On Tzin Yagur, Law Offices

Jacob Ben-Chitrit
Yigal Arnon & Co.

Jeremy Benjamin
Goldfarb Levy Eran Meiri Tzafrir & Co.

Marina Benvenisti
Ruth Cargo

Yitzchak Chikorel
Deloitte LLP

Koby Cohen
PwC Israel

Doron Cohon
Raveh, Ravid & Co. CPAs, member of Russell Bedford International

Danny Dilbary
Goldfarb Levy Eran Meiri Tzafrir & Co.

Ido Gonen
Goldfarb Levy Eran Meiri Tzafrir & Co.

Amos Hacmun
Heskia-Hacmun Law Firm

Roee Hecht
Shavit Bar-On Gal-On Tzin Yagur, Law Offices

Yossi Katsav
Ruth Cargo

Zeev Katz
PwC Israel

Vered Kirshner
PwC Israel

Adam Klein
Goldfarb Levy Eran Meiri Tzafrir & Co.

Gideon Koren
Gideon Koren & Co. Law Offices

Orna Kornreich-Cohen
Shavit Bar-On Gal-On Tzin Yagur, Law Offices

Michael Lagon
The Israel Electric Corporation Ltd.-Dan district

Aaron Lampert
Naschitz, Brandes & Co., with the support of Ernst & Young

Benjamin Leventhal
Gideon Fisher & Co.

Michelle Liberman
S. Horowitz & Co., member of Lex Mundi

Danielle Loewenstein
S. Horowitz & Co., member of Lex Mundi

Rotem Muntner
Ruth Cargo

Marcelle Noussimovitch
Raphael Katz & Co. Customs Brokers Ltd.

Meir Nussbaum
Deloitte LLP

Helen Raziel
Naschitz, Brandes & Co., with the support of Ernst & Young

Yoav Razin
Naschitz, Brandes & Co., with the support of Ernst & Young

Matt Rosenbaum
Hacohen & Wolf Law Offices

Liat Rothschild
Goldfarb Levy Eran Meiri Tzafrir & Co.

Gerry Seligman
PwC Israel

Amir Shani
Amit (Panalpina)

Edward Shtaif
The Israel Electric Corporation Ltd.- Dan district

Daniel Singerman
Business Data Israel + Personal Check

Ayelet Suissa
PwC Israel

Daphna Tsarfaty
Goldfarb Levy Eran Meiri Tzafrir & Co.

Eylam Weiss
Weiss-Porat & Co.

Zeev Weiss
Weiss-Porat & Co.

Dave Wolf
Hacohen & Wolf Law Offices

Shlomi Zehavi
PwC Israel

ITALY

Param Overseas

Studio dell'Avvocato Antich

Marianna Abbaticchio
Ristuccia & Tufarelli

Fabrizio Acerbis
TLS - Associazione Professionale di Avvocati e Commercialisti

Mario Altavilla
Unioncamere

Roberto Argeri
Cleary Gottlieb Steen & Hamilton LLP

Gaetano Arnò
TLS - Associazione Professionale di Avvocati e Commercialisti

Maria Pia Ascenzo
Bank of Italy

Romina Ballanca
TLS - Associazione Professionale di Avvocati e Commercialisti

Paola Barazzetta
TLS - Associazione Professionale di Avvocati e Commercialisti

Lamberto Barbieri
CRIF S. P. A.

Giuseppe Battaglia
Portolano Colella Cavallo

Sylvia Beccio
Studio Legale Sinatra

Alvise Becker
TLS - Associazione Professionale di Avvocati e Commercialisti

Susanna Beltramo
Studio Legale Beltramo

Stefano Biagioli
TLS - Associazione Professionale di Avvocati e Commercialisti

Gianluca Borghetto
Nunziante Magrone

Paola Calabrese
Calabrese Law Firm

Sergio Calderara
Almaviva S.p.A. - Direzione Affari Legali

Stefano Cancarini
TLS - Associazione Professionale di Avvocati e Commercialisti

Alessandro Cardia
Grieco e Associati

Alessandro Caridi
TLS - Associazione Professionale di Avvocati e Commercialisti

Cecilia Carrara
Legance

Ana Carretero
Studio Legale Sinatra

Gennaro Cassiani
GC Architecture Buro

Lucia Ceccarelli
Portolano Colella Cavallo

Giorgio Cherubini
Pirola Pennuto Zei & Associati

Domenico Colella
Portolano Colella Cavallo

Fabrizio Colonna
LCA - Lega Colucci e Associati

Mattia Colonnelli de Gasperis
Colonnelli de Gasperis Studio Legale

Fabio Corno
Studio Corno, member of Russell Bedford International

Barbara Corsetti
Portolano Colella Cavallo

Filippo Corsini
Chiomenti Studio Legale

Barbara Cortesi
Studio Legale Guasti

Massimo Cremona
Pirola Pennuto Zei & Associati

Salvatore Cuzzocrea
TLS - Associazione Professionale di Avvocati e Commercialisti

Elena Davanzo
Studio Legale Tributario Associato

Daniele de Benedetti
Studio Benessia - Maccagno

Antonio de Martinis
Spasaro De Martinis Law Firm

Francesca De Paolis
International Centre for Dispute Resolution

Claudio Di Falco
Cleary Gottlieb Steen & Hamilton LLP

Massimiliano Di Tommaso
Cleary Gottlieb Steen & Hamilton LLP

Iacopo Donati
Cleary Gottlieb Steen & Hamilton LLP

Sunil Dutt Sharma
Param Overseas

Emanuele Ferrari
Studio Notarile Ferrari

Maddalena Ferrari
Studio Notarile Ferrari

Paola Flora
Ashurst

Pier Andrea Fré Torelli Massini
Carabba & Partners

Linda Nicoletta Frigo
Gruppo Pam S.p.A.

Cristina Fugazza
Studio Legale Sinatra

Andrea Gangemi
Portolano Colella Cavallo

Enrica Maria Ghia
Ghia Law Firm

Lucio Ghia
Ghia Law Firm

Vincenzo Fabrizio Giglio
Giglio & Scofferi Studio Legale del Lavoro

Antonio Grieco
Grieco e Associati

Tommaso Gualco
Bre-engineering srl

Valentino Guarini
TLS - Associazione Professionale di Avvocati e Commercialisti

Federico Guasti
Studio Legale Guasti

Goffredo Guerra
Studio Legale Tributario Associato

Christian Iannacccone
Studio Legale Tributario Associato

Francesco Iodice
Cleary Gottlieb Steen & Hamilton LLP

Giovanni Izzo
Abbatescianni Studio Legale e Tributario

Paramjeet Kaur
Param Overseas

Ignazio la Candia
Pirola Pennuto Zei & Associati

Enrico Lodi
CRIF S. P. A.

Artemisia Lorusso
Tonucci & Partners, in alliance with Mayer Brown LLP

Paolo Lucarini
TLS - Associazione Professionale di Avvocati e Commercialisti

Stefano Macchi di Cellere
Jones Day

Matteo Magistrelli
Portolano Colella Cavallo

Donatella Martinelli
Alegal - International Law Firm

Pietro Masi
Portolano Colella Cavallo

Patrizia Masselli
Cleary Gottlieb Steen & Hamilton LLP

Gennaro Mazzuoccolo
Norton Rose

Stefano Merli
TLS - Associazione Professionale di Avvocati e Commercialisti

Andrea Messuti
LCA - Lega Colucci e Associati

Mario Miccoli
Notaio Miccoli

Federica Micoli
Lawyer

Nunzia Moliterni
Jones Lang LaSalle

Marco Monaco Sorge
Tonucci & Partners, in alliance with Mayer Brown LLP

Micael Montinari
Portolano Colella Cavallo

Valeria Morosini
Toffoletto e Soci Law Firm, member of Ius Laboris

Gianmatteo Nunziante
Nunziante Magrone

Francesco Nuzzolo
TLS - Associazione Professionale di Avvocati e Commercialisti

Ferdinando Offredi
Venosta R.E. S.rl

Fabiana Padroni
Ristuccia & Tufarelli

Marcella Panucci
Confindustria (National Business Association)

Luciano Panzani
Torino Court of First Instance

Paolo Pasqualis
Notary

Giovanni Patti
Abbatescianni Studio Legale e Tributario

Yan Pecoraro
Portolano Colella Cavallo

Federica Peres
Portolano Colella Cavallo

Davide Petris
Portolano Colella Cavallo

Martina Pivetti
TLS - Associazione Professionale di Avvocati e Commercialisti

Laura Prosperetti
Cleary Gottlieb Steen & Hamilton LLP

Sharon Reilly
Toffoletto e Soci Law Firm, member of Ius Laboris

Davide Rossini
APL Srl

Gianluca Russo
Cleary Gottlieb Steen & Hamilton LLP

Mike Salerno
KRCOM

Silvia Sandrin
Ashurst

Mario Scofferi
Giglio & Scofferi Studio legale del lavoro

Susanna Servi
Carabba & Partners

Massimiliano Silvetti
Nunziante Magrone

Carlo Sinatra
Studio Legale Sinatra

Pierluigi Sodini
Unioncamere

Piervincenzo Spasaro
Spasaro De Martinis Law Firm

Maria Antonietta Tanico
Studio Legale Tanico

Andrea Tedioli
Tedioli Law Firm

Francesca Tironi
TLS - Associazione Professionale di Avvocati e Commercialisti

Giacinto Tommasini
Alegal - International Law Firm

Luca Tufarelli
Ristuccia & Tufarelli

Rachele Vacca de Dominicis
Grieco e Associati

Mario Valentini
Pirola Pennuto Zei & Associati

Vito Vittore
Nunziante Magrone

Angelo Zambelli
Dewey & LeBoeuf

Filippo Zucchinelli
TLS - Associazione Professionale di Avvocati e Commercialisti

JAMAICA

Cheronne Allen
Jamaica Promotions Corporation (JAMPRO)

Roy K. Anderson
The Supreme Court of Jamaica

Paul Barton
Global Trading

Garfield Bryan
Office of Utilities Regulation

Mitzie W. Gordon Burke-Green
Jamaica Trading Services Ltd.

Nicole Foga
Foga Daley

Dave García
Myers, Fletcher & Gordon, member of Lex Mundi

David Geddes
Office of Utilities Regulation

Gavin Goffe
Myers, Fletcher & Gordon, member of Lex Mundi

Nicole Goodin
Jamaica Public Service Company Limited

Herbert Winston Grant
Grant, Stewart, Phillips & Co.

Errol Greene
Kingston and St. Andrew Corporation

Kerry-Ann Heavens
Myers, Fletcher & Gordon, member of Lex Mundi

Corrine N. Henry
Myers, Fletcher & Gordon, member of Lex Mundi

Hopeton Heron
Office of Utilities Regulation

Alicia P. Hussey
Myers, Fletcher & Gordon, member of Lex Mundi

Donovan Jackson
Nunes, Scholefield, DeLeon & Co. Attorney-at-Law

Joan Lawla
Manager, Academician

Noelle Llewellyn Heron
Tax Administration Services Department

Melinda Lloyd
Jamaica Public Service Company Limited

Zaila McCalla
The Supreme Court of Jamaica

Andrine McLaren
Kingston and St. Andrew Corporation

Sandra Minott-Phillips
Myers, Fletcher & Gordon, member of Lex Mundi

Deborah Newland
Lex Caribbean

Lorna Phillips
Nicholson Phillips, Attorneys-at-Law

Gina Phillips Black
Myers, Fletcher & Gordon, member of Lex Mundi

Judith Ramlogan
Companies Office of Jamaica

Hilary Reid
Myers, Fletcher & Gordon, member of Lex Mundi

Heather Rowe
Jamaica Public Service Company Limited

Lisa N. Russell
Myers, Fletcher & Gordon, member of Lex Mundi

Oneil Sherman
Global Trading

Arturo Stewart
Grant, Stewart, Phillips & Co.

Humprey Taylor
Taylor Construction Ltd.

Donovan Wignal
Mairtrans International Logistics Ltd.

Maliaca Wong
Myers, Fletcher & Gordon, member of Lex Mundi

JAPAN

Ernst & Young

Tokyo Electric Power Company Inc.

Miho Arimura
Hatasawa & Wakai Law Firm

Toyoki Emoto
Atsumi & Partners

Miho Fujita
Adachi, Henderson, Miyatake & Fujita

Tatsuya Fukui
Atsumi & Partners

Shinnosuke Fukuoka
Nishimura & Asahi

Mika Haga
Davis & Takahashi

Tamotsu Hatasawa
Hatasawa & Wakai Law Firm

Kan Hayashi
PwC Japan

Takashi Hirose
Oh-Ebashi LPC & Partners

Kenichi Homan
Adachi, Henderson, Miyatake & Fujita

Taro Honda
Atsumi & Partners

Hiroyasu Horimoto
City-Yuwa Partners

Michiya Iwasaki
Atsumi & Partners

Tomomi Kagawa

Aya Kamimura
Nishimura & Asahi

Yosuke Kanegae
Oh-Ebashi LPC & Partners

Hideki Thurgood Kano
Anderson Mori & Tomotsune

Chie Kasahara
Atsumi & Partners

Shigenobu Kataoka
Engineer, Inc.

Takahiro Kato
Nishimura & Asahi

Susumi Kawaguchi
Obayashi Corporation

Kohei Kawamura
Nishimura & Asahi

Yasuyuki Kuribayashi
City-Yuwa Partners

Yukie Kurosawa
O'Melveny & Myers LLP

Yoji Maeda
O'Melveny & Myers LLP

Nobuaki Matsuoka
Osaka International Law Offices

Kazuya Miyakawa
PwC Japan

Toshio Miyatake
Adachi, Henderson, Miyatake & Fujita

Tsuyoshi Mizoguchi
PwC Japan

Michihiro Mori
Nishimura & Asahi

Taeko Morita
Nishimura & Asahi

Masahiro Murashima
Kitahama Partners

Hirosato Nabika
City-Yuwa Partners

Yukie Nakagawa
Atsumi & Partners

Kazutoshi Nishijima
Adachi, Henderson, Miyatake & Fujita

Miho Niunoya
Atsumi & Partners

Takashi Saito
City-Yuwa Partners

Yuka Sakai
City-Yuwa Partners

Takefumi Sato
Anderson Mori & Tomotsune

Tetsuro Sato
Baker & McKenzie

Yoshihito Shibata
Bingham McCutchen Murase, Sakai & Mimura Foreign Law Joint Enterprise

Tomoko Shimomukai
Nishimura & Asahi

Hiroaki Shinomiya
Davis & Takahashi

Hisako Shiotani
Atsumi & Partners

Yuri Sugano
Nishimura & Asahi

Sachiko Sugawara
Atsumi & Partners

Yuri Suzuki
Atsumi & Partners

Hiroyuki Suzuki
PwC Japan

Shunji Suzuki
PwC Japan

Mikio Tasaka
Nittsu Research Institute and Consulting, Inc.

Atsushi Tempaku
Nippon Express Co., Ltd.

Junichi Tobimatsu
Mori Hamada & Matsumoto

Yoshito Tsuji
Obayashi Corporation

Masatoshi Ujimori
Atsumi & Partners

Kenji Utsumi
Nagashima Ohno & Tsunematsu

Jun Yamada
Anderson Mori & Tomotsune

Michi Yamagami
Anderson Mori & Tomotsune

Akio Yamamoto
Kajima Corporation

Yusuke Yukawa
Nishimura & Asahi

JORDAN
Ernst & Young

Tamara Abbadi
Hazboun & Co. for International Legal Business Consultations

Hassan Abdullah
The Jordanian Electric Power Co. Ltd. (JEPCO)

Hayja'a Abu AlHayja'a
Talal Abu Ghazaleh Legal (TAG-Legal)

Nayef Abu Alim
Premier Law Firm LLP

Osama Abu Rub
Law & Arbitration Centre

Ibrahim Abunameh
Law & Arbitration Centre

Maha Al Abdallat
Central Bank of Jordan

Arwa Al-Azzeh
Rajai Dajani & Associates Law Office

Tamara Al-Banna
Khalifeh & Partners

Eman M. Al-Dabbas
International Business Legal Associates

Omar Aljazy
Aljazy & Co. Advocates & Legal Consultants

Sabri S. Al-Khassib
Amman Chamber of Commerce

Mohamed Al-Kurdi
Gardenia Clearance

Mohammad Al-Said

Khaled Asfour
Ali Sharif Zu'bi, Advocates & Legal Consultants, member of Lex Mundi

Micheal T. Dabit
Michael T. Dabit & Associates

Anwar Elliyan
The Jordanian Electric Power Co. Ltd. (JEPCO)

Tariq Hammouri
Hammouri & Partners

George Hazboun
Hazboun & Co. for International Legal Business Consultations

Reem Hazboun
Hazboun & Co. for International Legal Business Consultations

Tayseer Ismail
East Echo Co.

Emad Karkar
PwC Jordan

Ahmed Khalifeh
Hammouri & Partners

Youssef S. Khalilieh
Rajai Dajani & Associates Law Office

Hussein Kofahy
Central Bank of Jordan

Rasha Laswi
Zalloum & Laswi Law Firm

Emad Majid
PwC Jordan

Firas Malhas
International Business Legal Associates

Nizar Musleh
Hazboun & Co. for International Legal Business Consultations

Amer Nabulsi
(NEN) Al Wagayan, Al Awadhi, Al Saif, member of DLA Piper Group

Ahmed Naiemat
Law & Arbitration Centre

Omar B. Naim
National Construction Company

Ridha Nasair
Law Gate Attorneys org

Laith Nasrawin
Aljazy & Co. Advocates & Legal Consultants

Khaldoun Nazer
Khalifeh & Partners

Mutasem Nsair
Khalifeh & Partners

Akram Obeidat
Khalifeh & Partners

Osama Y. Sabbagh
The Jordanian Electric Power Co. Ltd. (JEPCO)

Mohammad Sawafeen
Land and Survey Directorate

Ali Shishani
Crown Logistics

Stephan Stephan
PwC Jordan

Bassil Swaiss
International Business Legal Associates

Mohammed Tarawneh

Mahmoud Wafa
Customs Department

Azzam Zalloum
Zalloum & Laswi Law Firm

Faris Zaru
Faris and Faris

Malek Zreiqat
Ali Sharif Zu'bi, Advocates & Legal Consultants, member of Lex Mundi

Kareem Zureikat

KAZAKHSTAN

Yerkin Abdrakhmanov
PwC Kazakhstan

Askar Abubakirov
Aequitas Law Firm

Zulfiya Akchurina
Grata Law Firm

Aktan Akhmetov
First Credit Bureau

Aman Aliev
Assistance, LLC Law Firm

Jypar Beishenalieva
Michael Wilson & Partners Ltd.

Gulnur Bekmukhanbetova
BMF Group LLP

Assel Bekturganova
Grata Law Firm

Peter Burnie
PwC Kazakhstan

Yelena Bychkova
Aequitas Law Firm

Shaimerden Chikanayev
Grata Law Firm

Richard Chudzynski
Michael Wilson & Partners Ltd.

Walter Daniel
PwC Kazakhstan

Botakoz Dykanbayeva
Grata Law Firm

Ardak Dyussembayeva
Aequitas Law Firm

Vladimir P. Furman
BMF Group LLP

Sevil Gassanova
Macleod Dixon

Karina Iliusizova
PwC Kazakhstan

Semion Issyk
Aequitas Law Firm

Vladimir Ivlev
First Credit Bureau

Kamil Jambakiyev
Macleod Dixon

Dinara M. Jarmukhanova
BMF Group LLP

Thomas Johnson
SNR Denton Kazakhstan Limited

Elena Kaeva
PwC Kazakhstan

Marina Kahiani
Grata Law Firm

Assel Kazbekova
Michael Wilson & Partners Ltd.

Tatyana Kim
Marka Audit ACF LLP

Marina Kolesnikova
Grata Law Firm

Yerbol Konarbayev
SNR Denton Kazakhstan Limited

Anna Kravchenko
Grata Law Firm

Gulfiya Kurmanova
Halyk Bank Kazakhstan

Irina Latipova
Marka Audit ACF LLP

Aigerim Malikova
PwC Kazakhstan

Saule Marka
Marka Audit ACF LLP

Vsevolod Markov
BMF Group LLP

Bolat Miyatov
Grata Law Firm

Saule Mukhambetzhan
Marka Audit ACF LLP

Ruslan Murzashev
BMF Group LLP

Daniyar Mussakhan
Macleod Dixon

Assel Mussina
SNR Denton Kazakhstan Limited

Alina Mustafayeva
Signum Law Firm

Nazira Nurbayeva
PwC Kazakhstan

Zhanar Ordabayeva
BMF Group LLP

Yuliya V. Petrenko
BMF Group LLP

Olga Salimova
ORIS Law Firm

Ernur Seysenov
Desa EC

Gennadiy Shestakov
Kazakhstan Logistics Service

Karina Sultanaliyeva
Aequitas Law Firm

Amir Tussupkhanov
ORIS Law Firm

Zhaniya Ussen
Assistance, LLC Law Firm

Yekaterina V. Kim
Michael Wilson & Partners Ltd.

Marla Valdez
SNR Denton Kazakhstan Limited

Arlan Yerzhanov
Grata Law Firm

Dubek Zhabykenov

Liza Zhumakhmetova
PwC Kazakhstan

Sofiya Zhylkaidarov
Signum Law Firm

KENYA

George Akoto
Akoto & Akoto Advocates

Philip Aluku
SDV Transami

Oliver Fowler
Kaplan & Stratton

Hilary Gachiri
Kaplan & Stratton

Peter Gachuhi
Kaplan & Stratton

Francis Gichuhi
Prism Designs Africa

Edmond Gichuru
Post Bank

William Ikutha Maema
Iseme, Kamau & Maema Advocates

Shellomith Irungu
Anjarwalla & Khanna Advocates

Nigel Jeremy
Daly & Figgis Advocates

Karori Kamau
Iseme, Kamau & Maema Advocates

Benson Kamau
PwC Kenya

Judith Kavuki
KOKA Koimburi & Co.

Hamish Keith
Daly & Figgis Advocates

Morris Kimuli
B.M. Musau & Co. Advocates

Owen Koimburi
KOKA Koimburi & Co.

Nicholas Malonza
Sisule Munyi Kilonzo & Associates

Rosemary Mburu
Institute of Trade Development

James Mburu Kamau
Iseme, Kamau & Maema Advocates

Lilian Membo
SDV Transami

Richard Miano
Iseme, Kamau & Maema Advocates

Mansoor A. Mohamed
Ruman Ship Contractors Limited

Bernard Muange
Anjarwalla & Khanna Advocates

Davies Mugo
Lafarge

Benjamin Musau
B.M. Musau & Co. Advocates

Muteti Mutisya
B.M. Musau & Co. Advocates

Wachira Ndege
Credit Reference Bureau Africa Ltd.

Christina Ndiho
Kaplan & Stratton

Joseph Ng'ang'ira
Daly & Figgis Advocates

Kenneth Nganzi
Unilever Kenya Ltd.

Beatrice Bosibori Nyabira
Iseme, Kamau & Maema Advocates

Conrad Nyukuri
Chunga Associates

Julius Odawo
Lafarge

Gilbert Okello
Lafarge

Sam Omukoko
Metropol Corporation Ltd.

Tom Odhiambo Onyango
Ochieng, Onyango, Kibet & Ohaga

Robert Osiro
Lafarge

Cephas Osoro
Crowe Horwath EA, member Crowe Horwath International

Don Priestman
The Kenya Power and Lighting Company Ltd.

Sonal Sejpal
Anjarwalla & Khanna Advocates

Rajesh Shah
PwC Kenya

Deepen Shah
Walker Kontos Advocates

Christopher Siambe
Crown Agents Ltd.

David Tanki
Lan-x Africa Ltd.

Joseph Taracha
Central Bank of Kenya

Peter Wahome
PwC Kenya

Nicholas Wambua
B.M. Musau & Co. Advocates

Angela Waweru
Kaplan & Stratton

KIRIBATI

Kiribati Ports Authority (KPA)

Public Utilities Board

Kibae Akaaka
Ministry of Finance

Mary Amanu
Moel Trading Co. Ltd.

Neiran Areta
Ministry of Commerce, Industry and Cooperatives

Kenneth Barden
Attorney-at-Law

Rengaua Bauro
Ministry of Finance

Moanataake Beiabure
Ministry of Public Works and Utilities

Taake Cama
Ministry of Finance

Kiata Tebau Kahure
KK & Sons

Willie Karakaua Maen
Moel Trading Co. Ltd.

Tekeeua Kauongo
ANZ Bank (Kiribati) Ltd.

Iaokiri Koreaua
Kiribati Customs Service (KCS)

Terence Low
ANZ Bank (Kiribati) Ltd.

Paul McLaughlin
Ca'Bella Betio Construction

Debrah Mercurio
Office of the People's Lawyer

Tekaai Mikaer
Swire Shipping Ltd.

Lawrence Muller
Oceanic Shipping Service

Tetiro Semilota
High Court of Kiribati

Eliza Takotaake
Betio Town Council

Tieri Tamoa
Ministry of Commerce, Industry and Cooperatives

Martin Tekanene
Kiribati Provident Fund

Batitea Tekanito
Development Bank of Kiribati

Moaniti Teuea
Joyce Shipping Line

Reei Tioti
Ministry of Environment, Lands & Agriculture Development (MELAD)

KOREA, REP.

Yong Seok Ahn
Lee & Ko

Cheolhyo Ahn
Yulchon

Jong-Hyun Baek
Jeil Broker

Min-Sook Chae
Korea Credit Bureau

Min-Jeong Cho
Korea Credit Bureau

Hyeong-Tae Cho
Samil PricewaterhouseCoopers

Hyoung-Kyun Choi
Korea Customs Service

Han-Jun Chon
Samil PricewaterhouseCoopers

Eui Jong Chung
Bae, Kim & Lee LLC

Sang-goo Han
Yoon & Yang LLC.

C.W. Hyun
Kim & Chang

James I.S. Jeon
Sojong Partners

Goo-Chun Jeong
Korea Customs Service

In Beom Jin
Cheon Ji Accounting Corporation, member of Russell Bedford International

Bo Moon Jung
Kim & Chang

Sang Wook Kang
Korean Electrical Contractors Association

Sung Won Kim
Hanaro TNS

Se Jin Kim
Hwang Mok Park P.C.

Yoon Young Kim
Hwang Mok Park P.C.

Hyo-Sang Kim
Kim & Chang

Jung-In Kim
Korea Credit Bureau

Miok Kim
Kim & Chang

Yong-Chul Kim
Korea Customs Service

Kyu-Dong Kim
Samil PricewaterhouseCoopers

Wan-Seok Kim
Samil PricewaterhouseCoopers

Young-Sik Kim
Samil PricewaterhouseCoopers

S.E. Stephan Kim
Sojong Partners

Kwang Soo Kim
Woosun Electric Company Ltd.

Wonhyung Kim
Yoon & Yang LLC.

Joong Hoon Kwak
Lee & Ko

Ki Hyun Kwon
Cheon Ji Accounting Corporation, member of Russell Bedford International

Hye Jeong Lee
Ahnse Law Offices

Sung Whan Lee
Ahnse Law Offices

Jung-Un Lee
Kim & Chang

Seung Yoon Lee
Kim & Chang

Kyu Wha Lee
Lee & Ko

Hongyou Lee
Panalpina IAF Ltd.

Jin-Young Lee
Samil PricewaterhouseCoopers

Jong Ho Lee
Sojong Partners

Ji Woong Lim
Yulchon

Chul-Gue Maeng
Korea Customs Service

Ho Joon Moon
Lee & Ko

Yon-Kyun Oh
Kim & Chang

Joo Seok Paik
Sojong Partners

Ji Yeoun Park
Hwang Mok Park P.C.

Sang Il Park
Hwang Mok Park P.C.

Soo-Hwan Park
Samil PricewaterhouseCoopers

Jeong Seo
Kim & Chang

Brian Shim
Cheon Ji Accounting Corporation, member of Russell Bedford International

Won-Il Sohn
Yulchon

Bong Woo Song
Hanjin Shipping Co. Ltd.

Jiwon Suh
Ministry of Strategy and Finance

Kyung Hee Suh
Yulchon

Huh Uoung-uhk
KEPCO Economy Management Research Institute (KEMRI)

Dong-Suk Wang
Korea Credit Bureau

Jee Yeon Yu
Kim & Chang

KOSOVO

Kosovo Energy Corporation J.S.C.

Shyqiri Bytyqi VALA Consulting

Muhamed Disha
Kosovo Investment Promotion Agency

Sokol Elmazaj
Boga & Associates

Mirjeta Emini
Boga & Associates

Lorena Gega
PwC Albania

Maliq Gjyshinca
Intereuropa Kosova LLC

Mustafa Hasani
Kosovo Investment Promotion Agency

Ahmet Hasolli
Kalo & Associates

Virtyt Ibrahimaga
Avokatura I.O.T.

Bejtush Isufi
Interlex Associates l.l.c.

Besarta Kllokoqi
Boga & Associates

Agron Krasniqi
Boga & Associates

Sabina Lalaj
Boga & Associates

Abedin Matoshi
Interlex Associates l.l.c.

Fitore Mekaj
Boga & Associates

Dairida Metalia
PwC Albania

Ilir Murseli
Murseli Architects & Partners

Arben Mustafa
Intereuropa Kosova LLC

Gazmend Nushi
Kalo & Associates

Besim Osmani
Interlex Associates l.l.c.

Andi Pacani
Boga & Associates

Gazmend Pallaska
Pallaska & Associates

Loreta Peci
PwC Albania

Mehdi Pllashniku
Kosovo Business Registartion Agency

Vigan Rogova
Ethem Rogova Law Firm

Iliriana Osmani Serreqi
Avokatura I.O.T.

Flakron Sylejmani
Law Firm Ibrahimaga/Osamni/Tigani

Kreshnik Thaqi
Kosovo Investment Promotion Agency

Anita Tigani
Law Firm Ibrahimaga/Osamni/Tigani

Paul Tobin
PwC Bulgaria

Jeton Vokshi
Intereuropa Kosova LLC

Shaha Zylfiu
Central Bank of the Republic of Kosovo

KUWAIT

Credit Information Network

Ernst & Young

Freight Excel Logistics

Labeed Abdal
The Law Firm of Labeed Abdal

Hossam Abduel Fetouh

Mahmoud Abdulfattah
The Law Offices of Mishari Al-Ghazali

Hossam Abdullah
ASAR – Al Ruwayeh & Partners

Waleed Abdulrahim
Abdullah Kh. Al-Ayoub & Associates, member of Lex Mundi

Lina A.K. Adlouni
KIPCO Asset Management Company K.S.C

Abdullah Musfir Al Hayyan
Kuwait University

Faten Al Naqeeb
Ali & Partners

Fahad Al Zumai
Gust University

Aiman Alaraj
KEO International Consultants

Abdullah Al-Ayoub
Abdullah Kh. Al-Ayoub & Associates, member of Lex Mundi

Omar Hamad Yousuf Al-Essa
The Law Office of Al-Essa & Partners

Nada F. A. Al-Fahad
GEC DAR

Ammar Al-Fouzan
The Law Offices of Mishari Al-Ghazali

Mishari M. Al-Ghazali
The Law Offices of Mishari Al-Ghazali

Reema Ali
Ali & Partners

Akusa Batwala
ASAR – Al Ruwayeh & Partners

Christoph Birk
Panalpina World Transport (Kuwait) WLL

Nada Bourahmah
The Law Offices of Mishari Al-Ghazali

Luis Nene Cunha
ASAR – Al Ruwayeh & Partners

Paul Day
ASAR – Al Ruwayeh & Partners

Mahmoud Ezzat
Burgan Bank

Yaser Farook
GEC DAR

Sam Habbas
ASAR – Al Ruwayeh & Partners

Chirine Krayem Moujaes
The Law Offices of Mishari Al-Ghazali

Dany Labaki
The Law office of Al-Essa & Partners

Dany Labaky
The Law Office of Al-Essa & Partners

Amer Nabulsi
(NEN) Al Wagayan, Al Awadhi, Al Saif, member of DLA Piper Group

Anupama Nair
ABDULLAH KH. AL-AYOUB & ASSOCIATES, MEMBER OF LEX MUNDI

Mohammed Ramadan
AL MARKAZ LAW FIRM

Shafeek Rhaman
MAY INTERNATIONAL A-Z FREIGHT SOLUTIONS

Abdul Qayyum Saeed
GHF LAWYERS

David Walker
ASAR – AL RUWAYEH & PARTNERS

KYRGYZ REPUBLIC

Alexander Ahn
KALIKOVA & ASSOCIATES LAW FIRM

Shuhrat Akhmatakhunov
KALIKOVA & ASSOCIATES LAW FIRM

Gulnara Akhmatova
INTERNATIONAL BUSINESS COUNCIL

Niyazbek Aldashev
LORENZ INTERNATIONAL LAW FIRM

Nurlan Alymbaev
ANDASH MAINING COMPANY LLC

Iskender Batyrbekov
LORENZ INTERNATIONAL LAW FIRM

Richard Bregonje
PwC KAZAKHSTAN

Peter Burnie
PwC KAZAKHSTAN

Samara Dumanaeva
LORENZ INTERNATIONAL LAW FIRM

Akjoltoi Elebesova
CREDIT INFORMATION BUREAU ISHENIM

Leyla Gulieva
LORENZ INTERNATIONAL LAW FIRM

Saltanat Ismailova
PwC KAZAKHSTAN

Nurbek Ismankulov
M&M TRANSPORT LOGISTIC SERVICES

Elena Kaeva
PwC KAZAKHSTAN

Gulnara Kalikova
KALIKOVA & ASSOCIATES LAW FIRM

Assel Khamzina
PwC KAZAKHSTAN

Nurdin Kumushbekov
USAID BUSINESS ENVIRONMENT IMPROVEMENT PROJECT THE PRAGMA CORPORATION

Svetlana Lebedeva
LORENZ INTERNATIONAL LAW FIRM

Marina Lim
KALIKOVA & ASSOCIATES LAW FIRM

Asel Momoshova
KALIKOVA & ASSOCIATES LAW FIRM

Almas Nakipov
PwC KAZAKHSTAN

Karlygash Ospankulova
KALIKOVA & ASSOCIATES LAW FIRM

Nurbek Sabirov
KALIKOVA & ASSOCIATES LAW FIRM

Kanat Seidaliev
GRATA LAW FIRM

Temirbek Shabdanaliev
ASSOCIATION OF CARRIERS AND FREIGHT-FORWARDERS OF KYRGYZSTAN

Elvira Sharshekeeva
GRATA LAW FIRM

Maksim Smirnov
KALIKOVA & ASSOCIATES LAW FIRM

Aisuluu Sydygalieva
USAID BEI BUSINESS ENVIRONMENT IMPROVEMENT PROJECT (BY PRAGMA CORPORATION)

Ulan Tilenbaev
KALIKOVA & ASSOCIATES LAW FIRM

Kamila Tursunkulova
PwC KAZAKHSTAN

Gulnara Uskenbaeva
AUDIT PLUS

Azim Usmanov
GRATA LAW FIRM

Ali Ramazanovich Vodyanov
ELECTROSILA

LAO PDR

ENTERPRISE REGISTRY OFFICE

John Biddle
LS HORIZON LIMITED (LAO)

John Bowes
KPMG LAO CO. LTD.

Xaynari Chanthala
LS HORIZON LIMITED (LAO)

Sithong Chanthasouk

Aristotle David
DFDL MEKONG LAW GROUP

Sornpheth Douangdy

Daodeuane Duangdara
PRICEWATERHOUSECOOPERS (LAO) LTD.

William D. Greenlee, Jr.
DFDL MEKONG LAW GROUP

Somdy Inmyxay
SME PROMOTION AND DEVELOPMENT OFFICE

Latsamy Inthavong
EDL UTILITY AND NETWORKS

Ganesan Kolandevelu
KPMG LAO CO. LTD.

Litsamy Latsavong

Khamkhong Liemphrachan
R&T KHOUN MUANG LAO CO.,LTD.

Chris Manley
DFDL MEKONG LAW GROUP

Varavudh Meesaiyati
PRICEWATERHOUSECOOPERS (LAO) LTD.

Somlack Nhoybouakong
LAO FREIGHT FORWARDER CO. LTD.

Somphone Phasavath
LAO FREIGHT FORWARDER CO. LTD.

Khamphaeng Phochanthilath
DFDL MEKONG LAW GROUP

Ketsana Phommachanh
MINISTRY OF JUSTICE

Phasith Phommarak

Thavorn Rujivanarom
PwC THAILAND

Vichit Sadettan
LAO FREIGHT FORWARDER CO. LTD.

Ei Ei (Jessica) San
KPMG LAO CO. LTD.

Khamsene Sayavong
LAO LAW & CONSULTANCY GROUP

Siri Sayavong
LAO LAW & CONSULTANCY GROUP

Sivath Sengdouangchanh
CONSULTANT

Darika Soponawat
PRICEWATERHOUSECOOPERS (LAO) LTD.

Phonxay Southiphong
DESIGN GROUP CO. LTD.

Sengdara Tiamtisack
LAO FREIGHT FORWARDER CO. LTD.

Andrea Wilson
DFDL MEKONG LAW GROUP

LATVIA

ERNST & YOUNG

Ilze Abika
SKUDRA & UDRIS LAW OFFICES

Martins Aljens
RAIDLA LEJINS & NORCOUS

Laura Ausekle
LATVIJAS BANKA

Ieva Balcere
LAW FIRM SORAINEN

Ilona Bauda

Elina Bedanova
RAIDLA LEJINS & NORCOUS

Eva Berlaus
LAW FIRM SORAINEN

Andis Burkevics
LAW FIRM SORAINEN

Andis Čonka
LATVIJAS BANKA

Ingrida Dimina
PwC LATVIA

Valters Diure
LAWIN KLAVINS & SLAIDINS

Zane Džule
ATTORNEYS AT LAW BORENIUS

Zlata Elksnina-Zascirinska
PwC LATVIA

Valters Gencs
GENCS VALTERS LAW FIRM

Andris Ignatenko
ESTMA LTD.

Janis Irbe
LATVENERGO AS, SADALES TIKLS

Zinta Jansons
LAWIN KLAVINS & SLAIDINS

Helmuts Jauja
LATVIAN INSOLVENCY ADMINISTRATION

Sandis Jermuts
PUBLIC UTILITIES COMMISSION LATVIA

Aris Kakstans
EVERSHEDS BITĀNS

Dace Kalnmeiere
ATTORNEYS AT LAW BORENIUS

Irina Kostina
LAWIN KLAVINS & SLAIDINS

Gunda Leite
GENCS VALTERS LAW FIRM

Dainis Leons
LATVENERGO AS, SADALES TIKLS

Indrikis Liepa
ATTORNEYS AT LAW BORENIUS

Janis Loze

Irina Olevska
ATTORNEYS AT LAW BORENIUS

Sergejs Rudans
ATTORNEYS AT LAW BORENIUS

Lāsma Rugāte
LAW FIRM SORAINEN

Dace Silava-Tomsone
RAIDLA LEJINS & NORCOUS

Anita Sondore
GENCS VALTERS LAW FIRM

Mihails Špika
JSC DZINTARS

Sarmis Spilbergs
LAWIN KLAVINS & SLAIDINS

Zane Štālberga – Markvarte
MARKVARTE LEXCHANGE LAW OFFICE

Anatolij Strelin
COLLIERS INTERNATIONAL

Ruta Teresko
AZ SERVICE SIA

Maija Tipaine
RAIDLA LEJINS & NORCOUS

Ziedonis Udris
SKUDRA & UDRIS LAW OFFICES

Maris Vainovskis
EVERSHEDS BITĀNS

Krista Zariņa
LAWIN KLAVINS & SLAIDINS

Agate Ziverte
PwC LATVIA

Daiga Zivtina
LAWIN KLAVINS & SLAIDINS

LEBANON

ELECTRICITÉ DU LIBAN

ERNST & YOUNG

KORDAHI EST. COMPANY

Nadim Abboud
LAW OFFICE OF A. ABBOUD & ASSOCIATES

Hanan Abboud
PwC LEBANON

Nada Abdelsater-Abusamra
RAPHAËL & ASSOCIÉS

Wassim Abou Nader
MENA CITY LAWYERS

Wadih Abou Nasr
PwC LEBANON

Karen Baroud
PwC LEBANON

Jean Baroudi
BAROUDI & ASSOCIATES

Tarek Baz
HYAM G. MALLAT LAW FIRM

Katia Bou Assi
MOGHAIZEL LAW FIRM, MEMBER OF LEX MUNDI

Melynda BouAoun
BADRI AND SALIM EL MEOUCHI LAW FIRM, MEMBER OF INTERLEGES

Najib Choucair
CENTRAL BANK OF LEBANON

Sanna Daakour
MENA CITY LAWYERS

Aline Dantziguian
CHAMBER OF COMMERCE, INDUSTRY & AGRICULTURE OF BEIRUT

Michel Doueihy
BADRI AND SALIM EL MEOUCHI LAW FIRM, MEMBER OF INTERLEGES

Chadia El Meouchi
BADRI AND SALIM EL MEOUCHI LAW FIRM, MEMBER OF INTERLEGES

Sarah Fakhry
BADRI AND SALIM EL MEOUCHI LAW FIRM, MEMBER OF INTERLEGES

Dania George
PwC LEBANON

Abdallah Hayek
HAYEK GROUP

Antoine Hayek
RAPHAËL & ASSOCIÉS

Alexa Hechaime
HECHAIME LAW FIRM

Wajih Hechaime
HECHAIME LAW FIRM

Walid Honein
BADRI AND SALIM EL MEOUCHI LAW FIRM, MEMBER OF INTERLEGES

Maher Hoteit
MENA CITY LAWYERS

Dany Issa
MOGHAIZEL LAW FIRM, MEMBER OF LEX MUNDI

Marie-Anne Jabbour
BADRI AND SALIM EL MEOUCHI LAW FIRM, MEMBER OF INTERLEGES

Fady Jamaleddine
MENA CITY LAWYERS

Edgard Joujou
KPMG PCC

Elie Kachouh
ELC TRANSPORT SERVICES SAL

Georges Kadige
KADIGE & KADIGE LAW FIRM

Michel Kadige
KADIGE & KADIGE LAW FIRM

Najib Khattar
KHATTAR ASSOCIATES

Josephine Khoury
TALAL ABU GHAZALEH LEGAL (TAG-LEGAL)

Albert Laham

Georges Mallat
HYAM G. MALLAT LAW FIRM

Nabil Mallat
HYAM G. MALLAT LAW FIRM

Fares Moawad

Fadi Moghaizel
MOGHAIZEL LAW FIRM, MEMBER OF LEX MUNDI

Mario Mohanna
PATRIMOINE CONSEIL SARL

Rita Moukarzel
BADRI AND SALIM EL MEOUCHI LAW FIRM, MEMBER OF INTERLEGES

Andre Nader
NADER LAW OFFICE

Rana Nader
NADER LAW OFFICE

Toufic Nehme
LAW OFFICE OF ALBERT LAHAM

Hala Raphael-Abillama
RAPHAËL & ASSOCIÉS

Mireille Richa
TYAN & ZGHEIB LAW FIRM

Jihane Rizk Khattar
KHATTAR ASSOCIATES

Jihad Rizkallah
BADRI AND SALIM EL MEOUCHI LAW FIRM, MEMBER OF INTERLEGES

Samir Safa
BAROUDI & ASSOCIATES

Joseph Safar
HAYEK GROUP

Rached Sarkis
RACHED SARKIS - CONSULTANT

Antoine Sfeir
BADRI AND SALIM EL MEOUCHI LAW FIRM, MEMBER OF INTERLEGES

George Tannous
BEIRUT INTERNATIONAL MOVERS

Bassel Tohme
MENA CITY LAWYERS

Nady Tyan
TYAN & ZGHEIB LAW FIRM

Rania Yazbeck
TYAN & ZGHEIB LAW FIRM

LESOTHO

ERNST & YOUNG

HARLEY & MORRIS

WEBBER NEWDIGATE

Lebereko Lethobane
LABOUR COURT LESOTHO

Qhalehang Letsika
MEI & MEI ATTORNEYS INC.

Sechaba Makhabane
SELLO-MAFATLE ATTORNEYS

Bokang Makhaketso
MINISTRY OF JUSTICE

Thakane Makume
LESOTHO ELECTRICITY COMPANY (PTY) LTD.

Moeketsi Marumo
POWERCONSULT (PTY) LTD.

Andrew Marumo
SHEERAN & ASSOCIATES

Thandiwe Metsing

Molomo Mohale
SYSTEMATIC ARCHITECTS

Sentsuoe Lenka Mohau
REGISTRAR - GENERAL

M.R. Mokhethi
MASERU CITY COUNCIL

Phillip Mophethe
PHILLIPS CLEARING & FORWARDING AGENT
(PTY.) LTD.

Phelane Phomane

Duduzile Seamatha
SHEERAN & ASSOCIATES

Tiisetso Sello-Mafatle
SELLO-MAFATLE ATTORNEYS

Marorisang Thekiso
SHEERAN & ASSOCIATES

Phoka Thene

Mahlape Tjela
NEDBANK LESOTHO LTD.

LIBERIA

CENTRAL BANK OF LIBERIA

LIBERIA LAW SERVICES

Amos P. Andrews
ECOBANK

Gideon Ayi-Owoo
PwC GHANA

Christiana Baah
PwC GHANA

F. Augustus Caesar, Jr.
CAESAR ARCHITECTS, INC.

Henry Reed Cooper
COOPER & TOGBAH LAW OFFICE

Peter Doe-Sumah
GREHZON HOLDINGS (LIBERIA) INC.

Uzoma Ebeku
COOPER & TOGBAH LAW OFFICE

Patrick S. Fallah
ECOBANK

Christine Sonpon Freeman
COOPER & TOGBAH LAW OFFICE

Anthony Henry
CUTTINGTON UNIVERSITY GRADUATE
SCHOOL

Cyril Jones
JONES & JONES

Abu Kamara
MINISTRY OF COMMERCE & INDUSTRY

Elijah Karnley
MINISTRY OF PUBLIC WORKS

Samuel T. K. Kortimai
COOPER & TOGBAH LAW OFFICE

Mary Kwarteng
PwC GHANA

George Kwatia
PwC GHANA

Prossie Namakula
PwC GHANA

Miriam Nortey
PwC GHANA

Sylvanus O'Connor
AEP CONSULTANTS INC.

Sylvester Rennie
COOPER & TOGBAH LAW OFFICE

Bloh Sayeh
CENTER FOR NATIONAL DOCUMENTS &
RECORDS (NATIONAL ARCHIVES)

Yancy Seeboe
NATIONAL CUSTOM BROKERS ASSOCIATION
OF LIBERIA

Benjamin M. Togbah
COOPER & TOGBAH LAW OFFICE

Jerome Verdier
VERDIER AND ASSOCIATES

G. Lahaison Waritay
MINISTRY OF PUBLIC WORKS

T. Negbalee Warner
PIERRE, TWEH & ASSOCIATES

Darcy White
PwC GHANA

LITHUANIA

ERNST & YOUNG

Kęstutis Adamonis
LAW FIRM SORAINEN

Dovile Alekniene
GENCS VALTERS LAW FIRM

Dovile Aukstuolyte
ECOVIS MISKINIS, KVAINAUSKAS IR
PARTNERIAI ADVOKATU KONTORA

Pavel Balbatunov
UAB CONVENTUS

Petras Baltusevičius
DSV TRANSPORT UAB

Donatas Baranauskas
VILNIAUS MIESTO 14 - ASIS NOTARU
BIURAS

Kim Bartholdy
DSV TRANSPORT UAB

Vilius Bernatonis
TARK GRUNTE SUTKIENE

Andrius Bogdanovičius
JSC "CREDITINFO LIETUVA"

Ina Budelinaitė
LAW FIRM SORAINEN

Dovilė Burgienė
LAW FIRM LAWIN

Jurate Burnell
AMERINDE CONSOLIDATED, INC.

Dovile Cepulyte
LAW FIRM LAWIN

Giedre Cerniauske
LAW FIRM LAWIN

Robertas Čiočys
LAW FIRM LAWIN

Giedre Dailidenaite
VARUL

Lina Daruliene
AAA BALTIC SERVICE COMPANY - LAW
FIRM

Gintaras Daugela
BANK OF LITHUANIA

Goda Deltuvaitė
LAW FIRM SORAINEN

Giedre Domkute
AAA BALTIC SERVICE COMPANY - LAW
FIRM

Ieva Dosinaite
RAIDLA LEJINS & NORCOUS

Dalia Foigt-Norvaišienė
ATTORNEYS AT LAW BORENIUS

Valters Gencs
GENCS VALTERS LAW FIRM

Simas Gudynas
LAW FIRM LAWIN

Arturas Gutauskas
ECOVIS MISKINIS, KVAINAUSKAS IR
PARTNERIAI ADVOKATU KONTORA

Frank Heemann
BNT HEEMANN KLAUBERG KRAUKLIS APB

Indrė Jonaitytė
LAW FIRM LAWIN

Agne Jonaitytė
LAW FIRM SORAINEN

Povilas Junevičius
LAW FIRM LAWIN

Romualdas Kasperavičius

Jonas Kiauleikis
ATTORNEYS AT LAW BORENIUS

Jurgita Kiškiūnaitė
LAW FIRM ZABIELA, ZABIELAITE &
PARTNERS

Monika Knyzelyte
AMERINDE CONSOLIDATED, INC.

Kristina Kriščiūnaitė
PwC LITHUANIA

Ronaldas Kubilius
PwC LITHUANIA

Egidijus Kundelis
PwC LITHUANIA

Kęstutis Kvainauskas.
ECOVIS MISKINIS, KVAINAUSKAS IR
PARTNERIAI ADVOKATU KONTORA

Žilvinas Kvietkus
RAIDLA LEJINS & NORCOUS

Gytis Malinauskas
LAW FIRM SORAINEN

Linas Margevicius
LEGAL BUREAU OF LINAS MARGEVICIUS

Marius Matiukas
TARK GRUNTE SUTKIENE

Rūta Matonienė
VILNIUS CITY MUNICIPALITY

Vaidotas Melynavicius
AAA BALTIC SERVICE COMPANY -LAW
FIRM

Tomas Mieliauskas
LAW FIRM FORESTA

Bronislovas Mikūta

Jurate Misionyte
TARK GRUNTE SUTKIENE

Asta Misiukiene
MINISTRY OF ECONOMY OF THE REPUBLIC
OF LITHUANIA

Žygimantas Pacevičius
ATTORNEYS AT LAW BORENIUS

Rytis Paukste
LAW FIRM LAWIN

Algirdas Pekšys
LAW FIRM SORAINEN

Mantas Petkevičius
LAW FIRM SORAINEN

Angelija Petrauskienė
VILNIUS CITY MUNICIPALITY

Andrius Pilkauskas
ATTORNEYS AT LAW BORENIUS

Diana Puodziunaite
AMERINDE CONSOLIDATED, INC.

Amanda Revalde
GENCS VALTERS LAW FIRM

Marius Rindinas
LAW FIRM ZABIELA, ZABIELAITE &
PARTNERS

Rimantas Simaitis
RAIDLA LEJINS & NORCOUS

Egle Sliogeryte
AMERINDE CONSOLIDATED, INC.

Julija Solovjova
PwC LITHUANIA

Alius Stamkauskas
UAB ELMONTA

Jonas Stamkauskas
UAB ELMONTA

Marius Stračkaitis
LITHUANIAN NOTARY CHAMBER

Mindaugas Vaiciunas
ATTORNEYS AT LAW BORENIUS

Vilija Vaitkutė Pavan
LAW FIRM LAWIN

Adrijus Vegys
BANK OF LITHUANIA

Darius Zabiela
LAW FIRM ZABIELA, ZABIELAITE &
PARTNERS

Giedre Zalpyte
BNT HEEMANN KLAUBERG KRAUKLIS APB

Agnietė Žukauskaitė
LAW FIRM SORAINEN

Audrius Žvybas
GLIMSTEDT

LUXEMBOURG

ALLEN & OVERY LUXEMBOURG

INSTITUT LUXEMBOURGEOIS DE RÉGULATION

PAUL WURTH S.A. ENGINEERING &
PROJECT MANAGEMENT

Clemens Abt
KUEHNE + NAGEL KN LUXEMBOURG

Lara Aherne
BONN SCHMITT STEICHEN, MEMBER OF
LEX MUNDI

Guy Arendt
BONN SCHMITT STEICHEN, MEMBER OF
LEX MUNDI

Jalila Bakkali
PwC LUXEMBOURG

Louis Berns
ARENDT & MEDERNACH

Sabrina Bodson
ARENDT & MEDERNACH

Eleonora Broman
LOYENS & LOEFF

Olivier Buscheman
PwC LUXEMBOURG

Guy Castegnaro
IUS LABORIS LUXEMBOURG,
CASTEGNARO

Christel Dumont
OPF PARTNERS

Gérard Eischen
CHAMBER OF COMMERCE OF THE GRAND-
DUCHY OF LUXEMBOURG

Annie Elfassi
LOYENS & LOEFF

Martine Gerber Lemaire
OPF PARTNERS

Anabela Fernandes Gonçalves
PwC LUXEMBOURG

Alain Grosjean
BONN SCHMITT STEICHEN, MEMBER OF
LEX MUNDI

Véronique Hoffeld
LOYENS & LOEFF

Anthony Husianycia
PwC LUXEMBOURG

Renata Jokubauskaite
BONN SCHMITT STEICHEN, MEMBER OF
LEX MUNDI

Pierre-Alexandre Lechantre
LINKLATERS

Michaël Lockman
PwC LUXEMBOURG

Tom Loesch
LINKLATERS

Slke Metzdorf
KUEHNE + NAGEL KN LUXEMBOURG

Séverine Moca
PwC LUXEMBOURG

Charles Monnier
LINKLATERS

Peter Moons
LOYENS & LOEFF

Anne Murrath
PwC LUXEMBOURG

Laurent Paquet
PwC LUXEMBOURG

Simon Paul
LOYENS & LOEFF

Françoise Pfeiffer
SPEECHLY BIRCHAM PFEIFFER & PARTNERS

Wim Piot
PwC LUXEMBOURG

Judith Raijmakers
LOYENS & LOEFF

Jean-Luc Schaus
PIERRE THIELEN AVOCATS

Phillipe Schmit
ARENDT & MEDERNACH

Alex Schmitt
BONN SCHMITT STEICHEN, MEMBER OF
LEX MUNDI

Elodie Simonian
OPF PARTNERS

Alessandro Sorcinelli
LINKLATERS

Davide Visin
PwC LUXEMBOURG

Frank von Roesgen
SCHROEDER & ASSOCIÉS

Cynetta Walters
FITZWILLIAM STONE FURNESS-SMITH &
MORGAN

MACEDONIA, FYR

ERNST & YOUNG

Slavica Bogoeva
MACEDONIAN CREDIT BUREAU AD SKOPJE

PwC MACEDONIA

Zivko Ackoski
NOTARY OFFICE ACKOSKI

Mitko Aleksov
MACEDONIAN CHAMBERS OF COMMERCE

Nada Andonovska
IKRP ROKAS & PARTNERS

Zoran Andonovski
POLENAK LAW FIRM

Natasha Andreeva
NATIONAL BANK OF THE REPUBLIC OF
MACEDONIA

Zlatko Antevski
LAWYERS ANTEVSKI

Rubin Atanasoski
TIMELPROJECT ENGINEERING

Dragan Blažev
TIMELPROJECT ENGINEERING

Jela Boskovic
IKRP ROKAS & PARTNERS

Biljana Briskoska-Boskovski
MINISTRY OF JUSTICE, REPUBLIC OF
MACEDONIA

Biljana Čakmakova
CAKMAKOVA ADVOCATES

Tanja Cenova-Mitrovska
AGENCY FOR REAL ESTATE CADASTRE

Ema Cubrinovska
ENERGO DIZAJN

Aleksandar Dimić
POLENAK LAW FIRM

Josip Dimitrovski
LIKVIDAT DOOEL - BITOLA

Elena Dimova
CAKMAKOVA ADVOCATES

Dragi Dimovski
TP DRAGI ALEKSANDAR DIMOVSKI

Jakup Fetai
AGENCY FOR REAL ESTATE CADASTRE

Vesna Gavriloska
CAKMAKOVA ADVOCATES

Ljupco Georgievski
AGENCY FOR REAL ESTATE CADASTRE

Radica Lazareska Gerovska
MINISTRY OF JUSTICE, REPUBLIC OF
MACEDONIA

Marijana Gjoreska
CENTRAL REGISTRY OF THE REPUBLIC OF
MACEDONIA

Goce Gruevski
AGENCY FOR REAL ESTATE CADASTRE

Verica Hadzi Vasileva-Markovska
AAG - ANALYSIS AND ADVISORY GROUP

Ana Hadzieva
POLENAK LAW FIRM

Slobodan Hristovski
POLENAK LAW FIRM

Biljana Ickovska
LAW OFFICE NIKOLOVSKI & ASSOCIATES

Aleksandar Ickovski

Marjan Ivanov
EURO CONSULT

Nena Ivanovska
JUDICIAL REFORM IMPLEMENTATION PROJECT

Dragan Ivanovski
CUSTOMS ADMINISTRATION

Maja Jakimovska
CAKMAKOVA ADVOCATES

Ilija Janoski
CUSTOMS ADMINISTRATION

Dragana Jasevic
LAW OFFICE NIKOLOVSKI & ASSOCIATES

Biljana Joanidis
LAW & PATENT OFFICE JOANIDIS

Svetlana Jovanoska
REPUBLIC OF MACEDONIA, MUNICIPALITY OF GAZI BABA - SKOPJE

Aneta Jovanoska Trajanovska
LAWYERS ANTEVSKI

Aleksandar Kcev
POLENAK LAW FIRM

Dejan Knezović
LAW OFFICE KNEZOVIC & ASSOCIATES

Sead Kocan
MACEDONIAN CHAMBERS OF COMMERCE

Vancho Kostadinovski
CENTRAL REGISTRY OF THE REPUBLIC OF MACEDONIA

Lidija Krstevska
AGENCY FOR REAL ESTATE CADASTRE

Dragan Manailov
SINTEK

Irena Mitkovska
LAWYERS ANTEVSKI

Martin Monevski
MONEVSKI LAW FIRM

Valerjan Monevski
MONEVSKI LAW FIRM

Elena Mucheva
NATIONAL BANK OF THE REPUBLIC OF MACEDONIA

Gorgi Naumovski
CUSTOMS ADMINISTRATION

Svetlana Neceva
LAW OFFICE PEPELJUGOSKI

Ilija Nedelkoski
CAKMAKOVA ADVOCATES

Marina Nikoloska
CAKMAKOVA ADVOCATES

Marija Nikolova
LAW OFFICE KNEZOVIC & ASSOCIATES

Vesna Nikolovska
LAW OFFICE NIKOLOVSKI & ASSOCIATES

Goran Nikolovski
LAW OFFICE NIKOLOVSKI & ASSOCIATES

Zlatko Nikolovski
NOTARY CHAMBER OF R. OF MACEDONIA

Valentin Pepeljugoski
LAW OFFICE PEPELJUGOSKI

Sonja Peshevska
LAW OFFICE PEPELJUGOSKI

Nesa Petrusevska
AGENCY FOR REAL ESTATE CADASTRE

Kristijan Polenak
POLENAK LAW FIRM

Tatjana Popovski Buloski
POLENAK LAW FIRM

Zorica Pulejkova
REPUBLIC OF MACEDONIA NOTARY PUBLIC

Gligor Ralev
AGENCY FOR REAL ESTATE CADASTRE

Viktor Ristovski
CAKMAKOVA ADVOCATES

Ljubica Ruben
MENS LEGIS LAW FIRM

Biljana Saraginova
MONEVSKI LAW FIRM

Natasa Simonovska
IKRP ROKAS & PARTNERS

Tatjana Siskovska
POLENAK LAW FIRM

Dejan Stojanoski
LAW OFFICE PEPELJUGOSKI

Aleksandar Stojanov
AGENCY FOR REAL ESTATE CADASTRE

Ljupka Stojanovska
LAW OFFICE NIKOLOVSKI & ASSOCIATES

Zika Stojanovski
REPUBLIC OF MACEDONIA, MUNICIPALITY OF ILINDEN

Suzana Stojkoska
MARKOVSKA & ANDREVSKI

Margareta Taseva
CAKMAKOVA ADVOCATES

Dragica Tasevska
NATIONAL BANK OF THE REPUBLIC OF MACEDONIA

Zoja Andreeva Trajkovska
NOTARY OFFICE TRAJKOVSKA

Toni Trajkovski
REPUBLIC OF MACEDONIA, MUNICIPALITY OF GAZI BABA - SKOPJE

Vladimir Vasilevski
BETASPED DOO

Metodija Velkov
POLENAK LAW FIRM

Zlatko Veterovski
CUSTOMS ADMINISTRATION

MADAGASCAR

Rakotondrazaka Aina
MADAGASCAR CONSEIL INTERNATIONAL

Eric Robson Andriamihaja
ECONOMIC DEVELOPMENT BOARD OF MADAGASCAR

Tsiry Andriamisamanana
MADAGASCAR CONSEIL INTERNATIONAL

Josoa Lucien Andrianelinjaka
BANQUE CENTRALE DE MADAGASCAR

Andriamanalina Andrianjaka
OFFICE NOTARIAL DE TAMATAVE

Yves Duchateau
SDV LOGISTICS

Raphaël Jakoba
MADAGASCAR CONSEIL INTERNATIONAL

Hanna Keyserlingk
CABINET HK JURIFISC.

Pascaline R. Rasamoeliarisoa
DELTA AUDIT DELOITTE

Sahondra Rabenarivo
MADAGASCAR LAW OFFICES

Pierrette Rajaonarisoa
SDV LOGISTICS

Serge Lucien Rajoelina
JIRO SY RANO MALAGASY (JIRAMA)

Mamy Rakolonandria
POLES INTEGRES DE CROISSANCE

Danielle Rakotomanana
CABINET RAKOTOMANANA

Tojo Rakotomamonjy
ETUDE RAZANADRAKOTO RIJA

Heritiana Rakotosalama
LEGISLINK CONSULTING

Mamisoa Rakotosalama
LEGISLINK CONSULTING

Lanto Tiana Ralison
PwC MADAGASCAR

Gérard Ramarijaona
PRIME LEX

Michel Ramboa
MADAGASCAR LAW OFFICES

Tsiry Ramiadanarivelo
GROWIN' MADAGASCAR

Rivolalaina Randrianarisoa
PwC MADAGASCAR

William Randrianarivelo
PwC MADAGASCAR

Sahondra Rasoarisoa
DELTA AUDIT DELOITTE

Joseph Ratsimandresy
PRIME LEX

Mialy Ratsimba
PwC MADAGASCAR

Théodore Raveloarison
JARY - BUREAU D'ETUDES ARCHITECTURE INGENIERIE

Andriamisa Ravelomanana
PwC MADAGASCAR

Jean Marcel Razafimahenina
DELTA AUDIT DELOITTE

Rija Nirina Razanadrakoto
ETUDE RAZANADRAKOTO RIJA

Rivolala Razanatsimba
JIRO SY RANO MALAGASY (JIRAMA)

Louis Sagot
CABINET D'AVOCAT LOUIS SAGOT

Ida Soamiliarimana
MADAGASCAR CONSEIL INTERNATIONAL

MALAWI

ERNST & YOUNG

MANICA AFRICA PTY. LTD.

Binnie Banda
ESCOM

Kevin M. Carpenter
PwC MALAWI

Joseph Chavula
SDV LOGISTICS

W. Chigona
MALAWI REVENUE AUTHORITY

Brent Chikho
CITY BUILDING CONTRACTORS

Marshal Chilenga
TF & PARTNERS

Isaac Chimwala
ESCOM

Alan Chinula
WILLIAM FAULKNER

John Deans
SDV LOGISTICS

Wiseman Kabwazi
ESCOM

Gautoni D. Kainja
KANJA AND ROBERTS LAW FIRM

Chimwemwe Kalua
GOLDEN & LAW

Frank Edgar Kapanda
HIGH COURT OF MALAWI

Kalekeni Kaphale
KALEKENI KAPHALE

Alfred Majamanda
MBENDERA & NKHONO ASSOCIATES

James Masumbu
TEMBENU, MASUMBU & CO.

Joseph Malinga Moyo
QUANT CONSULT ASSOCIATES

Misheck Msiska
PwC MALAWI

Arthur Alick Msowoya
WILSON & MORGAN

Charles Mvula
DUMA ELECTRICS - CONTROL SYSTEMS AND ENERGY MANAGEMENT

Benard Ndau
SAVJANI & CO.

Remmie Ng'omba
WILSON & MORGAN

Davis Njobvu
SAVJANI & CO.

Grant Nyirongo
ELEMECH DESIGNS

Dinker A. Raval
WILSON & MORGAN

Duncan Singano
SAVJANI & CO.

MALAYSIA

ERNST & YOUNG

Nor Azimah Abdul Aziz
COMPANIES COMMISSION OF MALAYSIA

Abdul Karim Abdul Jalil
MALAYSIA DEPARTMENT OF INSOLVENCY

Sonia Abraham
AZMAN, DAVIDSON & CO.

Wilfred Abraham
ZUL RAFIQUE & PARTNERS, ADVOCATE & SOLICITORS

Sue Lyn Adeline Thor
RUSSELL BEDFORD LC & COMPANY, MEMBER OF RUSSELL BEDFORD INTERNATIONAL

Wee Ah Sah
SELANGOR FREIGHT FORWARDERS AND LOGISTICS ASSOCIATION (SFFLA)

Alwizah Al-Yafii Ahmad Kamal
ZAID IBRAHIM & CO. (ZICO)

Dato' Abdul Halim Ain
DEPARTMENT OF DIRECTOR GENERAL OF LAND & MINES

Dato' Sh. Yahya bin Sh. Mohamed Almurisi
MINISTRY OF HUMAN RESOURCE

Azmi Ariffin
COMPANIES COMMISSION OF MALAYSIA

Mohd Azlan B. Mohd Radzi
LAND & MINES OFFICE

Anita Balakrishnan
SHEARN DELAMORE & CO.

Shamsuddin Bardan
MALAYSIAN EMPLOYERS FEDERATION

Datuk Arpah Binti Abdul Razak
MINISTRY OF HOUSING AND LOCAL GOVERNMENT MALAYSIA

Hong Yun Chang
TAY & PARTNERS

Ar Teoh Chee Wui
ARCHICENTRE SDN BHD

Andrew Ean Vooi Chiew
LEE HISHAMMUDDIN ALLEN & GELDHILL

Meng Sim Chuah
RUSSELL BEDFORD LC & COMPANY, MEMBER OF RUSSELL BEDFORD INTERNATIONAL

Tze Keong Chung
CTOS SDN BHD

Nadesh Ganabaskaran
ZUL RAFIQUE & PARTNERS, ADVOCATE & SOLICITORS

Mohammed Rhiza Ghazi
RHIZA & RICHARD

Hashim Hamzah
FEDERAL COURT OF MALAYSIA

Mukhriz Hamzah
MINISTRY OF INTERNATIONAL TRADE AND INDUSTRY

Betty Hasan
MINISTRY OF HUMAN RESOURCE

Dato' Ir. Hamzah b. Hassan
LEMBAGA PEMBANGUNAN INDUSTRI PEMBINAAN MALAYSIA

Hj. Hasim Hj. Ismail
LAND & MINES OFFICE

Hung Hoong
SHEARN DELAMORE & CO.

Rohani Ismail
MAGISTRATE COURT KUALA LUMPUR

P Jayasingam
ZUL RAFIQUE & PARTNERS, ADVOCATE & SOLICITORS

Kumar Kanagasabai
SKRINE, MEMBER OF LEX MUNDI

Kumar Kanagasingam
LEE HISHAMMUDDIN ALLEN & GELDHILL

Kesavan Karuppiah
MINISTRY OF HUMAN RESOURCE

Azemi Kasim
DEPARTMENT OF DIRECTOR GENERAL OF LAND & MINES

Geeta Kaur
SDV TRANSPORT

Ng Swee Kee
SHEARN DELAMORE & CO.

Fong Keng Lun
SHIPPING ASSOCIATION OF MALAYSIA

Chuan Keat Khoo
PwC MALAYSIA

Richard Kok
RHIZA & RICHARD

Christopher Lee
CHRISTOPHER LEE & CO.

Mai Yeen Leong
PROFESSIONAL INNOVATORS SDN. BHD.

Seok Hua Lim
NORTH PORT (MALAYSIA) BHD

San Peen Lim
PwC MALAYSIA

Koon Huan Lim
SKRINE, MEMBER OF LEX MUNDI

Kok Leong Loh
RUSSELL BEDFORD LC & COMPANY, MEMBER OF RUSSELL BEDFORD INTERNATIONAL

Caesar Loong
RASLAN - LOONG

Len Toong Low
NORTH PORT (MALAYSIA) BHD

Daniel Musa MD. Daud
MINISTRY OF INTERNATIONAL TRADE AND INDUSTRY

Sze Mei Choong
PwC MALAYSIA

Rokiah Mhd Noor
COMPANIES COMMISSION OF MALAYSIA

Zuhaidi Mohd Shahari
AZMI & ASSOCIATES

Marina Nathan
COMPANIES COMMISSION OF MALAYSIA

Nor Rafidz Nazri
BANK NEGARA MALAYSIA

Oy Moon Ng
CTOS SDN BHD

Shahri Omar
NORTH PORT (MALAYSIA) BHD

Allison Ong
AZMAN, DAVIDSON & CO.

Hock An Ong
KPMG

Sabariah Othman
MAHKAMAH KUALA LUMPUR

Zulkifly Rafique
ZUL RAFIQUE & PARTNERS, ADVOCATE & SOLICITORS

Aminah BT Abd. Rahman
MINISTRY OF HOUSING AND LOCAL GOVERNMENT MALAYSIA

Sakaya Johns Rani
PwC MALAYSIA

Ashraf Rezal Abdul Manan
MAGISTRATE COURT KUALA LUMPUR

Sugumar Saminathan
MALAYSIA PRODUCTIVITY CORPORATION

Shaleni Sangaran
SKRINE, MEMBER OF LEX MUNDI

Tan Lai Seng
MINISTRY OF HOUSING AND LOCAL GOVERNMENT MALAYSIA

Andy Seo
FEDERATION OF MALAYSIAN MANUFACTURERS

Hadiman Bin Simin
MINISTRY OF HOUSING AND LOCAL GOVERNMENT MALAYSIA

Rishwant Singh
ZUL RAFIQUE & PARTNERS, ADVOCATE & SOLICITORS

Professor Dato Seri Dr Visu Sinnadurai
LAWYER

David Soong
RASLAN - LOONG

Muhendaran Suppiah
MUHENDARAN SRI

Kenneth Tiong
THE ASSOCIATED CHINESE CHAMBERS OF COMMERCE AND INDUSTRY OF MALAYSIA (ACCCIM)

Hock Chai Toh
BANK NEGARA MALAYSIA

Heng Choon Wan
PwC MALAYSIA

Keat Ching Wong
ZUL RAFIQUE & PARTNERS, ADVOCATE & SOLICITORS

Wei Kwang Woo
WONG & PARTNERS

Clifford Eng Hong Yap
PwC MALAYSIA

Norhazizah Yusoff
BANK NEGARA MALAYSIA

MALDIVES

ERNST & YOUNG

Jatindra Bhattray
PwC MALDIVES

Asma Chan-Rahim
SHAH, HUSSAIN & CO. BARRISTERS & ATTORNEYS

Mohamed Fizan
SHAH, HUSSAIN & CO. BARRISTERS & ATTORNEYS

Mohamed Hameed
ANTRAC PVT. LTD.

Dheena Hussain
SHAH, HUSSAIN & CO. BARRISTERS & ATTORNEYS

Laila Manik
SHAH, HUSSAIN & CO. BARRISTERS & ATTORNEYS

Ibrahim Nasir Mohamed
LYNX CHAMBERS-NASIR LAW OFFICE ADVOCATES

Ahmed Mohamed Jameel
RAAJJE CHAMBERS

Ahmed Murad
MAZLAN & MURAD LAW ASSOCIATES

Mazlan Rasheed
MAZLAN & MURAD LAW ASSOCIATES

Ahmed Rasheed
THE WIZ COMPANY

Aminath Rizna
SHAH, HUSSAIN & CO. BARRISTERS & ATTORNEYS

Shuaib M. Shah
SHAH, HUSSAIN & CO. BARRISTERS & ATTORNEYS

Mizna Shareef
SHAH, HUSSAIN & CO. BARRISTERS & ATTORNEYS

Hussain Siraj

MALI

Diaby Aboubakar
BCEAO

Oumar Bane
JURIFIS CONSULT

Amadou Camara
SCP CAMARA TRAORÉ

Céline Camara Sib
ETUDE ME CÉLINE CAMARA SIB

Boubacar Coulibaly
MATRANS MALI SARL

Sekou Dembele
ETUDE MAÎTRE SEKOU DEMBELE

Yacouba Diarra
MATRANS MALI SARL

Mohamed Abdoulaye Diop
SDV LOGISTICS

Djénéba Diop Sidibe
SCP D'AVOCAT DIOP-DIALLO

Kouma Fatoumata Fofana
ETUDE KOUMA FOFANA

Gaoussou Haïdara
ETUDE GAOUSSOU HAIDARA

Abdoul Karim Kone
CABINET BERTHE AVOCATS ASSOCIÉS

Amadou Maiga
MAIRIE DU MALI

Maiga Mamadou
AGENCE NATIONALE D'ASSISTANCE MEDICALE

Adeline Messou
PwC CÔTE D'IVOIRE

Bérenger Y. Meuke
JURIFIS CONSULT

Keita Zeïnabou Sacko
API MALI

Ousmane Samba Mamadou
BCEAO

Alassane T. Sangaré
NOTARY

Djibril Semega
CABINET SEAG CONSEIL

Mamadou Moustapha Sow
CABINET SOW & ASSOCIÉS

Perignama Sylla
ARCHITECT DE/AU

Dominique Taty
PwC CÔTE D'IVOIRE

Mahamadou Traore

Alassane Traoré
ICON SARL

Fousséni Traoré
PwC CÔTE D'IVOIRE

Emmanuel Yehouessi
BCEAO

MARSHALL ISLANDS

Kenneth Barden
ATTORNEY-AT-LAW

Benjamin Chutaro
BANK OF MARSHALL ISLANDS

Ben Graham
CONSULTANT

Jerry Kramer
PACIFIC INTERNATIONAL, INC.

James McCaffrey
THE MCCAFFREY FIRM, LTD.

Steve Philip
CHAMBER OF COMMERCE

Dennis Reeder
RMI RECEIVERSHIPS

Scott H. Stege
LAW OFFICES OF SCOTT STEGE

Bori Ysawa
MAJURO MARINE

Bori Ysawa
ROBERT REIMERS ENTERPRISES, INC.

MAURITANIA

Mohamed Salem Abdy
LAWYER

Sid'Ahmed Abeidna
SOGECO MAURITANIA

Esteit Mohamedou Amane
ETUDES RECHERCHES ET MAINTENANCE

Tidiane Bal
BSD & ASSOCIÉS

Ibrahim Camara

Mohamed Cheikh Abdallahi
A.F.A.C.OR SARL

Maroufa Diabira
LAWYER

Youssoupha Diallo
BSD & ASSOCIÉS

Fatoumata Diarra
BSD & ASSOCIÉS

Maouloud Vall El Hady Seyid
ETUDE HADY MAOULOUDVALL

Hamoud Ismail
SMPN

Cheikany Jules
CHEIKHANY JULES LAW OFFICE

Mohamed Lemine Salem Ould Béchir
EXACO

Abdou M'Bodj
COMMUNAUTÉ URBAINE DE NOUAKCHOTT

Fatimetou Mint Abdel Malick
COMMUNE DE TEVRAGH-ZEINA

Abdallahi Ould Abdel Vettah
DIRECTION DES DOMAINES

Bekaye Ould Abdelkader
MINISTÈRE DE LA FONCTION PUBLIQUE, DU TRAVAIL ET DE LA MODERNISATION DE L'ADMINISTRATION

Mine Ould Abdoullah
PRIVATE PRACTICE

Abdellah Ould Ahmed Baba
ATELIER ARCHITECTURE ET DESIGN

Ishagh Ould Ahmed Miské
CABINET ISHAGH MISKE

Mustafa Ould Bilal
TRIBUNAL DE COMMERCE DE NOUAKCHOTT

Moustapha Ould Bilal
TRIBUNAL DU COMMERCE

Mohamed Ould Bouddida
ETUDE MAÎTRE MOHAMED OULD BOUDDIDA

Ahmed Salem Ould Bouhoubeyni
CABINET BOUHOUBEYNI

Salimou Ould Bouhoubeyni

Abdellahi Ould Charrouck
ATELIER ARCHITECTURE ET DESIGN

Ahmed Ould Cheikh Sidya
PRIVATE PRACTICE AHMED OULD CHEIKH SIDYA

Brahim Ould Daddah
CABINET DADDAH CONSEILS

Brahim Ould Ebetty
LAWYER

Abdallahi Ould Gah
CABINET D'AVOCAT GAH

Mohamed Mahmoud Ould Mohamedou
GENISERVICES

Moulaye El Ghali Ould Moulaye Ely
AVOCAT

Ahmed Ould Radhi
BANQUE CENTRALE DE MAURITANIE

Abdel Fettah Ould Sidi Mohamed
SOCIÉTÉ MAURITANIENNE D'ÉLECTRICITÉ (SOMELEC)

Salah
COMMISSAIRE AUX COMPTES

Aly Ould Salihi
TRANSIT LOGISTIQUES TRANSPORT

Aliou Sall
ASSURIM CONSULTING

Cheikh Sall
ETUDE HADY MAOULOUDVALL

Ndeye Khar Sarr
BSD & ASSOCIÉS

Abdellahi Seyidi

Becaye Toure
BSD & ASSOCIÉS

Khalidou Traoré
COMMUNAUTÉ URBAINE DE NOUAKCHOTT

MAURITIUS

Ryan Allas
PwC MAURITIUS

Mohamed Iqbal Belath
BANK OF MAURITIUS

Jean-François Boisvenu
BLC CHAMBERS

André Bonieux
PwC MAURITIUS

Urmila Boolell
BANYMANDHUB BOOLELL CHAMBERS

Nicolas Carcasse
DAGON INGENIEUR CONSEIL LTÉE

D.P. Chinien
REGISTRAR OF COMPANIES AND BUSINESSES, OFFICE OF THE REGISTRAR OF COMPANIES

Vincent Chong Leung
JURISTCONSULT CHAMBERS

Sandy Chuong
GEROUDIS GLOVER GHURBURRUN

Chandansingh Chutoori
DAGON INGENIEUR CONSEIL LTÉE

Roland Constantin
ETUDE CONSTANTIN

Bert C. Cunningham
CUSTOMS AND EXCISE DEPARTMENT

Kalyanee Dayal
BANYMANDHUB BOOLELL CHAMBERS

Catherine de Rosnay
LEGIS & PARTNERS

Shalinee Dreepaul-Halkhoree
JURISTCONSULT CHAMBERS

Robert Ferrat
LEGIS & PARTNERS

Gavin Glover
GEROUDIS GLOVER GHURBURRUN

J. Gilbert Gnany
THE MAURITIUS COMMERCIAL BANK LIMITED

Darmalingum Goorriah
ETUDE ME DARMALINGUM GOORRIAH

Arvin Halkhoree
CITILAW

Marc Hein
JURISTCONSULT CHAMBERS

Nitish Hurnaum
GEROUDIS GLOVER GHURBURRUN

Anthony Leung Shing
PwC MAURITIUS

Stephen John Mendes
CUSTOMS AND EXCISE DEPARTMENT

Ramdas Mootanah
ARCHITECTURE & DESIGN LTD.

R. Mungly-Gulbul
SUPREME COURT

Loganayagan Munian
ARTISCO INTERNATIONAL

Suddul Oudesh
KROSS BORDER TRUST SERVICES LTD., MEMBER OF RUSSELL BEDFORD INTERNATIONAL

Marie Cristelle Joanna Parsooramen
BANYMANDHUB BOOLELL CHAMBERS

Siv Potayya
WORTELS LEXUS

Iqbal Rajahbalee
BLC CHAMBERS

Vivekanand Ramburun
MAURITIUS REVENUE AUTHORITY

Hurday Reshma
KROSS BORDER TRUST SERVICES LTD., MEMBER OF RUSSELL BEDFORD INTERNATIONAL

André Robert
ATTORNEY-AT-LAW

Gilbert Seeyave
BDO DE CHAZAL DU MEE

Gaetan Siew
L&S ARCHITECTS

Deviantee Sobarun
MINISTRY OF FINANCE & ECONOMIC DEVELOPMENT

Rajendra Sokoon
KROSS BORDER TRUST SERVICES LTD., MEMBER OF RUSSELL BEDFORD INTERNATIONAL

Chitra Soobagrah
GEROUDIS GLOVER GHURBURRUN

Shamina Toofanee
PwC MAURITIUS

Natasha Towokul-Jiagoo
JURISTCONSULT CHAMBERS

MEXICO

Ruben Almaraz
LOPEZ VELARDE, HEFTYE Y SORIA

Jesus Alvarado Nieto
BAKER & MCKENZIE

Salvador Alverdi Carmona
CAAAREM

Carlos Angulo
BAKER & MCKENZIE

Francisco Samuel Arias González
NOTARY PUBLIC 28

José Angel Becerril González
GOODRICH, RIQUELME Y ASOCIADOS

Gilberto Calderon
GALAZ, YAMAZAKI, RUIZ URQUIZA, S.C., MEMBER OF DELOITTE TOUCHE TOHMATSU LIMITED

Carlos Cano
PwC MEXICO

Josué Cantú Flores
SOLUCIONES INTEGRALES EN INFRAESTRUCTURA VERDE

María Casas López
BAKER & MCKENZIE

Tania Castellanos
PwC Mexico

Hector Castro
PwC Mexico

Hermilo Ceja
Comisión Federal de Electricidad

Alvaro Cepeda Eguibar
Baker & McKenzie

Jesus Chan
PwC Mexico

Carlos Chávez
Galicia y Robles, S.C.

Rodrigo Conesa
Ritch Mueller, S.C.

Fabio Corominas de la Pera
Baker & McKenzie

Eduardo Corzo Ramos
Holland & Knight-Gallástegui y Lozano, S.C.

Jose Covarrubias-Azuela
Solorzano, Carvajal, Gonzalez y Perez-Correa, S.C.

Cecilia Curiel
Sánchez DeVanny Eseverri, S.C.

Oscar de La Vega
Basham, Ringe y Correa, member of Ius Laboris

Franco del Valle Prado
Miranda & Estavillo, S.C.

Felipe Dominguez P.
Moore Stephens Orozco Medina, S.C.

Mariana Eguiarte Morett
Sánchez DeVanny Eseverri, S.C.

Dolores Enriquez
PwC Mexico

Luis Miguel Esparza
PwC Mexico

Miguel Espitia
Bufete Internacional

Roberto Fagoaga
Sánchez DeVanny Eseverri, S.C

Pedro Flores Carillo
Moore Stephens Orozco Medina, S.C.

Julio Flores Luna
Goodrich, Riquelme y Asociados

Manuel Galicia
Galicia y Robles, S.C.

Mauricio Gamboa
TransUnion de Mexico SA SIC

Joaquín A. García Hugues
COMAD, S.C.

Jose Garcia
Galaz, Yamazaki, Ruiz Urquiza, S.C., member of Deloitte Touche Tohmatsu Limited

Hans Goebel
Jáuregui, Navarrete y Nader, S.C.

Daniel Gómez Alba
CAAAREM

Teresa de Lourdes Gómez Neri
Goodrich, Riquelme y Asociados

Paloma Gomez Perez de Zabalza
Sánchez DeVanny Eseverri, S.C

Patricia Gonzalez
PwC Mexico

Eugenia González Rivas
Goodrich, Riquelme y Asociados

Luis Enrique Graham
Chadbourne & Parke LLP

Mario Alberto Gutiérrez
PwC Mexico

Yves Hayaux-du-Tilly
Jáuregui, Navarrete y Nader, S.C.

Roberto Hernandez Garcia
COMAD, S.C.

Juan Huitron
Sánchez DeVanny Eseverri, S.C.

Agustin Humann
Sánchez DeVanny Eseverri, S.C

Mauricio Hurtado
PwC Mexico

Jose Ricardo Ibarra Cordova
Sánchez DeVanny Eseverri, S.C.

Jorge Jimenez
Lopez Velarde, Heftye y Soria

Jorge Jiménez
Russell Bedford Mexico, member of Russell Bedford International

Diana Juárez Martínez
Baker & McKenzie

Alejandro Ledesma
PwC Mexico

Ricardo León-Santacruz
Sánchez DeVanny Eseverri, S.C.

Daniel Maldonado
Sánchez DeVanny Eseverri, S.C.

Gabriel Manrique
Russell Bedford Mexico, member of Russell Bedford International

Gabriel Manriquez
CAAAREM

Lucia Manzo
Galicia y Robles, S.C.

Esteban Maqueo Barnetche
Maqueo Abogados, S.C.

José Antonio Marquez González
Notary Public 28

Carlos Manuel Martinez
PwC Mexico

Edgar Francisco Martínez Herrasti
Goodrich, Riquelme y Asociados

Bernardo Martínez Negrete
Galicia y Robles, S.C.

Carla E. Mendoza Pérez
Baker & McKenzie

Carlos E. Montemayor
PwC Mexico

Guillermo Moran
Galaz, Yamazaki, Ruiz Urquiza, S.C., member of Deloitte Touche Tohmatsu Limited

Jorge Narváez Hasfura
Baker & McKenzie

Marco Nava
PwC Mexico

Mario Neave
Galaz, Yamazaki, Ruiz Urquiza, S.C., member of Deloitte Touche Tohmatsu Limited

Omar Nieto
PwC Mexico

Martin Pavon-Perez
Baker & McKenzie

Arturo Pedromo
Galicia y Robles, S.C.

Arturo Perdomo
Galicia y Robles, S.C.

Teresa Pérez
Russell Bedford Mexico, member of Russell Bedford International

Eduardo Perez Armienta
Moore Stephens Orozco Medina, S.C.

Gabriela Pérez Castro Ponce de León
Miranda & Estavillo, S.C.

Fernando Perez-Correa
Solorzano, Carvajal, Gonzalez y Perez-Correa, S.C.

Guillermo Piecarchic
PMC Asociados

Gerardo Prado-Hernandez
Sánchez DeVanny Eseverri, S.C.

David Puente-Tostado
Sánchez DeVanny Eseverri, S.C.

Monica Ramos
Jáuregui, Navarrete y Nader, S.C.

Eduardo Reyes Díaz-Leal
Bufete Internacional

Héctor Reyes Freaner
Baker & McKenzie

Claudia Ríos
PwC Mexico

Fernando Rivadeneyra
Rivadeneyra, Trevino & De Campo, S.C.

José Rodríguez Pérez
CAAAREM

Cecilia Rojas
Galicia y Robles, S.C.

Raúl Sahagun
Bufete Internacional

Adrián Salgado Morante
COMAD, S. C.

Ana Cristina Sanchez
Electricity Regulator Mexico

Jorge Sanchez
Goodrich, Riquelme y Asociados

Lucero Sánchez de la Concha
Baker & McKenzie

Cristina Sanchez Vebber
Sánchez DeVanny Eseverri, S.C

Cristina Sánchez-Urtiz
Miranda & Estavillo, S.C.

Francisco Santoyo
Comisión Federal de Electricidad

Monica Schiaffino Pérez
Basham, Ringe y Correa, member of Ius Laboris

Ernesto Silvas
Sánchez DeVanny Eseverri, S.C.

Pietro Straulino-Rodriguez
Sánchez DeVanny Eseverri, S.C

Yazbek Taja
Rivadeneyra, Trevino & De Campo, S.C.

Juan Francisco Torres Landa Ruffo
Barrera, Siqueiros y Torres Landa, SC

Maribel Trigo Aja
Goodrich, Riquelme y Asociados

Alfredo Valdés
Ritch Mueller, S.C.

Jose Villa Ramirez
COMAD, S.C.

Miguel Villalobos
Galaz, Yamazaki, Ruiz Urquiza, S.C., member of Deloitte Touche Tohmatsu Limited

Claudio Villavicencio
Galaz, Yamazaki, Ruiz Urquiza, S.C., member of Deloitte Touche Tohmatsu Limited

Humberto Zapien
Galaz, Yamazaki, Ruiz Urquiza, S.C., member of Deloitte Touche Tohmatsu Limited

MICRONESIA, FED. STS.
FSM Supreme Court

Kenneth Barden
Attorney-at-Law

Wayne Bricknell
E - CAD Project Management

Lam Dang
Congress of the FSM

Stephen V. Finnen
Stephen Finnen's Law Corporation

Kevin Palep
Office of the Registrar of Corporations

Ronald Pangelinan
A&P Enterprises, Inc.

Bendura Rodriquez
Foreign Investment Board, Pohnpei State Government

Salomon Saimon
Micronesian Legal Services Corporation

Joe Vitt
Pohnpei Transfer & Storage, Inc.

Larry Wentworth

MOLDOVA
ICS RED Union Fnosa S.A.

Brian Arnold
PwC Moldova

Eduard Boian
Intreprinderea cu Capital Strain PricewaterhouseCoopers Legal SRL

Vitsaliy Nikolaevich Bulgak
Self employed

Victor Burac
Victor Burac Law Firm

Octavian Cazac
Turcan Cazac

Svetlana Ceban
PwC Moldova

Vitalie Ciofu
Gladei & Partners

Bogdan Ciubotaru
Turcan Cazac

Anastasia Dereveanchina
PwC Moldova

Georgiana Descultu
PwC Romania

Igor Domente
Energonadzor Moldova

Sergiu Dumitrasco
PwC Moldova

Serghei Filatov
ACI Partners Law Office

Iulia Furtuna
Turcan Cazac

Roger Gladei
Gladei & Partners

Ion Gonta
Strengthen Policy Management Capacity Project in Moldova

Oxana Guțu
Ecorys in UK

Andrian Guzun
Schoenherr

Vladimir Iurkovski
Schoenherr

Roman Ivanov
Vernon David & associates

Fedor Kistol
Ofert-Construct S.R.L.

Vera Malancea
PwC Moldova

Georgeta Mincu
IOM

Marin Moraru
Intreprinderea cu Capital Strain PricewaterhouseCoopers Legal SRL

Alexandru Munteanu
Intreprinderea cu Capital Strain PricewaterhouseCoopers Legal SRL

Alexandr Muravschi
Dartax Consulting SRL

Igor Odobescu
ACI Partners Law Office

Aelita Orhei
Gladei & Partners

Ilona Panurco
Intreprinderea cu Capital Strain PricewaterhouseCoopers Legal SRL

Carolina Parcalab
ACI Partners Law Office

Vladimir Plehov
Maritimtrans

Olga Saveliev
Turcan Cazac

Alexandru Savva
Business Research Company

Foca Silviu
Biroul de Credit - Moldova

Viorel Sirghi
BSMB Legal Counsellors

Adrian Soroceanu
ACI Partners Law Office

Eugenia Stancu
DAI

Tatiana Stefanet
Gladei & Partners

Mariana Stratan
Turcan Cazac

Elena Talmazan
SC "Contabil Principal" SRL

Alexander Tuceac
Turcan Cazac

Irina Verhovetchi
ACI Partners Law Office

MONGOLIA
Ulaanbaatar Electricity Distribution Network Company

Telenged Baast
Monlogistics Worldwide LLC

Badarch Bayarmaa
Lynch & Mahoney

Richard Bregonje
PwC Kazakhstan

David C. Buxbaum
Anderson & Anderson

Baljinnyam Buyantogos
Anderson & Anderson

Batbayar Byambaa
GTs Advocates LLC

Khatanbat Dashdarjaa
Arlex Consulting Services

Zoljargal Dashnyam
GTs Advocates LLC

Enkhgerel Deleg
Anderson & Anderson

Emma Enkhriimaa
Tuushin Company Ltd.

Battsetseg Ganbold
Anderson & Anderson

Tuvshin Javkhlant
GTs Advocates LLC

D. Kang
Tsets

Damdinsuren Khand
Tsets

Unurbayar Khurelbaatar
Tuushin Company Ltd.

Daniel Mahoney
Lynch & Mahoney

Sebastian Merriman
PwC Mongolia

Bayartsetseg Nergui
Chono Corporation

Davaadorj Nomingerel
Anderson & Anderson

Maralgua Sharkhuu
Tsets

Baatarsuren Sukhbaatar
The Bank of Mongolia

Andrew Weber
Anderson & Anderson

L. Zolbayar
Tsets

Misheel Zorig
ARLEX CONSULTING SERVICES

MONTENEGRO

Bojana Andrić
ČELEBIĆ

Veselin Anđušic
ČELEBIĆ

Bojana Bjelicic
PwC SERBIA

Vasilije Bošković
LAW FIRM BOŠKOVIĆ

Bojana Bošković
MINISTRY OF FINANCE

Sebek Branislav
MONTINSPEKT D.O.O

Marija Crnogorac
KN KARANOVIĆ & NIKOLIĆ

Savo Djurovic
ADRIATIC MARINAS DOO

Vuk Drašković
BOJOVIĆ DAŠIĆ KOJOVIĆ

Danilo Gvozdenović
MINISTRY OF SUSTAINABLE DEVELOPMENT AND TOURISM

Ana Ivanović
MINISTRY OF FINANCE

Milorad Janjević
LAW OFFICE VUJAČIĆ

Maja Jokanović
MINISTRY OF ECONOMY

Nada Jovanović
CENTRAL BANK OF MONTENEGRO

Srđan Kalezić
TAX AUTHORITY MONTENEGRO

Darko Konjević
CEED

Ana Krsmanović

Sefko Kurpejević
MINISTRY OF FINANCE

Krzysztof Lipka
PwC SERBIA

Mirjana Ljumović
GOVERNMENT OF THE REPUBLIC OF MONTENEGRO REAL ESTATE ADMINISTRATION

Velizar Luković
VELMI-YUVEL

Nikola Martinović
ADVOKATSKA KANCELARIJA

Angelina Mijušković
URAL MONT

Jelena Miljkovic
PwC SERBIA

Mirjana Nikcevic
LAW OFFICE VUJAČIĆ

Nebojša Nikitović
PROINSPECT++

Goran Nikolić
MINISTRY OF ECONOMY

Milorad Peković
FINANCEPLUS

Nikola Perović
PLANTAŽE

Dragana Radević
CEED

Ana Radivojević
PwC SERBIA

Radmila Radoičić
LAW OFFICE VUJAČIĆ

Miladin Radošević
LAW FIRM RADOŠEVIĆ

Slobodan Radovic
BAST D.O.O

Slobodan Radovic
FINANCEPLUS

Ivan Radulović
MINISTRY OF FINANCE

Vesna Radunović
R&P AUDITING

Slađana Raičković
FINANCEPLUS

Dragan Rakočević
COMMERCIAL COURT OF PODGORICA

Savo Robović
K'VATRO PROJEKT

Danijela Saban
ČELEBIĆ

Tijana Saveljic
PRELEVIĆ LAW FIRM

Slaven Šćepanović
LEGAL CONSULTANT

Nino Scepovic
ZETATRANS

Lidija Šečković
TAX AUTHORITY MONTENEGRO

Slavko Simović
GOVERNMENT OF THE REPUBLIC OF MONTENEGRO REAL ESTATE ADMINISTRATION

Miloš Stojanović
ZETAGRADNJA

Velimir Strugar
EPCG AD NIKŠIĆ

Brane Tešović
PRIMASOFT D.O.O

Ana Vojvodic
LAW OFFICE VUJAČIĆ

Saša Vujačić
LAW OFFICE VUJAČIĆ

Jelena Vujisić
LAW OFFICE VUJAČIĆ

Lana Vukmirovic-Misic
HARRISONS SOLICITORS

Radovan Vulićević
ADVOKATSKA KANCELARIJA

MOROCCO

AGENCE URBAINE DE CASABLANCA

BANK AL-MAGHRIB

DIRECTION GÉNÉRALE DES IMPÔTS

ERNST & YOUNG

Benali Abdelmajid
EXPERIAN

Sidimohamed Abouchikhi
EXPERIAN

Samir Agoumi
DAR ALKHIBRA

Hanane Ait Addi
BASSAMAT & ASSOCIÉE

Lamya Alami
CABINET DE NOTAIRE ALAMI

Meredith Allen-Belghiti
KETTANI LAW FIRM

Karim Amroune
PwC ADVISORY MAROC

Younes Anibar
CABINET YOUNES ANIBAR

Redouane Assakhen
CENTRE RÉGIONALE D'INVESTISSEMENT

Adnane Bahija
DAR ALKHIBRA

Fassi-Fihri Bassamat
BASSAMAT & ASSOCIÉE

Linda Oumama Benali
CABINET NOTAIRE

Azel-arab Benjelloun
AGENCE D'ARCHITECTURE D'URBANISME ET DE DECORATION

Mohamed Benkhalid
CAISSE NATIONALE DE SÉCURITÉ SOCIALE

Mohamed Benkirane
ESPACE TRANSIT

Myriam Emmanuelle Bennani
AMIN HAJJI & ASSOCIÉS ASSOCIATION D'AVOCATS

Saad Beygrine
CABINET DE NOTAIRE ALAMI

Rachid Boubakry
AUDIT CONCEPT

Khalid Boumichi
TECNOMAR

Johan Bruneau
CMS BUREAU FRANCIS LEFEBVRE

Richard Cantin
JURISTRUCTURES – PROJECT MANAGEMENT & LEGAL ADVISORY SERVICES LLP

Mahat Chraibi
PwC ADVISORY MAROC

Sylvain Da Fonseca
PwC ADVISORY MAROC

Merieme Diouri
ETUDE DE NOTARIAT MODERNE

Michael Duhamel
COMANAV

Sarah El Couhen
ETUDE DE NOTARIAT MODERNE

Youssef El Falah
ABA RULE OF LAW INITIATIVE-MOROCCO

Mohssin El Makoudi
DAR ALKHIBRA

Hamid Elafdil
CENTRE RÉGIONALE D'INVESTISSEMENT

Driss Ettaki
ADMINISTRATION DES DOUANES ET IMPOTS INDIRECTS

Nadia Fajr

Adil Fasshii
LYDEC

Youssef Fassi Fihri
FYBA LAWYERS

Mustapha Fekkar
AGENCE NATIONALE DE LA CONSERVATION FONCIÈRE DU CADASTRE ET DE LA CARTOGRAPHIE (ANCFCC)

Nasser Filali
ZIMAG

Fatima Zahrae Gouttaya
ETUDE DE NOTARIAT MODERNE

Karima Hadrya
CAISSE NATIONALE DE SÉCURITÉ SOCIALE

Amin Hajji
AMIN HAJJI & ASSOCIÉS ASSOCIATION D'AVOCATS

Zohra Hasnaoui
HASNAOUI LAW FIRM

Ahmad Hussein
TALAL ABU GHAZALEH LEGAL (TAG-LEGAL)

Bahya Ibn Khaldoun
UNIVERSITÉ MOHAMED V

Ghiyta Iraqi
AUGUST & DEBOUZY AVOCATS

Naoual Jellouli
MINISTÈRE DE L'ECONOMIE ET DES FINANCES

Mehdi Kettani
KETTANI & ASSOCIÉS

Rita Kettani
KETTANI & ASSOCIÉS

Nadia Kettani
KETTANI LAW FIRM

Abdelmajid Khachai
BAKER & MCKENZIE

Nabyl Lakhdar
ADMINISTRATION DES DOUANES ET IMPOTS INDIRECTS

Adil Said Lamtiri
AVOCAT AU BARREAU

Beatrice Larregle
EXPERIAN

Wilfried Le Bihan
CMS BUREAU FRANCIS LEFEBVRE

Anis Mahfoud
ABOUAKIL, BENJELLOUN & MAHFOUD AVOCATS - AB AVOCATS & ASSOCIES

Amine Mahfoud
AMINE MAHFOUD NOTAIRE

Abdelkhalek Merzouki
ADMINISTRATION DES DOUANES ET IMPOTS INDIRECTS

Abdelaziz Messaoudi
MINISTÈRE DE L'ÉCONOMIE ET DES FINANCES

Mahboub Mohamed
ETUDE DE ME MAHBOUB

Alaoui Ismaili Mohammed
ADATRA

Anthony Mopty
YASSIR KHALIL STUDIO

Said Mouhcine
IMPACT ARCHITECTURE, MOROCCO

Tayeb Mohamed Omar
AVOCAT AU BARREAU DE CASABLANCA

Hicham Oughza
DAR ALKHIBRA

Nesrine Roudane
NERO BOUTIQUE LAW FIRM

Mehdi Salmouni-Zerhouni
SALMOUNI-ZERHOUNI LAW FIRM

Ghalia Sebti
AIT MANOS

Houcine Sefrioui
ETUDE DE NOTARIAT MODERNE

Marc Veuillot
CMS BUREAU FRANCIS LEFEBVRE

MOZAMBIQUE

Carolina Balate
PwC MOZAMBIQUE

José Manuel Caldeira
SAL & CALDEIRA ADVOGADOS, LDA.

Eduardo Calú
SAL & CALDEIRA ADVOGADOS, LDA.

Liliana Chacon
FURTADO, BHIKHA, LOFORTE, POPAT & ASSOCIADOS ADVOGADOS

Jonas Chitsumba
ELECTRICIDADE DE MOÇAMBIQUE E.P.

Pedro Couto
H. GAMITO, COUTO, GONÇALVES PEREIRA E CASTELO BRANCO & ASSOCIADOS

Avelar Da Silva
INTERTEK INTERNATIONAL LTD.

Thera Dai
FURTADO, BHIKHA, LOFORTE, POPAT & ASSOCIADOS ADVOGADOS

Alberto de Deus
FURTADO, BHIKHA, LOFORTE, POPAT & ASSOCIADOS ADVOGADOS

Carlos de Sousa e Brito
CARLOS DE SOUSA E BRITO & ASSOCIADOS

Fulgêncio Dimande
MANICA FREIGHT SERVICES S.A.R.L

Rita Donato
H. GAMITO, COUTO, GONÇALVES PEREIRA E CASTELO BRANCO & ASSOCIADOS

Pinto Fulane
BANCO DE MOÇAMBIQUE

Rita Furtado
FURTADO, BHIKHA, LOFORTE, POPAT & ASSOCIADOS ADVOGADOS

Xiluva Gonçalves Nogueira da Costa
SAL & CALDEIRA ADVOGADOS, LDA.

Jorge Graça
CGA - COUTO, GRAÇA E ASSOCIADOS, SOCIEDADE DE ADVOGADOS

Ássma Omar Nordine Jeque
SAL & CALDEIRA ADVOGADOS, LDA.

Annette Landman
PwC SOUTH AFRICA

Rui Loforte
FURTADO, BHIKHA, LOFORTE, POPAT & ASSOCIADOS ADVOGADOS

Gimina Luís Mahumana
SAL & CALDEIRA ADVOGADOS, LDA.

Vítor Marques da Cruz
FCB&A IN ASSOCIATION WITH LAW & MARK, ADVOGADOS E CONSULTORES LAW & MARK, LDA

João Martins
PwC MOZAMBIQUE

Camilo Mate
CGA - COUTO, GRAÇA E ASSOCIADOS, SOCIEDADE DE ADVOGADOS

Gonçalo Meneses
CARLOS DE SOUSA E BRITO & ASSOCIADOS

Auxílio Eugénio Nhabanga
FURTADO, BHIKHA, LOFORTE, POPAT & ASSOCIADOS ADVOGADOS

Rute Ramos
CARLOS DE SOUSA E BRITO & ASSOCIADOS

Malaika Ribeiro
PwC MOZAMBIQUE

Paula Castro Silveira
RAPOSO BERNARDO & ASSOCIADOS

NAMIBIA

ERNST & YOUNG

WOKER FREIGHT SERVICES

Joos Agenbach
KOEP & PARTNERS

Ronnie Beukes
CITY OF WINDHOEK ELECTRICITY DEPARTMENT

Clifford Bezuidenhout
ENGLING, STRITTER & PARTNERS

Benita Blume
H.D. BOSSAU & CO.

Hanno D. Bossau
H.D. BOSSAU & CO.

Lorna Celliers
BDO SPENCER STEWARD (NAMIBIA)

Jana-marie De Bruyn
BDO SPENCER STEWARD (NAMIBIA)

Ferdinand Diener
CITY OF WINDHOEK ELECTRICITY DEPARTMENT

Hans-Bruno Gerdes
ENGLING, STRITTER & PARTNERS

Amanda Gous
PwC NAMIBIA

Ismeralda Hangue
DEEDS OFFICE

Stefan Hugo
PwC NAMIBIA

Jaco Jacobs
ELLIS SHILENGUDWA

Sakaria Kadhila Amoomo
PEREIRA FISHING (PTY) LTD.

Herman Charl Kinghorn
HC KINGHORN LEGAL PRACTITIONER

Mignon Klein
G.F. KÖPPLINGER LEGAL PRACTITIONERS

Frank Köpplinger
G.F. KÖPPLINGER LEGAL PRACTITIONERS

Norbert Liebich
TRANSWORLD CARGO (PTY) LTD.

The Manager
NAMIBIA REAL ESTATE

John D. Mandy
NAMIBIAN STOCK EXCHANGE

Richard Traugott Diethelm Mueller
KOEP & PARTNERS

Brigitte Nependa

Coenraad Nolte
ENGLING, STRITTER & PARTNERS

Riana Oosthuizen
BDO SPENCER STEWARD (NAMIBIA)

Axel Stritter
ENGLING, STRITTER & PARTNERS

Marius van Breda
TransUNION

Hugo Van den Berg

Ockhuizen Welbert
*NAMIBIA WATER CORPORATION
(NAMWATER)*

Renate Williamson
KOEP & PARTNERS

NEPAL
Mahesh P. Acharya
NEPAL ELECTRICITY AUTHORITY

Sulakshan Adhikari
SHANGRI-LA FREIGHT PVT. LTD.

Lalit Aryal

Tulasi Bhatta
UNITY LAW FIRM & CONSULTANCY

Komal Chitracar
K.B. CHITRACAR & CO.

Basu Dahal
HIMALAYAN BANK

Nirmal Dhakal
*GOVERNMENT OF NEPAL MINISTRY OF
INDUSTRY*

Shivaraj Dhital
NEPAL FREIGHT FORWARDERS ASSOCIATION

Devendra Dongol
KATHMANDU METROPOLITAN CITY

Komal Prakash Ghimire
GHIMIRE & CO.

Tika Ram Ghimire
*MINISTRY OF LAND REFORM AND
MANAGEMENT*

Ajay Gupta
ATLAS GROUP

Rameswor K.C.
NEPAL FREIGHT FORWARDERS ASSOCIATION

Mahesh Kafle
KATHMANDU METROPOLITAN CITY

Gourish K. Kharel
KTO INC.

Satish Krishna Kharel
SAMAN LEGAL SERVICE

Parsuram Koirala
KOIRALA & ASSOCIATES

Tek Narayan Kunwar
KATHMANDU DISTRICT COURT

Hari Bahadur Kunwar
KATHMANDU METROPOLITAN CITY

Bharat Lamsal
KATHMANDU DISTRICT COURT

Hom Prasad Luitel
*GOVERNMENT OF NEPAL MINISTRY OF
INDUSTRY*

Amir Maharjan
*SAFE CONSULTING ARCHITECTS &
ENGINEERS PVT. LTD.*

Lumb Mahat
CSC & CO.

Surendra Kumar Mahto
PRADHAN & ASSOCIATES

Ashok Man Kapali
SHANGRI-LA FREIGHT PVT. LTD.

Purna Man Napit
NIC BANK

Nur Nidhi Neupane
KATHMANDU METROPOLITAN CITY

Matrika Niraula
NIRAULA LAW CHAMBER & CO.

Nav Raj Ojha
NEPAL ELECTRICITY AUTHORITY

Dev Raj Paudyal
*MINISTRY OF LAND REFORM AND
MANAGEMENT*

Egaraj Pokharel
LEGAL RESEARCH ASSOCIATES

Megh Raj Pokharel
LEGAL RESEARCH ASSOCIATES

Sakar Pradhan
INTER-SPACE DESIGN GROUP

Devendra Pradhan
PRADHAN & ASSOCIATES

Anup Raj Upreti
PIONEER LAW ASSOCIATES

Rajiv Shahi
ATLAS GROUP

Madan Krishna Sharma
CSC & CO.

Chiranjibi Sharma Paudel
NEPAL ELECTRICITY AUTHORITY

Rup Narayan Shrestha
DEVELOPMENT LAW ASSOCIATES

P. L. Shrestha
EVERGREEN CARGO SERVICES PVT. LTD.

Suman Lal Shrestha
EVERGREEN CARGO SERVICES PVT. LTD.

Deepak K. Shrestha
NEPAL INVESTMENT BANK

Rajeshwor Shrestha
SINHA - VERMA LAW CONCERN

Anil Kumar Sinha
SINHA - VERMA LAW CONCERN

Ram Chandra Subedi
APEX LAW CHAMBER

Ramesh Subedi
*GOVERNMENT OF NEPAL MINISTRY OF
INDUSTRY*

Nab Raj Subedi
*MINISTRY OF LAND REFORM AND
MANAGEMENT*

L.R. Tamang
*HYONJAN ELECTRICAL ENGINEERING
FABRICATOR P, LTD.*

Keshav Bahadur Thapa
*GOVERNMENT OF NEPAL MINISTRY OF
INDUSTRY*

Mahesh Kumar Thapa
SINHA - VERMA LAW CONCERN

Mdhusudan Yadav
NEPAL ELECTRICITY AUTHORITY

Sachidananda Yadav
NEPAL ELECTRICITY AUTHORITY

NETHERLANDS
Joost Achterberg
KENNEDY VAN DER LAAN

Andre Anders
TAKENAKA CORPORATION

W.R. Bremer
*MINISTRY OF HOUSING, SPATIAL PLANNING
AND THE ENVIRONMENT–GOVERNMENT
BUILDINGS AGENCY*

Karin W.M. Bodewes
BAKER & MCKENZIE

Mark Bodt
PwC NETHERLANDS

Sytso Boonstra
PwC NETHERLANDS

Roland Brandsma
PwC NETHERLANDS

Martin Brink
VAN BENTHEM & KEULEN NV

Stephan de Baan
BERKMAN FORWARDING B.V.

Margriet de Boer
DE BRAUW BLACKSTONE WESTBROEK

Rolef de Weijs
HOUTHOFF BURUMA

Hans de Wilde
*KAB ACCOUNTANTS & BELASTINGADVISEURS,
MEMBER OF RUSSELL BEDFORD
INTERNATIONAL*

Kees de Zeeuw
*CADASTRE, LAND REGISTRY AND MAPPING
AGENCY*

Henriette Derks
LIANDER

Myrna Dop
*ROYAL NETHERLANDS NOTARIAL
ORGANIZATION*

Mark Huijzen
SIMMONS & SIMMONS LLP

Niels Huurdeman
HOUTHOFF BURUMA

Alexander Kaarls
HOUTHOFF BURUMA

Marcel Kettenis
PwC NETHERLANDS

Edwin Kleefstra
*KAB ACCOUNTANTS & BELASTINGADVISEURS,
MEMBER OF RUSSELL BEDFORD
INTERNATIONAL*

Christian Koedam
PwC NETHERLANDS

Filip Krsteski
VAN DOORNE N.V.

Andrej Kwitowski
DHV B.V.

Stefan Leening
PwC NETHERLANDS

Allard Meine Jansen
ALLARD ARCHITECTURE

Matthias Noorlander
OFFICE OF ENERGY REGULATION

Hugo Oppelaar
HOUTHOFF BURUMA

Peter Plug
OFFICE OF ENERGY REGULATION

Johan Polet
SIMMONS & SIMMONS LLP

Willemieke Princée
DE BRAUW BLACKSTONE WESTBROEK

Mark G. Rebergen
DE BRAUW BLACKSTONE WESTBROEK

Helena Redons Schaatsheren
MUNICIPALITY OF AMSTERDAM

Hugo Reumkens
VAN DOORNE N.V.

Stefan Sagel
DE BRAUW BLACKSTONE WESTBROEK

Jan Willem Schenk
BAKER & MCKENZIE

Rutger Schimmelpenninck
HOUTHOFF BURUMA

Hans Londonck Sluijk
HOUTHOFF BURUMA

Stéphanie Spoelder
BAKER & MCKENZIE

Fedor Tanke
BAKER & MCKENZIE

Maarten Tinnemans
DE BRAUW BLACKSTONE WESTBROEK

Helene van Bommel
PwC NETHERLANDS

Kees van den Udenhout

Jos van der Schans
DE BRAUW BLACKSTONE WESTBROEK

Florentine van der Schrieck
DE BRAUW BLACKSTONE WESTBROEK

Emilia L.C. van Egmond-de
Wilde de Ligny
*FACULTY OF TECHNOLOGY MANAGEMENT,
EINDHOVEN UNIVERSITY OF TECHNOLOGY*

Gert-Jan van Gijs
VAT LOGISTICS (OCEAN FREIGHT) BV

Femke van Herk
DE BRAUW BLACKSTONE WESTBROEK

Sjaak van Leeuwen
STICHTING BUREAU KREDIET REGISTRATIE

Jan van Oorschot
LIANDER

Petra van Raad
PwC NETHERLANDS

Janine Verweij
OFFICE OF ENERGY REGULATION

Frank Werger
PwC NETHERLANDS

Michiel Wesseling
HOUTHOFF BURUMA

Hylda Wiarda
*BRONSGEEST DEUR ADVOCATEN, MEMBER
OF IUS LABORIS*

Marcel Willems
KENNEDY VAN DER LAAN

Christiaan Zijderveld
SIMMONS & SIMMONS LLP

NEW ZEALAND
Matthew Allison
VEDA ADVANTAGE

Jania Baigent
*SIMPSON GRIERSON, MEMBER OF LEX
MUNDI*

Geoff Bevan
CHAPMAN TRIPP

Kara Bonnevie
NEW ZEALAND COMPANIES OFFICE

Shelley Cave
*SIMPSON GRIERSON, MEMBER OF LEX
MUNDI*

Philip Coombe
PANALPINA WORLD TRANSPORT LLP

John Cuthbertson
PwC NEW ZEALAND

Vince Duffin
VECTOR ELECTRICITY

Koustabh Gadgil
*INVESTMENT NEW ZEALAND (A DIVISION OF
NEW ZEALAND TRADE AND ENTERPRISE)*

Tony Gault
PwC NEW ZEALAND

Don Grant
LAND INFORMATION NEW ZEALAND

Steffan Kelly
BELL GULLY

Matt Kersey
RUSSELL MCVEAGH

Greg King
JACKSON RUSSELL

Mahesh Lala
JACKSON RUSSELL

Leroy Langeveld
*SIMPSON GRIERSON, MEMBER OF LEX
MUNDI*

John Lawrence
AUCKLAND CITY COUNCIL

Brent Lewers
INLAND REVENUE DEPARTMENT

Mandy McDonald
MINISTRY OF ECONOMIC DEVELOPMENT

Shaun McMaster
MINTER ELLISON RUDD WATTS

Andrew Minturn
QUALTECH INTERNATIONAL LTD.

Nick Moffatt
BELL GULLY

Robert Muir
LAND INFORMATION NEW ZEALAND

Ciaron Murnane
BELL GULLY

Catherine Otten
NEW ZEALAND COMPANIES OFFICE

Ian Page
BRANZ

Mihai Pascariu
MINTER ELLISON RUDD WATTS

John Powell
RUSSELL MCVEAGH

Jim Roberts
HESKETH HENRY LAWYERS

Michael Slyuzberg
INLAND REVENUE DEPARTMENT

Neill Sullivan
LAND INFORMATION NEW ZEALAND

Mike Tames
PwC NEW ZEALAND

Howard Thomas
*LOWNDES ASSOCIATES - CORPORATE AND
COMMERCIAL LAW SPECIALISTS*

Murray Tingey
BELL GULLY

Amy Tiong
PwC NEW ZEALAND

Michael McLean Toepfer
WANAKA OFFICE AWS LEGAL

Ben Upton
*SIMPSON GRIERSON, MEMBER OF LEX
MUNDI*

Kay Warren
LAND INFORMATION NEW ZEALAND

Mike Whale
*LOWNDES ASSOCIATES - CORPORATE AND
COMMERCIAL LAW SPECIALISTS*

Sam Whiting
HESKETH HENRY LAWYERS

Richard Wilson
JACKSON RUSSELL

NICARAGUA
DISNORTE-DISSUR (UNION FENOSA)

Diana Aguilar
ACZALAW

Guillermo Alemán Gómez
ACZALAW

Bertha Argüello de Rizo
ARIAS & MUÑOZ

Carlos Barrantes
PwC COSTA RICA

Minerva Adriana Bellorín Rodríguez
ACZALAW

María José Bendaña Guerrero
BENDAÑA & BENDAÑA

Ricardo Bendaña Guerrero
BENDAÑA & BENDAÑA

Carlos Alberto Bonilla López
SUPERINTENDENCIA DE BANCOS

Orlando Cardoza
BUFETE JURIDICO OBREGON Y ASOCIADOS

Thelma Carrion
AGUILAR CASTILLO LOVE

Humberto Carrión
CARRIÓN, SOMARRIBA & ASOCIADOS

Ramón Castro
ARIAS & MUÑOZ

Ana Cecilia Chamorro
ARIAS & MUÑOZ

Dorisabel Conrado
CONSORTIUM TABOADA Y ASOCIADOS

Sergio David Corrales Montenegro
GARCÍA & BODÁN

Juan Carlos Cortes Espinoza
PwC NICARAGUA

Gloria Maria de Alvarado
*ALVARADO Y ASOCIADOS, MEMBER OF
LEX MUNDI*

Maricarmen Espinosa de Molina
MOLINA & ASOCIADOS CENTRAL LAW

Melvin Estrada
GARCÍA & BODÁN

Teodoro Flores Gonzalez
MULTITRANS

Terencio Garcia Montenegro
GARCÍA & BODÁN

Engelsberth Gómez
PRO NICARAGUA

Denis González Torres
G.E. ELECTROMECÁNICA & CIA LTDA.

Claudia Guevara
AGUILAR CASTILLO LOVE

Marianela Gutierrez
AGUILAR CASTILLO LOVE

Mario José Gutiérrez Avendaño
ACZALAW

Gerardo Hernandez
CONSORTIUM TABOADA Y ASOCIADOS

Rodrigo Ibarra Rodney
ARIAS & MUÑOZ

María Fernanda Jarquín
ARIAS & MUÑOZ

Mariela Jiménez
ACZALAW

Brenda Martinez
CONSORTIUM TABOADA Y ASOCIADOS

Fabiola Martinez
VENTANILLA UNICA DE INVERSIONES

Fernando Midence Mantilla
*ALVARADO Y ASOCIADOS, MEMBER OF
LEX MUNDI*

Alvaro Molina
MOLINA & ASOCIADOS CENTRAL LAW

Roberto José Montes Doña
ARIAS & MUÑOZ

Soraya Montoya Herrera
MOLINA & ASOCIADOS CENTRAL LAW

Michael Navas
PRO NICARAGUA

Jacinto Obregon Sanchez
BUFETE JURIDICO OBREGON Y ASOCIADOS

Róger Pérez
ARIAS & MUÑOZ

Mazziel Rivera
ACZALAW

Ana Teresa Rizo Briseño
ARIAS & MUÑOZ

Erwin Rodriguez
ACZALAW

Felipe Sanchez
UNICA

Felipe Sánchez
ACZALAW

Alfonso José Sandino Granera
CONSORTIUM TABOADA Y ASOCIADOS

Julio E. Sequeira
EVENOR VALDIVIA P. & ASOCIADOS

Arnulfo Somarriba
TRANSUNION

Rodrigo Taboada
CONSORTIUM TABOADA Y ASOCIADOS

Carlos Tellez
GARCÍA & BODÁN

Diana Zelaya
GARCÍA & BODÁN

NIGER

MAERSK S.A.

Diaby Aboubakar
BCEAO

Sidi Sanoussi Baba Sidi
CABINET D'AVOCATS SOUNA-COULIBALY

Joël Broux
SDV LOGISTICS

Moussa Coulibaly
CABINET D'AVOCATS SOUNA-COULIBALY

Elvis Danon
PwC CÔTE D'IVOIRE

Abdou Djando
EMTEF

Aïssatou Djibo
ETUDE DE MAÎTRE DJIBO AÏSSATOU

Boureïma Fodi
CABINET D'AVOCATS SOUNA-COULIBALY

Jean Claude Gnamien
PwC CÔTE D'IVOIRE

Souley Hammi Illiassou

Issoufou Harouna
CABINET D'AVOCAT HAROUNA ISSOUFOU

Bernar-Oliver Kouavoi
CABINET KOUAVOI

Marc Le Bihan
*ETUDE D'AVOCATS MARC LE BIHAN &
COLLABORATEURS*

Laouali Madougou
*ETUDE D'AVOCATS MARC LE BIHAN &
COLLABORATEURS*

Boubacar Nouhou Maiga
E.N.G.E.

Mamane Sani Manane
BUREAU D'ÉTUDES BALA & HIMO

Issaka Manzo
EGTC

Ibrahim Mounouni
BUREAU D'ÉTUDES BALA & HIMO

Mayaki Oumarou
DESS NOTARIAL

Ousmane Samba Mamadou
BCEAO

Abdou Moussa Sanoussi
E.N.G.E.

Ousmane Sidibé
*AUDIT CONSEIL SIDIBÉ & CONSEIL
(A.C.S.A.)*

Dominique Taty
PwC CÔTE D'IVOIRE

Idrissa Tchernaka
*ETUDE D'AVOCATS MARC LE BIHAN &
COLLABORATEURS*

Ramatou Wankoye
OFFICE NOTARIAL ETUDE WANKOYE

Hamadou Yacouba
ETUDE DE ME DODO DAN GADO HAOUA

Hamado Yahaya
*SOCIETE CIVILE PROFESSIONNELLE
D'AVOCATS YANKORI ET ASSOCIÉS*

Emmanuel Yehouessi
BCEAO

NIGERIA

ERNST & YOUNG

Ijeoma Abalogu
GBENGA BIOBAKU & CO.

Mohammed K. Abdulsalam
GITRAS LTD.

Oluseyi Abiodun Akinwunmi
*AKINWUNMI & BUSARI LEGAL
PRACTITIONERS*

Kunle Adegbite
CANAAN SOLICITORS

Olufunke Adekoya
*AELEX, LEGAL PRACTITIONERS &
ARBITRATORS*

Tolu Aderemi
PERCHSTONE & GRAEYS

Taiwo Adeshina
JACKSON, ETTI & EDU

Yetunde Adewale
*AKINWUNMI & BUSARI LEGAL
PRACTITIONERS*

Daniel Agbor
UDO UDOMA & BELO-OSAGIE

Tokunbo Agoro
JAIYE AGORO & CO.

Kunle Ajagbe
PERCHSTONE & GRAEYS

Olaoluwa Ajala
GBENGA BIOBAKU & CO.

Koyin Ajayi
OLANIWUN AJAYI LP

Bola Ajibola
LANDS REGISTRY ALAUSA

Funbi Akinwale
IKEYI & ARIFAYAN

Dafe Akpeneye
PwC NIGERIA

Overaye Brodrick Akpotaire
LIDUD NIGERIA LTD.

Barbara Ufuoma Akpotaire

Jonathan Aluju
OLANIWUN AJAYI LP

Segun Aluko
ALUKO & OYEBODE

Godwin Amadi
NNENNA EJEKAM ASSOCIATES

Tracy Amadigwe
ALKINGSHOLA CHAMBERS

Linda Arifayan
WTS ADEBIYI & ASSOCIATES

Esther Atoyebi
OKONJO, ODIAWA & EBIE

Akinshola Babatunde
ALKINGSHOLA CHAMBERS

Titilola Bamisile
GBENGA BIOBAKU & CO.

Ngozi Chianakwalam
LEGAL STANDARD CONSULTING

Stanley Chikwendu
*AELEX, LEGAL PRACTITIONERS &
ARBITRATORS*

Chinwe Chiwete
PUNUKA ATTORNEYS & SOLICITORS

Peter Crabb
NNENNA EJEKAM ASSOCIATES

Rebecca Dokun
ALUKO & OYEBODE

Oluwadamilola Durowaiye
OLANIWUN AJAYI LP

Ohireime Eboreime
UDO UDOMA & BELO-OSAGIE

Oyinda Ehiwere
UDO UDOMA & BELO-OSAGIE

Nnenna Ejekam
NNENNA EJEKAM ASSOCIATES

Mary Ekemezie
UDO UDOMA & BELO-OSAGIE

Nelson Ekere
1ST ATTORNEYS

Harrison Emmanuel
ABDULAI, TAIWO & CO.

Ebele Enedah
PUNUKA ATTORNEYS & SOLICITORS

Kenneth Erikume
PwC NIGERIA

Samuel Etuk
1ST ATTORNEYS

Anse Agu Ezetah
CHIEF LAW AGU EZETAH & CO.

Babatunde Fagbohunlu
ALUKO & OYEBODE

Olawale Fapohunda
IKEYI & ARIFAYAN

Olubunml Fayokun
ALUKO & OYEBODE

Bimbola Fowler-Ekar
JACKSON, ETTI & EDU

Adejoke A. Gbenro
ADEBANKE ADEOLA & CO.

Justice Idehen-Nathaniel
PERCHSTONE & GRAEYS

Afoke Igwe
UDO UDOMA & BELO-OSAGIE

Nduka Ikeyi
IKEYI & ARIFAYAN

Okorie Kalu
PUNUKA ATTORNEYS & SOLICITORS

Yetunde Kilanse
GBENGA BIOBAKU & CO.

Adetola Lawal
OKONJO, ODIAWA & EBIE

Emmanuel Egwuagu Nomso
OBLA & CO.

Chidnma Nwaogu
PUNUKA ATTORNEYS & SOLICITORS

Kenechi Nwizu
IKEYI & ARIFAYAN

Godwin Obla
OBLA & CO.

Abimbola Odeyemi
FORTIS LP

Oluwakemi Oduntan
JADE & STONE SOLICITORS

Godson Ogheneochuko
UDO UDOMA & BELO-OSAGIE

Alayo Ogunbiyi
ABDULAI, TAIWO & CO.

Ayokunle Ogundipe
PERCHSTONE & GRAEYS

Ayodele Ogunsemowo
CROWN AGENTS LTD.

Charity Ogwugwa
LAW, UNION & ROCK

Onyinye Okafo
UDO UDOMA & BELO-OSAGIE

Ogoegbunam Okafor
PERCHSTONE & GRAEYS

Ifedayo Oke-Lawal
PERCHSTONE & GRAEYS

Mathias Okojie
PUNUKA ATTORNEYS & SOLICITORS

Christine Okokon
UDO UDOMA & BELO-OSAGIE

Patrick Okonjo
OKONJO, ODIAWA & EBIE

Dozie Okwuosah
CENTRAL BANK OF NIGERIA

Stephen Ola Jagun
JAGUN ASSOCIATES

Adefunke Oladosu
*AKINWUNMI & BUSARI LEGAL
PRACTITIONERS*

Demilade Olaosun
IKEYI & ARIFAYAN

Titilola Olateju
OKONJO, ODIAWA & EBIE

Adebayo Ologe
PERCHSTONE & GRAEYS

Ayotunde Ologe
SYNERGY LEGAL PRACTITIONERS

Babatunde Olubando
BABATUNDE OLUBANDO & CO.

Patrick Omeke
*COLUMBIA UNIVERSITY, SCHOOL OF LAW,
NEW YORK*

Funke Onadeko
OLANIWUN AJAYI LP

Olayemi Onakoya
PwC NIGERIA

Fred Onuobia
*G. ELIAS & CO. SOLICITORS AND
ADVOCATES*

Donald Orji
JACKSON, ETTI & EDU

Christian Oronsaye
ALUKO & OYEBODE

Tunde Osasona
WHITESTONE WORLDWIDE LTD.

Kola Osholeye
ELEKTRINT (NIGERIA) LIMITED

Omotola Owoyemi
PERCHSTONE & GRAEYS

Abraham Oyakhilome
FIRST & FIRST INTERNATIONAL AGENCIES

Taiwo Oyedele
PwC NIGERIA

Titilola Rotifa
OKONJO, ODIAWA & EBIE

Taofeek Shittu
IKEYI & ARIFAYAN

Serifat Solebo
LAND SERVICES DIRECTORATE

Olufemi Sunmonu
FEMI SUNMONU & ASSOCIATES, SOLICITORS

Olubukola Thomas
PERCHSTONE & GRAEYS

Yvonne Udegbe
IKEYI & ARIFAYAN

Aniekan Ukpanah
UDO UDOMA & BELO-OSAGIE

Maxwell Ukpebor
WTS ADEBIYI & ASSOCIATES

Adamu M. Usman
F.O. AKINRELE & CO.

Edward Vera-Cruz
GBENGA BIOBAKU & CO

NORWAY

*ADVOKATFIRMAET HJORT DA, MEMBER OF
IUS LABORIS*

Eli Aasheim
WIERSHOLM LAW OFFICE AS

Anders Aasland Kittelsen
ADVOKATFIRMAET SCHJØDT DA

Ingvild Andersen
ADVOKATFIRMAET SCHJØDT DA

Sverre Ardø
EXPERIAN

Jan L. Backer
WIKBORG, REIN & CO.

Rannveig Bakke Tvedten
HOMBLE OLSBY ADVOKATFIRMA AS

Stig Berge
THOMMESSEN AS

Trine Bjerke Welhaven
HOMBLE OLSBY ADVOKATFIRMA AS

Jacob S. Bjønnes-Jacobsen
GRETTE LAW FIRM DA

Henrik Boehlke
*ADVOKATFIRMAET HJORT DA, MEMBER OF
IUS LABORIS*

Erik Børrud
EXPERIAN

Einard Brunes
RAEDER ADVOKATFIRMA

Elena Busch
Norwegian Mapping Authority, Cadastre and Land Registry, Centre for Property Rights and Development

Carl Arthur Christiansen
Raeder Advokatfirma

Lars Davidsen
Hafslund

Knut Ekern
PwC Norway

Simen Aasen Engebretsen
Deloitte LLP

Jan Erik Bauge
Simonsen Advokatfirma DA

Line Foss Hals
Wikborg, Rein & Co.

Amund Fougner
Advokatfirmaet Hjort DA, member of Ius Laboris

Jan Fougner
Wiersholm Law Office AS

Christian Friestad
PwC Norway

Geir Frøholm
Advokatfirmaet Schjødt DA

Mads Fuglesang
Advokatfirmaet Selmer DA

Ingenborg Gjølstad
Thommessen AS

Renate Iren Heggelund
Advokatfirmaet Selmer DA

Heidi Holmelin
Advokatfirmaet Selmer DA

Therese Høyer Grimstad
Advokatfirmaet Hjort DA, member of Ius Laboris

Odd Hylland
PwC Norway

Hanne Karlsen
Raeder Advokatfirma

Anne Kaurin
Kvale Advokatfirma DA

Bjørn H. Kise
Advokatfirma Vogt & Wiig AS

Charlotte Kristensen
PwC Norway

Bjarne Lothe
Nitter AS, member of Russell Bedford International

Ronny Lund
Wiersholm Law Office AS

Knut Martinsen
Thommessen AS

Ole Fredrik Melleby
Raeder Advokatfirma

Anders Midbøe
PwC Norway

Ernst Arvid Moe
Stavenger Bankruptcy Court

Karl Erik Nedregotten
PwC Norway

Halfdan Nitter
Nitter AS, member of Russell Bedford International

Ole Kristian Olsby
Homble Olsby advokatfirma AS

Helge Onsrud
Statens Kartverk

Camilla Schøyen Breibøl
Wiersholm Law Office AS

Ståle Skutle Arneson
Advokatfirma Vogt & Wiig AS

Simen Smeby Lium
Wikborg, Rein & Co.

Christel Spannow
PwC Norway

Bernt Olav Steinland
Advokatfirmaet Selmer DA

Svein Sulland
Advokatfirmaet Selmer DA

Ingvill Tollman Fosse
Advokatfirmaet Selmer DA

Kristin Tosterud Holte
Advokatfirmaet Hjort DA, member of Ius Laboris

Espen Trædal
PwC Norway

Oyvind Vagan
The Bronnoysund Register Center

Tore Walle-Jensen
The Bronnoysund Register Center

OMAN

Al Busaidy, Mansoor Jamal & Co.

Ernst & Young

Hamad Al Abri
Muscat Electricity Distribution Company

Zahir Abdulla Al Abri
Muscat Electricity Distribution Company

Zubaida Fakir Mohamed Al Balushi
Central Bank of Oman

Ahmed Al Barwani
SNR Denton & Co.

Salman Ali Al Hattali
Muscat Electricity Distribution Company

Zaid Al Khattab
Talal Abu Ghazaleh Legal (TAG-Legal)

Hanaan Al Marhuby
PwC Oman

Amer Al Rawas
Omantel

Eman Al Shahry
SASLO (formerly Said Al Shahry Law Office)

Said bin Saad Al Shahry
SASLO (formerly Said Al Shahry Law Office)

Majid Al Toky
Trowers & Hamlins

Azzan Al Yahmadi
SASLO (formerly Said Al Shahry Law Office)

Ibrahim Albri
Muscat Municipality

Khalid Khamis Al-Hashmi
Muscat Municipality

Leyan Al-Mawali
Trowers & Hamlins

Hilal Almayahi
Muscat Municipality

Ahmed al-Mukhaini
SASLO (formerly Said Al Shahry Law Office)

Mohamed Alrashdi
Muscat Municipality

Mohammed Alshahri
Mohammed Alshahri & Associates

Mona Taha Amer
Qais Al-Qasmi and Mona Amer Lawyers

Mohammed Ahmet Atieh
Amjaad Engineering Consultancy

Russell Aycock
PwC Oman

David Ball
SASLO (formerly Said Al Shahry Law Office)

Mahmoud Bilal
SASLO (formerly Said Al Shahry Law Office)

Sadaf Buchanan
SNR Denton & Co.

M.K. Das
Bank Muscat

Francis D'Souza
BDO Jawad Habib

Kobus Havemann
Driver Consult Oman LLC

Hussein
Muscat Electricity Distribution Company

Robert Kenedy
Curtis Mallet - Prevost, Colt & Mosle LLP

Philip Keun
SNR Denton & Co.

Andrew Kincaid
SASLO (formerly Said Al Shahry Law Office)

Kenneth Macfarlane
PwC Oman

Jose Madukakuzhy
Khimji Ramdas

Pushpa Malani
PwC Oman

Yashpal Mehta
BDO Jawad Habib

Subha Mohan
Curtis Mallet - Prevost, Colt & Mosle LLP

Ahmed Naveed Farooqui
Oman Cables Industry (SAOG)

Rachael Oxby
SNR Denton & Co.

Bruce Palmer
Curtis Mallet - Prevost, Colt & Mosle LLP

Raghavendra Pangala
Semac & Partners LLC

Khalid Al Riyami Dy.
Amjaad Engineering Consultancy

Hussain Salman
Oman Cables Industry (SAOG)

George Sandars
SNR Denton & Co.

Charles Schofield
Trowers & Hamlins

Paul Sheridan
SNR Denton & Co.

Rajshekhar Singh
Bank Muscat

Ganesan Sridhar
Bank Muscat

Tawfiq Ahmed Sultan
W J Towell & Co. LLC

Danielle Town
SASLO (formerly Said Al Shahry Law Office)

Alessandra Zingales
SASLO (formerly Said Al Shahry Law Office)

PAKISTAN

Georgetown University Law Center

Hagler Bailley Pakistan (Pvt) Ltd.

KESC

Shamim & Shams Co.

Ahmed Abbas
Surridge & Beecheno

Sh. Farooq Abdullah
Abraham & Sarwana

Ali Jafar Abidi
State Bank of Pakistan

Masooma Afzal
Haseeb Law Associates

Taqi Ahmad
A.F. Fergusons & Co.

Nasir Mehmood Ahmed
Bunker Logistics

Ahmad Syed Akhter
Pyramid Transportation Group

Hasnain Ashraf
AQLAAL Advocates

Muhammed Moeen Aslam
Bilal Rice Mills

Hyder Hussain Baig, Mirza
Haider Shamsi & Co., Chartered Accountants

Ali Javed Bajwa
Haseeb Law Associates

Akeel Bilgrami
Najmi Bilgrami Collaborative (Pvt) Ltd.

Waheed Chaudhary
LEGIS INN (Attorneys & Corporate Consultants)

Elizabeth Daniel
Zafar & Associates LLP

Faisal Daudpota
Khalid Daudpota & Co.

Junaid Daudpota
Khalid Daudpota & Co.

Khalid Daudpota
Khalid Daudpota & Co.

Zaki Ejaz
Zaki & Zaki (Advocates and Solicitors)

Salman Faisal
Haseeb Law Associates

Iram Fatima
Zafar & Associates LLP

Ikram Fayaz
Qamar Abbas & Co.

Khalid Habibullah
Abraham & Sarwana

Irfan Haider
Pyramid Transportation Group

Asim Harneed Khan
Ivon Trading Company Pvt. Ltd.

Asma Hameed Khan
Surridge & Beecheno

Sohail Hasan
A.F. Fergusons & Co.

Sana Hassan
Zafar & Associates LLP

Syed Ahmad Hassan Shah
Hassan Kaunain Nafees

Rashid Ibrahim
A.F. Fergusons & Co.

Fjaz Ishaq
AQLAAL Advocates

Fiza Islam
LEGIS INN (Attorneys & Corporate Consultants)

Muzaffar Islam
LEGIS INN (Attorneys & Corporate Consultants)

Masooma Jaffer
Abraham & Sarwana

Zahid Jamil
Jamil and Jamil

Saila Jamshaid
Securities and Exchange Commission of Pakistan

Tariq Nasim Jan
Datacheck Pvt. Ltd.

Zulfiqar Khan
Khursheed Khan & Associates

Arif Khan
Qamar Abbas & Co.

Aftab Ahmed Khan
Surridge & Beecheno

Muhammad Maki
Abraham & Sarwana

Farah Malik
Haseeb Law Associates

Muhammad Aslam Memon
United Agencies

Moazzam Mughal
Boxing Winner

Uzma Munir
Hassan Kaunain Nafees

Faiza Muzaffar
LEGIS INN (Attorneys & Corporate Consultants)

Saqib Naveed
Anaya Salt Crafts

Jamal Panhwar
Travel and Culture Services

Irshad Panhwer
Mohsin Tayebaly & Co., Corporate Legal Consultants, Barristers and Advocates

Zaki Rahman
Ebrahim Hosain, Advocates and Corporate Counsel

Abdul Rahman
Qamar Abbas & Co.

Fahad Hameedl Rana
LEGIS INN (Attorneys & Corporate Consultants)

Muhammad Saleem Rana
State Bank of Pakistan

Tariq Saeed Rana
Surridge & Beecheno

Abdur Razzaq
Qamar Abbas & Co.

Mudassir Rizwan
A.F. Fergusons & Co.

Abdul Salam
LEGIS INN (Attorneys & Corporate Consultants)

Jawad A. Sarwana
Abraham & Sarwana

Ghulam Haider Shamsi
Haider Shamsi & Co., Chartered Accountants

Muhammad Siddique
Securities and Exchange Commission of Pakistan

Mian Haseeb ul Hassan
Haseeb Law Associates

Baleegh Ur-Rehman
JWC Trucker Leather

Chaudhary Usman
Ebrahim Hosain, Advocates and Corporate Counsel

Saleem uz Zaman
Saleem uz Zaman & Co.

Sana Waheed
Zafar & Associates LLP

Muhammad Yousuf
Haider Shamsi & Co., Chartered Accountants

Ilyas Zafar
Zafar & Associates LLP

Asf Ali Zaidi
Pyramid Transportation Group

Xavier Zamurrad
XNRR Technologies

PALAU

Palau Public Utility Corporation

Kenneth Barden
Attorney-at-Law

Cristina Castro
Western Caroline Trading Co.

Yukiwo P. Dengokl
Dimdjtruk & Nakamura

Kevin N. Kirk
The Law Office of Kirk and Shadel

Kuniwo Nakamura
Belau Transfer & Terminal Co. Group

David Shadel
The Law Office of Kirk and Shadel

Neco Shao
Neco Construction Inc

Peter C. Tsao
Western Caroline Trading Co.

PANAMA

Ernst & Young

Panamá Soluciones Logísticas Int. - PSLI

Alejandro Alemán
Alfaro, Ferrer & Ramírez

Aristides Anguizola
Morgan & Morgan

Mercedes Arauz de Grimaldo
Morgan & Morgan

Renan Arjona
CAPAC (Cámara Panameña de la Construcción)

Gilberto Arosemena
Arosemena Noriega & Contreras

Amanda Barraza de Wong
PwC Panama

Luis Barría

Gustavo Adolfo Bernal
Sociedad Panameña de Ingenieros y Arquitectos

Carlos Klaus Bieberach
PwC Panama

Luis Chalhoub
Icaza, Gonzalez-Ruiz & Aleman

Julio Cesar Contreras III
Arosemena Noriega & Contreras

Jeanina Aileen Diaz
PricewaterhouseCoopers Corporate Legal Services

Manuel E. Espino
Fabrega, Molino & Mulino

Michael Fernandez
CAPAC (Cámara Panameña de la Construcción)

Enna Ferrer
Alfaro, Ferrer & Ramírez

Gina Gómez

Yamileth Herrera
Morgan & Morgan

Ricardo Lachman
Morgan & Morgan

Ivette Elisa Martínez Saenz
Patton, Moreno & Asvat

Gloria Moreno de López
Autoridad Nacional de Aduanas (ANA)

José Miguel Navarrete
Arosemena Noriega & Contreras

Ramón Ortega
PwC Dominican Republic

Sebastián Perez
Union Fenosa - EDEMET - EDECHI

Jorge Quijano
Arosemena Noriega & Contreras

Loreto Rivera
Nacional de Calificación, Registro y Certificación

Luz María Salamina
Asociación Panameña de Crédito

Verónica Sinisterra
Arosemena Noriega & Contreras

Michelle Solanilla
Arosemena Noriega & Contreras

Edwin Solis
Panalpina World Transport LLP

Ricardo Tribaldos Hernández
Panama Ministry of Economy and Finances

Marlaine Tuñón

Ramon Valdes
Arosemena Noriega & Contreras

Ramón Varela
Morgan & Morgan

PAPUA NEW GUINEA

Ernst & Young

Naomi Abel
IPA

Simon Bendo
Department of Lands and Physical Planning

Moses Billy
Billy Architects

Vincent Bull
Allens Arthur Robinson

David Caradus
PwC Papua New Guinea

Vanessa Geita
PwC Papua New Guinea

Loani R. Henao
Henaos Lawyers

Clarence Hoot
IPA

Gary Juffa
PNG Customs Service

Ambeng Kandakasi
Supreme Court of Justice

Stanley Kewa
PNG Power Ltd.

John Leahy
Peter Allan Lowing Lawyers

Bruce Mackinlay
Credit & Data Bureau Limited

Antonia Nohou
PwC Papua New Guinea

Ivan Pomaleu
IPA

Kapu Rageau
Rageau, Manua & Kikira Lawyers

Jason Reclamado
Eltech Engineering Services Ltd.

John Brian Sam
PNG Customs Service

Benjamin Samson
Department of Lands and Physical Planning

Ian Shepherd
Blake Dawson

Stuart Smith
Westpac PNG Limited

Lawrence Solomon
PNG Power Ltd.

Thomas Taberia
Peter Allan Lowing Lawyers

Stanley Timun
IPA

Alex Tongayu
IPA

PARAGUAY

Administración Nacional de Electricidad

Magalí Rodríguez Alcalá
Berkemeyer, Attorneys & Counselors

Perla Alderete
Vouga & Olmedo Abogados

Florinda Benitez
Notary public

Hugo T. Berkemeyer
Berkemeyer, Attorneys & Counselors

Luis Alberto Breuer
Berkemeyer, Attorneys & Counselors

Esteban Burt
Peroni, Sosa, Tellechea, Burt & Narvaja, member of Lex Mundi

Victoria Burt
Peroni, Sosa, Tellechea, Burt & Narvaja, member of Lex Mundi

Laura Cabrera
Vouga & Olmedo Abogados

Ramón Antonio Castillo Saenz
Informconf S. A.

María Debattisti
Servimex SACI

Giselle Deiró
Berkemeyer, Attorneys & Counselors

Lorena Dolsa
Berkemeyer, Attorneys & Counselors

Natalia Enciso Benitez
Notary public

Bruno Fiorio Carrizosa
Fiorio, Cardozo & Alvarado

Juan Bautista Fiorio Gimenez
Fiorio, Cardozo & Alvarado

Ana Franco
BDO Rubensztein & Guillén

Sergio Franco
PwC Uruguay

Jorge Guillermo Gomez
PwC Paraguay

Nadia Gorostiaga
PwC Paraguay

Carl Thomas Gwynn
Gwynn & Gwynn - Legal Counselling and Translations

Norman Gwynn
Gwynn & Gwynn - Legal Counselling and Translations

Carlos R. Gwynn S.
Gwynn & Gwynn - Legal Counselling and Translations

Jorge Jimenez Rey
Banco Central del Paraguay

Nestor Loizaga
Ferrere Attorneys

Karina Lozano
PwC Paraguay

Augusto César Mengual Mazacotte
Fiorio, Cardozo & Alvarado

María Esmeralda Moreno
Moreno Ruffinelli & Asociados

Roberto Moreno Rodríguez Alcalá
Moreno Ruffinelli & Asociados

Rocío Penayo
Moreno Ruffinelli & Asociados

Yolanda Pereira
Berkemeyer, Attorneys & Counselors

Beatriz Pisano
Ferrere Attorneys

Armindo Riquelme
Fiorio, Cardozo & Alvarado

Natalio Rubinsztein
BDO Rubensztein & Guillén

Belen Saldivar Romañach
Ferrere Attorneys

Federico Silva
Ferrere Attorneys

Ruben Taboada
PwC Paraguay

PERU

Superintendency of Banking, Insurance and Private Pension Fund Administrator

Walter Aguirre
PwC Peru

Marco Antonio Alarcón Piana
Estudio Luis Echecopar García S.R.L.

Alejandro Almendariz
Jorge Avendaño - Forsyth & Arbe Abogados

Pamela Arce
Rebaza, Alcazar & De Las Casas Abogados Financieros

Guilhermo Auler
Jorge Avendaño - Forsyth & Arbe Abogados

Milagros A. Barrera
Barrios & Fuentes Abogados

Raul Barrios
Barrios & Fuentes Abogados

Juan Domingo Barzola
Barzola & Asociados S.C., member of Russell Bedford International

Vanessa Barzola
PwC Peru

Maritza Barzola Vilchez
Barzola & Asociados S.C., member of Russell Bedford International

Manuel Aguilar Bermúdez
SUNARP

Giuliana Bonelli
Barzola & Asociados S.C., member of Russell Bedford International

Giancarlo Bracamonte
Ransa

Stephany Giovanna Bravo de Rueda Arce
Ransa

Jorge Calle

Liliana Callirgos
Barrios & Fuentes Abogados

Renzo Camaiora
Gallo Barrios Pickmann

Gaston Castillo
SUNARP

José Ignacio Castro
Rubio Leguía Normand

Fernando Castro Kahn
Muñiz, Ramírez, Peréz-Taiman & Luna Victoria Attorneys at Law

Cecilia Catacora
Estudio Olaechea, member of Lex Mundi

Alessandra Cocchella
Rubio Leguía Normand

Sandro Cogorno
Jorge Avendaño - Forsyth & Arbe Abogados

Luis Dávila
Department of Customs Procedures

Joanna Dawson
Estudio Olaechea, member of Lex Mundi

Ricardo de la Piedra
Estudio Olaechea, member of Lex Mundi

Alfonso De Los Heros Pérez Albela
Estudio Luis Echecopar García S.R.L.

Paula Devescovi
Barrios & Fuentes Abogados

Ana María Diez
Estudio Olaechea, member of Lex Mundi

Carlos Roberto Drago Llanos
SUNAT

Juan Carlos Durand Grahammer
Durand Abogados

José Espinoza
Department of Customs Procedures

Arturo Ferrari
Muñiz, Ramírez, Peréz-Taiman & Luna Victoria Attorneys at Law

Guillermo Ferrero
Estudio Ferrero Abogados

Carol Flores Bernal

Luis Enrique Narro Forno
SUNAT

Jorge Fuentes
Rubio Leguía Normand

Carlos Gallardo Torres
General Agency of Public Income Policy

Julio Gallo
Gallo Barrios Pickmann

Juan García Montúfar
Rubio Leguía Normand

Pamela Goyzueta
Equifax Peru S.A.

Gerardo Guzman
Delmar Ugarte Abogados

Cecilia Guzman-Barron
Barrios & Fuentes Abogados

Jose A. Honda
Estudio Olaechea, member of Lex Mundi

Diego Huertas del Pino
Barrios & Fuentes Abogados

Marco Iannacone
PwC Peru

Felipe Eduardo Iannacone Silva
SUNAT

César Ballón Izquierdo
Ransa

José Antonio Jiménez
Rebaza, Alcazar & De Las Casas Abogados Financieros

Rafael Junco
Camara Peruana de la Construccion

Juan Carlos Leon

Gianfranco Linares
Muñiz, Ramírez, Peréz-Taiman & Luna Victoria Attorneys at Law

Herles Loayza Casimiro
Camara Peruana de la Construccion

German Lora
Payet, Rey, Cauvi Abogados

Ursula Luna
Rubio Leguía Normand

Cecilia Manrique
PwC Peru

Milagros Maravi Sumar
Rubio Leguía Normand

Carlos Martinez Ebell
Rubio Leguía Normand

Jesús Matos
Estudio Olaechea, member of Lex Mundi

Milagros Mendoza
Rubio Leguía Normand

Marlene Molero
Rubio Leguía Normand

Juan Antonio Morales
Agencia de Aduana ANTANA

Javier Mori Cockburn
Equifax Peru S.A.

Claudio Mundaca
Barrios & Fuentes Abogados

Franco Muschi Loayza
Payet, Rey, Cauvi Abogados

L. Oliver
SUNARP

Lilian Oliver
SUNARP

Luis Orrego
Delmar Ugarte Abogados

Cristina Oviedo
Payet, Rey, Cauvi Abogados

Max Panay
SUNARP

Lucianna Polar
Estudio Olaechea, member of Lex Mundi

María José Puertas
Gallo Barrios Pickmann

Bruno Marchese Quintana
Rubio Leguía Normand

Carlos Javier Rabanal Sobrino
Durand Abogados

Fernando M. Ramos
Barrios & Fuentes Abogados

Jorge Reategui
Estudio Ferrero Abogados

Patricio Remon
Equifax Peru S.A.

Sonia L. Rengifo
Barrios & Fuentes Abogados

Alonso Rey Bustamante
Payet, Rey, Cauvi Abogados

Guillermo Acuña Roeder

Jose Rosas
Lima Chamber of Commerce

Renzo Rufasto Lira
Payet, Rey, Cauvi Abogados

Augusto Ruiloba Morante
Estudio Luis Echecopar García S.R.L.

Emil Ruppert

Carolina Sáenz Llanos
Rubio Leguía Normand

César Arbe Saldaña
Jorge Avendaño - Forsyth & Arbe Abogados

Adolfo Sanabria Mercado
Muñiz, Ramírez, Peréz-Taiman & Luna Victoria Attorneys at Law

Arturo Ruiz Sanchez
Rubio Leguía Normand

Paola Joselyn Sánchez Alfaro
Ransa

Victor Scarsi
Luz del Sur

Alvaro Delgado Schelje
SUNARP

Martin Serkovic
Estudio Olaechea, member of Lex Mundi

Hugo Silva
Rodrigo, Elías, Medrano Abogados

Ricardo Arturo Toma Oyama
SUNAT

Liliana Tsuboyama
Estudio Luis Echecopar García S.R.L.

Manuel A. Ugarte
Delmar Ugarte Abogados

Daniel Ulloa
Rebaza, Alcazar & De Las Casas Abogados Financieros

Carlos Urbina Ćarcamo
Ransa

Jack Vainstein
Vainstein & Ingenieros S.A.

José Antonio Valdez
Estudio Olaechea, member of Lex Mundi

Veronica Valverde
SUNARP

Carlos Vegas Quintana
Camara Peruana de la Construccion

Ana Vidal
Gallo Barrios Pickmann

Manuel Villa-García
Estudio Olaechea, member of Lex Mundi

Agustín Yrigoyen
Estudio Aurelio García Saván- Abogados

Gustavo Raúl Ytokazu Minami
PwC Peru

Gustavo Zanabria
General Agency of Foreign Economic Matters, Competition and Private Investment

Hector Zegarra
Payet, Rey, Cauvi Abogados

PHILIPPINES
Ernst & Young

Myla Gloria Amboy
Jimenez Gonzales Bello Valdez Caluya & Fernandez

Jazmin Banal
Romulo, Mabanta, Buenaventura, Sayoc & de los Angeles, member of Lex Mundi

Manuel Batallones
BAP Credit Bureau

Alexander Cabrera
Isla Lipana & Co.

Ciriaco S. Calalang
Calalang Law Offices

Ernesto Caluya Jr
Jimenez Gonzales Bello Valdez Caluya & Fernandez

Cecile Margaret Caro
SyCip Salazar Hernandez & Gatmaitan

Bryant Casiw
Baker & McKenzie

Joseph Omar A. Castillo
Puyat Jacinto Santos Law Office

Sandhya Marie Castro
Romulo, Mabanta, Buenaventura, Sayoc & de los Angeles, member of Lex Mundi

Pamela Ann T. Cayabyab
Jimenez Gonzales Bello Valdez Caluya & Fernandez

Kenneth Chua
Quisumbing Torres, member firm of Baker & McKenzie International

Barbara Jill Clara
SyCip Salazar Hernandez & Gatmaitan

Juan Paolo Colet
Castillo Laman Tan Pantaleon & San Jose

Von Bryan Cuerpo
SyCip Salazar Hernandez & Gatmaitan

Emerico O. de Guzman
Angara Abello Concepcion Regala & Cruz Law Offices (ACCRALAW)

Sheila S. De la Rosa
Puyat Jacinto Santos Law Office

Redel Domingo
MERALCO

Jaime Raphael Feliciano
Romulo, Mabanta, Buenaventura, Sayoc & de los Angeles, member of Lex Mundi

Rachel Follosco
Follosco Morallos & Herce

Catherine Franco
Quisumbing Torres, member firm of Baker & McKenzie International

Gilberto Gallos
Angara Abello Concepcion Regala & Cruz Law Offices (ACCRALAW)

Geraldine Garcia
Follosco Morallos & Herce

Andres Gatmaitan
SyCip Salazar Hernandez & Gatmaitan

Gwen Grecia-de Vera
PJS Law

Kathlyn Joy Guanzon
Jimenez Gonzales Bello Valdez Caluya & Fernandez

Tadeo F. Hilado
Angara Abello Concepcion Regala & Cruz Law Offices (ACCRALAW)

Jessica Hilado
Puyat, Jacinto & Santos Law Office

Jose Vicente E. Jimenez
Jimenez Gonzales Bello Valdez Caluya & Fernandez

Gene Nicholas A. Lee
Jimenez Gonzales Bello Valdez Caluya & Fernandez

Victoria Limkico
Jimenez Gonzales Bello Valdez Caluya & Fernandez

Eleanor Lucas Roque
Punongbayan & Araullo

Mel A. Macaraig
Castillo Laman Tan Pantaleon & San Jose

Redentor Marquez
MERALCO

Lory Anne McMullin
Jimenez Gonzales Bello Valdez Caluya & Fernandez

Yolanda Mendoza-Eleazar
Castillo Laman Tan Pantaleon & San Jose

Cheryll Grace Montealegre
Isla Lipana & Co.

Jesusito G. Morallos
Follosco Morallos & Herce

Freddie Naagas
SCM Creative Concepts Inc.

Alan Ortiz
Follosco Morallos & Herce

Carla Ortiz
Romulo, Mabanta, Buenaventura, Sayoc & de los Angeles, member of Lex Mundi

Emmanuel C. Paras
SyCip Salazar Hernandez & Gatmaitan

Lianne Ivy Pascua-Medina
Quasha Ancheta Pena & Nolasco

Zayber John Protacio
Isla Lipana & Co.

Senen Quizon
Punongbayan & Araullo

Janice Kae Ramirez
Quasha Ancheta Pena & Nolasco

Teodore D. Regala
Angara Abello Concepcion Regala & Cruz Law Offices (ACCRALAW)

Judy Alice Repol
Angara Abello Concepcion Regala & Cruz Law Offices (ACCRALAW)

Roderick Reyes
Jimenez Gonzales Bello Valdez Caluya & Fernandez

Ricardo J. Romulo
Romulo, Mabanta, Buenaventura, Sayoc & de los Angeles, member of Lex Mundi

Lea L. Roque
Punongbayan & Araullo

Rowena Fatima Salonga
Puyat Jacinto Santos Law Office

Neptali Salvanera
Angara Abello Concepcion Regala & Cruz Law Offices (ACCRALAW)

Froilan Savet
MERALCO

Abigail D. Sese
Castillo Laman Tan Pantaleon & San Jose

Felix Sy
Baker & McKenzie

Sheryl Tanquilut
Romulo, Mabanta, Buenaventura, Sayoc & de los Angeles, member of Lex Mundi

Maribel B. Tejada
Puyat Jacinto Santos Law Office

Anna Bianca Torres
Puyat, Jacinto & Santos Law Office

Ma. Melva Valdez
Jimenez Gonzales Bello Valdez Caluya & Fernandez

Shirley Velasquez
Puyat, Jacinto & Santos Law Office

Virginia B. Viray
Puyat Jacinto Santos Law Office

Maria Winda Ysibido
Isla Lipana & Co.

Redentor C. Zapata
Quasha Ancheta Pena & Nolasco

Gil Roberto Zerrudo
Quisumbing Torres, member firm of Baker & McKenzie International

POLAND
Allen & Overy, A. Pędzich sp. k.

Piotr Andrzejak
Sołtysiński Kawecki & Szlęzak

Jerzy Baehr
WKB Wiercinski, Kwiecinski, Baehr

Grzegorz Banasiuk
Gide Loyrette Nouel, member of Lex Mundi

Michal Bartłowski
Wardyński & Partners

Ewelina Batnik
MultiBank S. A

Michal Białobrzeski
Hogan Lovells (Warszawa) LLP

Anna Bochnia
DLA Piper Wiater sp.k.

Aleksander Borowicz
Biuro Informacji Kredytowej S.A.

Piotr Brzezinski
Gide Loyrette Nouel, member of Lex Mundi

Krzysztof Cichocki
Sołtysiński Kawecki & Szlęzak

Jan Ciećwierz
Wardyński & Partners

Bożena Ciosek
Wierzbowski Eversheds, member of Eversheds International Ltd.

Katarzyna Czarnecka-Zochowska
PwC Poland

Michał Dąbrowski
Ministry of Justice

Andrzej Dmowski
DZO Dmowski Zaremba Olczak Sp. z o.o., member of Russell Bedford International

Bartosz Draniewicz
Bartosz

Edyta Dubikowska
Squire Sanders Święcicki Krześniak sp. k.

Piotr Falarz
DLA Piper Wiater sp.k.

Agnieszka Fedor
WKB Wiercinski, Kwiecinski, Baehr

Krzysztof Feluch
Wierzbowski Eversheds, member of Eversheds International Ltd.

Klaudia Frątczak
WKB Wiercinski, Kwiecinski, Baehr

Jan Furtas
The SPIN Initiative Association

Joanna Gasowski
Wierzbowski Eversheds, member of Eversheds International Ltd.

Lech Giliciński
Wierzbowski Eversheds, member of Eversheds International Ltd.

Rafał Godlewski
Wardyński & Partners

Tomasz Grygorczuk
Hogan Lovells (Warszawa) LLP

Jakub Guzik
Sołtysiński Kawecki & Szlęzak

Monika Hartung
Wardyński & Partners

Łukasz Hejmej
White & Case W. Daniłowicz, W. Jurcewicz i Wspólnicy - Kancelaria Prawna sp.k.

Magdalena Jarosz
Wierzbowski Eversheds, member of Eversheds International Ltd.

Witold Jarzyński
Rymar and Partners

Jakub Jędrzejak
WKB Wiercinski, Kwiecinski, Baehr

Magdalena Kalinska
WKB Wiercinski, Kwiecinski, Baehr

Rafał Kamiński
White & Case W. Daniłowicz, W. Jurcewicz i Wspólnicy - Kancelaria Prawna sp.k.

Tomasz Kański
Sołtysiński Kawecki & Szlęzak

Iwona Karasek
Jagiellonian University Krakow

Beniamin Kiewra
Sołtysiński Kawecki & Szlęzak

Katarzyna Konstanty
Zacharzewski & Partners

Artur Kopijkowski-Gozuch
Ministry of Economy

Tomasz Korczyński
Wierzbowski Eversheds, member of Eversheds International Ltd.

Olga Koszewska
Chadbourne & Parke LLP

Ewa Łachowska - Brol
Wierzbowski Eversheds, member of Eversheds International Ltd.

Agnieszka Lisiecka
Wardyński & Partners

Wojciech Łuczka
Hogan Lovells (Warszawa) LLP

Firlej Marek
Ministry of Finance of Poland

Sebastian Michalik
Cargo-partner spedycja sp. z.o.o.

Agata Mierzwa
Wierzbowski Eversheds, member of Eversheds International Ltd.

Tomasz Misiak
PwC Poland

Radosław Moczadło
Gide Loyrette Nouel, member of Lex Mundi

Magdalena Moczulska
Wardyński & Partners

Michal Niemirowicz-Szczytt
bnt Neupert Zamorska & Partnerzy s.c.

Krystyna Olczak
DZO Dmowski Zaremba Olczak Sp. z o.o., member of Russell Bedford International

Krzysztof Pawlak
Sołtysiński Kawecki & Szlęzak

Weronika Pelc
Wardyński & Partners

Alexandra Pereira dos Reis
Raposo Bernardo & Associados

Łukasz Piebiak
VIII District Commercial Court in Warsaw

Jakub Pokrzywniak
WKB Wiercinski, Kwiecinski, Baehr

Bartłomiej Raczkowski
Bartłomiej Raczkowski Kancelaria Prawa Pracy

Anna Ratajczyk-Salamacha
Gide Loyrette Nouel, member of Lex Mundi

Piotr Sadownik
Gide Loyrette Nouel, member of Lex Mundi

Katarzyna Sarek
Bartłomiej Raczkowski Kancelaria Prawa Pracy

Karolina Schiffter
Sołtysiński Kawecki & Szlęzak

Zbigniew Skórczyński
Chadbourne & Parke LLP

Iwona Smith
PwC Poland

Ewelina Stobiecka
E|N|W|C Rechtsanwalte E.Stobiecka Kancelaria prawna sp.k.

Natalia Świderska
The SPIN Initiative Association

Izabela Szczygielska
WKB Wiercinski, Kwiecinski, Baehr

Łukasz Szegda
Wardynski & Partners

Anna Tarasiuk-Flodrowska
Hogan Lovells (Warszawa) LLP

Dariusz Tokarczuk
Gide Loyrette Nouel, member of Lex Mundi

Sylwia Tylenda
Raposo Bernardo & Associados

Dominika Wagrodzka
bnt Neupert Zamorska & Partnerzy s.c.

Radosław Waszkiewicz
Sołtysiński Kawecki & Szlęzak

Krzysztof Wierzbowski
Wierzbowski Eversheds, member of Eversheds International Ltd.

Anna Wietrzyńska
DLA Piper Wiater sp.k.

Robert Windmill
Windmill Gąsiewski & Roman Law Office

Jaroslaw Wisniewski
PwC Poland

Piotr Witecki
DLA Piper Wiater sp.k.

Gurba Włodzimierz
Ministry of Finance of Poland

Tomasz Zabost
ProLogis

Andrzej Zacharzewski
Zacharzewski & Partners

Malgorzata Zamorska
bnt Neupert Zamorska & Partnerzy s.c.

Grazyna Zaremba
DZO Dmowski Zaremba Olczak Sp. z o.o., member of Russell Bedford International

Tomasz Zasacki
Wardynski & Partners

Magdalena Zwolinska
Bartłomiej Raczkowski Kancelaria Prawa Pracy

PORTUGAL

EDP Distribuição - Energia, SA

Vieira de Almeida & Associados

Maria Isabel Abreu
Polytechnic Institute of Bragança

Paula Alegria Martins
Mouteira Guerreiro, Rosa Amaral & Associados - Sociedade de Advogados R.L.

Natália Garcia Alves
Abreu Advogados

Bruno Andrade Alves
PwC Portugal

Filipa Arantes Pedroso
Morais Leitão, Galvão Teles, Soares da Silva & Associados, member of Lex Mundi

Miguel Azevedo
J & A Garrigues, S.L.P

João Banza
PwC Portugal

João Nuno Barrocas
Barrocas Sarmento Neves

Manuel P. Barrocas
Barrocas Sarmento Neves

Mark Bekker
Bekker Logistica

Barbara Berckmoes
PwC Portugal

Nelson Bernardo
Raposo Bernardo & Associados

Marco Bicó da Costa
Credinformações/ Equifax

Rui Capote
PLEN - Sociedade de Advogados, RL

Ana Catarina Carnaz
PwC Portugal

Tiago Castanheira Marques
Abreu Advogados

Susana Cebola
Instituto dos Registos e do Notariado

Gabriel Cordeiro
Direcção Municipal de Gestão Urbanística

Maria Manuela Correia
Gali Macedo & Associados

Joana Correia
Raposo Bernardo & Associados

Marcelo Correia Alves
Barrocas Sarmento Neves

Ana Raquel Costa
PwC Portugal

Miguel de Avillez Pereira
Abreu Advogados

Maria de Lancastre Valente
SRS Advogados

João Cadete de Matos
Banco de Portugal

Carlos de Sousa e Brito
Carlos de Sousa e Brito & Associados

João Duarte de Sousa
J & A Garrigues, S.L.P

John Duggan
PwC Portugal

Jaime Esteves
PwC Portugal

Bruno Ferreira
J & A Garrigues, S.L.P

Sofia Ferreira Enriquez
Raposo Bernardo & Associados

Nuno Pimentel Gomes
Abreu Advogados

Paulo Henriques
University of Coimbra

Miguel Inácio Castro
Mouteira Guerreiro, Rosa Amaral & Associados - Sociedade de Advogados R.L.

Maria João Ricou
Cuatrecasas, Gonçalves Pereira

Andreia Junior
Gali Macedo & Associados

Caetano Leitão
Barros, Sobral, G. Gomes & Associados

Maria Manuel Leitão Marques
Secretary of State for Administrative Modernisation

Tiago Lemos
PLEN - Sociedade de Advogados, RL

Diogo Léonidas Rocha
J & A Garrigues, S.L.P

Jorge Pedro Lopes
Polytechnic Institute of Bragança

Helga Lopes Ribeiro
Mouteira Guerreiro, Rosa Amaral & Associados - Sociedade de Advogados R.L.

Tiago Gali Macedo
Gali Macedo & Associados

Ana Margarida Maia
Miranda Correia Amendoeira & Associados

Nuno Mansilha
Miranda Correia Amendoeira & Associados

Miguel Marques dos Santos
J & A Garrigues, S.L.P

Fernando Marta
Credinformações/ Equifax

Isabel Martínez de Salas
J & A Garrigues, S.L.P

Susana Melo
Grant Thornton LLP

Francisco Guimarães Melo
PwC Portugal

Joaquim Luis Mendes
Grant Thornton LLP

Gonçalo Meneses
Carlos de Sousa e Brito & Associados

José Carlos Monteiro
JMSROC, LDA, member of Russell Bedford International

Ana Pinto Morais
PwC Portugal

João Moucheira
Instituto dos Registos e do Notariado

António Mouteira Guerreiro
Mouteira Guerreiro, Rosa Amaral & Associados - Sociedade de Advogados R.L.

Rita Nogueira Neto
J & A Garrigues, S.L.P

Catarina Nunes
PwC Portugal

Vitorino Oliveira
Instituto dos Registos e do Notariado

Ema Palma
JMSROC, LDA, member of Russell Bedford International

Rui Peixoto Duarte
Abreu Advogados

Pedro Pereira Coutinho
J & A Garrigues, S.L.P

António Luís Pereira Figueiredo
Instituto dos Registos e do Notariado

Isabel Pinheiro Torres
Abreu Advogados

Acácio Pita Negrão
PLEN - Sociedade de Advogados, RL

Pedro Porto Dordio
António Frutuoso de Melo e Associados - Sociedade de Advogados, R.L.

Laurinda Prazeres Cardoso
FBL Advogados

Margarida Ramalho
Associação de Empresas de Construção, Obras Públicas e Serviços

Rute Ramos
Carlos de Sousa e Brito & Associados

Manuel Raposo
PwC Portugal

Filomena Rosa
Instituto dos Registos e do Notariado

César Sá Esteves
SRS Advogados

Francisco Salgueiro
Neville de Rougemont & Associados

Pedro Santos
Grant Thornton LLP

Raquel Santos
Morais Leitão, Galvão Teles, Soares da Silva & Associados, member of Lex Mundi

Filipe Santos Barata
Cuatrecasas, Gonçalves Pereira

Cláudia Santos Malaquias
Miranda Correia Amendoeira & Associados

Inês Saraiva de Aguilar
António Frutuoso de Melo e Associados - Sociedade de Advogados, R.L.

Angela Maria Silva
PwC Portugal

Eliana Silva Pereira
Gali Macedo & Associados

Manuel Silveira Botelho
António Frutuoso de Melo e Associados - Sociedade de Advogados, R.L.

Luís Filipe Sousa
PwC Portugal

Carmo Sousa Machado
Abreu Advogados

Bruna Sousa Pereira
PwC Portugal

João Paulo Teixeira de Matos
J & A Garrigues, S.L.P

Nuno Telleria
Barros, Sobral, G. Gomes & Associados

Liza Helena Vaz
PwC Portugal

PUERTO RICO (U.S.)

Viviana Aguilu
PwC Puerto Rico

Alfredo Alvarez-Ibañez
O'Neill & Borges

Vicente Antonetti
Goldman Antonetti & Córdova P.S.C

Salvador Antonetti
O'Neill & Borges

Juan Aquino
O'Neill & Borges

Antonio A. Arias-Larcada
McConnell Valdés LLC

Luis Ariza
ABF Freight Systems, Inc.

James A. Arroyo
TransUnion De Puerto Rico

Hermann Bauer
O'Neill & Borges

Nikos Buxeda Ferrer
Adsuar Muñiz Goyco Seda & Pérez-Ochoa, P.S.C

Edward Calvesbert
Departamento de Desarrollo Economico Puerto Rico

Jorge Capó Matos
O'Neill & Borges

Nydia Cardona
CMA Architects & Engineers LLP

Solymar Castillo-Morales
Goldman Antonetti & Córdova P.S.C

Samuel Céspedes Jr
McConnell Valdés LLC

Odemaris Chacon
William Estrella | Attorneys & Counselors

Walter F. Chow
O'Neill & Borges

Andrés Colberg
William Estrella | Attorneys & Counselors

Harry Cook
McConnell Valdés LLC

Miguel A. Cordero
Puerto Rico Electric Power Authority

Manuel De Lemos
Colegio de Arquitectos y Arquitectos Paisajistas de Puerto Rico

Miguel Del Rio
Del Rio Arquitectos

Myrtelena Díaz Pedora
Adsuar Muñiz Goyco Seda & Pérez-Ochoa, P.S.C

Francisco Dox
Goldman Antonetti & Córdova P.S.C

Antonio Escudero
McConnell Valdés LLC

Alberto G. Estrella

Ubaldo Fernandez
O'Neill & Borges

Dagmar Fernández
Quiñones & Sánchez, PSC

Bennett Díaz Figueroa
Colegio de Arquitectos y Arquitectos Paisajistas de Puerto Rico

Edwin Figueroa
McConnell Valdés LLC

David Freedman
O'Neill & Borges

Virginia Gomez
Puerto Rico Electric Power Authority

Pedro Janer
CMA Architects & Engineers LLP

Gerardo Jusino
CMA Architects & Engineers LLP

Héctor Lebrón
Ferraiuoli, LLC

Myrna I. Lozada-Guzmán
Goldman Antonetti & Córdova P.S.C

Antonio Marichal-Aponte
Marichal & Hernandez LLP

Hernan Marrero Calderon
McConnell Valdés LLC

Oscar O Meléndez - Sauri
Coto Malley & Tamargo, LLP

Juan Carlos Méndez
McConnell Valdés LLC

Rafael Pérez-Villarini
FPV & Galindez CPAs, PSC, member of Russell Bedford International

Edwin Quiñones
Quiñones & Sánchez, PSC

Eduardo Regis
TRG Architects

Thelma Rivera
Goldman Antonetti & Córdova P.S.C

Victor Rodriguez
Multitransport & Marine Co.

Victor Rodriguez
PwC Puerto Rico

Loudres Rodriguez-Morera

Edgardo Rosa
FPV & Galindez CPAs, PSC, member of Russell Bedford International

José Fernando Rovira-Rullán
Ferraiuoli, LLC

Jorge M. Ruiz Montilla
McConnell Valdés LLC

Patricia Salichs
O'Neill & Borges

Hector Silen
O'Neill & Borges

Eduardo Tamargo
Coto Malley & Tamargo, LLP

Jose Torres
Puerto Rico Electrical Contractors Association

Carlos Valldejuly
O'Neill & Borges

Laura Velez Velez
McConnell Valdés LLC

Travis Wheatley
O'Neill & Borges

QATAR

Diamond Shipping Services

Ernst & Young

National Shipping and Marine Services Company WLL

Qatar Credit Bureau

Sharaf Shipping Agency

Supreme Judiciary Council, Qatar

Abdelmoniem Abutiffa
Qatar International Law Firm

Hani Al Naddaf
Al Tamimi & Company Advocates & Legal Consultants

Rashed Albuflasa
Panalpina Qatar WLL

Monita Barghachieh
Patton Boggs LLP

Solymar Castillo-Morales
Goldman Antonetti & Córdova P.S.C

Ian Clay
PwC Qatar

Sleiman Dagher
Badri and Salim El Meouchi Law Firm, member of Interleges

Arnaud Depierrefeu
SCP d'avocats UGGC & Associés

Francisco Dox
Goldman Antonetti & Córdova P.S.C

Fouad El Haddad
Clyde & Co.

Chadia El Meouchi
Badri and Salim El Meouchi Law Firm, member of Interleges

Neyla El-Khazen
Badri and Salim El Meouchi Law Firm, member of Interleges

Sami Fakhoury
Al Tamimi & Company Advocates & Legal Consultants

Sarah Fakhry
Badri and Salim El Meouchi Law Firm, member of Interleges

Dalal K. Farhat Harb
Arab Engineering Bureau

Mohamed Fouad
Sultan Al-Abdulla & Partners

Antonio Ghaleb
Ahmed Tawfik & Co. Certified Public Accountant

Kamal Hafez
Al Tamimi & Company Advocates & Legal Consultants

Robert Hager
Patton Boggs LLP

Walid Honein
Badri and Salim El Meouchi Law Firm, member of Interleges

Tajedin Idris Babekir
MEEZA QSTP-LLC

Abdulla Omar Ismail Al-Dafaa
Qatar Petroleum

Daoud Adel Issa
Qatar Petroleum

Ahmed Jaafir
Al Tamimi & Company Advocates & Legal Consultants

Marie-Anne Jabbour
Badri and Salim El Meouchi Law Firm, member of Interleges

Marc Jreidini
Badri and Salim El Meouchi Law Firm, member of Interleges

Maryline Kalaydjian
Badri and Salim El Meouchi Law Firm, member of Interleges

Upuli Kasturiarachchi
PwC Qatar

Sajid Khan
PwC Qatar

Frank Lucente
Al Tamimi & Company Advocates & Legal Consultants

Elias Matni
Badri and Salim El Meouchi Law Firm, member of Interleges

Arnaud Montouché
SCP d'avocats UGGC & Associés

Rita Moukarzel
Badri and Salim El Meouchi Law Firm, member of Interleges

Ahmed Tawfik Nassim
Ahmed Tawfik & Co. Certified Public Accountant

Charbel Neaman
Clyde & Co.

Sujani Nisansala
PwC Qatar

Ziad Raheb
Badri and Salim El Meouchi Law Firm, member of Interleges

Lyka Rom
Ahmed Tawfik & Co. Certified Public Accountant

Sadek Sadek
Ahmed Tawfik & Co. Certified Public Accountant

David Salt
Clyde & Co.

Mohammad Sami
Al Sulaiti, Attorneys, Legal Consultants & Arbitrators

Zain Al Abdin Sharar
Qatar University

Abdul Aziz Mohammed Sorour
Ministry of Justice

Terence G.C. Witzmann
HSBC

Yuenping Wong
Al Tamimi & Company Advocates & Legal Consultants

ROMANIA

ANRE

Bitrans Ltd., member of World Mediatrans Group

Hercule Impex

Radu Tărăcilă Pădurari Retevoescu
SPRL in association with Allen & Overy

Adriana Almasan
STOICA & Asociații - Societate Civilă de Avocați

Cosmin Anghel
Badea Asociatii in association with Clifford Chance

Andrei Badiu
3B EXPERT AUDIT, member of Russell Bedford International

Emanuel Băncilă
D&B David și Baias Law Firm

Irina Elena Bănică
POP PEPA S C.A. Attorneys- at- Law

Alexandra Barac
POP PEPA S C.A. Attorneys- at- Law

Irina Barbu
D&B David și Baias Law Firm

Monica Biciusca
Anghel Stabb & Partners

Silvia Bohalteanu
Mușat & Asociații

Alin Buftea
DLA Piper Dinu SCA

Lucian Catrinoiu
STOICA & Asociații - Societate Civilă de Avocați

Adrian Cazan
DLA Piper Dinu SCA

Cezara Chirica
D&B David și Baias Law Firm

Mara Ciju
Lina & Guia S.C.A

Victor Ciocîltan
Oancea Ciocîltan & Asociatii

Andreea Ciorapciu
SALANS Moore & Asociatii SCA

Anamaria Corbescu
SALANS Moore & Asociatii SCA

Dorin Coza
Sulica Protopopescu Vonica

Ana Craciun
POP PEPA S.C.A. Attorneys- at- Law

Tiberiu Csaki
SALANS Moore & Asociatii SCA

Rebeca Dan
POP PEPA S.C.A. Attorneys-at-Law

Peter De Ruiter
PwC Romania

Adrian Deaconu
Taxhouse SRL

Georgiana Descultu
PwC Romania

Luminita Dima
Nestor Nestor Diculescu Kingston Petersen

Răzvan Dincă
STOICA & Asociații - Societate Civilă de Avocați

Adriana Dobre
D&B David și Baias Law Firm

Rodica Dobre
PwC Romania

Alexandru Dobrescu
Lina & Guia S.C.A

Ion Dragulin
National Bank of Romania

Laura Adina Duca
Nestor Nestor Diculescu Kingston Petersen

Serban Epure
Biroul de Credit

Corneliu Frunzescu
D&B David și Baias Law Firm

Adriana Gaspar
Nestor Nestor Diculescu Kingston Petersen

Monica Georgiadis
DLA Piper Dinu SCA

Gina Gheorghe
Leaua & Asociatii

Georgiana Ghitu
DLA Piper Dinu SCA

Sergiu Gidei
D&B David și Baias Law Firm

Ciprian Glodeanu
Wolf Theiss

Andra Gogulescu
DLA Piper Dinu SCA

Laura Gradinescu
DLA Piper Dinu SCA

Marius Grigorescu
Leaua & Asociatii

Mihai Guia
Lina & Guia S.C.A

Argentina Hincu
SALANS Moore & Asociatii SCA

Cristina Iacobescu
POP PEPA S.C.A. Attorneys- at- Law

Cristina Ibolea
Badea Asociatii in association with Clifford Chance

Diana Emanuela Ispas
Nestor Nestor Diculescu Kingston Petersen

Crenguta Leaua
Leaua & Asociatii

Cristian Lina
Lina & Guia S.C.A

Amalia Lincaru
SALANS Moore & Asociatii SCA

Edita Lovin
Retired Judge of Romanian Supreme Court of Justice

Smaranda Mandrescu
POP PEPA S.C.A. Attorneys- at- Law

Dumitru Viorel Manescu
National Union of Civil Law Notaries of Romania

Oana Manuceanu
PwC Romania

Gelu Maravela
Mușat & Asociații

Carmen Medar
D&B David și Baias Law Firm

Raluca Mihaila
PwC Romania

Mihaela Mihu
SALANS Moore & Asociatii SCA

Dan Minoiu
Mușat & Asociații

Dominic Morega
Mușat & Asociații

Razvan Nanescu
Nestor Nestor Diculescu Kingston Petersen

Adriana Neagoe
National Bank of Romania

Manuela Marina Nestor
Nestor Nestor Diculescu Kingston Petersen

Theodor Catalin Nicolescu
Nicolescu & Perianu Law Firm

Oana Niculescu
PwC Romania

Georgiana Nito
Badea Asociatii in association with Clifford Chance

Tudor Oancea
Oancea Ciocîltan & Asociatii

Delia Paceagiu
Nestor Nestor Diculescu Kingston Petersen

Marius Pătrăşcanu
Mușat & Asociații

Steven Pepa
POP PEPA S C.A. Attorneys- at- Law

Cosmin Petru-Bonea
SALANS Moore & Asociatii SCA

Eugen Pop
Enescu, Panait, Pop & Partners

Claudiu Pop
POP PEPA S.C.A. Attorneys- at- Law

Alida Popa
Mușat & Asociații

Cristina Popescu
Lina & Guia S.C.A

Alina Popescu
Mușat & Asociații

Mariana Popescu
National Bank of Romania

Cristian Predan
Gebrueder Weiss srl

Irina Preoteasa
PwC Romania

Monica Preotescu
Nestor Nestor Diculescu Kingston Petersen

Raluca Radu
SALANS Moore & Asociatii SCA

Laura Radu
STOICA & Asociații - Societate Civilă de Avocați

Cristian Radulescu
Taxhouse SRL

Ana Maria Ralea
D&B David și Baias Law Firm

Alexandra Rimbu
Mușat & Asociații

Anda Rojanschi
D&B David și Baias Law Firm

Angela Rosca
Taxhouse SRL

Andrei Săvescu
Săvescu si Asociatii

Valentin Serban
SALANS Moore & Asociatii SCA

Iulia Simion
Wolf Theiss

Alexandru Slujitoru
D&B David și Baias Law Firm

Ileana Sovaila
Mușat & Asociații

Oana Soviani
SALANS Moore & Asociatii SCA

David Stabb
Anghel Stabb & Partners

Alexandru Stanciu
Leaua & Asociatii

Cristiana Stoica
STOICA & Asociații - Societate Civilă de Avocați

Sorin Corneliu Stratula
Stratula Mocanu & Asociatii

Roxana Talasman
Nestor Nestor Diculescu Kingston Petersen

Florin Tineghe
DLA Piper Dinu SCA

Laura Tiuca
SALANS Moore & Asociatii SCA

Madalina Trifan
SALANS Moore & Asociatii SCA

Ionut Ursache
PwC Romania

Cristina Vedel
POP PEPA S C.A. Attorneys- at- Law

Cristina Virtopeanu
Nestor Nestor Diculescu Kingston Petersen

Roxana Vornicu
Nestor Nestor Diculescu Kingston Petersen

RUSSIAN FEDERATION
National Bureau of Credit Histories

RD Construction Management

Tax Service

Andrei Afanasiev
Baker & McKenzie - CIS, Limited

Marat Agabalyan
Herbert Smith CIS LLP

Dania Aknazarova
CMS Legal

Mike Allen
Russia Consulting

Alexey Almazov
Prosperity Project Management

Julia Andreeva
Capital Legal Services LLC

Anatoly E. Andriash
Macleod Dixon

Maxim Anisimov
Prosperity Project Management

Mikhail Anosov
Capital Legal Services LLC

Konstantin Baranov
CMS Legal

Marina Baranova
Mikhalilov & Partners, member of Russell Bedford International

Elena Barikhnovskaya
Salans

Alexander Batalov
CMS Legal

Derek Bloom
Capital Legal Services LLC

Fedor Bogatyrev
ALRUD Law Firm

Maria Bykovskaya
Gide Loyrette Nouel, member of Lex Mundi

David Cranfield
CMS Legal

Davidovskaya
Chamber of Tax Advisers of Russia

Andrey Demusenko
Russia Consulting

Grigory Domashenko

Andrey Dukhin
Gide Loyrette Nouel, member of Lex Mundi

Valery Fedoreev
Baker & McKenzie

Maria Gorban
Gide Loyrette Nouel, member of Lex Mundi

Inna Havanova
Chamber of Tax Advisers of Russia

Anton Kalanov
Interexpertiza LLC

Ekaterina Karunets
Baker & McKenzie - CIS, Limited

Darya Kazakova Podolskaia
Amerinde Consolidated, Inc.

Alexander Khretinin
Herbert Smith CIS LLP

Olga Konkova
ABU Accounting Services

Anastasia Konovalova
Macleod Dixon

Oksana Kostenko
CMS Legal

Georgy Koval
CMS Legal

Alyona Kozyreva
Macleod Dixon

Marina Krasnobaeva
Yukov, Khrenov & Partners

Alyona Kucher
Debevoise & Plimpton LLP

Ekaterina Evgenievna Lamanova
MOESK

David Lasfargue
Gide Loyrette Nouel, member of Lex Mundi

Andrey Lebedev
Yukov, Khrenov & Partners

Anastasiya Lemysh
CMS Legal

Maxim Likholetov
Magnusson

Stepan Lubavsky
Finec

Dmitry Lyakhov
Russin & Vecchi, LLC.

Igor N. Makarov
Baker & McKenzie - CIS, Limited

Anna Maximenko
Debevoise & Plimpton LLP

Lyudmila Merzlikina
ALRUD Law Firm

Yekaterina Migel
Interexpertiza LLC

Svetlana Minakova
Yukov, Khrenov & Partners

Dmitry Nikolaev
Maersk Line Russian Federation

Aleksandr Panarin
Logistic Service

Andrey Panov
Monastyrsky, Zyuba, Stepanov & Partners

Roman Peikrishvili
Globalink Logistics Group

Eugene Perkunov
Hogan Lovells

Oleg Petrov
CMS Legal

Ivan Podbereznyak
Debevoise & Plimpton LLP

Ekaterina Raykevich
Debevoise & Plimpton LLP

Mikhail Romanovsky
Finec

Andrey Savin
Capital Legal Services LLC

Maria Sinyavskaya
CMS Legal

Alexey Soldatov
ABU Accounting Services

Rainer Stawinoga
Mazars Russia

Tatiana Stepanenko
Russia Consulting

Valentina Subbotina
Interexpertiza LLC

Victoria Subocheva
Russin & Vecchi, LLC.

Ivetta Tchistiakova-Berd
Gide Loyrette Nouel, member of Lex Mundi

Pavel Timofeev
Hannes Snellman LLC

Sergey Tufar
ALRUD Law Firm

Olga Yudina
CMS Legal

Vladislav Zabrodin
Capital Legal Services LLC

Julia Zasukhina
Macleod Dixon

Andrey Zavalishin
CMS Legal

Andrey Zelenin
Lidings Law Firm

Nadezda Zenjutich
ABU Accounting Services

RWANDA
Barlirwa Ltd.

Alberto Basomingera
Cabinet d'Avocats Mhayimana

Guillermo Bolaños
Pierre Célestin Bumbakare
Rwanda Revenue Authority

Gasore Edward
National Bank of Rwanda

Duru Emmanuel
GML Ltd.

Claudine Gasarabwe
Gasarabwe Claudine & Associes

Patrick Gashagaza
Deloitte LLP

Jean Havugimana
SHP Consultants

Suzanne Iyakaremye
SDV Transami

Francois Xavier Kalinda
Université Nationale du Rwanda

Désiré Kamanzi
Kamanzi, Ntaganira & Associates

Théophile Kazeneza
Cabinet d'Avocats Kazeneza

Rodolphe Kembukuswa
SDV Transami

Nathan Loyd
DN International

Isaïe Mhayimana
Cabinet d'Avocats Mhayimana

Richard Mugisha
Trust Law Chambers

Virginie Mukashema
Virginie Mukashema

Léopold Munderere
Cabinet d'Avocats-Conseils

Claude Mutabazi Abayo
Mutabazi Abayo Law Firm

Pothin Muvara

Martin Nkurunziza
Deloitte LLP

Abel Nsengiyumva
Cabinet Abel Nsengiyumva

Jean Claude Nsengiyumva
Tribunal de Commerce de Musanze

Paul Pavlidis
Credit Reference Bureau Africa Limited

Damas Rurangwa
EWSA

Lucien Ruterana
EWSA

Etienne Ruzibiza

Sandrali Sebakata
Bureau d'Etudes CAEDEC

Patrick Sebatigita
Ugenje

Vincent Shyirambere
Office of the Registrar of Land Titles

Florence Umurungi
Freight Logistic Services (R) Ltd.

Ravi Vadgama
Credit Reference Bureau Africa Limited

SAMOA
Electric Power Corporation

Tiffany Acton
Quantum Contrax Ltd.

Hugo Betham
Betham Brothers Enterprises Ltd.

Mike Betham
Transam Ltd.

Lawrie Burich
Quantum Contrax Ltd.

Murray Drake
Drake & Co.

Ruby Drake
Drake & Co.

Fiona Ey
Clarke Ey Lawyers

Heather Filisita
Ministry of Natural Resources & Environment

Margaret Fruean
Ministry of Commerce, Industry and Labour

Siﬁlili Aumua Isaia Lameko
Ministry of Commerce, Industry and Labour

Namulauuul Lameko Viali
Land Transport Authority Samoa

George Latu
Latu Ey Lawyers

Tima Leavai
Leavai Law

Sala Isitolo Leota
Public Accountant

Leulua'iali'i Tasi Malifa
Sogi Law

Maiava Peteru
Law Firm Maiava V.R. Peteru

Peato Sam Ling
Samoa Shipping Services Ltd.

Faiiletasi Elaine Seuao
Ministry of Commerce, Industry and Labour

Sala Theodore Sialau Toalepai
Samoa Shipping Services Ltd.

Wilber Stewart
Stewart Architecture

Aleluia Taise
Planning and Urban Management Agency

Toleafoa RS Toailoa
Toa Law Office

Shan Shiraz Ali Usman
Tradepac Marketing Ltd.

Avalisa Viali-Fautua'alii
Ministry of Revenue

Sieni Voorwinden
Manager Legal

SÃO TOMÉ AND PRÍNCIPE
EMAE

António de Barros A. Aguiar
SOCOGESTA

Adelino Amado Pereira
Amado Pereira & Associados, Sociedade de Advogados

Rui Amaral
Miranda Correia Amendoeira & Associados

Eudes Aguiar
EBIC- CONSTRUÇÃO CIVIL

André Aureliano Aragão
Jurisconsulta & Advogado

Helder Batista
Despachante Oficial Helder Batista

Sukayna Braganca
Banco Internacional de São Tomé e Príncipe

Adelino Castelo David
Ministère du Plan et des Finances

Celiza Deus Lima
JPALMS Advogados

Ilza Maria dos Santos Mado Vaz
Direcção das Alfândegas

Alexandra Ferreira
ATS – Agência de Transitos Viagens e Logística Lda

Saul Fonseca
Miranda Correia Amendoeira & Associados

Eudes Gabriel
Supermaritime Sao Tome

Fidelio Lopes do Nascimento
EBIC- CONSTRUÇÃO CIVIL

Vítor Marques da Cruz
FCB&A in association with Posser da Costa & Associados

Idalina Martinho
Despachante Oficial Helder Batista

Raul Mota Cerveira
Miranda Correia Amendoeira & Associados

Hugo Rita
Terra Forma

Manuel Roque
Manuel Roque Ltda.

Ilma Salvaterra
Guiché Único Para Empresas

Vitor Santos
EBIC- CONSTRUÇÃO CIVIL

Cláudia Santos Malaquias
Miranda Correia Amendoeira & Associados

Peter Schouten
Supermaritime Sao Tome

Rui Veríssimo
Soares Da Costa

SAUDI ARABIA
Ernst & Young

Emad Fareed Abdul Jawad
Globe Marine Services Co.

Abdulaziz Abdullatif
Al-Soaib Law Firm

Asad Abedi
The Alliance of Abbas F. Ghazzawi & Co. and Hammad, Al-Mehdar & Co.

Omar Al Saab
Law Office of Mohanned Bin Saud Al-Rasheed in association with Baker Botts LLP

Ibrahim Al-Ajaji
The Law Firm Of Dr. Khalid Alnowaiser

Fayez Aldebs
PwC Saudi Arabia

Ali. R. Al-Edrees
Al-Bassam

Mohammed Al-Ghamdi
Fulbright & Jaworski LLP

Nader Alharbi
Al-Jadaan & Partners Law Firm

Abdullah Al-Hashim
Al-Jadaan & Partners Law Firm

Hesham Al-Homoud
The Law Firm of Dr. Hesham Al-Homoud

Abdulrahman Al-Ibrahim
Electricity & Co-Generation Regulatory Authority

Mohammed Al-Jadaan
Al-Jadaan & Partners Law Firm

Nabil Abdullah Al-Mubarak
Saudi Credit Bureau - SIMAH

Fayez Al-Nemer
Talal bin Naif Al-Harbi Law Firm

Lamia Abdulaziz Al-Ogailee
Fulbright & Jaworski LLP

Ayedh Al-Otaibi
Saudi Arabian General Investment Authority

Musaed Al-Otaibi
The Law Firm of Salah Al-Hejailan

Mohammed Al-Soaib
Al-Soaib Law Firm

Wicki Andersen
Baker Botts LLP

Abdul Moeen Arnous
Law Office of Hassan Mahassni

Wael Bafakih
Bafakih & Nassief

John Beaumont
Al-Jadaan & Partners Law Firm

Salah Deeb
Al Tamimi & Company Advocates & Legal Consultants

Abou Bakr Gadour
Toban, Attorneys at law & legal Advisors

Imad El-Dine Ghazi
Law Office of Hassan Mahassni

Rahul Goswami
Law Office of Hassan Mahassni

Shadi Haroon
Law Office of Mohanned Bin Saud Al-Rasheed in association with Baker Botts LLP

Kenny Hawsey
PwC Saudi Arabia

Hazim Karam
Bafakih & Nassief

Glenn Lovell
Al Tamimi & Company Advocates & Legal Consultants

Zaid Mahayni
Law Office of Hassan Mahassni

Abdulrahman M. Al Mohizai
Electricity & Co-Generation Regulatory Authority

Fadi Obiedat
Talal Abu Ghazaleh Legal (TAG-Legal)

K. Joseph Rajan
Globe Marine Services Co.

Mustafa Saleh
EMDAD Arriyadh

Abdul Shakoor
Globe Marine Services Co.

Peter Stansfield
Al-Jadaan & Partners Law Firm

Sameh M. Toban
Toban, Attorneys at law & legal Advisors

Natasha Zahid
Baker Botts LLP

Soudki Zawaydeh
PwC Saudi Arabia

Jean Benoit Zegers
The Law Firm of Salah Al-Hejailan

SENEGAL

SDV Logistics

Khaled Abou El Houda
Cabinet Kanjo Koita

Diaby Aboubakar
BCEAO

Adoul Aziz
Centre de gestion agréé de Dakar

Marie Ba
BDO S.A.

Ibrahima Diagne
Gainde 2000

Amadou Diouldé Diallo
Ministère de l'Urbanisme et de l'Assainissement

Fidèle Dieme
Senelec

Adiouma Dione
Proquelec

Issa Dione
Senelec

Amadou Diop
Gainde 2000

Andrée Diop-Depret
Ga 2 D

Khadijatou Fary Diop Thiombane
Cabinet Jurafrik Conseil en Affaires (JCA)

Amadou Drame
Cabinet d'Avocat

Cheikh Fall
Cabinet d'Avocat

Aïssatou Fall
PricewaterhouseCoopers Tax & Legal SA

Malick Fall
PricewaterhouseCoopers Tax & Legal SA

Bakary Faye
BDS

Mustapha Faye
Cabinet Sarr & Associés, Member of Lex Mundi

Balla Gningue
SCP Mame Adama Gueye & Associés

Antoine Gomis
SCP Senghor & Sarr, Notaires Associés

Matthias Hubert
PricewaterhouseCoopers Tax & Legal SA

Alioune Ka
Etude SCP Mes KA

Oumy Kalsoum Gaye
Chambre de Commerce d'Industrie et d'Agriculture de Dakar

Mahi Kane
PricewaterhouseCoopers Tax & Legal SA

Sidy Abdallah Kanoute
Etude Me idy Kanouté

Mouhamed Kebe
GENI & KEBE

Ousseynou Lagnane
BDS

Moussa Mbacke
Etude notariale Moussa Mbacke

Mamadou Mbaye
SCP Mame Adama Gueye & Associés

Ibrahima Mbodj
Avocat à la Cour

Pierre Michaux
PricewaterhouseCoopers Tax & Legal SA

Aly Mar Ndiaye
Commission de Régulation du Secteur de l'Électricité

Moustapha Ndoye
Avocat à la Cour

Madior Niang
Transcontinental Transit

Babacar Sall
BDS

Ousmane Samba Mamadou
BCEAO

Mbaye Sarr
SCP Mame Adama Gueye & Associés

Daniel-Sedar Senghor
SCP Senghor & Sarr, Notaires Associés

Fatma Sene
Cabinet Sarr & Associés, Member of Lex Mundi

Mbacké Sene
Senelec

Codou Sow-Seck
GENI & KEBE

Ousmane Thiam
Maersk Logistics

Ibra Thiombane
Cabinet Jurafrik Conseil en Affaires (JCA)

Sokna Thiombane
Cabinet Jurafrik Conseil en Affaires (JCA)

Baba Traore
Transfret

Emmanuel Yehouessi
BCEAO

SERBIA

Trimo inzenjering d.o.o.

Milos Andjelkovic
Wolf Theiss

Bojana Bjelicic
PwC Serbia

Marija Bojović
Bojović Dašić Kojović

Bojana Bregovic
Wolf Theiss

Milan Brkovic
Association of Serbian Banks

Branko Bukvić
Živković & Samardžić Law office

Marina Bulatovic
Wolf Theiss

Ana Čalić
Prica & Partners Law Office

Dejan Certic
Advokatska Kancelarija

Jovan Cirkovic
Harrison Solicitors

Nataša Cvetićanin
Law Offices Janković, Popović & Mitić

Vladimir Dabić
The International Center for Financial Market Development

Simon Dayes
CMS Cameron McKenna

Lidija Djeric
Law Offices Popovic, Popovic, Samardzija & Popovic

Uroš Djordjević
Živković & Samardžić Law office

Nemanja Djukic
Živković & Samardžić Law office

Bojana Djurovic
Wolf Theiss

Veljko Dostanic
Maric, Malisic & Dostanic o.a.d. correspondent law firm of Gide Loyrette Nouel

Vuk Drašković
Bojović Dašić Kojović

Jelena Edelman
Prica & Partners Law Office

Jelena S. Gazivoda
Law Offices Janković, Popović & Mitić

Danica Gligorijevic
Prica & Partners Law Office

Dejan Jeremić
Republic Geodetic Authority

Aleksandra Jovic
CMS Cameron McKenna

Branko Jovičić
Advokatska Kancelarija

Nemanja Kacavenda
A.D. InterEuropa, Belgrade

Tatjana Kaplanovic
JetSet Real Estate Agency

Nikola Kliska
Maric, Malisic & Dostanic o.a.d. correspondent law firm of Gide Loyrette Nouel

Emmanuel Koenig
PwC Serbia

Dubravka Kosić
Law Office Kosić

Vidak Kovacevic
Wolf Theiss

Dejan Krstic
Free Lance Legal Consultant

Zach Kuvizić
Kuvizić Law Office

Krzysztof Lipka
PwC Serbia

Rastko Malisic
Marić, Mališić & Dostanić o.a.d.

Aleksandar Mančev
Prica & Partners Law Office

Ines Matijević-Papulin
Harrison Solicitors

Jelena Miljkovic
PwC Serbia

Marko Mrvic
Law Office Kosić

Dimitrije Nikolić
Cargo T. Weiss d.o.o.

Jelena Obradović
Živković & Samardžić Law office

Darija Ognjenović
Prica & Partners Law Office

Vladimir Perić
Prica & Partners Law Office

Milan Petrović
Advokatska Kancelarija

Mihajlo Prica
Prica & Partners Law Office

Ana Radivojević
PwC Serbia

Branislav Ristić
Advokatska Kancelarija

Carol Santoni
Marić–Mališić–Dostanić oad correspondent law firm of Gide Loyrette Nouel

Stojan Semiz
CMS Cameron McKenna

Milan Stefanović
Regulatory Review Unit

Zoran Teodosijević
Law Offices Janković, Popović & Mitić

Jovana Tomić
Živković & Samardžić Law office

Snežana Tošić
Serbian Business Registers Agency

Sanja Vesic
A.D. InterEuropa, Belgrade

Andreja Vrazalic
Moravčević, Vojnović & Zdravković u saradnji sa Schönherr

Milenko Vucaj
PD "Elektrodistribucija Beograd" d.o.o.

Srećko Vujaković
Moravčević, Vojnović & Zdravković u saradnji sa Schönherr

Tanja Vukotić Marinković
Serbian Business Registers Agency

Miloš Vulić
Prica & Partners Law Office

Miloš Živković
Živković & Samardžić Law office

SEYCHELLES

Aquarius Shipping Agency

Public Utilities Corporation

Laura. A. Alcindor Valabhji
Sterling Offshore Limited

Bobby Brantley Jr.
Sterling Offshore Limited

Lucienne Charlette
Seychelles Registrar General

Brian Julie
Derjacques & Elizabeth Chambers

Conrad Lablache
Pardiwalla Twomey Lablache

Susan Morel
Ministry of Employment and Human Resource Development

Joe Morin
Mahe Shipping Co. Ltd.

Margaret Nourice
Stamp Duty Commission

Brian Orr
MEJ Electrical

Serge Rouillon
Attorney-at-Law

Divino Sabino
Pardiwalla Twomey Lablache

Kieran B. Shah
Barrister & Attorney-at-Law

Harry Tirant
Tirant & Associates

Melchior Vidot
Appleby Global

SIERRA LEONE

Bank of Sierra Leone

Fitz-Graham & Associates

Sierra Leone Commercial Bank

Alfred Akibo-Betts
National Revenue Authority

Gideon Ayi-Owoo
PwC Ghana

Christiana Baah
PwC Ghana

Abdul Akim Bangura
Association of Clearing and Forwarding Agencies Sierra Leone

Desmond Dalton Beckley
Daltech / DESMI Enterprises

Cheryl Blake
B & J Partners

Charles Campbell
Charles Campbell & Co.

Emile Carr
Leone Consultants

Paul Chiy
CLAS Legal

Leslie Theophilus Clarkson
Ahmry Services

Kpana M. Conteh
National Revenue Authority

Michaela Kadijatu Conteh
Wright & Co.

Abu Bakr Dexter
E.E.C. Shears-Moses & Co.

Mariama Dumbuya
Renner Thomas & Co., Adele Chambers

William L. Farmer
Ministry of Lands, Country Planning and the Environment

Pabai Fofanah
National Revenue Authority

Joseph Fofanah
OFFICE OF THE ADMINISTRATOR AND
REGISTRAR GENERAL (OARG)

Manilius Garber
JARRETT-YASKEY, GARBER & ASSOCIATES:
ARCHITECTS (JYGA)

Eke Ahmed Halloway
HALLOWAY & PARTNERS

Jacquie Hope
CLAS LEGAL

Christopher Jarrett
MINISTRY OF WORKS HOUSING AND
INFRASTRUCTURE (MWH&I)

Donald Jones
MINISTRY OF LANDS, COUNTRY PLANNING
AND THE ENVIRONMENT

Francis Kaifala
WRIGHT & CO.

Mariama Seray Kallay
GOVERNMENT OF SIERRA LEONE

Alimamy S. Kamara
NATIONAL REVENUE AUTHORITY

Raymond F. Kamara
NATIONAL REVENUE AUTHORITY

M.B. Kargbo
MINISTRY OF FINANCE

George Kawaley
BABADORIE CLEARING & FORWARDING CO.

Alieyah Keita

Adekunle Milton King
PETROLEUM RESOURCES UNIT

Mary Kwarteng
PwC GHANA

Millicent Lewis-Ojumu
CLAS LEGAL

Corneleius Max-Williams
DESTINY SHIPPING AGENCIES AND CLEARING
AND FORWARDING AGENCIES

Mohamed Pa Momoh Fofanah
EDRINA CHAMBERS

Prossie Namakula
PwC GHANA

Melron Nicol-Wilson
NICOL WILSON & CO.

Miriam Nortey
PwC GHANA

Christopher J. Peacock
SERPICO TRADING ENTERPRISES

Christian Pratt
MINISTRY OF LANDS, COUNTRY PLANNING
AND THE ENVIRONMENT

Ade Renner-Thomas
RENNER THOMAS & CO., ADELE CHAMBERS

Mohamed Salisu
MINISTRY OF FINANCE

Kargbo Santigie
A+S BUSINESS CENTRE

Augustine Santos Kamara
NATIONAL REVENUE AUTHORITY

Julia Sarkodie-Mensah

Horatio Sawyer
MINISTRY OF WORKS HOUSING AND
INFRASTRUCTURE (MWH&I)

Michaela Serry
WRIGHT & CO.

Edward Siaffa
NATIONAL REVENUE AUTHORITY

Fatmata Sorie
WRIGHT & CO.

Samuel Swarray-Lewis
CLAS LEGAL

Rodney O. Temple
EROD CONSTRUCTION & ENGINEERING
SERVICES

Valisius Thomas
ADVENT CHAMBERS

Mohamed Ahmad Tunis
AHMRY SERVICES

Darcy White
PwC GHANA

Franklyn Williams
SIERRA LEONE BUSINESS FORUM LTD.

Yada Williams
YADA WILLIAMS AND ASSOCIATE

Rowland Wright
WRIGHT & CO.

SINGAPORE

BUILDING & CONSTRUCTION AUTHORITY

ERNST & YOUNG

FIRE SAFETY & SHELTER DEPARTMENT

LAND TRANSPORT AUTHORITY

MINISTRY OF MANPOWER

THE NATIONAL ENVIRONMENT AGENCY

PUBLIC UTILITIES BOARD

SHOOK LIN & BOK IN ASSOCIATION WITH
ALLEN & OVERY

URBAN REDEVELOPMENT AUTHORITY

WONG TAN & MOLLY LIM LLC

Malcolm BH Tan
INSOLVENCY & PUBLIC TRUSTEE'S OFFICE

Paerin Choa
TSMP LAW CORPORATION

Douglas Chow
MINISTRY OF TRADE & INDUSTRY

Kit Min Chye
TAN PENG CHIN LLC

Leonard Goh
ACCOUNTING & CORPORATE REGULATORY
AUTHORITY, ACRA

Thomas Ho
ONG & ONG ARCHITECTS

Ashok Kumar

K. Latha
ACCOUNTING & CORPORATE REGULATORY
AUTHORITY, ACRA

Kwok Ting Lee
PARTNERS GROUP PTE LTD. (SINGAPORE)

Eng Beng Lee
RAJAH & TANN LLP

James Leong
SUBORDINATE COURTS

Yik Wee Liew
WONGPARTNERSHIP LLP

William Lim
CREDIT BUREAU SINGAPORE PTE LTD.

Kexin Lim
PwC SINGAPORE

Max Ng
GATEWAY LAW CORPORATION

Chee Siong Ng
SINGAPORE CUSTOMS

Mehul Patel
GLOBAL IMPEX LINK

See Tiat Quek
PwC SINGAPORE

Kannan Ramesh
TAN KOK QUAN PARTNERSHIP

Alan Ross
PwC SINGAPORE

Amitoj Saini
MONETARY AUTHORITY OF SINGAPORE

David Sandison
PwC SINGAPORE

Lee Chuan Seng
BECA CARTER HOLDINGS & FERNER (S.E.
ASIA) PTE. LTD.

Disa Sim
RAJAH & TANN LLP

Yong Tat Tan
ACCOUNTING & CORPORATE REGULATORY
AUTHORITY, ACRA

Douglas Tan
STEVEN TAN PAC, MEMBER OF RUSSELL
BEDFORD INTERNATIONAL

Nicole Tang
CREDIT BUREAU SINGAPORE PTE LTD.

Siu Ing Ieng
SINGAPORE LAND AUTHORITY

Keith Tnee
TAN KOK QUAN PARTNERSHIP

Stefanie Yuen Thio
TSMP LAW CORPORATION

SLOVAK REPUBLIC

ALLEN & OVERY BRATISLAVA, S.R.O.

Zuzana Lodova Amrichová
PwC SLOVAKIA

Martina Behuliaková
GEODESY, CARTOGRAPHY AND CADASTRE
AUTHORITY OF THE SLOVAK REPUBLIC

Peter Bollardt
ČECHOVÁ & PARTNERS, MEMBER OF LEX
MUNDI AND WSG

Todd Bradshaw
PwC SLOVAKIA

Miroslava Budínska
DEDÁK & PARTNERS

Ján Budinský
SLOVAK CREDIT BUREAU, S.R.O.

Katarína Čechová
ČECHOVÁ & PARTNERS, MEMBER OF LEX
MUNDI AND WSG

Kristina Cermakova
PETERKA & PARTNERS

Elena Červenová
WHITE & CASE

Tomas Cibula
WHITE & CASE

Ema Cveckova
DEDÁK & PARTNERS

Ondřej Dušek
PETERKA & PARTNERS

Matej Firicky
WHITE & CASE

Peter Formela
ABONEX, S.R.O.

Juraj Fuska
WHITE & CASE

Petronela Galambosova
PANALPINA SLOVAKIA, S.R.O.

Miroslava Terem Greštiaková
PwC SLOVAKIA

Simona Halakova
ČECHOVÁ & PARTNERS, MEMBER OF LEX
MUNDI AND WSG

Peter Hodál
WHITE & CASE

Radoslava Hoglová
ZUKALOVÁ - ADVOKÁTSKA KANCELÁRIA
S.R.O.

Vladimir Ivanco
WHITE & CASE

Miroslav Jalec
ZAPADOSLOVENSKA ENERGETIKA, A.S.

Tomáš Kamenec
DEDÁK & PARTNERS

Veronika Keszeliova
ČECHOVÁ & PARTNERS, MEMBER OF LEX
MUNDI AND WSG

Roman Konrad
PROFINAM, S.R.O.

Miroslav Kopac
NATIONAL BANK OF SLOVAKIA

Lukas Kvokacka
PwC SLOVAKIA

Soňa Lehocká
ALIANCIAADVOKÁTOV AK, S.R.O.

Katarina Leitmannová
GEODESY, CARTOGRAPHY AND CADASTRE
AUTHORITY OF THE SLOVAK REPUBLIC

Ľubomír Leško
PETERKA & PARTNERS

Jozef Malý
DETVAI LUDIK MALÝ UDVAROS

Maria Malovcova
PwC SLOVAKIA

Přemysl Marek
PETERKA & PARTNERS

Tomáš Maretta
ČECHOVÁ & PARTNERS, MEMBER OF LEX
MUNDI AND WSG

Lucia Miklasová
PETERKA & PARTNERS

Nadezda Niksova
GEODESY, CARTOGRAPHY AND CADASTRE
AUTHORITY OF THE SLOVAK REPUBLIC

Jaroslav Niznansky
JNC LEGAL S.R.O.

Veronika Pazmanyova
WHITE & CASE

Ladislav Pompura
MONAREX AUDIT CONSULTING

Zora Puškáčová
ZUKALOVÁ - ADVOKÁTSKA KANCELÁRIA
S.R.O.

Simona Rapavá
WHITE & CASE

Zuzana Šálková
ČECHOVÁ & PARTNERS, MEMBER OF LEX
MUNDI AND WSG

Gerta Sámelová-Flassiková
ALIANCIAADVOKÁTOV AK, S.R.O.

Ľubomír Šatka
WHITE & CASE

Zuzana Satkova
PwC SLOVAKIA

Christiana Serugova
PwC SLOVAKIA

Michal Šimunic
ČECHOVÁ & PARTNERS, MEMBER OF LEX
MUNDI AND WSG

Jaroslav Škubal
PRK PARTNERS S.R.O. ADVOKÁTNÍ
KANCELÁŘ

Michaela Špetková
GEODESY, CARTOGRAPHY AND CADASTRE
AUTHORITY OF THE SLOVAK REPUBLIC

Lubica Suhajova
PwC SLOVAKIA

Andrea Šupáková
DETVAI LUDIK MALÝ UDVAROS

Zdenka Švingalová
MONAREX AUDIT CONSULTING

Michal Toman
PwC SLOVAKIA

Stanislava Valientová
WHITE & CASE

Peter Varga
PRK PARTNERS S.R.O. ADVOKÁTNÍ
KANCELÁŘ

Lukas Vlnecka
PwC SLOVAKIA

Jakub Vojtko
JNC LEGAL S.R.O.

Martina Zdechovanova
PETERKA & PARTNERS

Dagmar Zukalová
ZUKALOVÁ - ADVOKÁTSKA KANCELÁRIA
S.R.O.

SLOVENIA

ENERGY AGENCY OF THE REPUBLIC OF
SLOVENIA

SODO D.O.O.

Teja Batagelj
AGENCY OF THE REPUBLIC OF SLOVENIA
FOR PUBLIC LEGAL RECORDS AND RELATED
SERVICES

Ana Berce
ODVETNIKI ŠELIH & PARTNERJI

Vesna Božič
ODVETNIKI ŠELIH & PARTNERJI

Nataša Božović
BANK OF SLOVENIA

Erika Braniselj
NOTARY OFFICE BRANISELJ

Mitja Černe
BDO EOS SVETOVANJE D.O.O.

Thomas Dane
PwC SLOVENIA

Miodrag Dorđevic
SUPREME COURT OF THE REPUBLIC OF
SLOVENIA

Nada Drobnic
KPMG

Marina Ferfolja Howland
FERFOLJA, LJUBIC IN PARTNERJI

Aleksander Ferk
PwC SLOVENIA

Ana Filipov
FILIPOV PETROVIČ JERAJ IN COOPERATION
WITH SCHÖNHERR

Nastja Gojtan
MIRO SENICA IN ODVETNIKI

Alenka Gorenčič
DELOITTE LLP

Hermina Govekar Vičič
THE BANK ASSOCIATION OF SLOVENIA

Damijan Gregorc
MIRO SENICA IN ODVETNIKI

Masa Grgurevic Alcin
SUPREME COURT OF THE REPUBLIC OF
SLOVENIA

Matej Grm
THE BANK ASSOCIATION OF SLOVENIA

Barbara Guzina
DELOITTE LLP

Rajko Hribar
ELEKTRO LJUBLJANA D.D.

Damjana Iglič
BANK OF SLOVENIA

Sabina Jereb
MINISTRY FOR ENVIRONMENTAL AND
SPATIAL PLANNING

Aleksandra Jemc
LAW OFFICE JADEK & PENSA D.N.O. - O.P.,
WITH THE SUPPORT OF ERNST & YOUNG

Jernej Jeraj
FILIPOV PETROVIČ JERAJ IN COOPERATION
WITH SCHÖNHERR

Roman Jesenko
ELEKTRO LJUBLJANA D.D.

Mia Kalaš
ODVETNIKI ŠELIH & PARTNERJI

Ermina Kamencic
CMS REICH-ROHRWIG HAINZ

Boštjan Kavšek
ODVETNIKI ŠELIH & PARTNERJI

Rok Kokalj
ROJS, PELJHAN, PRELESNIK & PARTNERJI,
O.P., D.O.O.

Vita Korinšek
CITY STUDIO

Miro Košak
NOTARY OFFICE KOŠAK

Vida Kovše
ODVETNIKI ŠELIH & PARTNERJI

Nevenka Kržan
KPMG

Vatovec Lea
CMS Reich-Rohrwig Hainz

Aleš Lunder
CMS Reich-Rohrwig Hainz

Marjan Mahnič
KPMG

Darja Malogorski
KPMG

Clare Moger
PwC Slovenia

Eva Mozina
Miro Senica in Odvetniki

Lojze Mrhar
Viator & Vektor

Mojca Muha
Miro Senica in Odvetniki

Siniša Nišavić
Data D.O.O.

Matic Novak
Rojs, Peljhan, Prelesnik & partnerji, o.p., d.o.o.

Blaž Ogorevc
Odvetniki Šelih & Partnerji

Irena Ostojic
City Studio

Grega Peljhan
Rojs, Peljhan, Prelesnik & partnerji, o.p., d.o.o.

Tomaž Petrovič
Filipov Petrovič Jeraj in cooperation with Schönherr

Natasa Pipan Nahtigal
Odvetniki Šelih & Partnerji

Petra Plevnik
Miro Senica in Odvetniki

Igor Podbelšek
Elektro Ljubljana d.d.

Bojan Podgoršek
Notariat

Jan Poniž
Data d.o.o.

Magda Posavec
KPMG

Jan Primec
Rojs, Peljhan, Prelesnik & partnerji, o.p., d.o.o.

Aleksander Rajh
Viator & Vektor

Savic Sanja
Deloitte LLP

Jaka Simončič
Law Office Jadek & Pensa d.n.o. - o.p., with the support of Ernst & Young

Andreja Škofič-Klanjšček
Deloitte LLP

Boštjan Špec
Law Office Jadek & Pensa d.n.o. - o.p., with the support of Ernst & Young

Maja Stojko
Miro Senica in Odvetniki

Gregor Strojin
Supreme Court of the Republic of Slovenia

Tilen Terlep
Odvetniki Šelih & Partnerji

Josip Tomac
Hidria Perles D.O.O.

Melita Trop
Miro Senica in Odvetniki

Lea Volovec
Law Office Jadek & Pensa d.n.o. - o.p., with the support of Ernst & Young

Katja Wostner
BDO EOS Svetovanje d.o.o.

Katja Šegedin Zevnik
Data d.o.o

Alojz Zupančič
Customs Administration of the Republic of Slovenia

SOLOMON ISLANDS

Dayson Boso
Office of the Chief Magistrar

Don Boykin
Pacific Architects Ltd.

Chris Harpa
Pacific Lawyers

John Katahanas
Sol - Law

John Keniapisia
Lawyer

Dentana McKinnie
Solomon Islands Government

Maurice Nonipitu
Kramer Ausenco

Andrew Norrie
Bridge Lawyers

Haelo Pelu
Ministry of Justice and Legal Affairs

Roselle R. Rosales
Pacific Architects Ltd.

Leonard Saii
Spark Electrical Services

Gregory Joseph Sojnocki
Morris & Sojnocki Chartered Accountants, with the support of Ernst & Young

John Sullivan
Sol - Law

Billy Titiulu
Pacific Lawyers

Whitlam K. Togamae
Whitlam K Togamae Lawyers

Pamela Wilde
Ministry for Justice and Legal Affairs

SOUTH AFRICA

ESKOM

Q & N West Export Trading House

Hajira Akhalwaya
PwC South Africa

Nicolaos Akritidis
Paradigm Architects

Ross Alcock
Edward Nathan Sonnenbergs Inc.

Mark Badenhorst
PwC South Africa

Claire Barclay
Cliffe Dekker Hofmeyr Inc.

Kobus Blignaut
Edward Nathan Sonnenbergs Inc.

Boitumelo Bogatsu
Garlicke & Bousfield Inc.

Ann Bonner
Baker & McKenzie

Matthew Bonner
Baker & McKenzie

Willem Cronje
B-Earth

Beric Croome
Edward Nathan Sonnenbergs Inc.

Haydn Davies
Webber Wentzel

Gretchen de Smit
Edward Nathan Sonnenbergs Inc.

Steve Donninger
Rawlins Wales & Partners

Daniel Francois Fyfer
Cliffe Dekker Hofmeyr Inc.

Tim Gordon-Grant
Bowman Gilfillan Inc.

Kim Goss
Bowman Gilfillan Inc.

Ryan Kraut
BDO Spencer Steward Southern African Co-Ordination (Pty) Limited

Annette Landman
PwC South Africa

Paul Lategan
Edward Nathan Sonnenbergs Inc.

Amanda Lea
Bowman Gilfillan Inc.

Robert Steven Gordon Linde
Sil-Gatty Trading Carriers and Consultants

Joey Mathekga
CIPRO (Companies & IPR Registration Office)

Burton Meyer
Cliffe Dekker Hofmeyr Inc.

Gabriel Meyer
Deneys Reitz Inc. / Africa Legal

Phetole Modika
Cliffe Dekker Hofmeyr Inc.

Glory Moumakwe
CIPRO (Companies & IPR Registration Office)

Lebogang Mphahlele
Mervyn Taback Incorporated

Sizwe Msimang
Bowman Gilfillan Inc.

Twaambo Muleza
Bowman Gilfillan Inc.

Emmanuel Ngubane
Lafarge

Sanelisiwe Nyasulu
Garlicke & Bousfield Inc.

Kerry Plots
Cliffe Dekker Hofmeyr Inc.

Eamonn David Quinn
Attorney-at-Law

Hansuya Reddy
Deneys Reitz Inc. / Africa Legal

Lucinde Rhoodie
Cliffe Dekker Hofmeyr Inc.

Andres Sepp
Office of the Chief Registrar of Deeds

Richard Shein
Bowman Gilfillan Inc.

Themba Sikhosana
Cliffe Dekker Hofmeyr Inc.

Arvind Sinha
RCS Pvt. Ltd. Business Advisors Group

Rajat Ratan Sınha
RCS Pvt. Ltd. Business Advisors Group

Jane Strydom
TransUnion

Andrew Theron
BDO Spencer Steward Southern African Co-Ordination (Pty) Limited

Muhammed Vally
Edward Nathan Sonnenbergs Inc.

Dawid Van der Berg
BDO Spencer Steward Southern African Co-Ordination (Pty) Limited

Nicky van der Weshuizen
Edward Nathan Sonnenbergs Inc.

Colin Van Rooyen
TransUnion

Anastasia Vatalidis
Werksmans Inc.

St Elmo Wilken
Mervyn Taback Incorporated

SPAIN

Allen & Overy

Promomadrid

Raposo Bernardo & Associados

Basilio Aguirre
Registro de la Propiedad de España

Marco Alcalde
Dr. Frühbeck Abogados S.L.P

Angel Alonso Hernández
Uría & Menéndez, member of Lex Mundi

Nuria Armas
Banco de España

Ana Armijo
Ashurst

Cristina Ayo Ferrándiz
Uría & Menéndez, member of Lex Mundi

Juan Antonio Barcelo Ramis

Santiago Barrenechea
Landwell PricewaterhouseCoopers Tax & Legal Services S.L.

Denise Bejarano
Pérez - Llorca

Alfonso Benavides
Clifford Chance

Juan Bolás Alfonso
Notariado

Vicente Bootello
J & A Garrigues, S.L.P

Agustín Bou
Jausas

Héctor Bouzo Cortejosa
Solcaisur S.L.

Teresa Camacho Artacho
Uría & Menéndez, member of Lex Mundi

Laura Camarero
Baker & McKenzie

Virginia Casado
Uría & Menéndez, member of Lex Mundi

Lorenzo Clemente Naranjo
J & A Garrigues, S.L.P

Francisco Conde Viñuelas
Cuatrecasas, Gonçalves Pereira

Jaume Cornudella i Marquès
PwC Spain

Juan Jose Corral Moreno
Cuatrecasas, Gonçalves Pereira

Sara Crespo
J & A Garrigues, S.L.P

Pelayo de Salvador
J & A Garrigues, S.L.P

Almudena del Río Galán
Colegio de Registradores de la Propiedad y Mercantiles de España

Agustín Del Río Galeote
Gómez-Acebo & Pombo Abogados

Iván Delgado González
Pérez - Llorca

Rossanna D'Onza
Baker & McKenzie

Antonio Fernández
J & A Garrigues, S.L.P

Luis Fernandez Arbex
Altius S.A. Vigo

Idoya Fernandez Elorza
Cuatrecasas, Gonçalves Pereira

Guillermo Frühbeck
Dr. Frühbeck Abogados S.L.P

Ignacio García Errandonea
J & A Garrigues, S.L.P

Valentín García González
Cuatrecasas, Gonçalves Pereira

Monica Garcia Prieto
Arquitecta Mónica Garcia Prieto

Borja García-Alamán
J & A Garrigues, S.L.P

Pedro Garrido Chamorro
Notariado

Juan Ignacio Gomeza Villa
Notario de Bilbao

Jorge Hernandez
Equifax Iberica

Joaquín Rodriguez Hernández
Colegio de Registradores

Alejandro Huertas León
J & A Garrigues, S.L.P

Montserrat Jané
Gómez-Acebo & Pombo Abogados

Igor Kokorev
Pérez - Llorca

Jaime Llopis
Cuatrecasas, Gonçalves Pereira

Joaquin Macias
Ashurst

Juan Carlos Marhuenda Gómez
TLACORP

Susana Marimón Charola
Gómez-Acebo & Pombo Abogados

Daniel Marín
Gómez-Acebo & Pombo Abogados

Ana Martín
J & A Garrigues, S.L.P

Jorge Martín - Fernández
Clifford Chance

Ignacio Martín Martín Fernández
Cazorla Abogados, SLP

Joaquim Martínez
Federal Logistic Services

Gabriel Martínez
Russell Bedford Espana, member of Russell Bedford International

José Manuel Mateo
J & A Garrigues, S.L.P

Eva Mur Mestre
PwC Spain

Nicolás Nogueroles Peiró
Colegio de Registradores de la Propiedad y Mercantiles de España

Ana Novoa
Baker & McKenzie

Alberto Núñez-Lagos Burguera
Uría & Menéndez, member of Lex Mundi

Jose Palacios
J & A Garrigues, S.L.P

Daniel Parejo Ballesteros
J & A Garrigues, S.L.P

Pedro Pérez-Llorca Zamora
Pérez - Llorca

Maria Redondo
Baker & McKenzie

Guillermo Rodrigo García
Clifford Chance

Déborah Rodríguez
Clifford Chance

Joaquín Rodríguez
Colegio de Registradores de la Propiedad y Mercantiles de España

Noemi Rodriguez Alonso
Sagardoy Abogados, member of Ius Laboris

Javier Rubio
Uría & Menéndez, member of Lex Mundi

Javier Ruz Cerezo

Álvaro Ryan Murua
Iberdrola S.A.

Iñigo Sagardoy de Simón
Sagardoy Abogados, member of Ius Laboris

Eduardo Santamaría Moral
J & A Garrigues, S.L.P

Ramón Santillán
Banco de España

Pablo Santos
Gómez-Acebo & Pombo Abogados

Catalina Santos
J & A Garrigues, S.L.P

Cristina Soler
Gómez-Acebo & Pombo Abogados

Francisco Téllez
J & A Garrigues, S.L.P

Adrián Thery
J & A Garrigues, S.L.P

Roberto Tojo Thomas de Carranza
Clifford Chance

Alejandro Valls
Baker & McKenzie

Juan Verdugo
J & A Garrigues, S.L.P

Marina Villanueva
Clifford Chance

Fernando Vives Ruiz
J & A Garrigues, S.L.P

SRI LANKA

APL

Ernst & Young

Freight Links International (Pte) Ltd.

Progressive Design Associates

Ayomi Aluwihare-Gunawardene
F.J. & G. De Saram, member of Lex Mundi

Shanaka Amarasinghe
Julius & Creasy

Gerard David
SJMS Associates

Savantha De Saram
D.L. & F. De Saram

Chamari de Silva
F.J. & G. De Saram, member of Lex Mundi

Sadhini Edirisinghe
F.J. & G. De Saram, member of Lex Mundi

Nilmini Ediriweera
Julius & Creasy

Chamindi Ekanayake
Nithya Partners

Anjali Fernando
F.J. & G. De Saram, member of Lex Mundi

Amila Fernando
Julius & Creasy

Lasantha Garusinghe
Tiruchelvam Associates

Jivan Goonetilleke
D.L. & F. De Saram

Naomal Goonewardena
Nithya Partners

Locana Gunaratna
Gunaratna Associates

P. Mervyn Gunasekera
LAN Management Development Service

Dharshika Herath Gunarathna
Sudath Perera Associates

Dharshanie Illukpitiya
F.J. & G. De Saram, member of Lex Mundi

Sonali Jayasuriya
D.L. & F. De Saram

Tudor Jayasuriya
F.J. & G. De Saram, member of Lex Mundi

Mahes Jeyadevan
PwC Sri Lanka

Yudhishtran Kanagasabai
PwC Sri Lanka

Neelakandan Kandiah
Murugesu & Neelakandan

Janaka Lakmal
Credit Information Bureau Ltd.

Ishara Madarasinghe
F.J. & G. De Saram, member of Lex Mundi

Sasikala Mayadunne
Sudath Perera Associates

Kaushalya Meedeniya
Sudath Perera Associates

Fathima Amra Mohamed
Sudath Perera Associates

Sudath Perera
Sudath Perera Associates

Lilangi Randeni
F.J. & G. De Saram, member of Lex Mundi

Hiranthi Ratnayake
PwC Sri Lanka

Sanath Senaratne
Ceylon Electricity Board

Shane Silva
Julius & Creasy

Priya Sivagananathan
Julius & Creasy

J.M. Swaminathan
Julius & Creasy

Dhanika Umagiliya
Tiruchelvam Associates

Shashi Weththasinghe
Julius & Creasy

Nihal Wicramasooriya
Ceylon Electricity Board

John Wilson
John Wilson Partners

ST. KITTS AND NEVIS

St. Kitts Electricity Department

Michella Adrien
Michella Adrien Law Office

Launlia Archibald
Customs and Excise Department

Rublin Audain
Audain & Associates

Nicholas Brisbane
N. Brisbane & Associates

Scott Caines
C & C Trading Ltd.

Idris Fidela Clarke
Financial Services Department

Neil Coates
PwC Antigua

Jan Dash
Liburd and Dash

Peter Davis
P.W.Davids & Associates

Kennedy de Silva
Customs and Excise Department

Renee Gumbs
Financial Services Department

Barbara L. Hardtman
Hardtman & Associates

K. Gregory Hardtman
Hardtman & Associates

Rodney Harris
Customs and Excise Department

Marsha T. Henderson
Henderson Legal Chambers

Dahlia Joseph
Daniel Brantley & Associates

Herman Liburd
Liburd and Dash

Tamara Malcolm
Liburd and Dash

Jeoffrey Nisbett
Jeffrey & Nisbetts

Mahailia Pencheon
PwC Antigua

Nervin Rawlins
Inland Revenue Authority

Larkland M. Richards
Larkland M. Richards & Associates

Reginald Richards
R & R Electrical Engineering Air Conditioning & Refrigeration Services Ltd.

Arlene Ross-Daisley
Webster Dyrud Mitchell

Tavo Sargeant
Customs and Excise Department

Anastacia Saunders
C & C Trading Ltd.

Warren Thompson
Construction Management and Consulting Agency Inc (CMCAI)

Charles Walwyn
PwC Antigua

Deidre N. Williams
WalwynLaw

ST. LUCIA

Lucelec

Ministry of Housing, Urban Renewal and Local Government

Thaddeus M. Antoine
Francis & Antoine

Clive Antoine
Ministry of Communications Works Transport and Public Utilities

Gerard Bergasse
Tropical Shipping

Candace Cadasse Polius
Nicholas John & Co.

Desma F. Charles
Registry of Companies and Intellectual Property

Shannon Chitolie
Gordon & Gordon Co.

Shonari Clarke
Francis & Antoine

Peter I. Foster
Peter I. Foster & Associates

Peterson D. Francis
Peterson D. Francis Worldwide Shipping & Customs Services Ltd.

Annick Gajadhar
Tropical Shipping

Carol J. Gedeon
Chancery Chambers

Claire Greene-Malaykhan
Peter I. Foster & Associates

Leevie Herelle
Herelle, Leevie & Associates

Simon Jeffers
Tropical Shipping

Anderson Lake
Bank of Saint Lucia Limited

Charlene Mae Magnaye
PwC St. Lucia

Duane C. Marquis
NLBA Architects

Stephen Mcnamara
Mcnamara & Co.

Bradley Paul
Bradley Paul Associates

Richard Peterkin
PwC St. Lucia

Eldris Pierre-Mauricette
Tropical Shipping

Kimberly Roheman
Mcnamara & Co.

Michael Sewordor
Ministry of Communications Works Transport and Public Utilities

Kim Camille St. Rose
Chong & Co.

Leandra Gabrielle Verneuil
Chambers of Jennifer Remy & Associates

Andie A. Wilkie
Gordon & Gordon Co.

Brenda M. Williams
BDO St. Lucia

ST. VINCENT AND THE GRENADINES

St. Vincent Electricity Services Ltd.

Kay R.A. Bacchus-Browne
Kay Bacchus - Browne Chambers

Allan P. Burke
Perry's Customs and Shipping Agency, Ltd.

Tamara Gibson-Marks
High Court Registrar

Sean Joachim
CaribTrans

Stanley John
Elizabeth Law Chambers

Cornelius Joseph
General & Maritime Agencies Ltd.

Errol E. Layne
Errol E. Layne Chambers

Isaac Legair
Dennings

Linton A. Lewis
Dr. Lewis Law Chambers

Charlene Mae Magnaye
PwC St. Lucia

Moulton Mayers
Moulton Mayers Architects

Floyd A. Patterson
International Liaison Partner BDO Eastern Caribbean

Richard Peterkin
PwC St. Lucia

Patrice Roberts-Samuel
Labour Department

L.A. Douglas Williams
Law Firm of Phillips & Williams

Andrea Young-Lewis
Commerce & Intellectual Property Office (CIPO)

SUDAN

Abu-Ghazaleh Intellectual Property (AGIP) TMP Agents Co. Ltd.

Design 2000 Ltd.

Omer Abdel Ati
Omer Abdel Ati Solicitors

Abdalla Abuzeid
Abdalla A. Abuzeid & Associates

Mohamed Ibrahim Adam
Dr. Adam & Associates

Al Fadel Ahmed Al Mahdi
Al Mahdi Law Office

Eihab Babiker
Eihab Babiker & Associates - Advocates

Elmugtaba Bannaga
Bin Suwaidan Advocates & Legal Consultants

Amani Ejami
El Karib & Medani Advocates

Asma Homad Abdellatif Ali
Mahmoud Elsheikh Omer & Associates Advocates

Mohamed Ibrahim
Somarain Oreintal Co.

Ahmed Mahdi
Mahmoud Elsheikh Omer & Associates Advocates

Tarig Mahmoud El Sheikh Omer
Mahmoud Elshfikh Omfr & Associates Advocates

Amel M. Sharif
Mahmoud Elsheikh Omer & Associates Advocates

AbdelGadir Warsama Ghalib
Dr. Abdel Gadir Warsama Ghalib & Associates Legal Firm

Tag Eldin Yamani Sadig
Montag Trading & Engineering Co. Ltd.

SURINAME

KPMG

G. Clide Cambridge
Paramaribo Custom Broker & Packer

Anoeschka Debipersad
A.E. Debipersad & Associates

Marcel K. Eyndhoven
N.V. Energiebedrijven Suriname

Johan Kastelein
KDV Architects

B.M. Oemraw
N.V. Global Expedition

Joanne Pancham
Chamber of Commerce & Industry

Adiel Sakoer
N.V. Global Expedition

Inder Sardjoe
N.V. Easy Electric

Prija Soechitram
Chamber of Commerce & Industry

Albert D. Soedamah
Lawfirm Soedamah & Associates

Radjen A. Soerdjbalie
Notariaat R.A. Soerdjbalie

Carol-Ann Tjon-Pian-Gi
Lawyer & Sworn Translator

Jennifer van Dijk-Silos
Law Firm Van Dijk-Silos

Carel van Hest
Carel van Hest Architecten N.V.

Dayenne Wielingen - Verwey
Vereniging Surinaams Bedrijfsleven, Suriname Trade & Industry Association

Perry D. Wolfram
BroCad N.V.

SWAZILAND

Office of the Registrar Swaziland

Robert Cloete
Cloete Henwood

Susanne DeBeer
MNS Group

Musa Dlamini
M.L. Dlamini Attorneys

Welile Dlamini
Standard Bank

Veli Dlamini

E.J. Henwood
M.L. Dlamini Attorneys

Phumlile Tina Khoza
Standard Bank

Paul Lewis
PwC Swaziland

Andrew Linsey
PwC Swaziland

Zodwa Mabuza
Federation of Swaziland Employers and Chamber of Commerce

Mangaliso Magagula
Magagula & Hlophe

Sabelo Masuku
Maphanga Howe Masuku Nsibande

Shadrack Mnisi
Sharp Freight SWD Pty. Ltd.

Bongani Mtshali
Federation of Swaziland Employers and Chamber of Commerce

Zakes Nkosi
Federation of Swaziland Employers and Chamber of Commerce

Kate Paton
TransUnion ITC

José Rodrigues
Rodrigues & Associates

P.M. Shilubane
P.M. Shilubane & Associates

Bob Sigwane
Sigwane and Partners

John Thomson
Mormond Electrical Contractors

Manene Thwala
Thwala Attorneys

Bradford Mark Walker
Brad Walker Architects

Diane Webb
Chambers Vilakati & Associates Architects

SWEDEN

UC AB

Stig Åkerman
Boverket- Swedish National Board of Housing, Building and Planning

Nicklas Anth
Panalpina AB

Ola Avdic
Advokatfirman Vinge KB, member of Lex Mundi

Nicolas Beaver
Amerinde Consolidated, Inc.

Martin Bergander
Gärde Wesslau Advokatbyrå

Mats Berter
MAQS Law Firm

Alexander Broch
Öresunds Redovisning AB

Magnus Graner
Advokatfirman Lindahl

Ingemar Gustafsson
Scheiwiller Svensson Arkitektkontor AB

Lars Hartzell
Elmzell Advokatbyrå AB, member of Ius Laboris

Emil Hedberg
Advokatfirman Vinge KB, member of Lex Mundi

Lukas Holmén
Advokatfirman Vinge KB, member of Lex Mundi

Erik Hygrell
Wistrand Advokatbyrå

Anders Isgren
Baker & McKenzie

Magnus Johnsson
PwC Sweden

Bengt Kjellson
Lantmäteriet

Niklas Körling
Setterwalls Advokatbyrå

Caroline Lagergréen
Elmzell Advokatbyrå AB, member of Ius Laboris

Jasmine Lawson
PwC Sweden

Johan Lindberg
Advokatfirman Lindahl

Anna Mansson
Vattenfall Eldistribution AB

Christoffer Monell
Mannheimer Swartling Advokatbyrå

Michael Nyman
Advokatfirman Lindahl

Ola Lo Olsson
Elmzell Advokatbyrå AB, member of Ius Laboris

Karl-Arne Olsson
Gärde Wesslau Advokatbyrå

Lennart Svantesson
PwC Sweden

Lars-Olof Svensson
Wistrand Advokatbyrå

Odd Swarting
Setterwalls Advokatbyrå

Bo Thomaeus
Gärde Wesslau Advokatbyrå

Robert Tischner
Baker & McKenzie

Erik Westman
PwC Sweden

Albert Wallfren

SWITZERLAND

Altenburger Ltd. Legal and Tax

SBV-SSE Société Suisse des Entrepreneurs

Beat M. Barthold
Froriep Renggli

Sébastien Bettschart
Abels Avocats

Myriam Büchi-Bänteli
PwC Switzerland

Lucas Bühlmann
PwC Switzerland

Antonio Calvo
Baker & McKenzie

Andrea Cesare Canonica
Swiss Customs

Sonia de la Fuente
Abels Avocats

Stefan Eberhard
Abels Avocats

Suzanne Eckert
Wenger Plattner

Jana Essebier
Vischer AG

Benjamin Fehr
PwC Switzerland

Peter Flueckiger
economiesuisse

Michael Gwelessiani
Commercial Register of the Canton Zurich

Olivier Hari
Schellenberg Wittmer

Jakob Hoehn
Pestalozzi, member of Lex Mundi

David Jenny
Vischer AG

Urs Klöti
Pestalozzi, member of Lex Mundi

Armin Marti
PwC Switzerland

Michel Merlotti
Notary & Consultant

Valerie Meyer Bahar
Niederer Kraft & Frey AG

Georg Naegeli
Homburger

Roland Niklaus
NCMB Notaires associés

Gema Olivar Pascual
PwC Switzerland

Daniela Reinhardt
PwC Switzerland

Patricia Roberty
Vischer AG

Marc Schenk
PwC Switzerland

Daniel Schmitz
PwC Switzerland

Roland Stadler
Migros-Genossenschafts-Bund

Andreas Staubli
PwC Switzerland

Daniel Steudler
Swisstopo, Directorate for Cadastral Surveying

Tanja Sussmann
Hosoya Schaefer

Beatrice Vetsch
PwC Switzerland

Meinrad Vetter
economiesuisse

Marc Widmer
Froriep Renggli

Pascal Wirth
PwC Switzerland

SYRIAN ARAB REPUBLIC

Ernst & Young

Sarkis & Associates

Talal Abu Ghazaleh Legal (TAG-Legal)

Maysa Abu Baker
Central Bank of Syria

Boulos Al Ashhab
Auditing Consulting Accounting Center

Mouazza Al Ashhab
Auditing Consulting Accounting Center

Rawaa Al Midani
Ministry of Economy & Trade

Kanaan Al-Ahmar
Al-Ahmar & Partners

Bisher Al-Houssami
AL-ISRAA Int'l Freight Forwarder

Serene Almaleh
Karawani Law Office

Anas Ghazi
Meethak - Lawyers & Consultants

Abdul Raouf Hamwi
Civil Engineering Office

Joumana Jabbour
Attorney-at-Law

Azzam Kaddour
International Legal Bureau

Osama Karawani
Karawani Law Office

Mazen N. Khaddour
International Legal Bureau

Loubna Khoury
Auditing Consulting Accounting Center

Moussa Mitry
University of Damascus / Louka & Mitry Law Office

Gabriel Oussi
Oussi Law firm

Housam Safadi
Safadi Bureau

Samer Sultan
Sultans Law

TAIWAN, CHINA

Tai E International Patent & Law Office

Olivier Beydon
Yangming Partners

Victor Chang
LCS & Partners

Jersey Chang
PricewaterhouseCoopers Legal

Eve Chen
Eiger Law

Yo-Yi Chen
Formosa Transnational

Nicholas V. Chen
Pamir Law Group

Edgar Y. Chen
Tsar & Tsai Law Firm, member of Lex Mundi

Christine Chen
Winkler Partners

Hui-ling Chen
Winkler Partners

Chun-Yih Cheng
Formosa Transnational

Chia Yi Chiang
PricewaterhouseCoopers Legal

Yu-Chung Chiu
Ministry of The Interior

Ying-Che Chiu
Taipei City Government

Cindy Chou
Chen, Shyuu & Pun

Dennis Chou
Eiger Law

Peter Dernbach
Winkler Partners

John Eastwood
Eiger Law

Rosamund Fan
PwC Taiwan

Philip T. C. Fei
Fei & Cheng Associates

Steven Go
PwC Taiwan

James Hong
Chen, Shyuu & Pun

Sophia Hsieh
Tsar & Tsai Law Firm, member of Lex Mundi

Katherine Hsu
Joint Credit Information Center

Tony Hsu
Pamir Law Group

Robert Hsu
SDV Logistics

T.C. Huang
Huang & Partners

Jack J.T. Huang
Jones Day

Margaret Huang
LCS & Partners

James J.M. Hwang
Tsar & Tsai Law Firm, member of Lex Mundi

Charles Hwang
Yangming Partners

Charlotte J. Lin
LCS & Partners

Joan Jing
PricewaterhouseCoopers Legal

Nathan Kaiser
Eiger Law

Yang Kun-Te
Yang & Associates Consulting Engineers

Vivian Lee
Huang & Partners

Michael D. Lee
Pamir Law Group

Chih-Shan Lee
Winkler Partners

Yu-Hsun Li
PricewaterhouseCoopers Legal

Justin Liang
Baker & McKenzie

Ming-Yen Lin
Deep & Far, Attorneys-at-Law

Lilian Lin
Financial Supervisory Commission,Banking Bureau

Nelson J Lin
Huang & Partners

Rich Lin
LCS & Partners

Emily Lin
Pamir Law Group

Yishian Lin
PwC Taiwan

Frank Lin
Rexmed Industries Co., Ltd.

Jennifer C. Lin
Tsar & Tsai Law Firm, member of Lex Mundi

Youlanda Liu
Pamir Law Group

Joseph Ni
Good Earth CPA

Mark Ohlson
Yangming Partners

Lawrence S. Ong
PricewaterhouseCoopers Legal

J. F. Pun
Chen, Shyuu & Pun

Lloyd G. Roberts III
Winkler Partners

Jasmine C. Shen
Pamir Law Group

Tanya Y. Teng
Huang & Partners

Bee Leay Teo
Baker & McKenzie

C.F. Tsai
Deep & Far, Attorneys-at-Law

Eric Tsai
PricewaterhouseCoopers Legal

Joe Tseng
LCS & Partners

Chao-Yu Wang
Yangming Partners

Robin J. Winkler
Winkler Partners

Ja Lin Wu
Council for Economic Planning & Development

Quiao-ling Wu
Deep & Far, Attorneys-at-Law

Stephen Wu
Lee and Li

Echo Yeh
Lexcel Partners

Shih-Ming You
Ministry of The Interior

TAJIKISTAN

National Bank of Tajikistan

Tajikhydroelektromontaj

Timur Abdulayev
Legal Consulting Group

Bakhtiyor Abdulhamidov
Akhmedov, Azizov & Abdulhamidov Attorneys

Shavkat Akhmedov
Akhmedov, Azizov & Abdulhamidov Attorneys

Nasira Avazova
MINISTRY OF LABOR & SOCIAL PROTECTION

Farhad Azizov
AKHMEDOV, AZIZOV & ABDULHAMIDOV
ATTORNEYS

Richard Bregonje
PwC KAZAKHSTAN

Jienshoh Bukhoriev
USAID BEI BUSINESS ENVIRONMENT
IMPROVEMENT PROJECT (BY PRAGMA
CORPORATION)

Peter Burnie
PwC KAZAKHSTAN

Ashraf Sharifovich Ikromov
SAMAD SOZ LLC

Elena Kaeva
PwC KAZAKHSTAN

Parviz Kamoliddinov
TSG - USAID REGIONAL TRADE
LIBERALISATION AND CUSTOMS PROJECT
(RTLC)

Manuchehr Kasimov
GLOBALINK LOGISTICS GROUP

Assel Khamzina
PwC KAZAKHSTAN

Parviz Kuliev
MASHVARAT LIMITED LIABILITY COMPANY

Umar Muhammadkarim
GLOBALINK LOGISTICS GROUP

Takhir Nabiev
AITEN CONSULTING GROUP

Mizrobiddin Nugmanov
GLOBALINK LOGISTICS GROUP

Jurabek Toshtemurovich Okhonov
LLC "MOVAROUNNAHR"

Ravshan Rashidov
LAW FIRM LEX

Firdavs Sadikov
SOMON CAPITAL JSC

Emin Sanginov
MINISTRY OF LABOR & SOCIAL PROTECTION

Marina Shamilova
LEGAL CONSULTING GROUP

Nurali Shukurov
LEGAL CONSULTING GROUP

Kamila Tursunkulova
PwC KAZAKHSTAN

Aliya Utegaliyeva
PwC KAZAKHSTAN

Abdurakhmon Yuldoshev
MINISTRY OF LABOR & SOCIAL PROTECTION

TANZANIA
ISHENGOMA, MASHA, MUJULIZI & MAGAI

UmmiKulthum Abdallah
AKO LAW

Patrick Ache
MKONO & CO. ADVOCATES

Albina Burra
MINISTRY OF LANDS & HUMAN
SETTLEMENTS DEVELOPMENT

Lydia Dominic
UNIVERSITY OF DAR ES SALAAM

Theresia Dominic
UNIVERSITY OF DAR ES SALAAM

Wayne Forbes
YARA TANZANIA LTD.

Santosh Gajjar
SUMAR VARMA ASSOCIATES

Kennedy Gastorn
MKONO & CO. ADVOCATES

Christopher Giattas
REX ATTORNEYS

Johnson Jasson
JOHNSON JASSON & ASSOCIATES
ADVOCATES

Jamhuri Johnson
TANESCO LTD.

Wilbert B. Kapinga
MKONO & CO. ADVOCATES

Cuthbert Kazora
CRB AFRICA LEGAL

Rehema Khalid-Saria
MKONO & CO. ADVOCATES

Jacktone Koyugi
MKONO & CO. ADVOCATES

Diana Kyobutungi
MKONO & CO. ADVOCATES

Victoria Makani
VELMA LAW CHAMBERS

Hyacintha Benedict Makileo
NATIONAL CONSTRUCTION COUNCIL

Lilian Maleko
YARA TANZANIA LTD.

David Mawalla
LAFARGE

Waziri Mchome
MKONO & CO. ADVOCATES

Lotus Menezes
AKO LAW

Sophia Mgonja
TANESCO LTD.

Lucia Minde
AKO LAW

Jimmy Mkenda
LAFARGE

Nimrod Mkono
MKONO & CO. ADVOCATES

Steven Mlote
ENGINEERS REGISTRATION BOARD

Angela Mndolwa
AKO LAW

Felchesmi Mramba
TANESCO LTD.

August Mrena
MKONO & CO. ADVOCATES

Octavianus Mushukuma
CRB AFRICA LEGAL

Alex Thomas Nguluma
REX ATTORNEYS

Cyril Pesha
CRB AFRICA LEGAL

Charles R.B. Rwechungura
CRB AFRICA LEGAL

Rishit Shah
PwC TANZANIA

Jaffery Shengeza
LAFARGE

Thadeus J. Shio
CQS SERVICES LIMITED

Christopher Siambe
CROWN AGENTS LTD.

Eve Hawa Sinare
REX ATTORNEYS

Aisha Ally Sinda
MKONO & CO. ADVOCATES

Filip Tack
MKONO & CO. ADVOCATES

Joseph T. Tango
CQS SERVICES LIMITED

David Tarimo
PwC TANZANIA

Mustafa Tharoo
ADEPT CHAMBERS

Sarah Thomas Massamu
ADEPT CHAMBERS

THAILAND
ALLEN & OVERY (THAILAND) CO., LTD.

APL

ASSOCIATION OF SIAMESE ARCHITECTS
UNDER ROYAL PATRONAGE

ERNST & YOUNG

THAI CONTRACTORS ASSOCIATION UNDER
H.M. THE KING'S PATRONAGE

Janist Aphornratana
PwC THAILAND

Roi Bak
DEJ-UDOM & ASSOCIATES

Chanakarn Boonyasith
SIAM CITY LAW OFFICES LTD.

Chalee Chantanayingyong
SECURITIES AND EXCHANGE COMMISSION

Phadet Charoensivakon
NATIONAL CREDIT BUREAU CO. LTD.

Thunyaporn Chartisathian
ALLENS ARTHUR ROBINSON / SIAM
PREMIER INTERNATIONAL LAW OFFICE
LIMITED

Warattaya Chiaracharuwat
VICKERY & WORACHAI LTD.

Chinnavat Chinsangaram
WEERAWONG, CHINNAVAT & PEANGPANOR
LTD.

Wachakorn Chiramongkolkul
PwC THAILAND

Kanphassorn Chotwathana
PwC THAILAND

David Duncan
TILLEKE & GIBBINS

Wongwaris Dunlayanitikosol
NATIONAL CREDIT BUREAU CO. LTD.

Frederic Favre
VOVAN & ASSOCIES

Seetha Gopalakrishnan
PwC THAILAND

Yothin Intaraprasong
CHANDLER & THONG-EK

Pimwasee Jaismut
SIAM CITY LAW OFFICES LTD.

Tanach Kanjanasiri
DLA PIPER (THAILAND) LIMITED

Tayvee Kanokjote
THAILAND LAND TITLING PROJECT OFFICE

Yingyong Karnchanapayap
TILLEKE & GIBBINS

Yongyuth Kenikanon
EEC LINCOLNE SCOTT CO. LTD.

Chaiwat Keratisuthisathorn
TILLEKE & GIBBINS

Suwat Kerdphon
DEPARTMENT OF LANDS

Chanida Leelanuntakul
SIAM CITY LAW OFFICES LTD.

William Lehane

Sakchai Limsiripothong
WEERAWONG, CHINNAVAT & PEANGPANOR
LTD.

Steven Miller
MAYER BROWN JSM

Sally Mouhim
TILLEKE & GIBBINS

Surapol Opasatien
NATIONAL CREDIT BUREAU CO. LTD.

Nipa Pakdeechanuan
DEJ-UDOM & ASSOCIATES

Tanadee Pantumkomol
CHANDLER & THONG-EK

Santhapat Periera
TILLEKE & GIBBINS

Sudthana Pilakasiri
NATIONAL CREDIT BUREAU CO. LTD.

Thawatchai Pittayasophon
SECURITIES AND EXCHANGE COMMISSION

Alexander Polgar
ANTARES CONSULTING LTD.

Ratana Poonsombudlert
CHANDLER & THONG-EK

Cynthia M. Pornavalai
TILLEKE & GIBBINS

Supan Poshyananda
SECURITIES AND EXCHANGE COMMISSION

Somboonpoonpol Pratumporn
SIAM CITY LAW OFFICES LTD.

Chitchai Punsan
TILLEKE & GIBBINS

Sutatip Raktiprakorn
SIAM CITY LAW OFFICES LTD.

Wanna Rakyao
THAILAND LAND TITLING PROJECT OFFICE

Anake Rattanajitbanjong
TILLEKE & GIBBINS

Suraphon Rittipongchusit
DLA PIPER (THAILAND) LIMITED

Thavorn Rujivanarom
PwC THAILAND

Boriboon Rungklan
PRICEWATERHOUSECOOPERS LEGAL & TAX
CONSULTANTS LIMITED

Sawat Sangkavisit
ALLENS ARTHUR ROBINSON / SIAM
PREMIER INTERNATIONAL LAW OFFICE
LIMITED

Maythawee Sarathai
MAYER BROWN JSM

Somchai Sathiramongkolkul
PRICEWATERHOUSECOOPERS LEGAL & TAX
CONSULTANTS LIMITED

Jeffrey Sok

Maprang Sombattha
DLA PIPER (THAILAND) LIMITED

Kowit Somwaiya
LAWPLUS LTD.

Pornchai Srisawang
TILLEKE & GIBBINS

Rachamarn Suchitchon
SECURITIES AND EXCHANGE COMMISSION

Picharn Sukparangsee
SIAM CITY LAW OFFICES LTD.

Siripong Supakijjanusorn
PRICEWATERHOUSECOOPERS LEGAL & TAX
CONSULTANTS LIMITED

Prasopchoke Suwanaroj
DEPARTMENT OF LANDS

Naddaporn Suwanvajukkasikij
LAWPLUS LTD.

Hunt Talmage
CHANDLER & THONG-EK

Jinjutha Techakumphu
SIAM CITY LAW OFFICES LTD.

Paisan Tulapornpipat
BLUE OCEAN LOGISTICS CO., LTD.

Sutharm Valaisathien
INTERNATIONAL LEGAL COUNSELLORS

Pattara Vasinwatanapong
VICKERY & WORACHAI LTD.

Harold K. Vickery Jr.
VICKERY & WORACHAI LTD.

Patcharaporn Vinitnuntarat
SIAM CITY LAW OFFICES LTD.

Pimvimol Vipamaneerut
TILLEKE & GIBBINS

Auradee Wongsaroj
CHANDLER & THONG-EK

TIMOR-LESTE
BIMAVI UNIPESSOAL LDA

EDTL

Martin Breen
CRA TIMOR

Jose Pedro Camoes
ASOSIASAUN ADVOGADO

Miguel Carreira Martins
NATIONAL UNIVERSITY OF TIMOR-LESTE
(UNTL)

Vital dos Santos
VSP - VITAL DOS SANTOS & PARTNERS

Jofino Ronuel Fernandes Reci
BANKING AND PAYMENTS AUTHORITY
OF TIMOR-LESTE CREDIT REGISTRY
INFORMATION SYSTEM (CRIS)

Renato Guerra de Almeida
MIRANDA CORREIA AMENDOEIRA &
ASSOCIADOS

Jackson Lay
PALM SPRING ESTATES

Aderito LCA de Araujo
ARCHTIMOR ENGINEERING CONSULTANT

Cornelio Pacheco
JVK INTERNATIONAL MOVERS

Tjia Soh Siang
TJIA & TCHAI ASSOCIATES

TOGO
BOLLORÉ AFRICA LOGISTICS

CABINET DE NOTAIRE KADJAKA-ABOUGNIMA

Diaby Aboubakar
BCEAO

Jean-Marie Adenka
CABINET ADENKA

Koudzo Mawuéna Agbemaple
AUTORITÉ DE RÉGLEMENTATION DU SECTEUR
DE L'ELECTRICITÉ

Kokou Gadémon Agbessi
CABINET LUCREATIF

Franck Akakpo
MAERSK LINE

Martial Akakpo
SCP MARTIAL AKAKPO & ASSOCIES

Richard Akpoto — Kougbleneou
L'ECOLE AFRICAINE DES MÉTIERS DE
L'ARCHITECTURE ET DE L'URBANISME
(EAMAU) STUDIO ALPHA A.I.C

Adzewoda Ametsiagbe
DIRECTION GÉNÉRALE DE L'URBANISME ET
DE L'HABITAT

Coffi Alexis Aquereburu
AQUEREBURU AND PARTNERS CABINET
D'AVOCATS

Cecile Assogbavi
ETUDE NOTARIALE ASSOGBAVI

Sylvanus Dodzi Awutey
CABINET LUCREATIF

Tiem Bolidja
COMPAGNIE ENERGIE ELECTRIQUE DU TOGO
(CEET)

Romain Dansou
AGENCE EPAUC NOUVELLE

Thomas Foli Doe-Bruce
ORDRE NATIONAL DES ARCHITECTES DU
TOGO, (ONAT)

Koffi Joseph Dogbevi
CABINET LUCREATIF

Firmin Kwami Dzonoukou
ETUDE NOTARIALE DZONOUKOU

Kodjo John Kokou
CABINET D'AVOCATS JOHN KOKOU

Atchroe Leonard Johnson
SCP AQUEREBURU & PARTNERS

Bleounou Komlan
AVOCAT À LA COUR

Hokaméto Kpenou
AUTORITÉ DE RÉGLEMENTATION DU SECTEUR
DE L'ELECTRICITÉ

Kofi Kumodzi
GLOBAL EXCEL INTERNATIONAL - DRH

Sibivi Elina Lawson-Atutu
SCP MARTIAL AKAKPO & ASSOCIES

Adeline Messou
PwC Côte d'Ivoire

Kissao Napo
Compagnie Energie Electrique du Togo (CEET)

Yawovi Negbegble
Autorité de Réglementation du Secteur de l'Électricité

Comlan Eli-Eli N'soukpoé
SCP Martial Akakpo & Associes

Adoko Pascal
Triangle Constructeur

Olivier Pedanou
Cabinet Lucratif

Ousmane Samba Mamadou
BCEAO

Galolo Soedjede
Cabinet de Maître Galolo Soedjede

Hoedjeto Tonton Soedjede
Cabinet de Maître Galolo Soedjede

Dominique Taty
PwC Côte d'Ivoire

Mouhamed Tchassona Traore
Etude Me Mouhamed Tchassona Traore

Inès Mazalo Tekpa
Cabinet Lucratif

Fousséni Traoré
PwC Côte d'Ivoire

Komi Tsakadi
Cabinet De Me Tsakadi

Bruno Dosseh Wodotzo
OMNITRA

Emmanuel Yehouessi
BCEAO

Edem Amétéfé Zotchi
SCP Martial Akakpo & Associes

TONGA
Supreme Court

Inoke Afu
Dateline Transam Shipping

Rosamond Bling
Ministry of Lands, Survey, Natural Resources & Environment

Lord Dalgety
Electricity Commission

Nailasikau Halatuituia

Aminiasi Kefu
Crown Law

Fisilau Leone
Kramer Ausenco Tonga

Ashleigh Matheson
Westpac Bank of Tonga

Lee Miller
Waste Management Ltd.

Laki M. Niu
Laki Niu Offices

Michael O'Shannassy
Inland Revenue Tonga

Sipiloni Raas
Jaimi Associates - Architects

Jemma San Jose
Electricity Commission

Dana Stephenson
Law Office

Ralph Stephenson
Law Office

Teimumu Tapueluelu-Schock
Westpac Bank of Tonga

Hiva Tatila
Tonga Development Bank

Fine Tohi
Dateline Transam Shipping

Lesina Tonga
Lesina Tonga Law Firm

John Fanua Uele
Ministry of Lands, Survey, Natural Resources & Environment

Christine Uta'atu
Uta'atu & Associates

Lepaola B. Vaea
Inland Revenue Tonga

Jone Vuli
Westpac Bank of Tonga

TRINIDAD AND TOBAGO
Customs and Excise Division of Trinidad and Tobago

Ernst & Young

Israiell Ali
Trinidad & Tobago Electricity Commission

Tara Mary Allum
Fitzwilliam Stone Furness-Smith & Morgan

Steve Beckles
Deloitte LLP

Cecil Camacho
Johnson, Camacho & Singh

Tiffanny Castillo
M. Hamel-Smith & Co., member of Lex Mundi

Stacy Lee Daniell
M. Hamel-Smith & Co., member of Lex Mundi

Anthony Farfan
Skyline Freight & Management Limited

Charisse Farfan
Skyline Freight & Management Limited

Hadyn-John Gadsby
J.D. Sellier & Co.

Sheryl Anne Haynes
Town and Country Planning Division

Nadia Henriques
M. Hamel-Smith & Co., member of Lex Mundi

Glenn A. Khan
Regulated Industries Commission

Keomi Lourenco
M. Hamel-Smith & Co., member of Lex Mundi

Ann-marie Mahabir
M. Hamel-Smith & Co., member of Lex Mundi

Rena M. Mahadeo
M. Hamel-Smith & Co., member of Lex Mundi

Kurt Andrew Anthony Miller
Fitzwilliam Stone Furness-Smith & Morgan

Celeste Mohammed
M. Hamel-Smith & Co., member of Lex Mundi

Jon Paul Dominic Mouttet
Fitzwilliam Stone Furness-Smith & Morgan

Dean Nieves
TransUnion

Marjorie Nunez
Lex Caribbean

Ronald Patience
Cargo Consolidators Agency Ltd.

Steven M. Paul
J.D. Sellier & Co.

Fanta Punch
M. Hamel-Smith & Co., member of Lex Mundi

Mark Ramkerrysingh
Fitzwilliam Stone Furness-Smith & Morgan

Ramdath Dave Rampersad
Deloitte LLP

Kelvin Ramsook
Trinidad & Tobago Electricity Commission

Danzel Reid
Trinidad & Tobago Electricity Commission

Myrna Robinson-Walters
M. Hamel-Smith & Co., member of Lex Mundi

Gregory Salandy
GSAL Designs Ltd.

Arun Seenath
Deloitte LLP

Stephen A. Singh
Johnson, Camacho & Singh

Jonathan Walker
M. Hamel-Smith & Co., member of Lex Mundi

Grantley Wilshire
M. Hamel-Smith & Co., member of Lex Mundi

Jude Xavier
Cargo Consolidators Agency Ltd.

Phillip Xavier
Cargo Consolidators Agency Ltd.

TUNISIA
Ernst & Young

Fakhfakh Abdellatif
Banque Centrale de Tunisie

Samir Abdelly
Abdelly & Associes

Mourad Abdelmoula
AFINCO, a member of NEXIA INTERNATIONAL

Ilhem Abderrahim
Société Tunisienne de l'Elecricité et du Gaz (STEG)

Mohamed Ammar
Société Tunisienne de l'Elecricité et du Gaz (STEG)

Leila Aouichri
AIT sarl

Mohamed Moncef Barouni
ACR

Adly Bellagha
Adly Bellagha & Associates

Hend Ben Achour
Adly Bellagha & Associates

Mohamed Salah Ben Afia
Orga Audit, member of Russell Bedford International

Ismail Ben Farhat
Adly Bellagha & Associates

Leila Ben Mbarek
Legalys

Miriam Ben Rejeb
CAF Juridique et Fiscal SARL

Abdelfetah Benahji
Ferchiou & Associés

Manel Bondi
PwC Tunisia

Elyes Chafter
Chafter Raouadi Law Firm

Zine el Abidine Chafter
Chafter Raouadi Law Firm

Kmar Chaïbi
Banque Centrale de Tunisie

Afef Challouf
Société Tunisienne de l'Elecricité et du Gaz (STEG)

Abdelmalek Dahmani
Dahmani Transit International

Mohamed Derbel
BDO

Mohamed Lotfi El Ajeri
El Ajeri Lawyers, Partenaire de DS Avocats

Yassine El Hafi
Adly Bellagha & Associates

Myriam Escheikh
Legalys

Cheiakh Faouzi
Banque Centrale de Tunisie

Abderrahmen Fendri
PwC Tunisia

Yessine Ferah
F&A Law Firm

Noureddine Ferchiou
Ferchiou & Associés

Slim Gargouri
CPA

Imene Hanafi
Legalys

Anis Jabnoun
Gide Loyrette Nouel, member of Lex Mundi

Atf Jebali Nasri
Legalys

Najla Jezi
ACR

Sami Kallel
Kallel & Associates

Larbi Kedira
Chafter Raouadi Law Firm

Mabrouk Maalaoui
PwC Tunisia

Dina Magroun
El Ajeri Lawyers, Partenaire de DS Avocats

Jomaa Mahmoud
CAF Juridique et Fiscal SARL

Mohamed Ali Masmoudi
CAF Juridique et Fiscal SARL

Emna Mazouni
CAF Juridique et Fiscal SARL

Sarah Mebazaa
Comete Engineering

Radhi Meddeb
Comete Engineering

Faouzi Mili
Mili and Associates

Mohamed Taieb Mrabet
Banque Centrale de Tunisie

Amel Mrabet
El Ajeri Lawyers, Partenaire de DS Avocats

Atf Nasri
Ferchiou & Associés

Imen Nouira
Conservation Foncière Tunisia

Othmane Olfa
Banque Centrale de Tunisie

Habiba Raouadi
Chafter Raouadi Law Firm

Lotfi Rebai
Cabinet Rebai

Hédi Rezgui
Société Tunisienne de l'Elecricité et du Gaz (STEG)

Koubaa Rym
CRK

Nizar Sdiri
Nizar Sdiri Law Firm

Imed Tanazefti
Gide Loyrette Nouel, member of Lex Mundi

Rachid Tmar
CAF Juridique et Fiscal SARL

Wassim Turki
AWT Audit & Conseil

Ben Afia Zied
Orga Audit, member of Russell Bedford International

TURKEY
Balkan Sulfur Ltd.

Ernst & Young

Emre Akarkarasu
PwC Turkey

Ceyda Akbal
Turunç Law Office

Sezin Akoğlu
Pekin & Pekin

Müjdem Aksoy
Cerrahoğlu Law Firm

Seza Ceren Aktaş
Basaran Nas Yeminli Mali Musavirlik A.S.

Simge Akyüz
Devres Law Office

Kenan Alpdündar
Central Bank of the Republic of Turkey

Ekin Altıntaş
PwC Turkey

Melsa Ararat
Corporate Governance Forum of Turkey, Sabanci University

Özlem Özgür Arslan
Talal Abu Ghazaleh Legal (TAG-Legal)

Ilkay Arslantaslı
KPMG

Ozgur Asik
INLAWCO Law Firm

Melis Atasagun
Pekin & Bayar Law Firm

Ozgecan Aydinsoy
Özel & Özel Attorneys At Law

Elvan Aziz
Paksoy Law Firm

Derya Baksı
Tarlan – Baksi Law Firm

Gokce Balcioglu
Özel & Özel Attorneys At Law

Z. İlayda Balkan
ADMD Law Firm

Naz Bandik
Çakmak Avukatlik Bürosu

Selin Barlak Gümrükçü
Paksoy Law Firm

Ayça Bayburan
ADMD Law Firm

Pelin Baysal
Mehmet Gün & Partners

Ayşe Eda Biçer
Çakmak Avukatlik Bürosu

Sinan Borovali
KarataşYildizBorovali

Yildirim Bozbiyik
Ministry of Finance

Melis Buhan
Pekin & Pekin

Zeynep Buharali
Basaran Nas Yeminli Mali Musavirlik A.S.

Burcu Çakallı
KPMG

A. Efe Çakmak
Deloitte LLP

Taylan Çalışkan
Pekin & Pekin

Esin Çamlıbel
Turunç Law Office

Burcu Canpolat
PwC Turkey

Maria Lianides Çelebi
Bener Law Office, member of Ius Laboris

Ipek Merve Celik
PEKIN & PEKIN

M. Fadlullah Cerrahoğlu
CERRAHOĞLU LAW FIRM

Fikret Çetinkaya
KPMG

Orçun Çetinkaya
MEHMET GÜN & PARTNERS

Dilek Çolakel
BASARAN NAS YEMINLI MALI MUSAVIRLIK A.S.

Niyazi Çömez
DELOITTE LLP

Alisya Bnegi Danisman
MEHMET GÜN & PARTNERS

Orkun Deniz
KREDIT KAYIT BUREAU

Pınar Denktaş
PEKIN & PEKIN

Chelsea Dereli
LAWYER

Rüçhan Derici
3E DANIŞMANLIK LTD. ŞTI.

Kazım Derman
KREDIT KAYIT BUREAU

Pia Deshpande
WEIL, GOTSHAL & MANGES LLP

Emine Devres
DEVRES LAW OFFICE

Ebru Dicle
TURKISH INDUSTRIALISTS' AND BUSINESSMEN'S ASSOCIATION (TUSIAD)

Başak Diclehan
KPMG

Tarık Dilek
BOLERO SOCKS

Irmak Dirik
PEKIN & PEKIN

Ahmet İlker Doğan
ÇAKMAK AVUKATLIK BÜROSU

Didem Doğar
PAKSOY LAW FIRM

Murat Volkan Dülger
DÜLGER LAW FIRM

Dilara Duman
SARIIBRAHIMOĞLU LAW OFFICE

Çisil Durgun
CERRAHOĞLU LAW FIRM

Pelin Ecevit
SERAP ZUVIN LAW OFFICES

Murat Emirhanoğlu
KPMG

Sedat Eratalar
DELOITTE LLP

Gökben Erdem Dirican
PEKIN & PEKIN

Hulya Ergin
INLAWCO LAW FIRM

Onur Erol
PwC TURKEY

Umurcan Gago
PwC TURKEY

Zeynephan Gemicioğlu
CERRAHOĞLU LAW FIRM

Nigar Gökmen
ÇAKMAK AVUKATLIK BÜROSU

Osman Nuri Gönenç
CENTRAL BANK OF THE REPUBLIC OF TURKEY

Sait Gözüm
DELOITTE LLP

Onur Gülsaran
CERRAHOĞLU LAW FIRM

Sezin Güner
PEKIN & PEKIN

Ahmet Güran
TURUNÇ LAW OFFICE

Ömer Gürbüz
MEHMET GÜN & PARTNERS

Ayşegül Gürsoy
CERRAHOĞLU LAW FIRM

Zeki Gunduz
PwC TURKEY

Remzi Orkun Guner
ADMD LAW FIRM

Salih Zeki Haklı
TOBB

Aydin Bugra Ilter
ILTER, TURAN & ARGUN

Gül Incesulu
ÇAKMAK AVUKATLIK BÜROSU

Şebnem Işık
MEHMET GÜN & PARTNERS

Baris Kalayci
MEHMET GÜN & PARTNERS

Ibrahim Kara
KREDIT KAYIT BUREAU

Ali Ozan Karaduman
MEHMET GÜN & PARTNERS

Bengi Su Karaköylü
BASARAN NAS YEMINLI MALI MUSAVIRLIK A.S.

Serhat Karakulaç
BASARAN NAS YEMINLI MALI MUSAVIRLIK A.S.

Sıddık Kaya
MINISTRY OF INDUSTRY & TRADE

Burak Kepkep
KEPKEP INTERNATIONAL LEGAL COUNSELING

Özlem Kızıl
ÇAKMAK AVUKATLIK BÜROSU

Çiğdem Koğar
CENTRAL BANK OF THE REPUBLIC OF TURKEY

Omruncegul Koyuncuoglu
BASARAN NAS YEMINLI MALI MUSAVIRLIK A.S.

Nergis Kundakçıoğlu
CERRAHOĞLU LAW FIRM

Sait Kurşuncu
CERRAHOĞLU LAW FIRM

Gülçin Kurt
CERRAHOĞLU LAW FIRM

Ümit Kurt
JONES LANG LASALLE

Zeki Kurtçu
DELOITTE LLP

Orhan Yavuz Mavioğlu
ADMD LAW FIRM

Charlotte McCrudden
PEKIN & PEKIN

Banu Mert
CERRAHOĞLU LAW FIRM

Sıla Muratoğlu
BAYIRLI & MURATOĞLU LAW FIRM

Yılmaz Nalçakar
MED SHIPPING LOGISTICS TRANSPORT & TRADE LTD. CORPORATION

Melis Oget Koc
SERAP ZUVIN LAW OFFICES

Gülçin Özlem Oğuzlar
TURUNÇ LAW OFFICE

Mert Oner
KPMG

Selin Özbek
OZBEK ATTORNEYS AT LAW

Selin Ozdamar
ÖZEL & ÖZEL ATTORNEYS AT LAW

Caner Özen
ÖZEL & ÖZEL ATTORNEYS AT LAW

Okşan Özkan
BASARAN NAS YEMINLI MALI MUSAVIRLIK A.S.

Tuba Özsezen
YASED - INTERNATIONAL INVESTORS ASSOCIATION

Özlem Özyiğit
YASED - INTERNATIONAL INVESTORS ASSOCIATION

Serkan Pamukkale
BIRSEL LAW OFFICES

Ferhat Pekin
PEKIN & BAYAR LAW FIRM

Ahmed Pekin
PEKIN & PEKIN

Batuhan Şahmay
BENER LAW OFFICE, MEMBER OF IUS LABORIS

Bilge Saltan
DÜLGER LAW FIRM

Hasan Sarıçiçek
KPMG

Simhan Savaşçın Başaran
TURUNÇ LAW OFFICE

Ahmet Can Seber
INLAWCO LAW FIRM

Duygu Şeftalici
CERRAHOĞLU LAW FIRM

Ayşe Sert
ÇAKMAK AVUKATLIK BÜROSU

Ömer Kayhan Seyhun
CENTRAL BANK OF THE REPUBLIC OF TURKEY

Aaron Shafer
BASARAN NAS YEMINLI MALI MUSAVIRLIK A.S.

M. Ufuk Söğütlüoğlu
DELOITTE LLP

Çağıl Sünbül
BASARAN NAS YEMINLI MALI MUSAVIRLIK A.S.

Esin Taboglu Yurtal
TABOGLU & DEMIRHAN

Aylin Tarlan Tüzemen
TARLAN – BAKSI LAW FIRM

Ferya Taş
TURUNÇ LAW OFFICE

Pınar Tatar
PwC TURKEY

Muge Temel
ÖZEL & ÖZEL ATTORNEYS AT LAW

Selen Terzi Özsoylu
PAKSOY LAW FIRM

Zeynep Tezcan
PEKIN & PEKIN

Elif Tezcan Bayırlı
BAYIRLI & MURATOĞLU LAW FIRM

Güzel Toker
BASARAN NAS YEMINLI MALI MUSAVIRLIK A.S.

Berna Toksoy
TURKISH INDUSTRIALISTS' AND BUSINESSMEN'S ASSOCIATION (TUSIAD)

Filiz Toprak
MEHMET GÜN & PARTNERS

Oya Tosunlar
PwC TURKEY

Noyan Turunç
TURUNÇ LAW OFFICE

Ibrahim Tutar
PENETRA CONSULTING AND AUDITING

Ebru Tuygun
DELOITTE LLP

N.Kerem Üler
ÖZEL & ÖZEL ATTORNEYS AT LAW

Furkan Ünal
PGLOBAL GLOBAL ADVISORY AND TRAINING SERVICES LTD.

Hakan Volkan

Selcen Yalçın
MEHMET GÜN & PARTNERS

Barış Yalçın
PwC TURKEY

Ayşegül Yalçınmani Merler
CERRAHOĞLU LAW FIRM

Begüm Yavuzdoğan
MEHMET GÜN & PARTNERS

Beril Yayla
MEHMET GÜN & PARTNERS

Cansu Yazıcı
MEHMET GÜN & PARTNERS

A.Çağrı Yıldız
ADMD LAW FIRM

Hülya Yılmaz
DELOITTE LLP

Aylin Yontar
CERRAHOĞLU LAW FIRM

Filiz Yüksel
CERRAHOĞLU LAW FIRM

Murat Yülek
PGLOBAL GLOBAL ADVISORY AND TRAINING SERVICES LTD.

Izzet Zakuto
SOMAY HUKUK BÜROSU

Serap Zuvin
SERAP ZUVIN LAW OFFICES

UGANDA

ERNST & YOUNG

KARGO INTERNATIONAL LTD.

Claire Amanya
KAMPALA ASSOCIATED ADVOCATES

Leria Arinaitwe
SEBALU & LULE ADVOCATES AND LEGAL CONSULTANTS

Bernard Baingana
PwC UGANDA

Matovu Emmy
MARMA TECHNICAL SERVICES

Ivan Engoru
A.F. MPANGA ADVOCATES

Sarfaraz Jiwani
SEYANI BROTHERS & CO. (U) LTD.

Lwanga John Bosco
MARMA TECHNICAL SERVICES

Charles Kalu Kalumiya
KAMPALA ASSOCIATED ADVOCATES

Richard Kamajugo
UGANDA REVENUE AUTHORITY

Francis Kamulegeya
PwC UGANDA

John Fisher Kanyemibwa
KATEERA & KAGUMIRE ADVOCATES

Phillip Karugaba
MMAKS ADVOCATES

Baati Katende
KATENDE, SSEMPEBWA & CO. ADVOCATES

Sim K. Katende
KATENDE, SSEMPEBWA & CO. ADVOCATES

Vincent Katutsi
KATEERA & KAGUMIRE ADVOCATES

Peter Kauma
KIWANUKA & KARUGIRE ADVOCATES

Muzamiru Kibeedi
KIBEEDI & CO.

Robert Komakec
ARCH FORUM LTD.

Brigitte Kusiima Byarugaba
SHONUBI, MUSOKE & CO. ADVOCATES

Ida Kussima
KATENDE, SSEMPEBWA & CO. ADVOCATES

Robinah Lutaaya
PwC UGANDA

Michael Malan
COMPUSCAN CRB LTD.

Paul Mbuga
SEBALU & LULE ADVOCATES AND LEGAL CONSULTANTS

John Mpambala
KAMPALA CITY COUNCIL

Cornelius Mukiibi
C.MUKIIBI.SENTAMU & CO. ADVOCATES

Andrew Munanura Kamuteera
SEBALU & LULE ADVOCATES AND LEGAL CONSULTANTS

Rachel Mwanje Musoke
MMAKS ADVOCATES

Peters Musoke
SHONUBI, MUSOKE & CO. ADVOCATES

Jimmy M. Muyanja
MUYANJA & ASSOCIATES

Plaxeda Namirimu
PwC UGANDA

Sophia Nampijja
KATENDE, SSEMPEBWA & CO. ADVOCATES

Diana Ninsiima
MMAKS ADVOCATES

Eddie Nsamba-Gayiiya
CONSULTANT SURVEYORS AND PLANNERS

Charles Odere
LEX UGANDA ADVOCATES & SOLICITORS

Harriet Wandira Rumanyika
SDV TRANSAMI

Kenneth Rutaremwa
KATEERA & KAGUMIRE ADVOCATES

Moses Segawa
SEBALU & LULE ADVOCATES AND LEGAL CONSULTANTS

Monica Kisubi Senjako
SDV TRANSAMI

Stephen Serunjogi
KATEERA & KAGUMIRE ADVOCATES

Alan Shonubi
SHONUBI, MUSOKE & CO. ADVOCATES

Christopher Siambe
CROWN AGENTS LTD.

Obed Tindyebwa
GRAND & NOBLE

Ronald Tusingwire
SYNERGY SOLICITORS & ADVOCATES

Isaac Walukagga
MMAKS ADVOCATES

UKRAINE

IBCH

Oleg Y. Alyoshin
VASIL KISIL & PARTNERS

Andrey Astapov
ASTAPOV LAWYERS INTERNATIONAL LAW GROUP

Ron J. Barden
PwC UKRAINE

Olena Basanska
CMS CAMERON MCKENNA

Anastasiya Bolkhovitinova
DLA PIPER UKRAINE LLC

Timur Bondaryev
ARZINGER & PARTNERS INTERNATIONAL LAW FIRM

Alexander Borisov
GRANT THORNTON LLP

Solomiya Borshosh
PwC UKRAINE

Lilia Boulakh
DLA PIPER UKRAINE LLC

Alexander Buryak
PwC Ukraine

Maryna Bychkova
DLA Piper Ukraine LLC

Serhiy Chorny
Baker & McKenzie

Dmytro Derkach
DLA Piper Ukraine LLC

Anna Deshko
Damco

Vladimir Didenko
Magisters

Lyudmyla Dzhurylyuk
DLA Piper Ukraine LLC

Svetlana Faieva
Grant Thornton LLP

Yuliya Goptarenko
KPMG

Sergiy Gryshko
CMS Cameron McKenna

Valeriia Gudiy
Ilyashev & Partners

Dirk Hagemann
BNT & partner

Maryana Hoy
PwC Ukraine

Oksana Ilchenko
Magisters

Olga Ivaniv
Vasil Kisil & Partners

Vitaliy Kazakov
Grant Thornton LLP

Natalya Kim
Chadbourne & Parke LLP

Andriy Kirmach
Chadbourne & Parke LLP

Natalia Koloskova
The Ukrainian Journal of Business Law

Maksym Kopeychykov
Ilyashev & Partners

Evgeniy Kornievskiy
Konnov & Sozanovsky

Natalia Kozyar
The Ukrainian Journal of Business Law

Tatyana Kuzmenko
Astapov Lawyers International Law Group

Natalia Levchuk
DLA Piper Ukraine LLC

Yulia Logunova
DLA Piper Ukraine LLC

Olga Lubiv
KPMG

Nellie Makary
Grant Thornton LLP

Oleksandr Maydanyk
Magisters

Tetiana Melnychuk

Arsenyy Milyutin
Magisters

Vadim Mizyakov
Asters

Anna Moliboga
KPMG

Oleksandr Mozheiko
Asters

Nataliya Mykolska
Vasil Kisil & Partners

Aleksandra Odynets
Grischenko & Partners

Sergiy Onishchenko
Chadbourne & Parke LLP

Oleksii Onishchenko
Grischenko & Partners

Oleksandr Padalka
Asters

Magdalena Patrzyk
PwC Ukraine

Iryna Pidlisna
Salans

Andriy Pozhidayev
Asters

Dmytro Pshenychnyuk
DLA Piper Ukraine LLC

Yuliana Revyuk
KPMG

Vadym Samoilenko
Asters

Marina Savchenko
Astapov Lawyers International Law Group

Vladimir Sayenko
Sayenko Kharenko

Olga Serbul
Law Firm IP & C. Consult, LLC

Dmytro Shevchenko
Arzinger & Partners International Law Firm

Alla Shevchenko
BNT & partner

Oleg Shevchuk
Proxen & Partners

Hanna Shtepa
Baker & McKenzie

Markian B. Silecky
Salans

Anna Sisetska
Vasil Kisil & Partners

Andriy Stetsenko
CMS Cameron McKenna

Yaroslav Teklyuk
Vasil Kisil & Partners

Olexander Tereschenko
Vasil Kisil & Partners

Svitlana Teush
Arzinger & Partners International Law Firm

Dmytro Tkachenko
DLA Piper Ukraine LLC

Anna Tkachenko
Salans

Zakhar Tropin
Proxen & Partners

Olga Usenko
The Ukrainian Journal of Business Law

Elina Vavryshchuk
DLA Piper Ukraine LLC

Olena Verba
Arzinger & Partners International Law Firm

Oleksandr Vygovskyy
Asters

Zeeshan Wani
Globalink Transportation & Logistics Worldwide LLP

Olexiy Yanov
Law Firm IP & C. Consult, LLC

Yulia Yashenkova
Astapov Lawyers International Law Group

Galyna Zagorodniuk
DLA Piper Ukraine LLC

Tatiana Zamorska
KPMG

UNITED ARAB EMIRATES
Ernst & Young

Intuit Management Consultancy

Karim Abaza
Shalakany Law Office, member of Lex Mundi

Moutaz Abddullat
Talal Abu Ghazaleh Legal (TAG-Legal)

Saeed Abdulla Al Hamiz
Central Bank of the UAE

Simon Adams
Clyde & Co.

Farid Ahmadi
National Trading and Development Est.

Yakud Ahmed
Orchid Gulf

Abdulla Al Kaabi
Department of Economic Development – Dubai

Essam Al Tamimi
Al Tamimi & Company Advocates & Legal Consultants

Saeed Al-Hamiz
Central Bank of the UAE

Yousef Al-Suwaidi
Dubai Courts

Joseph Altendorff
SNR Denton & Co.

Deepak Amin
Inchcape Shipping Services

Wicki Andersen
Baker Botts LLP

Sara Apostolides
SNR Denton & Co.

Manavalan Arumugam
Eros Group

Mohammed Ather
Farzana Trading

Ali Awais
Baker Botts LLP

T Suresh Babu
Landmark Group

Srinivas Balla
Green Port Shipping Agency

Prakash Bhanushali
Alsahm Al Saree Transport & Clearing

Hiten Bhatia
Silver Line Transportation

Jennifer Bibbings
Trowers & Hamlins LLP

Maryam Bin Lahej
Dubai Courts

Mazen Boustany
Habib Al Mulla & Co.

R. Chandran
Sea Bridge Shipping Co. LLC

Sudesh Chaturvedi
Gulf Agency Company LLC

Sarah Dahabiyeh
SNR Denton & Co.

Lisa Dale
Al Tamimi & Company Advocates & Legal Consultants

Shirish Deshpande
Arabian Automobiles

Ibrahim Elsadig
SNR Denton & Co.

Ashfat Farhan
Air Solutions Fze

Anthea Fernandes
Shalakany Law Office, member of Lex Mundi

Senil George
National Trading and Development Est.

Michael Hamway
PwC United Arab Emirates

Samer Hamzeh
Trowers & Hamlins LLP

Jayaram Hariharan
Vasco Global Maritime

Mohamed Hassan Ali Al Sherif
Farzana Trading

Sydene Helwick
Al Tamimi & Company Advocates & Legal Consultants

Raina Jain
Amerinde Consolidated, Inc.

Zaid Kamhawi
Emcredit

Mohammad Z. Kawasmi
Al Tamimi & Company Advocates & Legal Consultants

Jamal Khan
Amerinde Consolidated, Inc.

Naeem Khan
Mohammed Eshaq Trading Company

Khaled Kilani
Aramex Emirates LLC

Vipul Kothari
Kothari Auditors & Accountants

Solafa Kouta
Sharaf Shipping Agency

B.S. Krishna Moorthy
Landmark Group

Suresh Krishnamurthy
Al Khaleej Sugar

Rajiv Krishnan
Farzana Trading

John Kunjappan
Maersk Kanoo LLC

Ehab Lamie
Shalakany Law Office, member of Lex Mundi

Charles S. Laubach
Afridi & Angell, member of Lex Mundi

P.S. Liaquath
Sharaf Shipping Agency

Sohail Maklai
Mohammed Eshaq Trading Company

Premanand Maroly
Vasco Global Maritime

Sharnooz Mohammed
DHL Global Forwarding

Praveen Narikutty
Freightworks

Edward Nisbet
SNR Denton & Co.

Yasser Omar
Shalakany Law Office, member of Lex Mundi

Ravi Parambott
IAL Logistics Emirates LLC

Vijendra Vikram Singh Paul
Talal Abu Ghazaleh Legal (TAG-Legal)

Marjan Payan Tabari
Talal Abu Ghazaleh Legal (TAG-Legal)

Biju Pillai
DHL Global Forwarding

Jaya Prakash
Al Futtaim Logistics

V. Prakash
Al Tajir Glass Industries

Lal Premarathne
DHL Global Forwarding

Samer Qudah
Al Tamimi & Company Advocates & Legal Consultants

Yusuf Rafiudeen
Dubai Electricity and Water Authority

Sujaya Rao
DHL Global Forwarding

Basheer Hameed Rasheed
Professional Star Engineering Consultants

Dean Rolfe
PwC United Arab Emirates

Luke Sajan
Damco

Herbert Schroder
Emcredit

Kannan Senthilkumar
GLG Shipping

Mustafa Sharqawi
Dubai Courts

N.K. Sidharthan
National Trading and Development Est.

Sreekumar Sivasankaran
Globelink West Star Shipping L.L.C.

Wayne Smith
Al Futtaim Logistics

Suresh
X-Architects

Pervez Tatary
Green Port Shipping Agency

Mohammed Thani
Dubai Land Department

Hamad Thani Mutar
Dubai Courts

Raju V. Varghese
Al Yousuf L.L.C

Suresh Vallu
Diamond Shipping Services

Justin Varghese
Al Futtaim Logistics

Gary Watts
Al Tamimi & Company Advocates & Legal Consultants

Natasha Zahid
Baker Botts LLP

UNITED KINGDOM
Aerona Customs Clearing Agents Ltd.

Allen & Overy LLP

Experian Ltd.

Ofgem

White & Balck Legal LLP

Guy Bailey
CBI - The Confederation of British Industry

Jim Bligh
CBI - The Confederation of British Industry

David Bridge
Simmons & Simmons LLP

Sebastian Cameron
Cleary Gottlieb Steen & Hamilton LLP

Michael Canvin
Crown Agents Ltd.

Jonathan Dawe
HRO Grant Dawe LLP

Paul de Bernier
Mayer Brown LLP

Kirsten Dunlop
Shepherd & Wedderburn

Nick Francis
PwC United Kingdom

Laura Freestone
PricewaterhouseCoopers Legal LLP

Tony Grant
HRO Grant Dawe LLP

Donald Gray
Darwin Gray LLP

Stephen Gummer
PricewaterhouseCoopers Legal LLP

Helen Hall
DLA Piper UK LLP

Stephen Hall
PricewaterhouseCoopers Legal LLP

Jonathan Harries
PricewaterhouseCoopers Legal LLP

Jillian Hastings
Department for Communities and Local Government

Neville Howlett
PwC United Kingdom

Alice Isted
Simmons & Simmons LLP

Simon Jay
Cleary Gottlieb Steen & Hamilton LLP

Shahriar Khan
Crown Agents Ltd.

Rebecca Knight
PwC United Kingdom

Susan Knowles
Her Majesty's Land Registry

Shinoj Koshy
Cleary Gottlieb Steen & Hamilton LLP

Maria Llewellyn
Watson, Farley & Williams

Mushtak Macci
Lubbock Fine, member of Russell Bedford International

Helen Macdonald
PricewaterhouseCoopers Legal LLP

Christopher Mallon
Skadden, Arps, Slate, Meagher & Flom LLP

Emily Marshall
Cleary Gottlieb Steen & Hamilton LLP

Charles Mayo
Simmons & Simmons LLP

Forbes McNaughton
Tricor-ATC Europe LLP

Alexander Mehra
Cleary Gottlieb Steen & Hamilton LLP

Nnenna Morah
Lewis Silkin Solicitors, member of Ius Laboris

Matthew Percival
CBI - The Confederation of British Industry

Chris Perkins
PricewaterhouseCoopers Legal LLP

Stewart Perry
Clyde & Co.

David Pickstone
PricewaterhouseCoopers Legal LLP

Steve Pocock
Crown Agents Ltd.

Kate Pointer
Simmons & Simmons LLP

Anna Portsmouth
DLA Piper UK LLP

Eleanor Richardson
Davies Arnold Cooper LLP

Alex Rogan
Skadden, Arps, Slate, Meagher & Flom LLP

Andrew Shutter
Cleary Gottlieb Steen & Hamilton LLP

Sandra Simoni
Department for Communities and Local Government

Stacey-Jo Smith
Companies House

Paul Speirs
Experian Ltd.

Spencer Stevenson
British International Freight Association

Alice Steward
Simmons & Simmons LLP

Lance Terry
Glanvilles Solicitors

Angela Warrington
DLA Piper UK LLP

Carmel Weitzmann
PricewaterhouseCoopers Legal LLP

Christopher Wigley
London Building Control Ltd.

Sally Willcock
Weil, Gotshal & Manges LLP

Andrew Wilson
Andrew Wilson & Co.

UNITED STATES

Bemex International

Crown Agents Ltd.

TransUnion

Michael Aktipis
Cleary Gottlieb Steen & Hamilton LLP

Sam J. Alberts
Dickstein Shapiro LLP

Stephen Anderson
PwC United States

Phillip Anzalone
Atelier Architecture 64, PLLC

Pamy Arora
Cornell Group, Inc

Asheet Awasthi
Amerinde Consolidated, Inc.

Birute Awasthi
Amerinde Consolidated, Inc.

Luke A. Barefoot
Cleary Gottlieb Steen & Hamilton LLP

David Bartlett
Amerinde Consolidated, Inc.

Richard F. Broude

Elya Caplan
Legal Enforcement Service

Vaiva Cepukaityte
Amerinde Consolidated, Inc.

Victor Chiu
Cleary Gottlieb Steen & Hamilton LLP

Richard Conza, Esq.
Cleary Gottlieb Steen & Hamilton LLP

Brendan Cyr
Cleary Gottlieb Steen & Hamilton LLP

James Denn
New York State Public Service Commission

Joshua L. Ditelberg
Seyfarth Shaw LLP

Margareta Faris
Interdevelopment, Inc.

Irma Foley
Orrick, Herrington & Sutcliffe LLP

Daphney François
Cleary Gottlieb Steen & Hamilton LLP

Patrick Fuller, Esq.
Cleary Gottlieb Steen & Hamilton LLP

Greta Gerazirnaite
Amerinde Consolidated, Inc.

Robert Goethe
Cornell Group, Inc .

Boris Grosman
L & B Electrical International

Sonya H.S. Lee
Cleary Gottlieb Steen & Hamilton LLP

Adam Heintz
Morrison and Foerster

James Hough
Morrison and Foerster

Neil Jacobs
NI Jacobs & Associates

Edita Jauniute
Amerinde Consolidated, Inc.

Charles L. Kerr
Morrison and Foerster

Joshua Kochath
Comage Container Lines

Arthur Kohn
Cleary Gottlieb Steen & Hamilton LLP

Michael Lazerwitz, Esq.
Cleary Gottlieb Steen & Hamilton LLP

Macey Levington
Cleary Gottlieb Steen & Hamilton LLP

Bradford L. Livingston
Seyfarth Shaw LLP

Colin Lloyd
Cleary Gottlieb Steen & Hamilton LLP

Paul Marquardt
Cleary Gottlieb Steen & Hamilton LLP

Kerry Mohan
Seyfarth Shaw LLP

Robert Morris
PwC United States

Kelly Murray
PwC United States

David Newberg
Collier, Halpern, Newberg, Nolletti, & Bock

Samuel Nolen
Richards, Layton & Finger, P.A., member of Lex Mundi

Sean O'Neal
Cleary Gottlieb Steen & Hamilton LLP

Jeffrey Penn
Cleary Gottlieb Steen & Hamilton LLP

Sandra Rocks
Cleary Gottlieb Steen & Hamilton LLP

William Rucci
Rucci, Bardaro & Barrett, PC CPA's, member of Russell Bedford International

Manuel Santiago
Milrose Consultants, Inc.

Vincent Scott
Vincent Scott Enterprises

Helen Skinner
Cleary Gottlieb Steen & Hamilton LLP

Cole Smith
Cleary Gottlieb Steen & Hamilton LLP

David Snyder
Snyder & Snyder, LLP

Jantira Supawong
Cleary Gottlieb Steen & Hamilton LLP

F.W. Turner
Turner & Turner

Penny Vaughn
PwC United States

David Wilson
Holme Roberts & Owen LLP

Julie Yip-Williams
Cleary Gottlieb Steen & Hamilton LLP

URUGUAY

Isabel Abarno
Olivera Abogados

Juan Achugar
Banco Central del Uruguay

Marta Alvarez
Administración Nacional de Usinas y Transmisión Eléctrica (UTE)

Eduardo Ameglio
Guyer & Regules, member of Lex Mundi

Bernardo Amorín
Olivera Abogados

Sebastián Arcia
Arcia Storace Fuentes Medina Abogados

Rigoberto Paredes Ayllón
Rigoberto Paredes & Associates

Fernando Bado
Estudio Dr. Mezzera

Sofia Borba
Viñoles Arquitect Studio

Carlos Brandes
Guyer & Regules, member of Lex Mundi

Virginia Brause
Jiménez de Aréchaga, Viana & Brause

Ricardo Marcelo Bregani
Estudio Blanco & Etcheverry

Manuela Alejandra Bustillos García
Rigoberto Paredes & Associates

Irene Cao
Stavros Moyal y Asociados, member of Russell Bedford International

Mariana Caporale
Jimenez de Aréchaga Viana & Brause

Augusto Cibils
PwC Uruguay

Martín Colombo
Ferrere Internacional

Nicolas Constantinidi
Jiménez de Aréchaga, Viana & Brause

Leonardo Couto
Jose Maria Facal & Co.

Jorge De Vita
Jorge de Vita Studio

María Durán
Hughes & Hughes

Noelia Eiras
Hughes & Hughes

Agustín Etcheverry Reyes
Estudio Blanco & Etcheverry

Fabrizio Fava
Covidien Uruguay

Javier Fernández Zerbino
Bado, Kuster, Zerbino & Rachetti

Hector Ferreira
Hughes & Hughes

Juan Federico Fischer
Fischer & Schickendantz

Federico Florin
Guyer & Regules, member of Lex Mundi

Federico Formento
Fischer & Schickendantz

Sergio Franco
PwC Uruguay

Andres Fuentes
Arcia Storace Fuentes Medina Abogados

Diego Galante
Galante & Martins

Pablo Galmarini
Galmarini

Enrique Garcia Pini
Administración Nacional de Usinas y Transmisión Eléctrica (UTE)

Santiago Gatica
Guyer & Regules, member of Lex Mundi

Nelson Alfredo Gonzalez
SDV Uruguay

Andrés Hessdörfer
Arcia Storace Fuentes Medina Abogados

Marcela Hughes
Hughes & Hughes

Gonzalo Iglesias
Guyer & Regules, member of Lex Mundi

Ariel Imken
Superintendencia de Instituciones de Intermediación Financiera - Banco Central del Uruguay

Alfredo Inciarte Blanco
Estudio Pérez del Castillo, Inciarte, Gari Abogados

Cecilia Larrosa
Guyer & Regules, member of Lex Mundi

Andrea Medina
Arcia Storace Fuentes Medina Abogados

Ricardo Mezzera
Estudio Dr. Mezzera

Matilde Milicevic Santana
Equifax - Clearing de Informes

Robert Miller
Galante & Martins

Alejandro Miller Artola
Guyer & Regules, member of Lex Mundi

Matias Morgare
SDV Uruguay

Pablo Mosto
Administración Nacional de Usinas y Transmisión Eléctrica (UTE)

Pablo Moyal
Stavros Moyal y Asociados, member of Russell Bedford International

María Concepción Olivera
Olivera Abogados

Ricardo Olivera García
Olivera Abogados

María Cecilia Orlando
Guyer & Regules, member of Lex Mundi

Juan Orticochea
Guyer & Regules, member of Lex Mundi

Virginia Palleiro
Arcia Storace Fuentes Medina Abogados

Hugo Pereira
Arcia Storace Fuentes Medina Abogados

Ismael Pignatta Sánchez
Guyer & Regules, member of Lex Mundi

María José Poey
Guyer & Regules, member of Lex Mundi

Nathalie Polak
Fischer & Schickendantz

Mariana Saracho
Guyer & Regules, member of Lex Mundi

Eliana Sartori
PwC Uruguay

Enrique Schickendantz
Fischer & Schickendantz

Betania Silvera
Guyer & Regules, member of Lex Mundi

Leonardo Slinger
Guyer & Regules, member of Lex Mundi

Beatriz Spiess
Guyer & Regules, member of Lex Mundi

Dolores Storace
Arcia Storace Fuentes Medina Abogados

Miguel Angel Tambo Torrez
Rigoberto Paredes & Associates

Alvaro Tarabal
Guyer & Regules, member of Lex Mundi

Alejandro Taranto
Estudio Taranto

Martín Thomasset
Galante & Martins

Juan Ignacio Troccoli
Fischer & Schickendantz

Mariana Venturino
Arcia Storace Fuentes Medina Abogados

Horacio Viana
Jiménez de Aréchaga, Viana & Brause

Maria Noel Vidal
PwC Uruguay

Gerardo Viñoles
Viñoles Arquitect Studio

Ignacio Zubillaga
Arcia Storace Fuentes Medina Abogados

UZBEKISTAN

Globalink Logistics Group

Uzbekenergo

Askar K. Abdusagatov
OOO "Progress-Development"

Mels Akhmedov
BAS Law Firm

Rano Anvari
SNR Denton Wilde Sapte & Co.

Natalya Apukhtina
SNR Denton Wilde Sapte & Co.

Umid Aripdjanov
Grata Law Firm

Irina Gosteva
SNR Denton Wilde Sapte & Co.

Nail Hassanov
Leges Advokat Law Firm

Bakhodir Jabbarov
Grata Law Firm

Mouborak Kambarova
SNR Denton Wilde Sapte & Co.

Khurshid Kasimdzhanov
M & M

Tatyana Kasimova
M & M

Nurali Eshibaevich Khalmuratov
National Institute of Credit Information of Central Bank of the Republic of Uzbekistan

Davron Khasanov
Mukhamedjanov & Partners Law firm

Olga Kim
Grata Law Firm

Marina Kondratova
Marikon Audit LLC, member of Russell Bedford International

Ibrahim Mukhamedjanov
Mukhamedjanov & Partners Law firm

Behruz Nizamutdinov
M & M

Shavkat Radjabov
Fabis Consulting and Trading LLC

Laziza Rakhimova
Grata Law Firm

Ravshan Rakhmanov
Grata Law Firm

Alexander Samborsky
National Centre of Geodesy & Cartography

Vakhid Saparov
Grata Law Firm

Nizomiddin Shakhabutdinov
Leges Advokat Law Firm

Sofia Shakhrazieva
Grata Law Firm

Atabek Sharipov
Grata Law Firm

Petros Tsakanyan
Azizov & Partners

Aziz Turdibaev
M & M

Laziza Walter
Grata Law Firm

Nodir Yuldashev
Grata Law Firm

VANUATU

Barry Amoss
South Sea Shipping Ltd.

Loïc Bernier
Caillard & Kaddour

Garry Blake
Ridgeway Blake Partners

Andy Cottam
National Bank of Vanuatu

Paul de Montgolfier
Cabinet AJC

Frederic Derousseau
Vate Electrics

Julie Donald
Barrett & Partners

Roger Fabros
Genesis Shipping Services

Silas Charles Hakwa
Silas Charles Hakwa & Associates

David Hudson
Hudson & Sugden

Richard Ierongen
Barrett & Partners

Ari Jenshel
State Law Office

Frida Karie
Barrett & Partners

Chris Kernot
Fr8 Logistics Ltd.

Tony Lace
Fletcher Construction

Colin B. Leo
Colin Bright Leo Lawyers

John Malcolm

Philippe Mehrengerger
UNELCO

Edward Nalyal
Edward Nalyal & Partners

Serah Obed
Vanuatu Financial Services Commission

Juris Ozols

Harold Qualao
Qualao Consulting

Katoa Rezel
Department of Lands, Surveys & Records

John Ridgway
PLN Lawyers

Martin Saint Hilaire
Cabinet AJC

Mark Stafford
Barrett & Partners

Mandes K. Tangaras
Municipality of Port Vila

VENEZUELA, RB

Jorge Acedo-Prato
Hoet Pelaez Castillo & Duque

Tamara Adrian
Adrian & Adrian

Yanet Aguiar
Macleod Dixon

Juan Enrique Aigster
Hoet Pelaez Castillo & Duque

Servio T. Altuve Jr.
Servio T. Altuve R. & Asociados

Francisco Alvarez Silva
Travieso Evans Arria Rengel & Paz

Ramon Alvins
Macleod Dixon

Luís Andueza
Macleod Dixon

Carlos Bachrich Nagy
De Sola Pate & Brown, Abogados - Consultores

Edgar Eduardo Berroteran
Hoet Pelaez Castillo & Duque

Sergio Casinelli
Macleod Dixon

Diego Castagnino
Hoet Pelaez Castillo & Duque

Arturo De Sola Lander
De Sola Pate & Brown, Abogados - Consultores

Carlos Domínguez Hernández
Hoet Pelaez Castillo & Duque

Jose Fereira
Rodriguez & Mendoza

Francisco Gámez Arcaya

Jose Garcia
PwC Venezuela

Hector Garcia Corredor
Hoet Pelaez Castillo & Duque

Jose Alfredo Giral
Baker & McKenzie

Ybeth Gonzalez
Baker & McKenzie

Andres Felipe Guevara
Baker & McKenzie

Alfredo Hurtado
Hurtado Esteban & Asociados, member of Russell Bedford International

Maigualida Ifill
PwC Venezuela

Enrique Itriago
Rodriguez & Mendoza

Manuel Iturbe
Travieso Evans Arria Rengel & Paz

Ana Lugo
Hoet Pelaez Castillo & Duque

Andreina Lusinchi
Travieso Evans Arria Rengel & Paz

Luiz Ignacio Mendoza
Rodriguez & Mendoza

Maritza Meszaros
Baker & McKenzie

Patricia Milano Hernández
De Sola Pate & Brown, Abogados - Consultores

Lorena Mingarelli Lozzi
De Sola Pate & Brown, Abogados - Consultores

José Manuel Ortega Pérez
Palacios, Ortega y Asociados

Luis Esteban Palacios Wannoni
Palacios, Ortega y Asociados

John R. Pate
De Sola Pate & Brown, Abogados - Consultores

Thomas J. Pate Páez
De Sola Pate & Brown, Abogados - Consultores

Fernando Pelaez-Pier
Hoet Pelaez Castillo & Duque

Bernardo Pisani
Rodriguez & Mendoza

Eduardo Porcarelli
CONAPRI

Juan Carlos Pró-Rísquez
Macleod Dixon

Melissa Puga Santaella
CONAPRI

Wendy Quintero
Macleod Dixon

Jose Felix Ramirez G.
MIRKO Internacional

Laura Silva Aparicio
Hoet Pelaez Castillo & Duque

Raúl Stolk Nevett
Hoet Pelaez Castillo & Duque

Oscar Ignacio Torres
Travieso Evans Arria Rengel & Paz

John Tucker
Hoet Pelaez Castillo & Duque

Ricardo Useche
Electrificaciones Guayana CA

Carlos Velandia Sanchez
Asociación Venezolana de Derecho Registral "AVEDER"

Anhelisa Villarroel
CONAPRI

José Vivas
Self employed

Bernardo Wallis
Macleod Dixon

VIETNAM

DFDL Mekong Law Group

Panalpina World Transport LLP

Frederick Burke
Baker & McKenzie

Samantha Campbell
Gide Loyrette Nouel A.A.R.P.I., member of Lex Mundi

Giles Thomas Cooper
Duane Morris LLC

Thi Thu Quyen Dang
UNCTAD

Nguyen Dang Viet
Bizconsult Law firm

Van Dinh Thi Quynh
PwC Vietnam

Ngoan Doan
Grant Thornton LLP

Linh Doan
LVN & Associates

Dang The Duc
Indochine Counsel

Thanh Long Duong
ALIAT Legal

David Fitzgerald
PwC Vietnam

Ngoc Hai Ha
Baker & McKenzie

Quang Ha Dang
Gide Loyrette Nouel A.A.R.P.I., member of Lex Mundi

Giang Ha Thi Phuong
PwC Vietnam

Minh Ho Thi Hieu
Gide Loyrette Nouel A.A.R.P.I., member of Lex Mundi

Le Hong Phong
Bizconsult Law firm

Nguyen Thi Hong Van
YKVN

Kim Ngoan Huynh
Gide Loyrette Nouel A.A.R.P.I., member of Lex Mundi

Tuong Long Huynh
Gide Loyrette Nouel A.A.R.P.I., member of Lex Mundi

Anh Tuan Le
Credit Information Centre - State Bank of Vietnam

Phuc Le Hong
LuatViet - Advocates & Solicitors

Thuy Le Nguyen Huy
Indochine Counsel

Thuy Anh Le Phan
VILAF - Hong Duc Law Firm

Phuoc Le Van
Ho Chi Minh City Power Company

Le Thi Loc
YKVN

Tien Ngoc Luu
Vision & Associates

Duy Minh Ngo
DC Law

Quoc Phong Nguyen
ALIAT Legal

Hong Hai Nguyen
Duane Morris LLC

Dao Nguyen
Mayer Brown JSM

Huong Nguyen
Mayer Brown JSM

Linh D. Nguyen
VILAF - Hong Duc Law Firm

Tram Nguyen Huyen
Gide Loyrette Nouel A.A.R.P.I., member of Lex Mundi

Tam Nguyen Tinh
Gide Loyrette Nouel A.A.R.P.I., member of Lex Mundi

Ronald Parks
Grant Thornton LLP

Vu Anh Phan
Indochine Counsel

Viet D. Phan
Tran H.N. & Associates

Truong Nhat Quang
YKVN

Nguyen Que Tam
Chen Shan & Partners

Toby Nicholas Rees
Mayer Brown JSM

Yee Chung Seck
Baker & McKenzie

Huynh Tan Loi
Indochine Counsel

Dinh The Phuc
Electricity Regulatory Authority of Vietnam

Le Thi Nhat Linh
Ban Mai Co. Ltd.

Nhung Thieu Hong
PwC Vietnam

Tan Heng Thye
Chen Shan & Partners

Antoine Toussaint
Gide Loyrette Nouel A.A.R.P.I., member of Lex Mundi

Chi Anhi Traan
Baker & McKenzie

Thanh Ha Tran
Baker & McKenzie

Nguyen Anh Tuan
DP Consulting Ltd.

Nguyen Thu Thuy Vo
SDV Logistics

Chi Vo Ngoc Phuong
Gide Loyrette Nouel A.A.R.P.I., member of Lex Mundi

Thang Vu
Baker & McKenzie

Dzung Vu
LVN & Associates

Anh Thu Vu
Mayer Brown JSM

Le Vu Anh
PwC Vietnam

WEST BANK AND GAZA

Ernst & Young

Hani Abdel Jaldeh
Murad Abu Mwis
Ministry of National Economy

Ata Al Biary

Sharhabeel Al-Zaeem
Sharhabeel Al-Zaeem and Associates

Haytham L. Al-Zubi
Al-Zubi Law Office, Advocates & Legal Consultants

Moayad Amouri
Sa'adi Orfaly & Daher Certified Public Accountants

Khalil Ansara
Catholic Relief Services

Nada Atrash
ARCHITECTURE & DESIGN

Nizam Ayoob
MINISTRY OF NATIONAL ECONOMY

Ali Faroun
PALESTINIAN MONETARY AUTHORITY

George Handal
BETHLEHEM FREIGHT

Hiba I. Husseini
HUSSEINI & HUSSEINI

Mohamed Khader
LAUSANNE TRADING CONSULTANTS

Absal Nusseibeh
HUSSEINI & HUSSEINI

Michael F. Orfaly
SA'ADI ORFALY & DAHER CERTIFIED PUBLIC ACCOUNTANTS

Maysa Quod
PALESTINIAN MONETARY AUTHORITY

Wael Sa'adi
SA'ADI ORFALY & DAHER CERTIFIED PUBLIC ACCOUNTANTS

Samir Sahhar
OFFICE OF SAMIR SAHHAR

Husein Sholi
JUSTICE SECTOR ASSISTANCE PROJECT - JSAPII

YEMEN, REP.

Abdulalah A. Al karraz
LANDS & SURVEYING AUTHORITY

Tariq Abdullah
LAW OFFICES OF SHEIKH TARIQ ABDULLAH

Khalid Abdullah
SHEIKH MOHAMMED ABDULLAH SONS

Khaled Al Buraihi
KHALED AL BURAIHI FOR ADVOCACY & LEGAL SERVICES

Yaser Al-Adimi
ABDUL GABAR A. AL-ADIMI FOR CONSTRUCTION & TRADE

Fahdl M. Al-Akwa
COURT OF APPEAL FOR TORY OF SANA'A & AL-GOUF

Mohamed Taha Hamood Al-Hashimi
MOHAMED TAHA HAMOOD & CO.

Abdulkadir AL-Hebshi
ALCO - ADVOCACY AND LIGAL CONSULTATIANS OFFICE

Ali AL-Hebshi
ALCO - ADVOCACY AND LIGAL CONSULTATIANS OFFICE

Rashad Khalid Al-Howiadi

Ismail Ahmed Alwazir
ALWAZIR CONSULTANTS, ADVOCATES & LEGAL RESEARCH

Randall Cameron
KPMG

Abdulla Farouk Luqman
LUQMAN LEGAL ADVOCATES & LEGAL CONSULTANTS

Zayed Mohammed Budier
LANDS & SURVEYING AUTHORITY

Esam Nadeesh
ALCO - ADVOCACY AND LIGAL CONSULTATIANS OFFICE

Zuhair Abdul Rasheed
LAW OFFICES OF SHEIKH TARIQ ABDULLAH

Yousra Salem
LUQMAN LEGAL ADVOCATES & LEGAL CONSULTANTS

Khaled Mohammed Salem Ali
LUQMAN LEGAL ADVOCATES & LEGAL CONSULTANTS

Saeed Sohbi
SAEED HASSAN SOHBI

Taha Tawawala
AL SUWAIDI & COMPANY

Nigel Truscott
AL SUWAIDI & COMPANY

Khaled Hassan Zaid
YEMEN CHAMBER OF SHIPPING

ZAMBIA

ENERGY REGULATION BOARD (ERB)

Tinenenji Banda
CHIBESAKUNDA & COMPANY (PART OF DLA PIPER GROUP)

Chewe K. Bwalya
D.H. KEMP & CO.

Bonaventure Chibamba Mutale
ELLIS & CO.

Mwelwa Chibesakunda
CHIBESAKUNDA & COMPANY (PART OF DLA PIPER GROUP)

Sydney Chisenga
CORPUS LEGAL PRACTITIONERS

Emmanuel Chisenga Chulu
PwC ZAMBIA

Chiko Chuula
CHIBESAKUNDA & COMPANY (PART OF DLA PIPER GROUP)

Harjinder Dogra
PwC ZAMBIA

Arshad A. Dudhia
MUSA DUDHIA & COMPANY

Charles Haanyika
UTILINK LIMITED

Diane Harrington
SDV LOGISTICS

Chance Kaonga
NATIONAL COUNCIL FOR CONSTRUCTION

Namaala Liebenthal
CHIBESAKUNDA & COMPANY (PART OF DLA PIPER GROUP)

Mumba Makumba
PACRO

Bonaventure Mbewe
BARCLAYS BANK

Jyoti Mistry
PwC ZAMBIA

Namwene Mkadawire
SIKAULU LUNGU MUPESO LEGAL PRACTITIONERS

Gerald Mkandawire
SDV LOGISTICS

Mwape Mondoloka
BARCLAYS BANK

Henry Musonda
KIRAN & MUSONDA ASSOCIATES

Augustine Musumali
ZESCO LTD.

Francis Mwape
NATIONAL COUNCIL FOR CONSTRUCTION

Nchima Nchito
MNB LEGAL PRACTITIONERS

Solly Patel
CHRISTOPHER, RUSSELL COOK & CO.

Aleksandar Perunicic
SDV LOGISTICS

Miriam Sabi
ZRA- CUSTOMER SERVICE CENTER

Valerie Sesia
CUSTOMIZED CLEARING AND FORWARDING LTD.

Namakuzu Shandavu
CORPUS LEGAL PRACTITIONERS

Juliana Shoko Chilombo
MINISTRY OF LAND

Mildred Stephenson
CREDIT REFERENCE BUREAU AFRICA LTD.

Enos Zulu
PACRO

ZIMBABWE

ERNST & YOUNG

Richard Beattie
THE STONE/BEATTIE STUDIO

Tim Boulton
MANICA AFRICA PTY. LTD.

Peter Cawood
PwC ZIMBABWE

Onias Chigavazira
HLB RUZENGWE & COMPANY

Benjamin Chikowero
GUTU & CHIKOWERO

Grant Davies
MANICA AFRICA PTY. LTD.

Paul De Chalain
PwC SOUTH AFRICA

Beloved Dhlakama
DHLAKAMA B. ATTORNEYS

Canaan Farirai Dube
DUBE, MANIKAI AND HWACHA LEGAL PRACTITIONERS - DMH COMMERCIAL LAW CHAMBERS

Paul Fraser
LOFTY & FRASER

Obert Chaurura Gutu
GUTU & CHIKOWERO

Selby Hwacha
DUBE, MANIKAI AND HWACHA LEGAL PRACTITIONERS - DMH COMMERCIAL LAW CHAMBERS

Ali Imedi
CROWN AGENTS LTD.

Edwin Isaac Manikai
DUBE, MANIKAI AND HWACHA LEGAL PRACTITIONERS - DMH COMMERCIAL LAW CHAMBERS

R.T. Katsande
ZIMBABWE ELECTRICITY TRANSMISSION & DISTRIBUTION COMPANY

Abraham Kudzai Maguchu
DUBE, MANIKAI AND HWACHA LEGAL PRACTITIONERS - DMH COMMERCIAL LAW CHAMBERS

Annette Landman
PwC SOUTH AFRICA

Manuel Lopes
PwC ZIMBABWE

Immaculate Chipo Makone
MANICA AFRICA PTY. LTD.

Tavengwa Masara
V.S. NYANGULU & ASSOCIATES

Nunudzai Masunda
SCANLEN & HOLDERNESS

Lloyd Mhishi
DUBE, MANIKAI AND HWACHA LEGAL PRACTITIONERS - DMH COMMERCIAL LAW CHAMBERS

Sternford Moyo
SCANLEN & HOLDERNESS

Benjamin Mukandi
FREIGHT WORLD (PVT) LTD.

T. Muringani
SPEARTEC

Ostern Mutero
SAWYER & MKUSHI

Maxwell Ngorima
BDO KUDENGA & COMPANY

Vanani Nyangulu
V.S. NYANGULU & ASSOCIATES

Rudo Nyngulu
PERSPECTIVES CONSULTANTS

Anjuli Rebelo
SCANLEN & HOLDERNESS

Archford Rutanhirs
SCANLEN & HOLDERNESS

C.M. Ruzengwe
HLB RUZENGWE & COMPANY

Unity Sakhe
KANTOR & IMMERMAN

Aisha Thuliswa Tsimba
STANBIC BANK

Doing Business
THE WORLD BANK · IFC
2012

STANDING ORDER FORM
Standing orders are available to institutional customers only.

If you or your organization would like to automatically receive each new edition of *Doing Business* as it is published, please check the box below, complete your address details, and mail or fax this order form to us. This will establish a standing order for your organization, and you will be invoiced each year upon publication. You may also e-mail books@worldbank.org requesting your standing order for Doing Business. At any time you can cancel the standing order by sending an e-mail to books@worldbank.org.

☐ *I would like to automatically receive each new edition of Doing Business.*
I understand that I will be invoiced each year upon publication.

Name _____

Title _____

Organization _____

Address _____

City _____

State _____ Zip/Postal code _____

Country _____

Phone _____

Fax _____

E-mail _____

Institutional customers in the U.S. only: Please include purchase order

By mail
World Bank Publications
P.O. Box 960, Herndon
VA 20 172-0960, USA

Online
www.worldbank.org/publications

By fax
+ 1-703-661-1501

Questions?
E-mail us at books@worldbank.org

By phone
+1-703 -661-1580 or 800-645-7247

Available for US customers only, international customers please contact your local distributor to establish a standing order. Individuals interested in receiving future editions of *Doing Business* may ask to be added to our mailing list at books@worldbank.org. Please indicate in your e-mail that you would like to be added to the *Doing Business* e-mail list.